CHINA AND THE WTO
ACCESSION, POLICY REFORM, AND POVERTY REDUCTION STRATEGIES

CHINA AND THE WTO
ACCESSION, POLICY REFORM, AND POVERTY REDUCTION STRATEGIES

Editors

Deepak Bhattasali, Shantong Li,
and Will Martin

A copublication of the World Bank and Oxford University Press

9316768

© 2004 The International Bank for Reconstruction and Development / The World Bank
1818 H Street, NW
Washington, DC 20433
Telephone 202-473-1000
Internet www.worldbank.org
E-mail feedback@worldbank.org

The findings, interpretations, and conclusions expressed herein are those of the author(s) and do not necessarily reflect the views of the Board of Executive Directors of the World Bank or the governments they represent.

The World Bank does not guarantee the accuracy of the data included in this work. The boundaries, colors, denominations, and other information shown on any map in this work do not imply any judgment on the part of the World Bank concerning the legal status of any territory or the endorsement or acceptance of such boundaries.

Cover collage created by Tomoko Hirata using the following photographs:
© Michael S. Yamashita/CORBIS (farmer); © Enzo & Paolo Ragazzini/CORBIS (woman);
© Yang Liu/CORBIS (automobile factory); © How-Man Wong/CORBIS (man).

Library of Congress Cataloging-in-Publication Data

China and the WTO: accession, policy reform, and poverty reduction strategies / edited by
Deepak Bhattasali, Shantong Li, William J. Martin.
       p. cm. – (Trade and development series)
Includes bibliographical references and index.
ISBN 0-8213-5667-4
     1. China—Commercial policy. 2. World Trade Organization—China. 3. Foreign trade
Regulation—China. 4. Agriculture and state—China. 5. Poverty—Government policy—China.
6. China—Economic policy—2000-. I. Bhattasali, Deepak. II. Li, Shantong. III. Martin, Will, 1953-
IV. Series.

HF1604.C4426 2004
382'.3'0951—dc22   2004044097

CONTENTS

Part III. Impacts on Households and on Poverty   237

Boxes

Figures

Tables

FOREWORD

China's era of reform has seen enormous progress in reducing poverty at the same time as increasing integration with the world economy. The process of accession to the WTO contributed to a decisive deepening of the process of integration with the world and a move to a much stronger emphasis on rules-based reform. However, in recent years, there has been increasing concern about an increase in inequality within China and a rising gap between the fortunes of urban and rural families.

The aim of the project on which this book is based was to bring together information on the implications of China's WTO accession agreement—an enormous and complex watershed agreement—and to assess the overall impacts for households throughout China. This required the collection of information and the analysis of the policy reforms involved in the accession agreement, followed by an assessment of the effects of these policies on the major elements of the economy. Finally, drawing on this analysis, the impact of the reforms on individual households—and especially those of the poor—was evaluated. The results of the analysis provide a basis for recommending policies to capitalize on the benefits resulting from accession and to mitigate the adverse impacts.

The work on which this book is based has been disseminated in China through numerous presentations and seminars and through inputs into a number of training courses undertaken by the World Bank Institute and partner organizations in different parts of China. This book will provide a lasting reference to this major step in the evolution of the Chinese economy.

This book is the result of a number of years of work by a team of Chinese and foreign scholars. Just as China and her trading partners have benefited from the win-win nature of international trade, members of this team have benefited from one another's knowledge and understanding of different facets of this enormously complex and dynamic economy. The work is testimony to the success of the partnership between the World Bank and the Development Research Centre of State Council—a partnership that has contributed a great deal to both of our organizations. We look forward to even stronger cooperation between our two organizations in the future, as China enters the next phase of development.

François Bourguignon
Senior Vice President and Chief Economist
The World Bank

Wang Mengkui
Director
Development Research Centre of State Council

ACKNOWLEDGMENTS

We owe a debt of gratitude to the United Kingdom Department for International Development (DFID) for its generous support to this project. Particular thanks are due to the DFID staff who provided support and encouragement at critical times in the life of the project—in particular, Paul Whittingham for his encouragement in the original design; Catherine Martin for her continuing advice and encouragement from Beijing; and Fiona McConnon, Clare Roberts, and Kebur Azbaha for their assistance with the implementation of the project.

In addition to our authors—from the Development Research Center (DRC) of the State Council of China, the World Trade Organization, the World Bank, and other institutions around the world—we would like to thank numerous staff within the DRC, especially Sun Zhiyan and Liu Peilin, who assisted this project at every step, including the final dissemination workshop in Wuhan.

At the World Bank, we would like to thank Jianqing Chen, Leona Luo, and Rebecca Martin for the superb support and assistance they have provided throughout the life of the project. The assistance of the Beijing Office was invaluable also in organizing the many workshops and interim publications associated with this project.

Many others have assisted by commenting on drafts of this book, through participation in the workshops, or by providing advice. Among others, we would like to thank Long Yongtu, François Bourguignon, Christopher Hum, T. N. Srinivasan, Kong-Yam Tan, L. Alan Winters, Justin Yifu Lin, Wang Xinkui, Nicholas Lardy, Ke Binsheng, Wang Jun, Bernard Hoekman, Liu Xiaofan, Xu Lin, Wang Yan, Lu Feng, Yu Jianhua, Sarah Cook, Yang Guohua, Yu An, Sheng Laiyun, Wang Pingping, Wang Yongjuan, Huang Langhui, Li Yan, Chen Xiaodong, Zhang Xiangchen, Wang Kan, Nicholas Bridge, Gillian Cull, Yukon Huang, Charles Piggott, Jeffrey Liang, Li Shi, Edwin A.L.M. Vermulst, and Jianguang Shen for this help.

We are very grateful to Mary Fisk for her excellent editorial assistance and to Santiago Pombo-Bejarano for his enthusiastic support in converting the manuscript into a finished volume. We would also like to thank the anonymous reviewers, who provided excellent comments on the manuscript; may their tribe increase!

Deepak Bhattasali, Shantong Li, Will Martin

ABOUT THE EDITORS AND AUTHORS

Editors

Deepak Bhattasali, Lead Economist, Poverty Reduction and Economic Management Sector Development, World Bank, Beijing

Shantong Li, Director, Department of Development Strategy and Regional Economy, Development Research Center of the State Council, P.R. China, Beijing

Will Martin, Lead Economist, Development Research Group, World Bank, Washington, D.C.

Authors

Kym Anderson, Centre for Economic Studies, University of Adelaide, Adelaide, Australia

Min Chang, Graduate Student, Department of Agricultural and Resource Economics, University of California, Davis

Shaohua Chen, Senior Information Officer, Development Research Group, World Bank, Washington, D.C.

Christopher Findlay, Professor, Asia-Pacific School of Economics and Government, The Australian National University, Canberra

Joseph F. Francois, Professor, Tinbergen Institute, Rotterdam, and Fellow, Centre for Economic Policy Research, London

Jeffrey L. Gertler, Legal Affairs Division and former Secretary, Working Party on the Accession of China, World Trade Organization, Geneva

Thomas W. Hertel, Distinguished Professor, Department of Agricultural Economics, and Executive Director, Center for Global Trade Analysis, Purdue University, West Lafayette, Indiana

Jikun Huang, Director and Professor, Center for Chinese Agricultural Policy Institute for Geographical Sciences and Natural Resource Research, Chinese Academy of Sciences, Beijing

Athar Hussain, Department of Economics, London School of Economics, London

Elena Ianchovichina, Economist, Poverty Reduction and Economic Management, World Bank, Washington, D.C.

Wenping Luo, Professor, Shanghai Maritime University, Shanghai

Keith E. Maskus, Professor, Department of Economics, University of Colorado, Boulder

Aaditya Mattoo, Lead Economist, Development Research Group, World Bank, Washington, D.C.

Patrick A. Messerlin, Professor of Economics, Institutes d'Etudes Politiques, Groupe d'Economie Mondiale de Sciences Po, Paris

Debbie Mrongowius, Independent Researcher, Shanghai

Mari Pangestu, Director, Centre for Strategic and International Studies, Jakarta

Martin Ravallion, Research Manager, Development Research Group, World Bank, Washington, D.C.

Scott Rozelle, Professor, Department of Agricultural and Resource Economics, University of California, Davis

Terry Sicular, Associate Professor of Economics, University of Western Ontario, London, Ontario

Dean Spinanger, Professor, Institute for World Economics, Kiel University, Kiel

Zhi Wang, Economic Research Service, United States Department of Agriculture, Washington, D.C.

Chen Xiwen, Vice President (Vice Minister), Development Research Center of the State Council, Beijing

Fan Zhai, Department of Policy and Fiscal Affairs, Ministry of Finance, Beijing

Yaohui Zhao, Professor of Economics, Beijing University, Beijing

ACRONYMS AND ABBREVIATIONS

ADSL	asymmetric digital subscriber line	NME	non-market economy
AQSIQ	Administration for Quality Supervision, Inspection and Quarantine	NRP	nominal rate of protection
		OECD	Organisation for Economic Co-operation and Development
CAAC	Civil Aviation Administration of China	PBC	People's Bank of China
		PCT	Patent Cooperation Treaty
CGA	Customs General Administration	PTA	provincial telecommunications authority
CGE	Computable general equilibrium		
CHNS	China Health and Nutrition Survey	PTNR	permanent normal trade relations
CIRC	China Insurance Regulatory Commission	SARFT	State Administration of Radio, Film and Television
CJV	contractual joint venture	SCIO	State Council Information Office
CPI	consumer price index	SDPC	State Development Planning Commission
CSRC	Chinese Security Regulatory Commission		
		SETC	State Economic and Trade Commission
DDA	Doha Development Agenda	SEZ	special economic zone
EC	European Community	SILG	State Information Leading Group
EJV	equity joint venture	TCSC	Tariff Commission under the State Council
FDI	foreign direct investment		
GATS	General Agreement on Trade in Services	TDSCDMA	time division synchronous code division multiple access
GATT	General Agreement on Tariffs and Trade	3PL	third-party logistics
		TPS	transitional product-specific safeguard
GDP	gross domestic product		
GSM	global system for mobile communications	TRIPS	Trade-Related Aspects of Intellectual Property Rights
GTAP	Global Trade Analysis Project	TRQ	tariff-rate quota
HTS	Harmonized Tariff System	TVE	township and village enterprises
IP	Internet protocol	URAA	Uruguay Round Agreement on Agriculture
IPR	intellectual property rights		
ISDN	integrated services digital network	VAT	value-added tax
MEI	Ministry of Electronics Industry	VoIP	Voice over Internet Protocol
MFA	Multi-Fiber Arrangement	WCDMA	wideband code division multiple access
MFN	most favored nation		
MII	Ministry of Information Industry	WIPO	World Intellectual Property Organization
MOFTEC	Ministry of Foreign Trade and Economic Cooperation		
		WTO	World Trade Organization
MPT	Ministry of Posts and Telecommunications		

IMPACTS AND POLICY IMPLICATIONS OF WTO ACCESSION FOR CHINA

Deepak Bhattasali, Shantong Li, and Will Martin

After 15 arduous years as a candidate, China's application for membership in the World Trade Organization (WTO) was accepted at the WTO's Doha ministerial meeting in November 2001. As expected by observers such as Panitchpakdi and Clifford (2002), China has become an active and prominent member of the WTO, and has sharply increased its share of world trade since joining. Domestically, however, China faces many challenges, particularly in dealing with the widening gap between urban and rural incomes. The objective of this study is to analyze the impacts of China's accession to the WTO and the policy reforms needed to help facilitate China's economic development.

Of the many approaches that might be used to analyze China's accession to the WTO, an important one deals with the legal rights and responsibilities— that is, the challenges involved in meeting China's legal commitments and in ensuring that China's rights are maintained. Another focuses on the trade and policy changes required to open China's economy and integrate it into the global economy. Yet even though these are important, they are not a complete characterization of the implications of accession. For us, perhaps the most compelling aspect is one identified by Woo (2001): WTO accession as a key component in the restructuring of the Chinese economy.

There is every indication that China's policymakers see China's WTO accession agreement as a means to fulfilling broader goals. One broader strategic goal is to facilitate the peaceful emergence of China as a great trading nation—and to avoid the trade tensions associated with the emergence of major new traders in the past. Another goal is to accelerate the process of domestic reform—with the WTO acting, in the colorful words of Jin (2002), as a wrecking ball for what remains of the earlier closed economy (Jin 2002). The process of accession has also unleashed a massive process of reforming the laws covering trade issues (WTO 2002), with the result that many reforms go beyond those narrowly required by the WTO accession agreement. In addition, China's policymakers have also clearly recognized the need to deal with the yawning gap between urban and rural incomes—a gap that has become more evident since China's accession to the WTO (Wen 2004).

The importance of China's accession to the WTO has been widely recognized and studied. Both the *China Quarterly* (see Fewsmith 2001) and *China Economic Review* (see Chun, Fleisher, and Parker 2001) have published special issues on the topic, and it has been the subject of books, including those by Panitchpakdi and Clifford (2002) and Lardy (2002). Other investigators have undertaken quantitative studies of the effects of trade liberalization on China (McKibbin and Tang 2000; Ianchovichina and Martin 2001; Gilbert and Wahl 2002). Some studies, including those by Martin and Ianchovichina (2001) and Shafaeddin (2004) have looked into the implications of China's WTO accession for other countries and for the WTO system itself. The studies presented in this volume attempt to go beyond previous studies in examining, within an integrated framework, China's policy reforms and their implications for the Chinese economy and for individual households.

This volume is divided into three parts. The first part contains studies that cover the most important policy reforms associated with accession to the WTO. The second part consists of studies that examine the consequences of reform for the economy and for particular sectors. The studies in the third part build on the earlier studies and examine the implications of reform for households, and particularly for those households vulnerable to poverty. Only with the insights available from these three approaches is it possible to provide sound policy recommendations. In the remainder of this chapter, we review and summarize some of the key findings emerging from the entire set of studies.

China's Policies and the Reforms Associated with Accession

In chapter 2 of this volume, Jeffrey L. Gertler describes the long process that culminated in China's recent accession to the WTO. As in other accessions, the process involved bilateral negotiations on issues of market access and a multilateral process in which the accession agreement was formulated and the best market access given to any one member was extended to all other members under the most-favored-nation (MFN) rule.

The five basic principles of the General Agreement on Tariffs and Trade (GATT) and the WTO outlined by Gertler are useful in organizing our assessment of the implications of China's accession. The five principles are: (1) nondiscrimination, (2) market opening, (3) transparency and predictability, (4) undistorted trade, and (5) preferential treatment for developing countries. The agreement on Trade-Related Aspects of Intellectual Property Rights (TRIPS) incorporates some of these principles as well as others, such as striking a

balance between creating incentives for innovation and restricting competition by giving monopoly power to the inventor. The TRIPS agreement is discussed at the end of this section.

The general *principle of nondiscrimination* requires that WTO members give equal treatment to competing suppliers (the most-favored-nation principle), and that they not discriminate between domestically produced and imported goods or services in their internal markets. The application of this general principle to China involved some additional commitments, including the elimination of dual pricing systems, the phasing out of restrictions on trading, and the introduction of more uniform administrative arrangements and of judicial review. These commitments are important not just for the central authorities, but also for the lower tiers of government that deal with internal trade and regulation.

In China's accession, the *market opening principle* had three major dimensions: (1) commitments by China to abolish nontariff barriers, reduce tariffs, and open service sectors; (2) commitments by the importing countries to abolish the quotas on textiles and clothing originally imposed under the Multi-Fiber Arrangement (MFA); and (3) agreement by the United States and other countries to impose MFN tariffs on China. Analysis in chapter 13 by Elena Ianchovichina and Will Martin suggests that the tariff cuts offered by China were very substantial, and will result in a reduction in the weighted average tariff from 12 percent in 2001 to 6.8 percent at the end of the implementation period.[1] However, these reductions are quite small relative to the reduction of 29 percentage points between 1992 and 2001. The analysis reported by Aaditya Mattoo in chapter 8 suggests that China's commitments to liberalize trade in services are extremely large relative to those of almost all other countries. Indeed, Mattoo goes so far as to say that China's accession commitments on services constitute the most radical reform of trade in services ever undertaken under the WTO. He notes, however, that China's commitments were more frequently subject to qualifications or reservations than those of other countries. Details of the liberalization in specific sectors are considered in the next section, as a prelude to assessing the likely impact of accession on the Chinese economy.

Although most of the market opening agreed in China's accession, like in other WTO accession agreements, is to be carried out by the acceding country, China's trading partners made an important "concession" in agreeing to abolish the quotas on textiles and clothing originally imposed under the MFA. This agreement appears likely to be extremely important for China given its strong comparative advantage in textiles and clothing, although it is qualified by the ability of the importers to impose special textile and clothing safeguards for one year at a time during a transition period up to 2008. Another important "concession" by almost all existing members of the WTO was to refrain from invoking nonapplication provisions of the type widely invoked against Japan when it joined the GATT. As a result, China has received most-favored-nation treatment in virtually all markets. Clearly, this status is important because it frees China from onerous, one-sided review procedures,[2] such as the former annual review of MFN in the United States, and increases the confidence of investors in China's export industries that foreign markets will be available to them on a continuing basis.

The *transparency and predictability of trade policy* are enhanced through both the general WTO policy rules, such as the need to publish trade rules and regulations, and some of the specific commitments made by China, such as those on uniform application of the trade regime and independent judicial review, as well as the provision of a mechanism through which concerned parties can bring problems of local protectionism to the attention of the central government.[3] Another important contributing factor is China's binding of its entire tariff schedule for goods, almost always at tariff levels below prior applied rates. The transitional review held each year for eight years after China's accession provides additional information about China's trade regime and its reforms during that period.

China's commitments to phase out restrictions on trading rights for all products except a short list of commodities that may remain subject to state trading are important for increasing transparency. Commitments to allow entry into distribution and wholesale services provide further transparency as a side effect of liberalization of these important service activities.

The WTO *principle of undistorted trade* involves disciplines on issues such as subsidies and countervailing measures, antidumping, and safeguards.

China has made more stringent commitments, including one to refrain from using export subsidies on agricultural goods.

The issue of antidumping and safeguard measures is troubling, particularly because it concerns China's market access opportunities. As Patrick A. Messerlin notes in chapter 3, the WTO rules on antidumping are biased toward finding dumping, even where no economically meaningful dumping exists. The situation is worse for China than for other WTO members, because 70 percent of China's exports are products most vulnerable to antidumping measures. Furthermore, China will potentially remain vulnerable, for up to 15 years, to highly discriminatory non–market economy provisions. These provisions dramatically increase the probability that dumping will be found. And when antidumping duties are applied, they are generally much higher than when market economy provisions are used—in the United States, the average 40 percent duty applied using nonmarket economy provisions was more than 10 times as high when normal approaches were used.

A particularly worrying feature of the accession agreement is the product-specific transitional safeguard provisions that may be applied by any WTO Member, and may then trigger actions against diversion of Chinese exports to other markets (Panitchpakdi and Clifford 2002). These provisions are, in a sense, worse than the provisions on non–market economy treatment in that they introduce an entirely new form of protection, targeted specifically against China, more readily triggered than regular safeguards and available to China's trading partners for up to 12 years from the date of accession (Anderson and Lau 2001). The trade diversion measures allowed under this agreement are especially troublesome, because they provide even less procedural protection than is available under regular safeguards.

Messerlin believes that China has two major choices in responding to these measures: to retaliate by, for example, increasing use of antidumping and contesting safeguard actions in dispute settlement; or to mount a concerted campaign for reform of the rules in the Doha negotiations, most particularly in the area of antidumping. Clearly, China will have to contest unjustified actions through dispute settlement. However, a retaliatory approach of launching antidumping actions could be extremely costly to China's economy both by reversing liberalization and by increasing the degree of uncertainty about trade policy. Even though this approach is likely to be politically attractive, as is confirmed by the recent upsurge in antidumping actions in China—and the dramatic upsurge in these actions in developing countries such as Argentina, India, Mexico, and South Africa—the economic costs to China in particular suggest it needs be avoided as much as possible.

If China elects instead to lead a push for reform of the antidumping and safeguard rules that would reduce the abuses of these protectionist measures, it could greatly improve the performance of its own economy in the short run and the global trading system in the longer term. Here Messerlin provides two specific suggestions. On non–market economy treatment, he argues that China could press for new rules on the automatic granting of market economy status in a particular commodity as long as the country meets basic conditions such as low rates of protection, an absence of core gray-area measures, and an absence of state monopoly in the distribution of that good. On antidumping measures more generally, China could put forward, or strongly support, proposals to narrow the use of antidumping measures and to reduce their severity. China might also seek similar relief on the product-specific safeguards.

Preferential treatment for developing countries was a particularly vexing issue throughout the WTO accession negotiations. Although China is clearly a low-income country, because of its size and growth performance WTO members were reluctant to give it full developing-country treatment. In many areas of the agreement, it is likely to have full access to the developing-country provisions, although in some others—such as agriculture where it had to accept a limit of 8.5 percent on *de minimis* domestic support versus the usual 10 percent limit for developing countries—it faces tighter restrictions than other developing countries. At the same time, China obtained specific transitional arrangements in areas, such as the phasing out of quotas and licenses and phased entry of foreign enterprises, that are not generally available to developing-country Members. Special and differential treatment in the form of preferential access to industrial-country markets is not important for China, which increases the importance of multilateral trade reform as a means of creating market access opportunities.

A central aspect of the WTO agreement for China is the TRIPS agreement. In response to its recognized need to stimulate innovation in China and access foreign technology and in response to pressure from its trading partners, China has strengthened its intellectual property rights regime. Since 1990, China has updated its laws on copyrights, trademarks, patents, and trade secrets, and adopted protection for new plant varieties and integrated circuits.

Intellectual property rights involve a fine balance between creating the incentive to innovate and restricting competition in the market for the goods and services that result from innovation. The balance between these two objectives differs between developed and developing countries, so that implementing an appropriate intellectual property regime in a developing country is not simply a matter of emulating the state-of-the-art regime of a developed country. Such a regime may inhibit growth by limiting innovation and diffusion, and may result in excessive transfers to foreign producers of intellectual property. Appropriate regulations are needed to ensure that markets remain competitive without excessive reductions in the incentive to innovate. The TRIPS agreement generally appears to allow the needed flexibility, but taking advantage of such flexibility is a nontrivial task.

In chapter 4, Keith E. Maskus assesses China's intellectual property regime—that is, its provisions for patents, trademarks, trade secrets, and copyrights. He bases his assessment in part on a comparison of China's, intellectual property rights (IPR) with benchmark standards for middle-income developing countries (World Bank 2001, and on interviews with market participants). He concludes that China's TRIPS regime is broadly appropriate to China's situation. He believes, in particular, that China's policy of public procurement of pharmaceuticals at negotiated prices is appropriate for providing public health services. He also concluded that, with the reforms underway at accession, the regime would be fully consistent with TRIPS requirements.

Maskus does, however, raise some important concerns about China's policies related to TRIPS. For example, he believes proposals to extend patent protection to computer software—a level of protection currently provided only in the United States, Japan, and Australia—may be excessive in a young industry such as China's. Maskus also raises the serious problems of IPR enforcement, particularly of trademarks, patents, and trade secrets. He believes these enforcement problems will inhibit the transfer of technology in China and the development of innovative domestic businesses. A broader problem relates to China's current low allocation of resources to research and development and the therefore limited benefits of protecting Chinese innovations. Important issues for the future include enhancing pricing regulations on pharmaceuticals as patent protection becomes stronger and developing a broader competition policy regime to deal with abuses of IPRs such as monopoly pricing and restrictive licensing arrangements.

In chapter 5, Chen Xiwen explores the situation of the agricultural sector in China from the perspective of a senior policymaker. For basic foods, he emphasizes the shift from a supply-constrained environment to a demand-constrained environment. The demand for food has grown very slowly, while the growth of supplies has accelerated. Meanwhile, farmers' incomes grew very slowly in the second half of the 1990s. In this environment, Chen suggests that Chinese agricultural policymakers give priority to, among other things, improving the quality of food produced and moving toward higher-value labor-intensive commodities more suited to China's comparative advantage and to raising farmers' incomes. He sees very clearly that it is important to allow many farmers to leave the agricultural sector, and believes the coordinated expansion of cities and small towns is central to achieving this relocation of labor. Given that the shift from supply-constrained to demand-constrained has been, to a degree, fortuitous and unexpected, a key question is whether the traditional emphasis on food self-sufficiency will reemerge as a policy driver when imports of key agricultural commodities increase.

Economic Impacts of Accession

A comprehensive evaluation of the effects of major changes in trade policy must be based on an assessment of the stance of policy prior to accession—an assessment that was particularly difficult in

agriculture and services in China, and nontrivial in manufacturing. The evaluation must then take into account the implications of the policy measures being introduced. Only then can it take into account the impact of these measures on economic variables such as output and trade levels by sector, and on the income levels of people, and particularly poor people. We first examine the impacts on agriculture, then on manufacturing, then on services.

Agriculture

Many authors have raised concerns about the impact of WTO accession on China's agricultural sector and the many poor people engaged in this sector. Much of this concern has been based on comparisons of China's statutory tariffs on agriculture in the 1990s with the rates agreed in the accession process (e.g., Schmidhuber 2001). Other authors, such as Johnson (2000) and Lin (2000), have recognized that these statutory tariff rates bore little relationship to the protection (or taxation) actually experienced by China's agricultural sector. However, the evidence about the actual rates of protection applying to agriculture has remained extremely limited and frequently contradictory.

Agricultural trade in China has been influenced by a bewildering array of policies on imports and exports, including state trading, designated trading, quotas, licenses, tariffs, and tariff-rate quotas. Many studies have attempted to deal with this problem by summarizing the protective impact of agricultural trade policies through the price distortions created by these measures. The more restrictive the trade measure, in general, the larger will be the gap between the domestic price and the international price.

A number of studies have estimated the magnitude of the agricultural price distortions using the available series on domestic and international prices. Unfortunately, the results obtained have varied wildly. Huang, Chen, and Rozelle (1999), for example, estimated the protection applying to rice, wheat, and maize in the mid-1990s at 4 percent, 20 percent, and 25 percent, respectively. By contrast, Tuan and Cheng (1999) estimated these protection rates to be −29 percent, 62 percent, and 15 percent, respectively. Carter (2000, p. 80) relied on producer price data and found generally negative price distortions. More generally, Carter (2000) and

Martin (2001) believed that WTO accession would require relatively little agricultural liberalization in China, while Schmidhuber (2001) and many others believed that the agricultural liberalization required by accession would be dramatic. Clearly, when scholars reach such different conclusions from the same facts, a new approach is required, especially given that the policy implications are so large.

For this project, Jikun Huang, Scott Rozelle, and Min Chang adopted a new approach by basing their analysis of policy impacts on detailed interviews with participants in China's agricultural markets rather than on readily available price series (see chapter 6). This approach provides a much clearer indication of the implications of agricultural trade policies for product prices, and of the real-world impacts of policies, than would otherwise be possible. Their research reveals, for example, that a major source of the discrepancies in earlier research is differences in the quality of domestic products and those traded internationally. They also identify important features of the trade regime, such as export subsidies for maize and cotton, that have important impacts on product markets. Finally, they raise an important question about the implications of the manner in which the value-added tax (VAT) is collected, at a 13 percent rate, for imported agricultural commodities. It appears that, for administrative reasons, this tax is not collected on domestic agricultural output at the farm level. Rather, it is collected only on intermediate inputs into production.

Once the implications of agricultural policies have been assessed, it is possible to begin to assess the implications of China's accession commitments for agricultural markets. For those products protected by *ad valorem* tariffs, this evaluation is straightforward. The reduction in the tariff corresponds quite directly to the reduction in the domestic price of the good, and this change, together with information on the slope of the import demand curve, can be used to estimate the cost of protection. For those products protected by both a tariff and an export subsidy, it may be necessary to consider changes in both variables. The situation becomes considerably more complex, however, when products are being protected, or are to be protected, using tariff-rate quotas. In this situation, the impact depends greatly on whether the in-quota or out-of-quota tariff determines the price of the good. When the quota will be filled in some years but not in others, the average rate of protection may be a combination of the two tariff rates.

Some key assessments that have been made of the implications of the level of protection and the changes associated with WTO accession are given in table 1.1. The statutory tariff rates for 1998 used by Schmidhuber and others are given in the first column of the table; Huang, Rozelle, and Min's estimates of the actual protection provided in 2001 are

TABLE 1.1   Some Measures of Import Protection in China's Agricultural Sector (percent)

	1998 Statutory Tariffs	2001 Protection	Postaccession Protection
Rice	127	−3.3	−3.3
Wheat	133	12.0	12.0
Maize	130	32.0	32.0
Vegetables and fruits	15	−4.0	−4.0
Oilseeds	132	20.0	3.0
Sugar	30	40.0	20.0
Cotton	3	17.0	20.0
Livestock and meat	35	−15.0	−15.0
Dairy	46	30.0	11.0

Note: The third column of the table shows anticipated average rates of import protection after accession taking into account the reforms required by accession and likely market outcomes.

Sources: Average statutory rates taken from Schmidhuber (2001) and www.chinavista.com. Estimates of protection in 2001 provided by the authors.

given in the second column. The third column shows the anticipated average rates of import protection after accession taking into account the reforms required by accession and the likely market outcomes.

Huang, Rozelle, and Min estimated the average rate of protection for rice to be slightly negative, implying that China's system of state trading for rice operated to tax rice exports slightly in 2001. After accession this rate is expected to remain the same, because accession to WTO does not require reductions in such protection for a state-traded commodity. For wheat, protection averaged an estimated 12 percent. This rate of protection need not be greatly reduced, on average, because it seems likely that wheat imports will exceed the tariff-rate quota reasonably frequently (see Martin 2001), allowing imposition of a tariff of up to 65 percent. For maize, the rate of import protection utilized was higher, at 32 percent, because of an export subsidy. Although, on average, the level of import protection need not change greatly because there is a significant probability that the tariff-rate quota will bind by the end of the decade (Martin 2001), the export subsidy must be abolished, implying a potentially substantial reduction in the price support given to maize. Labor-intensive vegetables and fruits, like livestock products, experienced negative rates of protection in 2001, and the WTO accession commitments are unlikely to require changes in protection.

Oilseeds present an entirely different picture in which the principal form of protection has been a tariff, and the tariff is being reduced substantially. The protection provided to sugar must be reduced to meet China's commitments to a bound tariff of 20 percent. As for cotton, import protection will not change greatly, but export subsidies, such as the 10-percent export subsidy observed in 2001, are ruled out in the future. Protection of livestock and meat could remain negative as a consequence of export restrictions to markets such as Hong Kong. Finally, protection of dairy products can be expected to decline to meet China's tariff-binding commitments.

The reductions in protection between second and third columns of table 1.1 are just one possible outcome in a situation in which rates of agricultural protection can vary substantially, particularly if import levels exceed the tariff-rate quotas. However, the agricultural protection measures illustrate the importance of the discretion remaining to China's policymakers even after implementation of such comprehensive commitments on agriculture. Removal of the negative protection applying to labor-intensive products would also be consistent with WTO rules, and is likely to be particularly helpful for employment in rural areas, as well as economic efficiency.

Participation by China in the WTO agricultural negotiations being conducted under the Doha Development Agenda could potentially reinforce these benefits by opening large, and currently highly protected, markets for China's labor-intensive agricultural exports. Unfortunately, the high rates of agricultural protection that arose when GATT rules on agriculture were extremely weak mean that China faces barriers to its agricultural exports that are four times higher than those it faces on its other merchandise exports (Martin 2001).

In chapter 7, Kym Anderson, Jikun Huang, and Elena Ianchovichina examine the implications of China's agricultural commitments for agricultural protection and for the agricultural sector. They find that the basic WTO accession commitments to reduce agricultural import protection and eliminate agricultural subsidies will make those farm households dependent on agriculture worse off relative to urban households. If China elects as well to remove the negative protection of important commodities such as rice, vegetables, and meats, then returns to unskilled rural labor, and to farmland would rise slightly, and the impact of accession and the elimination of negative protection on rural wages would be −0.5 percent instead of the −0.7 percent observed in the accession case. They also highlight the importance of China pursuing improvements in agricultural market access, citing results from Yu and Frandsen (2002) that suggest that agricultural liberalization by member countries of the Organisation for Economic Co-operation and Development (OECD) would benefit China and improve its agricultural trade balance.

Industrial Products

In chapter 13, Ianchovichina and Martin examine the reductions in protection under way in manufacturing and services as well as in agriculture. Within industry, they find that accession builds on the substantial reductions in tariffs undertaken during the 1990s, when weighted average tariffs on manufactures fell from 46.5 percent in 1992 to 25 percent in 1995. By the time of accession in 2001, weighted average tariffs on manufactures had fallen to around 13 percent. With full implementation of China's accession commitments, they will fall to 6.9 percent. The six-percentage-point reduction in average tariffs to be implemented after accession is important, but very small relative to the 33-percentage-point reduction undertaken since 1992.

The largest reductions in industrial tariffs are required for beverages and tobacco—an almost 28-percentage-point reduction from 2001 levels. In automobiles, the reduction was just over 15 percentage points. Although large, these reductions were very much smaller than those undertaken since 1995. The reduction in protection to the automobile sector is particularly important because of the high profile of this industry and its pervasive linkages throughout the economy. Other industries in which substantial reductions in tariffs were required included textiles, clothing, electronics, and light manufactures. Many of these industries are relatively labor-intensive ones in which China has a comparative advantage and in which liberalization will help maintain efficiency and competitiveness.

The liberalization considered in this project is, apart from the export quotas on textiles and clothing, focused entirely on tariffs. This emphasis understates the degree of liberalization resulting from China's accession, because it ignores the abolition of nontariff barriers such as designated trading, quotas, and licenses. The seriousness of this exclusion is much less than it would have been in earlier years because of the dramatic reduction in the coverage of nontariff barriers in China—the frequency of import licenses, in particular, fell from almost half[4] in the late 1980s (Lardy 2002) to under 5 percent in 2001. Given the great uncertainty about the protective impacts of nontariff barriers in China and their limited remaining coverage, Ianchovichina and Martin concluded that it was perhaps better to use tariffs only when considering liberalization, and therefore to present something of a lower-bound estimate of the benefits of the liberalization associated with accession.

It is also important to take into account the reduction in the barriers facing China's exports of textiles and clothing. Because these barriers require an exporter to purchase an export quota—or to forego the opportunity to sell quotas already held—they impose a cost on exports that is similar to an export tax. Based on information on quota prices, this tax was estimated to be about 15 percent for clothing and 10 percent for textiles.[5]

The estimates of the extent of merchandise trade liberalization used in this study omit some important and potential elements of trade policy. One is the possibility of antidumping and safeguards measures being applied against China. Another is the increasing use of measures of this type in China. The potential use of the product-specific safeguards against China would be particularly important in this respect, because no such measure targeted specifically at China existed prior to China's accession. The risk that China will increase its use of antidumping and safeguard measures beyond the current levels is also a concern for development policy. Such an action would be a triumph of a rules-focused approach to WTO implementation—it is legal; therefore, we should do it!!!—over the sharp focus on promoting development that has characterized China's trade policy agenda since the beginning of the reform era.

Services

Trade in services was a key area in China's WTO accession negotiations. To obtain a clear understanding of the implications of China's commitments in this area, and the potential usefulness of the WTO process for China's economic development, we consider first Mattoo's overview of China's commitments in services (chapter 8), and then detailed case studies of logistics (chapter 9), telecommunications (chapter 10), and the financial sector (chapter 11).

Chapter 8 by Aaditya Mattoo compares the liberalization undertaken by China in services with that undertaken by other groups of countries, and it concludes that China's services reform is the most radical ever negotiated in the WTO. In cross-border trade (mode 1), consumption abroad (mode 2), and establishment trade (mode 3), China has made more commitments in more service sectors than the industrial countries, other developing countries, or the group of countries that recently acceded to the WTO. Of course, any assessment of the importance of these commitments depends on their implementation, which has drawn reservations from Whalley (2003). However, the first two reviews of China's services commitments at the WTO appear to indicate that considerable progress has been made (see WTO 2003a, 2003b).

Mattoo notes, however, that China's commitments to service market liberalization were not indiscriminate. The number of sectors with guaranteed unrestricted access is lower for the first two modes than that in most other countries, and essentially zero for mode 3. An important feature of China's commitments is that they focus on market access and provide national treatment in not discriminating between domestic and foreign suppliers.

Frequently applied restrictions on the establishment of services enterprises include:

- restrictions on the form of establishment
- restrictions on geographic scope
- regulatory requirements.

Restrictions on the form of establishment, such as requirements for joint ventures, have a long history in China and have frequently been justified as a means of achieving technology transfer or as means of obtaining a share of monopoly rents. Mattoo, however, points out that requirements to form joint ventures might inhibit the transfer of technology. He also points out that a more thorough approach to the problem of monopoly rents would be to ensure that competition between firms, whether domestic or foreign, eliminates these rents.

Restrictions on geographic scope also have a long history—from an era when experimentation with market-oriented approaches had to be isolated because of the inconsistencies between, for example, planned and market prices. Confining foreign ventures, such as insurance, to five cities for five years might encourage agglomeration of these activities in these cities that will not be reversed when the geographic restrictions are later lifted. Moreover, such an approach may reduce the opportunities for other parts of China, such as interior cities with a potential comparative advantage in these activities, to get started in these activities. Yet China's WTO commitments represent only a lower bound, and so they have not prevented

Chinese authorities from moving ahead faster than the minimum to which they have committed in some cases. Given the risks of exacerbating the already substantial inequalities between coastal and interior provinces, there would appear to be good development reasons to phase out these geographic restrictions more quickly than is required by the WTO commitments.

Imposing regulatory requirements is an important role of government. Some of the most important objectives of regulations are to make competition work, improve the availability of information to consumers, and ensure universal service. Making competition work is particularly important in network industries such as telecommunications, where individual firms frequently do not find it in their interest to allow interconnection by new firms. Improving the availability of information is especially important in financial services. Finally, developing efficient provisions on universal service is important for ensuring that all parts of China have access to telecommunications services.

In chapter 9, Wenping Luo and Christopher Findlay provide a detailed assessment of the reforms required by WTO accession in the range of service activities that make up the logistics chain. They note that although China has made substantial progress in many of the component activities, logistics costs are disproportionately high in China, and service quality is lower than is desirable, in part as an enduring legacy of the planned economy. Luo and Findlay conclude that logistics accounts for 30–40 percent of the wholesale cost of manufactured goods, as contrasted with 5–20 percent in the United States, implying that the scope for gain from liberalization is particularly large. High logistics costs are a particularly important problem for people in the poorer areas of China, whose ability to trade, and consequently their real incomes, are significantly reduced by these excessive costs.

China's WTO commitments on logistics apply to a range of specific General Agreement on Trade in Services (GATS) service sectors, including packaging and courier services; maritime and rail transportation; freight forwarding; and storage and warehousing services. The commitments made in these sectors promise to increase competition in some key areas, including road transport, rail transport, warehousing, and freight forwarding. The breadth of these commitments also provides a much stronger basis for development of integrated third-party logistics firms able to reduce the costs and increase the quality of logistics services in China. If the envisaged reductions in logistics costs are brought to fruition, Luo and Findlay conclude that the costs of a wide range of goods and services might be reduced by about 10 percent.

Yet the commitments outlined in the GATS agreement are not sufficient to achieve the full potential of logistics in China. Regulatory reforms are needed to remove discrimination against particular enterprise types, to separate local administrations from enterprises, and to eliminate local protectionism. In addition, substantial investments in infrastructure are needed to improve the timeliness and reduce the cost of providing logistics services.

In chapter 10, Mari Pangestu and Debbie Mrongowius explore China's commitments in telecommunications—commitments that take on particular importance given that China is expected to be the largest market for telecommunications in the world by 2010. These commitments are profound in that they allow foreign entry to a wide range of activities that are currently closed to foreign investment. Furthermore, this entry takes place in a sector that was monopolized by China Telecom until 1994 and is currently dominated by a small number of state-owned firms (see DeWoskin 2001).

In basic telecommunications, China has committed to the disciplines of the WTO reference paper on the regulatory framework for telecommunications. The objective is to create a competitive environment in which interconnection between systems is allowed under reasonable and nondiscriminatory conditions, and it allows for universal service provisions. It also requires the existence of a regulator independent of the telecom provider and sets criteria for licensing entry and for allocating scarce commodities such as the mobile telephone spectrum.

In the context of a basic telecommunications system governed in line with the regulatory paper, China's other GATS commitments cover value-added services such as voice mail and online information services; mobile voice and data services; and domestic and international services such as private leased circuit services. Most of these services are initially subjected to a combination of ownership restrictions and geographic restrictions within China. Although the geographic restrictions will be phased out over several years, China has not committed to allowing more than 49 percent foreign ownership for important services such as mobile telephony. Because allowing higher levels of foreign ownership would be consistent with China's GATS obligations, China may do so in the future if such a move appears to promise worthwhile gains in a particular activity.

Clearly, the challenge of establishing a telecommunications sector that makes the maximum contribution to China's overall growth and development will require further expansion of the regulatory framework. Pangestu and Mrongowius believe the central issues here will include ensuring the independence of the regulator, ensuring that interconnection works adequately, and making pricing regulations more flexible.

In chapter 11, Deepak Bhattasali examines the implications of China's commitments in the financial sector, including banking, security trading, fund management, and insurance. According to Bhattasali, reforms up to 1997 focused on institutional diversification and strengthened administrative oversight. Since 1997, reforms have addressed the portfolio problems of the banks and governance of the financial sector in preparation for WTO accession. In 2001, however, the four large state banks still accounted for 67 percent of bank deposits and 56 percent of total financial assets. The share of loans going to small and medium-size non–state enterprises—the most dynamic part of the economy—remains small, a finding evident in enterprise survey work reported by Dollar (2002). Another key concern is the dearth of the information needed to assess the performance of the financial sector.

Although a large number of foreign banks was active in China on the eve of accession, they operated almost exclusively on an offshore or enclave basis and accounted for less than 3 percent of bank assets. However, two years after accession they became able to provide local currency services to Chinese enterprises, and they will become eligible to offer these services to individuals within five years. Other areas of financial services, such as stockbroking, fund management, and insurance are also being opened up on quite short timetables.

Like other scholars such as Langlois (2001), Bhattasali believes that the reforms agreed upon in this vitally important sector were a clear attempt to increase competition, performance, and the range of products available in financial services. The key challenges will lie in managing the transition to a market-based system without serious problems or a financial crises. He believes that the state banks will come under serious pressures from their nonperforming loans, weak management systems, low operating margins, and the strong competition they will face. His assessment is that financial re-engineering and fairly radical actions to reduce operating costs will be required, but that, given suitable reforms, the rehabilitation of the state banks is unlikely to present major problems.

Impacts on the Economy

Because China's reforms are so broad-ranging, and their economy-wide interactions are so extensive, they must be evaluated on an economy-wide basis. In chapter 13, Ianchovichina and Martin assess the impacts of liberalization on agriculture, manufactures, and services. Previous research, however, revealed that undertaking any such assessment in a satisfactory manner required special attention to the motor vehicle sector. In an analysis in which they did not account for the restructuring of this industry, Ianchovichina and Martin (2001) found that output in this industry would decline absolutely over the period to 2007, despite the strong increases in the Chinese demand for automobiles and the shift in China's comparative advantage to more capital- and skill-intensive products such as motor vehicles.

In their contribution to this study, Joseph F. Francois and Dean Spinanger examine China's motor vehicle industry (chapter 12). Like previous studies such those by Harwit (2001) and the Chinese Academy of Engineering and National Academy of Engineering/National Research Council (2003), they conclude that it has been shaped by policies that have encouraged market segmentation and suboptimal plant size—a structure that is seen frequently in countries with highly protected automobile industries. As a result, the industry is very inefficient, with most plants operating well below global standards for efficient production. Unless these problems can be overcome, the industry is expected to respond to the fall in protection, and the increased competition for labor from expanding sectors such as textiles and clothing, with a

sharp decline in output achieved through widespread plant closures.

Francois and Spinanger conclude that restructuring in the industry to achieve scale economies in final assembly would reduce costs by about 20 percent. This reduction would more than reverse the negative impact on output of the reduction in protection from 1997 levels, allowing the industry to expand relative to the no-accession case—and to expand dramatically as China's growth and shifting comparative advantage shift resources into sectors such as motor vehicles. There also would be important changes within the motor vehicle sector. According to the analysis by Francois and Spinanger, the increase in efficiency of the final assembly industry relative to the production of intermediate parts is likely to increase the demand for imported parts substantially, with their share rising from 39 percent to 52 percent. If the restructuring of the industry is achieved successfully, exports of finished motor vehicles are projected to increase very rapidly, resulting in an increase in total exports of vehicles and parts of over US$4 billion[6] a year. Clearly, the reforms associated with accession will require major changes throughout the industry and considerable restructuring, although this process has perhaps been eased by the very rapid growth in demand during recent years.

In chapter 13, Ianchovichina and Martin analyze the impacts of liberalization associated with accession in agriculture, manufactures, and services,[7] and the opportunities arising from the elimination of the quotas against China's (and other countries') exports of textiles and clothing. Their analysis takes into account China's important export processing arrangements, and it builds on the labor market study by Sicular and Zhao (chapter 14), a study by Shi Xinzheng (2002) on labor markets, and the Francois and Spinanger analysis of automobile industry restructuring (chapter 12). The resulting changes in the specification of their model greatly increase the realism of their analysis and have very important implications for their results.

Ianchovichina and Martin divide the effects of WTO accession into a component of liberalization undertaken between 1995 and 2001 in preparation for accession and the remaining component to be undertaken after 2001 in order to meet China's accession commitments. The choice of 1995 as a starting period is somewhat arbitrary in view of the fact that China reformed its trade regime throughout the 1990s. However, 1995 was an important turning point, when China had to forgo its hope of resuming its seat in the GATT and apply as a newcomer to the WTO under a process much more focused on the commercial implications of the accession package. Ianchovichina and Martin recognize that China's product mix and the world's demand for China's exports are changing rapidly. They therefore superimpose the impact of liberalization on a situation in which China's industrial structure and output and trade patterns are veering sharply toward more capital- and skill-intensive goods in response to high rates of investment and rapid growth in educational levels.

The authors find that the liberalization associated with WTO accession results in substantial growth in trade relative to output, with the total volume of exports rising by 17 percent as a consequence of the liberalization after 2001. The most rapid growth in exports is in apparel; exports expand by over 100 percent in response to the abolition of the export quotas on clothing. Exports of most agricultural products rise because of a decline in agricultural input costs and constraints on the out-migration of labor from the agricultural sector. However, exports of plant-based fibers (predominantly cotton) are projected to fall in response to the increase in demand for use in export production. Feed grain exports also fall because of the abolition of the export subsidy on exports of maize. Exports of automobiles rise substantially because of the increase in the efficiency of the sector as it exploits economies of scale and the greater trade exposure of the industry in the more liberalized postaccession economy. None of the increases in exports takes into account the possible benefits to China of being able to expand its market access through participation in WTO negotiations. The expansion in textile and clothing exports is, in fact, a delayed benefit from the Uruguay Round, previously denied to China as a nonmember of the WTO.

Imports rise in a range of sectors in which there are substantial reductions in trade barriers, including beverages and tobacco, processed food, textiles, clothing, oilseeds, dairy products, and sugar. Because Ianchovichina and Martin have represented trade liberalization in services as reducing

trade barriers, there are also substantial increases in imports of services. The increase in imports of beverages and tobacco is the largest because of the sharp reduction in the tariffs for these commodities.

The biggest change in employment after accession is an increase in employment in the apparel sector of more than 50 percent. Employment in the textile sector and in plant fibers also increase to meet the demand from the apparel sector. Trade reform leads to small reductions in employment in most agricultural sectors and in manufacturing sectors such as petrochemicals, metals, and automobiles. Overall, however, the movements of labor between sectors are generally small relative to the changes in trade patterns.

The overall welfare gains to China are substantial, particularly from the liberalization undertaken between 1995 and 2001 to prove China's bona fides and to prepare for accession. The benefit from the liberalization undertaken during this period is estimated to be a continuing gain of about $30 billion per year. The smaller reduction in protection between 2001 and the end of the implementation period will generate incremental gains to China of $10 billion a year. The measured gains in export and income growth are very much lower-bound estimates in that they ignore the benefits from abolition of nontariff barriers and they involve serious aggregation biases. Moreover, models of this type appear to greatly understate the implications of major trade liberalizations, particularly those associated with the rapid emergence of new products (Kehoe 2002), which Martin and Manole (2003) have found to be a major feature of China's reform experience.

The gains from reform do not accrue evenly within China, with wages of skilled and unskilled urban workers rising modestly and wages for unskilled farm workers declining by 0.7 percent in real terms. Ianchovichina and Martin also examine the implications of some potential complementary policies that might be able to deal with this problem. Reform of the *hukou* system (a system of residence permits regulating movement between urban and rural residence) and other labor market barriers is highly desirable because of the inefficiencies and inequities associated with this segmentation of the labor market. However, such reform increases in importance after WTO accession because of the partial liberalization of the agricultural sector, which increases the pressures for workers to leave agriculture. Adding abolition of the *hukou* system to the policy package is found to result in an increase in rural wages of almost 17 percent. *Hukou* removal completely overwhelms the reduction in rural wages associated with trade liberalization, as an estimated 28 million agricultural workers leave the agricultural sector. Complete abolition of the *hukou* system would put downward pressure on unskilled wages in urban areas, although this reduction of an estimated 3.8 percent would be much smaller than the gain to rural workers.

Another complementary reform that Ianchovichina and Martin consider is an expansion in access to education—a change that would help to raise unskilled wages in both urban and rural areas. Improving agricultural technology is another policy option with potentially large benefits for poor rural households that are able to adopt the new production techniques.

The results of this quantitative analysis are highly stylized, because they assume that enterprises and households are able to adjust successfully to the changes in incentives created by WTO accession. As the OECD (2002) has pointed out, successfully making these changes is likely to require considerable strengthening of the economic system in areas such as enterprise governance and reform of the banking system.

Impacts on Households and on Poverty

The simplest possible approach to capturing the effects of WTO accession at the household level requires an assessment of its impacts on the prices consumers pay; on the prices that owners of labor, capital, and other factors receive for their resources; and on the government's ability to provide transfers or public goods. In addition, it is useful to be able to assess the ability of households to adjust to the changes resulting from accession, perhaps by changing occupations or activities.

Because ongoing work on trade and poverty has found that impacts through factor markets are consistently more important than impacts through consumer prices, it is important to examine factor market effects carefully. This is especially true in China because of the large income differences

between urban and rural workers and because of the explicit policy barriers resisting the movement of labor between urban and rural sectors.

In chapter 14, Terry Sicular and Yaohui Zhao examine the options that households in China face in selling their labor—the most important resource of the poor. They find substantial differences between the earnings of rural and urban households. Although some of these differences stem from differences in the quality of labor and other resources, much is attributable to differences in the earnings received for resources of the same quality—a finding that is consistent with the existence of substantial barriers between urban and rural labor markets. These barriers appear to be particularly strong for poorer households, contributing both to depressed income levels and to difficulty in adapting to changes in economic opportunities.

Another important feature of Chinese labor markets captured by Sicular and Zhao is the reluctance of China's farm households to transfer labor from agriculture to other sectors. Although such reluctance is frequently observed in countries that are attempting to transfer labor out of agriculture, it is exacerbated in China by restrictions on the sale of farmland usage rights. Permanent movement is likely to require families to relinquish their land rights without compensation. A main objective of the study by Sicular and Zhao is to provide estimates of the responsiveness of rural workers to changes in relative returns. They find rural households quite responsive to movements in agricultural returns relative to market wage rates, with an estimated response elasticity of 2.67, but the response to changes in the ratio of agricultural and nonfarm business returns is much lower. Although labor is not perfectly mobile between urban and rural labor markets, these results make clear that it is also far from immobile.

Two studies in this volume integrate the findings of the different studies and analyze their implications for poverty. They make these assessments by using general equilibrium models of China's economy to evaluate the implications of reform for the prices and factor returns faced by China's households and then examining the effects on particular households.

The study by Shaohua Chen and Martin Ravallion presented in chapter 15 considers the impact of WTO accession on income distribution and poverty drawing on the simulation model results provided by Ianchovichina and Martin. This study uses a sample of 84,000 households—17,000 urban and 67,000 rural—from surveys by China's National Bureau of Statistics. The price impacts implied by Ianchovichina and Martin's Global Trade Analysis Project (GTAP) model analysis are applied to the households, taking into account the impacts on the prices households must pay for their consumption goods and purchases of inputs, and the prices they receive for their sales of goods and of labor and other factors. The loss of government revenue from falling tariffs is restored very simply a tax that raises the price of all consumption goods to maintain government revenues.

Chen and Ravallion's analysis is focused on the short run, in which households are limited in their responses to changes in prices, and on the period after accession in 2001, when the impact on the average household and on poverty rates was very small. They consider the impacts on individual households and find sharp differences, particularly between urban and rural households. Most urban households, and especially the relatively poor urban households, gain from WTO accession, with the poorest urban group gaining by about 1.5 percent of initial incomes. This is not true for rural households. The very poorest rural households experience a sharp reduction in their living standards—about 6 percent for the poorest percentile. This reduction reflects a combination of falling rural wages and increases in the prices of consumption goods—items consumed in substantial quantities by members of this group. Overall, almost 90 percent of urban households gain from WTO accession, while over three-quarters of rural households lose, although the losses are generally quite small. The estimated losses to rural households are larger in the Northeast than in other areas, with average losses to rural households of over 2 percent in Heilongjiang and Jilin.

The study by Thomas W. Hertel, Fan Zhai, and Zhi Wang in chapter 16 uses a model of the Chinese economy that takes into account important features such as the duty exemptions for intermediate goods used in the production of exports. Because of limitations on the availability of household data for analytical purposes, it focuses on the three relatively diverse provinces of Liaoning, Sichuan, and Guangdong. This study

takes a longer-run perspective than the Chen and Ravallion study, and it assumes that households are more able to move labor between agriculture and other activities, with an elasticity of transformation of 2.67 for the movement of labor between agricultural and nonagricultural activities. Like Chen and Ravallion, the authors find that urban households benefit substantially more than rural households from WTO accession. However, in this longer-run analysis even agriculture-specialized households gain on average. Only in a shorter-run experiment, where households are much less able to move between sectors, do some agricultural households suffer small losses.

Hertel, Zhai, and Wang also consider a range of complementary policy reforms that might help to deal with adverse impacts on rural households. Abolition of the *hukou* system is found to be strongly beneficial for rural workers, as are expansions in education. Both of these reforms are found to be substantially favorable for rural households.

In chapter 17, Athar Hussain analyzes the Chinese system of social protection and its value as a safety net for shocks of the type involved in WTO accession. In his view, China's social protection systems should not attempt to compensate losers from the reforms; it is simply too difficult to determine the magnitude of compensation that is appropriate. Rather, Hussain believes the focus should be on preventing poverty. He notes that the wide distribution of land ownership by rural households has played an important role in maintaining living standards and providing insurance against adverse shocks, but views this insurance as less valuable against shocks to grain prices resulting from liberalization than against shocks such as the loss of an urban job.

Hussain observes that China's systems for income maintenance and poverty relief have three broad characteristics: a stark dichotomy between urban and rural systems; a focus on the reduction of absolute poverty; and a high degree of decentralization in financing. He finds the system in urban areas relatively comprehensive, but views the system in rural areas as seriously deficient. The locally funded system in place in many areas is unable to deal with a large-scale shock of the type likely to occur with accession to WTO—"the social safety net is full of holes." Hussain goes on to argue for extending basic safety net protection into rural areas. One first step might be to extend a mechanism like the urban unemployment insurance schemes to wage employees in township and village enterprises. However, Hussain believes the central element is the development of a national scheme, such as the Minimum Living Standard Scheme, that targets poor rural households.

Conclusions

China's WTO accession agreement calls for substantial reductions in protection, for a strengthening of intellectual property rights protection, and for adoption of a framework of trade rules at home and abroad to facilitate trade growth. While requiring many policy changes, it leaves open a wide range of policy choices and, in these, China should continue to focus strongly on its development needs—the central perspective that has guided the steady transformation of its trade regime, and its economy generally as it moves from a planned to a market economy.

One key concern in the accession agreement is the provisions on antidumping and safeguards. The nonmarket provisions that countries are permitted to invoke against China for up to 15 years are likely to result in antidumping duties substantially higher than those in other countries—in a situation in which China faces seven times as many antidumping actions per dollar of exports as the United States. The special product safeguards applicable against China for the next 12 years are a new form of protection, applicable only against China. The provisions on trade diversion lack even basic procedural restraints, and pose a potentially serious threat to China's export development. The temptation to retaliate, particularly with antidumping actions of its own, will be strong but would damage China more than other countries. A better option for China would be to seek reform of WTO rules in these areas.

China's TRIPS arrangements generally appear to have been implemented in a manner consistent with both the legal requirements of the agreement and China's development needs. They generally provide a reasonable balance between incentives to innovate and access to those innovations. Some concerns have emerged about proposals that might strengthen protection too much to allow access to innovations such as those for patent protection on

software and about problems with inadequate enforcement of IPRs that reduces the incentive to provide innovations.

Agriculture is being liberalized by less than was suggested by some earlier studies that began from the assumption that agricultural protection would be reduced from initial statutory tariff levels. Significant liberalizations have been achieved in areas such as maize, cotton, and sugar, and it appears that the adjustment pressures in these industries will be significant. There will, however, be opportunities to expand exports of some labor-intensive exports as part of a broader policy reform and by seeking increases in agricultural market access in the Doha negotiations.

The industrial sector will face substantial adjustment pressures in key sectors such as automobiles, and beverages and tobacco, where external protection is being substantially reduced. Restructuring of scale-intensive sectors such as the automobile sector will be essential and can generate substantial productivity gains. Overall, however, most of the adjustment in this industry has already occurred, and what remains is an expansion of both imports and exports.

China's GATS commitments represent perhaps the most thorough-going liberalization of the services trade ever undertaken in the GATT. The range of commitments is extremely broad, although some commitments involve restrictions on ownership, business scope, or region. Critical sectors such as telecommunications, logistics, and financial services are to be confronted with renewed competition, and they are likely to see a burst of innovation and productivity growth as restructuring proceeds.

The impacts of China's WTO commitments—and China's successful economic development—depend heavily on the ability of China's labor markets to reallocate labor from agriculture to other activities. Analysis reported in this volume concludes that these markets are adversely affected by a range of regulations such as the *hukou* system. Other features of the labor market, such as the "tie" to the land where households have use rights to land but cannot sell it because property rights are not sufficiently well defined, restrict the mobility of labor out of agriculture. These features of the economy inhibit the adjustment needed after accession and increase the vulnerability of poor people to downturns in agricultural prices.

We report in this volume two studies that evaluate the impacts of trade reform on poverty. Both studies find that the rural sector is more vulnerable to this reform than is the urban population, and both conclude that urban households benefit more than rural households from the package of reforms associated with accession. The study that looks at the shorter term finds rural households are more subject to negative shocks. Although these impacts are in general relatively small, they affect most rural households. The effects are largest in proportional terms among the poorest households, and tend to be geographically concentrated, particularly in the northeastern provinces such as Heilongjiang and Jilin. The second study provides a relatively optimistic longer-run picture, where virtually all households gain from the reform.

These models and the overall modeling studies suggest that the answer to mitigating these problems is to include reforms such as reductions in the barriers against movement of labor out of agriculture. Removal of the *hukou* system would increase rural wages substantially, with a relatively modest negative effect on higher-income households. A range of other policy options directed toward improving the welfare of rural people, such as rural research and development, improvements in rural infrastructure, expansion of educational opportunities in rural areas, and improvements in rural health services, are all fully WTO consistent and could have powerful beneficial effects in both the short and the long run. As an important WTO member, China also has an opportunity to press for greater market access opportunities for labor-intensive agricultural exports that could help generate employment in rural areas.

The network of social protection measures in China is quite underdeveloped and a constraint on the country's ability to grow while dealing with widely held concerns about the need to compensate the potential "losers" from the policy reforms. Particular attention should be given to strengthening the social welfare systems available to rural residents.

China's accession to the WTO was a defining moment for both China and the WTO. It necessarily moves the process of trade reform in China away from an incremental approach to one incorporating quite detailed rules for trade policy. It is important to combine the spirit of China's reform process—with its emphasis on continuing reform designed to improve economic performance—with the rules-oriented approach of the WTO. The benefits of accession to China will be substantial, but reaping them will require continuing reforms in the adventurous spirit of China's economic reforms—reforms that focus on economic development and go beyond trade policy into areas such as labor market reform and rural development.

Notes

1. See chapter 13 for a discussion of the methodology used for these computations.

2. Although China's transitional review at the WTO allows other WTO members to seek information and raise concerns about China's trade policies, the process is multilateral, and China can raise concerns about implementation of other Members' commitments in the protocol.

3. Although internal protectionism appears to have abated in recent years, survey results suggest that problems remain, particularly local government interventions in labor markets and administrative discrimination (DRC 2003). These interventions appear to hinder foreign investment (Amiti and Javorcik 2003).

4. Two-thirds of exports were also subject to licensing.

5. See www.chinaquota.com.

6. All dollar amounts are current U.S. dollars.

7. The estimated liberalization of services is very crudely approximated by halving the barriers to trade in these activities estimated by Francois.

References

The word *processed* describes informally reproduced works that may not be commonly available through libraries.

Amiti, M., and Javorcik, B. 2003. "Trade Costs and Location of Foreign Firms in China." Paper presented at Workshop on National Market Integration. Development Research Centre of State Council and World Bank. Beijing, September 6.

Anderson, S., and C. Lau. 2001. "Hedging Hopes with Fears in China's Accession to the World Trade Organization: The Transitional Special Product Safeguard for Chinese Exports." Powell, Goldstein, Frazer, and Murphy LLP, Geneva. Processed.

Carter, C. 2000. "China's Trade Integration and Impacts on Factor Markets." In Organisation for Economic Co-operation and Development, *China's Agriculture in the International Trading System, OECD Proceedings*. April.

Chinese Academy of Engineering and National Academy of Engineering/National Research Council. 2003. *Personal Cars and China*. Washington, D.C.: National Academies Press.

Chun, C., B. Fleisher, and E. Parker. 2001. "The Impact of China's Entry into the WTO: Overview." *China Economic Review* 11(4): 319–22.

DeWoskin, K. 2001. "The WTO and the Telecommunications Sector in China." *China Quarterly* 167: 630–54.

Dollar, D. 2002. "Improving the investment Climate in China." Presentation to the Conference on China's Investment Climate, Beijing, December 3.

DRC (Development Research Centre). 2003. "Measures, Objects and Degrees of Local Protection in the Chinese Market—An

Analysis Based on a Sample Survey." Paper presented at Workshop on National Market Integration. Development Research Centre of State Council and World Bank. Beijing, September 6.

Fewsmith, J. 2001. "The Political and Social Implications of China's Accession to the WTO." *China Quarterly* 167: 573–91.

Gilbert, J., and M. Wahl. 2002. "Applied General Equilibrium Assessments of Trade Liberalization in China." *World Economy* 25(5): 697–731.

Harwit, E. 2001. "The Impact of WTO Membership on the Automobile Industry in China." *China Quarterly* 167: 655–70.

Huang, J., M. Chen, and S. Rozelle. 1999. "Reform, Trade Liberalization and Their Impacts on China's Agriculture." Paper presented at International Agricultural Trade Research Consortium Symposium on "China's Agricultural Trade Policy: Issues, Analysis and Global Consequences." San Francisco, June 25–26.

Ianchovichina, E., and W. Martin. 2001. "Trade Liberalization in China's Accession to WTO." *Journal of Economic Integration* 16(4): 421–45.

Jin, Liqun. 2002. "China: One Year into the WTO Process." Paper presented at World Bank, Washington, D.C., October 22. Available at www.worldbank.org/wbi/B-SPAN/docs/IMF-WB_address_final.pdf.

Johnson, D. G. 2000. "The WTO and Agriculture in China." *China Economic Review* 11: 402–4.

Kehoe, T. 2002. "How Well Did Computable General Equilibrium Models Predict the Effects of NAFTA?" Paper presented at Conference on General Equilibrium Modeling. Cowles Foundation, Yale University. April.

Lardy, N. 2002. *Integrating China into the Global Economy.* Washington, D.C.: Brookings Institution Press.

Langlois, J. 2001. "The WTO and China's Financial System." *China Quarterly* 167: 610–29.

Lin, J. Y. 2000. "WTO Accession and China's Agriculture." *China Economic Review* 11: 405–8.

Martin, W. 2001. "Implications of Reform and WTO Accession for China's Agricultural Policies." *Economics of Transition* 9(3): 717–42.

Martin, W., and E. Ianchovichina. 2001. "Implications of China's Accession to the WTO for China and the WTO." *World Economy* 24(9).

Martin, W., and V. Manole. 2003. "China's Emergence as the Workshop of the World." Paper presented at Stanford Center for International Development Conference on Chinese Economic Policy Reform. Stanford University, September 18–20.

McKibbin, W., and K. Tang. 2000. "Trade and Financial Reform in China: Impacts on the World Economy." *World Economy* 23(8).

OECD (Organisation for Economic Co-operation and Development). 2002. *China in the World Economy: The Domestic Policy Challenges.* Paris.

Panitchpakdi, S., and M. Clifford. 2002. *China and the WTO: Changing China, Changing World Trade.* Singapore: John Wiley and Sons.

Schmidhuber, J. 2001. "Changes in China's Agricultural Trade Policy Regime: Impacts on Agricultural Production, Consumption, Prices, and Trade." In Organisation for Economic Co-operation and Development, *China's Agriculture in the International Trading System, OECD Proceedings.* April.

Shafaeddin, S. 2004. "Is China's Accession to WTO Threatening Exports of Developing Countries?" *China Economic Review,* forthcoming.

Shi Xinzheng. 2002. "Empirical Research on Urban-Rural Income Differentials: A Case of China." Peking University. Processed.

Tuan, F., and G. Cheng. 1999. "A Review of China's Agricultural Trade Policy." Paper presented at International Agricultural Trade Research Consortium Symposium on China's Agricultural Trade Policy: Issues, Analysis and Global Consequences. San Francisco, June 25–26.

Wen, J. 2004. "Report on the Work of the Government." Report delivered at the second session of the National People's Congress. Beijing, March 5.

Whalley, J. 2003. "Liberalization in China's Key Service Sectors Following WTO Accession: Some Scenarios and Issues of Measurement" NBER Working Paper 10143, National Bureau of Economic Research, Cambridge, Mass.

Woo, W. T. 2001. "Recent Claims of China's Economic Exceptionalism: Reflections Inspired by WTO Accession." *China Economic Review* 12: 107–36.

World Bank. 2001. *Global Economic Prospects 2002: Making Trade Work for the World's Poor.* Washington D.C: World Bank.

WTO (World Trade Organization). 2002. "Transitional Review under Article 18 of the Protocol of Accession of the Peoples' Republic of China." G/C/W/438. Geneva.

———. 2003a. "Report of the Meeting Held on 5 December 2003." Council for Trade in Services, S/C/M/69. Geneva.

———. 2003b. "Report of the Meeting held on 1 December 2003. Council for Trade in Financial Services, S/FIN/M/43. Geneva.

Yu, W., and S. E. Frandsen. 2002. "China's WTO Commitments in Agriculture: Does the Impact Depend on OECD Agricultural Policies?" Paper presented at Fifth Conference on Global Economic Analysis. Taipei, June 5–7.

PART I

POLICY REFORMS ASSOCIATED WITH ACCESSION

2

WHAT CHINA'S WTO ACCESSION IS ALL ABOUT

Jeffrey L. Gertler

With the gavelling of the accession package at the conclusion of the Working Party meeting on September 17, 2001, the negotiation on China's accession to the World Trade Organization (WTO) finally was concluded. The WTO Ministerial Conference subsequently approved the terms of China's accession in Doha, Qatar, on November 10, 2001, and the Chinese Government notified its acceptance on November 11. In line with customary practice and as set out in China's Protocol of Accession, China formally became a Member of the WTO 30 days later on December 11, 2001.

Each accession to the WTO is a unique event, but China's accession has been particularly noteworthy. China had been one of the 23 original contracting parties to the General Agreement on Tariffs and Trade (GATT) in 1948. However, the application process for readmission to the multilateral trading system took 15 years from its submission in July 1986, making it easily the longest and most arduous accession negotiation in the history of the GATT/WTO. A review of the application process contributes to an understanding of the overall process and highlights some key features of China's Accession agreement.

After China's revolution in 1949, the government in Taiwan (China) announced in 1950 that China would leave the GATT. Although the government in Beijing never recognized this withdrawal decision, nearly 40 years later, in 1986, China notified the GATT of its wish to resume its status as a contracting party and its willingness to renegotiate the terms of its membership.

A working party to examine China's status established in March 1987 met for the first time in October of that year. The GATT Working Party on China's Status met on over 20 occasions but without conclusion. With the formation of the WTO in 1995, the GATT Working Party was converted into a WTO Working Party on the Accession of China. The Working Party, chaired by Ambassador Pierre-Louis Girard of Switzerland, met 18 times.

Article XII of the Marrakesh Agreement Establishing the WTO (the "WTO Agreement"), which governs accessions, is striking in its brevity. The operative provision reads: "Any State or separate customs territory . . . may accede to this Agreement, on terms to be agreed between it and the WTO." By early April 2004, more than 20 new members had joined the WTO since its establishment, bringing membership to 146, including three separate customs territories (Chinese Taipei,[1] Hong Kong [China], and Macau). Cambodia and Nepal had been accepted for membership but were still in the process of completing ratification procedures.

The final stages of the China accession process can be classified rather naturally under three headings:

- conclusion of bilateral market-access negotiations
- conclusion of multilateral negotiations in the Working Party and the corresponding documents that together stipulate the terms of China's accession, including the draft Protocol and its Annexes, and the Working Party Report
- approval and acceptance of these terms of accession by WTO members and by China, respectively.

Before delving into a description of these three steps, it is worth reviewing briefly the many ups and downs China experienced in the course of the accession process. I refer in particular to significant progress made just prior to the Tiananmen "incident," followed by almost two-and-a-half years with virtually no accession activity, China's subsequent participation in the Uruguay Round negotiations, and its failure to conclude negotiations on its status as a GATT-contracting party in time to become an original member of the WTO. Next were the conversion of the GATT Working Party into a WTO accession working party in December 1995, the considerable optimism about an accelerated process in early 1997, the near-conclusion of a bilateral agreement with the United States in April 1999, the U.S. bombing of the Chinese Embassy in Belgrade the following month, and the conclusion of a bilateral agreement with the United States in November 1999. These developments were followed by a spate of additional bilateral agreements in the first half of 2000, including that with the European Union in May. Further hiccups occurred subsequently, including the downing of a U.S. spy plane over the Straits of Taiwan, the Bush administration's aggressive enthusiasm for a new form of the Strategic Defense Initiative called the Missile Defense System, and finally, the terrorist attack in the United States and the U.S.-led retaliatory actions since that time. Clearly, China and WTO members have been on a roller-coaster ride of major proportions over much of the accession period.

BILATERAL NEGOTIATIONS

China's importance as a trading nation generated considerable enthusiasm for its participation in the accession negotiations. Some 44 WTO members, including the 15 member States of the European Union as one entity, expressed interest in concluding bilateral market-access negotiations with China.

As these bilateral deals were struck and notified to the WTO, China's consolidated Schedule of Concessions and Commitments on Goods and its consolidated Schedule of Specific Commitments on Services were prepared with assistance from the WTO Secretariat. Thereafter, they were reviewed in the Working Party and multilateralized, that is, extended on a most-favoured-nation (MFN) basis to all WTO members, as China's Goods and Services Schedules, annexed to the Protocol of Accession. In this way, these bilateral commitments became part of the multilateral treaty terms of China's membership in the WTO.

China was only able to make rapid progress in concluding its bilateral negotiations with most other WTO member governments once it reached bilateral agreement with the United States in November 1999 and then with the European Communities in May 2000. Thereafter the negotiations proceeded apace.

Only in the final days of the Working Party was China able to conclude negotiations with Mexico, the last of the 44 WTO members seeking bilateral market-access commitments. The sticking point had been the hundreds of antidumping orders that Mexico continued to maintain against products of Chinese origin. Mexico eventually agreed to terminate these allegedly WTO-inconsistent measures six years after China's accession. In addition, El Salvador, which recognizes Taiwan (China) and not China (as is true of other WTO members), did not request bilateral negotiations with China and invoked the non-application provision of Article XIII of the WTO Agreement against China.

One element contributing to pressure on China and Members to conclude bilateral accords was the U.S. administration's agreement with China. As a *quid pro quo* for China's market-access concessions, the United States would provide China with permanent MFN status, thereby eliminating the annually renewed conditional MFN provided under the Jackson-Vanik Amendment to the U.S. trade act of

1974. After much debate, the U.S. Congress finally passed unconditional MFN status (what it calls permanent normal trade relations or PNTR) for China in September 2000.

MULTILATERAL STEPS

With the bilateral market-access negotiations nearing completion, members and China showed renewed interest in wrapping up the many outstanding multilateral elements of the accession package. In order to finalize the negotiated package and in recognition of the fact that much of the information China had submitted to the Working Party was incomplete or out of date, the Working Party requested that China submit updated information—including notifications of laws, regulations, and other policy measures—on all key aspects of China's trade regime.

Clearly, such information was indispensable to assessing the congruency of China's trade regime with WTO rules. It was also indispensable to finalizing negotiations on key provisions of the Protocol and the Report. Identifying the trouble spots and agreeing on the timing—including possible transition periods—for China to bring any WTO-inconsistent policy measures into compliance with WTO obligations, presented major challenges.

The final meeting of the Working Party in September 2001, with informal sessions the week of September 10 and the formal meeting on September 17, was devoted to completing the technical cleanup and verification of the Goods and Services Schedules, followed by an overall review of the documents to ensure consistency among the various elements of the accession package.

China and Working Party members finally reached agreement on all outstanding issues:

- preambular and general provisions
- the administration of the trade regime, including uniform administration, special economic areas, transparency, and judicial review
- nondiscrimination, special trade arrangements, state trading, nontariff measures, tariff-rate quota administration, import and export licensing, price controls, taxes and charges levied on imports and exports, export subsidies and domestic support in agriculture, and sanitary and phytosanitary measures

- trading rights
- standards and technical regulations.

Additional agreements were reached on the following:

- a special transitional provision lasting 15 years on price comparability in determining subsidies and dumping
- the establishment of both a transitional product-specific safeguard mechanism and a separate transitional textile safeguard
- immediate implementation of the Agreement on Trade-Related Aspects of Intellectual Property Rights (TRIPS)
- a transitional review mechanism to oversee compliance with the terms of the Protocol
- a host of technical sectoral issues in trade in services.

While China has reserved the right to exclusive state trading for products such as cereals, tobacco, fuels, and minerals, and to maintain some restrictions on transportation and distribution of goods inside China, many of the restrictions that foreign companies currently face in China will be phased out over a three-year transition period. During a 12-year period after accession, WTO members will have access to a transitional safeguard mechanism in cases where imports of products of Chinese origin cause or threaten to cause market disruption to member's domestic producers.

Upon accession China became a party to the Agreement on Textiles and Clothing; accordingly, as for all WTO members, quotas on textiles will end on December 31, 2004. However, a special, negotiated, safeguard mechanism will remain in place until the end of 2008, permitting WTO members to take action to curb imports in case of market disruption caused by Chinese exports of textile products.

Several areas of negotiation were problematic until very late in the process. First, there was lack of agreement on the availability to China of WTO provisions for developing countries in areas such as domestic support to agriculture and industrial subsidies. The United States, in particular, objected to providing China with the full benefit of developing country provisions in these areas. The matter eventually was resolved; China agreed not to resort to certain of these WTO provisions and accepted a cap of 8.5 percent on domestic support in agriculture, below the 10 percent available generally to developing country members under the WTO Agreement. Because this 8.5 percent cap is still well above existing budgetary outlays by the Chinese government, it is doubtful whether the cap will have a major impact on China's ability to help its farming sector adapt to the new and evolving conditions of competition.

A second area that was among the last resolved was the regime relating to trading rights. The basic regime eventually agreed to calls for a fully liberalized right for foreign companies to gain trading rights in China after a three-year transition period; state-traded products remain an exception.

A third area of considerable difficulty was agreement on China's handling of its regime dealing with technical regulations and standards; the key issue was how to ensure nondiscrimination (national treatment) in the application of this regime. After repeated urging spanning several years, China finally committed to unifying its administrative structure responsible for the inspection and conformity assessment procedures (under the Administration for Quality Supervision, Inspection and Quarantine [AQSIQ]) for both domestic and imported goods, thereby allaying many of the concerns raised by the dual and separate systems of inspection that previously existed.

As part of the concluding phase, the Working Party also reviewed and obtained amendments and clarifications to many of the transitional Annexes of the Protocol. This was done on the basis of updated and revised drafts of these Annexes provided by China. They included the following annexes:

- Products subject to state trading
- Products subject to designated trading
- Nontariff measures subject to phased elimination
- Products and services subject to price controls
- Notification and phase-out of subsidies
- Export taxes and charges
- Restrictions maintained against China
- Issues to be addressed in the transitional review
- the Schedule of Concessions and Commitments on Goods, as well as the Schedule of Specific Commitments on Services.

The Protocol and Working Party Report essentially contain a one-way set of commitments (from China's side only), although these documents also contain some "soft" commitments by Members, for example, regarding the non-abuse of domestic procedures in anti-dumping actions and restraint in the use of the special safeguard. Additionally, there is an unusual Annex to the Protocol, containing commitments by certain Members to phase out inconsistent measures maintained against China over a transition period lasting up to five years.

APPROVAL AND ACCEPTANCE

Once consensus was achieved in the Working Party on the final accession package, this was forwarded to the General Council for decision. Given the timing of the Fourth Ministerial Conference in mid-November 2001, it was decided that these documents should be forwarded to Doha for approval by Ministers, rather than be decided upon at the level of the General Council in Geneva.

In accordance with established procedures, the Ministerial Conference approved the Decision on Accession and the Protocol on the terms of China's accession on November 10, 2001. China accepted the WTO's Protocol of Accession on November 11, 2001, and became a Member of the WTO 30 days later. Notifying the Director-General that the Standing Committee of the People's Congress had ratified the terms of accession, China became the 143rd member of the WTO on December 11, 2001.[2]

Article XII:2 of the WTO Agreement provides that "the Ministerial Conference shall approve the agreement on the terms of accession by a two-thirds majority of the Members of the WTO." However, pursuant to Article IX:1 of the same agreement and a 1995 decision of the General Council, all accession decisions are to be approved by consensus (with possible recourse to voting only where consensus is not achievable). All 16 WTO accession decisions to date, including China's, have been taken by consensus.

CHINA'S ACCESSION IN THE CONTEXT OF THE WTO'S BASIC PRINCIPLES

It could be interesting to consider briefly how China's accession fits within the context of the five fundamental principles of the GATT and the WTO.

Simply put, these principles cover the following:

* Nondiscrimination
* Market opening
* Transparency and predictability
* Undistorted trade
* Preferential treatment for developing countries.

Non-Discrimination

Two types of nondiscrimination are of interest: the MFN principle and the national treatment principle. Under the MFN principle, a member may not discriminate between its trading partners: goods and services and service providers are to be accorded MFN, that is, equal, treatment. At the same time, a member must provide national treatment: it may not discriminate on its internal market between its own and foreign products, services, and nationals.

Where do things stand in terms of China's accession vis-à-vis the principle of nondiscrimination? China, like other members, has committed itself to abide by all WTO agreements, including those provisions requiring application of MFN and national treatment. In its Protocol of Accession, China has agreed to undertake additional commitments to ensure the smooth phasing in of these nondiscrimination principles. Of particular note are commitments to eliminate dual pricing practices and to phase out within three years most of the restrictions on importing, exporting, and trading currently faced by foreign enterprises. All foreign enterprises, including those not invested or registered in China, are to be accorded treatment no less favorable than that accorded to enterprises in China.

Market Opening

The principle of market opening is promoted in the WTO through successive rounds of multilateral trade negotiations aimed at the progressive lowering of trade barriers. New members are pressed to liberalize their trade regimes during accession negotiations. Trade ministers also initiated the latest round of multilateral negotiations at the Doha Ministerial Meeting in November 2001.

With respect to market opening, China has significantly reduced its tariff and nontariff barriers as part of its bid to join the WTO. The breadth and depth of the cuts are evident. China's willingness to progressively and substantially open up its services sectors to foreign competition also is undeniable. Moreover, China has already demonstrated its intention to play a significant role in the Doha Development Agenda.

Transparency and Predictability

These are key elements of the multilateral trading system. The basic transparency principle, contained in GATT Article X, calls on member governments to promptly publish all trade-related laws, regulations, judicial decisions, and administrative rulings of general application; to administer all such measures in a uniform, impartial, and reasonable manner; and to provide for independent judicial review procedures for the prompt review and correction of administrative actions. The predictability principle is ensured through a legal hierarchy giving preference to tariffs over less transparent and less secure non-tariff measures such as quotas and licences, and through encouraging members to "bind" their market opening commitments in goods and services. In the goods area, this binding amounts to setting ceilings on customs tariff rates.

China has committed to abide by the WTO's transparency obligations across the board—including with respect to uniform application of its trade regime and independent judicial review—and has made additional commitments in each of these areas. While difficulties may exist with respect to variations in treatment in different parts of China's customs territory, as well as with the perceived lack of independence of the judiciary, there can be little doubt that the Chinese government is committed to carrying through the necessary reforms to implement these obligations in a uniform and impartial manner. Also, as noted, China's accession commitments will be the subject of a special transitional review mechanism for the first 10 years of membership.

With China as a member, her producers and exporters will more confidently be able to make long-term business decisions on the expansion of their activities. The more open the Chinese economy becomes, the more China will benefit from the legal security of the rules-based trading system. Not just foreign investors, exporters, and importers, but also all Chinese citizens, will benefit from the more open, nondiscriminatory reforms China is undertaking.

In terms of producing a more predictable and secure trading environment, China has bound all its import tariffs in the goods area. China also has committed to the phased reduction and removal of tariff barriers, mostly by 2004, but no later than 2010. China's average bound tariff level will decrease to 15 percent for agricultural products, ranging from 0 to 65 percent, with the higher rates applied to cereals. For industrial goods, the average bound tariff level will go down to 8.9 percent, with a range from 0 to 47 percent, with the highest rates applied to photographic film and automobiles and related products. In services, China has made a more comprehensive set of initial commitments than those offered by most developed countries during the Uruguay Round. Of particular note are China's commitments in services sectors covering telecommunications, banking, and insurance.

Undistorted Trade

The WTO system also promotes undistorted trade through the establishment of disciplines on subsidies and dumping, allowing members to respond to unfair trade through the imposition of countervailing or antidumping duties. The treaty allows individual members to impose temporary safeguard measures, under strict rules, when faced with a sudden surge in imports causing serious injury to a domestic industry.

As in other areas, China has agreed to abide by all WTO disciplines relating to subsidies and countervailing measures, protection provided under rules for antidumping, and safeguard measures. As noted above, it has also committed not to use export subsidies on either industrial or agricultural goods and has accepted special provisions sought by other members in relation to determinations of dumping or subsidies, as well as a special product-specific safeguard mechanism and a separate textile safeguard. China has indicated its intention to join the plurilateral Agreement on Government Procurement, which is aimed at ensuring fair competition rules in purchases by government procurement agencies.

Preferential Treatment for Developing Countries

This principle permeates the entire WTO Agreement, providing transition periods to developing countries and countries in transition to market economies to adjust their systems to many of the new obligations resulting from the Uruguay Round. A Ministerial Decision gives additional flexibility to the least-developed countries in implementing the various Uruguay Round agreements and calls on developed country Members to accelerate their implementation of market access commitments on goods exported by the least-developed countries.

Although China has not been granted across-the-board preferential treatment as a developing country, it has negotiated specific transitional arrangements in certain areas of its trade regime. Examples include the phasing out of quotas and import licenses, and the phased liberalization of the right for foreign entities to trade in China. In contrast, despite the availability of more preferential treatment under the WTO agreements, China has accepted a special cap on its ability to provide domestic production subsidies in agriculture, has agreed not to use export subsidies, and has committed to immediate implementation of the TRIPS Agreement.

INSTITUTIONAL IMPLICATIONS

No one can contest that China's participation in the WTO will affect the operations of this organization in substantial ways and over the long term. China is joining as the seventh largest exporter and eighth largest importer of merchandise trade and as the twelfth leading exporter and tenth leading importer of commercial services. It has the largest population and largest potential market of any WTO member.

Undoubtedly, China's membership will have implications for the regular work of the WTO's many committees administering the many agreements of this institution. China will surely be active in the newly launched and future rounds of multilateral trade negotiations, in agriculture, and in services, but also in other areas of mutual concern. It will participate in fashioning the improved institutional operations of the WTO. Clearly, China's membership is likely to result in expanded recourse to the dispute settlement procedures of the WTO, both by China and by other members in relation to China's implementation of its WTO commitments. The first such case was that recently brought by

China, similar to that brought by many other WTO members, against the U.S. steel safeguard measures. We should, of course, expect to see some new faces in the Secretariat.

CONCLUDING REMARKS

Since the mid-1980s, the process of reform in China has matured considerably, and China's trade performance has reflected this maturation. China has become a very important player in international trade, on both the import and the export sides. Moving from an earlier phase of import planning to one of import licensing and then, more significantly, to one of import tariffs, has brought prices and the market mechanism into play as key determinants of China's future trade relations with the rest of the world.

Accession should allow China to lock-in the accumulated benefits of the trade reform process that the Chinese government has undertaken to date, and it should provide a platform from which China can sustain its reform process into the future.

By placing China's reforms within the broader context of trade liberalization by all WTO members, Chinese producers and exporters can increase the returns from trade reform in China through reciprocal market access abroad and help the Chinese government resist pressure domestically to reverse the process of reform.

For China, WTO accession will provide the 1.3 billion Chinese people with secure, predictable, and nondiscriminatory access to the markets of 143 trading partners. It will also give this same enormous population secure and nondiscriminatory access to the goods and services of these other WTO members.

However, from China's perspective, membership also for the first time commits this new WTO player at the international level to implement legal and domestic policy reform, ensuring much greater transparency and security on a uniform basis. China has made impressive strides at reform over the past 20 years. However, committing itself to abide by international treaty rules and the rule of law in the conduct of trade and in domestic policy reform is likely to take this process forward at an even more impressive pace.

Accession will also mean that China can replace the many risky and uncertain bilateral relationships

it has had to use until now, to shape its trade with its major trading partners, with a single, multilateral trade relationship with the rest of the world.

Of course, what lies beyond China's accession is the major, continuing, and, in many ways, imponderable task of implementation by China of its WTO accession commitments. A question uppermost in the minds of many Chinese and foreigners alike is whether and how China will be able to ensure uniform and impartial implementation of trade commitments.

At this stage, it is difficult to predict the speed with which WTO members and China will resort to the WTO's dispute settlement procedures. There is little doubt, however, that China and its trading partners will eventually take full advantage of WTO mechanisms to resolve trade disputes. While considerable emphasis has been placed on the 10-year transitional review mechanism provided in China's Protocol, this mechanism does not contain any enforcement provisions.

It is hard to overstate the difficulties many sectors of Chinese society will face in the months and years following accession. The impact on loss-making state industries, less developed agricultural communities, and myriad government-financed projects throughout the country will be dramatic. Moreover, the adjustment to new, more competitive market conditions, will, for many millions of individuals and families, mean unemployment and significant displacement. It will take many years for large segments of China to establish a new equilibrium, during which time many citizens may well face considerable hardships.

However, we should bear in mind that this adjustment process has already begun. The Chinese people are hardly strangers to this process. Already in the early 1990s China had introduced a bankruptcy law and other legislation making state industries in principle responsible for their own profits and losses. For at least the past decade, China has radically reduced state subsidies and encouraged development of private enterprise in many sectors. Since the mid-1990s in particular, and as a member of the International Monetary Fund, China has rationalized and liberalized handling of its foreign exchange market. In addition, China has progressively and dramatically reduced its import tariffs and other nontariff restrictions on foreign participation in the Chinese market.

The difficult adjustment is far from complete. At this stage, therefore, we can do little more than wish China and its people "bon courage" as they venture down the extremely challenging path that stretches before them.

Notes

1. The nation of Taiwan (China) became a member of the WTO as Chinese Taipei.

2. Chinese Taipei, whose terms of accession were approved by Ministers on 11 November 2001, became a WTO member on 1 January 2002.

3

CHINA IN THE WTO: ANTIDUMPING AND SAFEGUARDS

Patrick A. Messerlin

A few weeks prior to China's acceptance as a full member of the World Trade Organization (WTO), chief negotiator Long Yongtu had ranked stricter antidumping rules second among China's priorities in the WTO. Antidumping rules define the conditions under which a WTO member can, if it wishes, counter-balance dumping, that is, the fact that foreign firms exporting to the markets of this WTO member price their products more cheaply in these markets than in their own domestic markets. At that time, the United States was still fighting to exclude antidumping from the topics to be discussed at the WTO Doha Ministerial, and the European Community (EC) was adopting an ambiguous position.

In the early stages of the negotiations under the Doha Development Agenda (DDA), China finds itself in an unique situation on the antidumping and safeguard issues. (Safeguard rules define the conditions under which a WTO member can, if it wishes so, give a transitional relief to a domestic industry facing an unforeseen surge in competing foreign imports.) First, the WTO accession protocol of China includes very special provisions that China's trading partners may use against Chinese exports.

These include continued use of non-market economy (NME) status in antidumping investigations and the use of a special transitional product-specific safeguard (TPS) provision. These two provisions are scheduled to last 15 and 12 years, respectively.[1] Second, China, by far the main target of existing antidumping measures, to date is one of the smallest users of such measures. However, the past decade has shown how quickly large developing countries willing to use antidumping rules can become intensive users of this instrument, and the evolution of China's antidumping enforcement in 2002 and early 2003 raises legitimate concerns in this respect.

The chapter is organized as follows. The first section describes the current situation. Antidumping is used massively by only 10 countries (four industrial and six developing), and a strong asymmetry, best illustrated by China, exists between countries enforcing antidumping measures and those targeted by antidumping measures. The second section examines how China could minimize exposure to foreign antidumping cases—an option that would be a recipe for both trade success and China's leading role in reforming WTO antidumping rules. The third section analyzes China's antidumping

I would like to thank Mike Finger, Edwin Vermulst, Will Martin, and two anonymous referees for very useful comments on earlier drafts of this paper.

regulations and first cases, including their crucial relations with the existing web of the U.S. and EC antidumping cases. The fourth section examines the opportunities that the DDA offers to China for negotiating stricter disciplines both on WTO contingent protection, and on the use of the NME and TPS provisions by China's trading partners. The conclusion summarizes the crucial choices to be made by China with respect to antidumping and safeguard policies.

The Current Situation

During the November 2001 Doha WTO Ministerial Conference, antidumping was perceived as an issue pitting developing countries anxious to discipline the use of this instrument against the United States, which was (and still is) very reluctant to change its own antidumping regulations. However, a close examination of the current situation suggests a much more complex picture. This examination is based on the antidumping measures in force at the end of each year of the period 1995–2002 that are notified to the WTO Secretariat by members.[2]

Antidumping Users vs. Targeted Countries: A Key Asymmetry

Table 3.1, which presents the stock of antidumping measures in force by antidumping users, illustrates

two main results. First, worldwide antidumping enforcement is thus highly concentrated in less than a dozen countries. The top 10 antidumping users enforce 90 percent of the antidumping measures notified in the WTO; they represent 70 percent of the world GDP and 50 percent of world trade.

Second, the situation prevailing during the Uruguay Round—antidumping users were almost exclusively industrial countries—is no longer the case. Six "new" antidumping-intensive users (all of them developing countries: Argentina, Brazil, India, Mexico, South Africa, and Turkey) have almost caught up with the four major "old" users. These new users implement more than one-third of the total number of antidumping measures in force in 2002, compared with less than one-fourth in 1995. Meanwhile, the share of measures of the four old users has declined from more than two-thirds to half of the total number of antidumping measures in force during the period. A last worrisome sign is that the rest of the developing countries, while still small users individually, have doubled their global share of measures in force during the observation period.[3]

Table 3.2 presents the stock of antidumping measures in force by targeted country for the period 1995–2002. It shows a marked asymmetry

TABLE 3.1   Top 10 Antidumping Users, Measures in Force, 1995–2001

User Country	Number of Measures in Force[a]								Average Number per Import[b]	Average Applied Tariff[c]
	1995	1996	1997	1998	1999	2000	2001	2002		
U.S.	265	271	271	281	282	202	227	239	0.29	4.3
EC	140	138	138	139	159	175	175	183	0.19	4.6
Australia	78	46	40	49	39	44	59	38	0.77	5.8
Canada	79	78	78	65	72	71	85	83	0.38	4.8
Mexico	93	92	81	86	80	77	61	55	0.72	12.6
South Africa	12	29	42	56	87	96	94	80	1.81	15.0
India	13	15	24	44	58	94	115	181	1.28	39.6
Argentina	15	30	33	39	45	42	45	60	1.17	13.7
Turkey	37	37	34	34	35	14	16	30	0.61	12.7
Brazil	21	28	23	28	38	43	49	54	0.51	12.5
All Others	50	59	84	102	122	117	97	—	0.04	—
of which China	—	—	0	0	4	8	11	17	0.03	15.8
All countries	803	823	848	923	1017	975	1023	—	0.21	—

a. Antidumping duties and undertakings in force as of 31 December of the year.
b. Per thousand of US$ of the 1997 imports of the user country.
c. Average applied tariffs (WTO 2001).
Sources: WTO Reports on Antidumping (G/ADP/N series), WTO trade data 2001; Author's computations.

TABLE 3.2 Major Antidumping Targets, Measures in Force, 1995–2001

Targeted Countries	Number of Measures								Number per Export[b]
	1995	1996	1997	1998	1999	2000	2001	2002[a]	
U.S.	60	66	66	68	66	62	57	67	0.09
EC	77	88	89	102	132	149	99	(98)	0.13
Australia	5	6	5	6	5	5	5	5	0.08
Canada	19	19	19	19	20	18	8	8	0.08
Mexico	11	15	17	17	19	21	17	17	0.15
South Africa	7	10	11	11	12	15	16	24	0.39
India	15	15	15	21	29	35	42	44	0.72
Argentina	9	8	7	7	7	7	9	8	0.30
Turkey	9	9	6	8	10	13	12	18	0.37
Brazil	48	51	52	45	42	43	34	51	0.85
All others	543	536	561	619	675	611	724	—	0.29
of which China	143	148	180	193	202	207	199	212	0.99
All countries	803	823	848	923	1017	979	1023	—	0.22

a. Incomplete estimates for the EC.
b. Per thousand of US$ of the 1997 exports of the targeted country.
Sources: WTO Reports on Antidumping (G/ADP/N series); WTO trade data; Author's computations.

between antidumping users and targets. The top 10 users are the targets of less than one-third of all the measures in force, with a strong amplification of this gap in 2001 and 2002. In sum, antidumping is an instrument enforced by a few large countries against the smaller economies of the rest of the world—hence, the absence of incentives coming from the rest of the world that would induce the existing antidumping-intensive users to restrain their use of antidumping actions.

Combining tables 3.1 and 3.2 shows that for all top 10 antidumping users, with the exception of Brazil, the country's interests hurt by foreign antidumping measures are smaller than those benefiting from domestic antidumping protection. This is based on the well-known economic proposition that analyzes protection more as a conflict between domestic forces (namely export interests versus import-competing interests) than as a conflict between countries. To capture this aspect, one can calculate the number of foreign antidumping measures in force imposed on exports from a top user adjusted by the size of the country's exports (in thousands of U.S. dollars). Such a trade-adjusted number of measures (shown in table 3.2) mirrors the intensity of the foreign pressures imposed on the export interests of a country, giving

an indication of the incentives of these export interests to contribute to the opening of the markets of their country. These numbers can be usefully compared to the symmetrical numbers of antidumping measures in force by thousands of U.S. dollars imported by the country in question (shown in table 3.1), which can be interpreted as an indication of the strength of the incentives of these import-competing interests to induce their own government to use antidumping. The observed imbalance between export interests and import-competing antidumping beneficiaries in the top 10 antidumping users suggests that it also is unlikely that domestic coalitions are strong enough to support antidumping reforms in the WTO in users that are key WTO players.

This situation raises a question that should be carefully examined in the future. Table 3.1 suggests that one could reasonably argue that antidumping measures enforced by the six major developing country antidumping users impose welfare costs on their own domestic economies higher than the costs imposed on industrial economies by the developed country–imposed antidumping measures for two reasons. First is the marked difference between the number of measures imposed by developing countries and industrial countries, once adjusted by trade size. The average number of measures in force per thousands of U.S. dollars of goods imported in 1997 by an antidumping user is a better indicator of the potential harm done by antidumping on the domestic economy than the mere absolute number of measures. This indicator is much higher for developing countries than for industrial countries: it ranges from 0.5 (Brazil) to 1.8 (South Africa), whereas it ranges from 0.2 to 0.4 for industrial countries (with the exception of Australia). These differences would be much larger if the number of antidumping measures to be adjusted were to take into account the number of tariff lines concerned, since developing countries tend to cover many more tariff items with antidumping cases than industrial countries. The second reason for arguably higher welfare costs from antidumping measures in major developing country users is that available (though not systematic) information suggests that antidumping duties enforced by developing countries are, on average, more severe than those imposed by industrial countries—and economic analysis shows that welfare costs increase more rapidly than tariffs.

China's Special Situation

Table 3.2 shows that China has been the main target of all the antidumping measures enforced in the world—18 percent of the antidumping cases in 1995, almost 20 percent in 2001–2002. Table 3.3 refines this information by presenting the unadjusted number of antidumping measures imposed on Chinese exports by the top 10 antidumping users, and this number once adjusted by the trade value between each trade partner and China (in other words, the average number of cases imposed by foreign antidumping users per thousand U.S. dollars of exports from China to these users). Both sets of numbers show that China is much more targeted by the developing countries than by the industrial countries—especially when one looks at the figures adjusted for trade size. In fact, China is almost exclusively targeted by the top users, all of them relatively large economies.

The above information on antidumping users versus targets raises a key question about China's role in future world antidumping activities. Will China follow the same evolution as the other large developing countries, that is, will it increase rapidly

TABLE 3.3 Shares of Antidumping Measures in Force against Imports from China, 1995–2002

User Countries	Shares of Antidumping Measures Against China[a]								Average Share (excl. 2002)	Average Number per Export from China[a]
	1995	1996	1997	1998	1999	2000	2001	2002		
U.S.	12.8	13.7	15.1	14.6	14.5	16.5	18.5	18.0	15.1	1.72
EC	20.7	21.7	23.2	23.0	20.8	19.4	19.4	15.8	21.2	1.04
Australia	9.0	4.3	10.0	8.2	7.7	4.5	5.1	7.9	7.0	0.71
Canada	7.6	7.7	10.3	10.8	8.3	8.5	10.6	10.8	9.1	1.83
Mexico	33.3	28.3	40.7	38.4	36.3	35.1	44.3	41.8	36.6	60.27
South Africa	8.3	27.6	28.6	23.2	19.5	18.8	19.1	22.5	20.7	11.98
India	38.5	46.7	33.3	27.3	32.8	22.3	25.2	27.1	32.3	10.66
Argentina	33.3	20.0	30.3	35.9	31.1	21.4	15.6	20.0	26.8	9.98
Turkey	13.5	13.5	14.7	17.6	17.1	14.3	25.0	40.0	16.5	4.37
Brazil	14.3	14.3	21.7	28.6	28.9	25.6	22.4	20.4	22.3	4.67
All Others	34.0	28.8	26.2	22.5	18.9	12.8	15.5	—	22.7	—
Total (number)[b]	143	148	180	193	202	179	199	—	174	—
in % of total	17.8	18.0	21.2	20.9	19.9	18.3	19.5	—	19.4	—

a. in percent of the total number of antidumping measures in force imposed by the user country.

b. Per thousands of US dollars of the 1997 imports from China of the user country.

c. provisionally based on Lindsey and Ikenson 2001.

Sources: WTO Reports on Antidumping (G/ADP/N series). WTO trade data; Author's computations.

the number of antidumping cases? Or will China adopt a different approach, that is, will China minimize its own antidumping use and invest its negotiating strength in the WTO to obtain stricter antidumping rules, as claimed by its chief trade negotiator? Clearly, China's choice between these alternatives will have a decisive impact on the evolution of world antidumping enforcement and on WTO trade disciplines.

Minimizing China's Exposure to Foreign Antidumping

China's second alternative will be a difficult exercise, particularly in the coming years. The usual slowness of WTO negotiations means that China could not get reforms of WTO antidumping rules before two (and more likely four) years. In the interim, it will be hard for Chinese authorities to resist pressures from import-competing firms based in China that demand intensive use of China's antidumping procedures. This difficulty raises the following question: could China adopt policies minimizing, as quickly as possible, its exposure to foreign antidumping measures—thereby alleviating the political costs of playing a reforming role in WTO antidumping rules?

Trade problems are fundamentally domestic conflicts between export-oriented and import-competing industries. Country-based data, as those provided above, do not permit examination of this deeper aspect of protection. They can even be misleading. For instance, they can suggest that the strong asymmetry between antidumping users and targets observed in tables 3.1 and 3.2 would progressively disappear because each WTO member would be induced to introduce antidumping regulations and to enforce them—with such a worsening of the situation ultimately inducing WTO members to adopt collectively stricter disciplines. (Arguments have already been presented suggesting that the top antidumping users will be unlikely to follow this path.) Taking into account firms' behavior suggests that an even darker scenario is quite plausible. Firms that are the petitioners—hence the driving forces in antidumping enforcement—may well want to lodge similar antidumping complaints in several key countries to segment the world markets of their products through antidumping measures; evidence support-

ing this hypothesis is shown below. In such a case, the worldwide spread of antidumping regulations and the increase of antidumping measures are seen as a positive development by the firms in question, rather than as incentives to discipline antidumping use. Examining such deeper aspects of antidumping protection requires looking at the distribution of antidumping measures in force by sector or product rather than by country.

A Few "Antidumping-Intensive" Sectors

Table 3.4 provides a broad picture based on the number and average shares of antidumping measures in force by the most aggregated section of the Harmonized Tariff System (instead of specific products, as below). It shows that antidumping measures are concentrated in a handful of Harmonized Tariff System (HTS) sections. Antidumping measures in metals, chemicals, machinery and electrical equipment, textiles and clothing, and plastics and rubbers amount to 75 percent of the total number of measures, whereas trade in these sectors amounts to less than half of total world trade. These few HTS sections happen to be key sources of exports for dynamic developing countries in the first stages of their industrial development. Second, these HTS sections are characterized by a high proportion of relatively standard products and by oligopolistic market structures. The metals and chemicals sections clearly fit these features. The other HTS sectors require a closer look at subsectors. Few antidumping actions in the machinery and clothing subsectors are characterized by many firms and highly differentiated products, and most of the antidumping actions in the electrical equipment and textiles subsectors are characterized by relatively standard products and by oligopolistic firms. These features explain the wide use of antidumping measures in the textile subsector since the late 1980s, before any effective liberalization of the Multi-Fibre Arrangement quotas, as decided by the Uruguay Round (GATT, 1994).

Such a pattern strongly suggests that complaining firms use antidumping as an additional—cheap and powerful—instrument for segmenting the markets that ongoing or scheduled trade liberalizations aim at making more competitive. It also suggests that the spread of antidumping cases to certain sectors, such as clothing, should be expected to the extent that these markets will be increasingly

TABLE 3.4 Antidumping Measures in Force in the World by Sector, 1995–2000

Harmonized System Sections	Number of Anti-Dumping Measures						ADMs Pattern by HS Section	ADMs Growth Indexes[a]	Export Pattern	Import Pattern	China's Average Applied Tariff[b]	China's Tariff Lines with Tariffs <10%[c]
	1995	1996	1997	1998	1999	2000						
15 Metals, metal articles	276	290	305	316	372	401	33.5	117.0	6.7	9.2	9.6	68.6
6 Chemical, allied industry products	201	203	204	210	217	228	21.6	104.1	4.7	8.0	9.4	78.2
16 Machinery, electrical equip.	81	85	94	95	100	81	9.2	116.1	29.2	37.8	14.4	30.0
11 Textiles, clothing	48	60	61	54	70	79	6.4	114.2	19.8	7.4	21.0	12.6
7 Plasters, rubbers	53	54	55	53	66	74	6.1	108.4	3.2	7.3	15.9	18.0
17 Vehicles, transport equipment	42	40	40	42	43	30	4.0	101.6	3.7	2.8	23.8	43.4
13 Articles of stone, plaster, cement	34	37	37	42	44	40	4.0	115.5	1.6	0.8	17.7	12.1
10 Woodpulp, paper, paperboard	18	17	21	44	44	39	3.1	207.6	0.7	3.1	13.4	26.1
4 Prepared foodstuffs	35	31	29	31	28	27	3.1	88.9	2.1	0.8	28.4	15.7
2 Vegetable products	15	19	19	24	23	22	2.1	129.4	2.1	1.9	21.3	29.2
12 Footwear, headwear	21	16	9	17	13	16	1.6	70.3	4.8	0.2	23.2	0.0
18 Optical, cinema instruments	14	11	10	9	20	23	1.5	104.0	3.4	3.6	14.3	30.1
20 Miscellaneous manufactured articles	14	15	14	13	12	14	1.4	89.7	7.1	0.4	20.2	1.2
9 Wood, articles of wood	6	6	6	5	11	11	0.8	122.2	1.1	1.7	9.8	61.9
1 Live animals, animal products	4	3	4	6	7	7	0.5	161.9	1.7	1.0	18.9	21.5
3 Animal, vegetable fats, oils	9	9	9	2	1	1	0.5	44.4	0.1	0.5	40.6	5.9
5 Mineral products	0	0	0	9	9	9	0.5	—	3.7	10.9	4.1	96.3
19 Arms, ammunitions	3	3	3	3	0	0	0.2	66.7	0.0	0.0	13.0	0.0
8 Raw hides, skins, leather products	0	0	1	1	1	1	0.1	—	3.0	1.4	16.4	25.0
14 Gems, jewellery	0	0	0	0	0	0	0.0	—	1.0	0.5	12.6	67.2
21 Art objects	0	0	0	0	0	0	0.0	—	0.2	0.8	10.9	25.0
Total	874	899	921	976	1081	1103	100.0	112.0	100.0	100.0	15.8	38.7

a. Growth between 1998–2000 and 1997–1995. b. in 2001. c. in percent of total tariff lines, by sector.

Source: Lindsey and Ikenson 2001. In contrast with tables 3.1 to 3.3, ADMs imposed on imports of the same product by various EC member states are not systematically aggregated in one EC case.

subjected to product differentiation and imperfect competition (based on such factors as trademarks, goodwill, and distribution channels). In sum, the observed sectoral pattern of antidumping reflects the increasing privatization of trade policy by firms that enjoy enough initial oligopolistic power to fully use the pro-collusive bias embedded in antidumping regulations—a key lesson that should be kept in mind when implementing these regulations, in China as elsewhere.

China's Sensitivity to Antidumping-Intensive Sectors

Does China tend to import products pertaining to antidumping-intensive HTS sections (that is, to industries subjected to many antidumping measures in the world)? If that is the case, one should expect Chinese authorities to be under strong pressures for taking and enforcing antidumping measures on imports of such goods—that is, for participating to the worldwide segmentation game in this sector that constitutes the ultimate goal of antidumping enforcement. Table 3.4 shows that the five most antidumping-intensive HTS sections represent almost 70 percent of total Chinese imports, opening the possibility that Chinese firms or foreign firms producing in China could table antidumping complaints to segment world markets.

China's sensitivity to antidumping-sensitive sectors could also be assessed from an export perspective. Table 3.4 underlines how sensitive Chinese exports are to the worldwide antidumping activity, particularly in machinery-electrical equipment and in textiles and clothing. The above observations on the key role of economic characteristics (type of product, market structure) as the dominant factors driving world antidumping activity suggest China as a target of foreign antidumping measures much more because of the intrinsic economic features of her exported products (differentiation level and oligopolistic markets) than because it was not a WTO member.

Chinese Policies as the Best Ways to Minimize Exposure to Foreign Antidumping

A key corollary of this conclusion is that China should not expect to face less antidumping measures in the coming years because of her WTO acces-

sion but rather should expect to continue to face a large number of antidumping cases. Of course, WTO membership gives China access to the WTO dispute settlement mechanism, which could provide some relief to Chinese exporters harassed by foreign antidumping. However, this relief probably will be only marginal and short-lived. For instance, the 2001 WTO dispute settlement ruling banning the averaging method is already in the process of being circumvented by alternative procedures (hastily developed by creative petitioners) that may hurt the defendants differently, but not necessarily less than the condemned averaging method.

A more promising route for minimizing China's exposure to foreign antidumping measures may be Chinese policies—and pre-eminently China's own trade policy. If China still imposes high tariffs in antidumping-intensive sectors at the end of the accession period, it may not adopt many or severe antidumping measures on imports from the rest of the world in these products (though section 1 shows that the top developing country antidumping users have not hesitated to add high antidumping measures on the top of unfinished trade liberalization). However, such a costly tariff policy for China will not ensure less foreign antidumping cases against Chinese exports. On the contrary, high Chinese tariffs will facilitate the introduction of foreign antidumping measures against Chinese exports in antidumping-intensive sectors. This is because high Chinese tariffs will allow the existence of high prices in China, making the existence of dumping by Chinese exporters easier to prove, all the more because the Chinese exports in question consist mostly of basic products, for which Chinese exporters are likely to align their prices to those prevailing in foreign markets since there is minimal or no premium for differentiation.

Accordingly, a first way to minimize exposure to foreign antidumping measures would be the adoption by China of a relatively uniform and moderate tariff policy to reduce distortions in the domestic production pattern, foreign antidumping investigators interpret such distortions as sources of dumping as much as possible. Table 3.4 provides the average applied tariffs by HTS section that China imposed in 2001. Though averaging tariffs for such widely defined sectors gives very imperfect information on the tariff structure (peak tariffs within each sector are eroded by low tariffs), it suggests that tariff peaks in China are concentrated in HTS sections that are not antidumping-intensive activities, with the exception of textiles and clothing.

Implementing a uniform tariff policy may help China to shift export products away from antidumping-intensive sectors for another reason already observed in certain countries, such as Hong Kong (China), Japan, the Republic of Korea, Singapore, and Taipei. These five industrial countries have reduced their exposure to foreign antidumping measures by upgrading their exported products—to the point that one could argue that, in fact, foreign antidumping measures may have accelerated the economic development of these industrial countries by inducing them to shift faster to anticipated comparative advantages in highly differentiated products.

EC and U.S. Antidumping "Echoing" against China Exports

Table 3.4 relies on sectors too broad for capturing antidumping protection as embedded in the product strategies of a few large firms. This aspect requires information at the product level. Table 3.5 provides such detailed information for the EC and U.S. antidumping actions against China. More precisely, Table 3.5 provides the list of the EC and U.S. "echoing" cases, that is, those cases that have targeted the same products exported by China between 1980 and 1999. However, the European Community and the United States are the top antidumping users in terms of the absolute number of measures in force, and they represent the two largest markets for Chinese exports (15 and 21 percent, respectively).

Table 3.5 provides two general observations:

- First, the number of echoing cases is large: 58 cases, that is, 75 and 68 percent of the total number of antidumping cases initiated against Chinese exports by the United States and the European Community, respectively. All of these cases echo each other generally within a year or less, though of course they subsequently may follow different developments in these markets. All but three (cycles, hammers, and pocket lighters) resulted in antidumping measures of some kind. Such a large proportion of echoing cases and the similarity of their outcomes constitute signs that antidumping is a protectionist

instrument that petitioners are successfully using in a strategic way to segment the two largest world markets. This observation leads to an important corollary. Assessing the welfare costs of antidumping measures should take into account not only the severity of the measures *per se* (the high level of antidumping duties, or the restrictiveness of quantitative restrictions), but also the fact that the level of competition prevailing in the importing markets is dramatically reduced by such measures. "Indirect" welfare costs generated by antidumping-caused collusion compound the direct welfare costs generated by the antidumping duties.

- Second, U.S. antidumping duties are, on average, higher than EC duties: 104 percent and 38 percent, respectively. However, comparing in detail the measures in the EC and U.S. echoing cases is difficult because of the differences in regulations and the lack of sufficiently detailed information. For instance, some EC cases are terminated by the withdrawal of the complaint by the petitioners. The effective impact of such withdrawals is hard to assess. It may be limited to a "chilling" effect on Chinese exporters who may be forced to export less, or at higher prices, or both, to limit the risks of facing new antidumping complaints. However, withdrawals may merely reflect a lack of cooperation of the domestic industry or a failure to get the minimum number of EC member states to support an EC Commission proposal to impose measures. They also may reflect the fact that petitioners have been able to impose quantity or price restraints on Chinese exports on a "private" basis—with the corresponding full-fledged impact to be expected from these hidden restraints.

China's Antidumping Enforcement: At the Crossroads

The following first assessment of China's antidumping regulations and enforcement procedures should be taken as provisional because it is constrained by the limited number of ongoing cases to date; a substantial number of cases is often needed for a robust assessment of the effective antidumping enforcement by a country.

TABLE 3.5 EC and U.S. Echoing Antidumping Cases against Chinese Producers, 1980–99

Years	Initiating Country	Products	Dumping Margin (EC)	Positive EC	Positive U.S.	Negative EC	Negative U.S.	Antidumping Duties EC	Antidumping Duties U.S.
1992	EC	antimony trioxide	43.2			noi			
1991	U.S.	antimony trioxide					N		
1988	EC	barium chloride	50.1	D				25.8	
1982	EC	barium chloride	75.0	Ds					
1983	U.S.	barium chloride					N		
1983	U.S.	barium chloride			A				14.5
1999	EC	brushes, hair							
1992	U.S.	brushes, hair					T		
1986	EC	brushes, paint	100.0	Und					
1992	EC	brushes, paint				noi			
1985	U.S.	brushes, paint			A				127.1
1999	U.S.	brushes, paint							
1994	EC	coumarin	50.0	Ds					
1994	U.S.	coumarin			A				160.8
1991	EC	cycles	30.6	D				30.6	
1995	U.S.	cycles					N		
1984	EC	cycles, chains	45.0	Und				45.0	
1999	EC	cycles, forks							
1999	EC	cycles, frames							
1996	EC	cycles, parts	30.6	D				30.6	
1999	EC	cycles, wheels							
1992	EC	ferrosilicon	49.7	D				49.7	
1992	U.S.	ferrosilicon			A				137.7
1995	EC	furfuryl alcohol							
1994	U.S.	furfuryl alcohol			A				45.3
1999	EC	glycine							
1994	U.S.	glycine			A				155.9
1985	EC	handtools: hammers							
1990	U.S.	handtools: hammers			A				45.4
1994	U.S.	lighters, disposable					N		
1990	EC	lighters, pocket	16.9	D				16.9	
1991	EC	magnesium oxide	27.7	Und					
1994	U.S.	magnesium, alloy			A				79.4
1994	U.S.	magnesium, pure			A				108.3
1997	EC	magnesium, unwrought	31.7	D+Und				31.7	
1994	U.S.	manganese, metal			A				143.3
1992	EC	manganese, unwrought							
1996	U.S.	persulfates							
1994	EC	persulfates, peroxodisulfates	110.1	D				83.3	
1982	U.S.	polyester, cotton cloth			A				36.2
1990	EC	polyester, yarn	23.5	D				23.5	
1986	EC	potassium permanganate	94.5	D+Und				28.0	
1983	U.S.	potassium permanganate			A				39.6
1984	EC	silicon carbide	31.5	Und					
1993	U.S.	silicon carbide					N		
1989	EC	silicon, metal	38.7	Ds				18.7	
1991	EC	silicon, metal	178.0	Ds					
1990	U.S.	silicon, metal			A				139.5

TABLE 3.5   (Continued)

Years	Initiating Country	Products	Dumping Margin (EC)	Decisions Positive EC	Decisions Positive U.S.	Decisions Negative EC	Decisions Negative U.S.	Antidumping Duties EC	Antidumping Duties U.S.
1994	EC	steel, pipe or tubes fittings	58.6	D				58.6	
1999	EC	steel, pipe or tubes fittings	49.4	D				49.4	
1991	U.S.	steel, pipes			A				182.9
1985	U.S.	steel, pipes					N		
1988	EC	tungstate, ammon. para-	75.7	noi					
1988	EC	tungsten, carbide	73.1	D+Und					
1988	EC	tungsten, metal powder		noi					
1991	U.S.	tungsten, ore			A				151.0
1989	EC	tungsten, ores	50.3	D+Und					
1988	EC	tungstic, oxide & acid	85.8	D+Und					
Total	58	Average margins and duties	59.2	29	15	5	7	37.8	104.5

Sources: Bloningen 2001 for the U.S.; Official Journal of the EC.

Notes: EC decisions: D = ad valorem duty; Ds = specific duty; Und = undertaking; with = withdrawal; noi = no injury. ep = expired deadline.

U.S. decisions: A = affirmative; N = negative.

China's Antidumping Regulations

China adopted its first antidumping regulations on March 25, 1997, and the antidumping guidelines necessary for implementing the law later the same year. Following accession to the WTO, this "old" regulation was replaced by the "new" regulation in January 2002 with another set of guidelines (see, on the WTO website, G/ADP/N/1/CHN1 and G/ADP/ N/1/CHN2; see also Wang 2003 for a legal analysis).

Chinese regulations follow the usual structure of antidumping legislation, including proof of the existence and estimate of the magnitude of dumping and of material injury, and proof of the causal relation between dumping and injury. However, they have a few striking features. First, many details are left to the detailed guidelines or to case-by-case practices. This is often the case among countries that have recently adopted antidumping regulations. However, it has the great inconvenience of generating a high level of legal uncertainty in the process as a whole.

The second feature is that all the well-known protectionist biases of the WTO antidumping provisions are included in China's regulations, as shown by the following non-exhaustive list:

- use of the concept of "a major proportion" of the industry as the threshold level for accepting complaints (a condition that domestic monopolies, oligopolies, or cartels fit much more easily than do competitive industries)
- possibility of *ex officio* initiation of cases by the Chinese authorities
- screening of the complaints by the antidumping office, exposing this office to strong and hidden pressures by vested interests
- possibility of withdrawal by the petitioners, facilitating private collusion between them and the defendants
- cumulation of imports, facilitating the demonstration of injury and widening the geographical scope of protective measures
- recourse to constructed normal values, enabling manipulation of costs and reasonable profit in case of the absence of comparable prices in the exporting country
- broad definition of the confidentiality of the information limiting the rights of the defendants (and arguably having equal impacts on domestic and export firms)
- possibility of imposing undertakings as antidumping measures and the mandatory provision that antidumping duties shall be borne by the importers (the no-absorption provision)
- possibility of imposing retroactive antidumping duties in the case of a history of dumping, that is, recurrent antidumping complaints

- possibility of taking "appropriate" measures in case of circumvention of the antidumping measures by the foreign firms.

The third feature of the Chinese antidumping regulations prior to the 2003 government reform was a highly complex coordination of the various administrative agencies involved in antidumping investigations. The Fair Trade Administration for Import and Export (FTA) of the Ministry of Foreign Trade and Economic Cooperation (MOFTEC) received complaints, decided those it would accept or reject, and was involved in the whole investigation and process. The State Economic and Trade Commission (SETC) joined MOFTEC for determining the existence of injury at the preliminary stage and for the final investigations. The Customs General Administration (CGA) joined MOFTEC for some parts of the investigations. For the imposition of antidumping duties, MOFTEC made proposals to the Tariff Commission under the State Council (TCSC), which took the decisions. The merger of SETC and MOFTEC in early 2003 brought these two functions into one ministry.

Lastly, the Old Regulation included the following Article 40: "In the event that any country or region applies discriminatory antidumping or countervailing measures against the exports from the People's Republic of China, the People's Republic of China may, as the case may be, take counter-measures against the country or region in question." It is not known whether this provision has led to cases, but clearly it opened the possibility for China to use her antidumping rules as a retaliatory instrument. Interestingly, Article 56 of the New Regulation is only slightly more diplomatic: "Where a country (region) discriminatorily imposes antidumping measures on the exports from the People's Republic of China, China may, on the basis of the actual situations, take corresponding measures against that country (region)."

Antidumping Enforcement by China

Table 3.6 provides the list of the antidumping cases initiated by China between 1997 and May 2003, based on information provided by MOFTEC for the cases under the old regulation and on China's latest notification (G/ADP/N/105/CHN) to the

WTO for the cases under the new regulation. Sixty-nine cases have been initiated, with a very uneven time pattern: after a slow start in 1997–98, the number of cases has increased rapidly (some cases under the Old Regulation are left with unknown status), reaching 24 cases in 2002 and 11 cases for the first five months of 2003. This increase can only be a source of serious concern. It remains to be seen whether it simply mirrors cases that were "in the pipeline" for a long time, or whether China has begun to follow the drift observed in the six top developing country antidumping users and will soon become another antidumping intensive user, putting in danger her so-far successful liberalization.

Although it is too early to know whether China's first antidumping measures will be representative of future antidumping enforcement, these measures deserve a few observations. First is that antidumping measures have been taken in almost all the cases. This is a very high percentage, compared to generally observed levels of 60–70 percent in industrial countries. The second observation is the relatively high level of the measures adopted by the Chinese authorities, although it seems that the most recent measures are less severe than the ones taken under the Old Regulation. The main countries targeted are industrial and advanced developing countries—not quite the pattern observed for the other developing country antidumping users.

The cases initiated since 2001 deserve an additional remark. Their product pattern is closer to what is observed for the other antidumping users, as best illustrated by the steel cases (echoing the EC and U.S. safeguards) and by the ethanolamine cases (observed in several other antidumping users). This increasingly similar product pattern suggests that China's antidumping enforcement may be starting to be part of the ongoing process of segmenting world markets through worldwide antidumping activity. It also raises the issue of a progressive capture of China's trade policy by firms, similar to what is observed in the 10 major antidumping users. In this context, it would be important to know whether petitioners in China are Chinese firms (private or state-owned) or whether they are firms having strong links (such as joint ventures, technical relations, vertical integration) with foreign firms well experienced in "antidumping art."

TABLE 3.6   China's Antidumping Measures in Force and Investigations, as of 30 June 2003

Initiation Year	Country	Products	Provisional Antidumping Duties (percent)		Definitive Antidumping Duties (percent)	
			Minimum	Maximum	Minimum	Maximum
Cases initiated under the old regulation						
1997	Canada	newsprint	17.1	78.9	9.0	78.0
1997	Korea, Rep. of	newsprint	17.1	78.9	9.0	78.0
1997	U.S.	newsprint	17.1	78.9	9.0	78.0
1999	Russia	steel, cold-rolled silicon	11.0	73.0	0.6	62.0
1999	Korea, Rep. of	polyester film	21.0	72.0	13.0	46.0
1999	Japan	steel, cold-rolled stainless	4.0	75.0	17.0	58.0
1999	Korea, Rep. of	steel, cold-rolled stainless	4.0	75.0	17.0	58.0
1999	EC Germany	acrylates	24.0	74.0	0.0	0.0
1999	Japan	acrylates	24.0	74.0	31.0	69.0
1999	U.S.	acrylates	24.0	74.0	31.0	69.0
2000	EC Britain	methylene chloride	7.0	39.0	6.0	39.0
2000	EC France	methylene chloride	28.0	75.0	28.0	75.0
2000	EC Germany	methylene chloride	67.0	67.0	66.0	66.0
2000	EC Netherlands	methylene chloride	10.0	58.0	9.0	57.0
2000	Korea, Rep. of	methylene chloride	7.0	28.0	4.0	28.0
2000	U.S.	methylene chloride	49.0	58.0	49.0	58.0
2001	Japan	polystyrene	a	a	a	a
2001	Korea, Rep. of	polystyrene	a	a	a	a
2001	Thailande	polystyrene	a	a	a	a
2001	Indonesia	lysine	a	a	a	a
2001	Korea, Rep. of	lysine	a	a	a	a
2001	U.S.	lysine	a	a	a	a
2001	Korea, Rep. of	polyester, chips	a	a	a	a
Cases initiated under the new regulation						
2001	Korea, Rep. of	polyester, staple fiber	4.0	48.0	2.0	48.0
2001	Korea, Rep. of	pet chips	6.0	52.0	5.0	52.0
2001	Indonesia	acrylates	11.0	24.0	11.0	24.0
2001	Korea, Rep. of	acrylates	11.0	20.0	2.0	20.0
2001	Malaysia	acrylates	13.0	38.0	4.0	38.0
2001	Singapore	acrylates	46.0	49.0	30.0	49.0
2001	EC Belgium	caprolactam	6.0	16.0	6.0	16.0
2001	EC Germany	caprolactam	28.0	38.0	28.0	38.0
2001	EC Netherlands	caprolactam	9.0	18.0	6.0	18.0
2001	Japan	caprolactam	5.0	21.0	5.0	18.0
2001	Russia	caprolactam	6.0	29.0	7.0	16.0
2002	Korea, Rep. of	polyester, film	—	—	0.0	0.0
2002	India	anhydride, purified	33.0	33.0	b	b
2002	Japan	anhydride, purified	66.0	66.0	b	b
2002	Korea, Rep. of	anhydride, purified	14.0	33.0	b	b
2002	Japan	styrene butadiene	0.0	33.0	b	b
2002	Korea, Rep. of	styrene butadiene	10.0	27.0	b	b
2002	Russia	styrene butadiene	16.0	46.0	b	b
2002	Kazakstan	steel, cold-rolled products	21.0	48.0	b	b
2002	Korea, Rep. of	steel, cold-rolled products	9.0	40.0	b	b

TABLE 3.6 (Continued)

Initiation Year	Country	Products	Provisional Antidumping Duties (percent)		Definitive Antidumping Duties (percent)	
			Minimum	Maximum	Minimum	Maximum
2002	Russia	steel, cold-rolled products	9.0	29.0	b	b
2002	Taiwan (China)	steel, cold-rolled products	8.0	55.0	b	b
2002	Ukraine	steel, cold-rolled products	12.0	22.0	b	b
2002	Japan	polyvinyl chloride	32.0	115.0	b	b
2002	Korea, Rep. of	polyvinyl chloride	10.0	76.0	b	b
2002	Russia	polyvinyl chloride	34.0	82.0	b	b
2002	Taiwan (China)	polyvinyl chloride	10.0	27.0	b	b
2002	U.S.	polyvinyl chloride	25.0	83.0	b	b
2002	Japan	toluene	19.0	49.0	b	b
2002	Korea, Rep. of	toluene	6.0	22.0	b	b
2002	U.S.	toluene	23.0	28.0	b	b
2002	Japan	phenol	7.0	144.0	b	b
2002	Korea, Rep. of	phenol	10.0	10.0	b	b
2002	Taiwan (China)	phenol	7.0	20.0	b	b
2002	U.S.	phenol	29.0	29.0	b	b
2003	EC Germany	ethanolamine	b	b	b	b
2003	Iran	ethanolamine	b	b	b	b
2003	Japan	ethanolamine	b	b	b	b
2003	Malaysia	ethanolamine	b	b	b	b
2003	Mexico	ethanolamine	b	b	b	b
2003	Taiwan (China)	ethanolamine	b	b	b	b
2003	U.S.	ethanolamine	b	b	b	b
2003	EC	chloroform	b	b	b	b
2003	India	chloroform	b	b	b	b
2003	Korea, Rep. of	chloroform	b	b	b	b
2003	U.S.	chloroform	b	b	b	b
69	All cases	average antidumping duty	17.2	43.4	9.8	23.7

a. Status unknown; b. Ongoing investigations.
Sources: MOFTEC, WTO Semi-annual report G/ADP/N/105/CHN, 22 August 2003.

China's Options in the WTO Negotiations on Contingent Protection

China's antidumping enforcement needs to take into account an aspect that the six top developing country antidumping users have not had to address: China's WTO accession protocol incorporates specific provisions on antidumping and safeguards (for a legal analysis, see Vermulst 2000). The section argues that this special feature that is initially a handicap can be turned into a positive instrument. More precisely, it could induce China to negotiate, in the DDA, a more economically sound "interpretation" of the specific provisions on antidumping. Such an interpretation could create strong incentives in China for both restraining its own antidumping use and fighting for stricter WTO rules on antidumping. It also could give strong incentives to China's trading partners to ease China's transitional period of accession. It is fair to say that dealing with the provision on safeguards seems more difficult. This provision is so much in contradiction with the general WTO rules and spirit that its use will raise a large systemic risk for the whole WTO. However, various options are examined at the end of the section.

Linking China's Effective Liberalization to a Better Treatment of Exports by Antidumping Users

China's protocol of accession allows China's trading partners to use the non-market economy (NME) status in their investigations against allegedly dumped Chinese exports. This NME status, which is scheduled to last 15 years until 2017, allows foreign antidumping investigators to use proxies for estimating the home market prices or costs of Chinese exporters. Such proxies make the proof of the existence of antidumping much easier than under the antidumping rules for market economies, and they inflate the magnitude of the estimated antidumping margins compared to those, already high, imposed on market economies.

Table 3.7 gives a sense of the intrinsic biases of the NME procedure by summarizing the information available from 208 EC and U.S. antidumping cases initiated between 1995 and 1998 (Lindsey 1999; Messerlin 2000a). It shows that the further from pure price comparisons the methodology used for estimating dumping margins stays, the higher these margins have been: from 3 percent (U.S.) and 22 percent (EC) under pure price comparisons, to 14 percent (U.S.) and 24 percent (EC) under a mix of price comparisons and constructed values, and to 25 percent (U.S. and EC) under the various constructed value methods. Moreover, use of NME status is clearly linked to the highest dumping margins found (40 percent in the U.S. and 46 percent in the EC).[4]

It is almost impossible to eliminate a provision included in a country's protocol of accession. However, during the DDA, it may be possible to negotiate an economically sound interpretation of the use of the NME status by WTO members. The benefits from such an interpretation rely on the fact that China and her trading partners have a common interest in establishing the strongest possible link between Chinese effective liberalization and the elimination of the NME use by foreign antidumping authorities against Chinese exporters. It is important to underline that what is at stake is not the elimination of the NME provision itself (once again impossible to obtain) but its effective use in the future.[5]

The argument aims at mobilizing the export interests in both China and the rest of the world during the implementation period of China's accession to the WTO. On the one hand, if Chinese exporters know that they will face a less unfair treatment (i.e., that they will not be subject to the NME status) in foreign antidumping cases, they will be induced to monitor China's liberalization more closely—to check whether China is effectively opening her markets in accordance with her accession protocol—and to provide stronger support to it, including stricter use of China's antidumping regulations. On the other hand, if foreign exporters are convinced that they will get more effective and stable access to Chinese markets, they will be induced to fight for restraining the antidumping enforcement by their own authorities, in particular for limiting the use of the NME status.

Doing so could be achieved by implementing the following simple rule. Foreign antidumping investigators will *automatically* grant the market-economy status to Chinese exporters of any given

TABLE 3.7 Do Antidumping Investigations Really Look at Dumping?

Bases of Estimated Normal Values of Exporters	U.S. Cases (1995–98)		EC cases (1995–97)	
	Number of Cases Examined	Average Dumping Margins	Number of Cases Examined	Average Dumping Margins
Price comparisons only	5	3.2	8	22.7
Price comparisons and constructed values	33	14.2	33	24.4
Constructed values	20	25.1	12	25.1
Non-market economies	47	40.0	12	45.6
"Best available facts"	36	95.6	2	74.5
All cases examined	141	44.7	67	29.6

Sources: Lindsey 1999 for the U.S. cases; Messerlin 2000a for the EC cases.

product that would meet the three following conditions:

- The Chinese MFN tariff on the product involved is moderate (e.g., 10 percent or less). This threshold tariff will be one of the core components of a more economically sound "interpretation" of China's NME status to be agreed upon during the DDA. It could be stable over time, or it could increase as time passes—showing an increasing confidence in the ongoing Chinese liberalization process among China's trading partners.
- No "core grey measures" shall be imposed on the product in question by the Chinese authorities. The list of the core gray-area measures to be introduced in the interpretation agreement also should be negotiated during the DDA. It should be short (e.g., specific tariffs, quantitative restrictions, and minimum prices) and only the measures listed should be considered as parts of the conditions.
- No state-owned monopolies shall *distribute* in China the competing foreign and Chinese varieties of the product in question. Chinese state-owned sole *producers* are acceptable because, as shown by economic analysis, a protection granted exclusively by a moderate tariff eliminates the risk of monopoly power of the domestic sole producer.

Table 3.4 shows that Chinese *ad valorem* tariffs applied in 2001 lower than 10 percent amount to 38 percent of all the tariff lines. The fact that the Chinese tariff schedule has only roughly 7,000 tariff lines suggests that it does not offer many opportunities to create narrow niches of protection for carefully defined tariff items. Applying the above conditions thus would substantially reinforce the rights of Chinese exporters in the antidumping cases lodged in these two HTS sections. However, China should take some initiatives for improving the situation in the other antidumping-intensive HTS sections, in particular in textiles and clothing.

The rationale for the three conditions is that they make unlikely the fact that Chinese exporters would dump for other reasons than those economically sound, such as differences in demand pattern, and need to meet foreign demand and to make Chinese products known in foreign markets. Hence, the minimum that WTO China's trading

partners should grant to China is the unconditional benefit of market economy status in the antidumping investigations faced by the Chinese exports meeting these conditions.[6]

Three final observations are necessary. First, the negotiations on the improved implementation of the NME status for China should be as swift as possible. Second, the conditions can be easily defined on a tariff line (HTS) basis. For instance, China could notify the WTO, on a regular basis, of the tariff (HTS) lines for which these conditions are met; this procedure could readily be included in the general monitoring procedures of China accession process. Cross-notifications by China's trading partners could be added to the process, under the condition that they will not slow it. Finally, weaker variants of the above suggestions could be examined, if necessary. For instance, the NME status could only be eliminated for the goods notified after a specified period, for example, one year instead of immediately. Suggesting weaker variants is beyond the scope of this paper and is left to trade negotiators. However, it is worth noting that any weakening of the suggested approach may have huge costs in terms of decreasing incentives for export interests in both China and the rest of the world to support the transition process of the Chinese accession to the WTO.

Stricter Rules on Antidumping

Ambassador Long Yongtu's desire to introduce stricter rules on antidumping in the WTO is a "natural" extension of the negotiation on the NME use proposed above because it focuses on the antidumping rules faced by allegedly dumped exports from market economies. China's efforts to introduce stricter rules on WTO antidumping could follow two very different approaches.

A cautious approach would be to merely table a series of proposals or to support those already tabled in Geneva by a few WTO members for improving WTO-based antidumping regulations at the margin. For instance, the following suggestions, derived from proposals tabled by the Swedish Kommerzkollegium 1999, could receive China's support:

- Dumping should be the *principal* cause of material injury.

- *Double* protection (for instance, antidumping measures imposed on the top of quantitative restrictions) should not be allowed.
- Measures should last a maximum of five years (implying stronger limits to review).
- *Repeated* initiations in a short period of time should not be allowed.
- *Cumulation* of imports from different countries should be banned or severely restricted, unless they come from the same firms or from the subsidiaries of the same firms.
- Aggregating products under the "*one single product*" procedure should be severely restricted.
- All *zeroing* practices (only export transactions that have been found to be dumped are used to calculate dumping margins) should be banned; all export transactions should be included in the investigation.
- The antidumping authorities should produce *disclosure* documents.
- The use of the *de minimis* rule should be expanded in an economically sound way.

Alternatively, China could adopt a bolder approach. For instance, reforming antidumping could take, as often as possible, the form of negotiated "quantitative thresholds" (Messerlin 2000b). WTO members could agree that no antidumping measure should be imposed in cases where the level of injury losses is less than an agreed threshold of the complainants' revenues of the year(s) used as the reference (pre-dumping) period. An approach based on quantitative thresholds is conceptually equivalent to a tariffication process. This approach tends to give a sense of the magnitude of the concessions granted by both sides, bringing it more in line with usual WTO negotiating techniques. It is also flexible enough to permit incremental reforms and to deliver the progressive liberalization that WTO members seek through progressive increases of the thresholds, thereby avoiding the current deadlock of binary choices between fully enforcing antidumping regulations or rejecting them totally.

The TPS Provision and the General Issue of Contingent Protection in the WTO

Section 16 of the China Protocol of Accession creates the TPS mechanism. The TPS makes it legally much easier for WTO members to impose safeguard measures against Chinese exports during the next 12 years, until 2014 (for a detailed description from a legal perspective, see Andersen and Lau 2001). All the terms defining the use of a safeguard action in the traditional GATT-WTO context (under Article XIX) have been systematically weakened: no requirement of "unforeseen circumstances," no MFN requirement, the need for "material" rather than "serious" injury, fewer factors related to the condition of the domestic industry, a weaker causal link between increased imports and injury, the absence of a non-attribution causation analysis.

The most important—and potentially the most devastating for the WTO—provision of Section 16 of the WTO China Protocol states that WTO members have the unprecedented possibility to use a "trade-diversion" clause. This means that, as soon as one WTO Member implements a TPS measure against Chinese exports, all the others could enforce a similar measure at almost no cost in terms of legal procedures (e.g., no investigation, no prior notification, no input from Chinese parties). In short, the trade-diversion clause makes almost unchallengeable the hypothesis that Chinese exports will be diverted from the first closed market to the rest of the world.

All these features put the TPS largely in contradiction with the WTO's usual deep concerns about a fair balance of rights and obligations. It is a provision so unbalanced that one can fear that its use will trigger feelings in China close to those associated to the "Unequal Treaties" of the nineteenth century. As a result, it represents a serious systemic risk to the WTO regime.

One may argue that the TPS is such a politically aggressive instrument that one may wonder whether it will be ever used. This argument is far from convincing. Its politically explosive content makes the TPS unlikely to be initiated by a WTO member other than a very large industrial country (the United States, the European Community, or Japan). However, all the other WTO members that would have waited for such a move would benefit from the "trade diversion" clause as soon as a large industrial country takes the lead.

What are the possible actions left to China if the TPS were to be invoked? A first possibility would be to negotiate the same "preemptive" approach as for the NME provision by negotiating during the Doha

Round an interpretation agreement on the effective use of this procedure. WTO members would agree not to use the TPS when Chinese products would meet the three conditions listed above. Rather, they would use the normal WTO safeguard provision under Article XIX.

Putting antidumping and safeguard regulations on a par would make a lot of sense from the perspective of the global WTO architecture. Most WTO members use antidumping as a substitute for safeguards, with many antidumping measures in fact being safeguard actions dealing with industries in difficulties. In fact, the TPS provision expands China's strong stake in substantial improvements of antidumping rules to the whole WTO contingent protection regime—that is, antidumping *and* safeguard regulations. As a result, during the DDA, China may not only be very active in the antidumping negotiations but could also try to expand these negotiations to safeguards—so far not explicitly included in the Doha negotiating program—to make the whole WTO contingent protection regime more consistent.

A promising way to improve the current WTO Safeguard Agreements would require tying together the concept of temporary protection embedded in safeguards and the basic concept of renegotiation under GATT Article XXVIII (Messerlin 2000b). For instance, at the end of the second period of enforcing a safeguard measure allowed by the current Safeguards Agreement (based in turn on GATT Article XIX), the country shall be requested to choose between two alternatives: either to renegotiate the tariff of the product subjected to the safeguard measure in question, or to eliminate the safeguard measure (using then antidumping or any other trade remedy should be prohibited since all the instruments of contingent protection are substitutable). The logic of the mandatory aspect of such a choice is that current safeguard and antidumping procedures transform what should be transitory protection into permanent protection.

The possibility remains that such a global approach to antidumping, safeguards, and TPS measures may face entrenched hostility from WTO members, in particular from the top 10 antidumping users. In such a case, the remaining options for China would rely on some kind of threats of retaliation. The least aggressive approach would be for China to announce its intention to systematically use the dispute settlement mechanism as soon as a WTO member notifies TPS use to the WTO Secretariat. Lawyers tend to overstate the benefits of such an approach, by ignoring the full development of the trade conflicts. It is almost certain that WTO dispute settlement cases dealing with the TPS would leave the two parties in a difficult political situation. A more aggressive approach by China would be based on Article 56 of the New Regulation. However, such an approach should not ignore the basic principle of deterrence: trade deterrence, as nuclear deterrence, is good as long as it remains a threat—as long as it stops short of being an effective action.

Conclusion

The chapter provides two results of prime importance for China. First, the countries that would gain most from better disciplines on antidumping rules are the few developing countries which, since the 1995 Uruguay Round, are intensive antidumping users. Because antidumping measures imposed by these developing countries tend to be more frequent and severe than those imposed by industrial countries, they hurt developing countries' domestic economies much more than industrial country-imposed antidumping measures harm theirs. If China wants to continue to enjoy successful liberalization, it should not become an intensive antidumping user.

Second, few economic and political forces would introduce some automatic counterweights and restraints to the situation currently existing in terms of antidumping enforcement. Major current users have few incentives to reform their very discriminatory use of the antidumping instrument, mostly targeting other countries than the top 10 users if one accepts, of course, the economically sound welfare-based incentive that protection is harmful to the economy of the country imposing it. Meanwhile, smaller countries have few incentives to use the antidumping instrument in a retaliatory move.

As a result, China is at crossroads—and with China, so is the rest of the world, and in particular, the United States and the European Community, the world's largest economies. On the one hand, China may be increasingly tempted to use antidumping rules more intensively for several reasons: as a back door of old-time protection, at the risk of unraveling her scheduled trade liberalization; as a progressive integration in the worldwide collusive dimension of antidumping, used as an instrument for segmenting world markets for the benefit of large firms; and as a retaliatory instrument against foreign antidumping measures. This last reason is specific to China, and it deserves a comment. Retaliatory antidumping measures can have some appeal only for countries with markets large enough to generate some deterrence power. Chinese markets are not yet large enough to meet this condition. However, strong Chinese growth will change this situation relatively rapidly, and China's increasingly credible threat of antidumping retaliation implies that WTO disciplines on antidumping should become increasingly attractive to major trading partners (if the United States and the European Community are not myopic). Since WTO Rounds tend to last for extended periods, this evolution should be taken into account by the United States and the European Community as early as the current Doha Round—thereby triggering a potentially "virtuous" dynamic game.

On the other hand, being still a small antidumping user and a key target of foreign antidumping measures, China has expressed the desire to impose stricter WTO antidumping rules. It will be one of the main beneficiaries of such a move because it would allow it to preserve its successful trade liberalization. Such a move may have another key positive outcome: it will help China to negotiate an economically sound interpretation of the special provisions on antidumping and safeguard included in its WTO accession protocol. This new interpretation of these special provisions should be based on a few key and economically sound conditions to be met by China: low tariffs, no "core gray" measures, and no distribution monopolies. Such an interpretation relies on the following strong economic and political argument. China and its trading partners have a common interest in establishing the strongest possible link between Chinese effective liberalization and the elimination of the use of these special provisions by foreign authorities against Chinese exporters. In other words, the suggested interpretation of the specific antidumping and safeguard provisions included in China's accession protocol is an effort to mobilize the export interests in both China and the rest of the world during the difficult implementation period of the Chinese accession to the WTO.

Notes

1. In Spring 2002, the EC and the United States declared that they will consider Russia as a market economy for purposes of antidumping investigations. However, the case for the introduction of a TPS provision in Russia's accession protocol seems still open. It would be interesting to make a parallel between the conditions imposed on Japan's accession to GATT, and those imposed on China in its accession to the WTO.

2. Tables 3.1 to 3.3 treat measures taken against different individual member-states of the EC as one aggregated measure if adopted at the same time and for the same product (data for 2002 are still not totally complete). By contrast, table 3.4 follows the notifications of EC trading partners that vary in their treatment of the EC (as one entity or as a set of distinct member-states).

3. Are antidumping measures used by developing countries as a "safety valve" for softening the impact of their ongoing trade liberalizations? Rather, comparing the intensity of antidumping use with three indicators capturing key aspects (simplicity, irreversibility, and openness, as estimated by Laird and Messerlin (2002) of the trade policy of the six developing countries, which are intensive antidumping users, suggests a correlation between antidumping intensity and a flagging trade liberalization.

4. For instance, under the NME status, it is possible to use industrial countries (such as the United States or Sweden) as "reference" countries for China. That introduces systemic errors about the product and/or the production process. For instance, it makes no sense to consider, without deep economic analysis, the calcium metal produced in small quantities by a U.S. monopolist for its own use as similar to the calcium metal produced by China and Russia in large quantities for sales on international markets. The U.S. product is likely to have characteristics in terms of quality and/or availability making it very different from the Russian or Chinese calcium metal, and it is sold and bought in a market structure very different from the markets of its Russian and Chinese counterparts. In the same vein, trying to estimate production costs by combining input prices in industrial countries and input quantities used in a developing country makes little economic sense.

5. Antidumping authorities in the EC and the Untied States in some cases already adopt more liberal interpretations vis-a-vis Chinese exporters than the Protocol allows them. In the European Community, for example, this would be the case where the authorities accept individual treatment or market-economy status with respect to individual Chinese exporters.

6. It could be argued that market forces in China for these relatively unprotected products could be distorted by Chinese regulations on inputs for such goods (for instance, subsidies). However, there are WTO instruments for addressing such an argument (which could be applied to most China trading partners).

References

Andersen, Scott, and Christian Lau. 2001. "Hedging Hopes with Fears in China' Accession to the World Trade Organization: The Transitional Special Product Safeguard for Chinese Exports." Mimeo. Geneva: Powell, Goldstein, Frazer and Murphy.

Bloningen, Bruce. 2001. Database on U.S. Antidumping Cases. (*www.uoregon.edu*).

GATT Secretariat. 1994. *The Results of the Uruguay Round Multilateral Trade Negotiations.* Geneva: World Trade Organization.

Kommerzkollegium. 1999. Further Actions within the EU in the Field of Antidumping. Stockholm: Kommerzkollegium. Photocopy (17 June).

Laird, Sam, and Patrick A. Messerlin. 2002. "Trade Policy Regimes and Development Strategies: A Comparative Study." Mimeo. Washington, D.C.: InterAmerican Development Bank.

Lindsey, Brink. 1999. *The US Antidumping Law: Rhetoric versus Reality*. Washington, D.C.: Cato Institute.

Lindsey, Brink, and Dan Ikenson. 2001. *Coming Home to Roost: Proliferating Antidumping Laws and the Growing Threat to US Exports*. Washington, D.C.: Cato Institute.

Messerlin, Patrick A. 2000a. "An Economic Perspective on Antidumping and Safeguard." Seminar on Antidumping and Safeguards. Department of International Trade and Economic Affairs. Beijing: Ministry of Foreign trade and Economic Cooperation.

Messerlin, Patrick A. 2000b. "Antidumping and Safeguards." In Jeff Schott, ed. *The WTO After Seattle*. Washington, D.C.: Institute for International Economics.

Vermulst, Edwin. 2000. "Contingent Protection Provisions in China's Draft Protocol on Accession to the WTO." Seminar on Antidumping and Safeguards. Department of International Trade and Economic Affairs. Beijing: Ministry of Foreign Trade and Economic Cooperation.

Wang, Lei. 2003. "China's New Antidumping Regulations: Improvement to Comply with the WTO Rules." Mimeo (*1wang@ealawfirm.com*). Beijing: East Associates.

World Trade Organization (WTO). 2001. *Market Access: Unfinished Business, Post-Uruguay Round Inventory and Issues*. Special Studies 6. Geneva.

4

INTELLECTUAL PROPERTY RIGHTS IN THE WTO ACCESSION PACKAGE: ASSESSING CHINA'S REFORMS

Keith E. Maskus

After a long period of rapid growth and significant structural change, the Chinese economy increasingly makes use of advanced production technologies, while demand shifts toward higher-quality goods and services. Chinese enterprises place growing emphasis on developing brand-name recognition, reputation for quality, and product innovation. In such an environment, the provision and enforcement of intellectual property rights (IPRs) help promote further economic development. With substantial structural reform ongoing in Chinese enterprises, it is important to establish incentives for the development and expansion of businesses in high-growth sectors and to support innovation in consumer products. Properly structured, IPRs can help achieve these goals.

The Chinese central government recognizes the need for a workable IPRs system. Support is also growing among innovative Chinese enterprises, which are likely to suffer the largest losses from trademark and copyright infringement in the economy. Chinese enterprises understand that their access to new foreign technologies depends partially on IPRs.

In response both to changes in internal preferences and to considerable external pressure, China has undertaken a dramatic reform of its intellectual property laws. Since 1990 the government has updated its laws covering copyrights, trademarks, patents, and trade secrets (or "anti-unfair competition") and has adopted protection for new plant varieties and integrated circuits. The country has joined nearly all major international IPRs conventions and is a member of international agreements on classification of patents and trademarks and the deposit of microorganisms.

Most recently China made further revisions to conform to the requirements of the Agreement on Trade-Related Aspects of Intellectual Property Rights (TRIPS) in the World Trade Organization (WTO). In its accession agreement with WTO members, China agreed to implement intellectual property laws that are fully consistent with TRIPS. When legislative reforms are fully implemented, China will have a modern structure for IPRs on a par with many developed economies.

China also has established education and training programs in IPRs, upgraded its administrative and legal systems for enforcing these rights, and undertaken numerous anticounterfeiting programs. Nevertheless, problems remain in the areas of administration and enforcement. Victims of infringement complain about weak monetary and civil penalties, delays in administrative and court procedures, and "local protectionism" that makes enforcement difficult in regional jurisdictions.

The evolving system presents both opportunities and challenges for the Chinese economy. The opportunities arise from the improved environment for technical innovation, product development, and inward technology and investment flows. The challenges include moving resources out of infringing activities into legitimate businesses, coping with higher costs of imitating products and technologies, and absorbing the costs of administering a stronger system.

Over time, stronger IPRs will shift incentives away from encouraging static competition through copying and imitation toward promoting dynamic competition through innovation, technology absorption, and product design. The latter incentives are increasingly appropriate for China, which plans to become a leader in technology development. However, stronger intellectual property protection will place competitive pressures on lagging enterprises and will raise concerns about the distribution of costs and benefits among individuals, enterprises, and regions.

The ultimate objectives of an IPRs system are to increase competition through innovation and technology acquisition and to encourage innovators to make their products available to consumers. Strengthening IPRs improves such incentives but is not sufficient on its own. Rather, the system needs to be developed within a broader set of policies, including further enterprise reform, development of financial and innovation systems, expansion of educational opportunities, and means for sustaining competition in Chinese markets.

This chapter contains the following sections:

- a description of the progress in China's WTO commitments in the IPRs area
- an overview of the economic rationale for intellectual property rights
- a discussion of the intricate relationships between IPRs and economic development, including a review of available evidence on that subject and assessment of the potential of the China's regime to encourage growth
- an analysis of recent trends in the use of IPRs in China, considering both data and information learned from a series of interviews in 1998 and 2001, and some simple indications of how

Chinese economic development could be affected by stronger IPRs
- conclusions and recommendations.

WTO Commitments

Since the mid-1980s China has implemented a number of laws and administrative regulations covering intellectual property protection (see Lacroix and Konan 2002; Maskus, Dougherty, and Mertha 1998; Potter 2001). External pressure has been an important impetus for legal change. Many of these changes were made as a result of three agreements, each a Memorandum of Understanding, with the United States.

This regulatory process has culminated in the introduction of numerous changes in China's IPRs regime, both in anticipation of joining the WTO and in becoming fully compliant after the country's accession in late 2001. For example, a substantial second revision of the patent law was achieved in 2000, becoming effective in July 2001. This revision establishes full TRIPS compliance in patent regulations and clarifies and strengthens certain administrative and judicial procedures, including the use of preliminary injunctions. In June 2003 the government issued procedures for issuing compulsory licenses for patented inventions, consistent with TRIPS Article 31, while the patent law itself was revised in August 2003 (WTO 2003).

Similarly, in 1997 the government promulgated new rules on the protection of new plant varieties, establishing *sui generis*, TRIPS-consistent protection along the lines of the 1978 Union for the Protection of New Varieties of Plants (UPOV) treaty.[1] A new set of regulations for the protection of layout designs of integrated circuits came into force October 1, 2001.

Just prior to China's accession to the WTO at the Doha Ministerial in November 2001, some differences with required TRIPS standards remained.[2] Table 4.1 provides a list of areas in which standards are mandated, the norms (minimum standards) in TRIPS, the status of China's laws and regulations just before Doha, and China's actions in cases where a divergence exists. Most of these discrepancies arose in the trademark and copyright areas. For this reason, on October 27, 2001, the People's Congress enacted a substantial revision to its trademark and copyright laws to make both consistent with TRIPS obligations.[3]

TABLE 4.1   Substantive Requirements of the TRIPS Agreement in the WTO

	TRIPS Norm	Pre-WTO Status of Chinese Law	Actions
General Obligations			
National Treatment	Applied for persons	Discrimination in copyright enforcement, trademark agents, and trade secrets protection	Remove discrimination
Most Favored Nation	MFN with reciprocity exemptions for copyright	Member of Berne Convention; TRIPS-compliant	
Copyrights and Neighboring Rights			
Term of protection	Life + 50 years; 50 years corporate	TRIPS-compliant	
Computer software CR	Copyright	TRIPS-compliant	Discussing patents
Data compilations	Copyright	Not protected	Protect with copyright
Phonogram producer and performer rights	Right to prevent fixation, reproduction, or broadcasting for 50 years	Inconsistent with TRIPS	Clarify compensation system; strengthen rights
Broadcast rights	Right to prevent fixation, reproduction, or broadcasting for 20 years, or copyright	Inconsistent with TRIPS	Provide right of communication to public
Rental rights	Right to prohibit rental of computer programs and movies	Not protected	Provide rental rights
Discrimination in enforcement procedures	National Treatment	Foreigners could not use local copyright bureaus	Remove discrimination
Trademarks			
Well-known marks	Protected without requiring registration	No criteria for defining "well-known"; none granted to foreigners	Protect well-known marks; establish criteria
Use restrictions	Use not required for registration; import restraints cannot be used to invalidate use	Law is unclear on prior use	Comply with TRIPS
Symbols protected	Rights extend to distinguishing names, letters, numerals, colors	Certain signs are ineligible	Comply with TRIPS
Geographical Indications			
Basic protection	Prevent misleading claims of origin	Not protected	Comply with TRIPS
Wines and spirits	Prevent use of such words as "style" or "like"	Not protected	Comply with TRIPS
Patents			
Eligibility	Basic exemptions	Probably TRIPS-compliant	Clarify compatibility with TRIPS
Pharmaceutical products	Covered; interim marketing rights	TRIPS-compliant	
Living organisms	Micro-organisms and biological production processes covered; "higher-order" life optional	TRIPS-compliant; plant and animal varieties excluded	Considering patents
Term of protection	20 years from filing	TRIPS-compliant	

TABLE 4.1 (Continued)

	TRIPS Norm	Pre-WTO Status of Chinese Law	Actions
Patents			
Rights	Exclude others from production, use, or distribution	TRIPS-compliant	
Compulsory licenses	Wide scope for use with compensation and limiting conditions	TRIPS-compliant	
Burden of proof in process patent infringement	Falls on defendant	TRIPS-compliant	
Industrial Designs			
Term of protection	10 years from filing	TRIPS-compliant	
Textile designs	Covered	Protected by copyright	Considering design patents
Plant Varieties			
Basic protection	Plant breeders' rights to prevent commercial production or marketing of propagating material	Plant breeders' rights with farmer's privilege and research exemption (UPOV 1978)	
Stronger protection	Patents optional	No patents	
Integrated Circuits			
Term of protection	10 years from filing	TRIPS-compliant	
Rights	Prevent distribution of IC's or IC-using products	TRIPS-compliant	
Exceptions	Non-voluntary license	TRIPS-compliant	
Trade Secrets			
Protection from unfair disclosure	Defines boundaries of unfair practices	TRIPS-compliant	
Test data for pharmaceuticals and agricultural chemicals	Protection from disclosure for unspecified period and unfair use of undisclosed data	Unfair use not prohibited	Protection for six years from date of marketing approval
Control of Anti-Competitive Practices			
Compulsory licenses	Wide latitude for use subject to conditions and consultations	Weak consultation provisions	Comply with TRIPS
Exhaustion	No standard	Depends on form of IPR	
Enforcement			
Sanctions	Civil and criminal sanctions and border measures	In existence but weak enforcement action	Enhance enforcement
Provisional measures	Preliminary injunctions and seizures	Not fully available	Comply with TRIPS
Damages	Adequate to compensate victim of infringement	Generally low or no compensation	Comply with TRIPS
Administrative actions	Enforcement may be through administrative actions	Available but costly and tends to result in small fines	Enhance enforcement
Judicial review	Must be available	Not widely available	Enhance review procedures

The trademark law establishes the right of individual Chinese persons to apply to register trademarks. It clarifies the definition of collective marks, which are marks that several firms in a collective association (e.g., for producing fruits and vegetables of a given quality standard) may use jointly. It also establishes joint ownership and protects collective marks and certificate marks for the first time. It further broadens the range of symbols that may be used as a distinctive mark, extends protection of well-known trademarks to their unauthorized use on different products, and sets out criteria for ascertaining well-known marks. These regulations on well-known marks were further updated and adopted by the National Industrial and Commercial Administration in June 2003 (WTO 2003). The trade mark law also sets out protection for geographical indications in accordance with TRIPS.

The copyright law establishes a communication right over the Internet, sets out fair use limitations for electronic content consistent with two new treaties reached under the aegis of the World Intellectual Property Organization (WIPO), clarifies broadcast and rental rights, and recognizes that databases are copyrightable. Further changes were made in August 2002 with respect to rental rights, performance rights, rights of communication and broadcast, and database protection.

Both the trademark and copyright laws clarify the amounts of compensation available to plaintiffs and the methods for their calculation. In copyrights, foreign firms are now permitted to plead their cases with local copyright bureaus in addition to the National Copyright Administration, removing a prior form of discrimination. A number of clarifications regarding enforcement, administration, and penalties were made in 2002 and 2003 (WTO 2003).

This recent and ongoing activity should make China's IPRs legal regime fully consistent with TRIPS in the near term. It is evident that the promise of WTO membership significantly accelerated China's legal reforms in IPRs, because consistency with at least minimum TRIPS standards is a necessary condition for accession (Maskus 2000a). Moreover, China's commercial interests in innovation, development of consumer products, and access to high-level foreign technologies provided significant domestic motivation for such reforms. Nevertheless, because China remains a country with relatively low per-capita income and technological development has not spread widely through the economy, it is likely that significant problems with enforcement will remain for some time. China may become one focus of dispute resolution cases at the WTO as intellectual property interests from developed countries demand stronger enforcement and protection.

The Nature of Intellectual Property Rights

To analyze how IPRs influence economic development, it is important to understand their economic underpinnings. The need for IPRs arises from the social objective of promoting the creation of new types of information adding to the economy's knowledge base. These types of information include new products and technologies; new literary, musical, and artistic expressions; and indicators of product quality. An intellectual property right defines the extent to which its owners may legally prevent others from taking actions that infringe or damage the property. It also may be defined as the legal ability to set terms on which it may be used, subject to public-interest limitations on the scope of that ability. For example, patents provide exclusive use of a technology, but they are granted only for a fixed period of time and in return for disclosing sufficient technical information to allow competitors to understand it and try to improve on it.

Public intervention is needed because the outcome of some intellectual effort may be potentially valuable but also easily copied and used by others, leaving little incentive to incur the original investment costs or to improve it. Without public support for innovation, the economy suffers from insufficient incentives to develop new products, technologies, and cultural works, making citizens worse off in the long run. An additional problem is that the social value of information is often greater than its private value because there are external benefits from new inventions. Examples include spillover cost reductions from new technologies to input users and network efficiencies from software systems.

At the same time, IPRs generate costs. Legal excludability imposes a static cost on users, reflected by the excess of price over marginal production cost. In the case of intellectual creations, this distortion can be significant because the marginal cost of supplying additional blueprints, digital video discs (DVDs), and computer programs is small. Additional costs are incurred because IPRs encourage duplication of investment in research and development (R&D) through patent races, and generate wasteful efforts to assert and defend ownership rights and to extend those rights beyond the scope granted. Enforcement costs may be substantial.

Thus, there are complex tradeoffs facing the design of IPRs. China needs to strike an appropriate balance among the needs of creators, developers, and users, in accordance with minimum standards required by TRIPS.

One alternative to IPRs is direct government support for invention, including public monopolies in technology development, research institutes in agriculture and industry, and government subsidies to university research. Many such programs are important complements to IPRs in national innovation systems. However, the performance of China's public organizations and state-owned enterprises in commercializing products and services has been poor. This failure arose largely from inadequate incentives within public research institutions to focus on new and marketable inventions.

Intellectual Property Rights and Economic Development

Relationships between IPRs and economic development are extremely complex and available evidence is difficult to interpret (see Evenson and Westphal 1997). However there is a growing consensus that stronger IPRs can improve development prospects if they are structured properly.

Types of Intellectual Property Rights

It is useful to provide a brief description of the main forms of IPRs. Rights to exploit inventions with commercial uses are granted through patents, utility models or petty patents; these terms refer to short-term exclusive rights for small and incremental innovations, and industrial designs. Patents provide the right to prevent for a fixed time (20 years under TRIPS) the unauthorized making, selling, or using of the product or process described. Utility models provide exclusive rights for a shorter period to inventions that embody only a small inventive step. The scope of patent coverage is limited to uses of the novelty claimed by the inventor and recognized by patent examiners. The technology must meet technical criteria for novelty (or non-obviousness), inventiveness, and industrial utility and must survive procedures challenging validity. Patent applications are published for inspection by interested persons. The essential tradeoff in patents is to create a protected market position in return for disclosure of technical knowledge.

A related form of industrial property is plant breeders' rights (PBRs), which permit developers to control the marketing and use of new plant varieties. These rights operate much like patents, providing for fixed terms, requirements of distinctiveness in new plant strains, and disclosure rules. They are intended to encourage development of new seed strains for agricultural use.

Rights to market goods and services under exclusive names and symbols are protected by trademarks and service marks. Registration may be renewed indefinitely, subject to use requirements. An important related device is the geographical indication, which permits the use of a particular place name where a good was produced to ensure that the product embodies quality characteristics of that region. Trademarks provide incentives for firms to invest in brand-name reputation and product quality and for their licensees to produce and sell high-quality goods. If marks were not protected, rival firms would ruin their value by selling cheaper items under those marks. Thus, the social benefits from trademarks include greater product variety and lower consumer search costs due to the absence of confusion.

Firms develop technological know-how that is important for production but may not be patentable or may have greater economic value if it remains undisclosed. Such trade secrets are protected by legal rules against unfair misappropriation. There is no exclusive right to the process if it is discovered by fair means, such as reverse engineering. Trade secrets protection is important because it supports the introduction of sub-patentable technological processes into commerce and also promotes competition through reverse engineering.

Artistic and literary creations are protected by copyrights, which are exclusive privileges to copy and distribute particular creative expressions for a fixed term. Related IPRs include neighboring rights of performers and broadcasters and moral rights of original creators to prevent future alterations of their works. Copyrights are subject to limitations for social purposes, with the most prominent exception being the fair-use doctrine, under which others may use copies for scientific and educational purposes. Countries vary widely in the scope of their fair-use exceptions to copyrights, particularly with regard to reverse engineering of computer programs.

Some new technologies do not fit easily within this framework. Computer software contains elements of both literary expression and industrial utility, raising questions about whether it should be covered by copyrights or patents. The TRIPS standard is for copyright protection; the United States, Japan, and other countries also provide patent protection. Similar questions arise regarding semiconductor chip designs, which achieve a special form of protection under TRIPS. Electronic transmissions of Internet materials, databases, and broadcasts also raise concerns about the adequacy of copyright protection to encourage their development.

IPRs are enforced both to deter and punish infringement and to discipline rights holders that abuse their market power. Enforcement against basic infringement involves seizing unauthorized copies, destroying the associated facilities if necessary, and imposing fines and criminal sanctions. However, as claims about infringement or abuse, particularly in the patent realm, become more complicated, courts must decide on their legality, which requires considerable legal and scientific expertise.

How IPRs Stimulate Economic Development

IPRs protection can spur economic development and growth in several ways. A weak regime can stifle both invention and innovation even at low levels of economic development. Most inventions are specific to local market circumstances and can benefit from patent or utility model protection. Innovation usually involves minor adaptations of existing technologies, management systems, and quality control mechanisms, which can stimulate growth. Such investments tend to have high economic and social returns by raising productivity toward international levels. Evidence from Brazil and the Philippines suggests that effective systems of utility models can promote innovation (see Maskus and McDaniel 1999). Another study demonstrated econometrically that Japan's system of utility models contributed positively and significantly to its postwar rise in productivity (see Scotchmer et al. 1991).

Trademarks provide incentives for the entry of new firms and the development of new products, even in poor nations. Firms find it easier to innovate cumulatively as they grow larger and their trademarks are better recognized. This process has two positive effects on industrial development. First, it stimulates the entry of small and medium-sized enterprises into specific markets. Second, it encourages more successful enterprises to grow and take advantage of scale economies through interregional production and marketing. Some may even become significant exporters as they improve quality.

Similar comments apply to copyrights. Sectors that are dependent on copyrights, such as publishing, recorded entertainment, and software, will experience limited entry by local firms in their absence. Creation of new films, music, and software is expensive and little worth the investment by local entrepreneurs if their products will be copied. Accordingly, society's long-run cultural and economic development is impaired.

Innovation goes beyond developing new products to establishing marketing and distribution networks. It is difficult to do this in an environment of weak IPRs because rights holders cannot readily prevent infringement. IPRs improve the certainty of contracts, and permitting better monitoring and enforcement of rights at all levels of the supply network. In turn, both innovative firms and their distributors are more willing to invest in marketing and brand-name reputation.

As firms build reputations through trademarks, incentives grow to deter false use of those marks. Fake products sold under a misappropriated trademark can ruin reputations, particularly for new firms, and overcoming such damage can be costly. Thus, effective trademark enforcement should increase the average quality of products over time and permit consumers to be less wary of counterfeit goods. This is particularly important in cases of beverages, foodstuffs, and medicines.

Finally, IPRs can help disseminate knowledge. Patent claims are published, and competitors may use the disclosed technical knowledge to develop further inventions. This cumulative process of invention, which depends on the narrowness of patent claims, can be an important source of technical change (see Maskus and Penubarti 1995; Smith 1999). Moreover, patents provide a legal basis for trading and licensing technologies. Trademarks and trade secrets facilitate information exchange through ensuring that licensees do not abandon their contracts.

Considerable evidence suggests that international flows of technology depend on the strength of IPRs, among many other factors. For example, international trade in manufactures is positively affected by the strength of patent regimes in large developing countries (see Coe, Helpman, and Whoffmaister 1997). This trade often embodies technical knowledge that may be learned in recipient countries and adapted to local technological capabilities (see Maskus 1998a; Lee and Mansfield 1996).

Foreign direct investment, joint ventures, and technology-licensing contracts also transfer production knowledge. It is clear that the strength of IPRs influences choices by multinational firms on where to invest and whether to transfer advanced technologies. Studies of U.S.-sourced foreign direct investment (FDI) find evidence that firms limit their investments in countries with weak patents (see Mansfield 1995; Contractor 1980). Survey evidence indicates that the level of technology transferred depends on the ability to maintain control over the technology through defense of intellectual property (see Yang and Maskus 2001). Licensing also tends to rise with stronger IPRs because of reduced contracting costs and greater legal certainty.[4]

How IPRs Limit Economic Development

Tightened IPRs also impose economic costs. Poor countries may experience net losses in the short-run because the dynamic gains tend to take a long time to emerge.

The costs of administering and enforcing a modern IPRs system are high. For China they easily will amount to annual sums in excess of $10 million (see Watal 1999; Lanjouw 1998). These costs include training of examiners, judges, lawyers, and enforcement officers, along with the costs of running various offices. Many of these costs may be covered by administrative fees charged to apply for and register patents and trademarks, while others may be reduced by using international registration agencies such as the Patent Cooperation Treaty (PCT), as does China.

The most visible aspect of IPRs infringement in China is unauthorized copying of recorded entertainment and software and selling of products bearing counterfeit trademarks. Undoubtedly, significant amounts of labor are employed in copying and retailing illegitimate products in China, and an important short-run cost of stronger IPRs will be labor displacement. The adjustment costs tend to be smaller in economies with flexible labor markets

and rapid growth, making it easier to shift workers into legitimate activities. China has mixed prospects on this score, in part because of restrictions on internal labor mobility. It is conceivable that copyright and trademark enforcement will contribute significantly to looming unemployment problems associated with economic reform.

Because IPRs raise the costs of copying and imitating products and technologies, acquiring technological knowledge through simple imitation could become more expensive in China. Considerable anecdotal evidence suggests that firms operating in China lose technologies to potential rivals through such avenues as defection of technical personnel, misappropriation by input suppliers, and copying of blueprints. Without effective trade secret protection, these activities are common and help establish competition. However, some important practical effects are that foreign firms tend to transfer older technologies, engage in less technical training, hide key aspects of know-how from subcontractors and suppliers, and not establish first-rate R&D facilities.

Accordingly, stronger IPRs entail a balancing act. Stronger IPRs make uncompensated imitation more difficult but improve the quality of technology flows. Countries wishing to become significant technology developers should favor IPRs for that reason.

Stronger IPRs create market power, from which firms may be able to raise prices to monopolistic levels. This concern is particularly relevant in developing countries for two reasons. First, applications for protection come overwhelmingly from foreign firms, meaning that the associated profits are transferred abroad. Second, market competition may be weak, supporting monopolization. As will be discussed in the next section, China is in an intermediate position in this regard. Patent applications by domestic firms are rising rapidly but lag behind foreign applications. Broader economic reforms have improved competitive processes, but the economy remains far from a situation of free entry and vibrant competition in technology and product markets.

Chinese authorities may be especially concerned about the implications of patent rights for the prices of medicines. There is evidence that patents can support markedly higher prices for protected drugs than for copied and generic drugs.[5]

However, the extent of these price increases depends on the competitive aspects of markets. The more competitive the local drugs market is before patents are awarded, the larger is the share of drug production that consists of copies of patentable drugs; the more inelastic the demand for medicines is, the higher will be the price increases caused by patents. These conditions suggest that countries with extensive drug imitation and high demand could experience substantial price increases for protected drugs. In this regard, China's policy of public procurement at negotiated prices is appropriate for ensuring the continued provision of public health services.

Another area of concern is computer software. It is often claimed that software would be much more expensive with enforced copyrights because the current prices of legitimate copies in developing nations are very high compared to prices of unauthorized copies. However, in countries with high piracy rates software producers or their distributors tend to sell at low volumes and high markups, reflecting small markets with inelastic demand. In China such markets are largely limited to foreign-owned enterprises and government agencies. As markets broaden under copyright enforcement, foreign and domestic firms should supply more legitimate copies at lower prices, suggesting that ultimate price increases could be modest (see Potter 2001).

Thus, there are legitimate concerns about market power supported by IPRs. However, competitive markets and appropriate regulation can mitigate these impacts without unduly reducing innovative incentives. IPRs need to be introduced into markets in which other competitive processes, such as firm entry, labor flexibility, distribution systems, and international trade, are operating effectively.

Competition is important because IPRs may be abused, as shown by litigation problems in the United States, the European Union, and elsewhere. Such abuses include bad-faith lawsuits, hidden ownership of intellectual property, restrictive patent pooling agreements, refusals to license technologies, tie-in sales in related markets, and insistence on exclusive rights to competing technologies. Thus, China must develop mechanisms for ensuring competition maintenance in markets affected by IPRs.

A Scorecard for China's IPRs Regime

With this background it is useful to assess informally the legal standards China has adopted in terms of how these standards may affect prospects for technical change and the provision of certain public goods.[6] For this purpose, China's regulations in several critical areas are compared against benchmark standards consistent with TRIPS requirements for middle-income countries as set out by the World Bank (2001). China has characteristics of the dynamic middle-income countries, including a growing base of human capital and sophisticated capabilities in science and technology, suggesting that this comparison may be appropriate. However, it also suffers from substantial rural and urban poverty, and many of its enterprises use technologies that lag significantly behind those in the modern sectors. Accordingly, it is difficult to provide a definitive analysis of the nation's laws in this context, and the following analysis is offered largely for purposes of illustration and discussion.

An overview is provided in table 4.2. In the copyrights area, China provides TRIPS-standard terms of protection for creative goods, such as a once-renewable 25-year term for software copyrights (50-year maximum period). The essential question is whether the particular conditions of legal protection are appropriate for China's development prospects. For example, it is recommended that middle-income countries provide fairly wide exceptions for fair use of copyrighted materials in education and scientific research. China's Copyright Law embraces this concept, permitting free use of copyrighted material in journals, periodicals, and broadcast media for purposes of disseminating news. It also allows the uncompensated making of copies for classroom use and scientific research and allows a free right to translate works from Han into minority languages. In software, users are permitted a limited right of decompilation for purposes of developing new programs, which should help the industry remain fairly open to incremental innovation and competition. However, the government is considering extending patents to computer programs, a standard that would exceed TRIPS requirements and is found only in the United States, Japan, and Australia (see Caves 2000). For a software sector that remains young and subject to

TABLE 4.2   An Assessment of China's IPRs System for Development Purposes

Area of IPRs	Middle-Income Standards	China's Post-WTO Standards	Commentary
Copyrights			
Fair use exceptions	Liberal exceptions for education and research	Same	Important for research and technology access
Computer software	Copyrights with decompilation and fair use	Permit limited decompilation and fair use; considering patents	Patents may be overly protective
Market institutions	Improve collection societies and rights contracts	Weak institutions	Improvement would be beneficial
WIPO treaties	Adopt minimum standards	Considering ratification	Could improve internet content and access
Data compilations	Copyrights with creativity requirement	Same	Avoid EU-type protection
Trademarks			
Well-known marks	Narrow definition of sectoral coverage	Unclear	Clarify scope and recognize well-known marks
Domain names	Protect against fraudulent registration	Same	Important for promoting internet use
Confidential Information			
Test data	Short period of protection from disclosure	Six years of protection	Stronger than U.S. standard
Disclosure restraints	Limited restraints on what employees may reveal to new employers	Unclear limitation on "promise of gain"	Ambiguity may be detrimental
Patents			
Exemptions from eligibility	Exemptions for discoveries, algorithms, medical treatment methods, plants and animals	Same	Appropriate to retain exemptions
Novelty	Consider oral prior art	Oral prior art in China	Scope could be widened
Inventiveness	High step	Notable progress	Unclear
Scope of claims	Narrow claims and narrow doctrine of equivalents	Single claim; scope unspecified	Depends on examiners
Experimental use	Permit experimental use	Not permitted	May be overly strong
Exhaustion	International exhaustion	National exhaustion	Strong protection
Government use	For clear public interest	Same	Appropriate
Compulsory licenses	Permitted under TRIPS conditions	Same	Appropriate
Utility models and designs	Short duration, low inventiveness	10-year duration, same	Appropriate
Plant Varieties			
Farmers' privilege	Recognize farmers' privilege	Recognized	Appropriate
Breeders' exemption	Use for breeding and scientific research permitted	Permitted	Appropriate

considerable cross-fertilization through learning and reverse engineering, such a choice seems questionable for the medium term. Neither should China extend patents to methods of instruction or of doing business.

Other important issues exist in the copyright area. China has relatively weak complementary institutions for realizing economic returns to creative activity, including collection societies for licensing recorded music and gathering royalties. Indeed, only under the Amended Copyright Law of 2001 were copyright owners given the right to authorize collection associations to administer their rights. Further, because contract enforcement can be weak and uncertain, the ability of enterprises to allocate rights in creative works is limited. Such institutions are important for providing a full framework within which the development of artistic and literary work can grow beyond intermediate stages (see also Dahlman and Aubert 2001). To date China protects databases solely with copyright protection, as mandated by TRIPS, and clarifies that such protection cannot interfere with the independent rights of those who develop components of compilations. This minimum standard is appropriate for a country with a strong interest in access to information databases, and China should be wary of moving toward the much stronger standards of the European Union. Finally, ratification of the WIPO Copyright Treaty and the Treaty on Performances and Phonograms could be beneficial in sorting out copyright protection for Internet transmissions, so long as appropriate fair-use limitations are provided.

The Amended Trademark Law of 2001 clarifies the definition of well-known trademarks by setting out five criteria for achieving protection without registration. It remains to be seen whether these criteria will limit the unauthorized use of such marks by others, and the regulation is unclear about how widely the restrictions on use will apply across sectors of business. This law also recognizes that well-known marks should be applicable to domain names on the Internet, a provision that should promote wider content available to Chinese Internet users.

Protection of confidential test data from disclosure provides applicants for patents in pharmaceutical and chemical products a period of exclusivity in the use of results from clinical trial. It seems advisable for middle-income economies with domestic research capabilities in medicines and biotechnology to provide such exclusivity for some period, but TRIPS is silent on the length of any such requirement. Surprisingly, China has opted to protect it for six years from application date, in comparison to the U.S standard of five years. China's law may be overly protective from the standpoint of the encouragement of domestic competition. Next, China's law on unfair competition has no explicit language on the legality of restraints on the ability of employees to reveal technical secrets to rivals that may hire them, other than to declare void unfair "promises of gain." It is unclear what this statute covers, and the ambiguity

may be costly in terms of sorting out the scope of unfair competition in this area.

China does not patent higher-order life forms or biological research tools. In its 2001 patent law, China retains appropriate exemptions from coverage for discoveries of nature, mental methods of arriving at results (such as computer algorithms and mathematical formulas), diagnostic and surgical treatments, and plant and animal varieties. These limitations are widely advocated for developing countries with emerging biotechnology sectors in order to avoid locking up critical technologies that support additional research and learning. China's patent law does not permit experimental use of patented materials, however, which may be overly strong in the context of its development strategies. The country's standards covering government use, compulsory licenses, and utility models and designs are typical of middle-income economies.

Finally, China's plant variety law also seems appropriate for its needs. The patent law excludes such inventions from coverage, leaving them to variety protection. China's regulation permits the farmers' privilege to use propagating materials for re-planting and also permits experimental use for science and for rival breeders to develop new varieties.

The Issue of Enforcement

The largest remaining obstacle to effective use of IPRs in China is weakness in enforcement procedures. Recent legal changes increased the scope of enforcement considerably. As noted in table 4.1, criminal sanctions are now available for cases of willful infringement, while the maximum permissible monetary sanctions were increased. Preliminary injunctions and orders for seizure of suspected infringing goods may be issued, which are important components of timely relief for IPRs owners. Courts may order compensatory damages, though this standard is weaker than what might be required to deter infringement *a priori*. Finally, enhanced access to judicial review is provided, which is consistent with prior efforts by the Chinese government to strengthen its enforcement mechanisms.

Looking forward, perhaps the most significant issue for China with respect to IPRs and the WTO is that country's commitment to enforce against infringing activities and prevent exports of pirated and counterfeited goods. Because China remains a country with relatively low per-capita income and technological development has not spread widely through the economy, it is likely that significant problems with enforcement will remain for some time. Because the scale of activity in China is so large, weak enforcement against domestic infringement would attract the concerns of patent, trademark, and copyright holders. Thus, China may become one focus of dispute resolution cases at the WTO as intellectual property interests from developed countries demand stronger enforcement and protection.

Whether improvements in enforcement are liable to be in China's favor as a development issue depends on how economic agents respond to the changed incentives. As noted above, it is likely that this factor will generate higher equilibrium inflows of technology transfer. However, the essential question is whether it will expand incentives for local business development. The following section provides evidence that this expansion is likely to occur.

The IPRs Situation in China

Two sources of information about the current situation regarding the use and adequacy of IPRs provide more concrete perspective on the potential impacts of IPRs reform. First, the results of interviews of public officials, university scholars, and enterprise managers conducted in 1998 and 2001 paint a consistent picture that has not changed significantly over the three-year period. In fact, a number of interviewees described the situation with respect to enforcement of IPRs to have deteriorated in that period. Second, analysis of recent patent and trademark statistics in China suggest that the use of formal IPRs is growing rapidly but significant regional disparities exist. Overall the analysis suggests that the IPRs regime for invention and innovation is improving in China but significant problems remain.[7]

Discussion of Interview Findings

Management officials and intellectual property managers of enterprises from several IPR-sensitive industries were interviewed. The enterprises represented a mix of state-owned enterprises (SOEs), private Chinese enterprises, joint ventures with international firms, and majority-owned subsidiaries of multinational enterprises. Most firms in the last category are in high-technology sectors and have significant R&D programs in their home countries, although some undertake R&D in China as well. Thus, the sample is not representative of the bulk of Chinese industry at this time but is more focused on product and technology development.

Overwhelmingly, enterprise managers believe that the legal structure for IPRs in China has improved markedly and is adequate. However, the majority think the enforcement environment remains quite weak, while the rest find it to be weak but improving. Interestingly, Chinese enterprises tend to view the system as improving more rapidly than do foreign-owned enterprises and joint ventures. Many high-technology Chinese enterprises applaud the new legal climate, which allows them scope for defending their intellectual property.

Unquestionably, inadequate enforcement is the main problem facing firms wishing to exploit intellectual property in China. There can be long delays in enforcement actions and court rulings. Prior to the legislative changes in 2001, monetary penalties were small even in cases of significant infringement, and there was little scope for criminal prosecution of willful and ongoing violations. The new laws increase maximum fines and clarify the nature of criminal activity, but some interviewees thought these changes would be insufficient to deter infringement. Enforcement actions may be taken arbitrarily and may lack transparency. The central government and certain regional and municipal governments are taking steps to reduce these problems, and several enterprise managers in 2001 positively commented on this change.

There are several structural sources of weak enforcement:

- Trademark infringement and illegal copying remain profitable and face little opposition, especially in rural and inland regions.
- Enterprises engaged in infringement often are important employers and sources of revenue for local governments.
- Low salaries for public officials may reduce their effectiveness as enforcement agents, while administrative programs may be underfunded.

- Legal and technical expertise for administrative and judicial operations is limited despite the existence of special training programs in IPRs.

Among these problems, "regional protectionism" in IPRs is regarded as the most difficult to confront by enterprises suffering infringement. There is little coordination among regional bureaus of the Administration for Industry and Commerce (AIC). Moreover, the regional AICs have weak administrative powers and actions of municipal governments may supercede them. Municipal government officials may well have priorities that take precedence over IPRs enforcement.

Managers of both Chinese and foreign-affiliated enterprises expressed the view that weak enforcement of IPRs results in widespread copyright and trademark infringement. A major problem is that trademark violations often target innovative Chinese enterprises and thereby deter local business development. Examples were given of problems facing Chinese-brand producers of such consumer goods as medicines, soft drinks, processed foods, tobacco products, and clothing. Enterprises selling electronics products seemed particularly vulnerable. Once brand recognition is achieved, domestic enterprises find their trademarks applied to unauthorized products of lower quality, damaging the original enterprise's reputation. In some cases, Chinese enterprises either had to give up on their trademarks and become licensees of better-known enterprises or undertake extensive private and public enforcement actions. It is impossible to know the extent to which this problem hampers industrial development, but the impact could be significant.

Weak enforcement also impedes efficient use of patents and trade secrets. Patent infringement seems to be most common in utility models, which are easy to copy but are overwhelmingly owned by Chinese enterprises. Several foreign enterprises also claimed to have lost patented technologies through unfair means, such as the selling of design specifications and technical manuals by former employees. According to one industry association, such cases are becoming more common and increasingly targeted on sophisticated technologies. Interviewers claimed that many foreign companies are considering more carefully whether they wish to transfer advanced technologies into the Chinese economy.

Defection of technical and managerial employees remains a basic problem for both foreign-owned and Chinese enterprises. In economic terms a balance is needed between promoting mobility of skilled labor, which raises diffusion and competition, and discouraging uncompensated losses of technical knowledge, which can reduce competition over time. Both foreign and domestic enterprises attempt to manage the problem with temporary anti-disclosure clauses, but such contracts have been difficult to enforce in China and recent changes in the law have not clarified this issue.

Most respondents agreed that the environment for selling copyrighted materials is improving in China, although pirating of software, games, DVDs, and music remains common. While large foreign firms claim significant harm from such copying, it is likely that relatively larger losses are suffered by Chinese entertainment and publishing interests. For its part, the Chinese software industry is growing rapidly, largely because of a substantial base of skilled software engineers and managers. However, according to many interviewees, such firms concentrate on developing small-scale programs that attract less copying, such as business applications or limited-run games. This problem could delay the establishment of Chinese-developed software standards and networking software.

Significant differences exist between Chinese and foreign-owned businesses in their ability to deal with trademark and other IPRs-related violations. Foreign companies have more resources to combat infringement than domestic enterprises. Insofar as an enforcement action is a significant expense for a small or medium-sized Chinese operation, enforcement difficulties are biased against Chinese business development. Furthermore, foreign companies, particularly Western ones, are more inclined to seek legal solutions to IPRs problems.

Foreign companies may undertake more defensive actions in the presence of weak IPRs. Managers of most foreign enterprises indicated a reluctance to locate R&D facilities in China, although this is changing rapidly as the legal environment improves. Nearly all indicated that in the past they transferred technologies that are at least five years behind global standards in the expectation that those technologies would be lost to local competition, or they brought in technologies that would be obsolete quickly. Foreign enterprise managers are often reluctant to license technologies, preferring joint ventures and majority-owned subsidiaries in which they can exercise greater control of proprietary secrets. Enterprises are unlikely to integrate fully their Chinese operations, splitting various production processes among facilities in order not to reveal fully the underlying know-how.

Other defensive measures are used by both Chinese and foreign companies. One is to sell only to established customers that need assured quality, such as hospitals, large enterprises, and public agencies. This acts as a barrier to the entry of small firms needing the associated products or inputs. A second is to establish strict vertical supply and distribution chains to permit monitoring of quality. A third is to employ technical safeguards, such as software locks and encrypted source codes that must be decoded to operate software upgrades.

It is impossible to know how these distortions associated with weak IPRs contribute to economic inefficiency in China, although the effects presumably are significant. If so, stronger IPRs over time will generate important static and dynamic efficiencies.

Public officials often raise concerns about the potential impacts of stronger IPRs on prices and competition. Some officials also recognize that stronger IPRs need to be accompanied by other policy measures to build technological capacities and maintain competition. However, this recognition only recently has been translated into such policy initiatives as the Standards Office within the State Industry Commission, which will establish uniform national standards for information networks, including copyright provisions.

Patent and Trademark Activity in China

Despite these problems, data on patent and trademark use indicate that both foreign and domestic enterprises are applying for more protection. Table 4.3 presents figures on applications to the State Intellectual Property Organization for all three types of patents from 1994–2000. Domestic enterprises more than doubled their applications for invention patents, while foreign applications rose by 235 percent. From 1996 through 1999 foreign applications considerably exceeded domestic applications. A significant rise in Chinese domestic applications in 2000 virtually equalized the number for that year, however. Chinese enterprises now apply for nearly as many invention patents, with their higher inventive content, as do foreign enterprises.[8]

In contrast, applications for utility models and design patents overwhelmingly are filed by Chinese organizations. In both categories domestic applications rose far faster than foreign applications. Thus, these rewards aimed at encouraging small-scale invention seem to be having their desired effect on domestic innovation.

Table 4.4 shows data for patent grants and the ratio of cumulative grants to cumulative applications over the same period. Grants of invention patents to both domestic and foreign applicants increased rapidly, with the former nearly catching up to the latter by 2000. The aggregate grants ratios for invention patents are surprisingly low, perhaps reflecting long examination delays. Grant rates are much higher in utility models and

TABLE 4.3   Patent Applications by Type and Nationality, 1994–2000

	Invention Patents		Utility Models		Design Patents		Total Patents	
	Domestic	Foreign	Domestic	Foreign	Domestic	Foreign	Domestic	Foreign
1994	11,191	7,876	45,188	323	11,428	1,729	67,807	9,928
1995	10,018	11,618	43,429	312	15,433	2,235	68,880	14,165
1996	11,471	17,046	49,341	263	21,395	3,219	82,207	20,528
1997	12,713	20,953	49,902	227	27,456	2,957	90,071	24,137
1998	13,726	22,234	51,220	177	31,287	3,345	96,233	25,756
1999	15,596	21,098	57,214	278	37,148	2,905	109,958	24,281
2000	25,346	26,401	68,461	354	46,532	3,588	140,339	30,343
Growth	126.50%	235.20%	51.50%	9.60%	307.20%	107.50%	107.00%	205.60%
Total	100,061	127,226	364,755	1,934	190,679	19,978	655,495	149,138

TABLE 4.4   Patent Grants by Type and Nationality, 1994–2000

	Invention Patents		Utility Models		Design Patents		Total Patents	
	Domestic	Foreign	Domestic	Foreign	Domestic	Foreign	Domestic	Foreign
1994	1,659	2,224	32,611	208	5,507	1,088	39,877	3,520
1995	1,530	1,863	30,195	276	9,523	1,677	41,248	3,816
1996	1,383	1,593	26,961	210	11,381	2,252	39,725	4,055
1997	1,532	1,962	27,185	153	17,672	2,488	46,389	4,603
1998	1,655	3,078	33,717	185	26,006	3,248	61,378	6,511
1999	3,097	4,540	56,094	274	32,910	3,241	92,101	8,055
2000	6,177	6,506	54,407	336	34,652	3,267	95,236	10,109
Growth	272.30%	192.50%	66.80%	61.50%	529.20%	200.20%	138.80%	187.20%
Total	17,033	21,766	261,170	1,642	137,651	17,261	415,954	40,669
Grants Ratio	17.00%	17.10%	71.60%	84.90%	72.20%	86.40%	63.50%	27.30%

Source: State Intellectual Property Office 2000.

TABLE 4.5   Bilateral Invention Patent Applications, 1994–98

Country	1994		1996		1998	
	by China in Foreign	in China by Foreign	by China in Foreign	in China by Foreign	by China in Foreign	in China by Foreign
U.S.	190	8,105	246	14,892	436	25,634
Japan	137	3,742	145	7,212	373	11,301
Germany	172	2,094	210	3,631	624	6,599
U.K.	188	2,028	224	2,656	627	4,216
Australia	87	692	101	746	295	1,067
Korea, Rep. of	84	569	97	1,645	309	2,076
Brazil	85	20	100	39	290	104
India	21	8	54	6	15	21

design patents, which are easier to examine and carry shorter protection periods.

Tables 4.5 and 4.6 indicate trends in bilateral invention patenting activity between China and key trading partners.[9] Chinese patent applications abroad rose sharply between 1996 and 1998 in all countries listed except India, suggesting an increasing international orientation of Chinese innovation. However, China remains well behind most developed countries in terms of bilateral applications flows, with the United States and Japan together applying for some 37,000 patents in 1998 in that country. Despite the increase in Chinese applications abroad, only Japan actually granted rising numbers of invention patents to Chinese inventors.

Table 4.7 provides a breakdown of total domestic patent applications for the top 11 patenting regions

in China during 1985–96 and 2000. Residents of Guangdong applied for over 21,000 patents in 2000, while people in Hebei applied for less than 4,000. Better measures of inventive capacity are given in the final two columns as applications per million people and applications per million yuan of regional GDP. In these rankings Beijing is at the top of the list, with far more applications per capita and per unit of output than any other province. This reflects both Beijing's status as a technology developer and the fact that many patent registrations come through legal offices in the capital. Shanghai has the second highest applications per person but ranks sixth in applications per yuan of GDP. Fujian and Hebei rank low in both categories.

The middle column ranks these regions in terms of average income per capita. There are large

TABLE 4.6 Bilateral Invention Patent Grants, 1994–98

Country	1994 to China by Foreign	1994 by China to Foreign	1996 to China by Foreign	1996 by China to Foreign	1998 to China by Foreign	1998 by China to Foreign
U.S.	48	701	46	449	72	785
Japan	5	579	29	445	7	927
Germany	16	213	15	148	7	318
U.K.	21	94	29	66	12	133
Australia	4	24	5	20	14	36
Korea, Rep. of	0	48	0	49	2	149
Brazil	2	4	0	1	5	2
India	5	2	1	0	0	3

Note: Data include applications under Patent Cooperation Treaty.
Source: WIPO, various years.

TABLE 4.7 Patenting Indicators for Top Patenting Regions, 1985–96 and 2000

Region	Applications 1985–96	Applications 2000	2000 GDP per Capita, Yuan	2000 Applications per Million of Population	2000 Applications per Million Yuan of GDP
Guangdong	42,159	21,123	11,180.55	487.84	436.33
Shanghai	21,758	11,337	27,187.57	1,299.76	478.07
Beijing	54,348	10,344	17,936.32	3,932.56	2,192.51
Zhejiang	29,197	10,316	12,906.56	624.27	483.68
Shandong	37,082	10,019	9,408.97	408.44	434.09
Jiangsu	34,983	8,211	11,538.99	470.33	407.60
Liaoning	38,768	7,151	11,017.23	914.77	830.31
Sichuan	27,046	4,496	4,814.86	324.72	674.41
Fujian	11,027	4,211	11,293.86	317.69	281.29
Hunan	26,400	4,117	5,732.76	409.94	715.08
Hebei	20,584	3,848	7,545.91	305.22	404.48
Correlation with GDP per capita				0.54	0.78

Sources: The Patent Office, *Annual Report, 2000;* State Statistical Bureau, *China Statistical Yearbook 2000;*
Author's calculations.

regional disparities in income levels, ranging from Sichuan at the bottom to Shanghai at the top. The difference between them is a factor of 5.6, which is extraordinarily high for regions within a country. It is interesting to correlate per-capita GDP with the relative patent application figures; there is a strong positive correlation (0.54) between GDP per capita and patent applications per million people. Thus, richer provinces apply for more patents (develop more products) per person than poor provinces. The correlation between GDP per capita

and applications per million yuan of GDP is higher (0.78). Accordingly, higher incomes are associated with greater innovation propensities, which in turn raise regional economic growth.

Data for trademark registrations not shown here tell a similar story. In particular, trademark applications have risen rapidly since 1994, especially those through the Madrid Protocol. Far more domestic marks are registered than foreign ones, but foreign applications have increased at a faster pace. In terms of regional performance, Guangdong had the largest absolute number of applications in 2000, followed by Zhejiang and Jiangsu. Scaled by population, however, Shanghai ranked first by a large margin, followed by Beijing, Zhejiang, and Guangdong. There is a very high correlation (0.81) between per-capita GDP and per-capita applications, reflecting again that trademark applications rise with income levels.

Thus, the use of patents and trademarks is rising rapidly in China for several reasons:

- Laws have been strengthened and fees reduced, encouraging more applications.
- As trademark and patent infringement have increased, both domestic and foreign enterprises recognized the importance of establishing intellectual property protection, even in an environment of weak but improving IPRs.
- Chinese markets are getting deeper as income grows, despite the substantial barriers to interregional integration, And registration of IPRs is important for exploiting deeper markets.
- Chinese research organizations and enterprises are engaged in more inventions, and Chinese firms are undertaking more innovative activity.

Conclusions and Recommendations

In recent years China has made significant progress on the legislative end of intellectual property rights, especially in preparation for its entry into the WTO. The specific standards it has adopted across the range of intellectual property regimes are largely consistent with what might be recommended for middle-income developing countries with strong innovation potential. However, in some dimensions the new Chinese standards may be overly protective for an economy that remains largely a net importer of new technology and information. At the same time, China continues to experience severe enforcement problems. Enforcement is likely to be problematic for the intermediate term because of structural difficulties with the system and because costs of copying and counterfeiting remain small relative to prices of legitimate products.

China is undergoing a long process of increasing sophistication in technology use and development. Three important problems arise with IPRs that may influence the pace and characteristics of this transformation. First, inadequate enforcement of IPRs limits incentives to develop products and brand names, especially on the part of small and medium-sized domestic enterprises. This structural difficulty likely limits entry of new firms and the development of entrepreneurial skills. It also restricts the ability of enterprises to market nationally and to take advantage of economies of scale, and tends to reduce investment in quality improvements. Over time, this situation could make it increasingly difficult to break into export markets for high-quality and high-technology goods.

Second, Chinese enterprises and research organizations are engaging in more innovation, as suggested by the patent and trademark statistics. However, the country remains behind global standards in allocating resources to R&D and science (Maskus, Dougherty, and Mertha 1998). Moreover, interviewees noted that SOEs and state research institutions face structural difficulties in commercializing the results of invention. This points out the importance of continuing to develop a technology innovation system that encourages innovative activity.[10] The state has important roles to play in promoting pre-competitive research and removing disincentives to commercialization. China has made progress toward these goals, with support programs in information technology, biotechnology, and other important areas, along with efforts to raise the flow of knowledge from institutes and universities to producing enterprises. Nonetheless, ambiguities remain about effective ownership of intellectual property rights. This is another reason that the new system of IPRs should be an important component of the evolving innovation system.

Third, stronger IPRs alone are not sufficient to establish effective conditions for further technology development and growth. Rather, they must be embedded in a broader set of complementary initiatives that maximize the potential for IPRs to be pro-competitive over the long term. An important complement is development of human capital through education in science, technology, and law, and acquisition of skills through training in enterprises. Enterprises should be more willing to undertake such training under an improved IPRs regime. Both directly and indirectly, then, effective IPRs can help Chinese enterprises raise their technological capabilities, which is critical for adaptation of foreign technologies and innovation of new products.

Another supporting factor is to ensure that competition on domestic markets is sufficient to prevent stronger IPRs from becoming a damaging source of market power. Further enterprise reform and deregulation are important in this context. Over time the liberalization commitments made in the WTO will provide important competition as well.

Finally, China like other countries, has the right to safeguard its interests in competition and social objectives through effective regulation of IPRs as those rights become stronger. Thus, the government should further analyze the appropriate form of pricing regulations and compulsory licensing in its drug procurement programs as medicines receive stronger protection.

Moreover, an opportunity arises for China to consider what form of competition regime it will implement as it shifts further toward the market. Currently China tries to maintain competition through centralized regulation of market structure, ownership, and innovation, a system that will become increasingly incompatible with needs for technological change. A shift toward antimonopoly regulation of such IPRs abuses as monopoly pricing, restrictive licensing arrangements, and refusals to deal is important. China also may need to employ compulsory licenses for this purpose. To be effective, such regulation needs to be well defined, nondiscriminatory, and professionally applied by the competition authorities and courts. This points again to the need for building legal expertise in IPRs over the long term.

The authorities in China expect that the stronger IPRs regime set in place by new legislation and increased efforts at enforcement will support dynamic gains in technology acquisition and innovation. This outcome seems achievable in those regions and sectors that are technologically dynamic. At the same time, however, substantial differences in incomes, education, and entrepreneurship persist among regions, while much of the country remains poor. Developing a comprehensive approach to regulating the use of IPRs that helps bring these poorer regions and groups more fully into the modern commercial system will pose a significant challenge for China. In the long run, however, the technological dynamism that should be facilitated by the new IPRs regime will greatly assist the country in its efforts to spread widely the gains from competition.

Notes

1. See "Draft Protocol on the Accession of China," July 10, 2001.

2. For policies taken before 2003, the description in these paragraphs relies on information from an interview with a senior judicial official in Beijing and on Lehman, Lee and Xu, *China Intellectual Property Newsletter: Special Issue*, 2001.

3. For extensive reviews see Evenson and Westphal (1997), Maskus (2000a), and Primo Braga, and others (1998).

4. UNCTAD (1996) presents estimates of such costs in several developing countries.

5. Prices of copyrighted goods have fallen sharply in Taiwan since the aggressive crackdown on counterfeiting in the mid-1990s, in part because of additional competition from legitimate local developers.

6. The European Union has moved recently toward the provision of patent protection.

7. It is conceivable that the increase in Chinese applications come primarily from joint venture partners of foreign enterprises but unfortunately the available data do not make this distinction.

8. Because these data were taken from WIPO, they include applications made under the Patent Cooperation Treaty.

9. Dahlman and Aubert (2001) discuss this in detail.

10. See Maskus (2000a) for more detailed discussion.

References

Caves, Richard E. 2000. *Creative Industries*. Cambridge: Harvard University Press.

Coe, David T., Elhanan Helpman, and Alexander Whoffmaister. 1997. "North-South R&D Spillovers." *The Economic Journal* 107: 134–49.

Dahlman, Carl J., and Jean-Eric Aubert. 2001. *China and the Knowledge Economy: Seizing the 21st Century*. Washington, D.C.: World Bank.

Dougherty, Sean M. 1997. "The Role of Foreign Technology in Improving Chinese Productivity." MIT Science and Technology Initiative, Beijing.

Evenson, Robert E., and Larry E. Westphal. 1997. "Technological Change and Technology Strategy." In *Handbook of Development Economics: Volume 3*. Amsterdam: North-Holland.

Jiang, L. 1996. "Technological Innovation in Business Strategy." *Science and Technology International* 1: 60–3.

Lacroix, Sumner, and Denise Eby Konan. 2002. "Intellectual Property Rights in China: The Changing Political Economy of Chinese-American Interests." *The World Economy* 25: 759–88.

Lanjouw, Jean O. 1997. "The Introduction of Pharmaceutical Product Patents in India: 'Heartless Exploitation of the Poor and Suffering'?" Discussion paper no. 775. New Haven Connecticut, Economic Growth Center: Yale University.

Lee, Jeong-Yeon, and Edwin Mansfield. 1996. "Intellectual Property Protection and U.S. Foreign Direct Investment." *Review of Economics and Statistics* 28: 181–6.

Ma, Chi, and Gao Chang Lin. 1998. "Technological Innovation in China's Manufacturing," State Science and Technology Commission, Beijing, manuscript.

Mansfield, Edwin. 1995. "Intellectual Property Protection, Direct Investment, and Technology Transfer." Discussion paper 27. Washington: International Finance Corporation.

Maskus, Keith E. 1998. "The International Regulation of Intellectual Property." *Weltwirtschaftliches Archiv* 123: 186–208.

————. 2000a. *Intellectual Property Rights in the Global Economy.* Washington D.C.: Institute for International Economics.

————. 2000. "Intellectual Property Rights in Lebanon." In B. Hoekman and J. Zarrouk, eds. *Catching Up with the Competition.* Ann Arbor: University of Michigan Press.

Maskus, Keith E., and Christine McDaniel. 1999. "The Impacts of the Japanese Patent System on Post-War Productivity Growth." *Japan and the World Economy* 11: 557–74.

Maskus, Keith E., Sean Dougherty, and Andrew Mertha. 1998. "Intellectual Property Rights and Economic Development in China," manuscript.

Maskus, Keith E., and Mohan Penubarti. 1995. "How Trade-Related Are Intellectual Property Rights?" *Journal of International Economics* 39: 227–48.

Potter, Pitman B. 2001. *The Chinese Legal System: Globalization and Local Legal Culture.* London: Routledge.

Primo Braga, Carlos A., Carsten Fink, and Claudia Paz Sepulveda. 1998. "Intellectual Property Rights and Economic Development." Manuscript. Washington, D.C.: World Bank.

Scotchmer, Suzanne. 1991. "Standing on the Shoulders of Giants: Cumulative Research and the Patent Law." *Journal of Economic Perspectives* 5, Winter, 29–42.

Smith, Pamela J. 1999. "Are Weak Patent Rights a Barrier to U.S. Exports?" *Journal of International Economics* 48: 151–77.

UNCTAD (United Nations Conference on Trade and Development). 1996. *The TRIPS Agreement and Developing Countries,* Geneva: UNCTAD.

Watal, Jayashree. 1999. "Pharmaceutical Patents, Prices and Welfare Losses: A Simulation Study of Policy Options for India under the WTO TRIPS Agreement." Washington, D.C.: Institute for International Economics. Photocopy.

World Bank. 2001. *Global Economic Prospects 2002: Making Trade Work for the World's Poor.* Washington, D.C.: World Bank.

WTO (World Trade Organization). 2003. "Transitional Review Mechanism of China: Communication to the Council for Trade-Related Aspects of Intellectual Property Rights," IP/C/W/415.

Yang, Guifang, and Keith E. Maskus. 2001. "Intellectual Property Rights and Licensing: An Econometric Investigation." *Weltwirtschaftliches Archiv* 137, 1, 58–79.

5

CHINA'S AGRICULTURAL DEVELOPMENT AND POLICY READJUSTMENT AFTER ITS WTO ACCESSION

Chen Xiwen

At the time of its accession to the World Trade Organization (WTO), China was following the ninth Five-Year Plan for the Development of the National Economy and Society. The Plan required China to accomplish two major goals in its national economic and social development: to establish the system of the socialist market economy at the primary stage and to attain a higher standard of living. Accomplishing these two goals would provide an important foundation for reform and development and for the accomplishment of the third step, the strategic goal of modernization. While remarkable achievements had been made in agriculture and rural economy during the ninth Five-Year Plan, significant problems had developed that could not be ignored.

Agriculture and Rural Development during the Ninth Five-Year Plan

During this period, the gross value of agricultural production in China grew from RMB1199.3 billion in 1995 to RMB1421.2 billion in 2000, an average annual increase of 3.5 percent in constant prices, 0.5 percent lower than annual growth during the eighth Five-Year Plan. In 2000, the share of agriculture in Gross Domestic Product (GDP) decreased to 15.9 percent, 4.6 percent lower than in 1995. The reduced share of agriculture in the national economy, which is a normal development in a period of accelerated industrialization, does not alter the important position of agriculture in the national economy. The agricultural growth was remarkably higher than the population growth; annual population growth on average was 0.91 percent, having provided a reliable guarantee for improvements in the standard of living, especially diet and nutrition.

The agricultural and rural economic structures have improved gradually. In agricultural production, the share of forestry, animal husbandry, and fishery continued to increase compared to crop farming. Promoted by technical progress, the capacity of crop farming to ensure provision of farm produce and support agricultural restructuring is increasing (table 5.1).

At the same time, the percentage of farmers' incomes derived from secondary and tertiary industries has been increasing. In 1995, the average net income from secondary and tertiary industries accounted for 32.65 percent of the net productive incomes; this percentage increased to 46.65 percent in 2000. The value-added of township and village enterprises (TVEs) was equivalent to 121.7 percent of the gross value of agricultural production in 1995 and increased to 191.1 percent in 2000.

TABLE 5.1   Changes in Farm Output Value Shares (percent)

Year	Crop Farming	Forestry	Animal Husbandry	Fishery
1995	58.43	3.49	29.72	8.36
2000	55.68	3.76	29.67	10.89

Source: China Statistical Yearbook 2001.

The average standard of living of farmers continued to improve. In the ninth Five-Year Plan, even though the growth of farmers' income slowed down year by year, the per capita net income increased from RMB1,577.7 in 1995 to RMB2,253.4 in 2000, an average annual increase of 4.7 percent after adjustment for price changes. This growth exceeded the target of 4 percent set in the outline of the ninth Five-Year Plan. Farmers' standard of living also continued to improve. In 1995, spending on food made up 58.62 percent of per capita living expenses of farmers; this percentage was reduced to 49.13 percent in 2000. Compared with 1995, electric fans owned by every 100 farmers' households increased by 34 sets, black-and-white televisions by 38 sets, color televisions by 32 sets, refrigerators by 7 sets, washing machines by 12 sets, and motor cycles by 17 sets. The per capita housing space increased from 21 to 24.82 square meters.

The most remarkable achievements were the significant expansion of the production capacity of grain and other major farm produce and the historical transition from the long-standing short supply of major agricultural products to balance in aggregate and surplus in years of good harvests.

The achievements in grain production made during the ninth Five-Year Plan period are of historical significance to the development process of the Chinese economy and society. The pressure of population growth on demand for food has been a significant economic and social problem confronting China for close to 400 years. In the late Ming Dynasty and the early Qing Dynasty, China's population was less than 100 million and had 800 million mu of farmland. By 2000, the total population had grown to 1.266 billion, while the farmland area only expanded to 1.924 billion mu. The population grew over 11-fold, while the farmland area increased by a factor of little more than two. After the country's founding in 1949, "taking grain as the

key link" was stressed for years to alter the situation of food shortage, but the problem was not resolved. The grain rationing system was terminated as late as 1992, producing improvements in the food supply situation. Beginning in 1995, China had enjoyed good harvests in grain production for five consecutive years. In the first four years of the Plan period, the annual grain production surpassed 500 million tons, leading to a continuing situation of supply exceeding the demand.

Four causes contributed to the significant growth in grain production during the ninth Five-Year Plan period:

- *The basic rural policies were improved continuously.* The household contract responsibility system featuring a combination of centralization and decentralization played an important role in expanding grain production. In November 1993, the central government explicitly extended the land contract for another 30 years after the expiration of the original 15-year contract period. This policy gave farmers a sense of stability in terms of land contract rights and stimulated their initiative to increase investment in farmland. Many farmers have been digging motor-pumped wells and irrigation ditches on the contracted land and purchasing sprinkler irrigation devices to develop water-saving irrigation. The area of irrigated farmland increased by 68.55 million mu or 9.3 percent.

- *Increases in the contract purchase price for grain provided an incentive for farmers to increase production.* In 1994, consumer prices rose. To make up for the effect of these rises on farmers, the government raised the contract purchase price for grain by 40 percent; the price was further increased to 42 percent in 1996.

- *Scientific and technological progress has been responsible for nearly 40 percent of the agricultural growth in China.* The extension of several key technologies, in particular, played an important role in increasing grain production. The "seed project" introduced a large number of improved varieties and eliminated poor varieties that did not suit market needs. The "White Revolution" extended mulching technology in the cold and dry areas in the northern part of China to advance sowing time and prolong the period of crop production while improving soil moisture conservation and repressing weed growth. Water-saving irrigation technologies have been developed, and demonstration counties where these technologies are being applied have been designated. The flood irrigation practice has been replaced by wide application of spraying, trickle, and micro-irrigation methods to meet the needs of crop growth with less water.

• *Favorable climatic conditions produced adequate rainfall that alleviated long-standing drought conditions and facilitated increases in grain production.* The most serious threat to agricultural production in China traditionally has been drought.

Generally, the agricultural policies during this period were stable and explicit, and many of the scientific achievements facilitated growth in grain production. However, factors such as major rise in prices and favorable climatic conditions are inconsistent, and reliance on a confluence of such favorable factors in the future would be imprudent. Accordingly, the long-term development of grain production remains an issue meriting ongoing serious attention.

The Biggest Problem in China's Rural Economy: Raising Farmers' Incomes

The decreasing growth in farmers' income was the most outstanding problem during the ninth Five-Year Plan period. Changes in the patterns of supply and demand produced an excess of supply for most farm produce, leading to declines in prices and new difficulties in raising farmers' incomes. In 1996, farmers' net income increased by 9 percent, but the rate of growth declined to 4.6 percent in 1997,

4.3 percent in 1998, 3.8 percent in 1999, and 2.1 percent in 2000.

The decreasing growth in farmers' net income in recent years is only a symptomatic manifestation of the problem. The severity of the problem lies primarily in the sustained decrease of income from agricultural production. Table 5.2 shows the composition of and changes in per capita net income of farmers from 1997 to 2000.

It can be clearly seen from Table 5.2 that, while the productive net income of farmers in 2000 increased by RMB142 over 1997, the net income from agricultural production decreased by 132, a reduction of 10.4 percent. Between 1998 and 2000, the average farmer's income from agricultural production declined progressively, decreasing by RMB30 between 1998 and 1997, RMB57 between 1999 and 1998, and further by RMB44 between 1999 and 2000. According to the statistics in the agricultural survey, 59 percent of the rural households in China are "pure farmer households" (i.e., the family members are mainly engaged in farming), and another 18 percent are "farmer households with combined occupations" (i.e., the number of family members engaged in farming is more than those engaged in nonfarm occupations). These two types of households with farming as their main source of income account for 78 percent of households in rural China. Accordingly, due to the progressively reduced income from agriculture in the last three years, the per capita net income of the households with farming as the main source of income actually declined.

It was under just such circumstances that part of the agricultural provinces and the western provinces with underdeveloped nonfarm industries faced a severe reduction in the per capita income of

TABLE 5.2 Sources of Farmers' Incomes, 1997–2000

Year	Productive Net Income (Yuan/Person)	Net Income from Primary Industry (Yuan/Person)	Net Income from Secondary Industry (Yuan/Person)	Net Income from Tertiary Industry (Yuan/Person)
1997	1987	1,268	438	281
1998	2040	1,237	499	303
1999	2079	1,180	564	334
2000	2130	1,136	598	395
2000 vs. 97	+142	−132	+160	+113

TABLE 5.3   Declines in Per Capita Farm Incomes in Six Key Provinces

	Yuan	Yuan	Yuan	Yuan	Yuan	Yuan
Reduction in income in 1999	Shanxi 86	Liaoning 79	Jilin 123	Heilongjiang 87	Gansu 36	Xinjiang 127
Reduction in income in 2000	Guangxi 184	Liaoning 145	Jilin 238	Heilongjiang 18	Shaanxi 12	Ningxia 30

TABLE 5.4   Changes in Farm Household Spending, 1997–2000

Year	Total Spending (Yuan/Person)	Household Operation Spending (Yuan/Person)	Living Expenses (Yuan/Person)	Spending on Food (Yuan/Person)	Spending on Garments (Yuan/Person)
1997	2,537	706	1617	890	109
1998	2,457	652	1590	850	98
1999	2,390	600	1577	829	92
2000	2,652	654	1670	821	96

farmers. In 1999 and 2000, farmers in six provinces and regions experienced decreases in their per capita net income over the previous year. Table 5.3 shows the provinces and amounts of the reduction in income.

Per capita income decreased for two consecutive years in the provinces of Liaoning, Jilin, and Heilongjiang. The reduction in Jilin was as much as RMB361 in the same period, and per capita income in the province was 15 percent lower in 2000 than in 1998.

The net income from farming declined for years running, while the tax burden on farmers' households mainly included taxes on agricultural and animal products, taxes on special products, and a contract land deduction. These factors have deepened the feeling of households in which farming is the main source of income that "income can not go up and burdens can not come down." This situation has forced some farmers to seek work from other sources to offset payment of agricultural taxes and fees with income; more farmers have had to reduce their spending on production and living expenses. Since 1998, the per capita spending on operation and living expenses has decreased or stopped increasing. Table 5.4 shows the changes in this regard.

There were successive declines in 1998 and 1999 in per capita spending on farm household operations, with a cumulative 15 percent reduction between 1997 and 1999 (a reduction of RMB106). The increase in per capita spending on farmer household operations in 2000 constituted something of a recovery, but it still left spending over 7 percent lower than in 1997. On the other hand, this increase was indirect, the result of increases in drought relief expenses and the rise in prices for fuels.

The changes in the per capita consumer spending of farmers have similar characteristics: successive declines in 1998 and 1999, with spending in 1999 at 2.5 percent (RMB40) below the level in 1997. Although the per capita living expenditures increased by RMB93 in 2000 compared with the previous year, the change was to a large extent passive. First, the per capita spending on food continued to decrease after the successive decrease for two years, while per capita spending on garments increased slightly but was still lower than the levels in 1997 and 1998. Second, much of the spending increase resulted from the rise in service prices, such as medical expenses that increased by RMB18 or 25 percent, transport by RMB24 or 35.5 percent, and education and entertainment devices and

TABLE 5.5   Share of Farmers in Consumer Spending at County and Lower Levels (percent)

Year	Percent
1996	40
1997	39
1998	39
1999	39
2000	38

services by RMB18 or 11 percent. The above expenditure increases, which were basically passive, increased by RMB60 or 65 percent of the total increase in living expenses. Therefore, even though farmers' per capita spending on living had increased, the amount of the spending that could be used to improve their quality of life was very limited.

The data on per capita expenditures on production and living of farmers are only national averages, and, very often, average figures conceal many disparities. The situation was more serious in terms of the reduction in spending for most of the farmer households that mainly depend on farming for incomes. This is one of the major reasons for the decline in farmers' share of rural consumption evident in table 5.5.

Thus it can be seen that the decrease and stagnation in farmers' spending has actually produced negative impacts on the expansion of the domestic market and healthy development of the national economy. As the central government pointed out at the Central Working Conference on Rural Issues, the issue of increasing tangible benefits to farmers is central to the continuation of the progress achieved in agriculture productivity. If the purchasing power of farmers does not continue to improve, the policy for expanding domestic demand will not achieve the desired results. If farmers' living standards cannot be improved, the risk of increased social instability in the rural areas will increase. If the ability of agriculture to save and accumulate cannot be constantly strengthened, it will be difficult for China's agricultural products to compete in the global marketplace. If Chinese agriculture experiences major setbacks, the development of the whole national economy and society will be affected adversely.

WTO Accession and the New Stage of Development of Chinese Agriculture and Rural Economy

The Initiation of the New Stage and its Central Tasks

In October 1998, the Third Plenary Session of the 15th Central Committee of the Communist Party of China (CPC) adopted the Decisions of the CPC Central Committee on Major Issues of Agriculture and Rural Work. The judgment of balance in aggregate and surplus in harvest years for grain and other major agricultural products was made in the Decisions. Based on this judgment, the central government stated at the National Conference on Rural Work at the end of 1998 that the development of Chinese agriculture and rural economy had entered a new stage. The main basis for the new stage thinking is the major change in the pattern of agricultural supply and demand. One of the key features of the situation is that the quantitative contradictions in the supply of and demand for agricultural products have been relieved. Another is that past agricultural production had been restricted by natural resources; presently, however, restrictions of market demand on production have become more acute. What farmers are worrying about is not whether enough products can be produced, but whether the products can be sold at good prices. Precisely because of such changes, the central government explicitly directed at the end of 1999 that the central task for agriculture and rural economy in the new stage should be implementation of strategic restructuring.

The Crux of the Strategic Restructuring of Agriculture and Rural Economy

Since China adopted reform and open economic policies, Chinese agriculture has experienced restructuring. The starting point of the strategic restructuring lies in the adjustment of variety and quality instead of quantity. The adjustment in the area of crop sowing is no more than which crop should have more sowing area and which should have less. This kind of adjustment was effective in the past, is effective at the present, and will be effective in the future. However, adjustment in quantity has major limitations. For example, judging from the existing production level and consumer demand for grain in China, the total sowing area for grain crops should be maintained at 1.65 billion mu to 1.7 billion mu, with only about 50 million mu as a margin for adjustment.

Strategic restructuring differs substantially. Adjustment can be made on every piece of land within more than 2.3 billion mu of sowing area, such as replacing the unmarketable poor quality varieties with high quality marketable ones. Adjustment can be made not only on cultivated land, but also in forest products, fruits, animal products, and aquatic products. Accordingly, adjustments emphasizing optimizing varieties, improving quality, and efficiency can be made everywhere. Only by such strategic restructuring focused on quality and efficiency can the overall quality of Chinese agriculture be improved to meet the requirements and challenges posed by WTO accession and economic globalization, to ensure improvement in the people's living standards, and to accelerate the process of agricultural modernization in China.

The Fundamental Objective of the Strategic Restructuring

The new stage of strategic restructuring was initiated early in 2001 when the central government specified that the fundamental objective of the strategic restructuring is to ensure increases in farmers' income. After entering the new stage and basically solving the quantitative contradiction in agricultural supply and demand, increasing farmers' income has increasingly become a priority of the Chinese central government. In November 2000, Secretary General Jiang Zemin and Premier Zhu Rongji stressed at the National Economic Conference that increasing farmers' income should be a key goal in the entire economic work program.

The government has paid close attention to issues concerning agriculture, rural areas, and farmers, with the focus on increasing farmers' income. The fundamental objective set at the Central Working Conference on Rural Affairs at the beginning of 2001 was to achieve growth in farmers' income. In mid January 2001, the central government convened a National Conference on Agricultural Science and Technology, at which a group of agricultural scientists was commended and the Outline for the Development of Agricultural Science and Technology in the Next 10 Years was adopted. In February 2001, the State Council held a working conference in Anhui Province on the reform experiment in rural taxes and fees to explore fundamental solutions to the burdens on farmers. At the turn of the century, the central government held a series of major conferences on rural restructuring, increasing farmers' income, and alleviating burdens on farmers.

Securing income growth for farmers is by no means a simple matter. The most important immediate cause of the slow increase in farmers' income is the current difficulty in selling agricultural products and the declines in prices. However, problems of product sales and price declines are not only evident in agriculture, but in most other industries as well. Therefore, the current difficulties facing farmers' income are to a great extent related directly to the economic cycles at both home and abroad. Achievement of sustained growth in farmers' income is a complicated project of system engineering. One or two specific policies cannot be expected to provide fundamental solutions. The key is to make great efforts in all aspects of agricultural and rural work. This also depends to a large degree on the improvement in the national economy as well as the world economy so as to create a broader market for the agricultural development.

The Basic Direction of the Strategic Restructuring of Agriculture and the Rural Economy

As directed by the Chinese government, the central task of the new stage of agricultural development is to implement strategic restructuring of agricultural production. This restructuring is strategic for two reasons. The first is to put the long-standing practice of pursuing quantitative growth in agricultural products on the track of stressing optimized variety and improved quality and efficiency. The second is that the ongoing development of Chinese agriculture needs to continue to consider the constraints on the resource side and to pay more attention to constraints from demand side. To achieve this, the regulation of agricultural production by market forces should be expanded.

It can clearly be seen that WTO accession will accelerate agricultural restructuring and adjustment in agricultural policies. The agricultural restructuring consistent with the above goals will require changes in the relevant policies. Although these policy adjustments primarily resulted from major changes in the patterns of agricultural supply and demand in China, they are fundamentally consistent with the direction of China's WTO commitments. Even if no WTO accession issues are presented, such adjustments in agricultural policies would be required.

The restructuring of agriculture and rural economy, revealed at the end of the ninth Five-Year Plan, has five major orientations:

1. Optimize varieties of farm produce and improve the overall product quality. Optimization of varieties and improvement in quality and efficiency should be the main orientation of adjustment for all agricultural production, including crop farming, animal husbandry, fishery, forestry, and fruit production. With the issue of quantity in agricultural supply and demand resolved, optimizing varieties and improving quality will constitute an objective requirement for the current stage of agricultural development facing supply and demand changes. It is preferable in agricultural production to have smaller quantities of higher quality products to avoid wasting the human, financial, and material resources of farmers. To this end, the central government announced the termination of purchasing at protective prices for long-grained nonglutinous rice, northeastern spring wheat, southern winter wheat, and other unmarketable varieties, starting in 2000. The purpose of this reform was to guide farmers to replace inferior varieties with superior ones.

2. Expand processing of agricultural products. Agricultural processing will become more and more important in agricultural development in China. With continuous increases in people's incomes and living standards, the Engel coefficients and income elasticity of demand can be expected to fall, which could pose a grave challenge to the continued development of agriculture.

Currently, the main factor restricting the growth of farmers' income is the decrease of income from agricultural production. This is related to the stage of social and economic development in China. Profound changes have taken place in the current consumption structure of residents. One is the decrease of the Engel coefficient and the associated decline in the income elasticity of demand for food. In 1991, the Engel coefficients of China's urban and rural residents were 54 percent and 58 percent, respectively. These declined to 38 percent and 48 percent in 2001.

The decline in the propensity of households to spend their income on food is evident in Table 5.6. Between 1996 and 2001, per capita disposable income increased by RMB2 021 and consumer expenditure increased by RMB1,390, while food expenditure only increased by RMB109, even though expenditures on food eaten outside the home increased by RMB128. Thus, the urban resident expenditures on grain, oil, meat, and vegetables decreased by RMB131.

Only by expanding farm produce processing and encouraging the consumption of higher quality, more nutritious, and safer food can the

TABLE 5.6   Changes in Urban and Rural Resident Income and Spending, 1996–2001

	2001 (Yuan)	1996 (Yuan)
Per capita disposable income	6,860	4839
Per capita consumer expenditure (total)	5,309	3919
Food	2,014	1905
Grain	188	272
Oil	59	69
Meat, poultry, and products	413	439
Aquatic products	152	132
Vegetables	194	207
Tobacco	104	84
Liquor and beverage	104	85
Fresh and dried fruits	131	118
Dining out	314	186

continued expansion of agricultural markets be achieved. Food processing can not only increase the value of agricultural products, but it also can guide consumption and develop new markets to make it possible to continuously increase farmers' income. Two concepts should be altered in terms of developing agricultural processing industry. First, food processing should not be regarded as an industry with low-technology content and without the need for substantial investment. On the international market, brand-name and marketable processed foods all have high-technology content. These products simply can not be produced without the application of advanced technology. Second, it should not be believed that unsaleable fresh products can be processed into high-quality processed products. The raw materials for food processing should be special-purpose farm produce, such as special wheat and special grapes, which are distinctive from those directly used for food. Therefore, adjustments should be made in the varieties of agricultural products to achieve better results from food processing.

3. Bring into play the local comparative advantages in agriculture. In the past, widespread shortages of agricultural products left localities with no choice but to pursue higher degrees of self-sufficiency. Now that the supply and demand situation has changed, local authorities should be liberalized from such traditional thinking and bring into play local comparative advantage in agriculture. Particularly, the coastal regions and suburbs of large and medium cities should make use of capital and technology-intensive techniques. These localities should properly reduce their grain production and develop higher value-added animal husbandry, fishery, and horticulture so as to give more market space to the main grain-producing regions in a pattern of mutual benefit and relative complementarity. At the same time, the various localities should be encouraged to develop their own agriculture with distinctive features.

To promote restructuring of the regional distribution of agriculture, the central government decided in 2001 to liberalize grain markets in the main coastal grain-consuming regions, including Beijing, Tianjin, Shanghai, Jiangsu, Zhejiang, Fujian, Guangdong, and Hainan. Particularly, in the face of the challenges and opportunities after WTO accession, much more attention should be paid to giving play to local comparative advantage in agriculture. China has a large population and little land. Most of the land-intensive agricultural products, such as grain, cotton, and edible oil are relatively high-cost in China. Most labor-intensive agricultural products, such as animal and poultry products, aquatic products, and horticultural products (fruits, vegetables, flowers, and bonsai), have a comparative advantage in international markets. Currently, there is an urgent need for Chinese agriculture to foster strengths and circumvent weaknesses and to give full play to China's comparative advantage in international market competition. To tap the comparative advantage of Chinese agriculture on the international market, it is first necessary to bring into full play the agricultural comparative advantages of different domestic regions. In this way, it will be possible to create a pattern of mutual benefit and complementarity between regions to improve the competitiveness of Chinese agricultural products on international markets and to promote the development of China's agriculture as a whole.

4. While continuing to support the development of TVEs, make positive and steady efforts to advance urbanization. In the second half of the ninth Five-Year Plan period, the per capita net income of farmers increased, although income from farming declined. This increase depended almost entirely on income growth from nonfarm sectors. This shows that the fundamental way to enrich farmers is to reduce the number of farmers. Agricultural resources are limited and efforts should be made to transfer rural labor and population to allow the farmers remaining on the land to expand their scale of production. The township and village enterprises (TVEs) in the countryside have provided 130 million job opportunities to farmers, and their role in alleviating the unemployment problem can hardly be replaced. TVEs should be guided to conduct restructuring and institutional innovation to promote their further development and to make a greater contribution to increasing the employment and income of farmers.

Another major source of income growth of farmers during the ninth Five-Year Plan was transient employment of farmers in towns and cities. This part of income has provided an increasing share in the net income of farmers. According to an estimation by Sichuan, 6 million farmers in the province seek transient employment and remit nearly RMB30 billion each year. The transient employment of farmers, which should be encouraged, should be managed to keep it orderly. However, many large and medium cities have set up various restrictions and rules on employing farmers, and many of these rules and regulations are both unreasonable and ineffective. On one hand, these transient farmer workers should be guided to flow in an orderly manner and to abide by relevant laws and regulations. On the other hand, the various rules and regulations restricting farmers seeking jobs in urban areas should be reviewed so as to alleviate the burden on the transient farmers. In the process of economic development in China, the transient employment of farmers will certainly be a long-term process. A large number of farmers will be transferred to nonfarm employment, but the transition to settlements in towns will occur over time and will require an extended period of transient employment. Conscientious research should be conducted, and effective policies should be adopted to guide and manage such a large scale and long-term population flow.

Developing small towns is an important way to transfer rural population and accelerate the process of urbanization in China. In the decisions adopted at the Third Plenary Session of the 15th Central Committee of the Chinese Party Congress, it was specified that developing small towns would be a major strategy for the development of the rural economy and society.

There are two schools of thought on the specific ways in which urbanization should be advanced. The first places the emphasis on large and medium cities. Through a host of analyses and researches, many scholars think that large cities can generate higher economic benefits and provide a large number of job opportunities. The second school of thought stresses the effect of developing small towns. Its advocates believe that the basic goal of urbanization at the current stage is to speed up the transfer of rural surplus labor and rural population, and these advocates view developing small towns as a more effective means of achieving this goal.

The path to urbanization should be one with Chinese characteristics, featuring coordinated development of large and medium cities and small towns. Medium and small cities should be developed, the regional center cities should have distinctive features, and large cities should bring into play their leading role and growth pole functions. However, measured with the goal of transferring the rural population, developing small towns is more realistic. Presently, large and medium cities frequently provide job opportunities for transient farmers and opportunities for them to accumulate capital, but it is very difficult for these farmers to settle in these cities. After a certain period of capital accumulation, rural residents typically leave the large cities, but not all of them return to rural areas. Some of them settle in small towns. This process of resettlement will provide practical opportunities for the development of small towns. However the development of small towns should not rush headlong into mass action and "blossom" everywhere, or the results will be counterproductive. There are about 45,000 towns and townships in China, in which 19,000 are governmentally nominated townships. Considerations of how many small towns should be established should proceed from realistic assessments of China's actual conditions and national strength. Towns with better basic conditions and development potential should be given priority in construction. The most important precondition for the development of small towns is a prosperous local economy.

Construction of small towns differs from that of residential quarters. A residential district can accommodate several thousand residents and has sound living environments and complete living facilities; however, most of the residents are not employed within the district, that is, residential districts have no function to create job opportunities. The basic function of small towns is to attract the transferred farmers and provide job opportunities. Accordingly, emphasis should be laid on giving play to functions of towns; the basic function is to create a prosperous local economy and to provide employment. The most basic judgment on whether conditions exist for constructing a town is whether a planned town can become a source of economic growth. Only by making this judgment can we achieve the goal of accelerated transfer of rural surplus labor and population, provide better conditions for agricultural and rural development, and provide more opportunities for income growth of farmers.

5. Intensify the construction of ecological environment and implement sustainable development. In ecologically vulnerable regions such as those along the upper reaches of major rivers and arid areas, the government should provide financial aid for farmers to return grain plots to forestry to conduct ecological construction including re-vegetation and soil and water conservation. Starting in 1999, experiments on returning grain plots to forestry were conducted in some provinces and regions. By the end of 2001, 11 million mu of grain plots had been returned to forestry nationwide. In 2002, the central government officially adopted policies for returning grain plots to forestry. The government will subsidize 300 jin of grain to farmers in the southern part of China and 200 jin to farmers in the north for every 1 mu of grain plots returned to forestry, plus RMB50 for each mu incurred in sapling and grass seed expenses and RMB20 in living expenses. Under this policy, implementation of returning grain plots to forestry not only can recover balance of ecology effectively, but it also can offer opportunities for farmers to receive direct benefits. By the end of 2002, the total area of returning grain plots to forestry reached 34 million mu and is expected to reach 100 million mu during the whole tenth Five-Year Plan.

Policy Orientations for Promoting Restructuring of Agriculture and the Rural Economy

To promote the strategic restructuring of agriculture and rural economy and to improve the overall quality and international competitiveness of Chinese agriculture, the government is accelerating a series of policy readjustments to meet the needs of current agricultural development. The main readjustments include the following:

- accelerate the establishment of market information systems for agricultural products and provide farmers with timely, comprehensive, accurate, and authoritative market information on agricultural products
- accelerate the establishment of quality, security, and standards systems, and improve the means of inspection and testing for agricultural products, particularly food products, guiding the

farmers to produce high-quality, low-residue, and safe farm produce
- adjust the existing supportive and protective policies for agriculture and establish a domestic protective system for agriculture that conforms to WTO rules
- accelerate the innovation of agricultural management system; develop an integrated agricultural management system with "company plus farmer households" as the main form to improve farm organization and farmers' access to markets
- further reform and perfect the circulation system for grain and other major agricultural products to reduce circulation expenses and improve competitiveness
- further restructure the rural financial system and explore the establishment of an agricultural insurance system that suits the national conditions in China
- restructure the agricultural science and technology research and extension systems and intensify international cooperation and technology import to accelerate technical progress in agriculture
- reform the household registration system in small towns and encourage the rural population that has met necessary conditions to settle in small towns.

Remaining Policy Issues

A number of policy issues needs to be examined in more detail in the future. Some of the most important of these issues are as follows:

- *Correct analysis of price issues for staple agricultural products, particularly grain, soybeans, and cotton.* The relationship among producer prices, wholesale prices, and retail prices should be distinguished, and the actual gap between prices for China's staple agricultural products and international market prices should be analyzed objectively. Monopoly still exists in the circulation of staple agricultural products. Therefore, it is absolutely possible to reduce the circulation expenses of China's staple agricultural products by further reforming the agricultural circulation system to reduce the gap between the Chinese and international market prices.

- *The comparative advantages of Chinese agricultural products; labor costs give China a clear comparative advantage in many animal and aquatic products.* However, given the aggravated "green barriers" in international agricultural trade, low labor costs are not enough to constitute international competitiveness. The key is to find ways to produce agricultural products that meet international quality and safety standards. At the same time, the question remains whether other WTO members will open their markets to Chinese agricultural products.
- *Reforming the foreign trade system for agricultural products.* The key is to properly resolve the problems in giving nonstate firms that have met the necessary conditions of foreign trade rights for importing and exporting agricultural products.
- *Both tariff concessions and tariff-rate quotas for imports of agricultural products are hard to bear in the transitional period.* However, it is crucial to study how to deal with the pressures from the international agricultural markets. Both research and preparations for the new round of WTO agricultural negotiations are inadequate. The central government should set up special bodies to intensify research on the relevant policy recommendations.

References

"The Outline of the Ninth Five-Year Plan (1996–2000) for National Economic and Social Development and the Long-range Objectives to the Year 2010." Delivered at the Fifth Plenary Session of the 14th Central Committee of the Communist Party of China. Xinhua News Agency, September 28, 1995.

National Bureau of Statistics. *Statistical Yearbook of China 2002.* Beijing. China Statistics Press.

National Bureau of Statistics. *Statistical Yearbook of China 2001.* Beijing. China Statistics Press.

"The Decisions of the CPC Central Committee on Major Issues of Agriculture and Rural Work." Delivered at the Third Plenary Session of the 15th Central Committee of the Communist Party of China. *People's Daily.* October 15, 1998.

The Outline for the Development of Agricultural Science and Technology in the Next 10 Years: 2001–2010. People's Daily. May 24, 2001.

6

THE NATURE OF DISTORTIONS TO AGRICULTURAL INCENTIVES IN CHINA AND IMPLICATIONS OF WTO ACCESSION

Jikun Huang, Scott Rozelle, and Min Chang

The initiation of economic liberalization and structural change in 1978 has produced substantial growth in China's economy. The annual growth rate of gross domestic product (GDP) was 8.5 percent from 1979–84 and 9.7 percent from 1985–95. Despite the Asian financial crisis, the GDP growth continued at 8.2 percent annually from 1996 to 2000.

Although reform has penetrated the entire economy since the early 1980s, most of the successive transformations began with, and to some extent were dependent on, growth in the agricultural sector (Nyberg and Rozelle 1999). After 1978, decollectivization, price increases, and the relaxation of local trade restrictions on most agricultural products accompanied the substantial growth of the agricultural economy from 1978 to 1984. Grain production increased by 4.7 percent per year. Even higher growth was enjoyed in horticulture, livestock, and aquatic products. Although agricultural growth decelerated after 1985 after the one-time efficiency gains from decollectivization, the country still enjoyed agricultural growth rates that have outpaced the rise in population. New opportunities in the off-farm sectors have allowed farm families to shift part of their household labor out of the agricultural sector into higher paying off-farm jobs.

Despite the healthy expansion of agriculture, the sector still faces serious challenges. According to the World Bank (2000), more than 100 million people fell below the poverty line in the late 1990s, earning less than one dollar (U.S.) per day in purchasing power parity (PPP) terms. Some regions of the nation remain highly dependent on crop production, including farmers in some Northeast provinces (maize and soybeans) and the North China Plain (wheat and maize) (Ministry of Agriculture 2001). In recent years, expanding supplies and increased liberalization have pushed real agricultural prices to their lowest levels in history (Park and others 2002). With the retreat of the state

The authors would like to thank the research assistance of Yuping Xie. This work could not have been done without him. We also acknowledge the helpful comments and suggestions of Kym Anderson, Fred Crook, Tom Hertel, Elena Ianchovichina, Will Martin, Francis Tuan, and participants in the World Bank-sponsored meeting on the impact of WTO accession on China. We acknowledge the financial support of the World Bank's Trade and Rural Development units.

occurring in many sectors of the economy, such as rural health care and provision of welfare services (Nyberg and Rozelle 1999), large numbers of people remain poor and vulnerable to even relatively minor income shocks.

Agriculture has been at the center of discussion of China's entry into the World Trade Organization (WTO), due in part to the vulnerability of parts of the rural economy and in part to the importance of agriculture in the political economy of a number of developed nations with whom China negotiated its accession to the WTO. However, the likely shifts in China's future agricultural policy and their impacts are not well understood, and debates on the future of China's agriculture continue. Some argue that the impact of WTO accession on China's agriculture will be substantial, adversely affecting hundreds of millions of farmers (Carter and Estrin 2001; Li and others 1999). Others believe that, although some impacts will be negative and even severe in specific areas, the overall effect of accession on agriculture will be modest (Anderson and Peng 1998). In part, the confusion about the ultimate impact of WTO accession on agriculture can be traced to a general lack of understanding of the policy changes that accession will engender (Martin 2002). However, in perhaps an even greater way, the lack of clarity of the debate can be traced to a lack of understanding of the fundamental facts about the nature of the distortions to China's economy on the eve of its WTO entry.

In this chapter, we provide an approach to help researchers and trade officials better understand how trade liberalization will affect agricultural prices and how the price changes will be experienced in different parts of the nation. First, we describe a new way of collecting data that can be used to design more accurate, disaggregated measures of protection (specifically, nominal rates of protection NRPs). Then, we use price determination and market integration analyses to study the nature of domestic markets to begin to understand how price shifts at the borders that arise from trade liberalization measures affect producers in different parts of the country.

We report the results of a case study of the impact of China's WTO accession on agricultural prices. Since many of China's poor rural households live in remote regions and tend to rely more than any other group on the income earned from cropping, they are the ones most likely to be affected by the WTO's liberalizing measures (Chen and Ravallion 2004). In conducting our case study, we focus on the effects of the WTO accession on agricultural prices even though the other effects on the rural population are likely to be at least as important as cropping (Zhao and Sicular 2002). We do not want to quantify the total welfare effect; instead, we focus primarily on the qualitative effects on China's farmers to illustrate how to approach assessing the effects of trade liberalization on agricultural prices.

The rest of the chapter is organized as follows. First, after providing a brief context for our analysis and discussing our data, we present measures of NRPs for a set of commodities for China. Next we discuss how these distortions to agricultural prices should be expected to change as China implements its WTO obligations and gains access (or not) to the promises that were made to China. The next section analyzes the transmission of prices through the economy, and the final section discusses the implication of the findings.

Gradual Opening and Remaining Distortions

Although agriculture has been at the center of China's negotiations over its WTO entry, the likely shifts in future agricultural policy and its impacts are not well understood. Debates on future food security are growing. The fundamental confusion about the ultimate impact of WTO accession in part can be traced to a widespread lack of understanding of the policy changes that may result from China's WTO accession (Martin 2002). Traditionally, analysts have focused on four sets of trade policies, measures that are most frequently used by other countries to protect their agricultural sectors. In examining the previous work (e.g., CARD 2001; Tuan and Cheng 1999; OECD 2001), we find that almost all of the discussion is directed at tariffs, quotas and licensing, state trading, and traditional non-tariff barriers (NTBs). It is implicitly assumed that the WTO agreement is focused solely on these policies, that these policies are responsible for most if not all of the protection that China enjoyed prior to accession, and that accession represents China's initial assault on protection at the border. In fact, while at one time these policies were the source of high distortions, some of the worst distortions caused by these policies have already disappeared after nearly two decades of reform in the external economy. The experience of China's agricultural tariff policy illustrates the gradual but dramatic changes that China has experienced in the past two decades. In the late 1970s and early 1980s, the domestic wholesale price of China's four major commodities, converted at the official exchange rate far exceeded the world price measured at China's border (table 6.1). For example, in 1978, China's rice price was 10 percent above the world market price. The nation's wheat and maize prices exceeded the world price by approximately 90 percent. However, over the next two decades, the NRP for rice fell to −6 percent and to about 30 percent for wheat and maize. Although the NRP for soybeans fell similarly between the late 1980s and the mid 1990s, the rate rose in the late 1990s before falling to less than 20 percent in 2001 (table 6.1; Xie 2002). During this period, the intervention by state traders and the use of NTBs also fell gradually (Martin 2002).

Falling protection and changes in international trade and domestic marketing policies have resulted in dramatically shifting trade patterns. Disaggregated, crop-specific trade trends show how exports and imports increasingly are moving in a direction that is more consistent with China's comparative advantage. For example, the proportion of grain

exports in the 1990s, approximately 20 percent of total agricultural exports, is less than half of what it was in the early 1980s (Huang and Chen 1999). By the late 1990s horticultural products and animal and aquatic products accounted for about 80 percent of agricultural exports. These trends are even more evident when reorganizing the trade data grouping them on the basis of factor intensity (table 6.2). The

TABLE 6.1 Changes in Nominal Rates of Protection Over Time of China's Major Agricultural Commodities, 1978–2000[a]

	Nominal Rates of Protection (Percent)			
	Rice	Wheat	Maize	Soybean
1978–79	10	89	92	40
1980–84	9	58	46	44
1985–89	−4	52	37	39
1990–94	−7	30	12	26
1995–97	−1	19	20	19
1998–00	−6	26	32	49
1998	−6	22	40	37
1999	−9	30	33	67
2000	−2	26	23	44

[a]Nominal rates of protection (NRPs) measured as difference (percentage) between average border prices and average domestic wholesale (market) prices.
Source: Huang 2001.

TABLE 6.2 China's Agricultural Trade (US$ millions) by Factor Intensity, 1985–97

Year	Land Intensive Products		Labor Intensive Products		Labor/Capital Intensive Products	
	Value (US$ Million)	Share (Percent)	Value (US$ Million)	Share (Percent)	Value (US$ Million)	Share (Percent)
Agricultural exports						
1985	2,119	36.4	2,199	37.8	1,497	25.7
1990	1,689	17.7	4,971	52.1	2,881	30.2
1995	875	6.0	7,095	48.4	6,704	45.7
1997	2,158	14.1	6,538	42.6	6,642	43.3
Agricultural imports						
1985	1,072	43.8	680	27.8	695	28.4
1990	4,032	71.9	642	11.5	935	16.7
1995	6,575	54.5	3,278	27.2	2,216	18.4
1997	4,644	47.3	2,179	22.2	2,987	30.5

Source: Huang and Chen 1999.

imports of land-intensive bulk commodities, such as grains, oilseeds, and sugar crops, have risen (or net exports have fallen); while exports of higher-valued, more labor-intensive products, such as horticultural and animal (including aquaculture) products, have risen (table 6.2).

Nontraditional Sources of Trade Liberalization or Protection

Based on the preceding discussion, two facts become clear. First, distortions have declined significantly in the past 20 years. Considering this fact, the current episode of policy reform that accompanied China's accession to the WTO should be considered an extension of past efforts. Second, much of the falling protection has come from decentralizing authority and relaxing licensing procedures for some crops (e.g., moving oil and oil seed imports away from state trading firms), reducing the scope of NTBs, relaxing real tariff rates at the border, and changing quotas (Huang and Chen 1999). It is perhaps for these reasons that much research on China's entry into the WTO focuses on the policies responsible for much of the earlier progress and studying these policy tools might be beneficial. Undoubtedly, changes in China's tariff regimes, state trading system, and matrix of NTBs will play a continuing role in creating or eliminating distortions in China's agriculture. However, partly because many of the gains from traditional trade reforms have already been experienced, China may be able to affect further trade liberalization via other, less discussed policies. Even if traditional policies are still important, the gains from these other policy reforms may be as important as those from traditional trade reform.

For example, China also has used its taxation policy to protect its agriculture, especially in certain sectors, such as soybeans, that have been most liberalized. In the early 1990s, leaders radically revised China's fiscal system, making it much more reliant for revenue generation on a value-added tax system (Nyberg and Rozelle 1999). The theory of the tax is that it is assessed on value added in all goods during their manufacture and sales process from the time the raw material comes out of the ground until it reaches the consumer. National regulations state that imported goods that are not for immediate re-export also are to be assessed the value-added tax. Although rates vary, the typical value-added tax rate ranges from 13 to 17 percent.

For a variety of political and tax collection reasons, in the early stages of the implementation of the tax, authorities decided to exempt farmers when they sold their products into the market. Traders that purchased grain, for example, from a farmer in his home or in a local market would not have to pay the value-added tax. When the good was resold in a downstream wholesale market, the value-added tax was assessed, but the trader only owed the tax on the amount of the marketing margin, or the difference between the procurement price and sale price. Xie (2002) and Rozelle (2003) found that in China's competitive marketing regime, the marketing margins (the difference between the buying and selling prices) are extremely low. For shipments from markets that are 500 to 1,500 kilometers from the port, traders report margins that range from 10 to 20 percent. Assuming an average of 15 percent, the real tax rates on domestic agricultural goods are only 15 percent of those on imported goods.

Such a tax system can provide some of China's farmers with significant protection. For example, in the case of soybeans, there is only a 3-percent tariff on imports. In recent years, however, many traders have been given the right to import soybeans. Theoretically, then, the international price of soybeans upon arrival at China's borders should differ by only 3 percent. However, as soybeans enter the country, soybean importers also must pay a 13-percent tax to meet their value-added tax obligation. Domestic soybeans, in contrast, are taxed, on average, at less than 3 percent. Through this means, then, China's soybean producers have an added 10 percent of price protection.[1]

China also has used export subsidies in recent years to increase exports of some commodities, thereby increasing protection by raising the price of domestic commodities (table 6.3). Maize and cotton are the two crops that have received the most substantial export subsidies. In general, the subsidies are paid out of the national budget on approval of the State Council. Only approved state trading organizations are authorized to export with the subsidies. During interviews in the field during 2001, we found that maize exporters, especially

TABLE 6.3   Subsidies and Tax Rebates for Exports of Selected Agricultural Commodities in China, 2001

Commodity	Export Subsidies (Percent)	Rebate of Value-Added Tax for Exported Agricultural Commodities (Percent)
Rice	<1	0
Cotton	10	0
Maize	34	0
Pork	0	5.2
Beef	0	5.2
Chicken	0	13

Source: Authors' survey.

those in Northeast China, received subsidies that *averaged* 34 percent of export price (row 3). For example, one trader said that for each ton of maize that his company exported in 2001, it received back 378 yuan per ton (45.7 US$ per ton) after producing an export bill of sale with the export sales price. With a sale price of 104 US$ per ton, the trading company received a subsidy of 44 percent, 10 percentage points above the average. The total payment received (export earnings plus subsidy) was 1,240 yuan per ton, which was about 90 yuan higher than what could have been earned in the domestic market (1,150 yuan). We also discovered that cotton exporters received fairly large subsidies when they exported raw cotton, up to 10 percent or more (table 6.3). Finally, in several isolated cases, rice exporters reported that they received small subsidies (though no more than 5 percent for any single trade) from municipal and prefectural governments, a subsidy that we only documented in south China (although it should be noted that we did not have the opportunity to interview many rice traders in north China—that is, ones that might be exporting japonica varieties into the northeast Asia market). Most of the rice traders we spoke with received no subsidy for their exports, meaning the average subsidy almost certainly was less than 1 percent (table 6.3).

Because of the higher numbers of meat exporters and the private or commercialized public nature of the companies, subsidies are not provided; however, tax policies help exporters compete on an equal basis in international markets. Based on the trade ministry's estimate of the average value-added tax paid on the products exported by meat traders, when a meat exporter executes a contract, the company can receive a rebate equal to the estimated value of the value-added tax (table 6.4). For example, pork and beef exporters receive a rebate equal to 5.2 percent of the value of their transaction (rows 4 and 5). Poultry exporters received 13 percent rebates (row 6). When international prices for meat commodities are higher than those inside China, rebates encourage domestic producers and traders to export, since the perceived price gap between the domestic and international price will be greater (which, of course, will also help raise China's domestic price as exports rise).

In summary, then, as China enters the WTO, those officials interested in liberalizing China's trade will face a number of challenges. Alternatively, China also has a number of instruments that it has been using and may continue to use (legally or not) in managing its domestic economy. In addition to traditional trade policies, tariffs, quotas and licensing, state trading, and NTBs, China has protected and/or has the potential to protect its agriculture with a number of other policy measures. In particular, our analysis has shown that taxation policy may still be a tool that China could try to use to protect or further open its agricultural sector. It may also use other policies, such as sanitary and phytosanitary (SPS) regulations. In the past, it also has used export subsidies and rebates (when used for commodities on which the domestic value-added tax is not assessed) to create wedges between the domestic and international prices of importable commodities and to decrease the domestic price relative to the world price of exportable goods. While export rebates can still be used legally (assuming the taxes that are being rebated have been paid domestically), some instruments will not be able to be used in the future (such as, export subsidies).

New Estimates of China's Nominal Rates of Protection

In this section, we estimate a new set of NRPs on the eve of China's accession to the WTO. These estimates will attempt to overcome some of the previous problems faced by researchers. In particular, we try to understand in a more disaggregated way the part of certain markets (in terms of varieties or commodity type) that China is protecting. Such an analysis should help us more accurately assess what the impacts will be after China implements it WTO obligations. To do so, we first explain how we collected our data. Next, we look at the disaggregated results. Finally, to make the information more useful to policy makers and other researchers, we create a series of more aggregate NRPs. The aggregation of our disaggregated NRPs into a single crop-specific figure allows us to assess how our methods would have changed had we used traditional methods of estimating NRPs. Appendix A summarizes some of the difficulties that practitioners face when trying to measure NRP for China's agriculture.

To overcome the shortcomings of previous NRP studies, we conducted a set of interviews and surveys with the stated goal of precisely identifying the differences in prices at a precise point of time and a particular location between an imported good on one side of the border (outside China) and a domestic good of identical quality on the other side (inside China). Similarly, we also wanted to identify the same price gap between exportable domestic goods as they leave the country and the same goods from other countries that are being traded in international markets. Conducted in 2001, the enumeration team was in the field more than three months, from August to November. The team visited seven coastal cities—Guangzhou, Shenzhen, Ningbo, Shanghai, Lianyungang, Qinghuangdao, and Dalian—and the two more inland cities of Beijing and Changchun. In each port, a number of "sampling frames" was used to select a sample of domestic traders, importers and exporters, wholesalers, grain and oilseed users, trade regulators, agents, and other grain and fiber officials. More than 100 people were interviewed;[2] less than 10 percent of those contacted refused to be interviewed.[3]

Disaggregated NRPs for Selected Agricultural Commodities in China

The results of our analysis clearly illustrate the problems with a strategy of NRP estimation that attempts to come up with a single rate of protection for a commodity. For example, it is difficult to provide one single NRP of wheat in China, one of the world's largest importers of wheat (table 6.4). Traders reported that the price of very high quality wheat from North America was 20 to 50 percent higher in the domestic markets of China's major ports than when it was on a ship in China's port ready to be brought into the country (table 6.4). More precisely, the average trader told us that if a ton of Canadian Number 3 hard white wheat were brought in and auctioned off in October 2001, the competitive bid price would have been 20.5 percent higher than the international price on a cost, insurance, and freight (CIF) basis. The same traders told us that the competitive bid price of high quality U.S. wheat would have been 50 percent higher. Hence, based on this price gap, one would have to assume that China's protection price is high, and if it were to open its markets completely, wheat prices would plummet and import volume soar.

However, traders were quick to point out that they did not think that even with open markets China's wheat price would fall anywhere near 50 percent even if there was no effect on the world price; they were not considering the impact of China's imports on the world price.[4] According to our interviews, the market for baking-quality wheat, the main use for hard white wheat from North America, is actually relatively small in China, at most only several million metric tons (MMTs). We also were told that few users in China outside those who demanded flour for making cakes, pastries, and high-quality breads would use this type of wheat and that only a small group of farmers and processors inside China could supply this type of wheat. If this is in fact the case, this would mean that even in a world free of any trade restrictions, imports would come into China until demand was filled and the domestic price for that variety fell to international levels.

Alternatively, it could be the case that all production of that particular variety would shift out of China if all of China's farmers abandoned them because they could not make a profit. In such an extreme case, with few domestic supplies and with little or no substitution of the baking-quality wheat for other domestic uses, the price impact on most domestic producers would be small. Growers of the high-quality wheat would lose; they would have to

TABLE 6.4   Disaggregated Nominal Rates of Protection for Selected Grains in China, October 2001

Variety or Quality	Comparable Domestic Price		Border Prices (US$/Ton)		NPR (%)
	Yuan/Ton	US$/Ton	C.I.F	F.O.B	
Estimated at official exchange rate[a]					
Rice Weighted average					−3
Thai jasmine rice	3,690	446	380		17
High-quality japonica	2,930	354		398	−11
Medium-quality indica	1,519	184		185	−0.5
Wheat Weighted average					12
US DNS	2,350	284	190		49
Canadian #3	1,800	218	181		20
Australian soft	1,625	196	175		12
US hard red	1,550	187	169		11
UK	1,350	163	145		12
China high quality	1,350	163	145		12
China medium quality	1,250	151	140		8
China low quality	1,100	133	133		−0.1
Soybean Common variety	1,950	236	205		15
Maize Common variety	1,150	139		105	32

C.I.F.   Cost, insurance, and freight
F.O.B.   Free on board
[a]The estimated official exchange rate is 8.28.
Source: Authors' survey.

keep growing at a lower price, switch to another wheat variety, or change cropping patterns. Since the quantities of such grain are so small, however, the overall impact would be minimal.

While not as extreme as the case for North American baking-quality wheat, traders reported that arbitrage possibilities in other markets (table 6.4). With a remarkable degree of consistency, the CIF price of medium-quality wheat imports from Australia, England, and the Pacific Northwest of the United States (hard red) was reported to be 10 percent lower than the price that they believed the same wheat would command in China's domestic market. Used for more common bread, cheaper pastries, industrial uses, and high-quality noodles, interviewees believed that this market accounted for approximately 10 to 15 percent of China's wheat demand. However, unlike the case of the highest-quality baking wheat, production was greater in China. In fact, in 2001 domestic producers supplied most of the wheat of this quality into this segment of China's wheat market. In

China's domestic market, however, this wheat was considered to be high-quality Chinese wheat. Interestingly, evidence that medium-quality wheat on international markets is the same as high-quality wheat supplied by China's farmers is found in the answer to the question that we asked our interviewees: if China's higher-quality wheat were sold on international markets, how much *loss* would a trader incur? Our survey found that this rate, 10 percent, was almost exactly the same as the premium importers would make from bringing in medium-quality grain from the international market.

Finally, although there have been no imports of low- or lower-medium quality wheat from international markets, it appears that China's medium-quality wheat, by far the biggest part of China's production (estimated to be more than 60 percent) is only marginally protected (table 6.4). Our survey found that traders believed if China's medium-quality wheat was sold on the international market in late 2001, it would sell at a discount

TABLE 6.5   Average Nominal Protection Rates for Major Imports and Exports in China, October 2001

Major Imports and Exports	Domestic Price (Yuan per Ton)	Nominal Rate of Protection (Percent)
Imports		
Wheat[a]	1,250	12
Maize	1,150	32
Soybeans	1,950	15
Cotton	9,500	17
Sugar	2,612	40
Exports		
Rice[a]	1,954	−3
Pork[a]	11,442	−30
Beef[a]	13,743	−10
Poultry[a]	9,904	−17
Fresh fruits	5,472	−4

[a]Average Nominal Rates of Protection are created by summing the NRP rates of individual varieties weighting with the sown area (production) share.

Source: Authors' survey.

of about 8 percent. Another way to interpret this result is that if international traders can ship this quality of wheat to China, it would command a premium of 8 percent. It is likely that imports of wheat will increase after WTO accession because of the persistent price gap. The effect, however, appears to be less than 10 percent. China's lowest quality of wheat (about 10 to 15 percent of its harvest) is at the world's feed wheat price (table 6.5). China did export some feed wheat into international markets in 2001 (mostly to Asia, according to an interviewee). Similar differences in the size of the price gap among varieties of a single grain are found for rice, though not for wheat and maize, which are more homogeneous products.

New NRPs for China

Although differences exist among major types of any individual agricultural commodity, by weighting them by their sown area (for crops) and production (for meats) shares, a set of by crop aggregate NPRs can be created (table 6.5). Wheat, for example, has an NRP of 12 percent (row 1) when the individual NRPs from table 6.4 are

weighted by their area shares. On average, the prices of all varieties of domestically produced wheat sold in the domestic markets of China's major port (and inland) cities are 12 percent above the average CIF price of all types of imported wheat varieties. Rice, on the other hand, is implicitly taxed at 3 percent. The aggregate figures, although helpful (and perhaps needed for analysis that is only disaggregated to the crop level), are less interesting and provide much less insight into which groups of farmers in which areas are producing which varieties will be hurt or helped if trade liberalization reduces the distortions.

However, to the extent that certain commodities have less intracrop quality differences, the aggregate measures have more inherent interest. For example, maize, soybeans, cotton, and sugar have far less quality differences among varieties than rice and wheat. This is partly due to the fact that maize and soybeans are rarely consumed directly (as are rice and wheat, making them more sensitive to human tastes and preferences). Instead, maize and soybeans are used mostly as feed or are processed. As a consequence, in our analysis we only examine aggregate crop NRPs for maize, soybeans, cotton, and sugar.[5]

Our findings show not only that significantly positive rates of protection exist for a number of China's major field crops, but also that they vary over the nation and according to the position in which China finds itself as a net importer or as a net exporter. Maize prices, according to exporters, were more than 30 percent, on average, above world prices. In other words, they would have lost more than 30 percent of the value of their shipment if the government had not paid a subsidy. Protection rates for maize as an import differed. For example, traders in the northeast told our survey team that if they were not exporting and foreign maize was to come into China, the importer could gain 21 percent since the price of imported maize is 21 percent lower than the domestic maize price. Our interviews in south China, however, found that the price gap between imported maize (CIF) and maize being traded in the domestic market in and around Guangzhou was more than 30 to 40 percent. Aggregated across areas on the basis of meat consumption shares, we estimate that China's maize NRP was 32 percent in 2001 (table 6.5).

TABLE 6.6 Percentage of Market Pairs that Test Positive for Being Integrated based on Dickey-Fuller Test in Rural China, 1988 to 2000

Commodity	1989–95	1996–2000
	(Percent of Market Pairs)	
Maize	28	89
Soybeans	28	68
Japonica Rice (Yellow River Valley)	25	60
Indica Rice (Yangtse Valley and South China)	25	47

Note: Results for two periods from same data set. For results from 1989–95 for maize and rice, see Rozelle and others (2000). Rice results are for the whole country in 1989–95. Results from soybeans for 1989 to 1995 and all results from 1996 to 2000 are by authors.

Interviewees also reported that despite the large volume of increase of soybean imports in recent years, a difference remains between the CIF and domestic price in the port (table 6.6). The average difference between the domestic price and the international price was 15 percent. In one sense, the fact that there is a remaining price gap is remarkable given that China imported almost 15 MMT of soybeans in 2001, the official tariff is only 3 percent, and the commodity is freely traded without securing a license or quota allocation. On the other hand, the remaining price gap reminds us that there may be other reasons for distortions beyond tariffs and state trading.

Our results also demonstrate that cotton and sugar were fairly highly protected in October 2001 (table 6.5). The case of cotton, however, is an example of how fast the NRP can change across time. The NRP was measured at 17 percent in October 2001. When our team returned for follow-up work at the end of November, the domestic price of cotton had fallen from 9,500 yuan per ton in October to less than 8,000 yuan per ton. With this fall, the NRP went to less than zero. However, later in the year, the international price of cotton also dipped, a fact that would lead to a higher NRP. Being less variable in 2001 in both China's and international markets, the

NRP of sugar remained about 40 percent throughout the year.

Assessing the New Methodology

Since one of our objectives was to use a new data source and method for aggregating NRPs data to generate crop specific NRPs, it would be interesting to analyze what would have happened had we not used this time- and data-intensive survey methodology. To conduct such an experiment we used the same methodology, data sources, and assumptions that many people use for calculating NRPs to calculate an NRP for China in 2001.[6] Although the two approaches give almost the same answers for some commodities, such as soybeans and maize (though soybeans were still overstated, in part because of difference in prices over the entire year—China's domestic prices fell sharply over the year, suggesting that the NRP in late 2001 was lower than it was in early 2001), the answers vary considerably for other commodities. For example, the national average price for wheat in 2001 reported from the Ministry of Agriculture reporting system was 1,113 yuan per ton. The average price of imports calculated by dividing total import value by total import quantity was 1,393 yuan per ton. In other words, the domestic price of wheat using these sources of data about prices is 21 percent below the CIF price of imports. From this standard methodology, one would come to the conclusion that wheat, rather than being protected (by 12 percent—see tables 6.4 and 6.5), was actually being taxed by trading policies. Yet, as we have seen the main reason for generating a negative rate of protection is that China is importing almost exclusively very high-grade, baking-quality wheat, while its domestic consumers use mostly medium- and lower-quality wheat. The wrong conclusion is reached when one uses the specialty prices for imports as an international reference price for types of wheat that are much lower quality and are lower priced.

The same problem is found for rice. Because China imports only high-quality jasmine rice from Thailand, the international price of rice (3,908 yuan per ton—that is calculated by total import value divided by total import quantity) appears to be more than 150 percent higher than the average domestic price (1464 yuan per ton). In fact, as shown in table 6.5, China's average price protection (tax) rate, calculated on a variety-by-variety basis, is almost zero (−3).

Thus, according to this illustrative example, we can see the necessity of approaching the estimation of NRPs in a more careful way for some commodities. Using the traditional approaches work fairly well for commodities that are relatively homogenous in their quality characteristics, such as maize and soybeans. We have seen for the case of wheat and rice for China in 2001, however, that comparing average prices inside and outside of the nation can lead to misleading results. Based on this example, one might conjecture that traditional estimates of NRP for some products, such as sugar and edible oils, may be fairly reliable. Those for meat products, cotton, and horticulture crops, however, could be misleading.

WTO Effects Away from the Border

While important in determining the size of the shock at the border, the broader magnitude of the effect of the WTO agreement on China's farmers depends not only on the size of the distortion, but also on the size of the area across which it will be felt. This second factor, in turn, is a function of the size and nature of China's market. In fact, there are at least three factors:

- policy safeguards that limit market forces from fully equilibrating domestic and international prices
- household responses by which households are able to move into the production of higher profitability commodities and away from those that experience price falls
- high transaction costs that possibly can serve to buffer the effects of liberalization policies on those who live in rural areas in China.

The policy safeguards are discussed elsewhere in this volume. The effects of household responses are discussed in Taylor (1998) and Huang and Rozelle (2002). In this section, we focus on the nature of markets.

Ultimately, the distributional impacts of WTO will depend on the nature of China's markets. If large areas of the country are isolated from coastal markets where imports land, then the effects of WTO may be circumscribed to restricted parts of the country and should not be expected to have highly adverse impacts on the poor who are largely located in inland areas far from major urban centers. While being isolated from negative external shocks is a plus, there is also a cost. Those living in poor, isolated areas also would not benefit from price rises and opportunities to export, and they are potentially vulnerable to price shocks as regional production and consumption demand change. However, if markets exist that link together distant regions with the coast and price changes in one part of the economy quickly ripple through the economy, even though imports are infused into (and exports flow out of) areas concentrated around a few large coastal cities, they could have ramifications for poor households thousands of kilometers away.

To the extent that there are high transaction costs inside China and to the extent that certain domestic markets are isolated from others in the country—especially those inland areas isolated from port regions where imports land—the impact of WTO policies may not be evenly distributed. In previous work done on China's agricultural markets (e.g., Park and others 2002), it was found that, in general, China's markets were becoming fairly integrated by the mid-1990s. However, this conclusion should be qualified. First, although markets improved greatly during the early 1990s, the analysis still found large parts of the country, especially poorer areas, were not completely integrated into national markets in all years. Moreover, the study's dataset is dated. Since the final year of the available data, more than seven years have passed. It is unclear whether markets have matured since that time or whether the actions taken by leaders have led to greater fragmentation (Nyberg and Rozelle 1999). Surprisingly, given the fragile nature of reforming China's agricultural markets, almost no recent work addresses these questions.

Assessing the Determination of Price and Market Integration in China

To assess the state of the integrated and developed markets in rural China in the late 1990s and 2000, we first describe the data. Second, we test for integration and conduct direct tests of how well prices in different markets move together and if prices are integrated between the market town and China's villages. Finally, we measure the degree of price transmission.

Data The data come from a unique price dataset collected by China's State Market Administration Bureau (SMAB). Nearly 50 sample sites from 15 of China's provinces report prices of agricultural commodities every 10 days. The prices are the average price of transactions that day in the local rural periodic market. The Ministry of Agriculture assembles the data in Beijing, making them available to researchers and policymakers.

We examine rice, maize, and soybean prices from 1996 to 2000 (except for maize that was only available only through 1998). The three crops are produced and consumed in nearly every province in China. Rice price data are available for 31 markets. Because of quality differences among rice varieties in different regions of China, we look at price integration between markets within four regions, South China, the Yangtse Valley, the North China Plain and Northeast China. For the provinces included in the sample, rice prices are available for over 90 percent of the time periods. Prices for maize and soybean data are available for 13 and 20 markets, respectively.[7] Product homogeneity makes it possible to include a broader geographic range of buyers and sellers in a single analysis, and we are able to assess the integration of markets spread out over thousands of kilometers. We compare these results to results from 1988 to 1995 that were produced with the same data and published in Park and others (2002).

Integration Tests In this section we use more formal tests of market integration. To do so, we apply the Engle-Granger cointegration approach to test for the integration of China's grain markets. Two or more price series are cointegrated (even if each is individually nonstationary) if a linear combination of the variables (e.g., the differences of the prices) is stationary. Following Engle and Granger (1987), we apply a two-step residual-based test. The first step uses the ordinary least square (OLS) regression of one price series on another:

$$P_t^i = \alpha + \lambda t + \beta P_t^j + e_t, \qquad (6.1)$$

where t is the common trend of the two price-series and where e_t is the error term. The main reason for running the first step is that it provides the

residuals, e_t, for the second step. The second step then tests for the stationarity of the residuals from equation (6.1) using the augmented Dickey-Fuller test:

$$\Delta e_t = \delta e_{t-1} + \sum_{j=2}^{N} \gamma \Delta e_{t-j} + \xi_t \qquad (6.2)$$

If the test statistic on the δ coefficient is less (i.e., more negative) than the relevant critical value from the Dickey-Fuller (D-F) table, the null hypothesis may be rejected and the two series are said to be cointegrated of order (1,1). When the series are cointegrated this way, it implies that the two markets from which the price series come are integrated. The absolute value of the test statistics should be greater than 3 at 10% significant level. In our paper, we are conducting only the unit root test, where j equals zero, since the error term from equation (6.1) is an AR(1) process.

The results of the cointegration analysis support both our descriptive findings and the conclusions of the determinants of commodity price analysis in the previous page, especially when they are compared to the findings of research on market integration in the late 1980s and early 1990s (table 6.6). In middle part of the reform era (1988–1995), a time when markets were starting to emerge, between 20 to 25 percent of markets showed signs the prices were moving together during the study periods and sub-periods. According to their findings, although there were many market pairs in which prices did not move together, between the late 1980s and mid-1990s, there was evidence of rising integration.

Using the results from the early 1990s as a base line, our current analysis shows that during the late 1990s, China's markets continued along their previous path of maturation; markets in China, especially those for maize, are remarkably integrated. In the late 1990s, examining the co-movement of prices between pairs of markets in our sample, we see a large increase in the number of integrated markets. In the case of maize, for example, in 89 percent of the cases, prices in one market move at the same time as in another (table 6.6). This is up from only 28 percent of the time in the early 1990s. The number of pairs of markets for soybeans, japonica, rice, and indica rice shows similar increases (table 6.6). The integration of these markets is notable because, in many cases, the pairs of markets are separated by more than a 1000 kilometers. For example, we find prices in almost all years to be integrated between markets in Shaanxi and Guangdong provinces and between those in Sichuan province and southern Jiangsu.

Despite the significant progress in terms of integrations, our results also show pairs of markets during different years that are not integrated. For example, in one third of the cases, japonica rice prices moved in one market but did not in another. The case of indica rice trade is even more notable. In the case of more than half the time (and places), prices do not move together in China's indica rice producing and consuming regions. One explanation for such a result is that there is some kind of institution (policy or infrastructure/communication) breakdown that is creating China's fragmentation, as shown in Park and others (2002). It is also the case that since every province in China has rice production and consumption, if during a certain year in a certain area, supply in that region is just equal to demand and price differentials between regions stay within the band between regional "export" and "import" prices, moderate price movements in another area may not necessarily induce a flow into or out of the region that is in equilibrium.

Even with the nontrivial number of cases in the late 1990s in which market prices in pairs of markets do not move together, based on each of the market performance analyses, one must conclude that the impacts of WTO on China's agriculture will be experienced across wide regions of the nation from coastal to inland areas. However, this is only half of the story. The discussion of table 6.6 demonstrates a remarkable degree of integration between markets on the coast and those inland, such an analysis is still not sufficient to ensure that many of China's villages will be affected by the shocks that hit the coast and are transmitted inland.

To do so, in this part of this section we examine the extent to which villages are integrated into regional markets. Our test of integration will essentially identify if farmers in China's villages are price takers or are villages isolated, making prices determined by local supply and demand. In briefest terms, if variables that affect local supply significantly affect prices, we will assume villages are isolated and markets are not integrated to the village level; in contrast, if the local supply shock does not affect the price, villagers are price takers and markets will be thought to be integrated.

The data for this study were collected in a randomly selected, nearly nationally representative sample of 60 villages in six provinces of rural China the China National Rural Survey (CNRS). To accurately reflect varying income distributions within each province, one county was randomly selected from within each income quintile for the province, as measured by the gross value of industrial output. Two villages were randomly selected within each county. The survey teams used village rosters and our own counts to randomly choose twenty households, both those with their residency permits (*hukou*) in the village and those without. A total of 1,199 households was surveyed. The CNRS project team gathered detailed information on both the production and marketing behavior of all of the farmers in the sample and the characteristics of each village and its relationship to the nearest regional market. From each respondent in the survey in each village, we identified the price and timing of the sale for each commodity. From these data, we construct an average village price for each month in yuan per kilogram. In a community questionnaire, we know how far the village's center is from the nearest paved road and the distance to the county market in kilometers. Finally, for each crop that the farmer cultivated, we know whether the farmer's crop suffered a shock, recording both the incidence and the percentage by which the yield fell. We do not include any variable that controls for the presence of a community buffer stock system, primarily because such an institution is almost never observed in modern China.[8] In addition, sales among farmers within a village are rare (according to our data, less than 5 percent of sales). County dummies hold quality constant.

Our regression analysis clearly shows markets in China are integrated down to the village level (table 6.7). The signs and level of significance of the coefficients on variables, such as the distance that a village is from the market, demonstrate that the farther a village is from a market, the lower the price the farmer receives, which is the expected result. More importantly for our purposes, the

TABLE 6.7 Soybean, Corn, and Wheat Village Price Regression, 2000

Explanatory Variable	Soybean Price	Corn Price	Wheat Price
Distance to the nearest country market	−0.029	−0.00064	−0.0095
	(2.37)**	(−1.63)*	(3.24)**
Village-level shock to production	−0.04	0.12	0.081
	(−0.17)	(−1.34)	(−1.02)
Other variables not shown	timing of sales/net purchase or seller		

t-ratios of the coefficients of the village supply shock variables are all less in absolute value terms than 1.35, signifying that the output of the local village's crops do not affect the local price. One implication of this result is that factors outside the village affect the price that farmers receive, making them price takers. In other words, farmers, even in China's remote villages, are linked to the markets of its main commodities.

Price Transmission Coefficients

While integrated markets mean that inland markets will experience price changes in the direction of the price movements at the ports (for those crops that are imported and exported), frictions in the marketing system may shield inland producers from some of the effects.[9] Moreover, despite the rise of price integration in China's domestic markets during the reform period, there are still a significant number of market pairs during certain years that do not move together. Hence, when assessing the impact of WTO-induced price shocks at the border on farmers inland, we need to examine the degree of transmission of these effects.

To examine the proportion of the price changes that would be experienced in regions away from the port, we conducted a series of analyses to try to measure the extent of the change of prices inland for a percentage change at the port. We do the analysis for the two major crops for which we have complete data series: rice and maize. In the first

analysis, we stack the price data from various markets for the last three years (1998–2000) and regress the price of the inland market (in logs in time period t) on the price at the port market (in logs in time period t) and three lags (t-1; t-2; and t-3—table 6.8). The sum of the coefficients on the port variables provide an intuitive measure for the total transmission of price shocks in percentage terms. The price transmission coefficients range from 42 to 51 percent for rice (the lower range being a measure of the price impact that does not include coefficients with t-ratios under 1.580 (table 6.8). According to these measures, about half of the price change at the port is transmitted to the inland market. The transmission coefficients for maize range from 51 to 57 percent (table 6.8). This means that if

TABLE 6.8 Transmission Coefficients for Rice and Maize Measuring the Percentage of Price Shock at Port that Is Transmitted to Inland Markets in China, 1996–2000[a]

	Maize	Rice
Standard Vector Autogression Model (VAR)[b]	51–57	42–51
VAR with corrections for autocorrelation.	49	10–13
Vector Autogression Model with Impulse Response Simulation[d]	20–35	12–25

[a]The transmission coefficient is interpreted at the average proportion of a price shock in the port market that is experienced by the markets inland.
[b]Standard Vector Autoregression Analysis stacks the price data from various markets for the last three years (1998 to 2000) and regresses the price of the inland market (in logs in time period t) on the price at the port market (in logs in time period t) and three lags (t-1; t-2; and t-3). The sum of the coefficients on the port variables is a measure of the total transmission of price shocks in terms of proportions.
[c]This uses the same model as in row 1, but also includes lags of the dependent variable for t-1, t-2 and t-3. Simulation analysis proceeds by shocking the price at the border and following the price from port to inland, holding the own market's price generation constant.

maize prices fell 10 percent at the border due to the import of an amount up to China's quota limits, the price of maize inland would fall around 5 percent.

The analysis in the above paragraph, however, does not account for the fact that the error term in the equation could be subject to autocorrelation. The corrected transmission coefficients fall only modestly for maize, declining to 49 percent (table 6.8). In other words, even after accounting for autocorrelation, if the price at the border (or port) changes by 10 percent, the inland price falls by nearly 5 percent. After the same treatment in the rice equations, however, the price transmission coefficient falls sharply (to around only 10 percent (table 6.8)). According to this result, we find that rice markets are subject to much more friction than those for maize, a result that may result from the inherent differences between rice (a commodity with a wide range of qualities) and maize (a more homogeneous commodity). In other words, when we are observing a price shock in the port market, it may be caused by the new inflow or shortage of a particular type of rice. For example, when a certain type of rice in Guangzhou suffers a shock (e.g., the harvest in one of the production bases is greatly reduced, although the price in another production base that produces that variety may move, the price in an area that does not produce that variety may not change. In the case of maize, however, its homogeneous nature means that most of the price shock in one market is passed through by traders.

A third analysis confirms the finding of the more traditional price transmission model (table 6.8). Using a impulse response analysis (which basically uses the price transmission model and adds a set of lagged own prices the price in the inland market in period t-1, t-2 and t-3), we find that a 10 percent price change in the port price of maize changes the inland price by up to 35 percent and up to 28 percent in the case of rice.

Conclusions

The purpose of our study is to examine the effects of China's accession to the WTO on the agricultural sector. Although there are many possible effects, we have focused on the impact of trade policy changes on agricultural prices. Moreover while trade will also affect other subsectors of the rural economy, this study's focus on the agricultural sector showed that there will be an impact. However, like other effects, those in the agricultural sector may not all be negative. Our findings, based on new methods to collect data and create NRPs, show that indeed for some crops WTO accession will likely lead to a fall in prices and a rise in imports. Maize and cotton may be most affected. It is possible that soybeans and sugar could be significantly affected in the longer run. There are also commodities in which China has considerable comparative advantage— for example, rice, meats, and horticultural products and, hence, WTO accession could provide benefits to those engaged in these activities. The prospect of increased imports of feed grains (e.g., maize and soybeans) at lower prices means that livestock producers could become even more competitive.

The extent to which prices fall from rising imports or rise from rising exports in part depends on how China executes its WTO obligations. Although there may be room for footdragging (which could delay that negative effects), the nature of the agreement also provides many means to limit the downside effects. Likewise, China's benefits are going to depend on how well trading partners honor their commitment and provide better access to global markets. We suggest that rather than footdragging on its own reforms, China would be better to use some of its capital and goodwill to fight measures in its trading partners, such as Japan's safeguards against mushrooms. Here, China has already had a huge, unheralded win by getting Japan to move from its original way of conducting bilateral trade with China (based on blatantly WTO–illegal measures to safeguards that are transparent and temporary. China also should realize that, as a WTO member, it now has a means to file a protest if it believes it is being treated unfairly. When countries use the WTO enforcement organizations to fight unauthorized trade barriers, complainants tend to have a high success rate. In general, to gain the most in the long run from this agricultural agreement, both China and its partners need to endeavor to live up to their agreements.

We also found that unlike the case of Mexico, it appears as if most of China's markets may be well-integrated into the economy. This is good news and bad news for poor farmers. The good news is that they can benefit from falling input prices and rising export opportunities. The bad news is that unlike a large number of maize farmers in Mexico who were not affected by the North American Free Trade Agreement reduction in maize import restriction, if our results are correct for large parts of China, its farmers will be affected. The problem, although it is a short-run one, may be that it is this group of rural households that are most dependent on agriculture and least able to be flexible. As a consequence, our findings should be taken as a warning to government leaders that they need to be concerned about the welfare of these susceptible groups.

Our results also generate findings that show the close relationship that exists among the degree of integration of an economy, the size of the price effect, and the amount that fraction of the TRQ that will be imported. If China's markets are really so integrated, and leaders do not artificially delay the ability of traders to execute TRQs, our findings suggest that the price effects may not be too large because they will be spread out across a large area of the country. However, if the price effects for a given quantity of imports are not large, the volume of imports may be larger than predicted by some and the bindings may be more likely to take effect. We do not expect in any circumstance that imports will ever exceed the limits put on by the TRQs.

Appendix: Challenges and Issues in Measuring Nominal Protection Rates

Although measuring the difference in price between an economy's domestic price and the international price, the wide range of estimates of NPRs that exist for China demonstrate it is not a straightforward process. In fact, a number of issues complicate NPR measurement. First, confusion may stem from the way analysts have asked their question about NPRs. Policy makers and researchers have sought to summarize the impact of various commodities with a single number. Trade modelers need a single number to make their analytical frameworks tractable. People want to know what is *the* price of wheat in China and compare that to *the* world price of wheat. With this information, the

NPR of a commodity is simply the difference of these two numbers.

However, more careful observation shows the search for a *single* number may be one of the main reasons different analysts can come to *so many different* conclusions. In fact, there are many prices for wheat in China. Prices vary across time within a year. Prices vary across regions within a time period. When calculating the NPR, does one look at the price of corn in a Guangzhou feedlot or the price of corn sitting in storage in a farmer's home-made silo in Northeast China? Moreover, rice is not rice is not rice. There are many different varieties and types, all of which command different prices at different places at different times during the year. In fact, for some commodities, such as rice, China is exporting one type at the same time it is importing another. The same sets of issues face analysts when they attempt to choose a price series (or more difficult yet, the single price) to represent the international price. Which price should an analyst choose? Should it be FOB or CIF? Should it be the average annual price or a price during one particular period? If there are many different types of imported varieties, which type should be chosen?

In part because previous studies have not dealt with these issues (at least explicitly), it is unsurprising that different research efforts have generated different estimates of NPRs. For example, Tuan and Cheng (1999) estimated quite high and variable nominal rates of protection for agricultural commodities. Their estimates for wheat, maize, and soybeans in 1997 were 62, 15, and 140 percent respectively. On the other hand, Carter and Estrin (2001) find generally negative price distortions. Huang (2001) provides sets of estimates that show some products are highly protected and in other cases there are negative rates of protection.

Notes

1. Some scholars in China have also pointed out that since part of the value of agricultural commodity production uses inputs on which the value added tax has been assessed, the "real" tax rate on agricultural commodities is actually higher. Although certainly this is the case, the maximum that could be added would only be an additional 2 to 4 percentage points (15 percent times the share of the inputs that were taxed—about 10 to 30 percent—depending on the commodity, the technology, and region of production).

2. Because of the absence of a single central authority that manages grain flows, the enumeration team chose its sample in a number of ways. In each location, we first visited the local grain bureau and obtained access to a list of all grain bureaus, the firms that they were running on a commercial basis, and their subsidiaries. We interviewed an official in the grain marketing division and transportation division. We also chose three firms that were owned directly by the grain bureau and three that were affiliated with the grain bureau. In several cities, the grain bureau had a list of large grain trading and grain using firms (e.g., mills and feed lots). In others, this was obtained from the market administration bureau. Five firms were chosen on the basis that they were private and had yearly sales that exceeded one million yuan. We interviewed at least two flour or rice mills and feed mills in each location. Finally, we visited the wholesale market and randomly chose five stalls to interview. The team also visited a number of other entities, such as the grain reserve, the local COFCO agency, and supermarket chains. In some cases, the managers of these entities knew the grain trade business well enough to answer our questions; in other cases they did not.

3. During the interviews, a survey instrument was filled out documenting the scope of the interviewee's participation in China's domestic and international food and fiber trade. We were particularly concerned with understanding the transactions that the interviewees were involved with or knew about that concerned imported or exported grains, fiber, meat and other goods. The survey recorded the characteristics of the commodities that were involved in trade in the immediate marketing area during the fall of 2001. Enumerators then asked the interviewee a series of questions about commodities about which the traders were most familiar. For imported commodities, interviewees first told the enumerators the international CIF price of the good. Second, the interviewee then told enumerators what the good would sell for if auctioned of in a competitive auction. In other words, we elicited a series of price gaps for a carefully defined set of goods. Since, on average, each interviewee had information about a number of commodities, we had several hundred observations. A similar set of questions was asked about exportable goods, including maize, rice, cotton, and meat products.

4. The assertion that consumption will be limited is based on the assumption that tastes will not change. It could be, however, that when the changes in consumption due to rising incomes are added to those due to changing tastes as higher quality products become cheaper, the scope for much greater penetration of the domestic market clearly seems possible. After years or centuries of consuming certain foods, the Chinese might find as others have that better quality bread or noodles are desirable options, in some cases offering nutritional advantages as well.

5. We should stress, however, our survey was conducted the same way. In most cases, interviewees told us that there were not a lot of quality differences among maize varieties. Moreover, there was only a slight (2 to 3 percent) of price difference between imported and domestic soybeans from quality.

6. These are computed by comparing the domestic wholesale price with the average implicit price of trade. For the importable (exportable) it is total value of import (export) divided by total volume of import (export).

7. Since we use data over time, we need to convert prices to a real basis. Nominal prices from our data set are deflated using monthly consumer price indices calculated and reported by the China National Statistical Bureau. Deflation facilitates transaction cost comparisons across time and allows us to disregard transaction cost increases within periods associated with inflation.

8. We do, however, in an alternative specification (not shown here) include a variable that controls for the average amount of private grain storage in the village. It is not significant and its inclusion does not affect the results.

9. It is also possible that there could be transmission elasticities greater than unity. Producers in an exporting region may find their price moves proportionally more than in the port. For example, consider the case if the CIF price was 100 and the interior price was 50. If the marketing margin were additive, the rise in the world price of 10 percent.

References

Anderson, K., and C. Y. Peng. 1998. "Feeding and Fueling China in the 21st Century." *World Development* 26(8): 1413–29.

CARD. 2001. "Effect of WTO on Agriculture." Paper Presented at the 2001 annual meetings of the American Agricultural Economics Association, August 5–8. Chicago, IL.

Carter, C. A., and A. Estrin. 2001. "China's Trade Integration and Impacts on Factor Markets." Mimeo. Department of Agricultural and Resource Economics, University of California, Davis.

Chen, Shaohua, and Martin Ravallion. 2004. "Welfare Impacts of China's Accession to the WTO." In D. Bhattasali, S. Li, and W. Martin, eds., *China and the WTO: Accession, Policy Reform, and Poverty Reduction Strategies*. Washington, D.C.: World Bank and Oxford University Press.

Huang, Jikun. 2001. "Agricultural Policy and Food Security." Working paper, Center for Chinese Agricultural Policy, Chinese Academy of Sciences. Beijing.

Huang, Jikun, and C. Chen. 1999. "Effects of Trade Liberalization on Agriculture in China: Institutional and Structural Aspects." Working Paper 42, United Nations ESCAP CGPRT Centre, Bogor, Indonesia.

Huang, Jikun, and Scott Rozelle. 2002. "Market Distortions and the Impact of WTO on China's Rural Economy." Working Paper, University of California, Davis, CA.

Li, S., F. Zhai, and Z. Wang. 1999. "The Global and Domestic Impact of China Joining the World Trade Organization, A Project Report." Development Research Center, the State Council, China.

Martin, W. 2002. "Implication of Reform and WTO Accession for China's Agricultural Policies." *Economies in Transition* (forthcoming).

Ministry of Agriculture. 2001. *China Statistical Yearbook*. Beijing: China Agricultural Press.

Nyberg, A., and S. Rozelle. 1999. *Accelerating China's Rural Transformation*. World Bank, Washington, D.C.

OECD. 2001. "Implications of Trade and Investment Liberalization for China's Agriculture." Working Paper, Organization for Economic Cooperation and Development, Paris.

Park, A., H. Jin, Scott Rozelle, and Jikun Huang. 2002. "Market Emergence and Transition: Transition Costs, Arbitrage, and Autarky in China's Grain Market," *American Journal of Agricultural Economics*. Forthcoming.

Rozelle, Scott. 2003. "After Accession to the WTO: Corn Trade Within China and Between China and the Rest of the World." A Report written for the U.S. Grains Council, Beijing, China.

Rozelle, Scott, Albert Park, Jikun Huang, and Hehui Jin. 2000. "Bureaucrat to Entrepreneur: The Changing Role of the State in China's Transitional Commodity Economy," *Economic Development and Cultural Change* 48, 2: 227–52.

Taylor, J. Edward. 1998. "Trade Liberalization and the Impact on Small Holders in Rural Mexico," Working Paper, Department of Agricultural and Resource Economics, University of California, Davis.

Tuan F.C., and Cheng, G. 1999. "A Review of China's Agricultural Trade Policy," paper prepared for the IATRC Summer Meeting. June 25–26. San Francisco.

Xie, Yuping. 2002. "WTO and China's Agricultural Trade and Impact on Domestic Markets," Unpublished Masters Thesis.

Center for Chinese Agricultural Policy, Chinese Academy of Sciences, Beijing.

World Bank. 2000. "An Assessment of China's Poverty Policy." Working Paper, World Bank, Washington, D.C.

Zhao, Yaohui, and Terry Sicular. 2002. "Affects of WTO Accession on China: Labor Market Responses." Working Paper, Center for Chinese Economic Reform, Peking University, Beijing.

PART II

ECONOMIC IMPACTS OF ACCESSION

7

THE IMPACTS OF WTO ACCESSION ON CHINESE AGRICULTURE AND RURAL POVERTY

Kym Anderson, Jikun Huang, and Elena Ianchovichina

After 15 years of negotiations, China acceded to the World Trade Organization (WTO) at the end of 2001. During those negotiations, China was continually opening up and reforming its economy, and further reforms will be introduced over the next few years to fulfill its legal obligations under its WTO Protocol of Accession. Such reform necessarily involves structural adjustments by households, firms, and bureaucracies, and although the economy as a whole can gain substantially from those adjustments, losses and even hardship can result for some households unless complementary domestic policies are in place to facilitate adjustment or compensate losers. This situation underscores the importance of first analyzing the likely distributional consequences of the reforms themselves and then considering what complementary policies are needed to provide adequate safety nets for potential losers.

Of particular concern in China's case is that the reforms may cause farm incomes to fall, exacerbating the rise since the mid-1980s in farm–nonfarm and inland–coastal aggregate income inequality and possibly reversing the decline since the late 1970s in rural poverty (reported in Kanbur and Zhang 2001). So high is the level of concern that at its first WTO ministerial meeting in Cancún in September 2003, China joined a new group of more than 20 developing countries that demanded that member countries of the Organisation for Economic Co-operation and Development (OECD) reform their agriculture sectors without requiring developing countries to lower their farm trade barriers.

The policy changes that China still must make to fulfill its WTO obligations include major changes in its farm trade policies by 2005—that is, cuts in protection that appear to be far greater, and faster, than those imposed on any other developing country in the Uruguay Round Agreement on Agriculture. With one-quarter of rural households in China living on less than $1 a day in 1999 (versus 1 percent of urban households) and more than three-quarters of all poor Chinese people living in rural areas, concerns about the impact of WTO accession on rural poverty are understandable. Yet reduced protectionism also may boost output and exports of some labor-intensive farm products in which China still has a comparative advantage.[1] In

Our thanks are extended to the World Bank and Australian Research Council for their financial support and to Will Martin, Tom Hertel, Scott Rozelle, and three referees for helpful comments on earlier versions of this chapter. The usual disclaimer applies.

addition, farm households will be affected indirectly by many of the other commitments China has made in its WTO Accession Protocol. Especially important will be the arrangements for phasing out the "voluntary" export restraints on China's textile and clothing trade and the reductions in protection of the motor vehicle and parts industry. Those changes, together with the promised increase in a wide range of agricultural imports, will allow China to exploit more fully its strong comparative advantage in unskilled labor-intensive products—both farm and nonfarm.

An assessment of the impacts on farmer incomes and on rural areas of the remaining reforms required to meet China's commitments to WTO membership is best conducted by seeing those impacts in the context of ongoing economic growth and structural change. This chapter therefore begins with a brief summary of rural developments since the initial reforms began in the late 1970s, of recent policies affecting rural households, and of the pertinent reforms still to be delivered as part of China's WTO commitments. With that background, the chapter then provides some indication of the likely effects of the reforms to be implemented between 2002 and 2007 on the welfare of different factor markets and thus different types of farm households. Because even the direction, let alone the magnitude, of some of the effects cannot be discerned from theory (McCulloch, Winters, and Cirera 2001), we use the numerical simulation model known as GTAP (named after Purdue University's Global Trade Analysis Project) to address these issues. Our experimental design, which is detailed in the companion paper by Ianchovichina and Martin (2004), goes beyond previous studies (see the survey by Gilbert and Wahl 2002) in several respects: (a) it focuses just on the liberalization required to meet China's WTO accession commitments from 2002 (by projecting the GTAP database to 2001 with China's prior reforms and all countries' Uruguay Round commitments implemented); (b) it incorporates new estimates of nominal rates of agricultural protection as of 2001 and at the end of accession; (c) it takes account of existing duty drawbacks so that it avoids overstating the extent of reform; (d) it binds the government budget by adding a uniform consumption tax to offset the loss of tariff revenue; (d) it takes account of differences between farm and nonfarm unskilled labor; and (e) it examines the real income effects on different types of farm households. The chapter concludes by drawing out implications for Chinese policymakers wishing to preempt any increases in food insecurity or rural poverty.

The Setting

To put prospective changes in perspective, it is helpful to review rural developments over the past 25 years and then the policies that have affected those changes.

Rural Developments since the Late 1970s

China's decision in December 1978 to open up its economy acted as a major stimulus to economic growth: the pre-reform rate of growth in the per capita gross domestic product (GDP) of 3.1 percent a year more than doubled, and it has remained above 7 percent for the past two decades (see last row of table 7.1). Rapid economic growth is normally accompanied by a relative decline in the farm sector, but in China that decline was initially tempered by introducing the farm household responsibility system (which led to replacing collective farms with individually managed holdings) and by raising the prices received by farmers. So began the process of moving away from taxing agriculture relative to other sectors—a process followed by most of the advanced economies in the early stages of their industrialization (Anderson and others 1986; Lindert 1991).

Agriculture grew nearly as rapidly as industry from 1979 to 1984. However, the one-off efficiency effects of moving to the household responsibility system and raising relative prices for farm products were mostly reaped by the mid-1980s, after which agriculture grew at only one-third the pace of industry and less than half that of the services sector as industrialization boomed on the eastern seaboard (table 7.1). Meanwhile, the employment, output, and exports of rural township and village enterprises also boomed (see the first three columns of table 7.2). Despite that migration of farm workers to rural industrial and service activities (not to mention the temporary unauthorized migration to urban jobs such as those in construction), the average area per farm worker has fallen steadily since the late 1970s, while the share of farm household income from nonfarm sources has risen (see last two columns of table 7.2). Table 7.3 shows

TABLE 7.1   Growth Rates of China's Economy, 1970–2000 (percent per year)

	Pre-Reform 1970–78	Reform Period		
		1979–84	1985–95	1996–2000
Gross domestic product[a]	*4.9*	*8.8*	*9.7*	*7.9*
Agriculture	2.7	7.1	4.0	3.4
Industry	6.8	8.2	12.8	9.6
Services	n.a.	11.6	9.7	8.3
Food production volume				
Grain	2.8	4.7	1.7	0.03
Oilseed crops	2.1	14.9	4.4	5.6
Fruit and vegetables	6.6	7.2	12.7	8.6
Red meat	4.4	9.1	8.8	6.5
Fish	5.0	7.9	13.7	10.2
Value of output of nonfarm rural enterprises	*n.a.*	*12.3*	*24.1*	*14.0*
Population	1.80	1.15	1.43	0.9
Per capita GDP	*3.1*	*7.7*	*8.3*	*6.9*

n.a. Not applicable.

[a]Figures for GDP in 1970–78 are the growth rate of national income in real terms. Growth rates are computed using the regression method. Growth rates of individual and groups of commodities are based on volume of production data; sectoral growth rates refer to value added in real terms.

Sources: National Bureau of Statistics of China, various issues; Ministry of Agriculture, *Agricultural Yearbook of China,* various issues.

TABLE 7.2   Farm and Rural Enterprise (RE) Developments in China, 1980–99

	RE's Share of Total Rural Labor (%)	RE's Share of Total GDP (%)	RE's Share of Total Exports (%)	Farmland Size (Hectares/Farm)	Share of Farm Household Income from Nonfarm Sources (%)
1980	9	4	0	0.56	17
1985	19	9	15	0.51	25
1990	23	14	43	0.43	26
1995	34	25	48	0.41	37
1999	35	30	48	0.40	47

Sources: National Bureau of Statistics of China, a, b; various issues.

the slowdown in the decline in agriculture's shares of GDP and employment in the 1980s and its subsequent acceleration in the 1990s.

Income growth has boosted the demand for foods that are high in protein and nutrients relative to those high in carbohydrates, which in turn has stimulated major structural changes within agriculture as farmers respond to the changes in domestic demand. For example, livestock and fish increased their share of agricultural output from less than 20 percent in the late 1970s to 30 percent by the late 1990s (table 7.3). Within the crop subsector, fruit and vegetable production grew two to three times as fast as grain output (table 7.1). The prices and marketing of grain and oilseed products have continued to be highly regulated, whereas the markets for horticultural, livestock, and fish products have been greatly liberalized. This liberalization has accentuated the growth in the output of the latter group relative to grain and oilseed output

TABLE 7.3 Changing Structure of China's Economy, 1970–2000 (percent, based on current prices)

	1970	1980	1985	1990	1995	2000
Share of GDP						
Agriculture	40	30	28	27	20	16
Industry	46	49	43	42	49	51
Services	13	21	29	31	31	33
Share of employment						
Agriculture	81	69	62	60	52	49
Industry	10	18	21	21	23	23
Services	9	13	17	19	25	28
Share of agricultural output						
Crops	82	76	69	65	58	56
Livestock	14	18	22	26	30	30
Fish	2	2	3	5	8	10
Forestry	2	4	5	4	3	4
Share of population that is rural	83	81	76	72	71	64

Sources: National Bureau of Statistics of China, a, b; various issues.

TABLE 7.4 China's Grain Production, Trade, and Consumption, 1980–2000 (million metric tons)

	1980–89	1990–94	1996–2000
Production	332	396	389
Net imports	8	−1	−3
Change in stocks	1	11	12
Consumption	339	384	374
Food—urban	35	42	41
Food—rural	177	190	177
Feed	64	86	91
Other (seed, industrial use, waste)	63	66	65

Source: Huang 2001, based on China National Statistics Bureau publications and the Center for Chinese Agricultural Policy's database.

since the mid-1980s (table 7.1). Meanwhile, the direct consumption of grain by both rural and urban households has virtually ceased growing (table 7.4)—a consequence not only of incomes rising but also of population growth slowing to less than 1 percent a year and of cuts in the implicit consumption subsidy for food grains.

The use of grain for animal feed continues to grow. To date, that increase has been supplied almost completely by rising domestic production, so that the trend level of grain self-sufficiency has remained close to 100 percent. Table 7.5 shows that there are nevertheless considerable changes from year to year in grain exports and imports. It also shows that, overall, China has remained a net exporter of food and feed, with meat, fish, and fruits and vegetables providing most of the growth in net export earnings.[2]

TABLE 7.5 Structure of China's Food and Feed Trade, 1980–99 (millions of US$)

	SITC	1980	1985	1990	1995	1999
Exports						
Live animals	00	384	304	430	473	374
Meat	01	361	448	791	1,349	1,054
Dairy products	02	71	57	55	61	71
Fish	03	380	283	1,370	2,875	2,969
Grains	04	423	1,065	614	281	1,273
Fruits and vegetables	05	746	825	1,759	3,399	3,150
Sugar	06	221	79	317	321	214
Coffee and tea	07	328	435	534	523	561
Animal feeds	08	58	241	623	351	239
Other foods	09	49	66	107	290	541
Oilseeds	22	—	—	—	522	373
Vegetable oils	4	—	—	—	454	132
Total food		3,021	3,803	6,600	10,899	10,951
Imports						
Live animals	00	5	18	14	18	22
Meat	01	1	6	54	97	503
Dairy products	02	5	31	81	60	160
Fish	03	13	44	102	609	890
Grains	04	2,458	982	2,353	3,631	574
Fruits and vegetables	05	48	52	83	185	384
Sugar	06	316	274	390	935	183
Coffee and tea	07	56	40	30	74	72
Animal feeds	08	14	83	182	423	620
Other foods	09	2	23	46	92	182
Oilseeds	22	—	—	—	110	1,531
Vegetable oils	4	—	—	—	2,596	1,352
Total food		2,918	1,553	3,335	8,828	6,474
Net exports						
Live animals	00	379	286	416	455	352
Meat	01	360	442	737	1,252	551
Dairy products	02	66	26	−26	1	−89
Fish	03	367	239	1,268	2,266	2,079
Grains	04	−2,035	83	−1,939	−3,350	663
Fruits and vegetables	05	698	773	1,676	3,214	2,766
Sugar	06	−95	−195	−73	−614	31
Coffee and tea	07	272	395	504	449	489
Animal feeds	08	44	158	441	−72	−381
Other foods	09	47	43	61	198	359
Oilseeds	22	—	—	—	412	−1,158
Vegetable oils	4	—	—	—	−2,142	−1,220
Total food		103	2,250	3,265	2,071	4,477

— Not available.

SITC = Standard International Trade Classification.

Source: Mathews 2001, based on UN COMTRADE statistics.

*Recent and Prospective Policies Affecting
Rural Areas*

As in most developing countries,[3] agriculture in
China was squeezed at the early stages of industrialization when gross fiscal contributions to the sector
were more than outweighed by implicit taxation in
the form of depressed prices for farm products, neglect of public infrastructure in rural areas relative to
that in urban areas, and capital outflows via the
financial system (Huang and Ma 1998). Then, agriculture experienced the introduction of price and
other market reforms associated with China's policy
shift from a socialist to a market-oriented economy,
starting with nonstrategic commodities such as vegetables, fruits, fish, livestock, and oil and sugar crops.
The early reforms were aimed at raising farm-level
prices and gradually deregulating the market. As the
right to private trading was extended to include surplus output of all categories of agricultural products
after contractual obligations to the state were ful-
filled, the foundations of the state marketing system
began to be undermined (Rozelle and others 1997).
Despite periodic stop-go cycles in the reform
process, the proportion of retail commodities sold
at market prices has continued to rise. According
to Lardy (2002), the share for agriculture was just
6 percent in 1978, but had risen to 40 percent by
1985, 79 percent by 1995, and 83 percent by 1999.

What have these policies meant for the nominal
rates of agricultural protection in China (the percentage by which domestic prices exceed prices at the
country's border)? Table 7.6 shows new estimates by
Huang, Rozelle, and Chang (2004) of nominal protection rates for key agricultural commodities for
some recent years. It suggests that rice, meat, fish, and
fruits and vegetables have been priced at less than
border prices, while other grains, oilseeds, sugar,
cotton, and milk have been priced at 20–40 percent above border prices. Maize and cotton also
enjoyed export subsidies in 2001, amounting to one-
third and one-tenth of f.o.b. prices, respectively.

Table 7.6 also shows China's commitments in its
WTO Protocol of Accession: the tariff-rate quota
will apply to grains, sugar, and cotton whose out-of-
quota tariffs are quite high, but, otherwise, after the
phase-in period the tariffs range between just 1 and
15 percent—representing substantial liberalizations
over 2001 levels. As well, producers of major crops
may continue to be affected by commodity-specific
policies of government procurement of a portion of
the crop at lower-than-market prices as in the past
(see Sicular 1988) or at higher-than-market prices,
as in 1998 (see Huang 1998).

What will those reforms mean for agricultural
trade? Many analysts expected China to become
ever more dependent on agricultural imports in the
course of the economy's rapid industrialization
over the past two-plus decades. Some extremists
(e.g., Brown 1995) even suggested that China could
seriously deprive other developing countries of
food. Yet, as reported earlier in this chapter, growth
in net food imports has not yet happened, at least

**TABLE 7.6 Nominal Rates of Protection (NRP, Applied Tariff or Tariff Equivalent),
Agricultural Products: China, 1995–2007 (percent)**

	1995	1997	2001	2007 In-Quota Tariff	2007 Out-of-Quota Tariff	Assumed NRP in 2007 (Core Scenario)
Rice	−5	−5	−3	1	65	−3
Wheat	25	17	12	1	65	12
Coarse grains	20	28	32	1	65	32
Fruits and vegetables	−10	−8	−4	11	11	−4
Oilseeds	30	28	20	3	3	3
Sugar	44	42	40	15	50	20
Cotton	20	17	17	1	40	20
Meats	−20	−19	−15	12	12	−15
Milk	30	30	30	11	11	11

Source: Based on research subsequently reported in summary form in Huang, Rozelle, and Chang 2004.

not in a sustained way, and China has continued to be a net exporter of meat, fish, and fruits and vegetables. Indeed, on occasion in the latter 1990s China also was a net exporter of grain and cotton. How much of that situation was attributable to government policies that constrained domestic demand, including occasional export subsidies, is a moot point. *accession blight*

In its WTO Protocol of Accession (WTO 2001), China agreed to have no agricultural export subsidies and to limit its domestic support for farmers to 8.5 percent of the value of production (compared with 10 percent for other developing countries). The import market access commitments China has made to WTO members look substantial on paper. Tariff-rate quotas (TRQs) will be retained only on wheat, rice, maize, edible oils, sugar, cotton, and wool—the domestic production of which in aggregate makes up only about one-sixth of China's agricultural GDP. The quota volumes are to grow over 2003–05 at annual rates ranging from 5 to 19 percent. China has also agreed to weaken the monopolies previously held by state trading enterprises, except for tobacco. Even though some state trading enterprises will continue to operate, there will be some competition from private firms in the importing and exporting of farm products, at least within the tariff-rate quotas.

Farmers and the rural sector more broadly will also be affected by China's commitment to provide improved and WTO-bound market access for industrial products. Mineral and manufacturing tariffs will be bound and generally reduced on a broad basis, with many tariffs falling to 10 percent or less. Tariffs were to be cut on accession, and further cuts will be phased in by 2005 (with just a few exceptions). Furthermore, for industrial products China will reduce significantly its nontariff measures and will eliminate all quotas, tendering, and import licensing on nonfarm merchandise by no later than 2005. Quotas on Chinese imports of automobiles and parts will grow by 15 percent annually, from a level of about US$6 billion[4] in 2000, and these quotas will be eliminated by 2005. For textiles and clothing, however, the current "voluntary" export restraints will be phased out by the end of 2004, although importing countries will be able to reimpose quotas under a special textile safeguard mechanism until the end of 2008. China also has made commitments to open up its services markets.

Over the 1990s the average scheduled tariff rates for manufacturing initially exceeded those for agriculture, but later fell more than those for agriculture. By 2010 the manufacturing average will be well below that for agriculture (a simple average of 9 percent versus 16 percent for agriculture—see WTO 2003: Appendix Table IIB). However, these numbers do not give a true indication of the extent of change in protection that is taking place, because in the 1990s many manufactures were entering China at reduced or zero tariffs via duty drawbacks to encourage foreign investment in the processing of imported intermediate goods for subsequent export. Some agricultural products also have entered at less than the scheduled rate, including through smuggling.

What all this information means for incentives for each industry is difficult to discern precisely, but it is better information than has been available to date for analyzing empirically the economic effects of the reforms associated with China's WTO accession, including the impacts on factor rewards and prices from which inferences about income distributional effects can be made. We make these inferences bearing in mind the marked differences in per capita incomes between eastern, central, and western provinces, and between urban and rural areas (as shown in tables 7.7 and 7.8).

Applying the GTAP Model

Version 5 of the computable general equilibrium model of the global economy known as GTAP is used here.[5] As an economy-wide model, GTAP describes both the vertical and horizontal linkages between all product markets within the model's individual countries and regions as well as between countries and regions via their bilateral trade flows. For present purposes, the 1997 database is aggregated to 25 sectors and 20 regions and projected forward first to 2001 and then to 2007, using World Bank projections of population, income, and endowments of productive factors (agricultural land, other natural resources, unskilled labor, skilled labor, and other capital). The initial base case assumes that China retains its protection policies as of 1995 and that Taiwan (China) retains its protection as of 1997, but that all other countries fully implement their Uruguay Round obligations on schedule before 2005. China's trade policy

TABLE 7.7   Rural Income, Employment, and Food Output by Region: China, 2000

	Western Provinces	Central Provinces	Eastern Provinces
Rural income per capita (yuan)	1,557	2,030	2,994
Share of population that is rural (%)	81	75	71
Share of rural labor force in agriculture (%)	75	73	61
Share of farm household income from off-farm (%):			
Wages	20	22	36
Total	38	35	58
Share of national agricultural GDP (%)	17	34	49
Share of regional food output (%) from:			
Rice	8	11	6
Wheat	5	5	4
Maize	5	5	3
Fruits and vegetables	11	10	14
Oilseeds	4	6	3
Sugar	0	0	1
Cotton	3	2	1
Dairy products	2	1	1
Other livestock products	20	19	17
Fish products	2	6	20
Other food, agricultural, and forest products	40	35	30
Total	100	100	100

Sources: Center for Chinese Agricultural Policy's CAPSIM Model; China National Statistics Bureau, *China Rural Statistical Yearbook* 2001.

TABLE 7.8   Income and Its Distribution: Rural and Urban China, 1980–99

	Real Per Capita Income Index		Income Disparity	
Year	Rural Average	Poorest 20 Percent	Gini Coefficient	Urban/Rural Income Ratio
1980	100	100	0.24	3.4
1985	175	157	0.23	2.2
1990	183	154	0.31	2.3
1995	239	179	0.34	2.8
1999	330	224	0.32	2.9

Sources: China National Statistics Bureau (CNSB), *China Statistical Yearbook* 1989–2000; CNSB's rural household income and expenditure surveys.

changes between 1995 and 2001 are assumed to have been in anticipation of the requirements of, and thus part of, China's WTO accession. These changes are analyzed in detail in Ianchovichina and Martin (2004), together with the effects of implementing over the next few years the remainder of China's commitments as recorded in its WTO Protocol of Accession.[6] In this chapter we focus just on the additional reform commitments to be implemented after 2001, relative to the revised base case in which China's reforms only up to 2001 are in place and there are no further reforms to 2007. For key agricultural import policies, these remaining reform commitments are assumed to shift the nominal rates of protection (NRPs) from column 3 to column 6 of table 7.6. As well, the export subsidies in place in 2001 (34 percent for maize, 10 percent for cotton) are eliminated, and we assume no new farm production subsidies are introduced.[7] The choices of new agricultural NRPs fall into three categories:

- no change if they were negative in 2001 (rice, meats, fruits and vegetables
- a move to part way between the in-quota and out-of-quota tariffs if the TRQs become binding on imports (wheat, coarse grains, sugar, cotton)
- a move down to the new in-quota tariffs (oilseeds, milk).

The sensitivity of the results for the first two categories is explored in the results section later in this chapter.

If this reform were to require a movement of unskilled labor out of farm activities, three impediments have to be kept in mind. The first is that those farm workers would be less than perfect substitutes for those already in nonfarm pursuits. Econometric work by Sicular and Zhao (2004) suggests that restraints on mobility could be approximated via a constant elasticity of transformation (CET) function with an elasticity of transformation of 1.32.[8] Accordingly, we have incorporated that function in the GTAP model for China. The second impediment to off-farm migration is that urban social welfare benefits such as subsidies for housing, food, education, and health care are not available to nonurban people, except by purchasing a residence permit or *hukou* (Zhao 1999). And the third impediment is that farm workers who permanently cut their ties with agriculture may lose entitlement to returns from their family's land, and even the direct support and assistance of family members (Hussain 2004). These latter two impediments have contributed to the persistence of a large gap in farm versus nonfarm returns to unskilled labor. We model that gap as a "tax" wedge that raises the cost of labor to urban employers, with urban unskilled workers receiving the tax-inclusive wage.

The closure adopted is a long-run one in which, in addition to the earlier assumptions about unskilled labor, we assume agricultural land is mobile between industries within the agriculture sector, and skilled labor and capital are mobile within and between sectors. This closure contrasts with the short-run closure used by Chen and

Ravallion (2004). It keeps the aggregate trade balance and government tax revenue as a fixed share of GDP (with little change in net international capital flows), and holds employment constant so that wages adjust endogenously.

What Do the Results Show?

We begin with the bottom line of the main scenario before revealing the details.

The Core WTO Accession Scenario

The core empirical results suggest that WTO accession will increase farm–nonfarm income inequality. The main reason for this greater inequality is that the relative producer prices of farm products are projected by the GTAP model to fall more than the prices of labor-intensive nonfarm products after the completion of WTO accession reforms (table 7.9).

The removal of the "voluntary" export restraint on sales of textile products to the United States and European Union is not the only boost to unskilled labor off farms. There is, in addition, a lower cost structure in unskilled, labor-intensive manufacturing activities for three reasons:

- The lower demand for labor on farms lowers the cost of unskilled labor in manufacturing.
- Import taxes on the intermediate inputs used in those manufacturing activities are lower because of the accession process.
- The real exchange rate effect of the tariff reductions lowers the cost of nontraded goods and other factors used as inputs into manufacturing production.

As a result, the quantity of unskilled nonfarm labor demanded is greater (by 0.8 percent). However, lower farm product prices mean the quantity of unskilled farm labor demanded is less (by 1.7 percent), resulting in a 0.7 percent fall in the real wage for unskilled farm labor and a rise in real wages for unskilled nonfarm labor of 1.2 percent, after adjusting for the change in the aggregate cost of living. Farmers are also made worse off by the lower demand for farmland, the return from which is 5.5 percent lower in 2007 after WTO accession reforms. Meanwhile, the real wages of skilled labor

TABLE 7.9   Sectoral Volume Effects of China's WTO Accession Reforms (Core Case), 2002–07

	Output (%)	Employment (%)	Household Consumption (%)	Exports (%)	Imports (%)	Trade Balance (Millions of U.S. Dollars)	Producer Prices (%)	Consumer Prices (%)
Rice	−2.1	−2.3	−0.1	6.1	−7.1	64	−0.9	0.9
Wheat	−2.0	−2.3	0.0	18.9	−10.1	174	−1.7	0.4
Feed grains	−2.3	−2.6	−0.1	−77.8	−2.4	−596	−1.9	1.9
Fruits and vegetables	−3.4	−3.7	0.1	14.6	−6.3	214	−1.9	−0.1
Oilseeds	−7.9	−8.4	0.9	29.8	20.9	−789	−2.8	−4.7
Sugar	−6.5	−7.4	0.6	13.9	24.1	−73	−1.9	−3.1
Plant-based fibers	15.8	16.4	−0.6	−51.8	7.7	−189	0.1	3.1
Livestock and meat	1.3	1.1	0.0	15.5	−8.9	837	−1.6	0.2
Dairy	−2.0	−2.4	0.0	13.5	23.8	−143	−1.5	0.2
Other food	−5.9	−6.4	0.4	11.4	62.6	−3460	−1.7	−1.8
Beverages and tobacco	−33.0	−33.1	1.5	9.7	112.4	−14,222	−1.8	−6.9
Extractive industries	−1.0	−1.3	−0.2	7.5	−4.4	2,088	−0.7	1.2
Textiles	15.6	15.5	0.7	32.7	38.5	−10,366	−1.7	−3.2
Apparel	57.3	56.1	0.5	105.8	30.9	49,690	−0.5	−1.9
Light manufacturing	3.7	3.7	0.0	5.9	6.8	1,786	−0.9	0.0
Petrochemical industry	−2.3	−2.3	−0.2	3.1	11.8	−8,810	−0.7	0.8
Metals	−2.1	−2.1	−0.3	3.7	6.8	−1,893	−0.4	1.3
Automobiles	1.4	−2.2	1.0	27.7	24.0	516	−3.9	−4.2
Electronics	0.6	0.4	0.5	6.7	6.8	453	−1.3	−1.7
Other manufactures	−2.1	−2.2	−0.2	4.1	18.9	−11,291	−0.5	0.8
Trade and transport	0.0	0.0	−0.3	0.8	−0.4	493	−0.2	1.6
Construction	0.9	0.9	−0.4	2.7	17.5	−436	−0.2	1.7
Communication	−0.5	−0.5	−0.4	−0.5	10.9	−56	0.1	1.9
Commercial services	−2.0	−2.0	−0.5	−0.4	35.4	−1,749	0.2	1.9
Other services	−1.7	−1.8	−0.3	1.4	33.6	−1,525	−0.1	1.6

Source: Authors' GTAP results.

increase by 0.8 percent, and the rewards to nonfarm capital are 1.3 percent higher.

Together, these results suggest that the owners of nonfarm capital gain almost the same in proportional terms as unskilled laborers in nonfarm employment, but the latter do better than skilled workers. Therefore, on balance, income inequality may improve slightly among nonfarm households dependent mainly on labor income.[9]

However, income distribution can be expected to worsen slightly, just as between farm and nonfarm households, although the degree depends on the proportion of farm household income earned off the farm. With only 1.7 percent (or about 6 million) of unskilled farm workers leaving agriculture for nonfarm work and with land returns depressed by 5.5 percent in addition to farm labor returns being 0.7 percent lower, the gap between farm and nonfarm incomes even within rural areas—and

certainly between rural and urban areas—appears poised to increase slightly unless remedial policy action is forthcoming. For farm households entirely dependent on earnings from agriculture (type A in table 7.10), income would fall 1.6 percent on average. This decrease would differ little across the three regions identified in table 7.7, because product shares for farm output—when fish products are ignored—are reasonably similar in the western, central, and eastern provinces.[10] For farm households earning 30 percent of their income from nonfarm unskilled work, however, that income fall is only half as large (0.8 percent), and for farm households earning 60 percent of their income from nonfarm unskilled work, their incomes would not decline at all (types B and C, respectively, in table 7.10, rows 7 and 8).

The sectoral details of the GTAP results are summarized in table 7.9. The real consumer prices,

TABLE 7.10 Change in China's Real Factor Prices and National Economic Welfare Attributable to WTO Accession, 2001–07 (percent)

	Core Accession Case	Alternative 1: Greater Agricultural Protection Cuts	Alternative 2: Core Case Plus Also Removing Negative Agricultural Protection
Farm unskilled wages	−0.7	−0.9	−0.5
Rental price of land	−5.5	−6.4	−4.7
Nonfarm unskilled wages	1.2	1.4	1.1
Skilled labor wages	0.8	1.0	1.5
Rental price of capital	1.3	1.5	1.5
Farm household[a] income–A	−1.6	−1.9	−1.3
Farm household[a] income–B	−0.8	−0.9	−0.6
Farm household[a] income–C	0.1	0.1	0.1
National economic welfare (increase in billions of 1997 US$)	9.56	9.57	9.87

[a]According to the GTAP database, 57 percent of farm income from agriculture comes from unskilled labor, 26 percent from land, and 17 percent from capital. In 1999 on average 51 percent of rural household income in China was earned outside agriculture, mostly from unskilled labor. Therefore, to illustrate the importance of those off-farm earnings, three types of farm households are shown in this table: type A, where it is assumed that nonfarm unskilled labor contributes 0 percent of farm household income; type B, 30 percent; and type C, 60 percent. It is assumed that all households have the same expenditure pattern, and so all changes are net of the consumer price index change.
Source: Calculated from the authors' GTAP results.

relative to the consumer price index (CPI) driven lower the most by WTO accession are those for motor vehicles, oilseeds, and sugar (and for beverages and tobacco, although if China was using import taxes on those items as a form of consumption tax and their decline were to be matched by an increase in domestic sales taxation, those price declines may not materialize). The prices for textile products, and to a lesser extent clothing, are driven lower as well. Among the farm products, consumer prices rise slightly for livestock products, somewhat more for grains, and significantly for cotton (plant-based fibers).

Producer prices (also shown relative to the CPI in table 7.9) fall more than consumer prices because of a uniform consumption tax of 1.9 percent that is levied to compensate for the loss of import tariff revenue. The prices of farm products fall more than those of most other products except autos, and farm output is down for all but cotton and meat. Moreover, feed grain exports shrink by three-quarters and cotton exports by half with the abolishment of export subsidies. The difference in the effects on production and consumption shown in table 7.9 reveal that

China's food, feed, and fiber self-sufficiency will be reduced at least slightly by these reforms. But the extent is really quite minor: the trade balance column in table 7.9 suggests that for all agricultural and food products net imports would be greater because of the remaining accession reforms by only $3.96 billion a year by 2007 (in 1997 U.S. dollars), which represents only 1 percent of total imports.

The results described here depend as always on the assumptions in the model. To check the sensitivity of some of those assumptions, two alternative scenarios—one with greater agricultural protection cuts and the other removing negative agricultural protection—were run to compare their results with those in the base accession scenario.

Alternative Scenario 1: Greater Agricultural Protection Cuts

In this scenario the grain, sugar, and cotton NRPs drop to the in-quota tariff levels shown in table 7.6. In the additional GTAP simulation run, the differences for factor rewards are not huge in the aggregate, but they would be in the direction of worsening income inequality: unskilled farm wages would fall 0.9 instead of 0.7 percent, and, on the one hand, rewards to farmland would fall 6.4 instead of 5.5 percent, while, on the other, nonfarm wages would rise 1.4 instead of 1.2 percent for unskilled workers and 1.0 instead of 0.8 percent for skilled workers (table 7.10). These changes would attract only another million workers from farms. Even though agricultural incomes would be lower, farm household income would not fall if at least 60 percent of income comes from wages of non-farm unskilled labor (see row 8 of table 7.10). Domestic production of grains, sugar, and cotton would, however, be less, and domestic consumption would be greater, so that self-sufficiency in those products would be slightly lower. Even so, the net imports of all food and agricultural products would be greater by only $1.5 billion a year by 2007 ($5.43 billion instead of $3.96 billion). Such an import increase would be within the tariff-rate quotas for those items, with the possible exception of maize (depending on the extent to which other feed grains that are not TRQ-restricted, such as barley, are substitutable for maize). National economic welfare would be only very slightly greater in this case as compared with the core scenario (see bottom row of table 7.10).

Alternative Scenario 2: Removing Negative Agricultural Protection

If the negative NRPs for rice, meats, and fruits and vegetables were to be raised to zero, the income distributional effects would go in the direction opposite to that in the first alternative scenario—that is, toward less inequality between farm and nonfarm households. The changes are not great though, even though these products account for nearly 40 percent of the value of food and agricultural output in China. A comparison of columns 1, 2, and 3 of table 7.10 reveal they would involve about as much improvement in income distribution as the previous alternative scenario would worsen it. This case involves a 3 percent larger national economic welfare gain than the core case (bottom row of table 7.10).

Conclusions and Policy Implications

Our initial analysis suggests that rural nonfarm incomes will rise on average absolutely and possibly even faster than urban incomes for households

depending just on labor income (assuming urban laborers are more skilled). However, some farm households facing increased import competition may be worse off in this case, other things being equal, if they are

conditional factors

- unable to send household members to jobs in expanding industrial and service industries
- too poorly served with infrastructure to attract such activities to their own region
- unable to diversify into producing farm goods whose relative prices have risen
- lacking relatives who are able to repatriate non-farm earnings to them.

Thus in the core scenario the incidence of rural nonfarm poverty will fall mainly because of the growth in wages for unskilled workers in rural non-farm activities, while poverty may well increase in agriculture-based hinterland provinces a long way from markets and in regions poorly served by the infrastructure needed to attract investment in expanding activities such as textiles and clothing.

The first alternative scenario shows that this situation would be exacerbated slightly if the TRQ-protected items (grains, sugar, and cotton) were to become even less protected than we initially assumed. By way of contrast, the second alternative scenario suggests that the situation could be ameliorated slightly by removing the negative protection affecting rice, meats, and fruits and vegetables. But both of these alternatives involve only small changes to the magnitudes of effects rather than altering the sign of those effects, and both add only a small amount to the aggregate gains from trade liberalization.

National self-sufficiency in farm products would decrease slightly, particularly for feed grains and cotton as demand for livestock products grows, driven by the income gains from trade reform, and as the production of natural fiber-based textiles and clothing expands. But, overall, most of the declines in domestic agricultural production as a consequence of the remaining postaccession reforms are relatively tiny in magnitude, especially when compared with the growth in farm output that would occur as a result of normal economic growth (compare columns 1 and 5 of table 7.11).

What should be done if some farmers' incomes worsen relative to those of nonfarm households,

TABLE 7.11   Changes in China's Farm Output, Employment, and Trade Volumes: Without WTO Accession, 1995–2007, and Resulting from China's WTO Accession Reforms, 2002–07 (percent)

	Changes Without WTO Accession, 1995–2007				Changes Due to WTO Accession, 2002–07			
	Output	Employment	Exports	Imports	Output	Employment	Exports	Imports
Rice	63.8	−11.5	134.7	−8.8	−2.1	−2.3	6.1	−7.1
Wheat	81.4	6.4	−15.2	126.3	−2.0	−2.3	18.9	−10.1
Feed grains	109.5	23.8	−0.6	95.9	−2.3	−2.6	−77.8	−2.4
Fruits and vegetables	98.2	16.8	−10.8	122.1	−3.4	−3.7	14.6	−6.3
Oilseeds	100.9	18.4	−36.0	151.7	−7.9	−8.4	29.8	20.9
Sugar	112.5	14.5	109.4	88.7	−6.5	−7.4	13.9	24.1
Plant-based fibers	137.2	41.1	−8.5	146.1	15.8	16.4	−51.8	7.7
Livestock and meat	121.9	25.6	12.8	135.3	1.3	1.1	15.5	−8.9
Dairy products	122.5	18.8	60.5	100.3	−2.0	−2.4	13.5	23.8
Other food	110.8	−1.5	76.8	58.5	−5.9	−6.4	11.4	62.6

Source: Authors' GTAP results.

and if there is concern about the fall in agricultural self-sufficiency? Rather than argue against trade reform, policymakers should seek the best ways to deal with those concerns (and with any transitory unemployment that might follow reform). The most efficient policy responses are likely to involve investments in rural human capital, rural infrastructure, and agricultural research and development (Fan, Zhang, and Zhang 2002); improvements in the land tenure system and rural financial markets; reductions in the informal taxes/levies on farmers by local governments; and changes in grain marketing.

First, the government might consider further investments in basic rural education and health services to reduce the adverse effects of trade reform on the incidence of poverty and perceived food security. Better education and health for farmers' children not only boosts their farm productivity should they choose to stay on the farm after finishing school, but also increases their capacity to find more lucrative off-farm work and to adjust to nonagricultural employment and living (Schultz 1975; Zhang, Huang, and Rozelle 2002). In addition to those longer-term benefits, there could also be an immediate poverty-alleviating effect if the government were to cut basic school fees and make up the shortfall with a bigger direct grant to rural primary and middle schools.

Second, improvements in rural infrastructure such as roads and rail mean that a larger share of the price eventually received at the end of the marketing chain for farm products can be passed back to farmers. Such improvements also lower the barrier for off-farm work by members of farm households, making it easier for them to take advantage of expanding employment opportunities in rural townships.

Third, agricultural research and development can ease both urban and rural poverty (see Fan, Fang, and Zhang 2001; Hazell and Haddad 2001). A boost in agricultural productivity could significantly offset the 2–8 percent drop in agricultural production that is estimated in the core scenario to result from WTO accession. An important policy issue here is whether China should deny itself the use of genetically modified organisms in food production.[11]

Fourth, improvements in the land tenure system would not only increase the incentive to invest more in land but would also enhance the collateral of farm households. If accompanied by improvements in rural financial markets, investments by farmers back into agriculture would rise. They would rise even further if returns were increased via reductions in the informal taxes/levies imposed by local governments on farmers.[12]

Finally, the government might reduce its regulation of grain marketing and, in particular, cease compulsory procurement from farmers at less than market prices and reduce the provision of grain to urban consumers at less than market prices. De-emphasizing the governors' grain responsibility system (provincial self-sufficiency) would allow more exploitation of comparative advantage within China as well.

If all these measures proved insufficient to support the incomes of the poorest farm households, short-term adjustment assistance via inframarginal (and therefore not output-inducing) producer price subsidies could be provided as an efficient way to boost those households' incomes without boosting farm output in an equal but opposite way to that used to tax farmers in earlier decades (see Shea 2003). Such an intervention could well be deemed WTO-consistent because of its decoupled nature. In any case, if it just targets poor farmers it is unlikely to ever exceed 8.5 percent of the value of China's output of the product concerned (China's *de minimis* exemption limit for product-specific support under Article 6.4 of the WTO's Agreement on Agriculture).

Finally, now that China is in the WTO it can take part in the new rounds of multilateral trade negotiations and thereby seek increased market access for its exports of farm (and other) products abroad. Although this factor is not taken into account in the analysis described here, if WTO membership enhances China's chances of expanding its access to agricultural more than other markets abroad in the future, that would be a positive benefit of WTO accession for China's farmers and rural areas. Martin (forthcoming) points out that Chinese farm exports face particularly high barriers abroad, so this potential benefit is nontrivial in principle (although in practice it may be difficult to secure, especially if the main barriers are sanitary and phytosanitary measures). That proposition is tested by Yu and Frandsen (2002), also using the GTAP model. They find that reductions in barriers to agricultural imports and in domestic support to farmers in OECD countries reduce the extent to which China's farm output would fall with WTO accession, and that in some cases they lead to expansion rather than contraction of outputs. As a consequence, China's agricultural imports would fall slightly and its agricultural exports would be greater. These changes are reflected in table 7.12. It shows that not only would China's food self-sufficiency be higher with than without agricultural protection in the European Union, United States, and Japan, but that the difference is in most cases more than enough to offset the fall in self-sufficiency that is projected to result from China's WTO accession. Such reform in the OECD would clearly benefit farm households in China, providing a further pro-poor consequence of trade reform.

TABLE 7.12   **Effect on Agricultural Self-Sufficiency of China's WTO Accession without and with Cuts in Agricultural Protection in OECD Countries (domestic production as a percentage of domestic consumption)**

	Base Case (No WTO Accession for China)	China's WTO Accession with No Change in OECD Policies	China's WTO Accession with EU, United States, and Japan Removing Agricultural Tariffs, Exports Subsidies, and Domestic Support
Rice	99.9	99.4	99.6
Wheat	93.0	88.2	89.1
Feed grains	98.1	98.1	99.6
Fruits and vegetables	99.7	99.7	99.9
Oilseeds	81.0	81.3	82.3
Sugar	77.2	77.4	82.9
Plant-based fibers	83.8	83.7	83.9
Ruminant meat	88.5	88.2	89.4
Nonruminant meat	97.7	97.8	98.9
Dairy products	81.8	80.0	84.9

Source: Yu and Frandsen 2002, table 4.

Notes

1. The difficulties China has had in exporting food products to, for example, Japan, the Republic of Korea, and the United Kingdom in recent years because of those countries' quarantine and sanitary and phytosanitary measures should ease after WTO accession, or at least be challengeable under WTO dispute settlement provisions. Because those measures are notoriously difficult to predict, they are ignored in our empirical analysis (as are prospective changes to other nontariff measures that may limit China's access to foreign markets for farm or nonfarm products). Also ignored is the possibility that China itself may use quarantine measures to limit its imports of farm products.

2. However, soybean imports grew substantially when the government (in anticipation of WTO accession) lowered the tariff on soybeans from 114 percent to 3 percent in 2000.

3. See Sah and Stiglitz (1992) and Anderson (1995).

4. All dollar amounts are current U.S. dollars.

5. The GTAP model is a multiregional, static, applied general equilibrium model based on neoclassical microeconomic theory, including full employment of all factors of production, constant returns to scale, and perfect competition. For a discussion of the prospect of greater unemployment during the accession period, see Zhai and Wang (2002). The numeraire is the world price of exports. See Hertel (1997) for comprehensive documentation. The Version 5 database is described at www.gtap.org.

6. A particularly important feature of their analysis is the inclusion of China's duty exemptions in the base scenario, because, otherwise, the model would overstate the gains from tariff reductions. Tariff cuts are from the 2001 applied rates to the postaccession bound rates (or zero if the latter exceed the former). In this application the aggregate trade balance and government tax revenue are both assumed to remain a fixed share of GDP. The 2001 trade data are from the UN's COMTRADE database, and the 2001 applied tariffs for China are from CDS Consulting Co. (2002).

7. Three nonfarm reforms are worthy of mention. The "voluntary" export restraint on China's textile and clothing exports to the United States and European Union, expressed in the base scenario as taxes on those exports, are removed; restructuring of the motor vehicle and parts industry after WTO accession is modeled as a 20 percent productivity boost to vehicle assembly, following François and Spinanger (2004); and liberalization of China's services trade also follows François and Spinanger (2004).

8. In a subsequent analysis, Sicular and Zhao (2004) provide estimates of 2.67 for the "push" elasticity of transformation from changes in agricultural returns to changes in the supply of labor out of agriculture, but only 0.6 from changes in nonagricultural returns. Ianchovichina and Martin (2004) conducted sensitivity analysis on the implications of changes in these parameters, and they found the results are not altered greatly.

9. Wages of skilled workers might increase more than suggested here because we do not capture the endogenous productivity growth resulting from the substantial liberalization of the service sectors. For a recent study that does incorporate that effect using a dynamic version of the GTAP model, see Ianchovichina and Walmsley (2003).

10. However, in the northern and southern provinces of China the differences could be large because wheat, maize, soybean, and cotton are planted primarily in northern China, and rice, horticultural products, livestock, and fish are raised mostly in southern China.

11. For an empirical analysis using GTAP of the impact of the adoption or nonadoption of genetically modified varieties of first maize and oilseeds and then rice and wheat on China, India, and other countries, see Anderson and Jackson (2003).

12. According to Lin and others (2002), such levies amount to as much as one-quarter of the net incomes of poorer farmers in the hinterlands.

References

The word *processed* describes informally reproduced works that may not be commonly available through libraries.

Anderson, K. 1995. "Lobbying Incentives and the Pattern of Protection in Rich and Poor Countries." *Economic Development and Cultural Change* 43 (2): 401–23.

Anderson, K., Y. Hayami, and [others]. 1986. *The Political Economy of Agricultural Protection: East Asia in International Perspective.* Boston, London, and Sydney: Allen and Unwin (also available in an expanded Chinese language edition translated by F. Cai. Tianjin: People's Publishing House, 1996).

Anderson, K., and L. A. Jackson. 2003. "Standards, Trade and Protection: The Case of GMOs." Paper presented at a seminar at the World Bank, October 2. Washington, D.C.

Brown, L. R. 1995. *Who Will Feed China? Wake-up Call for a Small Planet.* New York: Norton.

CDS Consulting Co. 2002. "Applied Tariffs in China, 2001." Washington, D.C.

Chen, S., and M. Ravallion. 2004. "Household Welfare Impacts of China's Accession to the WTO." In D. Bhattasali, S. Li, and W. Martin, eds., *China and the WTO: Accession, Policy Reform, and Poverty Reduction Strategies.* Washington, D.C.: World Bank and Oxford University Press.

Fan, S., C. Fang, and X. Zhang. 2001. "How Agricultural Research Affects Urban Poverty in Developing Countries: The Case of China." Environment and Production Technology Discussion Paper 83. International Food Policy Research Institute, Washington, D.C.

Fan, S., L. Zhang, and X. Zhang. 2002. *Growth, Inequality, and Poverty in China: The Role of Public Investments.* IFPRI Research Report 125. Washington, D.C.: International Food Policy Research Institute.

Francois, J., and D. Spinanger. 2004. "Regulated Efficiency, WTO Accession and the Motor Vehicle Sector in China." In D. Bhattasali, S. Li, and W. Martin, eds. *China and the WTO: Accession, Policy Reform, and Poverty Reduction Strategies.* Washington, D.C.: World Bank and Oxford University Press.

Gilbert, J., and T. Wahl. 2002. "Applied General Equilibrium Assessments of Trade Liberalization in China." *World Economy* 25 (5): 697–731.

Hazell, P., and L. Haddad. 2001. "Agricultural Research and Poverty Reduction." Food, Agriculture, and the Environment. Discussion Paper 34. International Food Policy Research Institute, Washington, D.C.

Hertel, T. W., ed. 1997. *Global Trade Analysis: Modeling and Applications.* Cambridge and New York: Cambridge University Press.

Huang, J. 1998. "Evaluation of Current Three-Grain-Policy." CCAP's Working Paper WP-00-C01. Center for Chinese Agricultural Policy, Chinese Academy of Agricultural Sciences, Beijing.

———. 2001. "Agricultural Policy and Food Security in China." Center for Chinese Agricultural Policy, Chinese Academy of Sciences, Beijing. Processed.

Huang, J., and H. Ma. 1998. "The 20-Year Reform and the Role of Agriculture in China: Capital Flow from Rural to Urban and from Agriculture to Industry." *Reform* 5: 56–63.

Huang, J., S. Rozelle, and M. Chang. 2004. "The Nature of Distortions to Agricultural Incentives in China and Implications of WTO Accession." In D. Bhattasali, S. Li, and W. Martin, eds., *China and the WTO: Accession, Policy Reform, and Poverty Reduction Strategies*. Washington, D.C.: World Bank and Oxford University Press.

Hussain, A. 2004. "Coping and Adapting to Job Losses and Declines in Farm Earnings." In D. Bhattasali, S. Li, and W. Martin, eds., *China and the WTO: Accession, Policy Reform, and Poverty Reduction Strategies*. Washington, D.C.: World Bank and Oxford University Press.

Ianchovichina, E., and W. Martin. 2004. "Economic Impacts of China's Accession to the WTO." In D. Bhattasali, S. Li, and W. Martin, eds., *China and the WTO: Accession, Policy Reform, and Poverty Reduction Strategies*. Washington, D.C.: World Bank and Oxford University Press.

Ianchovichina, E., and T. Walmsley. 2003. "Impact of China's WTO Accession on East Asia." Policy Research Working Paper 3109. World Bank, Washington, D.C.

Kanbur, R., and X. Zhang. 2001. "Fifty Years of Regional Inequality in China: A Journey through Evolution, Reform and Openness." CEPR Discussion Paper No. 2887. Centre for Economic Policy Research, London.

Lardy, N. 2002. *Integrating China in the Global Economy*. Washington, D.C.: Brookings Institution Press.

Lin, Y. F., R. Tao, M. Liu and Q. Zhang. 2002. "Rural Direct Taxation and Government Regulation in China: Economic Analysis and Policy Implications." Working Paper. China Center for Economic Research, Beijing University.

Lindert, P. 1991. "Historical Patterns of Agricultural Protection." In P. Timmer, ed. *Agriculture and the State*. Ithaca: Cornell University Press.

Martin, W. Forthcoming. "Implication of Reform and WTO Accession for China's Agricultural Policies." *Economies in Transition*.

Mathews, A. 2001. "The Possible Impact of China's WTO Accession on the WTO Agricultural Negotiations." Trinity Economic Papers No. 15. Department of Economics, Trinity College, Dublin.

McCulloch, N., L. A. Winters, and X. Cirera. 2001. *Trade Liberalization and Poverty: A Handbook*. London: Centre for Economic Policy Research.

Ministry of Agriculture. *China's Township and Village Enterprise Statistical Yearbook*. Beijing: China Statistics Press.

National Bureau of Statistics of China a. *China Statistical Yearbook* (various issues). Beijing: China Statistics Press.

National Bureau of Statistics of China b. *China Rural Statistical Yearbook*. Beijing: China Statistics Press.

Rozelle, S., A. Park, J. Huang, and H. Jin. 1997. "Liberalization and Rural Market Integration in China." *American Journal of Agricultural Economics* 79 (2): 635–42.

Sah, R., and J. E. Stiglitz. 1992. *Peasants versus City-Dwellers: Taxation and the Burden of Development*. Oxford: Clarendon Press.

Schultz, T. W. 1975. "The Value of the Ability to Deal with Disequilibria." *Journal of Economic Literature* 13 (3): 827–46.

Shea, Y. P. 2003. *The Political Economy of China's Grain Policy Reform*. Ph.D. diss., University of Adelaide.

Sicular, T. 1988. "Plan and Market in China's Agricultural Commerce." *Journal of Political Economy* 96 (2): 383–87.

Sicular, T., and Y. Zhao. 2004. "Earnings and Labor Mobility in Rural China: Implications for China's WTO Entry." In D. Bhattasali, S. Li, and W. Martin, eds., *China and the WTO: Accession, Policy Reform, and Poverty Reduction Strategies*. Washington, D.C.: World Bank and Oxford University Press.

WTO (World Trade Organization). 2001. *Report of the Working Party on the Accession of China.*, WT/MIN(01)/3. Geneva.

———. 2003. *World Trade Report 2003*. Geneva.

Yu, W., and S. E. Frandsen. 2002. "China's WTO Commitments in Agriculture: Does the Impact Depend on OECD Agricultural Policies?" Paper presented at the Fifth Conference on Global Economic Analysis, Taipei, June 5–7.

Zhai, F., and Z. Wang. 2002. "WTO Accession, Rural Labor Migration, and Urban Unemployment in China." *Urban Studies* 39 (12): 2199–217.

Zhang, L., J. Huang, and S. Rozelle. 2002. "Employment, Recessions, and the Role of Education in Rural China." *China Economic Review* 114: 1–16.

Zhao, Y. 1999. "Leaving the Countryside: Rural-to-Urban Migration Decision in China." *American Economic Review* 89 (2): 281–86.

8

THE SERVICES DIMENSION OF CHINA'S ACCESSION TO THE WTO

Aaditya Mattoo

The fulfillment of China's accession commitments will lead to one of the most dramatic episodes of services sector liberalization seen in any country. Over the space of some six years, one of the most closed services markets has promised to become one of the most open. This chapter begins by describing China's policy commitments, and it then asks whether the disciplines implied by these commitments are desirable and, more important, how the process of implementing these commitments is best managed.

Successful reforms will lead to significant improvements in the services markets themselves in terms of prices, quality, product variety, and the availability of new products.[1] More efficient provision of telecommunications, transport, and other services will also advance the integration of the Chinese economy with that of the rest of the world and within the country itself—provided access to improved services is not limited to the coastal enclaves. The poor are also likely to be affected—in the product market, as efficiency increases but cross-subsidization ends, and in the factor markets, as the scale of activity expands but surplus labor is shed. It is, unfortunately, not easy to quantify these effects.

It is possible, however, to analyze a key determinant of these changes: how the transition to more open markets is managed. Already known are the policy status quo and the destination as specified in the commitments, but how much discretion does China retain in its choice of policy? China's schedule of commitments specifies not only the terminal situation, but also how many of the modifications of policy will be phased in. Even though changes in the degree of competition and the pattern of ownership are largely prespecified, they can be accelerated—commitments in the General Agreement on Trade in Services (GATS) do not prevent a country from liberalizing faster than it has said it would. More important, China retains much freedom in designing domestic regulation, and reforms in this area will crucially affect the magnitude and distribution of gains from liberalization.

The views contained in this paper are those of the author and should not be attributed to the World Bank. This paper has benefited greatly from the comments of Carsten Fink and two anonymous referees. Antonia Carzeniga, Stijn Claessens, Caroline Freund, Christina Lund, Will Martin, Cristina Neagu, Randeep Rathindran, and Beata Smarzynska also made valuable contributions.

The chapter begins by describing China's accession commitments. It then examines whether the implied loss of policy discretion is desirable and whether China's commitments promote good policy. Finally, the chapter identifies the priorities for complementary reform and offers some conclusions.

China's Accession Commitments

The GATS Framework and Services Liberalization

The GATS covers all measures taken by members of the World Trade Organization (WTO) affecting trade in services and all service sectors.[2] The agreement is unusual in taking a wide view of what constitutes trade, and it defines trade in services as the supply of a service through any of four modes. Mode 1, *cross-border supply,* is analogous to trade in goods and arises when a service crosses a national frontier, for example, the purchase of software or insurance by a consumer from a supplier located abroad. Mode 2, *consumption abroad,* arises when the consumer travels to the territory of a service supplier to purchase, for example, tourism, education, or health services. Mode 3, *commercial presence,* involves foreign direct investment—for example, when a foreign bank or telecommunications firm establishes a branch or subsidiary in the territory of a country. And mode 4, *movement of individuals,* occurs when independent service providers or employees of a multinational firm temporarily move to another country.

Certain GATS obligations apply across the board, while others depend on the sector-specific commitments assumed by individual Members. The most important of the general obligations are *transparency* and the *most-favored-nation* (MFN) principle. The transparency obligation requires, among other things, that each member publish promptly "all relevant measures of general application" (that is, measures other than those involving only individual service suppliers) to trade in services. The MFN obligation prevents members from discriminating among their trading partners. The agreement, however, permits members to list temporary exemptions to MFN status.

The liberalizing content of the GATS depends on the extent and nature of sector-specific commitments assumed by individual members. The core provisions of the GATS in this context relate to *market access* (Article XVI) and *national treatment*

(Article XVII). These provisions apply only to sectors explicitly included by a member in its schedule of commitments—a "positive list" approach—and these sectoral commitments, too, are subject to the limitations that the member has scheduled. GATS commitments are guarantees, and the absence of such guarantees need not mean that access to a particular market is denied in practice.

The *market access* provision prohibits six types of limitations, unless they have been inscribed by a Member in its schedule. These are as follows:

- limitations on the number of suppliers
- limitations on the total value of service transactions or assets
- limitations on the total number of service operations or on the total quantity of service output
- limitations on the total number of natural persons (i.e. individuals rather than juridical persons) that may be employed
- measures that restrict or require specific types of legal entity or joint venture
- limitations on the participation of foreign capital.

In scheduled sectors, the existence of any of these limitations has to be indicated with respect to each of the four modes of supply described earlier.

In the traditional manner followed by the General Agreement on Tariffs and Trade (GATT), n*ational treatment* is defined under Article XVII as treatment no less favorable than that accorded to like domestic services or service suppliers. In contrast to the GATT approach, however, members may inscribe limitations on national treatment in their schedules with respect to each of the four modes of supply, as in the market access provision.

Numerical Overview of Commitments: How Different Is China?

This section compares China's services commitments with those of other WTO members. It begins with a brief look at the state of access today, before China's liberalization commitments have been phased in, for a representative sample of sectors. Figure 8.1 compares China's commitments for each mode with those of industrial, developing, and acceding countries. On consumption abroad

FIGURE 8.1 Country Services Commitments by Mode

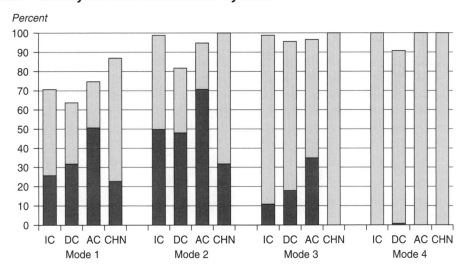

IC = industrial countries, DC = developing countries, AC = acceding countries, CHN = China.
Note: Calculated on the basis of a sample of 37 sectors deemed representative for various service sectors. See chapter appendix table 8.3 for details on China and WTO (1999) for details on other countries. The upper part of each bar represents partial commitments, the lower part full commitments.
Source: WTO.

(mode 2), commercial presence (mode 3), and the presence of natural persons (mode 4), China has made at least partial commitments in all the sectors, and on cross-border supply (mode 1) for over 80 percent of the sectors. This situation compares favorably with the commitments of all other country groups. However, the number of sectors with a guarantee of full access in China's schedule today is less than those for the other country groups, with a very significant difference for mode 3.

The picture changes quite drastically when looking at the period after all the liberalization has been phased in. Three indicators are computed by Ianchovichina, Martin, and Wood (2001) for both market access and national treatment commitments:

- "unweighted average count," indicating the number of sector/mode-of-supply combinations where a commitment was made about the maximum number possible
- "average coverage," providing an arithmetic weighted average of the weights (0 for no commitment, 1 for a full commitment, and 0.5 for all partial commitments) allocated to each cell
- the "no-restriction commitments share" in a country's total commitments as well as in the maximum possible commitments.

Overall for China, the coverage of market access commitments (i.e., the unweighted average count) was 57.4 percent (table 8.1). This coverage is much more extensive than the commitments offered in the Uruguay Round by any other group of countries (including high-income ones). The "average coverage," a measure of coverage that better reflects the extent of liberalization of services, was 38.1 percent for China—again showing more openness than that of even the high-income countries. China's share of completely liberal commitments (i.e., no restrictions) of the maximum possible was 23.1 percent, which is much higher than that for any other group of developing countries but somewhat lower than that for high-income countries. China's commitments on national treatment are deeper and wider than those of all other country groups.

A Closer Look, Sector by Sector

Typical Restrictions In some respects, China's commitments resemble those made by other countries. For most sectors, modes 1 and 2 are either fully open or unbound and are not subject to specific restrictions. Commitments on mode 4, specified horizontally rather than sector by sector, are also standard: entry is guaranteed only for managers, executives, and specialists—who must be

TABLE 8.1 Coverage of Specific Commitments by China to Services in Trade (percent)

	High-Income Countries	Low- and Middle-Income Countries	Large Developing Nations	China
Market access				
Unweighted average count (sectors/modes listed as a share of maximum possible)	47.3	16.2	38.6	57.4
Average coverage (sectors/modes listed as a share of maximum possible, weighted by openness or binding factors)	35.9	10.3	22.9	38.1
Coverage/count (average coverage as a share of the average count)	75.9	63.6	59.3	66.4
No restrictions as a share of total offer (unweighted count)	57.3	45.5	38.7	40.2
No restrictions as a share of maximum possible	27.1	7.3	14.9	23.1
National treatment				
Unweighted average count (sectors/modes listed as a share of maximum possible)	47.3	16.2	38.8	57.4
Average coverage (sectors/modes listed as a share of maximum possible, weighted by openness or binding factors)	37.2	11.2	25.5	45.0
Coverage/count (average coverage as a share of average count)	78.6	69.1	66.1	78.4
No restrictions as a share of total offer (unweighted count)	65.1	58.0	52.3	63.5
No restrictions as a share of maximum possible	30.8	9.4	20.2	36.5
Memo item				
No restrictions on market access and national treatment as a share of maximum possible	24.8	6.9	14.3	29.8
Number of sectors committed	293.0	100.0	239.0	356.0

Source: Ianchovichina, Martin, and Wood 2001.

Note: The breadth and depth of commitments by other countries are understated because their more recent commitments in telecommunications and financial services have not been taken fully into account.

either intracorporate transferees or employees of foreign invested enterprises—and for services salespersons on exploratory business visits. No commitments are made on other categories of natural persons such as unskilled personnel or movement not linked to a commercial presence.

It is for the commitments on commercial presence that a range of restrictive measures emerge. They are related to the following:

- *Form of establishment.* The typical restriction is the requirement to form a joint venture that is either an equity joint venture (EJV) or a contractual joint venture (CJV). Foreign ownership in EJVs is frequently restricted to specified levels, ranging from minority ownership

(49 percent or less), to 50 percent ownership, to majority ownership, to full ownership. There is no commitment to allowing establishment of branches by foreign enterprises, except in specific sectors.
- *Geographic scope.* Business activity may be allowed only in specified cities (e.g., Shanghai) or in special economic zones (SEZs).
- *Business scope.* Transactions may be permitted only with a subset of consumers or restricted in some other way.
- *Regulatory requirements.* Foreign firms may be required to possess a certain minimum amount of assets and be established as a representative office for a certain period of time before commencing full business operations.

Interestingly, most restrictions pertain to market access; relatively few limitations affect national treatment.[3] In fact, one of the striking aspects of China's schedules is the country's willingness to commit across modes and sectors to full national treatment for foreign providers.

Commitments: Past, Present, and Future   How much has China's trade policy already changed, and how much will it change over the next few years? China's schedules of commitments provide a first source of information. China participated in the Uruguay Round services negotiations and submitted a schedule under GATS in April 1994. Because China did not become a member of the WTO at this time, this schedule did not have legal status. More important, it is not clear how much this schedule reflected the actual openness of Chinese services markets at that time. Nevertheless, it does provide the basis for an interesting comparison with the final schedule.

China's schedule of commitments under GATS has had legal status ever since China became a WTO member, and it is the outcome of the toughest services negotiations undertaken in the WTO. Whereas most WTO members have merely bound the policy status quo or even less, China agreed to allow significant liberalization to be implemented either immediately or in the near future. One consequence is that the schedule describes the state of actual policy at the time of accession and over the next few years.

Relying on these two schedules, table 8.2 reveals a rough picture of the state of "policy" at three points of time: 1994; 2001, the date of accession; and 2008, the date by which all liberalization commitments will have been phased in (i.e., seven years after accession). The earlier date shows how far China has already come, and the latter date shows how far it is committed to go.

Professional Services   Today, commitments on professional services are far more liberal than in 1994, and the sector will be highly liberalized over the next few years. Unlike in 1994, China is now committed to allowing the cross-border supply of professional services; quantitative limitations no longer apply to accountancy firms; taxation services can be offered outside of "economically

developed areas"; and there are meaningful commitments in urban planning and legal services.

By 2007 geographic and quantitative limitations will be eliminated in legal services, and fully owned foreign subsidiaries can operate in accounting, taxation, architecture, engineering, and urban planning services. But some restrictions will persist, especially in legal and medical services. Foreign firms are not allowed directly to participate in legal activity in China and are only entitled to work on legal affairs related to their home country or to entrust work to Chinese firms on behalf of their clients. In medical services, hospitals cannot be fully foreign-owned and are still subject to quantitative limitations in line with China's assessed needs.

Computer and Related Services   This is the one sector where some commitments have actually become less liberal. In 1994 there were no restrictions on establishment in software implementation, systems and software consulting, and systems analysis. Now establishment can only take place through joint ventures, although foreign majority ownership is permitted. Cross-border delivery in these services remains unbound, but it is fully open in all other computer and related services. No future liberalization has been specified.

Telecommunications   Much change is anticipated in this sector over the next few years. Today foreign providers can provide value added and mobile services in and between Shanghai, Guangzhou, and Beijing through joint ventures, subject to stringent restrictions on foreign ownership. By 2004 fixed-line services can be provided on similar terms in and between the same cities. By 2007 all geographic restrictions will be eliminated and equity restrictions will be relaxed. But even at the end of the period majority foreign ownership will not be allowed in any area. Furthermore, there is no commitment to allow cross-border any of these services.[4]

Construction and Engineering Services   Whereas commercial presence was unbound in 1994, today it is allowed through joint ventures with foreign majority ownership permitted, but only in foreign-invested construction projects. By 2004 full foreign

TABLE 8.2   China's Commitments: Past, Present, and Future

Sector	1994	2001	2008
Professional services			
Legal services	No commitments	Modes 1 and 2: None Mode 3: Only through one rep. office which is allowed to engage in profit-making activities, but only in specified cities. Business scope restricted to home country legal affairs for Chinese and China-based clients and to entrusting, on behalf of foreign clients, Chinese law firms to deal with Chinese legal affairs.	CONTINUED RESTRICTIONS ON BUSINESS SCOPE. Mode 3: Geographic and quantitative limitations were to be eliminated by 2002.
Accounting, auditing, and bookkeeping services	Modes 1 and 2: Unbound Mode 3: Through branch offices and CJVs subject to limitations on minimum size, aggregate number (15), and geographic scope (SEZs). Auditing reports are only valid if a Chinese CPA title is obtained.	FULLY LIBERALIZED except that partnerships and incorporated accounting firms are limited to CPAs licensed by Chinese authorities.	
Taxation	Mode 1: None Mode 2: Unbound Mode 3: Through branch offices subject to limitations on minimum size and geographic scope (SEZs).	Mode 2: None Mode 3: Only through CJVs, with majority foreign ownership permitted.	FULLY LIBERALIZED Mode 3: None; wholly foreign-owned subsidiaries permitted by 2007.
Architecture and engineering	Mode 1: Unbound Mode 2: None Mode 3: Only through an EJV or CJV. Registered in own country.	Mode 1: None for scheme design; otherwise, cooperation with Chinese professional organizations is required. Mode 3: Only through an EJV or CJV. Registered in own country and engaged in architecture/ engineering services in home country.	FULLY LIBERALIZED EXCEPT FOR MODE 1 RESTRICTIONS. Mode 3: Wholly foreign-owned subsidiaries permitted by 2006.
Urban planning (excluding general urban planning)	Mode 1: Unbound Mode 2: None Mode 3: Unbound	Mode 1: None for scheme design; otherwise, cooperation with Chinese professional organizations is required. Mode 3: Only through an EJV or CJV.	FULLY LIBERALIZED EXCEPT FOR MODE 1 RESTRICTIONS. Mode 3: Wholly foreign-owned subsidiaries permitted by 2006.
Medical and dental services	Mode 1: Unbound Mode 2: Unbound Mode 3: Only through an EJV or CJV with a quantitative limitation based on a needs test and approval by the Ministry of Public Health and Ministry of Foreign Trade and Economic Cooperation. CJV or EJV solely responsible for foreign exchange balance and profits and losses. Majority of personnel must be Chinese. Mode 4: Foreign doctors can provide services for six months (may extend to a year) provided a license is obtained at provincial level and they are contracted by Chinese medical institutions.	Mode 1: None Mode 2: None Mode 3: Foreign majority ownership explicitly permitted. Not required to accept sole responsibility for foreign exchange balance and profits and losses, but still subject to quantitative limitations based on a needs test. Mode 4: Licenses can be obtained from the Ministry of Public Health, and a contract is not required.	FULL FOREIGN OWNERSHIP NOT ALLOWED AND NEEDS-BASED QUOTAS.

TABLE 8.2   (Continued)

Sector	1994	2001	2008
Computer and related services			
Consultancy services related to the installation of computer hardware Data processing and tabulation Time-sharing	Mode 1: Unbound Mode 2: None Mode 3: None Mode 4: Qualifications: B.A. and five years of experience.	Modes 1–3: FULLY LIBERALIZED Mode 4: Qualifications: B.A. and three years of experience.	
Software implementation Systems and software consulting Systems analysis	Mode 1: Unbound Mode 2: None Mode 3: None Mode 4: Qualifications: B.A. and five years of experience.	Mode 1: Unbound Mode 2: None Mode 3: Only through JVs with foreign majority ownership permitted. Mode 4: Qualifications: B.A. and three years of experience.	
Systems design Programming Systems maintenance Data processing Input preparation	Mode 1: Unbound Mode 2: None Mode 3: Through EJV only. Mode 4: Qualifications: B.A. and five years of experience.	Mode 1: None Mode 2: None Mode 3: Only through JVs with foreign majority ownership permitted. Mode 4: Qualifications: B.A. and three years of experience.	
Telecommunications			
Value added	No commitments	Mode 1: Unclear Mode 2: None Mode 3: Through JVs with a foreign investment limit of 30 percent only in Shanghai, Guangzhou, and Beijing.	By 2002 expansion in geographic area and foreign investment limit to 49 percent. By 2003 no geographic restriction and FOREIGN INVESTMENT LIMIT TO 50 PERCENT.
Basic telecommunications: mobile voice and data	No commitments	Mode 1: Unclear Mode 2: None Mode 3: Through JVs with a foreign investment limit of 25 percent only in and between Shanghai, Guangzhou, and Beijing.	By 2002 expansion in geographic area and foreign investment limit to 35 percent. By 2004 FOREIGN INVESTMENT LIMIT TO 49 PERCENT. By 2006 no geographic restriction.
Basic telecommunications: fixed-line services	No commitments	Mode 1: Unclear Mode 2: None Mode 3: Unbound	By 2004 through JVs with a foreign investment limit of 25 percent only in and between Shanghai, Guangzhou, and Beijing. By 2006 expansion in geographic area, and foreign investment limit to 35 percent. By 2007 no geographic restriction and FOREIGN INVESTMENT LIMIT TO 49 PERCENT.

TABLE 8.2 (Continued)

Sector	1994	2001	2008
Construction			
Construction and related engineering	Mode 1: Unbound Mode 2: None Mode 3: Unbound	Mode 1: Unbound Mode 2: None Mode 3: Through JVs with foreign majority ownership permitted and only foreign-invested construction projects.	RESTRICTIONS ON BUSINESS SCOPE OF FULLY FOREIGN-OWNED ENTERPRISES. Mode 3: By 2004 fully foreign-owned enterprises permitted but only in projects financed by foreign investment and/or grants, or by loans from international financial institutions, or those projects that are technically difficult for Chinese enterprises.
Distribution			
Commission agents and wholesale trade, and a full range of subordinated services, including after-sales services.	No commitments	Mode 1: Unbound Mode 2: None Mode 3: Foreign-invested enterprises are permitted to distribute their products manufactured in China.	LIBERALIZED EXCEPT CROSS-BORDER DELIVERY AND TWO PRODUCTS. Mode 3: By 2002 through JVs subject to restrictions on products, to be phased out by 2006 (except salt and tobacco). By 2003 foreign majority ownership allowed and no geographic or quantitative restrictions.
Retailing and a full range of subordinated services, including after-sales services.	No commitments	Mode 1: Unbound except for mail order. Mode 2: None Mode 3: Through JVs (not foreign majority controlled) in five SEZs and eight cities subject to quotas (e.g., four in Beijing and Shanghai), restrictions on products (not books, newspapers, pharmaceuticals, pesticides, chemical fertilizers, etc.).	CONTINUED RESTRICTIONS ON LARGE CHAIN STORES. Mode 3: By 2003 all provincial capitals open. By 2004 no more geographic restrictions. By 2006 no restrictions on products. Foreign majority control allowed except in chain stores with more than 30 outlets selling a range of products.
Franchising	No commitments	Mode 1: None Mode 2: None Mode 3: Unbound	FULLY LIBERALIZED BY 2004. Mode 3: By 2004 none.
Educational and environmental services			
Educational services, excluding special education (e.g., military and political) and national compulsory education	Mode 1: Unbound Mode 2: None Mode 3: Unbound Mode 4: Subject to licensing from the State Bureau of Foreign Experts (SBFE) and State Education Commission (SEC), and possession of M.A. and professional title.	Mode 1: None Mode 2: None Mode 3: Only through JVs with foreign majority ownership permitted (national treatment: unbound). Mode 4: Subject to invitation or employment by Chinese institution and possession of B.A., two years of experience, and professional title.	
Environmental services	No commitments	Mode 1: Unbound except for consultation services. Mode 2: None Mode 3: Through JVs with foreign majority ownership permitted.	

TABLE 8.2   (Continued)

Sector	1994	2001	2008
Financial services			
Insurance (except statutory insurance)	Mode 1: Unbound Mode 2: Unbound Mode 3: Through a branch or JV only in Shanghai, subject to minimum local and global asset and local presence (as rep. office) requirements.	Mode 1: Unbound except for international maritime, aviation, and transport insurance and reinsurance, and certain types of brokerage. Mode 2: None, but unbound for brokerage. Mode 3: Form of establishment: non-life: through a branch or JVs with 51 percent foreign ownership; life: through JVs with 50 percent foreign ownership. Geographic limitation: only in five cities. Business scope: only selected forms of non–life insurance. Life only to individuals, not groups. Licenses: no quotas but subject to minimum asset and duration of establishment requirements. Upon accession, a 20 percent cession required of all lines of the primary risks for non-life, personal accident, and health insurance business with an appointed Chinese reinsurance company.	By 2004, FULLY LIBERALIZED EXCEPT 50 percent FOREIGN OWNERSHIP LIMIT IN LIFE INSURANCE. Mode 3: By 2003 no establishment restrictions in non-life. By 2004 no geographic restrictions. By 2004 no restrictions on business scope By 2005 no cession requirement.
Banking	Mode 1: Unbound Mode 2: Unbound Mode 3: Through a branch, subsidiary JV only in specified regions, subject to minimum asset and local presence (as rep. office) requirements; acceptance of deposits only from nonresidents in foreign currencies (with some exceptions) and no loans to Chinese citizens.	Mode 1: Unbound except for provision of data, advice, etc. Mode 2: None. Mode 3: Geographic limitation: none for foreign currency business, but local currency only in four cities. Interregional supply of services permitted. Clients: only foreign currency business. Licenses: only prudential criteria.	FULLY LIBERALIZED BY 2006. Mode 3: Geographic limitations phased out gradually by 2006. Clients: local currency business with Chinese enterprises by 2003 and all clients by 2006.
Securities	No commitments	Mode 1: Unbound except B share business. Mode 2: None Mode 3: Unbound, except rep. offices may become special members of the Chinese Stock Exchange (CSE)s, and through JVs with up to 33 percent foreign ownership to conduct domestic securities investment fund management business.	Mode 3: By 2004 49 percent foreign ownership in JVs to conduct domestic securities investment fund management business, and through JVs with up to 33 percent foreign ownership to underwrite A shares and underwrite and trade B and H shares, as well as government and corporate debts, launching of funds.
Tourism and travel-related services			
Hotels	Mode 1: Unbound Mode 2: None Mode 3: Through JVs subject to needs test at central and local levels.	Mode 1: Unbound Mode 2: None Mode 3: Through JVs with foreign majority ownership permitted.	FULLY LIBERALIZED BY 2005.
Travel agency and tour operator	No commitments	Mode 1: Unbound Mode 2: None Mode 3: Through JVs subject to geographic and business scope restrictions.	FULLY LIBERALIZED BY 2007.

TABLE 8.2   (Continued)

Sector	1994	2001	2008
Transport services			
MARITIME TRANSPORT			
International transport	Mode 1: None Mode 2: None Mode 3: Unbound	Mode 1: None Mode 2: None Mode 3: Through JVs subject to 49 percent foreign ownership limits to operate only a Chinese flag fleet	
Auxiliary services	Mode 1: Unbound Mode 2: None Mode 3: Through JVs only.	Mode 1: Unbound Mode 2: None Mode 3: Through JVs only with foreign majority ownership permitted.	
INTERNAL WATERWAYS	Mode 1: Only international shipping in ports open to foreign vessels permitted. Mode 2: None Mode 3: Unbound	As in 1994.	
AIR TRANSPORT			
Aircraft repair and maintenance	No commitments	Mode 1: Unbound Mode 2: None Mode 3: Through Chinese controlled JVs and subject to an economic needs test.	
Computer reservations	No commitments	Mode 1: By connection with Chinese computer reservation system, etc. Mode 2: None Mode 3: Unbound	
SPACE TRANSPORT	No commitments	No commitments	
RAIL TRANSPORT	No commitments	Mode 1: None Mode 2: None Mode 3: Through JVs with a foreign ownership limit of 49 percent.	FULLY LIBERALIZED BY 2007. Mode 3: Majority ownership by 2004.
ROAD TRANSPORT (FREIGHT)	Mode 1: Unbound Mode 2: None Mode 3: Through JVs subject to an economic needs test.	Mode 1: None Mode 2: None Mode 3: Through JVs with a foreign ownership limit of 49 percent.	FULLY LIBERALIZED BY 2004. Mode 3: Majority ownership by 2002.
SERVICES AUXILIARY TO ALL MODES OF TRANSPORT Storage and warehousing	Commitments only for maritime transport, as above.	Mode 1: Unbound Mode 2: None Mode 3: Through JVs with a foreign ownership limit of 49 percent.	FULLY LIBERALIZED BY 2004. Mode 3: Majority ownership by 2002.
Freight forwarding agency services	Commitments only for maritime transport, as above.	Mode 1: None Mode 2: None Mode 3: Through JVs with a foreign ownership limit of 50 percent and subject to minimum capital requirements.	FULLY LIBERALIZED BY 2005. Mode 3: Majority ownership by 2002.

JV = joint venture; CJV = contractual joint venture; EJV = equity joint venture; SEZ = special economic zone; CPA = certified public accountant.

Source: Compiled by the author from China's schedules of commitments under the GATS.

ownership will be permitted but subject to certain restrictions on business scope.

Distribution Services No commitments at all were shown in the 1994 schedule. Substantial liberalization has already taken place, but restrictions persist on establishment (only through joint ventures), geographic scope (retailing in only five special economic zones) and products sold (e.g., not books, newspapers, pharmaceuticals, and pesticides). By 2006 the sector will be largely open. Perhaps most strikingly, China has agreed to open up the whole logistical chain of related services, including inventory management; assembly, sorting, and grading of bulk lots; breaking bulk lots and redistributing into smaller lots; delivery services; refrigeration, storage, warehousing, and garage services; sales promotion, marketing and advertising; and installation and after-sales services, including maintenance and repair and training services. No WTO member has made such deep commitments in this sector.

Some restrictions will remain. Salt and tobacco are excluded from the scope of commitments on commission agents and wholesalers. Furthermore, majority foreign ownership will not be allowed in retail chain stores that sell multiple products and different brands of products such as books, newspapers, pharmaceuticals, and chemical fertilizers and have more than 30 outlets. There are no commitments on the cross-border supply of commission agents' services and delivery of wholesale trade services. More interestingly, cross-border supply of retail services is allowed only through mail order, which presumably covers electronic commerce.

Educational Services Cross-border delivery was unbound in 1994, but it is now fully open. Commercial presence was also unbound, but it now can be established through joint ventures with foreign majority ownership permitted. National treatment is not, however, guaranteed for foreign educational institutions.

Financial Services The 1994 commitments specified that insurance services could be supplied through a branch or joint venture only in Shanghai, subject to conditions pertaining to minimum capital and prior presence, globally (30 years as an insurance company) and locally (three years as a

representative office). On accession, non–life insurers are permitted to open a branch or joint venture with 51 percent foreign ownership, whereas life insurers are permitted 50 percent ownership of a joint venture with a partner of their choice. Non–life insurers can provide "master policy" insurance and insurance of large-scale commercial risks without geographic restrictions, and insurance of enterprises abroad as well as property insurance, related liability insurance, and credit insurance of foreign-invested enterprises in five cities: Shanghai, Guangzhou, Dalian, Shenzhen, and Foshan. Life insurers are permitted to provide individual (not group) insurance to foreigners and Chinese citizens in the same five cities. By 2004 all restrictions will disappear except the foreign ownership limit on life insurers. Licenses are to be awarded solely on the basis of prudential criteria, with no application of quantitative limitations or economic needs tests.

Under the 1994 commitments, foreign banks could only operate in specified regions, accept deposits only from nonresidents and only in foreign currencies (with some exceptions), and make no loans to Chinese citizens. On accession, geographic and client limitations will be eliminated for the foreign currency business. Even though the schedule states that on accession local currency business will be allowed in four cities (Shanghai, Shenzhen, Tianjin, and Dalian), there seems to be a binding restriction on clients that will only be relaxed in two years. The entire banking sector will be fully liberalized by 2006. As for insurance, licenses are to be awarded solely on the basis of prudential criteria, with no quantitative limitations or economic needs test applied.

There were no commitments on securities in 1994. On accession, joint ventures with up to 33 percent foreign ownership will be allowed to conduct business in domestic securities investment fund management. By 2004 foreign ownership of such ventures will be allowed to increase to 49 percent. Furthermore, joint ventures with up to 33 percent foreign ownership will be allowed to underwrite domestic equity issues and underwrite and trade in international equity and all corporate and government debt issues.

Grandfather Provisions One of the key difficulties in the accession negotiations arose because of the presence in the Chinese insurance market of firms that enjoyed better conditions than China was prepared to guarantee to new entrants. In particular, the U.S. life insurance firm AIG was established in Shanghai with full foreign ownership; Allianz (German), Axa (French), and Manulife (Canadian) were 51 percent foreign-owned. As noted earlier, the best China was prepared to offer new entrants was entry through joint ventures that were 50 percent foreign owned. Apparently this asymmetry in itself was generally acceptable and led to the following grandfather provision in China's schedule:

> The conditions of ownership, operation and scope of activities, as set out in the respective contractual or shareholder agreement or in a license establishing or authorizing the operation or supply of services by an existing foreign service supplier, will not be made more restrictive than they exist as of the date of China's accession to the WTO.

The problem arose because of the implications for branching rights. The key element of China's commitment was the guarantee that "internal branching for an insurance firm will be permitted consistent with the phase out of geographic restrictions." In effect, AIG would be able to expand operations through branches of its fully owned subsidiary in China, whereas other new firms could only do so through branches of their 50 percent–owned joint ventures. This situation was apparently not acceptable to the European Union. The eventual compromise was a rather convoluted footnote in the schedule, which states:

> Any further authorization provided to foreign insurers after accession under more favorable conditions than those contained in this schedule (including the extension of grandfathered investments through branching, sub-branching or any other legal form), will be made available to other foreign service suppliers which so requested.

This solution is messy and could lead to a dispute. If AIG is denied the right to branch from its fully owned subsidiary, the United States can claim that the assurance contained in the grandfather and internal branching commitments is not being respected. If AIG is allowed the right to establish branches and the European Union is denied the right to establish fully owned subsidiaries, then the latter can claim that the assurance contained in the footnote is not being respected.[5]

Transport Services Liberal commitments had already been made in international maritime transport and certain supporting services, even in 1994. The major change is that the greater depth of commitments across the whole range of transport and auxiliary services will significantly facilitate the provision of multimodal transport services. In road, rail, and key auxiliary services, notably storage and warehousing and freight forwarding agency services, restrictive or no commitments will be replaced on accession by the requirement to enter as joint ventures, and by 2007 there will be full liberalization. The exception will be hard rights in air transport, which are excluded from the scope of the GATS.

Do China's Commitments Promote Good Policy?

The commitments just described imply a dramatic loss of discretion in policymaking. China has promised to give up over the next few years much of the freedom it had to restrict new entry and foreign ownership, to discriminate between trading partners and in favor of its own firms, and, more broadly, to change its mind. The central argument of this section is that, for the most part, the discipline implied by the commitments is desirable. However, the persistence of restrictions on foreign ownership may deprive China of the full benefits of foreign investment, and the scheduled sequence of liberalization across regions may accentuate regional inequalities. Moreover, as discussed in the next major section, the size and distribution of the gains from liberalization will depend on how China uses the freedom it still has to strengthen its regulatory framework and choose an appropriate sequence of reform. Given the limited empirical evidence and the uniqueness of China's experience, these issues are at this stage not much more than plausible hypotheses that define an agenda for future research.

Eliminating Discretion

In many areas the Chinese government has been reluctant to liberalize immediately. Some of the protection is probably a consequence of political economic pressures from vested interests. In some cases, the government evidently has felt the need to protect the incumbent suppliers from competition because of infant industry–type arguments, to facilitate an "orderly exit," or to allow complementary reforms sufficient time—all of which are arguments for temporary protection. But protection once granted can be difficult to remove. The failure of infant industry policies in the past and the innumerable examples of perpetual infancy (or senility) are attributable in part to the inability of the Chinese government to commit itself to liberalize at some future date and thus to confront incumbents with a credible deadline. The binding commitments under the GATS to provide market access by a precise future date should play a valuable role in overcoming the credibility problem. Failure to honor these commitments creates an obligation to compensate those who are deprived of benefits, making the commitment more credible than a mere announcement of liberalizing intent in the national context. The price in terms of the loss of flexibility would seem to be worth paying.

It is also worth emphasizing that GATS commitments represent only a ceiling on protection and not a floor. China has given up the freedom to liberalize more slowly than specified in its GATS commitments, but it still has the freedom to move faster.

Eliminating Discrimination

Discrimination either between trading partners or in favor of domestic firms results in economically costly distortions, and so its prohibition is generally desirable. The two pillars of nondiscrimination under the GATS are the MFN and national treatment obligations, but both allow exceptions to be listed. China's MFN exemptions are relatively narrow. The only one listed applies to international maritime transport: to permit cargo-sharing agreements only with certain countries and to allow joint ventures and wholly owned shipping subsidiaries to be formed on the basis of bilateral agreements. In any case, because China has committed to full market access and national treatment on cross-border supply, there seems to be little scope for discriminatory cargo sharing.

There are also surprisingly few limitations on national treatment, and so, for the most part, China

has given up the right to offer preferential treatment to domestic enterprises through *any measure* affecting the supply of services. Virtually no scope exists for discriminatory taxation, and discriminatory subsidies can be awarded only in aviation, audiovisual, and medical services—and there, too, only to the extent that such subsidies already exist. The other instances of discriminatory provisions are the following: all legal representatives are required to be resident in China for no less than six months each year; a majority of doctors in joint venture hospitals must be Chinese; the existing registered capital requirements for joint venture construction enterprises are slightly different from those of domestic enterprises; joint venture travel agencies are not allowed to provide services to Chinese traveling abroad; and foreign insurers are subject to a 20-percent cession requirement with a Chinese reinsurance company, to be phased out in four years.

Although the scope for explicit discrimination has shrunk, the nature of measures affecting trade in services does offer considerable scope for implicit discrimination. First, there is the possibility of variable treatment through *domestic regulations* such as licensing, recognition of qualifications, and various other technical regulations. Such discretion is likely to be constrained, but probably not eliminated, by the assurance that licenses in financial services will be issued solely on the basis of prudential criteria and by the requirement for transparency of licensing criteria and decision processes in other areas. Furthermore, Article VII of the GATS, which deals specifically with recognition agreements pertaining to educational qualifications, licenses, and such, strikes a delicate balance by allowing such agreements, provided they are not used as a means of discrimination, and third countries have an opportunity to accede or demonstrate equivalence.

Second, China has retained the freedom to impose explicit *quantitative restrictions* on the number of providers in legal, medical, and retailing services. De facto quotas also may exist in some areas, such as those imposed by the scarcity of radio spectrum needed for the provision of mobile telecommunications services and the scarcity of space needed for department stores or airports in a city. Apart from the general MFN obligation, no specific rules are in place to ensure the nondiscriminatory allocation of quotas in services (WTO rules are, however, in place for goods). In the past, this lack of rules was not a major issue because commitments reflected the status quo, and quotas, particularly those for service suppliers, were descriptions of the existing market structure. But when genuine liberalizing commitments are made, like those by China, the nondiscriminatory allocation of quotas is bound to be an important issue. The instinctive candidate for a nondiscriminatory rule is an auction, which also has the virtue of transferring quota rents to the government. It remains to be seen whether the Chinese regulators can resist the temptation to resort to other, more discretionary methods of allocating quotas.

Adhering to the principle of nondiscrimination is important, even though it may seem at first sight that there is no real cost to granting preferential treatment in services. Because the protective instrument is often a restrictive regulation that does not generate revenue (or rents), there is no cost to granting preferential access because there is no revenue (or rents) to lose. When the protective instrument is a quota, the implications of preferences depend on who appropriates the rents. Where rents are appropriated by exporters or dissipated, preferential liberalization is again necessarily welfare-enhancing for the importing country.

Preferences in services may, however, impose other, more subtle costs. The cost of trade diversion may well be the establishment of poorer-quality providers, not just in terms of poorer-quality services but also in terms of smaller social benefits in the form of knowledge and technological spillovers. Furthermore, the greater importance of sunk costs in some service sectors, ranging from basic telecommunications to financial services, suggests that preferential liberalization may have more durable consequences than in the case of goods. For example, allowing the second-best provider to establish a business may mean that a country is stuck with such a provider even when it subsequently liberalizes on an MFN basis.[6]

These considerations suggest that China would do well to resist the reported pressure to grant preferential access to the service suppliers of certain WTO members. Such pressure resulted in, for example, the grandfather provisions in China's commitments on insurance services, described earlier in this chapter. These provisions reflect an emphasis on

guaranteeing the rights of incumbents. Insofar as they provide the benefits of security to investors who are already present in the market rather than to *new* investors, they may not do enough to make markets more contestable. New entrants may even be placed at a competitive disadvantage insofar as differences in ownership and legal form affect firm performance. For example, larger equity shares may make it easier to exercise effective control over the operations of a firm and ensure efficient production, and the marginal cost of providing a service through a branch may be lower than through a subsidiary. Fortunately, the fact that several foreign and domestic firms are already competing in the market may limit the impact of these grandfather provisions.

Eliminating Barriers to Entry

Apart from the few instances just noted, China has chosen not to limit the number of service providers. The only barrier to new entry is the requirement to enter as a joint venture, which is discussed in the next section. But two questions arise: Is it good policy to allow unrestricted entry in all service sectors? Will China's commitments deprive the government of an important policy instrument? One reason for entry restrictions might be the existence of significant economies of scale. For example, networks incur substantial fixed costs, and competitive entry could lead to inefficient network duplication.[7]

For several reasons, however, entry restrictions are increasingly difficult to defend in principle in the face of technological change and in the face of mounting evidence that competition works. First, entry restrictions change the nature of interaction between incumbents and may well make collusion more likely. Second, such restrictions dampen the impact of competition on productive efficiency. Third, the regulator is usually not better placed than the competitive process to determine the optimal number of firms in the market, especially given the difficulty of obtaining information about the cost structure of firms and other sources of regulatory failure. Fourth, technological advances have significantly lowered network costs, even in a sector like fixed-line telecommunications, and vertical separation (e.g., through network unbundling) has widened the scope for competitive entry (Smith 1995). Inefficiencies introduced by the duplication of networks may be small compared with the operational inefficiencies that can result from a lack of competitive pressure.[8] On this basis, it would seem that there is little reason to worry about excessive entry; rather, the priority should be eliminating the barriers to entry where they remain (e.g., in medical services and retailing).

Eliminating Restrictions on Foreign Ownership

The most important restriction on foreign presence in China is the requirement to enter as a joint venture, often with limits on the extent of foreign ownership. In most areas these limits on ownership are being gradually phased out, but in some areas such as telecommunications and life insurance they will remain even after all the liberalization commitments have been phased out. What is the rationale for such restrictions, and what are their implications? Furthermore, what are the consequences of the manner in which they are being phased out?

Joint ventures may, of course, be the preferred choice of the foreign investor if, for example, local firms have specific assets that can be accessed only through collaboration. However, binding ownership restrictions may adversely affect firm performance, because the incentive to undertake costly transfers of technology and improvements in management is related to the expected gains, which in turn are related to an owner's share of the profits of. Moreover, changes in the permissible share of ownership in the vicinity of 50 percent (e.g., from 49 percent to 51 percent) may have a particularly large impact on performance as a firm obtains fuller control of its operations and has greater freedom to make the changes it deems necessary.

At this stage the evidence available is not sufficient to evaluate the magnitude of these effects, but the plausibility of their existence raises the question of why the Chinese government is willing to bear such costs. Four reasons are possible. First, limitations on ownership may seek to balance the efficiency enhancing and the rent-appropriating aspects of foreign investment. However, rent appropriation could to some extent be prevented by ex ante auctions of equity or ex post taxation of profits.[9] A more basic question is why rent-generating restrictions on competition continue to exist. Second is the "infant entrepreneur" argument: foreigners are induced to form EJVs so that local investors

can learn by collaborating. As with all such arguments, it is difficult to judge whether the current costs are likely to be offset by the eventual benefits. Third is the adjustment cost argument: an immediate transfer of control could lead to drastic cuts in surplus labor, which gradual reductions in ownership help prevent. A central issue is whether it is possible to address these adjustment costs through direct support to the affected factors rather than by staggered liberalization. Finally, the most important reason is probably a purely political reluctance to allow foreign control of an essential service. Again, these political concerns should diminish if multiple competing foreign firms, not just one foreign monopolist, are providing the service.

Eliminating Restrictions Gradually Across Regions

A remarkable feature of China's dramatic expansion in international trade over the past two decades has been the concentration of export-oriented industries in coastal regions. Three coastal provinces (Guangdong, Jiangsu, and Fujian) and Shanghai have been the main recipients of outward-oriented foreign investment, with the remaining portion going either to other coastal provinces or to regions adjoining coastal areas. Thus, although China's economic reforms have been successful in raising living standards for a considerable share of the population, a large number of Chinese people in inland provinces have benefited substantially less.

A factor responsible for coastal agglomeration has been the inefficiencies in China's internal service systems, most obviously transport and telecommunications, but also financial, business, and other services. Transport infrastructure disparities between the coastal and inland provinces narrowed considerably after policies were adopted in 1990 aimed at promoting more regionally balanced economic development. However, there is evidence to suggest that it is not the availability of transport infrastructure per se that has precluded inland provinces from actively participating in foreign trade. Rather, the inadequacies associated with transport services have been the more serious binding constraints on better integrating China's hinterland economy.[10]

The geographic limitations on liberalization commitments in certain sectors could well accentuate these interregional inequalities, even though the limitations do not apply to transport services and most are to be phased out over time. The existing enclaves of development are likely to see faster improvements in service quality from early liberalization, and these improvements will cause even more economic activity to gravitate to these areas. Eventually, though, liberalization of services in the hinterland may lead to greater diffusion of activity. Yet insofar as sunk costs are important, the earlier agglomeration is unlikely to be completely reversible and inequalities may persist. The importance of these considerations needs to be established through further empirical research, but at least intuitively would seem to strengthen the case for eliminating the geographic restrictions simultaneously rather than sequentially.

What Are the Priorities for Complementary Domestic Reform?

If China is to make the most of the liberalization it is now committed to undertake, improving the regulatory framework is critical. Regulation in services, as in goods, arises essentially from the need to remedy market failure—attributable to the problems of natural monopoly and inadequate consumer information—and to ensure equitable access.

Efficient Regulation: Making Competition Work

The first regulatory priority arises in the so-called locational services. These markets are concentrated because of the large fixed costs required to create specialized distribution networks: roads and rails for land transport, cables and satellites for communications, and pipes for sewage and energy distribution (UNCTAD and World Bank 1994). Unless the appropriate regulatory mechanisms are put in place, the incumbent can frustrate competition by denying rivals access to essential facilities such as distribution networks and terminals.

China has accepted the regulatory principles specified in the Telecommunications Reference Paper. Thus it has committed to instituting an independent regulator for basic telecommunications services to ensure that the incumbent supplier does not undermine market access by charging prohibitive rates for interconnection to its established networks.[11] Since 1998 the Ministry of Information

Industry (MII) has been the regulator of telecommunications and other information technology-related products and services, including data communications, wireless communications, electronics, computers, the Internet, and software. In August 2001 the high-profile State Council Information Office (SCIO) was formed with a mandate to develop and implement information policy in China (see chapter 10). Similar steps may need to be taken in a variety of other network services, including transport (terminals and infrastructure) and energy services (distribution networks).

The creation of a regulator is only a first step. Persuading the dominant interest groups to concede control is fraught with difficulty. For example, in India a conflict between the Department of Telecommunications (DOT) and the Telecommunications Regulatory Authority of India (TRAI), as it was initially constituted, hampered progress toward an efficient telecom infrastructure.[12] Absent a truly independent regulator empowered to rebalance tariffs, enforce fair interconnection agreements, and ensure rapid, equitable issuance of radio spectrum, the benefits of a sector opened to allow private participation and foreign investment could be significantly limited.

In certain market segments it may not be possible to create conditions for effective competition in the supply of certain telecommunications, transport, and financial services, even if all barriers to entry are eliminated. Two related factors are likely to be involved. First, unlike for goods, national markets are often segmented from the international market by the infeasibility of cross-border delivery. Second, changing technologies may have reduced the optimal scale of operation as well as the sunk costs in these sectors, but not enough for small markets to sustain competitive market structures. Some form of final price regulation may therefore be needed.

Regulation to Remedy Inadequate Consumer Information

In China's increasingly open markets, priority must be given to strengthening the quality of prudential regulation in intermediation and knowledge-based services, where consumers have difficulty securing full information about the quality of service they are buying (UNCTAD and World Bank 1994). For example, consumers cannot easily assess the competence of professionals such as doctors and lawyers, the safety of transport services, or the soundness of banks and insurance companies. When such information is costly to obtain and disseminate and consumers have similar preferences about the relevant attributes of the service supplier, the regulation of entry and operations in a sector could increase social welfare. However, the establishment of institutions competent to regulate well is a serious challenge, as revealed by the difficulties in the financial sectors elsewhere—not only in various developing countries but also in the United States, Sweden, and Finland in the 1980s and 1990s.

A separate problem is that domestic regulations to deal with market failure may themselves become impediments to competition and trade as a result of differences across jurisdictions in technical standards, prudential regulations, and qualification requirements in professional, financial, and numerous other services. For example, China requires foreign doctors to obtain a license from the Ministry of Public Health and foreign accountants to pass the Chinese national certified public accountant examination. In many instances the impact on trade is an incidental consequence of the pursuit of a legitimate objective, but in some instances regulation can be a particularly attractive means of protecting domestic suppliers from foreign competition. Multilateral trade rules on domestic regulations may contribute to domestic reform by helping to sift the legitimate from the protectionist. To this end, negotiations are under way to develop GATS rules for domestic regulations. The core of these disciplines may well be the so-called necessity test, which seeks to establish whether a particular regulation is more burdensome than necessary to achieve a legitimate objective.

Regulation to Ensure Universal Service

Opening up essential services to foreign or domestic competition could have an adverse effect on the poor—a point that is often cited as a reason for the persistence of public monopolies. A more efficient solution is to have regulations with a social purpose.

Where China is a relatively inefficient producer of a service, liberalization and the resulting foreign competition are likely to lead to a decline in domestic prices and improvements in quality. However, there is a twist. Frequently, the prices before liberal-

ization were not determined by the market, but were set administratively and then kept artificially low for certain categories of end users or types of service products. Liberalization threatens these arrangements. The elimination of restrictions on entry implies an end to cross-subsidization, because it is no longer possible for firms to make extranormal profits in certain market segments. And privatization could mean the end of government support.

Reform programs can accommodate universal service obligations by imposing this requirement on new entrants in a nondiscriminatory way. Thus in several countries such obligations have been part of the license conditions for new entrants into fixed network telephony and transport. Often, however, subsidies have proved more successful than direct regulation in ensuring universal access (Estache, Foster, and Wodon 2001). The Chilean government adopted a scheme that permitted it to leverage over $2 million in public funds into $40 million in private investment. As a result, telephones were installed in 1,000 localities at about 10 percent of the cost of direct public provision. Public subsidies can also be directed to the consumer rather than the provider (Cowhey and Klimenko 1999). The choice of appropriate instrument will have to be made on a sector-by-sector basis.

Addressing Adjustment Costs

Different modes of supply have different effects on factor markets. Cross-border trade and consumption abroad resemble the goods trade in their implications. The impact of the movement of factors depends critically on whether they are substitutes or complements for domestic factor services. Given the structure of factor prices in China, liberalization would typically lead to an inflow of capital and skilled workers. Such inflows would tend to be to the advantage of the unskilled poor—increasing employment opportunities and wages.[13] Interestingly, it has been shown that even when foreigners compete with local skilled workers in a service sector, the productivity boost to the sector from allowing foreigners access could lead to an increase in the demand for domestic skilled workers—that is, the scale effect could outweigh the substitution effect (Markusen, Rutherford, and Tarr 2000). Given these predictions, why are workers in China sometimes skeptical about the benefits of liberalization?

One concern is the possible reduction in employment in the formerly public monopolies that have frequently employed surplus labor.

Evidence suggests that such pessimism may not always be justified. For example, some developing countries have managed to maintain or even increase employment in their liberalized telecommunications sectors. Because China still has a low teledensity outside the big cities (about 10 lines per 100 people), much of telecom investment is being directed toward building wire line and mobile networks that are labor-intensive and that are probably helping to maintain or raise employment levels. The introduction of competition should help. For example, Petrazzini and Lovelock (1996) found in a study of 26 Latin American and Asian economies that telecom markets with competition were the only ones that consistently increased employment levels, while two-thirds of the countries with monopolies saw considerable declines in their telecom work force. Despite these optimistic projections, it is likely that reform programs will require complementary policies to mitigate any social and economic costs of adjustments in factor markets.

Sequencing Regulatory Reform and Trade and Investment Liberalization

Regulatory improvements take time. Changes in the patterns of competition and ownership can be implemented instantaneously in principle, but China, like many other countries, has chosen to introduce changes gradually. One question that arises in this context is: How does the impact of different elements of reform depend on the extent to which other reforms have been implemented—that is, how does the *interaction* of the different elements of policy reform affect performance? The other, more subtle question is: Does the *sequence* of reforms have transitory and permanent effects on performance? Some preliminary observations on these questions, which are relevant to the design of transition strategies, are presented in the sections that follow.

Telecommunications   Figure 8.2 depicts the sequence of telecommunications liberalization in nine Asian countries. China is among the few that have allowed some degree of competition (in long-distance services) before allowing a change of ownership in the incumbent supplier and creating an independent regulator. Fink, Mattoo, and Rathindran

(2001), in a study of telecommunications reform in Asia, Africa, and Latin America, found that although each element of reform has a positive impact on performance, the effect of each is magnified when others are also implemented. Moreover, privatizing the incumbent after introducing competition (the Chinese route) is likely to lead to a higher level of mainline penetration than the opposite sequence.

Although China has chosen the preferred sequence in telecommunications, it must still make important choices in other areas, such as postal and air transport services. Introducing privatization before introducing competition may create a privileged incumbent that has a first-mover advantage in the market. Among other things, the incumbent may be able to make certain strategic decisions or indulge in lobbying to affect the eventual form of competition.[14] For example, in South Africa foreign and domestic shareholders in the privatized telecommunications monopoly managed to persuade the government to allow only one new entrant rather than the planned two. Regulating the terms of access to essential facilities for new entrants may also be more difficult in an arm's length relationship with a private provider whose costs are difficult to observe than with a public provider whose cost information may be easier to access. Entry may be easier on symmetric terms with an inefficient public incumbent than on asymmetric terms with an efficient private incumbent.

Financial Services   In financial services, internationalization raises several concerns: the threat to the survival of local banks and financial companies; the loss of monetary autonomy; and the increased volatility of capital flows. Many of these concerns do not relate just to the internationalization of financial services, but also to the processes of financial deregulation and capital account liberalization. However, the extent of the benefits and costs of internationalization depend to a great extent on how it is phased in with these other two types of financial reform, and, in particular, the strengthening of prudential regulation and supervision.

Many countries that have had successful experiences opening up to foreign financial firms (Brazil, Chile, Hungary, Ireland, Poland, Portugal, and Spain, among others) also engaged in a process of domestic deregulation and consequently reaped substantial gains (World Bank 2001). The experience

FIGURE 8.2   Sequence of Telecommunications Reform in Nine Asian Countries, 1989–99

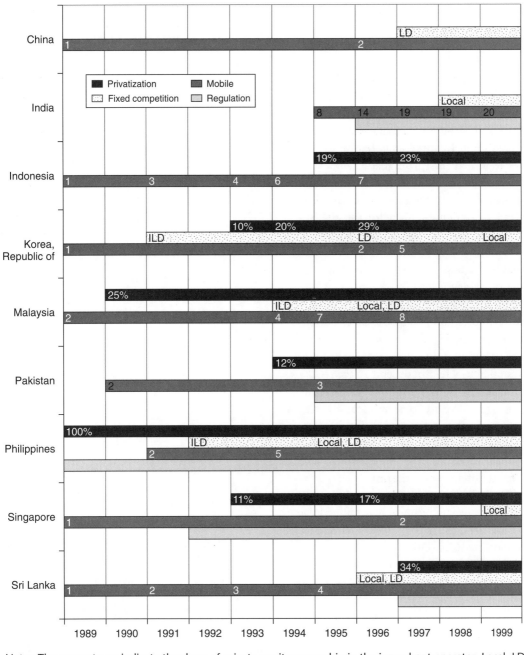

Notes: The percentages indicate the share of private equity ownership in the incumbent operator. Local, LD, and ILD refer to the local, long distance, and international fixed-line service segments, respectively. The number(s) in the mobile row corresponds to the number of cellular operators in the country. "Regulation" only captures the existence of a separate regulatory agency.

Source: World Bank/ITU telecommunications policy database.

of the countries acceding to the European Union suggests that internationalization and domestic deregulation can be mutually reinforcing. Increased foreign entry bolstered the financial sector framework by creating a constituency for improved regulation and supervision, better disclosure rules, and improvements in the legal and regulatory framework for the provision of financial services. It also added to the credibility of rules.

Most of these considerations are relevant to China. As discussed by Bhattasali in chapter 11, on-performing loans account for a large fraction of the assets of the big four banks, which account for more than two-thirds of the assets of the banking sector. The big four are already thought to be insolvent (Fitch and Moody's). One of the main reasons for the many bad loans is that interest rates are still controlled by the People's Bank of China (PBC). They are unusually low to make it easier for state-owned enterprises to borrow funds at well below the market-clearing equilibrium rate of interest.[15] This situation has been responsible for a huge transfer of wealth from individual savers to state-owned enterprises. Two-thirds of credit resources went to state-owned enterprises that generate only one-third of industrial output. The official target of 2003 for interest rate liberalization has already been pushed back to 2005 unofficially for fear that the ensuing competition for deposits will drive business away from the four large banks, which would then collapse, leading to a serious banking crisis (*Business China*, May 7, 2001).

Although the two reform processes (internationalization and domestic financial deregulation) are mutually reinforcing, they are not sufficient in themselves. More than in other sectors, the gains and costs of financial reform depend on the regulatory and supervisory framework (Barth, Caprio, and Levine 2001). Experience shows that it is vital to strengthen the supporting institutional framework in parallel with domestic deregulation and internationalization. In the absence of such strengthening, foreign entry may entail risks. Foreign bank entry can destabilize local banks by taking away the lowest-risk business—including large exporting firms—leaving local banks to venture further out on the risk frontier.

The benefits of a supportive institutional framework are even more obvious when it comes to capital account liberalization.[16] Experiences in recent years, most recently in Asia, have shown that achieving the potential gains, and avoiding the risks, of capital account liberalization depend to a great extent on whether domestic institutions and prudential authorities have developed sufficiently to ensure that foreign finance will be channeled in productive directions (Eichengreen 2001).

Conclusions

China's GATS commitments represent the most radical services reform program negotiated in the WTO. China has promised to eliminate over the next few years most restrictions on foreign entry and ownership, as well as most forms of discrimination against foreign firms. Trading partners are naturally interested in the market access dimension of these commitments and are keen to see them fully implemented.[17] However, realizing the gains from, and perhaps even the sustainability of, liberalization will require the implementation of complementary regulatory reform and the appropriate sequencing of reforms.

Although China's commitments, for the most part, promote good policy, two elements raise some concern. First, restrictions on foreign ownership—temporary in most sectors, but more durable in telecommunications and life insurance—may dampen the incentives for foreign investors to improve firm performance. The rationale for these restrictions merits greater scrutiny. Second, initial restrictions on the geographic scope of services liberalization could encourage the further agglomeration of economic activity in certain regions—indeed, to an extent that is unlikely to be reversed completely by subsequent country-wide liberalization. It may therefore be worth examining whether these restrictions could be phased out more quickly.

This chapter has identified three main priorities for complementary reform. First, improved prudential regulation and measures to deal with the large burden of nonperforming loans by state banks are necessary to realize the benefits of liberalization in financial services. Second, in basic telecommunications and other network-based services meaningful liberalization will be difficult to achieve without strengthened pro-competitive regulation. Finally, in virtually every important service sector, an effective universal service policy must be put in place because liberalization alone will not deliver improved access for the poor.

Appendix: Structure of China's Market Access Commitments

TABLE 8.A.1

Sector	Mode 1			Mode 2			Mode 3			Mode 4		
	F	P	N	F	P	N	F	P	N	F	P	N
Business services												
Legal services	0	1	0	0	1	0	0	1	0	0	1	0
Accounting/auditing/ bookkeeping	1	0	0	1	0	0	0	1	0	0	1	0
Architectural services	0	1	0	0	1	0	0	1	0	0	1	0
Medical and dental services	1	0	0	1	0	0	0	1	0	0	1	0
Data processing services	0	1	0	0	1	0	0	1	0	0	1	0
RandD services (natural sciences)	0	1	0	0	1	0	0	1	0	0	1	0
Advertising services	1	0	0	1	0	0	0	1	0	0	1	0
Management consulting services	0	1	0	0	1	0	0	1	0	0	1	0
Communication services												
Courier services	0	1	0	0	1	0	0	1	0	0	1	0
Voice telephone services	0	1	0	0	1	0	0	1	0	0	1	0
Private leased circuit services	0	1	0	0	1	0	0	1	0	0	1	0
Electronic mail	0	1	0	1	0	0	0	1	0	0	1	0
Online info and database retrieval	0	1	0	1	0	0	0	1	0	0	1	0
Audiovisual services	0	1	0	0	1	0	0	1	0	0	1	0
Construction, engineering												
Construction work (building)	0	0	1	0	1	0	0	1	0	0	1	0
Construction work (civil engin.)	0	0	1	0	1	0	0	1	0	0	1	0
Distribution												
Wholesale trade	0	1	0	0	1	0	0	1	0	0	1	0
Retailing services	0	1	0	0	1	0	0	1	0	0	1	0
Educational services												
Secondary education	0	0	1	0	1	0	0	1	0	0	1	0
Adult education	0	0	1	0	1	0	0	1	0	0	1	0
Environmental services												
Sewage services	0	1	0	0	1	0	0	1	0	0	1	0
Refuse disposal	0	1	0	0	1	0	0	1	0	0	1	0
Financial services												
Non–life insurance	0	1	0	0	1	0	0	1	0	0	1	0
Acceptance of deposits	0	1	0	0	1	0	0	1	0	0	1	0
Lending of all types	0	1	0	0	1	0	0	1	0	0	1	0
Trading in securities	0	1	0	1	0	0	0	1	0	0	1	0
Health-related, social services												
Hospital services												
Social services												
Tourism services												
Hotels and restaurants	1	0	0	1	0	0	0	1	0	0	1	0
Travel agencies	1	0	0	1	0	0	0	1	0	0	1	0
Recreational services												
Entertainment services												
News agency services												
Transport services												
Maritime (freight)	0	1	0	0	1	0	0	1	0	0	1	0
Rail (passenger)												
Rail (freight)	1	0	0	1	0	0	0	1	0	0	1	0
Road (passenger)												
Road (freight)	1	0	0	1	0	0	0	1	0	0	1	0
Total number (31 subsectors)	7	20	4	10	21	0	0	31	0	0	31	0
Percent	23	64	13	32	68	0	0	100	0	0	100	0

F = full commitment; P = partial commitment; N = no commitment.

Sources: WTO services database.

Notes

1. See, for example, chapter 9 by Luo and Findlay, chapter 10 by Pangestu and Mrongowius, and chapter 11 by Bhattasali.

2. The only explicit sectoral exclusion from the GATS is certain "hard" rights in the aviation sector.

3. Note that a GATS scheduling rule requires that discriminatory quantitative restrictions be listed as market access restrictions even though they are also inconsistent with national treatment.

4. The commitment on mode 1 indicates a cross reference to mode 3, the meaning of which is not clear.

5. It was reported in the *Financial Times* of December 6, 2001, that a compromise had been reached on this issue. Apparently, AIG would be given permission to open two more 100 percent–owned branches, but would thereafter have to abide by the same 50 percent rule as all other foreign insurers in the Chinese market. The deal was seen as consistent with WTO rules because the two extra licenses were to be awarded to AIG before China entered the WTO on December 11, 2001. The licenses were to be granted for the cities of Suzhou, near Shanghai, and Beijing, the capital.

6. Where this happens will depend on the importance of sunk costs relative to differences in costs and quality.

7. One such possibility is in the "nonsustainability" of a natural monopoly. This situation could arise, for example, under some natural monopoly cost conditions, when there exist no prices that will not attract entry, even though supply by a single firm is efficient. Armstrong, Cowan, and Vickers (1994, p. 106) conclude: "Notwithstanding the logical possibility of this happening, we are doubtful whether it provides a good case for entry restrictions in the utility industries, which are not for the most part remotely contestable and where there is little evidence that cost conditions give rise to non-sustainability."

8. Interesting evidence in this context is available from the Indian telecommunications sector. Das (2000) estimates a frontier multiproduct cost function for the incumbent fixed-line operator, covering 25 years from 1969 to 1994. The study finds the existence of very high economies of both scale and scope in the technology used—the parameter estimates even suggest that telecommunications in India is a natural monopoly. However, the incumbent operator displays great inefficiency, leading to a 26 percent increase in the operator's cost of production. Based on these findings, Das concludes that India's market liberalization program, started in the mid-1990s, is justified, but he argues that there may be a need to regulate entry in order to reduce the unnecessary duplication of common costs. Moreover, with continued improvements in technology, the fixed costs of entrants are likely to fall, reducing losses of scale economies and thus increasing the costs of entry restrictions.

9. The fear of creating a disincentive for investors might be a reason to refrain from taxation.

10. For example, although there has been a significant increase in the volume of container traffic in China since 1990, the increase is largely confined to coastal regions and associated with the ocean-going leg of travel. Container traffic in inland areas is much less, with no significant change in the percentage of seaborne containers traveling beyond port cities and coastal provinces. Truck rates for moving a container 500 kilometers inland are estimated to be about three times more, and the trip duration five times longer, than they would be in Europe or United States. The intermodal transport system was found to be poorly integrated, with no streamlined procedures to support the continual movement of containers between the coast and inlands.

11. Several countries have found it difficult to create open, competitive telecommunications sectors because of a weak regulatory environment. Poland opened up its telecommunications sector to private competition as early as 1990. There was a rush to invest, and about 200 licenses were awarded in the first six years of the newly liberalized regime. However, the dominant state operator, operating in a weak regulatory system, limited access to its network and benefited from unequal terms for revenue sharing. By 1996 only 12 of the 200 licenses were still being used by the few competitive operators to survive.

12. The Indian government announced a new telecommunications policy on March 26, 1999, that addressed several of these key outstanding issues.

13. Because the poor are likely to be unskilled, the question arises as to which service sectors are likely to employ them? Data on the skill composition of the work force in service sectors are available only at a rather aggregate level. Still, a certain pattern can be inferred. Construction, distribution, and personal services tend to be unskilled labor–intensive, whereas communications, financial, and business services tend to be skilled labor–intensive.

14. A public sector provider could also behave in this way, but presumably if the government's objective is liberalization, it is somewhat easier to draw along a public provider.

15. In 1995 savings deposits received a paltry 3.15 percent in interest, while loans for working capital were made at only 11 percent—they should have been made at about 21 percent after factoring in the rate of inflation. The current one-year rate on savings deposits is about 2.25 percent.

16. Because China has made only limited commitments on cross-border trade in financial services, its GATS commitments do not require it to allow a high degree of capital mobility, except insofar as capital inflows are required to establish commercial presence.

17. In fact, in the WTO's Services Council the United States has already raised the issue of whether China's current rules for express delivery services and branching by non–life insurance companies conform to its GATS commitments (*Inside US Trade*, March 29, 2002).

References

The word *processed* describes informally reproduced works that may not be commonly available through libraries.

Armstrong, M., S. Cowan, and J. Vickers. 1994. *Regulatory Reform: Economic Analysis and British Experience.* Cambridge, Mass.: MIT Press.

Barth, J. R., G. Caprio Jr., and R. Levine. 2001. "Bank Regulations and Supervision: What Works Best?" Paper presented at Thirteenth Annual World Bank Conference on Development Economics, April.

Cowhey, P., and M. M. Klimenko. 1999. "The WTO Agreement and Telecommunication Policy Reforms." Draft report for the World Bank. Graduate School of International Relations and Pacific Studies, University of California at San Diego, March.

Das, N. 2000. "Technology, Efficiency and Sustainability of Competition in the Indian Telecommunications Sector." *Information Economics and Policy* 12: 133–54.

Eichengreen, B. 2001. "Capital Account Liberalization: What Do the Cross-Country Studies Tell Us?" *World Bank Economic Review* 15 (3): 341–65.

Estache, A., Vivian Foster, and Quentin Wodon. 2001. "Accounting for Poverty in Infrastructure Reform: Learning from

Latin America's Experience." WBI Development Studies No. 23950. World Bank Institute, Washington, D.C.

Fink, Carsten, Aaditya Mattoo, and Randeep Rathindran. 2001. "Liberalizing Basic Telecommunications: The Asian Experience." Policy Research Working Paper 2718. World Bank, Washington, D.C., November.

Ianchovichina, E., W. Martin, and C. Wood. 2001. "Economic Effects of the Vietnam–US Bilateral Trade Agreement." World Bank, Washington, D.C. Processed.

Markusen, James, Thomas F. Rutherford, and David Tarr. 2000. "Foreign Direct Investment in Services and the Domestic Market for Expertise." Policy Research Working Paper 2413. World Bank, Washington, D.C., August.

Petrazzini, B. A., and P. Lovelock. 1996. "Telecommunications in the Region: Comparative Case Studies." Paper presented at International Institute for Communication Telecommunications Forum, April 22–23. Sydney, Australia.

Smith, P. 1995. "End of the Line for the Local Loop Monopoly." Public Policy for the Private Sector, Note No. 63. World Bank, Washington, D.C.

United Nations Conference on Trade and Development (UNCTAD) and World Bank. 1994. *Liberalizing International Transactions in Services: A Handbook.* New York and Geneva: United Nations.

World Bank. 2001. "Finance for Growth: Policy Choices in a Volatile World." *World Bank Policy Research Report.* World Bank and Oxford University Press.

WTO (World Trade Organization). 1999. "Structure of Commitments for Modes 1, 2 and 3." *Background Note by the Secretariat,* Council for Trade in Services, S/C/W/99, March.

LOGISTICS IN CHINA: IMPLICATIONS OF ACCESSION TO THE WTO

Wenping Luo and Christopher Findlay

Study of the geography of poverty has revealed how changes in transport costs, even when they make up a small share of the value of a product, can lead to large changes in value added and in growth rates (see Radelet and Sachs 1998 and Redding and Venables 2000). The rate at which transport costs accumulate over distance is usually taken as given in this research, and the questions asked are about the links between location and rural producer incomes. Policy prescriptions then usually refer to processes under direct government control such as port operations or customs procedures. However, in this chapter we stress that policy reform, especially through commitments to the World Trade Organization (WTO), can have significant effects not just on transport prices, but also on the other costs of getting goods to market in the form that consumers prefer. These effects are important both in international trade and in trade within an economy. Reductions in this set of costs can add to value added, especially in remote, poor areas.

We illustrate these points in this study of the logistics sector in China and of the impact of China's accession to the WTO on the performance of that sector. The concept of logistics continues to evolve, and recently it became a "hot" topic in China, with logistics services eliciting strong interest from both businesses and policymakers. Moreover, a significant part of seminar and management training time in China is now devoted to developing what might be called the "logistics way of thinking." There is an appreciation that systems, processes, and perspectives—that is, the software of the business—are just as important as the physical assets, if not more so, in the growth of enterprises that are internationally competitive in logistics.

We argue in this chapter that WTO accession has significant implications for the logistics sector. Although there is no easy match between the various categories of the General Agreement on Trade in Services (GATS) and the modern scope of logistics, it is possible to make a concordance. We complete that work in order to comment on the implications of China's accession commitments. The requirement to make these associations illustrates an important feature of scheduling commitments under GATS in emerging business areas.

The next section of this chapter reviews the definition of logistics services. It is followed by an overview of their evolution in China.[1]

The authors thank the editor of this volume and seminar participants for comments. Errors remain their own.

We then outline the WTO commitments made by China related to this sector, and reach a set of conclusions on their direct effects and their indirect implications. The direct effects, we emphasize, include substantial savings in real resources and not just transfer differences that represent relatively small gains in efficiency.

The indirect effects include reference to policy-making processes and administrative structures. The analysis here highlights the value of complementary reforms in domestic institutions and regulatory agencies and their processes in order to maximize the gains from liberalization.

The chapter then continues with a discussion of the likely orders of magnitude of the effects of a more open logistics sector on total logistics costs, and discusses the significance of these changes for poor areas in China. We pay special attention to the role of the gains in increasing the value added in production processes in poor areas. Some of the main points are revisited in the final section of the chapter.

Logistics Defined

Logistics is the process of planning, implementing, and controlling the efficient flow and storage of goods, services, and related information from the point of origin to the point of consumption to meet customers' requirements. The provision of logistics services requires inputs from various service providers, including the providers of transport and warehousing as well as other value-adding activities.

The concept of logistics has undergone many significant changes. Coyle, Bardi, and Langley (1996) divided the development of logistics into three stages:

- Stage 1: physical distribution or outbound logistics system (during 1960s and 1970s). Businesses attempted to manage systematically a set of interrelated activities, including transportation, distribution, warehousing, finished goods, inventory levels, packaging, and materials handling, to ensure the efficient delivery of finished goods to customers.
- Stage 2: integrated logistics management (during the 1970s and 1980s). Companies began to recognize the additional opportunities for savings by combining the inbound side (materials management) with the outbound side (physical distribution). Initially, savings was achieved by

having a single transportation manager who could coordinate inbound and outbound transportation. Then companies became aware of the opportunities to view the whole process, from raw materials to work-in-process inventory to finished goods, as a continuum that, managed from a systems perspective, could lead to more efficient operation.
- Stage 3: supply chain management (from 1980s to 1990s). Companies expanded their perspective on the logistics processes to include all the firms involved, making use of partnerships/alliances between manufacturing companies and their suppliers/vendors, customers (channels of distribution), and other logistics-related parties such as transportation and public warehousing companies.

The concentration on fewer carriers operating under long-term contracts and on outsourcing the whole package of services stimulated the development of third-party logistics (3PL) firms. As noted, several subsectors are involved in logistics—the transport sector (including different modes of transportation), the warehousing sector, and related providers of value-added services. The 3PL business is complex, because it operates across all the subsectors involved.

Luo and Findlay (2001) reviewed developments in each subsector in China, including the basic facts of capacity, volume, and growth; evolution and reform of the subsectors; subsector infrastructure and organization; and administrative, regulatory, and policy issues. Some of the results relevant to this chapter are outlined in the next section.

The Logistics Sector in China

Growth of the logistics sector in China has been dramatic. Freight turnover in China increased from 76 billion ton-kilometers in 1952 to 4,381 billion ton-kilometers in 2000. The volume increased by 3.8 times between 1980 and 2000.

Evolution of Transport Services

In the political and economic environment of the early 1950s, China gave priority to heavy industries. A precondition for their development was a supply of cheap raw materials. This development in turn demanded a supply of cheap transport, and rail and

FIGURE 9.1   Choice of Transport Modes: China, 1970–2000

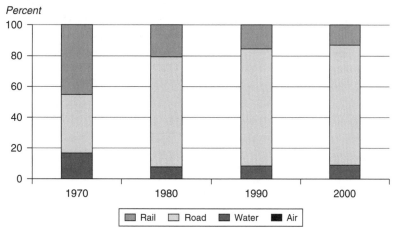

Freight traffic by mode (metric tons)

Source: Luo and Findlay 2001.

water were two modes of transportation that could provide transport services for large volumes at a relatively low price.

Figure 9.1 shows the composition of freight carried by mode (measured in weight) from 1970 to 2000. After 1978 the transport system in China was characterized by the rapid development of road and air transportation. The market shares of water and rail transport decreased sharply, reflecting the shift from the traditional heavy industries to light industries that demanded speedy, flexible transportation services and that could bear a higher transport service price. Figure 9.1 shows the rising share of road transport and the fall in the shares of rail and water in the total tonnage. Although it is not evident, data for air transport were included in the construction of the chart. Those numbers are very small compared with those for other modes, and therefore are not evident in the columns of the chart, but air freight volumes are growing fastest among all modes. As for trip lengths, they vary significantly by mode. The length of road trips is relatively short on average. Rail and water show longer trip lengths and therefore account for much higher shares of the transport task measured in terms of ton-kilometers. But even in these terms, the road share continues to grow, mainly at the expense of rail.

Constraints on Development

China's program of economic reform has gradually changed the ownership of its enterprises, especially in the manufacturing sector. But in the transportation sector the change has been relatively small; large, state-owned enterprises still dominate the sector. In recent years, the use of joint ventures has increased, especially in the container berth, container freight station, and motor carrier activities. However, these firms still account for only a small portion of the total number of enterprises. Road transport and shipping were deregulated in 1986, and rail and air transportation were also decentralized to some extent. The ownership structure has changed to different degrees in different modes of transportation. The road and inland shipping companies are dominated by collective and private enterprises, and coastal and international shipping, rail, and air transportation enterprises are still mostly state-owned.

The transport sector is still a weak link in China's economy:

- The number of either rail or road trunk lines linking regions is insufficient. The major railway lines are overloaded. The trunk lines of the highway system linking provinces are not well networked and cannot meet the demand. These impediments also contribute to differences in growth rates between regions.
- The coordination between different modes requires planning and development. Within each mode of transport, there are imbalances. In the rail sector, the mixing together of passenger trains with cargo trains on the busy lines leads to slower speeds and low efficiency. In the air

sector, there is an imbalance between the trunk and feeder lines and in the number of big and small aircraft. In the road sector, the construction of the national-level trunk road system has been accelerated, but in the rural areas the road network is far less developed.

- Service quality is generally low, as is the technical level of the equipment. For example, in the rail sector double lines and electrified lines represent a relatively small share of the total length of lines. Less than 20 percent of the freight trucks can carry containers.

The warehousing and storage system in the planned economy before reform was characterized by department or sector administration and operations—that is, sectors built and owned their own warehousing and storage facilities and served their own demands only. Many sectors formed their own closed warehousing systems.[2] Meanwhile, each local government at the provincial, city, and county levels established their own warehousing system to serve their local economy. Overall, therefore, government administration and enterprise functions are not separated, which constrains enterprise performance; the administration is fragmented in both vertical and horizontal dimensions, which inhibits the integration of services; and in some activities the quality of the physical infrastructure is insufficient.

Demand for 3PL Services

The demand for specialized logistics or 3PL services has begun to grow faster in recent years, especially that originating from the multinational companies, the leading Chinese state-owned companies, and some of the private companies, as well as that arising from the e-commerce sector. In the recent years, quite a few 3PL companies have appeared, including (a) international companies such as Maersk, UPS, and TNT; (b) traditional Chinese transport, warehousing, and forwarding companies such as COSCO and Sinotrans; and (c) emerging companies such as the Bao Gong Logistics Group.

Relevant departments in the central government have paid greater attention from different perspectives to the logistics sector and its development, and they have studied policies that they expect will promote it. Local governments such as Shenzhen,

Beijing, Tianjing, Shanghai, Guandong, and Shandong have also paid attention to the development of their local logistics sectors.

Most of logistics activities are still operated in-house, and demand for 3PL services is low among traditional Chinese firms. State-owned companies in China have inherited an operating model based on the provision of services in-house, including logistics. According to investigations by the China Warehousing and Logistics Council, a third party undertakes only 18 percent of the inbound logistics. As for outbound logistics, 59.8 percent is operated together with a 3PL firm, and only 16.1 percent is operated totally by a 3PL firm. Most Chinese firms keep their own logistics assets and personnel (Luo and Findlay 2001).

Although many 3PL firms have appeared in the marketplace, most of them offer a low standard of service and efficiency. For one thing, most of the firms provide only simple delivery and warehousing services: value-added services such information services, inventory management, logistics cost control, or logistics system design are not offered. For another, the scale of the firms is usually small, and most of them come from among traditional firms with weak network and organizational capabilities.

Moreover, modern logistics facilities such as transshipment facilities for different modes of transport, public warehousing and transport facilities, and logistics centers are not available. At low levels are the technology used for logistics equipment and the extent to which facilities are standardized and information technology is applied. Finally, logistics facilities are distributed unevenly—for example, transport facilities are less developed in the middle and western parts of the country.

An important constraint on the capacity of service providers to offer integrated services lies in the administration system—in particular, in the vertical and horizontal separations in the administrative systems that have carried over from the planning system, the self-protection that remains, the mixing of the enterprise with administration functions, and the lack of transparency in policy measures. All these issues, and the extent to which they impede the scope to gain from reform in the logistics sector, are examined in more detail after a review of the implications of China's WTO accession for the sector.

Accession to the WTO and Implications for the Logistics Sector

To provide integrated logistics services, a logistics sector must cover the following service elements: international and domestic transport (all modes); warehousing and storage; international and domestic freight forwarding; other value-added services such as logistics information (tracing and tracking), packaging and labeling, and quality control/inspection; and third-party logistics services.

Various GATS categories must be examined in order to incorporate the scope of logistics services as just defined. Although these categories are listed in the appendix to this chapter, this list is not comprehensive, and in some cases the impact of logistics activities must be inferred from packages of more specific commitments—for example, in relation to 3PL services.

Another issue related to the definition of the sector is coverage of the GATS category called "distribution." Distribution includes some activities that might normally be associated with logistics, such as warehousing and inventory management.[3] It appears, therefore, that some parts of a logistics sector, as might be defined in ideal terms, are already included in the category of distribution. However, distribution refers to these activities when undertaken in the context of wholesaling and retailing. Thus their coverage is much narrower than that which is relevant here.

Our assessments of the effects of the likely policy changes associated with WTO accession are divided into two types: direct and indirect. Direct effects are those on the costs and quality of services provided. Indirect effects are those on the regulatory or administrative environment.

Direct Effects

The direct effects of WTO accession on the logistics sector are presented in the appendix to this chapter and are summarized in tables 9.1–9.3. The tables show the starting position (table 9.1) and the impacts of the commitments one year after accession (table 9.2) and in the period three years after accession (table 9.3).

In general, China's accession to the WTO will have a positive affect on performance in the logistics services sector as a whole. Of the elements listed in the tables, only the air transport and water transport sectors are isolated from a significant change in policy. The commitments in many areas extend existing policy (e.g., customs clearance, container depot services, maritime agency services, road transport, rail transport, warehousing and forwarding, courier services). In others, the commitments bind current policy (international shipping). In some cases, geographic limits apply—in internal waterway transport, foreign firms can operate only on routes to ports open to foreign shipping.

TABLE 9.1   Starting Position of China's Logistics Sector

Area	Starting Position
Air transport	Relatively closed in both domestic and international routes
Water transport	Inland shipping open to domestic companies; coastal and international shipping relatively closed
Road transport	No restriction for domestic entry; foreign entry only by joint ventures
Rail transport	State monopoly
Forwarding	International forwarding: licensing system applies; foreign participation only via a joint venture
	Domestic forwarding: relatively open for domestic companies; not open to foreign companies
Storage and warehousing	No restriction for domestic entry; foreign entry only by joint ventures
Integrated services (3PL)	Determined by the above
Other (packaging)	No restriction for domestic entry; foreign entry only by joint ventures
Courier service	No restriction for domestic entry; foreign entry only by joint ventures

Source: The authors.

TABLE 9.2   Position of China's Logistics Sector One Year after WTO Accession

Area	Evaluation of Direct Impacts		
	High	Medium	Low
Air transport			✓
Water transport			✓
Road transport		✓	
Rail transport		✓	
Forwarding		✓	
Storage and warehousing		✓	
Integrated services (3PL)		✓	
Courier service		✓	
Other (packaging)		✓	

Source: The authors.

TABLE 9.3   Position of China's Logistics Sector Three Years after WTO Accession

Area	Evaluation of Direct Impacts		
	High	Medium	Low
Air transport			✓
Water transport			✓
Road transport (3)	✓		
Rail transport (6)	✓		
Forwarding (4)	✓		
Storage and warehousing (3)	✓		
Integrated services (3PL)	✓		
Courier service	✓		
Other (packaging)	✓		

Note: The numbers in parentheses show the number of years after accession when wholly owned foreign establishments will be permitted.
Source: The authors.

Discrimination against foreign suppliers will continue (mainly in terms of rules on the forms of establishment) for varying periods, which delays the benefits of reform. A schedule might be designed to capture some of the rents created in the transition to full openness. It also might be designed to slow down the transition and therefore (it is hoped) reduce the costs of adjustment. The consequence, however, may only be one of delaying those costs and adding to the risks of backsliding. Another goal may be to limit for a longer time foreign ownership in sensitive sectors. However, costs would be incurred, including the imposition on

foreign suppliers of second-best forms of participation in the market (joint ventures instead of wholly owned operations).

As discussed earlier, the demand for integrated services (3PL) is increasing, and so, more and more, logistics service firms are trying to provide or control the whole chain of the services. Therefore, a 3PL firm needs to have access to all the relevant licenses, which could include those for international freight forwarding, different modes of transportation (air, international shipping, domestic shipping, road, rail), storage and warehousing, container station and depot services, and courier services. The opening up of the different sectors in logistics, as discussed earlier, would have a significant impact on the ability of logistics firms to provide the whole chain of services.

Indirect Effects

This section assesses the indirect effects on the logistics sector of the reforms associated with China's accession to the WTO. These effects are summarized in table 9.4.

Local Protectionism Vertical and horizontal divisions within administrative systems constrain development of the logistics sector. For example, the administrative system that applies to transportation is divided according to the mode of transport, and the same systems operate at both the local and higher levels of government. The result is overlapping responsibility and power between the departmental and district administrations. These administrative structures are no longer suitable for the development of logistics activities for several reasons:

- Coordination of the different modes of transport services is difficult because the separation of different modes has resulted in differences in organization, service standards, and technical and equipment standards. This lack of consistency leads to the difficulties in developing multimodal services.
- Coordination of the construction of infrastructure is poor, which leads both to duplication of investments and to neglect of the development of transshipment centers.

- Self-protection is evident at the departmental and district levels. Policies and regulations are often designed according to the self-interest of the department, sector, or district involved. A local logistics firm will often seek protection from competition through the application of policy by departmental or district agencies, which hampers the development of cross-department or cross-district logistics networks (see box 9.1 for an example of local protectionism).

Reform of the administrative system will have to be accelerated to meet WTO rules. The more rapid reform will break down the scope to apply protection at the departmental and district levels, and it will facilitate competition in the market at a national level. Bosworth (2002) points out, however, that the obligations under the GATS covering subnational governments are weaker than those applying to national governments. The requirement is that WTO members take only "reasonable measures" to ensure that subnational governments meet their obligations. However, China's commitments under its Protocol of Accession specifically require that it maintain a uniform system of administration. Furthermore, the central government is required to establish a mechanism whereby those concerned about problems of regional protection can bring their concerns to its attention. These specific provisions seem likely to make the disciplines on China stronger than those under general WTO rules.

Separation of Government Administration from Enterprises Some government departments are still directly or indirectly involved in enterprise

TABLE 9.4 Summary of Indirect Effects of WTO Accession on China's Logistics Sector

Area of Existing Problems	Evaluation of Indirect Impact
Local protectionism	GATS obligations also apply at subnational government level.
Mixing of government administration and enterprise management	State-owned enterprises are under pressure to transform to a market-oriented operation, and government administration can be separated from enterprise management.
Inadequate infrastructure and facilities/equipment	Sector likely to attract more foreign investment.
Lack of research and professional skills	Foreign-invested enterprises will bring know-how, innovation, technology, and management.

Source: The authors.

BOX 9.1 Local Policies and Their Implications for Logistics Operations

The Jia Yu Freight Group Company is a new private transport and logistics services company. Its more than 20 branches cover most of the country to provide road express service in a fast-growing business. The company manager, Mr. Zhai, complains about the business environment, especially the local protection:

> We face many obstacles in operating our business and providing our services to customers. Transport needs both registration in the Administration Bureau of Industry and Commerce of the local government and a license from the Road Administration Bureau [RAB]. Each local RAB has a different practice. Some cities like Changzhou in Jiangsu Province and Wenzhou in Zhejian Province do not issue licenses to companies from other regions. Our trucks are not allowed to enter these cities. If we carry cargoes from their cities, we will be fined. Some cities are not so extreme in their treatment of the outside

transport companies, but we have to follow their special practice. For example, in Guangzhou we have to rent their designated office room with a higher rental in a specified place. Otherwise, we are not allowed to enter the market. In Guangzhou, we have to deposit a larger amount of money and administration fee. But whenever we meet difficulties, there is no assistance from them.

In general, local governments do not have identical rules and regulations. The road sector has been deregulated, but the local government always wants to protect its local companies by various means, which limits the development of cross-regional logistics services. "The strange thing is the more developed the region, the more restrictions there are on the outside firms. For example, in Chongqing we haven't met much difficulty in establishing our presence and operating our business," Mr. Zhai added.

Source: Author interviews.

activities. As already noted, in the railway and air sectors state ownership is still dominant. Port administration is mixed with port enterprise operations. These situations not only affect government functioning, but also weaken the competitiveness of the enterprises.

Logistics Infrastructure and Facilities/Equipment
The scale of the infrastructure and the quality of facilities and equipment available to logistics services suppliers are relatively poor. The assessment by the Hong Kong Trade Development Council (2002) is that the airport infrastructure is a "major impediment to aviation industry growth." Furthermore, there is an imbalance in development between the eastern and western parts of the country. Road and rail transport, storage and warehousing, container station and depot services, and airports are some of the areas that could attract more foreign investment after accession.

Human Resources Research on logistics, especially among business firms, is rare, and the professional education system has so far included little logistics training. Foreign investment and establishments in the logistics services sector will bring with them technology and management know-how. The

relevant know-how includes not only the operation of particular segments of the logistics operation, but also the manner in which the elements fit together, as well as the management of the relationships between all the suppliers and the customers. Opening other service sectors, such as education, will also raise the quality of options available for education and training in this sector.

Cost Savings in the Third-Party Logistics Sector

Little empirical work has been conducted on the efficiency of the logistics sector in China or on the impacts of reform. Some ideas about methodology and some indicators of the scale of impacts are available, however, from work done in other markets—for example, on the effects of the integration of transport markets in Europe (European Commission 1997).[4]

Those studying the European logistics services markets identified eight input-oriented measures of logistics performance: (1) customer orientation; (2) integrated long-range planning; (3) supplier partnerships; (4) cross-functional operations; (5) continuous improvement process; (6) employee empowerment; (7) integrated information technology (IT) systems; and (8) measurement, comparison, and action.

Different stages of development of the logistics sector can be identified through the use of these indicators. Higher levels of performance, as measured by these indicators, lead to better performance in terms of the costs of each element of the service and in terms of other indicators such as on-time delivery, order completeness, invoice accuracy, and damage-free delivery. All these features can therefore be summarized in the total cost of logistics services, which refers to the sum of inventory, administrative, warehousing, and transportation costs. Not only does market opening lower the prices of the direct inputs (e.g., transport), but it also raises services quality and thereby lowers other costs (e.g., warehousing or inventory, or allowances for losses).

Transport is usually the single major component of logistics costs. For example, in 1992 in Europe logistics costs were on average 10.1 percent of revenue, down from 14.3 percent in 1987. The 1992 share comprised 3 points for transport, 2.3 points for warehousing, 1.9 points for administration, and 2.9 points for carrying inventory. The logistics cost share of revenue was expected to fall to 9.1 percent in 1997. In the firms regarded as leaders in the operations of logistics, the logistics share of revenue was estimated to be as low as 6.5 percent (1992), 36 percent lower than the overall average. The largest decreases over this period in Europe were observed in the component associated with inventory costs, followed by those linked with administration, warehousing, and transportation. Transport, even in those leading companies, remains the largest single component of total logistics costs.

The significance of logistics costs varies between sectors of the economy as illustrated in table 9.5.

According to Gibson (2001), electronics is associated with a significantly higher share of logistics costs in total revenue than textiles. Gibson also notes that in some sectors, such as fresh food, logistics costs can be 50–60 percent of total revenue.

The table also illustrates the variation in the significance of logistics costs in Asia and those in Europe—the latter are lower by 24 percent. Gibson (2001) suggests that in China logistics could account for 30–40 percent of the total cost of manufactured goods. Another source suggests that "supply-chain-related costs can be 30% to 40% of wholesale prices in China, compared to 5% to 20% in the U.S."[5] The Hong Kong Trade Development Council (2002) refers to an assessment that logistics account for 40 percent of general production costs and that "logistics . . . takes 90% of the whole production cycle time."

A key factor in the performance of the logistics sector is the damage rate. One source reports that for fast-moving consumer goods, the damage rate is 5 percent in China compared with "well below" 1 percent in developed economies.[6] High rates of product loss lead to requirements for higher inventory levels. The costs of inventory and product loss can be significant, which reduces the relative importance of the transport component of the total cost of distribution. Switching to a higher-quality logistics service, even one that charges higher fees, for example, a foreign provider can then lower overall logistics costs if the costs associated with product loss are reduced sufficiently.

Boillot and Michelon (2000) provide a breakdown of the total logistics costs in China. They report that losses and damage account for 48 percent of the total, compared with 21 percent for transport activities. They also quote industry

TABLE 9.5   Logistics Costs as a Share of Total Revenue, Europe and Asia, 2001 (percent)

Sector	Europe	Asia
Textile	8.7	11.5
Automotive	8.9	13.5
Chemicals	10.2	13.8
Fast-moving consumer goods	10.4	14.0
Electronics	12.6	14.0
Average	10.4	13.7

Source: Gibson 2001.

estimates that total logistics costs could fall by 37 percent if the current arrangements for managing logistics were replaced by a subcontracting approach. The bulk of this reduction appears, in their assessment, to be attributable to the reduction in losses and damage rather than a reduction in profit margins. Management fees may increase to reflect the higher costs of the higher levels of management inputs in time and experience.

In summary, a more open market for logistics services that transfers the technology for the redesign and management of integrated services is likely to have significant effects on total logistics costs in China. The composition of those costs will change—for example, management fees will increase, but this change will be offset by reductions in other items, not necessarily in the transport component but more likely in the costs associated with damage, losses, and inventory.

To summarize this discussion, if total logistics costs are 30–40 percent of wholesale prices in China, as suggested earlier, and if those costs fall by 35 percent, then logistics costs as a share of wholesale prices would fall by 10–14 percentage points, to 20–26 percent of wholesale prices. But even this assessment may be conservative, because logistics costs as a share of the wholesale price in China is still above the average for Asia in table 9.5. It also lies above that observed in developed market economies, although there are limitations on the extent to which comparisons of these ratios can be made across countries.[7]

Implications for Less-developed Areas in China

As noted in the previous section, reforms associated with China's accession to the WTO could result in a fall in logistics costs equal to 10–14 percent of wholesale prices in China. In an example developed by Radelet and Sachs (1998), suppose that a region of China faces a perfectly elastic demand for its output and a perfectly elastic supply of purchased intermediate inputs that come from outside the region. Suppose that the share of purchased inputs in gross value is 30 percent. If then logistics costs are 35 percent of the value of output and inputs, the value added is 24.5 percent of the value of output. If logistics costs fall to 23 percent of the value of output, the value added rises by 64 percent, to reach 40 percent of the value of

output. Changes in logistics costs even in the range suggested here can make a significant difference in the value added available for distribution to the factors of production. If the payment to capital is fixed, then the amount of valued added available to labor changes by an even greater proportion.[8] This example illustrates the significance of logistics efficiency for inland areas of China.

A more efficient logistics sector will benefit people living in poor areas in several ways. For example, as implicit in the example just given, their terms of trade will improve; the costs of items they buy from the rest of China will be less, and the prices they receive for the items they export to the rest of China will be higher. The impact of reform, which reduces logistics costs, also generates extensive real gains: the impacts on real incomes are greater than those of the removal of a tax, for example. The impact of tax removal includes transfer effects, but when logistics costs are reduced, resources are saved. In other words, the rectangle effects are gains, not just transfers (see Deardorff 2001).

Reductions in transport costs can also lead to significant increases in trade orientation. Some of the orders of magnitude involved in these effects are illustrated by the work on Africa by Limao and Venables (2001) who estimate the response of trade to reductions in transport costs. They find an elasticity of 2.5, which could be applied to the reduction of 35 percent in logistics costs, according to the assessment reported earlier.

The opening up of markets stemming from improvements in transport and logistics services also can have effects on competition in the local markets. And competition itself has additional effects. One is the impact on the rents available. The suppliers who previously had monopoly power are constrained by the options now available to their customers to seek supplies from outside the region. Thus not only does regulatory reform lower costs, but also its competitive effects force the passing on of those cost reductions to consumers in business and in households.[9] Firms that previously earned rents from their protected position are clearly worse off, but overall the region will realize a welfare gain from the introduction of competition. In terms of the welfare of those people living in the poor area, this effect is even larger when those who captured the rents were not local firms.

Competition, and a greater foreign (both from out of the country and out of the region) presence in all markets within a poor area, also could have a dynamic effect on, for example, the transfer of technology and productivity growth. This effect is likely to be greater in those services markets where an establishment is required to deliver the activity, and where there is therefore more interaction between the new supplier and local firms.

After markets become more competitive, some localities may continue to lack services of a quality typical of those in more developed areas. Governments often respond to this situation by subsidizing the provision of services. Subsidies might be arranged within the sector (supported by a regulatory structure that facilitates these transfers between consumers), or through explicit payments from the budget. The design of these policies includes important efficiency considerations, both on the funding side and in the manner in which the subsidies are applied.

Gruen (2001) has questioned and proposed options for the management of service obligations. The popular approach to a service obligation policy is to use cross-subsidies between consumer groups to provide specific services (e.g., a rail link) to all residents in a particular area. Gruen suggests instead strategies in which services are provided to well-defined target households and where the recipients have options for the manner in which they receive that support ("cashing out," for example, or at least substitutability between modes of supply—in this case, of transport services). Analysis of costs and benefits of alternatives is important—for example, those of building a road to an existing community or implementing an option for relocating that community.[10]

An important consideration in the design of policies to support provision of services to poor areas is their consistency with obligations under the WTO on subsidies. Models for the design of these policies are available, however—for example, in the WTO's April 1996 reference paper on basic telecommunications, which notes:

> Any Member has the right to define the kind of universal service obligation it wishes to maintain. Such obligations will not be regarded as anti-competitive per se, provided they are administered in a transparent, non-discriminatory and competitively neutral manner and are not more burdensome than necessary for the kind of universal service defined by the Member.[11]

China can learn much from the considerable experience in the rest of the world with community service obligation policies, and the scope for China to innovate in policy development in this field is great.

Conclusions

The China experience illustrates that the design of commitments in the GATS is complicated in new business areas. For example, the GATS categories do not match exactly the business structures used to provide logistics services. However, it is possible to make a concordance: China's commitments, which are significant and which in most parts go beyond a binding of current policy, provide a template that other developing economies may consider for this sector.

China's experience also illustrates how WTO commitments can open up the component activities of the logistics sector, including areas that in the past might have been regarded as nontradeables. The commitments thereby also facilitate the growth of third-party logistics providers. The design and management of the provision of services in this field is important; not just the extent and quality of physical capacity matters. The presence of foreign providers of these integrating services will be facilitated by the WTO commitments.

A feature of the set of commitments reviewed here was the application of timetables for their implementation. Some motivations for that approach can be identified, but it comes at some cost, including the higher risks of backsliding and the use of inefficient forms of business organization by firms that enter in anticipation of further market opening—for example, where joint ventures are permitted but full foreign ownership is not.

One of the challenges, however, is to promote complementary administrative and regulatory reform. The China case highlights the risks associated with administrative structures, even at the central level, that add to the complexity of establishing the most efficient business structures (e.g., for intermodal transfers of freight). Perhaps an even more important issue is to translate national commitments to the WTO into local government policy, especially in regions where there has been a tradition of using regulatory instruments to protect local businesses. Implementation of the principles of transparency and nondiscrimination in the application of business regulation are important elements of the extent to which markets are actually opened to foreign competition.

A more open logistics sector, especially through the growth of 3PL providers, can lead to significant cost reductions. One estimate, based on assessments of the state of logistics services in China by industry commentators, is that the more widespread presence and use of efficient and internationally competitive 3PL providers could lower costs by an amount equivalent to at least 10 percent of the wholesale price of manufactured goods on average. The impact on these relative terms may be even higher for fresh food produce. These amounts are not simply transfers, but real gains associated with the saving of resources. For example, an important source of gains is the lower wastage rates in transport and warehousing.

Changes of these magnitudes in the quality of transport services could have important effects for poor areas. Their lack of access to markets in the rest of the country and in the rest of the world is an important constraint on their development. A more open and competitive logistics sector will remove some of the impediments to their participation in trade within the economy and with the rest of the world. The effects of lower logistics costs on value added and on the total value of wages paid and available for distribution to workers are significant. In an example reported here, a 12 percentage point reduction in the logistics costs in the wholesale value of goods leads to an increase in value added of more than 60 percent.

However, some impediments remain to the supply of services in remote areas. Policies to support the provision of services where these impediments apply are not inconsistent with the GATS, but they should be evaluated against alternative strategies for promoting the income growth of those communities.

Appendix: China's Commitments on Logistics Services–Related Sectors and Their Implications

Air Transport

Air transport remains quarantined from GATS coverage except for a limited number of complementary services.[12] Even in these areas, China's commitments are relatively limited.

1. Aircraft Repair and Maintenance Services

COMMITMENT

Foreign service suppliers are permitted to establish joint venture aircraft repair and maintenance enterprises in China. The Chinese side should hold a controlling share or be in a dominant position in the joint ventures. Licenses for the establishment of joint ventures are subject to an economic needs test.

IMPLICATIONS

The commitment effectively binds current policy. Two joint venture aircraft repair and maintenance service firms are already located in China: AMECO (founded in July 1989) with a 40 percent foreign share and GAMECO (founded in August 1989) with 50 percent share. Binding policy may reduce uncertainty from the perspective of potential entrants. Further entry would add to competition and may facilitate the introduction of new technology and management expertise in aircraft repair and maintenance, so that a higher volume of qualified services are made available within China.

2. Computer Reservation System (CRS) Services

COMMITMENT

For cross-border supply:

- Foreign computer reservation systems, when having agreements with Chinese aviation enterprises and the Chinese computer reservation system, may provide services to Chinese aviation enterprises and Chinese aviation agents by connecting with the Chinese computer reservation system.
- Foreign computer reservation systems may provide services to representative offices and sales offices established in the destination cities in China by foreign aviation enterprises that have the right to engage in business under the bilateral aviation agreements.
- Direct access to and use of foreign computer reservation systems by Chinese aviation enterprises and agents of foreign aviation enterprises are subject to the approval of the general administration of the Civil Aviation Administration of China (CAAC).

IMPLICATIONS

The commitment refers only to foreign connection with the Chinese system. The commitment confirms policy as it is now. Chinese carriers have code-sharing arrangements with carriers in more than 10 foreign countries, but direct foreign participation in the provision of CRS services is not allowed. Commercial presence by foreign providers is still not permitted.

Water Transport (International and Domestic Shipping)

1. Maritime Transport Services: International Transport (Freight and Passengers, (CPC 7211 and 7212 Less Cabotage Transport Services)

COMMITMENT

Registered companies may be added for the purpose of operating a fleet under the national flag of China. Foreign service suppliers are permitted to establish joint venture shipping companies, but the foreign investment shall not exceed 49 percent of the total registered capital of the joint venture. The chairman of the board of directors and the general manager of the joint venture shall be appointed by the Chinese side.

IMPLICATIONS

The commitment is the same as current policy.

2. Auxiliary Services: Maritime Services (CPC 741), Customs Clearance Services for Maritime Transport

COMMITMENT

Foreign participation is possible only in the form of joint ventures, but foreign majority ownership is permitted.

IMPLICATIONS

Joint ventures are already allowed, but currently the maximum foreign share is 49 percent. The commitment relaxes that constraint.

3. Container Station and Depot Services

COMMITMENT

Foreign participation is possible only in the form of joint ventures, but foreign majority ownership is permitted.

IMPLICATIONS

Joint ventures are already allowed, but currently the maximum foreign share is 49 percent. The commitment relaxes that constraint.

4. Maritime Agency Services

COMMITMENT

Foreign participation is permitted in the form of joint ventures, but the foreign equity share may not exceed 49 percent.

IMPLICATIONS

Maritime agency services are not presently open, so this commitment is significant. The level of foreign ownership remains constrained, however.

5. Internal Waterways Transport: Freight Transport (CPC 7222)

COMMITMENT

For cross-border supply: international shipping is possible on routes to ports that are open to foreign vessels.

IMPLICATIONS

This policy will apply only in ports open to foreign shipping. In 1999 there were 130 such ports.

Road Transport

Road Transport Services: Freight Transportation by Road in Trucks or Cars (CPC 7123), Storage and Warehousing Service (CPC 742)

COMMITMENT

Foreign participation is permitted in the form of joint ventures, but the foreign equity share may not exceed 49 percent. Within one year of China's accession, foreign majority ownership is permitted. Within three years of China's accession, wholly foreign-owned subsidiaries are permitted.

IMPLICATIONS

In the road transport sector joint ventures are allowed at present, but foreign partners are allowed only a minor share (less than 49 percent). This sector is now very competitive with low margins because it was subject to domestic deregulation in 1986. Road transport is an essential link of the logistics chain and, of all the transport sectors, plays the most important role. Moreover, of the four modes of transport, the road sector is the fastest growing. Foreign logistics firms might have an interest in participating in the road transport sector by either providing new capacity (perhaps in special road transport services) or buying an existing fleet. Some of the effects of deregulation include greater use of subcontracting and larger-scale and lower-cost operations.

Rail Transport

Rail Transport Services: Freight Transportation by Rail (CPC 7112)

COMMITMENT

Foreign participation is permitted in the form of joint ventures, but the foreign equity share may not exceed 49 percent. Within three years of China's accession, foreign majority ownership will be permitted and within six years of accession wholly foreign-owned subsidiaries will be permitted.

IMPLICATIONS

Railway transport continues to be monopolized by the government. China's WTO commitment in this sector reveals its intention to open this transport up to the outside world. The process is, however, slower than that in the road sector. Only six years after China's accession to the WTO will wholly foreign-owned subsidiaries be permitted. Some parts of the rail sector are profitable, and others are not (e.g., in rural areas). Foreign firms will take an interest in the profitable lines or regions.

Evidence from other markets indicates that productivity in rail is related to government policy. Key factors include degree of managerial autonomy and the extent of subsidies made available. Higher levels of private (and foreign) ownership would be expected to add to productivity in this sector. One important issue is how the unprofitable lines can be maintained if that is required to meet service obligations. The effects of reform in this area could be significant. According to one source, "Most logistics companies and distribution managers continue to argue that there is never a good reason to use rail for transport." Factors in this view include damage rates, delays, slow speed, lack of information and booking requirements, and lack of route flexibility.[13]

Warehousing and Storage

Storage and Warehousing Services (CPC 742)

COMMITMENT

Foreign participation is permitted in the form of joint ventures, but the foreign equity share may not exceed 49 percent. Within one year of China's accession, foreign majority ownership is permitted,

and within three years of accession wholly foreign-owned subsidiaries are permitted.

IMPLICATIONS

Storage and warehousing are an important link in logistics services. Joint ventures are allowed at present, but foreign partners are allowed only a minor share. The margins in this sector are low. There also appears to be excess capacity, but the service standard is low, and the mix of services available does not match demand. The opening up of the market could help foreign-owned logistics suppliers establish their own presence in this sector by either building new warehouses or buying the existing warehouses that are appropriate.

Forwarding

Freight Forwarding Agency Services (CPC 748 and 749, Excluding Freight Inspection)

COMMITMENT

Upon China's accession, foreign forwarding agencies that have at least three consecutive years of experience are permitted to set up freight forwarding agency joint ventures in China, with foreign investment not to exceed 50 percent. Within one year of China's accession, foreign majority ownership is permitted. Within four years of accession, wholly foreign-owned subsidiaries will be permitted. The minimum registered capital for a joint venture is to be no less than US$1 million. With four years of accession, national treatment will be accorded in this respect. The term of the joint ventures shall not exceed 20 years. After one year of operating in China, the joint venture can set up branches, but another US$120,000 should be added to the original registered capital of the joint venture for the setup of each branch. Within two years of China's accession to the WTO, this rule on an additional registered capital requirement will be implemented on the national treatment basis. A foreign freight forwarding agency may set up a second joint venture after its first joint venture has been in operation for five years. Within two years of China's accession to WTO, this requirement will be reduced to two years.

IMPLICATIONS

Joint ventures are allowed at present, but the foreign partner is allowed only a minor share. Within four years of China's accession, wholly foreign-owned subsidiaries will be permitted. Foreign-owned firms could enter the market easily after the restriction is lifted. Many firms have already presented themselves in the market in the form of a joint venture. Although, according to the regulations, only a minor share is allowed, the foreign partner actually may control the business. Some firms enter the market by using the "shell" of a domestic company. Complete opening of the market will reduce for these firms the costs of providing forwarding services and also enhance their ability to provide "whole of chain" services.

Related Areas

Courier Services (CPC 75121, Except Those Currently Specifically Reserved to Chinese Postal Authorities by Law)

COMMITMENT

Upon China's accession, foreign service suppliers are permitted to establish a joint venture, with foreign investment not exceeding 49 percent. Within one year of accession, foreign majority ownership is permitted. Within three years of accession, foreign service suppliers are permitted to establish wholly foreign-owned subsidiaries.

IMPLICATIONS

Courier services are an important part of logistics services. A joint venture is allowed at present, but only with a minor share for foreigners. The opening up of this sector could bring up more competition in this market, and there is already evidence of the interest of foreign firms in this sector.

Packaging Services (CPC 876)

COMMITMENT

Foreign service suppliers will be allowed to establish a joint venture in China. Within one year of China's accession, foreign majority ownership is permitted. Within three years of China's accession, foreign service suppliers are permitted to establish wholly foreign-owned subsidiaries.

Notes

1. These sections are summaries of the material in Luo and Findlay (2001). For a review of developments in the logistics sectors in three East Asian economies, including China, see Heaver (2001).

2. These systems operated in these sectors: raw material and components *(wu zi)*, manufactured consumer products *(shang ye)*, rural area suppliers and distributors *(gong xiao)*, foreign trade goods *(wai mao)*, railway, road, and water transportation *(jiaotong)*, military, and basic food *(liang shi)*.

3. Distribution (trade) is different from logistics. But the related subordinated services are increasingly likely to be included in the logistics sector, because the sector has taken on more and more of the value-added services demanded by shippers. As defined, distribution trade services are composed of four main subsectors: commission agents' services, wholesaling, retailing, and franchising. The principal services rendered in each subsector can be characterized as reselling merchandise, accompanied by a variety of related subordinated services, including inventory management; assembly, sorting, and grading of bulk lots; breaking bulk lots and redistributing into smaller lots; delivery services; refrigeration, storage, warehousing, and garage services; sales promotion, marketing, and advertising; and installation and after-sales services, including maintenance and repair and training services (covered by CPC [Central Product Classification] 61, 62, 63, and 8929).

4. The experience of regulatory reform in the United States can be used as another comparator. A longer time-series of data on the European experience may also now be available.

5. Andrew Tanzer quoting McKinsey & Co. in "Chinese Walls," *Forbes Global*, November 12, 2001. Available at www.forbes.com/global/2001/1112/091.html.

6. Economic Intelligence Unit, China Hand (database), December 1999, Chap. 12, Sec. 1.

7. The ratio of logistics costs to wholesale prices in different countries will depend not only on the characteristics of the product, but also on the factor intensities of the different production processes of both the logistics services and the manufactured products and the relative factor prices in the economy concerned.

8. For example, if the cost of payments for capital is 20 percent of the value of output, the funds available for the wage bill rise by a factor of 3.5 as logistics costs fall from 35 to 23 percent of wholesale prices.

9. According to anecdotal evidence, this effect has appeared in markets for light industrial products made in the past by township and village enterprises. Brand-name products from suppliers based in eastern China are now much more widespread.

10. Gruen also discusses the value of broadening the funding base for service obligation policies.

11. Available at www.wto.org/english/tratop_e/serv_e/telecom_e/tel23_e.htm.

12. See Hong Kong Trade Development Council (2002) for another review of China's WTO commitments in transportation and logistics.

13. Economic Intelligence Unit, China Hand (database), December 1999, chap. 12, sec. 3.

References

Boillot, Jean-Joseph, and Nicholas Michelon. 2000. "The New Economic Geography of Greater China." *China Perspectives* 30 (July–August): 18–30.

Bosworth, M. 2002. "Most-Favoured-Nation Treatment and National Treatment in the GATS." In Sherry Stephenson and Christopher Findlay, with Soonhwa Yi, eds., *Services Trade Liberalisation and Facilitation.* Canberra: Asia Pacific Press, ANU.

Coyle, J. J., E. J. Bardi, and J. C. Langley. 1996. *The Management of Business Logistics.* 6th ed. St. Paul, Minn.: West Publishing Co.

Deardorff, A. 2001. "International Provision of Trade Services, Trade, and Fragmentation." *Review of International Economics* 9 (2): 233–48.

European Commission. 1997. *Impact on Services: Transport Networks*. The Single Market Review, subseries II, vol. 11. Luxembourg: Office for Official Publications of the European Communities.

Gibson, Ken. 2001. "Analysing the Trends: Predicting the Future of Logistics in Asia." Presentation to the conference "Toward the Final Frontier: Logistics and the Efficient Supply Chain." September 27. Available at www.dnmstrategies.com/presentation/tnt/sep_2001/KenGibsonV1.0-0945.pdf.

Gruen, N. 2001. "Beyond the Safety Net—A View from Outside." Presentation to the APEC Telecommunications Working Group, Canberra, March.

Heaver, T. 2001. "Logistics in East Asia." Development Economic Research Group, World Bank, Washington, D.C.

Hong Kong Trade Development Council. 2002. "China's WTO Accession: Enhancing Supply Chain Efficiency—Transportation and Logistics." Hong Kong.

Limao, N., and T. Venables. 2001. "Infrastructure, Geographical Disadvantage and Transport Costs." *World Bank Economic Review* 15: 315–43.

Luo W., and C. Findlay. 2001. "Analysis of Logistics Service Sector in China: Accession to the WTO and Its Implications." Paper prepared for Authors' Workshop on WTO Accession and Poverty Reduction, Beijing, October 26–27.

Radelet, S., and J. Sachs. 1998. "Shipping Costs, Manufactured Exports and Economic Growth." Paper presented at American Economic Association Meetings, Harvard University. Processed. Available at www2.cid.harvard.edu/hiidpapers/shipcost.pdf.

Redding, S., and T. Venables. 2000. "Economic Geography and International Inequality." CEPR Discussion Paper Series No. 2568. Centre for Economic Policy Research, London, September.

WTO (World Trade Organization). 1996. Telecommunications services: Reference Paper, Negotiating Group on basic telecommunications. WTO, Geneva. Available at http://www.wto.org/english/tratop_e/serv_e/telecom_e/tel23_e.htm.

10

TELECOMMUNICATIONS SERVICES IN CHINA: FACING THE CHALLENGES OF WTO ACCESSION

Mari Pangestu and Debbie Mrongowius

Despite some significant reforms, China's telecommunications sector since the country's accession to the World Trade Organization (WTO) remains one of the most restricted and regulated of those in the major developing countries in the region. During the WTO negotiations, liberalization of this sector was a critical issue both because of its growth potential and because it was considered one of China's "key national industries."[1] By the end of the decade, China is projected to become the largest market for telecommunications services in the world, creating a strong incentive for foreign players to enter the market.[2]

Reforms were sought before and in association with China's WTO accession, as well as in response to technological advances and the gradual commoditization of services.[3] However, competition remains constrained, and obstacles include lack of clear and concise legislation, regulatory implementation, and regulatory independence. The key challenge for China is to ensure that regulatory reforms and new institutions will create greater competition that will maximize the benefits for the Chinese economy as well as meet equity objectives.

This chapter has several goals. The first major section seeks to examine the pace and progress of change in China's telecommunications services sector and to assess China's position at the beginning of

the five-year phase-in period under its WTO accession agreement. The second section sets out to analyze the effects of current reforms on greater efficiency, reduced costs, improved quality, and greater access in the sector. The third and fourth sections evaluate the post–WTO accession environment faced by China and analyze the possible direct and indirect implications. The final section draws general conclusions and policy implications about the telecommunications sector in China.

The Landscape of the Telecommunications Industry before WTO Accession[4]

In anticipation of the liberalization commitments it would have to make upon its accession to the WTO, China began in 1994 to undertake reforms to increase competition in its telecommunications sector. It took tentative first steps in 1994 to change the monopoly structure, but only in the last five years, beginning in 1998, has it undertaken major reforms.

Tentative First Steps: Constrained Competition

Up to 1994 China Telecom was the sole basic telecommunications services provider in China. New market entry was prohibited, and the Ministry of Posts and Telecommunications (MPT) not only regulated the sector but also operated telecommunications services. In 1994 the China United Telecommunications Corporation (Unicom) was created to improve service quality by introducing managed competition (see chapter appendix). However, pricing policies, such as service fees, remained under the MPT, and individual operators were not able to compete through the price mechanism. Unicom faced an uphill battle in its early years.[5]

The biggest problem faced by Unicom was getting access to the backbone infrastructure controlled by China Telecom. When Unicom was first granted fixed-line services in some provinces, the local China Telecom operators refused to allocate phone numbers to Unicom, which held up interconnection for over a year. Another problem was securing access to capital, which Unicom did largely by using "gray area" measures, the most well known of which was the Chinese-Chinese-Foreign (*Zhong-Zhong-Wai* or CCF) joint venture enterprise structure, to circumvent the ban on foreign direct investment (FDI) in the sector. The government subsequently initiated an investigation into the legality of CCF ventures in light of the 1993 directive forbidding foreign investment in the sector. The investigation resulted in restrictions on CCF arrangements: a mandatory limit on agreements of 15 years, a five-year limit on profit sharing, and transfer of 90 percent of all network assets to the Chinese party.

Another company, Jitong, was created in 1994 as part of the "Golden Bridge Network"—a government initiative to develop a series of information networks. Jitong's original objective was to provide data services via satellite connections, and it was intended to compete with China Telecom. Most of Jitong's services have now been shifted to an Internet protocol (IP) network infrastructure. These services include Internet access and gateway services; value-added services such as Web site hosting, server management, and e-commerce solutions; and VoIP (Voice over Internet Protocol). In early 1999 Jitong was the first Chinese operator to offer VoIP, and it became at once a dominant player in the market.

The reforms undertaken up to 1998 were significant first steps, but the competition remained constrained, the service quality poor, and the prices uncompetitive by global standards. Prices were still set by the MPT, the State Pricing Board, and the

State Development Planning Commission (SDPC). In response to the inefficiency in the telecommunications system and its inability to provide connection, rural communities began to finance and establish their own systems to provide basic service in their areas. These town and village enterprises (TVEs) then merged into larger organizations providing wider coverage and eventually set up administrative relationships with the local office of the MPT. In addition, various networks had also evolved within separate industries and institutions in order to compensate for the supply shortage in the public network maintained by the MPT. These networks included those for the academic and research communities, the military, the railways, and the oil industry.

To separate the regulatory and operational function of the MPT, as well as to respond to changes in technology and administrative reforms, the Chinese government created the Ministry of Information Industry (MII) in March 1998.[6] This "super agency" was created by merging the MPT; the Ministry of Electronics Industry (MEI); and parts of the State Administration of Radio, Film and Television (SARFT), China Aerospace Industry Corporation, and China Aviation Corporation. The MII worked closely with the State Economic and Trade Commission (SETC) in setting policies for the information industry about the introduction of foreign investment and technologies, as well as in establishing industry strategic development plans. However, the independence of the MPT and China Telecom was not convincingly demonstrated, in part because many of the senior staff at the MII came from the MPT.

Breaking Up the China Telecom Monopoly

The MII's fear that the monopoly it enjoyed would be sacrificed as a "pawn" for China's accession to the WTO, and its conviction that national interests would be compromised if China's telecom industry did not survive the resulting competition, galvanized the ministry into devising a survival plan, beginning in 1998. This strategy involved creating a favorable policy environment for China Unicom and breaking up the China Telecom monopoly.

In 1999 the MII launched major restructuring efforts by splitting China Telecom into three state-owned companies and reinvigorating Unicom. The three companies emerging from China Telecom were: China Telecom for fixed-line business; China Mobile Communications Corporation (CMCC or China Mobile) for mobile phone business; and China Satellite (ChinaSat) for satellite communications. In addition, a new company, China Netcom Corporation (CNC) was established to build a broadband Internet protocol network. The division of enterprises by subsector reflected MII's plan to speed up the development of individual service sectors.

In 2000 a license was also given to Railcom, which was part of the Ministry of Railways, to provide all basic telecommunications services except mobile. Thus, together with Jitong, at the end of 2001 there were seven major operators in the telecommunications sector. More than 3,000 different enterprises are engaged in Internet-related and other value-added businesses, which enjoy greater operational freedom and are market-oriented. Current operators are only granted licenses that specify the type of telecom service they may offer (table 10.1).

Only Unicom has a license to undertake all services except for satellite. Although mobile telephony is the most rapidly growing sector in the industry, currently there are only two mobile phone licensees and no clear indications about whether an additional license will be issued despite much speculation that China Telecom will be awarded the coveted license. Other advantages of Unicom include being allowed to charge 10 percent lower rates than China Mobile, the right to operate a code division multiple access (CDMA) mobile phone system[7] and to list its shares on the Hong Kong (China) stock exchange. Unicom also has a modern management structure, because it did not inherit an existing state-owned enterprise structure.

China Mobile has listed shares from its most profitable subsidiaries through China Mobile Group (Hong Kong) Co. Ltd. The latter company listed 24.4 percent of its shares on the Hong Kong and New York stock exchanges. Its stated development strategy is to shift from traditional circuit-switched networks to broadband packet-switched IP networks and to diversify from pure wireless voice service to mobile image and data services. Its competitive edge over Unicom in the mobile sector is its financial resources, geographic coverage, and brand name.

China Telecom owned most of the backbone infrastructure and leased it to the others. Only China Telecom and China Mobile, which originally was part of China Telecom, operated in all provinces. As for mobile phone market, Unicom has been given a boost since its first uphill struggle due to some of the advantages mentioned above, and it has reached a market share of about one-third. Even though other operators are covering some areas, Unicom's coverage appears to be quite extensive, with expansion plans in place.

TABLE 10.1   Network Operators and Licensing, China (end of 2001)

Company	Fixed-Line	Cellular	Paging	VoIP	Data[a]	International Gateway	Satellite
China Telecom	✓		✓	✓	✓	✓	
Unicom	✓	✓	✓	✓	✓	✓	
China Mobile		✓		✓	✓[b]	✓	
China Netcom				✓	✓	✓	
Jitong[c]				✓	✓	✓	✓[d]
Railcom[e]	✓			✓	✓		✓
ChinaSat							✓

[a]Data includes fax and Internet transmission.
[b]Only mobile data transmission.
[c]Jitong serves only corporate clients and has since merged with China Netcom and part of China Telecom.
[d]Only VSAT.
[e]Although Railcom is licensed to provide services other than fixed-line, it has yet to develop the capability to do so.
Source: Compiled by authors.

TABLE 10.2 Network Operators in China: Description of Network and Coverage

Company	Networks		Coverage	
	Own	Lease[a]	Current	Planned
China Telecom	✓		All provinces	Add capacity for 18.5 million new telephone subscribers and 7.1 million data communication users.
Unicom	✓	✓	180 cities; mobile: 322 cities	CDMA coverage for 200 cities
China Mobile	✓		All provinces; GPRS service in 25 cities and 16 provinces	GPRS for all provinces
China Netcom	✓	✓	18 major cities	Add 15,000 km of fiber-optic cable
Jitong	✓	✓	120 cities; 30 cities covered by city-area networks; 1,000 VSAT stations	180 cities by 2002
Railcom	✓		28 cities, 14 provinces	100 cities, all provinces
ChinaSat	✓		All provinces[b]	n.a.

n.a. Not available.

Note: GPRS = general packet radio service.

[a]Although all operators have built their own backbone networks, China Telecom still maintains a monopoly over end local loops throughout the country. Currently, interconnection fees must be negotiated individually at every China Telecom province administration.

[b]This includes 120 duplex remote stations providing access to remote regions such as Guangxi, Guizhou, Inner Mongolia, Qinghai, Tibet, and Yunnan.

Source: Compiled by the authors.

As for universal service obligations (USOs), all operators are subject to these obligations, but there are no clear implementing regulations. Because China Telecom is the primary owner of the functional local end loops, some believe it eventually will be the major deliverer of universal service. Already required to provide telecommunications services to government organizations and emergency services, it has implicitly been the one given the task of providing universal service.

Regulatory Framework

Since 1998 the Ministry of Information Industry has been the regulator of telecommunications and other information technology–related products and services, including data communications, wireless communications, electronics, computers, the Internet, and software. The MII reports to the State Council and is a member of the State Information Leading Group (SILG), which is the government agency that links the central government (State Council) and the MII and other government bodies in charge of information security and enforcement. The SILG was created in the mid-1990s in response to the growth of Internet service and computer crimes. The group wields much control and influence over the development of the sector, and approves and modifies the framework for industry regulations and the future direction for the industry, and measures to implement policy. The State Council Informatization Office (SCIO) was formed under the SILG in August 2001 as the executive arm with a mandate to explain and carry out government policy. SCIO is a high-profile organization, and it plays a more direct role than SILG in developing and implementing information policy in China.

Because the Internet involves information flows to the public, which raises issues of censorship and security, other relevant authorities are the State Secrets Bureau, Ministry of Public Security (network security), and the State Administration for Industry and Commerce, which is responsible for registering Internet service providers (ISPs) and

Internet content providers (ICPs). The MII, State Development Planning Commission, and Ministry of Finance (MOF), with approval from the State Council, determine prices and rates.

Prior to the reforms that began in 2001, various issues arose about the regulatory framework. One was the independence of MII from the incumbent telecom operators, since the latter still comprised of officials from the Ministry of Post and Telecommunications (MPT) structure and still influential in the new MII structure. Other issues are that although the MII supervises the telecom network, SARFT presides over cable markets, and other departments regulate the Internet. Given the number of authorities in charge of the overall sector, it is often not clear who is in charge of policies and guidelines for the sector. Another general problem—not just for regulation of the Internet but more generally—is the gap between national and local policies. Shanghai, for example, has taken the lead in encouraging e-commerce, and local authorities have forged ahead without approval from the central government.

To address the problems between national and regional policies, provincial telecommunications authority (PTA) offices were set up in 2001 to conduct the regulatory function within each province.

Performance of the Sector: Impact of Reforms Prior to WTO Accession

The effects of reforms and the introduction of competition, albeit controlled by the government, are expected to include lower prices, better quality of service, high growth and telecom penetration rates, and major changes in the structure of the industry.

Decline in Prices

Prices for basic telecom services have come down considerably in the last few years, but more because of mandated price reductions than pure competition. After all, the MII retains a considerable degree of control over the sector through price controls as well as through licensing. The MII justifies its control of prices by pointing to its desire to maintain stability in the market and avoid disruptive price wars. The procedure for telecom rate changes begins when an operator submits a proposal, which is followed by State Council department and ministry discussions. Public hearings on the proposed prices must then be held before the prices are resubmitted to the State Council for final approval and implementation. In practice, basic telecommunications service fees have come down since 1999.

In 1999 the MII slashed service fees, in part to address consumer complaints, but also to increase consumer access to advanced technology and to rationalize the fee structure in anticipation of China's WTO entry. The move was also part of a strategy to provide universal service. The drastic cuts accelerated telephone popularization in rural areas, doubled the number of Chinese accessing the Internet, and enabled Chinese Internet service providers to expand their business and telecom facilities, which in turn benefited Chinese Internet content providers. Reducing long-distance rates was intended to cut down on "information smuggling"—that is, channeling calls to China through Hong Kong (China), where rates were lower.

In early 2001, the MII, the SDPC, and the MOF jointly announced massive cuts in telecommunications and Internet usage fees. Those cuts were followed by a second round of cuts in July 2001. Local phone charges per unit dropped from being charged at three minute to one minute intervals, and the charge was set at 0.10 yuan ($0.01[8]) per minute. Monthly service fees for fixed-line telephones also dropped from 24 yuan ($2.90) to 18 yuan ($2.17), and fixed-line phone installation fees were eliminated completely. Domestic long-distance charges have been standardized at 0.70 yuan ($0.08) per minute and additional charges on long-distance calls will no longer apply. Long-distance charges for calls to Hong Kong, Macao, and Taiwan were standardized at 2 yuan ($0.24) per minute, while the rate for international calls was set at about 8 yuan ($0.97) per minute. Initial installation fees have been eliminated as well, and the price to lease lines from China Telecom was lowered by 72.8 percent.

On top of the mandated price cuts, several operators continued to announce further rate cuts of up to 40 percent for domestic long-distance calls, while doubling the rates for local calls to maintain their operational profits. At the local level, individual operators have underpriced themselves slightly when they have felt local conditions required it. Most competition in pricing takes place through packaging mechanisms, which are not subject to the constraints of the established price ranges.

An example of price competition and its effect on reducing prices is evident in those services, such as IP telephony, where the government does not have price controls. There, intense competition has led to reductions in the price of long-distance calls. A price war on IP telephony was introduced in 2001 by China Netcom. The IP phone card, a prepaid device for long-distance calling, became very popular because it can save callers up to 70 percent on their long-distance call charges. CNC then further reduced their charges by another 50 percent, pricing IP domestic long-distance calls at 0.3 yuan ($0.036) per minute and overseas calls at 2.4 yuan ($0.28) per minute. When the other operators—China Telecom, Unicom, Jitong, and China Mobile—followed suit and reduced their IP prepaid cards, the government had to lower long-distance rates in the face of such competition.

Most of these rates appear to be artificially low and to require significant rebalancing before the sector can become fully competitive. IP card rates may be the only ones that closely reflect the true costs of these services.

Profitability of the Industry

The resulting decline in prices for long-distance calls had a serious effect on China Telecom's overseas listing plans, because China Telecom holds a franchise on fixed-line phone service and makes most of its money from long-distance calls. China Mobile (listed in Hong Kong) and Unicom should be able to benefit significantly from the changes because both companies lease lines from China Telecom for their voice and Internet businesses. By contrast, China Mobile, Unicom, China Netcom, and Jitong could be adversely affected by the changes in Internet protocol telephony. With China Telecom's rates falling, the discount margin for using IP telephony has been narrowed significantly, removing much of the attraction for using the service in the first place. In 2001 China Mobile's average revenues per user fell by 35 percent, leading to a fall in its share prices and those of Unicom's. The additional users of mobile are not subscribers; they are using prepaid cards for which the cost of administration and use is much lower.

It remains unclear how profitable each operator is under current conditions. Those operators who have partially listed on the stock exchange must regularly reveal the financial conditions of the listed subentities, but a significant portion of their businesses remains undisclosed. Corporatization has not severed the state connection, and it is not possible to discern exactly how much support they still receive from their shareholders and how many are actually sustained purely by generated revenues. Furthermore, many board members and top-level management continue to be closely connected with the state authorities. The support that these relationships could continue to generate, in any terms, is utterly unquantifiable. China Telecom, China Mobile, Unicom, and China Netcom claim that they are no longer subsidized by the state and are able to run a stand-alone operation profitably.

Licensing and the forced divestiture of China Telecom's mobile and paging components have reduced cross subsidization between products or interproduct subsidization, although this possibility has not been eliminated entirely.

Growth and Competition in the Different Subsectors

Fixed-Line   The number of fixed-line subscribers has increased substantially in recent years, especially in the post-1998 reform era. In 1996 there were 54.9 million fixed-line subscribers—a number that had doubled to 108.8 million by 1999. By the end of 2002 this number had almost doubled again, with the number of users reaching 180.4 million. By the end of 2003 the number of fixed-line users reached 210 million (figure 10.1) or slightly lower than the number of mobile users. This increase represents a growth rate of 27 percent p.a. or per year over the 1996–2003 period. The penetration rates of the population for fixed-line telephony have gone up from 10 percent in 1998 to 14 percent in 2003, still leaving considerable scope for growth. Even though Unicom and Railcom had licenses to provide fixed-line services, China Telecom remained the dominant provider with 99 percent of the market.

Mobile Phones   Mobile telephony began to increase significantly with the introduction of the GSM (global system for mobile communications) networks in 1995. Domestic and international roaming capability was introduced in 1996. The

FIGURE 10.1   Mobile and Fixed-Line Use in China, 1996–2003 (millions)

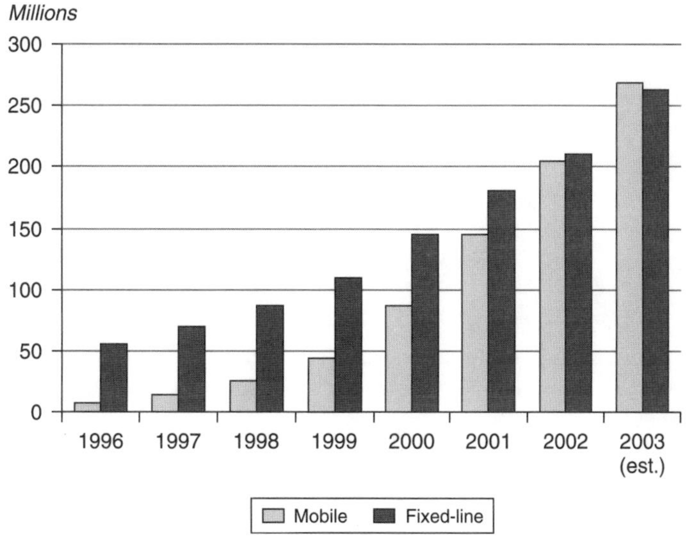

Source: Ministry of Information Industry.

number of mobile subscribers in China grew from 7.3 to 44.3 million over the 1996 to 1998 period, and surpassed the number of users in the United States in 2001, reaching 144.8 million (compared with 120 million in the United States) (figure 10.1).[8] Growth has continued, and the number of subscribers reached 268.7 million by the end of 2003, and for the first time was slightly higher than the number of fixed-line users at 263.3 million. This increase represents a dramatic growth rate of 86 percent over the 2001–2003 period. As a result, the penetration rates have also increased. An important contributing factor to the increase in the number of mobile phone users has been the introduction of prepaid cards, which do not require subscriptions or monthly user fees.

Of the only two licensed mobile phone operators in China, both are state-owned companies. Although the market share of UNICOM has increased, China Mobile's share of the market is still dominant at about two-thirds. In this mobile telephony market, the two participants in the duopoly have been reluctant to work together. For example, lack of number portability eliminates much of the incentive for consumers to switch service operators. Newly attained market share rarely comes at the expense of the incumbent; instead, most of the uptake comes from new sub-

scribers. In an effort to eliminate this type of "arbitrage" opportunity between operators, the MII has begun to standardize.

The issuance of additional mobile licenses is the subject of great debate. It remains unclear whether the government will issue new licenses, despite indications that such plans are under way to increase competition in the sector and despite the need to have new licenses issued to operators during the transition to third-generation (3G) technology. However, it is unclear which technology standards and which 3G technology should be used. A time division synchronous code division multiple access (TDSCDMA) was recently created within China, with standards parallel to those of the wideband code division multiple access (WCDMA) standard favored by European and Japanese companies. TDSCDMA was also approved by the International Telecommunication Union's telecom division as one of the three international 3G standards.

Internet   The number of Internet users[9] in China has also increased rapidly, rising 20-fold—from about 1.2 million in 1997 to reach 22.5 million in 2000 (figure 10.2). By the end of 2002 the number had more than doubled again, to 59.1 million. About two-thirds are dial-up users, and the remainder are connected through leased-line

FIGURE 10.2   Internet Users in China, 1996–2002

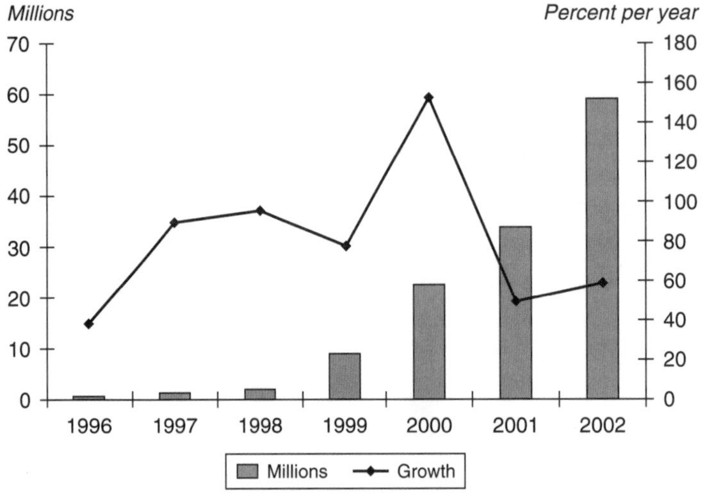

Source: Ministry of Information Industry 2003.

connections or use both dial-up and leased lines. Despite the high growth rates, China is a long way from being considered a "wired" nation.

The chief bottlenecks for further expansion of Internet use include high costs and slow speeds in most areas. The maximum transmission rate of the telephone lines used by most people to access the Internet is only 56 kilobits per second, making downloading and uploading very time-consuming. Although an integrated services digital network (ISDN) was introduced in 1998, it remains costly and is still of insufficient bandwidth to allow for more sophisticated online usage and programs.

Shanghai has been able to benefit by using the more advanced asynchronous digital subscriber line (ADSL) services since the beginning of 2000.[10] ADSL is not the only broadband technology available. More mature technologies include hybrid fiber/coax (HFC), digital subscriber line access (DSLx), local multipoint distribution service (LMDS), and fiber-optic cable. HFC has to date been applied in only a few selected pilot project locations. Much of the difficulty in getting this technology installed in a wider area arises from issues of convergence. The HFC broadband access technology is the cable modem, which allows transmission of data to computers and television sets at the same time. Regulatory reforms are required for this technology to be approved on a nationwide basis.

Perhaps one of the more interesting developments in the industry—and a step on the way to convergence—is the evolution of Voice over Internet Protocol (VoIP) services. Despite significant resistance from existing operators and the MII, the possibility of providing reduced long-distance costs, up to 70 percent less than conventional long-distance rates over the fixed line provided by China Telecom, led to intense competition for the provision of this service. In recognition that it would be difficult to control this development, MII legalized VoIP, and incumbents such as China Telecom have seen their revenues drop by an estimated $130 million because of the increase in VoIP usage. This increase in competition could come about very quickly because IP networks can be built and deployed more rapidly than other networks. The MII was forced to create a framework to allow the incumbents to provide these services as well. Currently, five of the six telecommunications carriers are licensed to provide VoIP services. Foreign network providers and local paging companies have come together in alliances to seek a share of the lucrative market.[11]

Competition and Improvements in Quality of Service

Five regulations governing the quality of services have been promulgated by the MII in the last few years related to periodic reports about the quality of service, frequency of publication, and service quality maintenance, including how to manage

TABLE 10.3   Impacts of Reforms on China's Telecommunications Industry, 1998–2003

	1998	1999	2001	2003
Backbone optical cable line (yuan per thousand km)	180.8	194.1	340	
Fixed asset investment (billions of yuan)	168.1	151.8		
Telecom services business volume (10 million of yuan)	226.49	313.24	350 (est.)	
Price (yuan)			June 1	
Fixed (LAN) line installation (analog)	1,010	725	Free	Free
Domestic leased lines (digital, per month)				
For telecommunications services		9,000	3,000	1,500
For Internet services		4,500	2,000	1,000
International leased lines (per month)				
Hong Kong, Macao, and Taiwan (China)		27,400	2,800	
Other Asia		28,900	14,000	
Other		30,800	15,000	
Domestic long-distance fee (per minute)		0.5–1.00 (depending on range)	0.7 (flat fee)	
Internet connection fee (per minute)			0.02	
Mobile network access fee	800	500	Free	
Users (millions)				
Fixed-line	87.4	108.8	180.4	263.3
Urban	62.6	74.6		171.3
Rural	24.8	34.1		92.0
Mobile phones[a]	23.9	43.2	144.8	268.7
Fixed-line penetration (per 100 people)	10.5	13	18.9	21.2
Computers with Internet access	2	8.9	22.5	
Competition				
Number of players	2	5	7	6[b]
Mobile	2	2	2	2
Fixed-line	2	2	3	3
Data	1	2	2	2
VoIP	0	1	5	5
Market share of China Mobile (percent)	95	89	75	68
Market share of Unicom mobile (percent)	5	11	25	32

[a]Various estimates say mobile phone use will hit 300 million by 2005.

[b]After the breakup of China Telecom into north and south, with north and Jitong being absorbed by ChinaNetCom.

Source: Various issues of *China Daily* and MII.

complaints from customers. It is difficult to measure whether the limited increase in competition to date has led to improvements in quality. However, interviews do reveal that there has been a change in attitude at China Telecom, which is servicing its customers better.

Since 2000, the Telecom Consumer Complaints Handling Center under MII has made public all complaints made against telecom companies. Notices on complaint handling will be published every three months. Service quality reports submitted regularly by the telecom agencies to the MII will be published every six months. The results of surveys and evaluations of customer satisfaction will be published annually. All other information related to service quality will be published irregularly and according to circumstance. Recently, telecom companies were warned that if they do not provide good service, they will be given a warning by the MII or will face losing their license altogether. However, the effectiveness of this mechanism on the quality of service remains to be seen.

China's WTO Commitments and Changes in the Regulatory Framework

A series of reforms and regulatory changes preceded China's accession to the WTO on December 11, 2001, and reforms continue in line with meeting China's WTO commitments, which are to be completed over the next five years. However, delays in completion of the regulatory framework prompted some of China's fellow WTO Members to express concerns during China's transitional review (WTO 2003).

WTO Commitments

China's WTO commitments in the telecommunications sector open up the telecom market to foreign participation, and bring the domestic regulatory and business environment in line with international standards (box 10.1). The commitments have two main components. The first is removal of limitations on market access by allowing right of establishment and removal of limitations on national treatment. Foreign investment is allowed to enter, but initially at a lower ownership level and with geographic restrictions. Over a period—two years for value-added services, five years for mobile telephony; and six years for domestic and international services—the geographic restrictions are removed. However, foreign ownership is capped at 50 percent for value-added services and 49 percent

---

BOX 10.1   Summary of China's WTO Commitments

The main commitments are to open up for foreign entry, which is currently prohibited. The opening up is undertaken in phases for geographic area and percentage of foreign ownership, and agreement to give national treatment to foreign firms. China also has to abide with the WTO's April 1996 reference paper on basic telecommunications.

Value-added services (electronic mail, voice mail, online information and database retrieval, electronic data interchange, enhanced facsimile services, code and protocol conversion, online information and data); paging services: no limitations on cross-border supply except for right of establishment, no limitations on consumption abroad, and no limitations on national treatment. On right of establishment, upon accession joint ventures with up to 30 percent foreign ownership will be allowed to provide services in Beijing, Guangzhou, and Shanghai. Within one year, this arrangement will be expanded to Chengdu, Chongqing, Dalian, Fuzhou, Hangzhou, Nanjing, Ningbo, Qingdao, Shenyang, Shenzhen, Xiamen, Xian, Taiyuan, and Wuhan. The amount of foreign investment is not to exceed 49 percent. Within two years, there will be no geographic restriction, and foreign ownership can be up to 50 percent.

Mobile voice and data services (analog/digital/cellular services, personal communications services): no limitation on cross-border supply except under right of establishment, no limitations on consumption abroad, and no limitation

on national treatment. On right of establishment, upon accession joint ventures will be allowed in Beijing, Guangzhou, and Shanghai, with foreign ownership of up to 25 percent. Within one year, areas will be expanded to include services in Chengdu, Chongqing, Dalian, Fuzhou, Hangzhou, Nanjing, Ningbo, Qingdao, Shenyang, Shenzhen, Xiamen, Xian, Taiyuan, and Wuhan, with foreign investment allowed up to 35 percent. Within three years of accession, foreign investment will be no more than 49 percent, and within five years the geographic restriction will be removed.

Domestic and international services (voice, packet-switched, circuit-switched, facsimile, domestic private leased circuit services, international closed user group voice and data services): no limitation on cross-border supply except under right of establishment, no limitations on consumption abroad, and no limitation on national treatment. On right of establishment, upon accession joint ventures will be allowed in Beijing Guangzhou, and Shanghai, with foreign ownership of up to 25 percent. Within five years, areas will be expanded to include services in Chengdu, Chongqing, Dalian, Fuzhou, Hangzhou, Nanjing, Ningbo, Qingdao, Shenyang, Shenzhen, Xiamen, Xian, Taiyuan, and Wuhan, with foreign investment allowed up to 35 percent. Within six years of accession, foreign investment will be no more than 49 percent, and the geographic restriction will be removed.

for mobile telephony and domestic and international services, indicating that a foreign majority is not desired. The second component requires China to adhere to the WTO's April 1996 reference paper on basic telecommunications, which sets out principles on the regulatory framework for basic telecommunications services.

September 2001 Regulations

Prior to China's formal accession to the WTO in December 2001, some observers had been anticipating the introduction of a telecommunications law, because work on one had been under way since 1986, with earlier attempts dating back to the early 1980s. However, the law was not announced prior to China's accession and provisional telecommunications regulations were issued in September 2001 in line with China's WTO commitments in the telecom sector.[12] These regulations and some follow-up regulations are a very important first step toward developing a comprehensive and pro-competitive regulatory framework, but many issues of interpretation, clarity, and implementation remain, and some areas have not been adequately addressed. Moreover, as regulations, they do not have the full effectiveness of a true telecommunications law. The

major elements of the regulations are described in the following sections.

Defining Coverage The working definition used in the WTO schedule is that basic telecom service encompasses local, long-distance, and international services for public and non-public use; may be provided on a facilities basis or by resale; and may be provided through any means of technology (e.g., cable, wireless, satellite). In anticipation of this working definition, the 2001 regulations defined telecom services as services provided by means of carrying, sending, or receiving sound, data, images, or any other information through a hard-wired or wireless system. This definition is intended to cover broadcast networks, the Internet, and related services in order to provide the legal basis for the "convergence" of information technologies (Horsley 2000). A summary of definition of coverage is provided in box 10.2.

Foreign Investment Foreign investment issues are not explicitly addressed in the regulations, although a schedule for phasing in foreign ownership was set out in China's protocol of accession to the WTO. In addition, Regulations for the Administration of Foreign Invested Telecom Enterprises

---

BOX 10.2 Coverage and Definition of China's Telecommunications Sector

Basic telecommunications services are fixed-line local and long-distance telephony; mobile telecommunications including analog and digital trunk systems, analogue cellular services, second (2G) and third (3G) generation mobile telecommunication services; satellite communications; Internet, and information transmission; sale or lease of bandwidth, wavelength, fiber optics, cable, or any other network elements; network access and out-sourcing; international telecommunications infrastructure and international telephony business; wireless paging; and resale of basic telecom services.

Value-added services refers to services in which the supplier adds value to the information by enhancing its content or providing storage and retrieval. These include nine categories: e-mail, voice mail, online information database and retrieval, electronic data exchange, online data processing and transaction handling, value-added fax, Internet access service, Internet information service, and videoconferencing.

An additional five categories were introduced in 2001: fixed-line-based, value-added telecom services, including telephone information, paging, message recording, and restoring and video conferencing services; mobile phone value-added telecom services; satellite value-added telecom services; Internet value-added telecom services, including Internet access, data center, information, analog private network, videoconferencing imaging, and other Internet-based services; and other data transmission and network telecom services, including computer information, electronic data exchange, messaging, e-mail, fax restoring and forwarding, and analog private network services.

Source: Telecom Service Classification Catalogue (annex to PRC Telecommunication Regulations, October 1, 2000) and Notice Regarding Adjustment of the Telecom Service Classification Catalogue, June 21, 2001.

(FITE Regulations) came into effect on January 1, 2002. An additional MII directive was issued in early January 2002. The Administrative Measures for Telecommunications Business Operating Permits defined changes in registered capital requirements, permit applications, and approvals processes, as well as operating and annual auditing requirements.

Responding to the Requirements of the Reference Paper   The September 2001 regulations also incorporated many of the specific requirements on creating pro-competitive regulations and administration that are contained in the WTO Agreement on Basic Telecommunications Services. The main elements of pro-competitive regulations and procedures contained in the regulations are as follows.

Competitive safeguards are incorporated to prohibit unreasonable cross-subsidization of other businesses, actions that limit subscribers from using services of other operators, and the provision of below-cost services. In addition, an operator is not allowed to restrict subscribers to using only services or equipment specified by the operator, refuse or delay service without justification, increase rates or items for which it charges fees without the approval of the regulator or customer, provide misleading information, or refuse to carry out its commitment to subscribers.

As for *licensing*, all telecom service providers need a license and have to meet the transparency requirements and the criteria of eligibility for a license. A time limit has been set for making decisions on licensing applications and for making available the reasons for denial. In issuing the license, the issuing agency must consider its impact on national security, network safety, the sustainability of telecom resources, environmental protection, and competition. The pending issues here are the implementing regulations and details on how the MII and the provincial regulators will evaluate these factors and handle issues such as auctions.

The provisions related to *domestic interconnection* are in line with the reference paper in requiring major operators not to refuse other operators' requests for interconnection and the use of nondiscriminatory and transparent interconnection procedures, including how disputes should be resolved. The operators must also "unbundle" the network elements they sell so that the supplier only pays for the network components or facilities required.

Universal service is to be provided in a transparent, nondiscriminatory, and competitively neutral way, and operators should carry out any relevant national provisions for universal service. The regulations refer to some form of subsidy or cost recovery without being specific and linking it to the competitive safeguards. However the regulations did not make clear how universal service will be implemented.

Resource allocation of scarce resources such as frequencies are to be done in an objective, transparent, timely, and nondiscriminatory way. The regulations in fact go beyond the reference paper by referring to the establishment of an auction-based system of allocating telecom resources including frequencies and network numbers. Leading operators are required to ensure that such users can utilize their network resources. However, it is not clear what form the implementing regulations will take.

Restructuring of the regulation and administration of the telecom sector in line with the reference paper requirement to have an independent regulator has begun, but it is still unclear what the final outcome will be and how long the process will take. The reference paper calls for the regulator to be separate and not accountable to operators and suppliers, and be impartial and nondiscriminatory in dealing with all market participants.

In the September 2001 regulations the MII remained the institution designated "to oversee and control the telecommunications industry of China." Surveillance and control of the sector were to abide by the following principles: "the separation of administrative departments and enterprises; the breakdown of monopolies and the encouragement of competition, transparency, fairness and just practice." The official position is that the operational and regulatory functions were separated through the creation of the MII in 1998 (WTO 2003: para. 78). How objective and impartial MII can be in dealing with China Telecom and China Mobile remains a source of concern, given close associations between the incumbents and MII.

In September 2001 the government set up a new commission to decide on major policies for the telecommunications sector and prepare the new law. The MII will be in charge of implementing those rules and administering standards (Dow Jones Newswire, September 20, 2001). The setting up of the commission is intended to lead to the required objective changes in policies and laws and will pave the way for the independent regulatory body. However, since at present MII is still charged with implementing the rules and administrative standards, one has to wait for the implementing regulations and mechanisms to be in place to assess how objective the outcomes will be.

Other provisions in the telecom regulations address the provision and quality of telecom services, network construction, and security. Requirements of greater transparency imply that there could be a greater role for the nongovernment sector—operators, users, and other relevant parties—in providing input to rates, as well as implementation of regulations, setting of standards, and so on.

Regulations Regarding Internet and E-Commerce[13]

Given the rapid development of this segment of the industry and of technology, regulations are still catching up with current conditions. Currently, China has over 300 Internet service providers and over 600 Internet content providers. Of the ISPs, only 53 have MII approval to provide nationwide services, and the remainder are approved by the local provincial telecommunications authorities, or PTAs, to provide restricted services. The latest regulations require ISPs to obtain permits to do business and require ICPs to register and record within the MII/PTA system currently in place. ISPs must no longer require foreign investors to find a Chinese partner in order to gain approval.

Regulations issued in 2001 on Internet information services, electronic bulletin board services, and online news publishing specify registration procedures for providers. Even though the rules exist, local authorities have reiterated the rules, and in some cases extended the deadlines, for the necessary approvals. In conjunction with the Ministry of Public Security, the Ministry of Culture, and the State Administration for Industry and Commerce (SAIC), the MII also issued in 2001 new measures for the "Administration of Places that Provide Internet Access Services"—that is, they govern Internet cafes. Those cafes that have already been approved by the relevant authorities are now required to apply for reexamination and approval. For example, Internet cafes may not set up within a 200-meter radius of primary and middle schools and are forbidden to set up in a residential building.

Whereas for E-Commerce the issue of whether to tax e-commerce has not been resolved, and

China's State Administration of Taxation has set up a strategy and research group to discuss the issue of e-commerce taxation and conduct research on the logistics of an e-commerce tax policy. The group's findings will be the basis for new e-commerce regulations to meet the requirements of China's Internet economic development, differentiate and standardize business activities on the Internet, enhance the government's role in the sector, protect the lawful rights and interests of enterprises and consumers, crack down on illegal business activities, maintain the socioeconomic order, and establish an e-commerce operations registration system.[14]

Recent Changes in Institutional Structure and Preparation of a New Telecommunications Law

The MII minister was appointed director of the State Council Informatization Office in June 2003—the first time one person was placed in charge of both MII and SCIO. Some say it is a step closer to merging the two agencies to oversee the country's telecom, electronics, and information technology industry and become the new independent regulatory agency. However, at this stage it is not clear how and when the regulatory agency will be set up.

Meanwhile, the telecommunications law was still being drafted in late 2003 (WTO 2003: para. 71); policy reforms and rapid changes in technology had forced revisions of the drafts before they were even issued. There have been various updates and clarifications since the September 2001 regulations and they are going in the right direction. This includes greater transparency such as specification of deadlines for approval of licenses in basic telecom (180 days) and value added services (60 days) and requiring the authorities to provide an explanation for decisions. In August 2003 the State Council announced its "opinion" on the broad framework for telecommunication market administration as part of the results of the commission set up to look into telcom regulations.[15] This included strengthening and facilitation interconnection policy with fees to be based on costs incurred by the operator, and sanctions and penalties on violation of interconnection. This issue is important in light of the disagreements on interconnection pricing between mobile and fixed line networks. The scope of the telecommunication law confirms that the authorities have convergence in mind, that so, that

FIGURE 10.3   Restructuring of China's Telecommunications Industry, 1994–2003

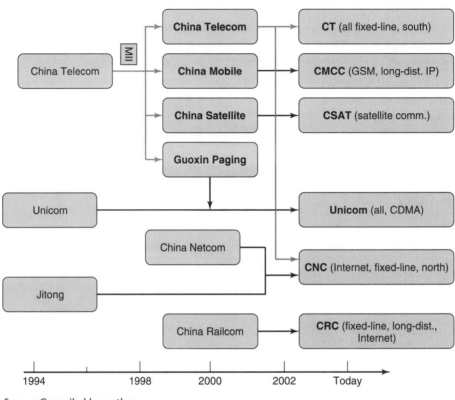

Source: Compiled by authors.

the framework law is intended to include operations of telephony, internet, and cable TV indicating that all of the subsectors will come under one framework law. However, even though the organization and administration of the new regulatory authority was announced in broad terms, it was not clarified how the responsibilities between MII and SARFT will be reallocated. Other issues addressed with greater transparency and market based principles in mind, were implementing regulations for market entry, distribution and administration of scare resources (e.g. frequencies), service fees, quality standards, and information security.

Restructuring: Government-Driven Mergers and Consolidation

Other than regulatory changes, the authorities have also restructured the sector through government rather than market driven mergers and consolidations. In 2002 China Telecom was split along regional lines. Operations covering the northern 10 provinces were merged with China Netcom and Jitong to form the China Netcom Communications Group Corporation. The 21 southern operations retained the China Telecom name and operate as a separate entity. Figure 10.3 shows the restructuring efforts since 1994 up to the last change.

Corporatization efforts to improve the performance of the sector and raise capital continue. In November 2002 China Telecom listed the four profitable networks in Guandong, Jiangsu, Shanghai, and Zhejiang in the Hong Kong and New York capital markets, raising $1.5 billion. Meanwhile, China Netcom is still undertaking internal reorganization in merging the three separate entities (China Telecom north, Jitong, and the original China Netcom), and, as a result, its plans to list shares on the capital markets have been delayed, with a public offering now planned for 2004.

The Potential Direct Impact of Reforms and Outstanding Issues

What is the expected impact of the current set of reforms and WTO accession commitments on the telecommunications sector? First, the sector will be challenged to be competitive and efficient before the likely entry of foreign investment stemming from China's WTO commitments, and it will face increased pressure to meet customer satisfaction, as well cope with the restructuring that is under way domestically. Second, the industry has to respond to rapid changes in technology. Meeting these challenges will require further restructuring of the sector, new investments from both the government and private sector, and the transfer and development of the appropriate technology and infrastructure (hard and soft). The evolution of the sector should be managed carefully, because there is the danger of over investment and over capacity, which will be influenced by the regulatory environment facing the sector. The sections below address the potential competition and impact on the different subsectors, and issues related to developing the appropriate regulatory environment.

The Potential for New Entrants and Managing Competition

It is unlikely that China would have opened up its telecommunications sector to foreign entry without the pressure it faced in bargaining for WTO accession (Mueller and Lovelock 2000; Zhang 2001). Now, even though the schedule allows new entry and permits foreign investors to come in over the next few years under the WTO commitments, it is unlikely that a flood of new foreign entrants will materialize. Because of the large size of the investment and the higher risks of an uncertain regulatory environment, foreign interest will be limited unless there is a credible commitment from the regulators to implement the planned regulations. In any event, foreign majority ownership will not be allowed in key areas, and foreign ownership is capped at 49–50 percent, with entry still based on obtaining a license to operate.

Interviews with foreign telecom operators and industry people conducted from mid-2001 to mid-2002 indicate that capping foreign ownership was not a major disincentive, but the lack of specificity on the regulations for foreign investors was. An important barrier to entry to fixed-line operators is the dominance of the incumbent, China Telecom; the lack of certainty surrounding interconnection to its backbone infrastructure; and the drastic

decline in prices and the fall in monopoly rents with the commoditization[16] of fixed-line use. The only area in which prices could decline further is international rates, which will face increased pressures to fall given the advent of VoIP. Perhaps a more important concern is that most foreign telecom operators are currently not in a position to undertake huge investments in China.

Thus it is unlikely that new entrants will enter the fixed-line subsector, except possibly in segments requiring low capital requirements. Increased competition in fixed-line is unlikely to come from liberalization or privatization, because the majority ownership is expected to remain with the state. Rather, the priority will be on creating the regulatory framework, including the institution, to create the pro-competitive operating environment and complete the corporatization process so that China Telecom and China Netcom will operate more efficiently. The government-driven process of mergers and consolidations is likely to continue to be the modus operandi.

As for mobile phone services, the rapid progress of technology in this subsector, combined with declining costs and an infrastructure cost lower than that for fixed-line telephony, make it attractive to investors. Yet toppling the major barrier to entry, obtaining a license, remains elusive. Licenses to operate mobile services, as with any other basic service, are issued at the discretion of the central authorities, and although the procedures for greater transparency in the issuance of licenses were laid out in the September 2001 regulations, there is no indication when new licenses will be opened. Additional licensing to operate mobile services has so far been linked to technology such as 3G and standards such as those represented by UNICOM's CDMA, although a decision on the technology standard has yet to be made.

The mobile telephone market is still a duopoly with very little competition in this subsector. Backdoor attempts at entering the market by, for example, mobiles that operate from the fixed-line network within limited areas have been halted indefinitely.[17] Moreover, because the applications for value-added services that use the latest technology do not yet exist in China, technology alone will not provide enough of a catalyst for users to switch. Another problem for competition is that as yet there is no number portability—that is, users cannot

FIGURE 10.4 **Share of Revenue by Operator, 2001 and 2002**

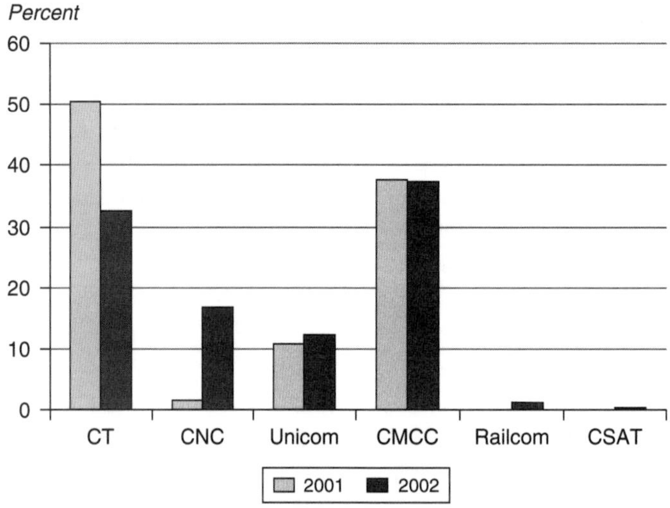

Source: Ministry of Information Industry.

switch services without switching their numbers. Therefore, the technology alone does not provide enough of an incentive to switch services. The attractiveness of mobile telephony is also reduced because roaming charges are based on the caller pay party principle.

The main challenge facing the mobile industry in China—as everywhere—is the commoditization of call fees as the average revenue per user continues to decline. To find new revenue streams, mobile operators need to seek out new partnerships with value-added service providers. One model is the cooperation between Unicom and ICPs (e.g., Montro). Another value-added service that is booming is the short messaging service (SMS). Foreign and new entrants are likely to take part in the value-added and specialized services segments of this subsector.

Another issue is what will happen to the existing internal networks that developed in response to the inefficiencies and high cost of using China Telecom? Many ministries such as the State Power Commission and the Ministry of Railways built their own internal networks. One of the important government-supported networks is the one developed by the agency that administers the state radio, SARFT. The network already has 90 million users and is planning to connect all existing networks.

Finally, the government also plans to upgrade the CATV network so that it can also transmit Internet data. The first broadband services system using television cable was recently introduced in Daqing City in Heilongjiang Province. The opening of the system on CATV represents a major break-through in the country's broadband progress. The benefits to the industry could be substantial, if the government can come to a final decision on how fast it wants convergence to take place.

Development of Internet and the New Economy

Although certain barriers such as low credit card penetration and an underdeveloped distribution infrastructure will exist for some time in China, Internet usage and everything associated with it, including e-commerce, are expected to continue to grow rapidly. Although foreign companies will be able to enter this market to provide value-added services, it seems likely that partnerships between the two will become the order of the day. The foreign companies will provide the technology, brand-name reputation, and skills, and the Chinese companies will provide the local connections, language abilities, and legal foundations for the new venture's existence. Again, however, as the recent changes in regulations have demonstrated, the lack of regulatory certainty, including on cross-border taxation, security, and content, have to be resolved before the subsector can really take off.

Overall, then, China does not yet have the infrastructure needed to take advantage of the new economy, and the chief bottlenecks to such development are less in the technology than in finance and logistics. Much needs to be done in terms of developing these sectors of China's old economy before it can leapfrog its way into the new global economy. This constraint also points to the need for a comprehensive approach in developing the services sector. Currently, the only real possible use of new economy systems in China rests with the foreign multinationals that have already implemented various supply chain management systems, customer relations management systems, and other e-solutions systems throughout their global operations. In many cases, China continues to be the one country in which their operations cannot be fully implemented.

Managing Policy Reforms and Increased Competition

The discussion in this chapter thus far clearly points to the importance of creating an appropriate regulatory environment to attain the emergence of healthy competition and an efficient telecommunications sector. Some of the key regulatory issues related to policies on convergence, government-mandated restructuring, consolidation of the state-owned enterprises, and the creation of pro-competitive regulations are described in this section.

Cable and Convergence Issues   China's cable television network now reaches about 90 million subscribers throughout the country, and it is expected to eventually be the largest in the world. Major recent regulatory reforms have enabled fixed-line operators such as China Telecom, Unicom, CNCC, and Railcom to offer cable television over their broadband networks. Cable TV companies were also looking forward to being able to deliver Internet and voice services over their networks. However, until there is an implementation schedule on convergence, explicitly indicating what is or is not permissible for cable operators, the cable industry remains reluctant to see convergence because it fears broadband would significantly erode its current subscriber base.

The MII has remained generally unsupportive of convergence. Regulations introduced in 2002

required joint ventures between existing telecom operators and new partners to seek new telecom licenses and to adhere strictly to the business category and geographic area of operation specified by the telecom license already in hand.

Toward a Pro-Competitive Regulatory Framework and Institutions   Given the nature of and developments in the telecommunications sector, it is unlikely that increased competition will come from liberalization or privatization. In any case, studies have shown that privatization will flow from the introduction of competition, but that the reverse is not necessarily true (Petrazinni 1996; Fink, Mattooo, and Rathindran 2001). In China, inefficiency has stemmed not from government ownership per se, but from a lack of competition and ineffective government regulation (Stiglitz 1998). Given that the major operators in basic telecom are state-owned and that the situation is unlikely to change even in the short term despite the liberalization of the sector through WTO accession as already outlined, the key challenge for China's telecom sector is to ensure that the few and predominantly state-owned players will be competing in a pro-competitive environment.

The September 2001 regulations go some way toward responding to some of the obligations for pro-competitive regulations and institutions as set out in the WTO agreement on basic telecommunications, but there are still areas of uncertainty, issues of implementation, and lack of a timetable for implementation. Given the current political institutions and structure in China, it is unrealistic to expect full regulatory independence in the near term. Not only does the Communist Party have overall responsibility for policy, but the MII still has a strong and complex relationship with the major operators. This situation gives rise to specific and major challenges to the creation of a truly independent regulator (Zhang 2001: 47). If regulatory reform continues to proceed slowly, the impact of WTO accession on liberalization of China's telecommunications market could end up being limited.

The problems and the issues surrounding the creation of an independent regulatory agency are not just confined to China, but also are being replayed in most developing countries attempting to open up their telecom sector. Therefore, careful thought should be given to the sequence of steps taken in developing such an institution. The first steps should be adopting transparency and training human resources adequately, as well as setting administrative guidelines as to just what constitutes an "independent" agency. These measures could be followed by a step-by-step phase-in of a more independent regulatory agency.

Provision of Universal Service to Poor and Isolated Areas[18]

As in other countries, before reforms China Telecom was the only operator in China and had an obligation to provide universal service. The model adopted for China Telecom was the traditional cross-subsidization model in which subsidization flowed from the eastern and more developed coastal areas to the western provinces of China and from wireless and long-distance services to local services. The need to provide all households and small firms with telecommunications was used as a reason to defend monopolistic telecom companies. Furthermore, it was believed that profit-maximizing private firms would not go to poor and remote areas. However, experience with protected state monopolies has shown that the outcome is likely to be one of inefficiency and underinvestment, with little or no service actually provided to the poor areas. Indeed, many developing countries have paid capital costs of $4,000 per line, or three to four times the achievable cost (Stiglitz 1998). Evidence also suggests that liberalization in the form of greater competition or privatization will generally increase network availability (Petrazinni 1996, p. 37).

With the restructuring of the China's telecom sector, the authorities are shifting from the traditional cross-subsidization model to the provision of universal service by popularizing access through significant price reductions. By means of such actions, it is hoped that telecom services will gradually become more accessible, despite the lack of an explicit universality mandate. The growth rates of fixed-line and mobile phone users have indeed been dramatic, leading to penetration rates of about 20 percent and 21 percent of the population, respectively, based on 2003 estimates. This average is, however, misleading, because a much lower rate of teledensity—only about 6 percent—prevails in rural areas and western provinces (MII statistics). Furthermore, in large areas of the country the basic infrastructure for telecommunications connectivity still does not exist, and mobile stations are limited to serving only the large cities.

The objective of the universal service obligation is to ensure that the public has access to affordable telecommunications services, including people living in high-cost service areas such as rural and remote regions as well as low-income groups. The authorities have not yet assigned the delivery of universal service to any of the current operators, although the expectation is that China Telecom will remain the major provider for the less developed areas and the poor regions.

The WTO reference paper on basic telecommunications services does not provide guidelines on universal service, although it does make clear that it should be implemented in an anticompetitive fashion, that it should be administered in a transparent, non-discriminatory, and competitively neutral manner, and that it should be no more burdensome than necessary for the kind of universal service defined by the WTO Member.

The experience of and lessons learned by other countries in implementing universal service programs have yielded some caveats and models that China could consider (World Bank 2000, Box 10.3). First, it is important that the definition of the universality target is clear and that it is linked to realistic implementation measures, including how it should be funded. The universality target differs from country to country, depending on local economic and sector conditions, the distribution of the population, geographic considerations, and security issues. *Universal service* refers to individual or private access, whereas *universal access* refers to community or public (shared) access (e.g., a phone booth in every village), and in developing countries the latter is more important.

There are several common models for achieving universal access: applying market-based reforms through privatization, competition, and cost-based pricing; requiring operators, including new entrants, to assume mandatory service obligations; implementing cross-subsidies between and within services provided by incumbent operators; using access deficit charges paid by telecommunications operators to subsidize the access deficit of incumbents; and creation of a fund to provide for universal service (World Bank 2000). Other models and combinations of these approaches are available, but the choice depends on country-specific issues and conditions.

BOX 10.3   Experiences of Chile, Peru, South Africa, and Hong Kong (China) with Universal Access

Chile

After market opening and privatization of its telecommunications sector, Chile introduced policy intended especially to provide universal access to people living in low-income and rural areas. The supporting funds, which came from the central government budget, took the form of targeted subsidies to private operators for the installation of public telephones in the unserved areas. The process included competitive bidding and the funds were not linked to the rollout obligations of operators to provide services in certain areas Over the period 1993–99, a total of 183 projects to serve almost 6,000 localities were approved. Competition between bidders reduced the actual subsidies paid, although there were some delays in installation. The targets are now to finance community Telecenters that have access to the Internet and other new information and communications technology.

Peru

Peru imposed rollout obligations as part of privatization and established universal access telecommunications funds, whose revenues were taken from the 1 percent of the gross revenues of the telecommunications sector. The funds were used to meet the target of extending services to 5,000 unserved localities by the year 2003. Universal access was defined as services provided by public operators and available to a majority of users, including voice telephony, low-speed fax and data, and free emergency calls. Criteria for the selection of localities were set as rural towns (300–400,000 population), district capitals, and towns in high social interest areas. Several innovations were introduced in the bidding process such as, for economies of scale, allowing a single operator to bid simulta-

neously on three projects and permitting bidders to bid on any combination of three projects. In 2000 Peru modified its target to fund access to the Internet and other advanced services, and to allow for funding the operation and maintenance of designated services, not just installation.

South Africa

In South Africa, rollout obligations are imposed on operators in underserved areas and combined with a universal service fund. The fund is generated by annual contributions from all telecommunications licensees, and is used to provide direct subsidies to a targeted priority population to subsidize the higher costs of telecommunications and to subsidize the cost of network rollout to underserved areas by operators. The network rollout, service quality targets, and pricing are closely monitored by the responsible agency. The funds have been used to assign priority to the setting up of telecenters in partnership with communities and donor agencies. The telecenters typically contain telephones, fax and photocopy machines, personal computers, and access to the Internet.

Hong Kong (China)

In Hong Kong, the cost-based universal service regime is funded through charges on external (i.e., international) traffic. The designated service provider has the obligation to provide PSTN (public switched telephone network) access service in Hong Kong and receives a fair contribution from other licensees toward the net cost of serving customers and providing public telephones. In 1999 the funds accounted for about 1 percent of total sector revenues.

Source: Kerf, Schiffler, and Torres 2001; Wellenius 1997.

Cross-subsidization has traditionally been used when a state has one dominant provider. The disadvantages, however, are by now well known, such as inefficiency and not reaching the target group. China has used this model in the past, and so now must rethink how to deliver universal access.

The MII plans to set up a universal service fund that will be used for developing the western and

rural regions, which currently lag far behind their eastern coastal counterparts. The fund is intended to separate government administration from enterprise management in the sector, shifting responsibility for infrastructure, operations, and fund-raising to the telecom companies themselves. Because the costs of these activities are high and have low returns, the MII is proposing tax incentives and investment, financing, and human resource policies for the industry, in tandem with the continued opening of pricing issues toward full market force management. However, the plan is still under discussion. In February 2003 the government announced that it would reinstate the universal service fund with would require contribution from all domestic operators to subsidize the construction of telecom infrastructure in China's rural areas. However the details on the size of contributions, how they will be disbursed and managed remains unclear.[19]

The approach of using universal funds has the advantage of being most effective in providing targeted subsidies to expand or support uneconomic services, such as the basic telecommunications services needed in the underdeveloped western provinces and rural areas. Indeed, it is potentially the most efficient and transparent approach, but much depends on how it is structured and administered. The scheme can be administratively complex, so that the transaction cost are higher than the subsidy, and there is the potential for bad governance if accountability and monitoring mechanisms are not built in and implemented. Furthermore, it is often difficult to predict the associated costs and revenues.

Experience has produced important lessons for anyone using the universal funds approach to provide universal access. First, the target must be clearly specified (e.g., high-cost regions such as the western provinces of China, rural areas without any access, a low-income population). Second, the financing, be it from direct government funding, contributions from operators, or proceeds from privatization, must be transparent. Third, the body that administers and disburses the funds must be independent from the operators. It also should be market-neutral in that it does not favor the incumbent vis-à-vis new entrants, and it must seek competitive bidding. Fourth, the subsidies given (i.e., in the form of a fiscal or investment incentive) should cover only the uneconomic portion of the cost of providing the services, and the operators, whether private or government, should finance the rest of the cost from their revenue.

Conclusions

In recent years the view of the telecommunications sector has changed—from that of a natural monopoly with large fixed costs to that of a set of more complex and competitive activities. New technologies have lowered unit costs dramatically. Since the mid-1990s, there has been a tendency toward a convergence of telecommunications, computing, and broadcasting. New services, such as the Internet, mobile, and wireless telecom, use different platforms and transmit through various media, and they provide alternatives to traditional wire line telephony at a much lower cost. These services have developed beyond regulators' control and can bypass the public switched network and control of the incumbent. These changes have also meant moves away from traditional forms of ownership and the market structure of state monopoly to one of joint ventures, strategic alliances, and new and foreign entrants (Petrazzini 1996, p. 24; Intven 2000). In addition the justification of maintaining state monopoly in telecom and undertaking cross subsidization has lost ground.

China's reforms in the last few years have been quite dramatic compared with the situation in other countries, and currently the telecom services sector in China is moving in this direction also. Increased competition has occurred, although it has been "managed" by the government through introducing new state owned players, breaking up the state monopoly and restructuring as well as consolidation efforts, and through government driven price reductions. Increased competition has in turn led to greater efficiency, price reductions beyond the government mandates, competition through better service and product differentiation, and greater penetration rates. Even though many challenges lie ahead, considering the dramatic changes that the sector has witnessed since 1998 and the unstoppable pace of global technological change, it seems reasonable to expect that the sector will continue to liberalize.

Whilst a number of foreign players have entered and will continue to enter value added services, as already discussed above, even after basic telecom sector is opened up under China's commitments, competition will remain between domestic (which will remain largely state owned) companies. Therefore to reach the desired level of fair competition and efficiency, and attract new investments, much depends, however, on the ability of the authorities to come up with a solid legislative framework that fosters a stable business environment by ensuring and enforcing a level industry playing field and private property rights, and how the state owned companies will be "corporatized" to be managed in a commercially viable manner. In 1999 the MII issued a statement that a telecom law would be finished prior to accession, but in December 2003 this law was still being drafted. Given that even the United States, considered to be the most wired nation, continues to have considerable difficulty with creating and updating regulations on various subsectors of the telecom industry, it is perhaps not surprising that the process of drafting this legislation has been so time-consuming. A number of issues related to the new telecommunications law such as interconnection policy, the creation of an independent regulatory authority and convergence appear to be moving in the right direction. However, a number of other issues still need to be clarified:

- Regulate and enforce a level playing field for private and foreign investment. Although hedging against risk is an inherent part of good business practice, the current environment creates a major disincentive for investment of the foreign and private funds needed to develop the industry.
- Consider implementation of less interventionist and government driven price mechanism, such as introducing price caps, that incorporate quality and other self-regulating factors. Current prices reflect an effort to broaden the use of telecommunications services, and significant sector and geographic rebalancing will be required. But they will affect cross-subsidization and will not reflect true costs.
- Decide, like all other countries, which 3G technology standard to adopt. The debate over which 3G technology to use contributes to the environment of uncertainty and has the potential to hold back investments.
- Adopt a clear and concise, but flexible, framework for the regulation of value-added services, including e- and m-commerce platforms.
- Devise anticollusion mechanisms given the likelihood of mergers between the current major market players. Such mechanisms become particularly important once the MII is relieved of its control over the industry and pricing issues are left to market forces.
- Establish an independent regulatory agency. Given past experience, it is likely that this will

take some time and the issue of how "independent" the regulator will be from the domestic operators, if the regulator emerges out of MII, will continue. However, it is important that China addresses these issues by beginning with the introduction of greater transparency. For instance, by establishing a clear and transparent scheme within which licenses can be allocated. The deadlines provided for consideration of license approval are welcome, but more details are needed with regard to the criteria for eligibility of licenses.

Other than the regulatory framework and implementation thereof to ensure greater transparency and a level playing field, another major challenges facing the sector of providing universal service. China is already moving in the right direction by recognizing that separate policies are needed to address this social objective and not being burdened on the objective of developing an efficient and competitive telcom sector. China should take note of the experience of other countries, and choose what will be appropriate for its conditions. Given China's size and vast differences between provinces, more than one model is likely to work depending on the existing conditions and geographical location in question. However, the principles and lessons from other countries should be borne in mind—especially with respect to it being market based, transparent and with the right incentive structure—when designing the policy.

Appendix: Summary of WTO Reference Paper on Basic Communications (Annex to Fourth Protocol of General Agreement on Trade in Services [GATS], Agreement on Basic Telecommunications, Effective January 1, 1998)

China's WTO accession commitments in telecommunications oblige it to also adhere to the principles of the WTO reference paper. The paper provides for a pro-competitive environment of policy and regulation.

Competitive Safeguards

Prevention of Anticompetitive Practices in Telecommunications Appropriate measures shall be maintained for the purpose of preventing suppliers who, alone or together, are a major supplier from engaging in or continuing anticompetitive practices.

Safeguards   Anticompetitive practices include, in particular, engaging in anticompetitive cross-subsidization, using information obtained from competitors with anticompetitive results, and not making available to other services suppliers on a timely basis technical information about essential facilities and commercially relevant information that are necessary for them to provide services.

Interconnection

Interconnection is to be provided under nondiscriminatory terms, conditions, and rates, and in a timely fashion, and, upon request, at points in addition to the network termination points offered to the majority of uses. The procedures applicable for interconnection to a major supplier will be made publicly available, and a major supplier will make publicly available either its interconnection agreements or a reference interconnection offer. An independent domestic body will resolve interconnection disputes.

Universal Service

Any Member has a right to define the kind of universal service obligation it wishes to maintain. Such obligations would not be considered anticompetitive as long as they are administered in a transparent, nondiscriminatory, and competitively neutral manner.

Licensing Criteria

The following should be made publicly available: all licensing criteria and the period of time required to reach a decision on a license application, the terms and conditions of individual licenses, and the reasons for denial of a license.

Independent Regulators

The regulatory body should be separate from and not accountable to any supplier of basic telecommunications services. The decisions of and procedures used by regulators shall be impartial to all market participants.

Allocation and Use of Scarce Resources

Allocation of scarce resources such as frequencies, numbers, and rights of way will be carried out in an objective, timely, transparent, and nondiscriminatory way. The current state of allocated frequency bands will be made publicly available.

Notes

1. For the United States, European Union, and Japan, opening up telecommunications services was a major point of contention during their bilateral negotiations with China. China's rejection of foreign direct investment (FDI) in telecommunications services was unusual when compared with its stance in other economic sectors or with that taken by other countries at a similar level of development.

2. About 40 foreign operators lost up to US$1.4 billion when the government cracked down on investments that circumvented the FDI ban in the sector. Despite this, the U.S. company AT&T recently entered into a joint venture to form Shanghai Symphony Telecommunications, and all other major foreign operators remain in China, awaiting further entry opportunities.

3. A decline in average revenue per unit without increasing usage.

4. See Gao, Pin, and Kalle (2000); Perkins (2001), Price Waterhouse Coopers (2001), World Bank (1992, 2000) and Zhang (2000) for greater detail and background.

5. The lack of cooperation is not surprising, because Unicom was created by the rival Ministry of Electronics and an official in the State Council—not by MPT. Unicom's original objective was to share 10 percent of the fixed-line market and 30 percent of the mobile phone market with China Telecom by 2000 (Asian Communications, September 1998).

6. Creation of the agency was part of the institutional reorganization undertaken at the Ninth National People's Congress.

7. In 1998 the government forced the People's Liberation Army (PLA) to divest itself of all of its business interests as part of a government crackdown on corruption and forced a handover of Great Wall Telecom Corporation, which had the right to operate a CDMA system, to Unicom.

8. As reported in *China Daily*, 5 August 2001.

9. The Chinese Internet Network Information Center (CNNIC) semiannual survey defines Internet users in China as Chinese citizens who use the Internet at least one hour a week.

10. ADSL employs the existing double twisted copper telephone lines to provide broadband network access, enabling a downstream rate of 8 megabits per second and an upstream rate of 760 kilobits per second. However, transmission quality can be maintained only within a distance of 5 kilometers, thus requiring one base site every 5 kilometers, and with heavy initial investment by telecom operators in network construction. Since ADSL was first introduced, charges have dropped from about 450–500 yuan to about 130 yuan per month.

11. Companies such as AT&T and Edge2net Inc. have already entered the market. The latter has teamed up with China Motion Telecom to create Shenzhen China Motion Telecom.

12. The regulations have since been updated with a revised catalogue of value-added services in June 2001.

13. See Baker and McKenzie (2000); Liu He, Qin Hai, and Lu Yanrong (2001) for more details.

14. New regulations were announced in early 2003 that covered the legal definition of E-Commerce as trading, production,

and services provided over the electronic network (e.g. information search, ordering, and payment) and authentication of e-signatures. They did not as yet discuss the issue of taxation.

15. State Council, Opinions Regarding Further Strengthening the Supervision and Administration of Telecom Market, August 2003.

16. A decline in average revenue per unit without an adequate increase in minutes of usage.

17. After essentially being cut out of the mobile market with its divestiture of CMCC, China Telecom tried to enter the mobile business by introducing a mobile phone that functioned essentially as an extension of its fixed-line networks. Therefore, the mobiles only functioned within a limited geographic area around the line. Nevertheless, 2.5 million lines in about 50 cities were already installed when the MII, in response to the lobbying by two licensed mobile operators, ordered China Telecom to cease such operations. The attraction for users was that handsets cost about half the price of normal handsets.

18. See Petrazinni (1996); Smith (1997a, 1997b); Stiglitz (1999); and Wallenius (1997) for more information.

19. It was recently announced under the Rural Communication and Universal Services Initiative that, by 2005, 40,000 villages will be reached and each of the six major telecom operators will be asked to cover certain regions: China Telecom (Shanxi); China Netcom (Inner Mongolia autonomous region); China Mobile (Sichuan); Unicom (Guanxi autonomous region); China Satcom (Sichuan); and China Railcom (Henan).

References

Baker and McKenzie. 2000. Asia Information Associates, E-Commerce in China.

McKinsey Quarterly. China Statistics Yearbooks 1998–2000. Beijing, China Statistics Press.

Fink, Carsten, Aaditya Mattoo, and Randeep Rathindran. 2001. "Liberalizing Basic Telecommunications: the Asian Experience." Paper presented at the Conference on Trade, Investment and Competition Policy in the Global Economy; the case of the International Telecom Regime. Germany, January.

Gao, Pin, and Lyytinen, Kalle. 2000. "Transformation of China's Telecommunication Sector: A Macro-perspective." *Telecommunications Policy* 24: 719–30.

Intven, Hank, ed., "Telecommunications Regulation Handbook." 2000. Infodev, World Bank.

Klein, Michael, and Philip Gray. "Competition in Network Industries—Where and How to Introduce It." Public Policy for the Private Sector, World Bank.

Liu He, Qin Hai, and Lu Yanrong. 2001. "E-Commerce in China" (First Draft).

Mueller, Milton, and Peter Lovelock. 2000. "The WTO and China's Ban on Foreign Investment in the Telecommunications Sector: A Game-theoretic Analysis." *Telecommunications Policy* 24: 731–59.

Perkins, Tony, and Steven Shaw. 2000. "China and the WTO: What Will Really Change?" *McKinsey Quarterly* no. 2.

Petrazinni, Ben A. 1996. "Competition in Telecoms—Implications for Universal Service and Employment." Public Policy for the Private Sector. World Bank Group, Washington, D.C., October.

Price Waterhouse Coopers. 2001. "Briefing Overview of China Telecommunications Sector," February.

Qiang, C.Z.W., and Xu, L.C. 2000. "Reforming China Telecom," World Bank DECRG.

Smith, Peter. 1997. "What the Transformation of Telecom Markets Means for Regulation." Public Policy for the Private Sector. World Bank Group, Washington, D.C., July.

Smith, Warrick. 1997. "Utility Regulators—The Independence Debate." Public Policy for the Private Sector. World Bank Group, Washington, D.C. October.

Stiglitz, Joseph. 1998. "Creating Competition in Telecommunications." Paper presented at World Bank Conference on Managing the Telecommunications Sector Post-Privatization, Washington, D.C., April.

Stiglitz, Joseph. 1999. "Promoting Competition and Regulatory Policy: With Examples from Network Industries." Washington, D.C., World Bank, Beijing, July.

Wellenius, Bjorn. 1997. "Extending Telecommunications Service to Rural Areas—The Chilean Experience." Public Policy for the Private Sector. World Bank, Washington, D.C., February.

World Bank. 1992. "People's Republic of China Telecommunications Sector Study: Survey, Assessment and Strategy Recommendations." Report No. 9413-CHA, February.

World Bank. 2000. "China: Services Sector Development and Competitiveness." Washington, D.C., December.

World Bank. 2001. "Seizing the 21st Century: Using Knowledge for China's Development." Washington, D.C., June.

WTO (World Trade Organization). 2003. "Report of the Meeting held on 5 December 2003: Note by the Secretariat." Council for Trade in Services. WTO, Geneva.

Zhang, Bing. 2001. "Assessing WTO Agreements on China's Telecommunications Regulatory Reform and Industrial Liberalization." TPRC.

11

ACCELERATING FINANCIAL MARKET RESTRUCTURING IN CHINA

Deepak Bhattasali

Close to the date of China's entry into the World Trade Organization (WTO) in December 2001, several events appeared to perk up the domestic financial market. A leading international bank announced that it would charge a small monthly fee if the amount in an individual bank deposit fell below US$5,000.[1] A leading local bank then pointed out that about 20 percent of its savings deposits were in the amount of 100 yuan or less and hinted that this situation was uneconomical. The China Bank Association then wrote a detailed proposal that reportedly was discussed with the People's Bank of China (PBC)—the central bank—before submission for approval to the State Development Planning Commission. The proposal recommended that banks be allowed to levy fees for about 40 different services that traditionally they had provided free of charge.

A little earlier, fierce competition had broken out among Shanghai banks when they slashed buy/sell margins on foreign currency transactions to 10 basis points (from an average of 40 basis points in 2001), but order was quickly restored by the Shanghai Banking Association. In parallel developments, a foreign-invested bank and a fully owned foreign bank received their first Chinese customers. Meanwhile, a major local financial conglomerate opened a new life insurance company in

a joint venture with one of the largest foreign life insurance firms, which led to a further round of new associations between Chinese financial enterprise groups and foreign insurance companies. A similar pattern of mergers, acquisitions, and partnerships has emerged in investment banking, funds management, securities houses, and housing finance. In another development, a leading foreign manufacturing firm entered into an innovative agreement with a wholly owned foreign bank for loans against its receivables and promptly used the funds to pay off outstanding credits to two large local banks. To cap it all, data available during the first quarter of 2002 suggested that a credit crunch had occurred in the second half of 2001, as banks tightened lending in order to improve their portfolios to meet the post–WTO accession challenge.

By the standards of most financial markets, these events were unremarkable, either singly or together. However, to observers of China's financial market it was clear that something momentous was happening; the genie was out of the bottle, competition was about to break out! Members of China's moribund financial community, especially bankers, saw these events as the first signs of the imminent destruction of the domestic financial system, justifying the fears of protectionists who had argued against many of the liberal measures included in China's accession agreement (see table 11.2). Against this backdrop it is interesting to assess the following issues: How did the accession agreement threaten the status quo in the domestic banking market?[2] If the policymakers were aware of the threat, why did they agree to take such radical measures to permit the entry of foreign banks? What are some likely scenarios for the evolution of the banking sector in China during the period of accession and beyond?

The next section of this assessment describes the structure and behavior of the Chinese banking industry at the time that the final WTO-related negotiations were under way. It is followed by a description of China's WTO accession commitments. The final section examines the likely impact of foreign entry on China's banking sector and related policy issues.

Initial Conditions

The post-1978 economic reforms in China—when agriculture and industry began to grow rapidly in response to improved incentive systems—led to a large increase in incomes, savings, and bank deposits. For the most part, deposits were channeled to state-owned enterprises (SOEs) through the state-owned banking system, with insufficient regard for credit quality. Although investment decisions were controlled by the central government in theory, in practice subnational governments enjoyed remarkable degrees of freedom in choosing investments and appropriating finance from the local branches of the state banks.

The banking system, and later the securities market, played an even more important role in supporting the level of economic activity in the early 1990s, as the government budget became increasingly constrained by a drop in revenues. Revenues fell from about 34 percent of the gross domestic product (GDP) in the early to mid-1980s to below 12 percent by the mid-1990s. However, the legacy of poor loans began to affect the profitability of banks acutely by the mid-1990s, although the propensity of Chinese households to save a large part of their income (averaging 28 percent of GDP), the relative absence of alternative savings vehicles, and the implicit deposit guarantees at the state banks provided high levels of liquidity to the banking system, helping to mask its problems. The rapid growth of household savings in the domestic banking system has also been possible because of capital controls

and the successful nationalization of capital flight through the creation of an onshore foreign currency deposit and loan market. Uncertainties about the solvency of pension plans, the absence of a mortgage market (until 1999), and funds for education needs and purchases of other services are also believed to have stimulated savings in the form of bank deposits. However, this proposition has not yet been tested rigorously.

Financial Sector Reform

China's attempts to modernize its financial market have been steady, but, beyond an occasional flurry of precautionary measures introduced after the mini-crises of the 1990s, they have focused mainly on institutional diversification and strengthened administrative oversight. It is possible to distinguish four distinct phases of institutional reform in China in the 22 years leading up to WTO accession.

The *first phase* (1979–86) was characterized by the breakup of the mono-bank system. PBC became the central bank, and the Industrial and Commercial Bank of China (ICBC) was created to handle urban commercial banking, thus joining other specialized institutions for large-scale construction (China Construction Bank [CCB]), foreign exchange transactions and international trade (Bank of China [BOC]), and rural lending (Agricultural Bank of China [ABC]). Foreign banks were initially allowed to open representative offices, but by the end of this phase they also were permitted to establish commercial branches, albeit with tight geographic, product, and customer restrictions.

The *second phase* (1987–91) was marked by a reduction in administratively governed specialization among institutions, the rapid growth of non-bank financial intermediaries, the establishment of the first joint stock universal bank (Bank of Communications [BOCOM]), the establishment of two state-owned insurance companies (in addition to the People's Insurance Company of China [PICC] established in 1949), and the beginnings of a capital market by the introduction of secondary market trading in government securities.

The *third phase* (1992–96) saw even greater diversification in the financial market. Stock exchanges were established in Shanghai and Shenzhen, the interbank market was developed, some interest rates became flexible, and life and non–life insurance licenses were extended to foreign firms, but with tighter product and geographic restrictions than for domestic providers.

In the *final* pre-WTO accession phase of reform (1997–2001), the emphasis shifted to addressing the portfolio problems of the commercial banks and governance of the financial market as a whole. In a sense, the preparations for WTO accession effectively began during this period. They entailed restructuring the PBC, attempting to improve bank supervision and the recognition of bad loans in the portfolios of state banks, creating four asset management companies (to segment a portion of such loans), clarifying the roles of the China Securities Regulatory Commission (CSRC) and the China Insurance Regulatory Commission (CIRC), and diversifying financial instruments to meet the emerging needs of savers

(e.g., mortgage loans and automobile finance to accompany the rapid growth of newly created housing markets and the anticipated increase in car buying as their prices dropped after China's accession to the WTO). Moreover, the pressure to improve corporate governance within financial institutions and increase the transparency of financial information provided by listed companies and banks was notched up, using a combination of sanctions, personnel movements, moral suasion, and new regulations.

Preaccession Situation

Despite these measures, China's financial services industry seemed far from ready for increased competition from abroad at the time of WTO accession (table 11.1).[3] The size of the Chinese financial

TABLE 11.1   China's Financial Services Industry, 2001

Type of Institution	Size (Trillions of Yuan)			Share (%)		
	Assets	Loans	Deposits	Assets	Loans	Deposits
Deposit money banks	15.0	10.7	13.1	100.0	100.0	100.0
State banks	10.1	7.2	8.7	67.3	67.3	66.4
Other banks	1.9	1.2	1.6	12.7	11.2	12.2
Foreign funded banks	0.4	0.2	0.01	2.7	1.9	0.1
Urban credit cooperatives	0.8	0.6	0.8	5.3	5.6	6.1
Rural credit cooperatives	1.6	1.3	1.7	10.7	12.1	13.0
Finance companies	0.2	0.2	0.3	1.3	1.9	2.2
Other deposit institutions	1.1	1.4	0.2			

	Size (Trillions of Yuan)		Prevalence	
	Assets	Premium Income	Depth (%)	Penetration (Yuan)
Insurance companies	0.46	0.21	2.2	169

	Trading Volume (Trillions of Yuan)				
	Overnight	7 Days	30 Days	90 Days	Total
Interbank market	0.10	0.56	0.04	0.005	0.81

	Size		
	Market Capitalization (Trillions of Yuan)	Turnover (Trillions of Yuan)	Trading Volume (Trillion Shares)
Securities market	4.4	3.8	31.5

	Size (Trillions of Yuan)			Share (%)		
	Treasury	Financial	Corporate	Treasury	Financial	Corporate
Bond market	1.95	0.69	0.03	73.2	25.7	1.1

Sources: People's Bank of China 2002–03; *Almanac of China's Finance and Banking* 2002, Yearbook of China's Insurance 2002.

market was remarkable. Total deposits in banks reached the exceptionally high level of 150 percent of GDP in 2001. China had the second-largest securities market in Asia, with 1,189 listed companies, about 60 million brokerage accounts, and a market capitalization approaching 45 percent of GDP. The four large state banks—which had been transformed into universal banks and constituted the core of the financial system—accounted for 67 percent of deposit bank assets and 56 percent of total financial assets.

Nearly 77 percent of the annual financial savings of households was deposited in the banking system during 1998–2001. Consequently, banks handled most of the finance available to enterprises and the government, of which the share held by small and medium nonstate enterprises—the most dynamic segment of the Chinese economy—was tiny. Moreover, the rural finance system was malfunctioning, with the Agricultural Development Bank of China (policy bank), the Agricultural Bank of China, and the rural credit cooperatives facing the severest repayment problems in the banking sector. During 2001, total bank loans expanded by 1.3 trillion yuan, while both new equity issues and corporate bond issues were a negligible fraction of this amount. Corporate (i.e., state enterprise) sector leverage was very high; equally, a high proportion of loans taken by state enterprises was nonperforming. Government estimates placed the nonperforming loans (NPLs) of the four large state banks at about 27 percent of their loans outstanding, which excluded the NPLs transferred in 2000 to four asset management companies (nearly 20 percent of loans outstanding at the four banks at that time). Unofficial estimates of the remaining NPLs in the state banks have run as high as 40–50 percent of loans outstanding.[4] In addition, it is likely that the other domestic banks have a larger proportion of NPLs.[5] However, neither the application of existing loan classification systems nor the current state of management information systems within the banks gives analysts any reason to believe that the various estimates present an accurate picture of the condition of bank portfolios.

Current accounting, auditing, and reporting standards and practices do not provide sufficient information for making judgments about the profitability of China's financial institutions, the adequacy of their capital bases, and the efficiency of their operations.[6] The information available on the condition of their portfolios or in balance sheets and income statements can, at best, help only in understanding broad changes in the direction of these parameters over time. However, the information available on the operating practices of Chinese financial institutions is sufficient to develop a set of characterizations to describe the state of the major industry segments on the eve of WTO accession.[7]

Each of China's four state banks is big—they have an average asset size of more than $400 billion, average employment of over 415,000 people, and from 15,000 to 58,000 branches (see Almanac of China's Finance and Banking 2002). These numbers suggest that, at least in terms of resources, they are large enough to compete against most foreign banks, even after factoring in the potential entry of major international players that have grown rapidly in recent years through aggressive mergers and acquisitions.

The core institutional problem, however, is the relative lack of profitability and insolvency of the four state banks, which undermines the many benefits that could result from size, incumbency, and reach.[8] Furthermore, although improving, the banks have limited capacity to make lending decisions based purely on the commercial appraisal of repayment ability and credit risk. Until recently, the PBC-regulated spread between deposit and lending rates (about 400 basis points, which are high by international standards but not unusual by developing country standards) was sufficient to sustain the reported profitability of banks, but it removed incentives to extend credit to underserved but relatively dynamic segments of the economy, such as small enterprises. The competitive prospects of the state banks are further undermined by their relative inability so far to implement efficiency reforms—for example, by cutting staff as much as required or closing unprofitable branches. Since 1997, the state banks have reportedly closed 29 percent of their offices and cut staff by 15 percent; not only are these measures considered insufficient, the feasible limits under current ownership conditions seem to have been reached. Thus, as of the end of 2001, the pace of *innovation* in retail banking—where such banks would normally be expected to have an advantage—was unsatisfactory, despite the fact that such services are relatively underdeveloped in China, where they have massive potential.[9] Finally, these banks' lack of experience with international banking—and their unfamiliarity with internationally benchmarked banking practices, technology, and management—is a handicap.[10]

If information about the state banks is scanty, that on the other parts of the banking industry, with the exception of the four listed commercial banks, is even more deficient. The published data do not engender much confidence, and little systematic research has been undertaken into their operating conditions. In general, however, it is believed that the urban and rural credit cooperatives (as well as some city commercial banks) are insolvent and mostly illiquid, with periodic reports of failures among them. In addition to poor management and banking practices, the rural credit cooperatives have been affected adversely by the stagnation of the rural economy since the mid-1990s. Although the ABC generally withdrew from subcounty-level banking in 1996, leaving the field clear for the cooperatives, the franchise value of rural banking did not rise, and may have declined in the face of large-scale rural distress.

The other development of note in the period immediately preceding accession to the WTO was the transfer of a significant portion of directed lending to the three policy banks.[11] It is not immediately apparent that this transfer reduced the level of credit risk in the banking industry, because there is little evidence that these banks are better placed than the state banks to evaluate such risks. Moreover, directed lending has played an important role in the support state banks have given to the fiscal stimulus program introduced in 1998 and currently under implementation. Finally, because the two main policy banks (China Development Bank and China Import and Export Bank, or Eximbank) fund themselves mainly through the issuance of long-term local currency bonds, the majority of which are sold to the state banks, covariant risk exists among the major players in the banking system.

Despite these weaknesses, other segments of the banking market show potential for growth and innovation. Although deposit growth at the state banks continues to be strong—rising nearly 26 percent during 1999–2001—joint stock and other commercial banks, with a significantly smaller reach in terms of branch networks, have made rapid gains. Thus, despite the implicit guarantee that deposits at state banks are thought to enjoy, and the widespread belief among banking analysts that concerns about financial sector solvency would result

in a flight of deposits to the big banks, the nonstate banks saw an increase in deposits of 77 percent over the same period. The same is true of loans, with these banks accounting for 42 percent of the increase over the period, compared with 21 percent for the state banks. Agility in trawling for savings in urban areas, combined with deft exploitation of the non-SOE segment of the corporate market, produced such outcomes. Both areas of concentration represent the fastest-growing parts of the Chinese economy. Therefore, it is likely that, unless they prove to be equally dexterous, the state banks will have a smaller market share in 2006, by which time all of China's existing WTO commitments on banking liberalization are expected to come into force.

On the eve of WTO accession, the 191 foreign banks in China operated almost as off-shore or enclave banks.[12] The foreign bank penetration rate, if measured by the number of banks or branches, seemed quite high—52 percent and 14 percent of the total Chinese banking industry, respectively. However, they accounted for less than 3 percent of assets, 2 percent of loans, and about 0.1 percent of deposits. Despite these low numbers, several foreign banks were able to become profitable within 12–18 months of entering the Chinese market, although market reports also suggest that they had nonperforming assets equal to 20 percent of their total assets (and some as high as 90 percent), and their business was almost exclusively with enterprises with foreign investment. Because foreign banks were being limited mostly to foreign currency transactions—commanding a 24 percent market share in foreign currency loans and 45 percent share in international settlements—such banks had co-located with their clients, the overwhelming majority of whom were foreign-domestic joint ventures in the coastal belt of China. Only a handful of banks—mainly with strong Hong Kong (China) or other Asian institutional presence—had developed longer-term strategies aimed at other local market segments. The banks operated in an environment that was radically different from that for the domestic banks. They had to deal with onerous location, product, and investment restrictions, and a vastly different supervisory and tax regime (foreign banks are taxed at a 33 percent rate, while local banks are taxed at a 50 percent rate). Overall, few linkages exist between foreign and domestic banks—which limited technological spillover and competition in the domestic banking industry.

China's WTO Commitments in Financial Services

China's commitments to liberalizing its financial services industry, and indeed its General Agreement on Trade in Services (GATS) commitments as a whole, are possibly the most radical offerings ever negotiated in the history of the WTO and in the Uruguay Round (see table 11.2). Although hazardous, it is interesting to speculate briefly about the possible motivation for such a fundamental attempt to liberalize the financial services industry.

At the time the Chinese government was negotiating its specific commitments, a significant body of literature had been building up on the effect of foreign entry into developed and developing country financial markets. Issues related to the survival of domestic financial institutions and the possibility of more complex macroeconomic risks and management demands were known and debated. At the same time, the evidence of a favorable impact on financial market efficiency was equally impressive, especially because it was based on very careful analysis

TABLE 11.2   China's WTO Commitments in the Financial Services Sector

Subsector	Commitment
Banking	*Location:* Upon accession, foreign currency business is allowed without geographic restriction. Geographic restrictions on the local currency business of foreign banks will be phased out over five years; four cities will be opened upon accession, four additional cities thereafter. *Products:* Within two years of accession, China will permit foreign banks to provide local currency services to Chinese enterprises; within five years, to all Chinese. *Investment:* Within five years of accession, all current nonprudential measures regarding the ownership, operation, and establishment of foreign banks, as well as those concerning their branches and restrictions on issuing licenses, will be eliminated (national treatment).
Securities	*Product:* Foreign securities companies may engage directly in B share business. *Investment:* Within three years of accession, foreign investment banks will be permitted to establish joint ventures, with foreign ownership not exceeding 33 percent, to engage (without Chinese intermediary) in underwriting domestic shares (A shares) and underwriting and trading in foreign currency denominated securities (B and H shares, government and corporate debts). Representative offices of foreign securities companies may become special members of Chinese stock exchanges.
Fund management	*Investment:* Upon accession, the establishment of joint venture fund management companies will be permitted, with foreign ownership not exceeding 33 percent, to conduct domestic fund management business. Foreign investment shall be increased to 49 percent after three years.
Insurance	*Location:* All geographic restrictions will be lifted in three years after the entry. *Product:* Upon accession, foreign life insurers will be permitted to provide individual (nongroup) life insurance services. Two years after entry, they will be permitted to provide health insurance, group insurance, pension insurance, and annuities to Chinese and foreign customers. Reinsurance is completely open upon accession, with no restrictions. *Investment:* Upon accession, foreign life insurers will be allowed to hold 50 percent ownership in joint ventures. They may choose their own joint venture partners. For nonlife, China will allow branching or 51 percent foreign ownership upon accession and wholly owned subsidiaries in two years after the entry (i.e., no restriction on the form of enterprise establishment). Licenses will be granted solely on the basis of prudential criteria with no economic needs test or quantitative limits on the number of licenses granted.

Source: Ministry of Commerce 2002.

of country experience and microdata.[13] China's decision to join the WTO was a clear attempt to benchmark its economic activities to international standards and to ensure that the future growth of the economy was along the lines of its comparative advantage. Within this broader context, and given certain institutional and political considerations relevant to the financial sector, the evidence on foreign entry and efficiency seems to have been compelling.

The basic impulse for financial sector liberalization seems to have been based less on the effects it was likely to have on the mobilization of a greater volume of financial savings and the promotion of a higher level of investment—which in standard models appears to lead to a temporary increase in the aggregate growth rate of the economy—than on the need for technical innovation that would lower the cost of financial services and permanently boost growth. Moreover, in recent years Chinese policymakers have expressed greater concern about the efficient allocation of resources in the economy. This concern has manifested itself in pricing, competition, and fiscal measures, as well as financial sector reform. The rapid liberalization of many real sectors—for example, housing and other services—provided the opportunity to apply a similar competition policy model in banking reform, although less so in other financial market segments which, because of their infancy, attracted stronger protectionist sentiment.

Equally important, given the size of the dominant players in the banking market, the information gaps and span of control problems that accounted for their ineffective management, and the difficulties of severing or weakening the links between SOEs and banks, fairly strong procompetitive measures had to be employed. Foreign entry, suitably phased to provide a manageable adjustment process, addressed many of the perceived problems with the financial services industry in China. The expected diversification of financial instruments for saving, liquidity management, and financing of economic activity would also support the transition to market finance. Guidance from the recent Sixteenth National Congress of the Communist Party on active promotion of the private sector is bound to be translated into demands for a significant redirection of debt and equity flows. More significant, it sets China inexorably on the path toward market-based finance

and highlights the need to manage the transition actively.

Major Issues and Implications

This concluding section examines briefly some of the major banking issues related to WTO accession that will have to be addressed in the transition to market-based finance. It is useful to start with the likely effect on general economic management, because accession to the WTO is likely to result in a significant remapping of the flow of funds in the financial market.

Interestingly, many of the factors traditionally thought to have permitted relatively uncomplicated financial and macroeconomic management, despite inadequate economic information, weak accountability of institutions, and distortions in market signals, are likely to become high-pressure points in the transition period. They include control over major interest rates, capital flows, and the level of the exchange rate. The ability to capture and retain within the financial system a large proportion of household savings, then to channel it to enterprises and government directly or indirectly to support fiscal policy with quasi-fiscal stimulus through the financial system, is likely to be affected the most. As foreign banks and other financial institutions are allowed to offer a broader range of domestic and foreign currency savings instruments, the excess liquidity of local banks will shrink. If expectations about the selective credit reach of foreign institutions are realized, the liquidity position for meeting the burgeoning needs of the domestic banks' large customer base is likely to tighten. Finally, the need to correct disparities that have resulted from using an unbalanced growth model to promote coastal provinces represents a special challenge. The effects of geography and favorable government policies toward such provinces have been reinforced by lopsided financial sector development, which discriminates against the growth of the interior and western provinces of China.[14] The geographic liberalization built into China's WTO accession commitments will tend to foster more rapid development of the financial services industry—and the benefits to savers and investors that stem from it—in these same regions.

A central issue related to financial stability and the future of the banking system is the fate of the state banks. Clearly, rapid development of the non-bank financial market will erode the role of all banks—a particular concern with respect to their ability to capture household savings and maintain lending in the face of declining levels of liquidity. This problem could, of course, be mitigated partly by removing gradually and according to satisfactory prudential control the current investment restrictions on banks—for example, by permitting prudent participation in equity markets and investment funds. However, the recent portfolio problems of banks will also limit their future risk-bearing capacity, and possibly their ability to compete with foreign banks on the development of new financial instruments. State banks are particularly vulnerable because their high operating costs and inability to reduce NPLs stem as much from weak management as from domestic political economy pressures.[15] Despite recent attempts to cut the number of branches and attract new sources of equity (as, for example, in the recent initial public offering by the BOC), it is unlikely that small changes in macro-economic parameters, banking behavior, or the level of nonperforming loans will restore the health of their balance sheets.

Extrapolations from published data on the state bank income statements and balance sheets and a variety of assumptions about macroeconomic parameters are shown in box 11.1. They suggest that, without fairly radical actions to reduce

---

BOX 11.1   Modeling State Bank Performance: Can the State Banks Survive Liberalization?

Within the limitations of the data, it is useful to assess the prospects of China's main banks after the post-WTO accession period. The official and industry response to banking system liberalization hinges critically on whether the banks are able to earn their way out of their current difficulties while facing foreign entry and associated changes. The results of a simple financial projections exercise, which draws on publicly available information on the condition of the portfolios of the four state-owned commercial banks, their accounts, and assumptions about key macro-economic parameters, suggest the following broad trends:

- By the end of the accession period in 2007, the banks will not, either individually or as a group, be able to cope with their current and prospective nonperforming loans (a level of 30 percent is used for the base case, ranging from 25 to 40 percent for the individual banks). It is likely that all but one bank will have negative capital by 2007, and that, as a group, the four banks will have negative capital.
- The operating margins are too low throughout the post-accession period, and not only do the banks not make profits during the transition period, but their capital turns even more negative over time.
- Changes in assumptions about the current stock of nonperforming loans make a significant difference to the results of the base case. However, within a zone of 20 percent around the base case assumption (about 5 percentage points above and below the 30 percent nonperforming loan level assumed in the base case), the banks as a group are likely to still have negative capital by 2007.
- Competitive pressures, either in the form of rising interest rates to protect deposit bases or shrinking loan margins, would worsen the base case results.
- The group results are not affected significantly by *small changes* in the assumptions about macroeconomic growth, inflation, or the operating costs of banks. However, the effect on individual banks could differ substantially. Also, even large changes in macroeconomic variables—for example, higher credit growth resulting from 50 percent higher output growth in the economy—will be inadequate for stopping the erosion of the capital base of the banks.

The conclusion to be drawn from this simple financial modeling exercise is that the state banks will come under severe pressure during post–WTO accession liberalization. Fairly substantial changes in operating costs would be required to improve the condition of the banks. Failing this, because they are unlikely to be able to simply "grow out of their problems"—that is, they will be unable to recapitalize themselves from provisions and retained earnings—a recapitalization of the state banks from outside sources is likely to be required. A combination of instruments most probably will be used to restore the health of the state banks' balance sheets. These results support broadly the findings of other, similar modeling exercises related to China's state banks (see, for example, Li and Ma 2001).

operating costs, the banks will be unable to earn their way to improved health. In such an event, to avoid a loss of confidence in the state banks or a sharp erosion of their competitive position with respect to foreign and smaller domestic banks, financial reengineering will have to accompany the needed changes in banking practices. Toward this end, it is possible that bolder actions to inject new capital from private and public sources will have to be taken. Private capital would be preferable, especially if it is bundled with access to new banking technologies and financial expertise, but many market analysts believe that the use of public capital is unavoidable. If so, the internal reform of the banks should be speeded up and strengthened, so they can move toward self-sufficiency. Reforms will reduce the size of the public capital infusion that will be needed which, given many other claims on government finances, would help smooth post-WTO accession and structural adjustment elsewhere in the Chinese economy.

Notes

1. All dollar amounts are current U.S. dollars.

2. This chapter focuses on banking, although it refers to other financial market segments where relevant.

3. Domestic banks compete vigorously in extending credit to the larger corporate customers. One indicator of price competition is the tendency to make full, but one-sided, use of the leeway allowed by the PBC on loan rates (from 10 percent below to 30 percent above the base rate). Because banks have little experience with the estimation of risks, when they charge more than the base rate it is usually for the full amount allowed, which is 30 percent, rather than for some amount in-between that would suggest finer differences among their customers.

4. See, for example, Lardy (2000).

5. These banks comprise 10 national commercial banks (accounting for 12 percent of banking assets), 99 city commercial banks, 1,695 urban credit cooperatives (5 percent of banking assets), 39,255 rural credit cooperatives (10 percent of banking assets), and 3 policy banks (10 percent of banking assets). The other financial institutions were 12 financial leasing companies, 100 trust and investment companies and regional policy banks, 98 securities firms, 13 insurance companies, 191 foreign-funded financial institutions, and 71 enterprise group finance companies.

6. China's WTO accession agreement for the financial services industry does not seem to have relied significantly on technical calculations of profitability or solvency. Instead, broad product/client/geographic criteria were used to give domestic institutions and labor markets time to adjust. In this sense, the financial services sector is radically different from other sectors, such as agriculture, where the information base was much stronger and permitted disaggregated calculations of impacts, to which a host of finely sequenced market opening measures were tied.

7. The literature on which to draw is vast. See, for example, Lardy (1998), Cheng (1999), Bonin and Huang (2001a, 2001b), Fang (2001), OECD (2002).

8. Given their role and their dominance of the financial market, the current health and future performance of the state banks cannot help but be a major source of uncertainty about the prospects for development of the financial services industry and China's economy.

9. Most indicators—number of checking accounts, share of personal loans, mortgages or automobile finance in total credit or normalized by GDP, automated teller machines per capita—show that Chinese banks lag substantially when compared with those in neighboring East Asian countries. By contrast, China's retail banking through the postal system has expanded rapidly, managing over $46 billion in 110 million accounts at the end of 1999 through a network of 66,649 postal branches nationwide. The Postal Savings Bank, reconstituted in 2000, has established transactions links with more than 17 countries and boasts a better electronic network than most state banks. See Leong (2000).

10. Almost all of the expertise was located within the BOC, which accounted for 80 percent of China's financial sector abroad, 40 percent of international trade settlement, and 85 percent of foreign exchange clearing.

11. They are the Agricultural Development Bank, China Development Bank, and China Export and Import Bank, which together accounted for 11 percent of assets, 13 percent of loans, and less than 1 percent of deposits. They have mostly funded their operations through long-term local currency bonds, mainly purchased by the state banks.

12. Of these, 92 percent were branches of foreign banks, and the remainder were locally registered banks with full foreign ownership or joint venture arrangements. In addition, 263 representative offices of foreign banks were situated in China.

13. See, for example, the excellent collection of papers presented at the Third Annual International Financial Markets and Development Conference, entitled "Open Doors: Foreign Participation in Financial Systems in Developing Countries." Sponsored by the World Bank, International Monetary Fund, and Brookings Institution, it was held April 19–21, 2001, in New York City. The papers by Mathieson and Roldos (2001) and Pomerleano and Vojta (2001) contain useful overviews of the issues. Also see Claessens, Demigurc-Krunt, and Huizinga (1998).

14. See Boyreau-Debray (2002) and Hu and Zhou (2001) for analyses of regional disparities in financial development.

15. In addition, the risks that could arise from a change in market conditions should be considered. For example, given the very generous debt-service-to-household-income criteria in the rapidly growing home mortgage market where state bank exposure is rising, an increase in market interest rates could spark defaults among households.

References

The word *processed* describes informally reproduced works that may not be commonly available through libraries.

Almanac Editorial Board. 2002. *Almanac of China's Finance and Banking.* Beijing.

Bonin, John P., and Yiping Huang. 2001a. "Dealing with the Bad Loans of the Chinese Banks." *Journal of Asian Economics* (summer).

———. 2001b. "Foreign Entry into Chinese Banking: Does WTO Membership Threaten Domestic Banks?" Paper presented at an international conference on Greater China and the WTO, March 22–24, Hong Kong.

Boyreau-Debray, Genevieve. 2002. "Financial Intermediation and Growth: Chinese Style." World Bank, Washington, D.C., March. Processed.

Cheng Hang-Sheng. 1999. "Can China Achieve Bank Marketization without Bank Privatization? Paper presented at World Bank, March. Washington, D.C.

Claessens, Stijn, Asli Demigurc-Kunt, and Harry Huizinga. 1998. "How Does Foreign Entry Affect the Domestic Banking Market?" Policy Research Working Paper 1918. World Bank, Washington, D.C., May.

Fang Xinghai. 2001. "Reconstructing the Micro-Foundation of China's Financial Sector." Paper presented at Conference on Financial Sector Reform in China, Harvard University, Cambridge, Mass., September.

Hu Angang, and Li Zhou. 2001. "Market Openness and Good Governance: The Changing Regional Disparity of Financial Development in China (1978–1999)." Paper presented at Conference on Financial Sector Reform in China, Harvard University, Cambridge, Mass.

Lardy, Nicholas R. 1998. *China's Unfinished Economic Revolution.* Washington, D.C.: Brookings Institution and Institute for International Economics.

———. 2000. "When Will China's Financial System Meet China's Needs?" Revised version of paper presented at Conference on Policy Reform in China, February. Stanford University.

Leong, Elaine. 2000. "China's Postal Savings Service Challenges State Banks." *FinanceAsia* (September).

Li Kui-Wai, and Jun Ma. 2001. "China's Accession to the World Trade Organization and Policy Options for Banking Reform." Paper presented at Greater China and the WTO Conference, March. City University of Hong Kong, Hong Kong.

Mathieson, Donald J., and Jorge Roldos. 2001. "The Role of Foreign Banks in Emerging Markets." Paper presented at Third Annual International Financial Markets and Development Conference. April 19–21. Sponsored by the World Bank, International Monetary Fund, and Brookings Institution, New York.

Organisation for Economic Co-operation and Development (OECD). 2002. *China in the World Economy: The Domestic Policy Challenges.* OECD: Paris.

People's Bank of China. *People's Bank of China Quarterly Bulletin.* 2002–03. Vol. 27.

Pomerleano, Michael, and George J. Vojta. 2001. "What Do Foreign Banks Do in Emerging Markets? An Institutional Study." Paper presented at Third Annual International Financial Markets and Development Conference, April 19–21. Sponsored by the World Bank, International Monetary Fund, and Brookings Institution, New York.

Yearbook of China's Insurance. 2002. Beijing: Insurance Yearbook Editorial Board.

12

WTO ACCESSION AND THE STRUCTURE OF CHINA'S MOTOR VEHICLE SECTOR

Joseph F. Francois and Dean Spinanger

An automobile industry has often been a symbol of economic prestige in the developing world. Brazil, China, India, Indonesia, and Malaysia, among other countries, have all promoted, and sometimes even showcased, the development of a domestic motor vehicle industry. In China, which has a huge population together with a surface area roughly as large as that of the United States and almost 15 percent larger than that of Brazil (see table 12.1), almost every province has its own motor vehicle factory and satellite factories. Yet, among the world's major economies, China has the largest number of people per vehicle. Even Indonesia, with a 30 percent lower per capita income than China, has over 50 percent fewer people per automobile.

China's situation is the result of a series of policy measures dating from 1949 (see box 12.1). Further distorting an efficient structuring of the automobile industry have been the internal measures that have limited and even prohibited trade through local protectionism (analogous to inter-provincial

trade restrictions in Canada). The Chinese government has also set prices and limited competition through a raft of import restrictions, which have included quotas, high tariffs, and differential taxes that favor local suppliers (see, for example, Li 2003). The limitation of trade has encouraged inefficient production and has allowed market segmentation.[1]

The integration of Greater China (Mainland China and Chinese Tapei) into the World Trade Organization (WTO), and thus into most-favored-nation (MFN) principles, has important implications for the Chinese economy, not least of all for the motor vehicle sector. For example, the accession agreements specify major changes in tariffs, the elimination of quotas as well as local content requirements, and changes in the rules governing foreign investment. The perception of the Chinese market by outside investors has already changed, because the application of WTO rules covering the treatment of foreign firms has reduced uncertainty

This paper builds on Francois and Spinanger (forthcoming 2004). Special thanks are extended to Zhang Wenkui for help with data, to L. Alan Winters and Will Martin for detailed comments on an earlier draft, and to five anonymous referees, who offered valuable suggestions. Thanks also go to the participants in a World Bank-sponsored conference in Beijing for their helpful discussion. Finally, the authors would like to thank each other for their individual efforts to improve the quality of the output. Unfortunately, no agreement has been reached on who accepts final responsibility for errors or misinterpretations, and so we blame each other for any shortfalls.

TABLE 12.1   GNP, Population, and Stocks of Cars: Selected Countries, 2000

	PPP GNP per Capita (2002 U.S. Dollars)	Population (Millions, 2001)	Stocks of Cars/Trucks (Millions, 2001)	People per Car	Surface Area (1,000 sq. km)
India	2,570	1,032.4	6.3/5.9	163.2	3,287
Indonesia	2,990	209.0	3.0/2.4	68.8	1,905
China	**4,390**	**1,271.8**	**8.5/15.4**	**149.0**	**9,598**
Colombia	5,870	43.0	1.8/0.8	23.4	1,139
Turkey	6,120	66.2	4.5/1.6	14.6	775
Thailand	6,680	61.2	2.9/4.1	21.4	513
Brazil	7,250	172.4	15.8/4.0	10.9	8,547
Russia	7,820	144.8	21.2/5.1	6.8	17,075
Malaysia	8,280	23.8	4.2/1.0	5.6	330
Mexico	8,540	99.4	12.2/5.6	8.2	1,958
South Africa	9,870	43.2	41.0/2.5	1.1	1,221
Argentina	9,930	37.5	5.4/1.6	7.0	2,780
Rep. of Korea	16,480	47.3	8.9/4.0	5.3	99
Chinese Taipei	17,730	22.4	4.8/0.9	4.6	36
Spain	20,460	41.1	18.2/4.2	2.3	506
Italy	25,320	57.9	33.2/3.8	1.7	301
United Kingdom	25,870	58.8	27.8/3.4	2.1	243
Japan	26,070	127.0	53.5/19.9	2.4	378
France	26,180	59.2	28.7/5.9	2.1	552
Germany	26,220	82.3	44.4/3.6	1.9	357
Canada	28,070	31.1	17.1/0.7	1.8	9,971
United States	35,060	285.3	128.7/88.0	2.2	9,629
Total	**9,224**	**4,017.1**	**492.2/184.3**	**8.2**	**71,200**
Low and middle income	4,682	3,274.4	140.6/54.9	23.3	49,263
High income	29,248	742.7	351.6/129.4	2.1	21,937

PPP GNP = GNP adjusted for purchasing power parity exchange rate differences.
Sources: World Bank, *World Development Indicators*, various issues; VDA, various issues.

about the general economic climate, thereby inducing notable increases in investment and prompting new decisions to enter the market.

This chapter assesses the effect of these broad changes on the Chinese motor vehicle sector. It emphasizes the role of administratively imposed inefficiencies within the sector and the role of such inefficiencies in structural adjustment. We call these *regulated efficiencies*. A 1993 World Bank report pointed out that "it cannot be too much emphasized that in the long run the Chinese automotive sector will have a most efficient industrial organization when its development, dictated by international competition and state participation in the sector, is eventually replaced by entrepreneurial ownership" (World Bank 1993, xix).

The industry itself anticipates significant change. In recent years, growth in the motor vehicle sector has been very rapid, with output expanding at an annualized rate of 13 percent in the four years ending in 1999, at a 26 percent rate in the three years to 2002, and at more than 52 percent in 2003. In view of the new, modern plants that came on line in 2001 and 2002 and the additional facilities expected to increase capacity by over 150 percent from 2002 to 2005, a large, discrete change in production levels is expected.

At the same time, WTO membership implies lower prices and steeper foreign competition in the sector. The response to this shift in the competitive landscape will be shaped by continuing problems with local government protection, lack of

BOX 12.1   Summary of Developments in China's Automotive Sector

The following summary is based on the authors' survey of the literature:

1953–65: Self-Reliance Policy

- About 60,000 vehicles were produced each year.
- Production relied on Soviet technologies.
- Sector had no other international contacts.
- Provincial governments set up production units.
- By 1960, 16 auto producers and 28 assembly companies were in place.

1966–80: Security-Oriented Policy

- Government invested heavily in western regions (Sichuan, Shanxi, and Hubei).
- Remote locations caused severe problems and overcapacity.
- Focus was on heavy vehicles for military purposes.
- Car demand increased rapidly and capacities were expanded to 160,000 units per year.
- By 1980, 58 carmakers, 192 assembly companies, and 2,000 spare parts producers were operating in China.

1981–98: Initial Fruits of the Open Door Policy

- The Open Door policy adopted in 1978 kick-started the industry.

- From 1983 to 1985, the number of automotive companies almost doubled, from 65 to 114 units.
- By 1998, roughly 2,500 production units were in place.
- Provincial governments further regionalized production.
- Major international firms began to invest, and then toward 1998 began to invest quite rapidly.
- Volkswagen had already established operations in China—in 1978.
- These joint ventures accounted for about 60 percent of production during the period 1981–98.

1999– Opening Up and Beyond

- Major investments have been initiated by foreign companies.
- All major Japanese companies now have operations in China.
- All major German producers now have operations in China.
- French and Italian producers are nominally present.
- U.S. producers also are nominally present.
- Currently, the expansion is rapid; capacity is now close to 2.5 million units.
- Capacity is especially growing in coastal areas.

automobile infrastructure such as roads, parking, and service facilities, and related factors that act as constraints on growth of the sector. Even so, the industry itself expects continued strong growth.[2]

Notwithstanding industry expectations about its prospects, what is really likely to happen once the competitive landscape has changed in critical ways? The primary approach employed here to explore this question is general equilibrium, involving the application of a computational model. The next section discusses some basic issues about the structure of China's motor vehicle industry, in particular the impact of government intervention on its efficiency. A brief description of the model framework and then the experiments themselves follow. Conclusions are offered in the final section.

China's Auto Industry

Because of China's own national and regional policies, the country's motor vehicle industry is highly fragmented and inefficient by global standards. This situation is not just the result of the introduction of Soviet-style industrialization in the 1950s, when firms were merely production units and questions about efficiency were irrelevant because the dictated output was all that mattered. As noted by Zhang and Taylor (2001), the First Automobile Works (FAW) provides ample evidence of the impact evolving from the various policies in place in China over the past 50 years. Between 1959 and 1981, FAW produced "a mere 1,542 units, an average 67 units per annum." As Zhang and Taylor also note, in 1970 the production cost of a particular

FIGURE 12.1   China's Production of Motor Vehicles since Adoption of the Open-Door Policy

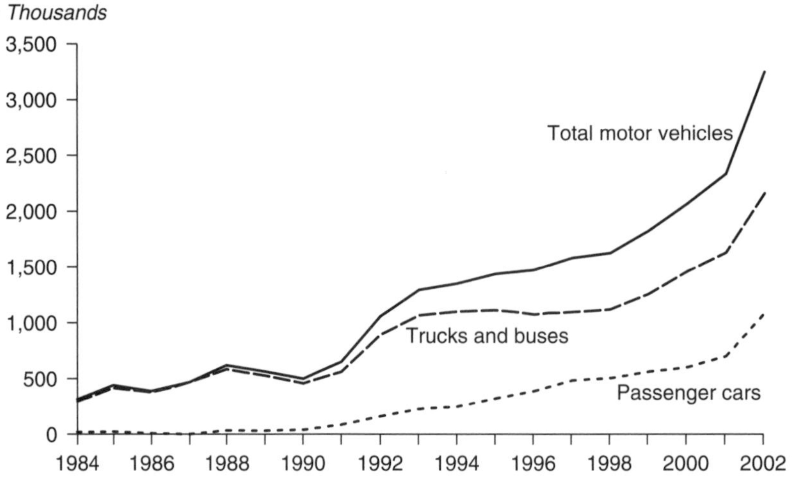

Sources: Bessum 2002; VDA, various issues.

model (the CA72) was 220,000 yuan, but "the sales price was only 40,000 yuan. . . . In the absence of competition, all production units ran at low levels of productivity and efficiency. . . . The legacy left by Mao's regime loomed well into the 1980s. By 1980 the number of automotive enterprises had risen to 2,379, consisting of 56 vehicle manufacturers . . . [producing, among other things] 5,418 cars."

China's fragmented and inefficient automotive industry is also the result of import substitution policies, together with cooperation agreements made with foreign companies beginning in the 1980s that were meant to fill the increasing gap between production and the rapidly expanding demand for automobiles. After all, the major thrust of policies until then had been to build trucks.[2] These trends are depicted in figure 12.1.

Thus China's automotive companies are operating with cost structures well within the global frontier, and the plants are producing considerably below global standards for efficient scale. This observation is illustrated in table 12.2 for the sedan industry, assuming that plants of minimum efficient scale (MES) for final assembly of cars are those that produce at least 200,000 units a year of one model (see Huang 2002, p. 543). China's entire sedan production in 1998 was 507,000 vehicles, produced by 13 factories. The fact that only two factories produced more than 100,000 sedans each implies that fewer than 40,000 sedans were produced by each of the other factories.

Actually, a great deal of variation in plant scale exists around this average (see table 12.2). The leading producer, Shanghai-Volkswagen, made 248,000 sedans in 2002 (and therefore operated at MES levels if producing one model). Several other plants had production runs of less than 20,000. In this sense, there are strong parallels to the situation in Mexico prior to implementation of the NAFTA in which protected, inefficient factories operated well within the global technology frontier (see Lopez de Silanes, Markusen, and Rutherford 1994). Overall, China's motor vehicle industry has about 2,400 industrial enterprises. In 1998, these included 122 motor vehicle manufacturing plants, 520 auto-refitting factories, 130 motorcycle factories, 62 car engine factories, and 1,589 auto and motorcycle spare parts factories. Annual production capacity exceeds 2.3 million motor vehicles and 10 million motorcycles. Since 1995, the general pattern has been closure of the smaller plants (generally relegated to the "other" category in table 12.2) and expansion of production runs in the larger plants. With foreign investment and the rapid growth in the industry, the number of plants producing at least 25,000 vehicles rose from 3 in 1995 to 11 in 2002 (see U.S. and Chinese National Academies of Engineering 2003).

Import and domestic shipment data in value terms are summarized in table 12.3 (the data are for 1997, which serves as the "pre-accession" reference point). Import tariff protection is summarized

TABLE 12.2 Auto Production by Plant in China, 1995–2002

Rank 2002/1995	Plant	1995	1996	1997	1998	1999	2000	2001	2002[a]
1/1	Shanghai-VW	160,070	200,222	230,443	235,000	230,946	221,524	230,378	248,000
2/4	FAW-VW	24,553	44,825	46,405	66,000	81,464	94,147	101,622	131,000
3/n.a.	Shanghai-GM	—	—	—	—	—	30,024	58,548	106,000
4/2	Tianjin Xiali (Daihatsu)	65,258	88,232	95,155	100,021	101,828	81,951	41,703	93,000
5/5	FAW-Audi-Hongqi	19,350			15,000	15,731	31,225	52,667	78,000
6/9	Shenlong (Citroen)	3,797	9,228	30,035	36,240	40,200	53,900	52,850	68,000
7/6	Chang'an (Suzuki)	17,770	16,420	35,160	36,239	44,583	48,235	50,573	64,000
8/n.a.	Guangzhou-Honda	—	—	—	2,246	10,008	32,228	51,153	60,000
9/n.a.	Shanghai-Qirui	—	—	—	—	—	2,767	30,085	47,000
10/n.a.	Geely Group	—	—	—	—	—	14,594	21,702	38,000
11/n.a.	Dongfeng Fengshen	—	—	—	—	—	3,159	8,000	32,000
12/n.a.	Haima (Nainan-Mazda)	—	—	—	—	—	3,059	7,800	20,000
13/n.a.	Yuedo-KIA	—	—	—	—	—	2,423	6,210	16,000
14/n.a.	Qinchuan	—	—	—	—	—	5,380	5,686	16,000
15/n.a.	Nanya	—	—	—	—	—	1,000	8,000	13,500
16/3	Beijing (Jeep)	25,127	26,051	19,377	8,344	9,294	4,867	4,663	4,400
17/7	Guizhou Yunque (Subaru)	7,105	798	1,000	—	—	859	1,253	2,100
18/n.a.	Tianjin-Toyota	—	—	—	—	—	—	—	2,000
n.a./8	Guangzhou-Peugeot	6,698	2,416	1,557	8,013	31,312	17,930	—	—
	Other	22,570	—	22,479					1,900
	Total	352,298	388,192	481,611	507,103	565,366	649,272	732,883	1,040,900
	Number of plants producing >25,000	3	4	5	5	5	8	9	11
	Number of plants producing >50,000	2	2	2	3	3	4	7	8
	Number of plants producing >100,000	1	1	1	2	2	1	2	3

— Not available because plants have closed or were not yet opened.

n.a. Not applicable.

[a]The 2002 values are based on company projections.

Sources: Bessum 2002; Chinese Motor Vehicle Documentation Center 2002.

TABLE 12.3 Import and Domestic Shipment Values of China's Motor Vehicle Industry, 1997 (millions of US$)

	Value
Imported motor vehicles and parts, world prices	3,607.71
Imported motor vehicles and parts, internal prices	4,849.31
Imported parts, internal prices	3,239.45
Imported motor vehicles, internal prices	1,609.86
Domestic intermediates and parts	32,812.46
Domestic intermediate parts	10,896.15
Industry consumption of motor vehicles	21,625.50
Final consumption of motor vehicles	290.81

Source: Global Trade Analysis Project (GTAP) version 5 database.

TABLE 12.4 Tariffs on Chinese Motor Vehicles (percent)

	Base Rate	Final Rate
Finished motor vehicles	70.5	25
Motor vehicle parts	23.4	10
Electronic vehicle parts	12.0	10
Average, vehicles and parts	34.7	15

Sources: China's WTO accession schedule; GTAP data; Office of the U.S. Trade Representative.

in table 12.4. China's pre-accession average tariff on auto products (vehicles and parts and electronics) was 35 percent. The rate for vehicles averaged 70 percent, with sedans subject to tariffs of between 80 percent and 100 percent. Motor vehicle parts were subject to an average tariff of only 23 percent. Import shares were relatively low, averaging perhaps 3 percent in the years 1995–2002. Officially, only 20,000 sedans were imported.[3] Government policy encouraged the use of domestic parts, and, better yet, locally produced parts. For new investments, domestic content rules applied, stipulating 80 percent domestic content by the third year. All this is reflected as well in the low share of automotive parts imports in total production. As for the ownership of companies, even after full implementation of the WTO, foreign ownership will be limited to 50 percent.[4]

China's tariff rates are scheduled to come down substantially (table 12.4)—25 percent for vehicles and 10 percent for parts on an MFN basis as part of

WTO accession. In addition, quotas on automobiles and on key components will be phased out by 2006, after being expanded by 15 percent a year until then. Likewise, domestic content requirements have already been removed. (Both of these nontariff measures violate basic WTO rules.) Clearly, these changes in the structure of protection will have significant implications for the structure of the automotive sector. Critically, other WTO obligations imply free movement of imported autos (free of import quotas) within the China market. This situation implies tremendous pressure for a breakdown of internal barriers for domestic production and for a rationalization of the domestic industry. The internal barriers to trade simply cannot be sustained if China's new WTO obligations are to be taken seriously.

The government has itself recognized this situation. Official and industry sources have signaled their intention to support only a small number of domestic production groups, perhaps including the

Shanghai group (Volkswagen), China's First Auto Works (Volkswagen), Shanghai-GM (Buick), and the Dongfeng Group (Citroën). These groups with their foreign partners already account for over 70 percent of production in China. Such a sharp rationalization would undoubtedly be painful, but it could allow the industry to consolidate production and work its way down the average cost curve for vehicle production.

The Modeling Framework

The next section sketches a quantitative assessment of the possible impact of WTO accession on China's motor vehicle industry—an assessment made by applying the computable general equilibrium (CGE) model. This section provides a brief overview of the model. More technical details and references are provided in Francois and Spinanger (2001) and in the technical annex available for downloading with the model files.[5] For multi-sector policy initiatives (such as WTO accession) in which interactions between sectors have a major effect on results, the use of CGE models has become a relatively standard approach (see François 2000). We recognize that the results of these exercises are hampered both by the assumptions made and by the quality of the data available. Even so, we believe their utility in estimating the possible overall pattern of the effect of broad policy changes—both direct and indirect—is well proven.

The Model Data

The model data, taken from a variety of sources, were organized into 23 sectors and 25 regions. (Note that we included some detail on the value-added chain, linking fibers with textile and clothing production to better capture the initial impact of the Agreement on Textiles and Clothing [ATC] on our base scenario.) The sectors and regions for this 23 × 25 aggregation of the data are detailed in table 12.5.

Data on production and trade are based on national accounting data linked through trade flows and drawn directly from the Global Trade Analysis Project (GTAP) version 5 data set (McDougall 2001). The GTAP version 5 data set is benchmarked to 1997, and it includes detailed national input-output, trade, and final demand structures. We modified the basic database. In particular, we updated the data set to better reflect actual import protection for goods and services.

The basic data on current tariff rates are drawn from United Nations Conference on Trade and Development (UNCTAD) and WTO data on the schedules of applied and bound tariff rates, and they are integrated into the core GTAP database. They are supplemented with data from the Office of the U.S. Trade Representative and the U.S. International Trade Commission on regional preference schemes in the Western Hemisphere. For agriculture, protection is based on Organisation for Economic Co-operation and Development (OECD) and U.S. Department of Agriculture (USDA) estimates of agricultural protection, as integrated into the GTAP core database. Tariff and nontariff barrier estimates are further adjusted to reflect remaining Uruguay Round commitments, including the phaseout of remaining textile and clothing quotas under the ATC. Data on post–Uruguay Round tariffs are taken from recent estimates reported by Francois and Strutt (1999). These estimates are taken primarily from the WTO's integrated database, with supplemental information from the World Bank's recent assessment of detailed pre– and post–Uruguay Round tariff schedules. All of this tariff information has been matched to the current model sectors. Services trade barriers are based on the estimates described in the technical annex and are shown in table 12.6. (The basic GTAP database includes no information at all on trade barriers for services, for example.)

Although the basic GTAP data set is benchmarked to 1997 and reflects applied tariffs actually in place in 1997, we want to work with a representation of a post–Uruguay Round world. To accomplish this, before conducting any policy experiments we run a "pre-experiment" in which we implement the remaining Uruguay Round tariff cuts. Most of these cuts are already in place in the 1997 benchmark data set. At the same time, the data are adjusted to reflect regional preference schemes in Latin America (not represented in the core GTAP database). The data set we work with for actual experiments is therefore a representation of a notional world economy (values are in

TABLE 12.5 Regional and Sectoral Breakdown of the Model

Model Regions/Economies		Model Sectors	
Economy	Description	Sector	Description
Hong Kong	Hong Kong (China)	Wool	Wool
China (PRC)	People's Republic of China	Other natural fibers	Natural fibers (cotton, etc.)
Chinese Taipei	Chinese Taipei	Primary food	Primary food production
Japan	Japan	Other primary production	Other primary production
Korea, Rep. of	Korea, Rep. of	Sugar	Sugar
ASEAN5	ASEAN5 member states[a]	Processed foods	Processed foods, tobacco, and beverages
Vietnam	Vietnam		
India	India	Textiles	Textiles
Bangladesh	Bangladesh	Clothing	Wearing apparel
Other South Asia	Other South Asian economies[b]	Leather goods	Leather products
Australia	Australia	Chemicals, rubber, and refinery products	Chemicals, refinery products, rubber, plastics
New Zealand	New Zealand	Primary steel	Steel refinery products
Canada	Canada	Primary nonferrous metals	Nonferrous metal products
United States	United States of America	Motor vehicles and parts	Motor vehicles and parts
Mexico	Mexico	Electronics	Electronic machinery and equipment
Brazil	Brazil	Other machinery and equipment	Other machinery and equipment
MERCOSUR, other	MERCOSUR[c]	Other manufactures	Other manufactured goods
CBI	Caribbean Basin Initiative economies[d]		
ATP	Andean Trade Pact economies[d]	Wholesale and retail trade	Wholesale and retail trade services
Chile	Chile[d]	Transport services	Transportation services (land, water, air)
Other Latin America	Other Latin America[d]	Communications	Communications services
European Union(15)	European Union, 15 economies	Construction	Construction
Turkey	Turkey	Finance, insurance, and real estate	Finance, insurance, and real estate services
Africa, Mideast	Africa and the Middle East	Commercial services	Other commercial services
Rest of world	Rest of world	Other services	Other services (public, health, etc.)

[a]ASEAN5 = Philippines, Thailand, Indonesia, Singapore, and Malaysia.
[b]Pakistan, Sri Lanka, and Nepal.
[c]MERCOSUR = Argentina, Paraguay, Uruguay. Brazil is represented separately.
[d]Not treated in tables and figures.
Source: The authors.

1997 U.S. dollars), with full implementation of Uruguay Round tariff cuts. We then examine both the ATC phaseout and Greater China accession with reference to this post–Uruguay Round tariff benchmark.

Model Structure

We turn next to the basic analytical features of the model. Except for automobiles, we use a very standard CGE model structure. On the production side,

TABLE 12.6 Mainland China's Pre- and Post-WTO Accession Tariff Rates (as modeled)

Sector	Model Base Rate	Accession Rate	New Bound Rate
Merchandise			
Wool	14.76	42.00	38.00
Natural fibers (cotton, etc.)	3.14	17.38	13.58
Primary food production	58.80	58.13	46.83
Other primary production	0.48	6.94	5.08
Sugar	29.49	30.00	20.00
Processed food, tobacco, and beverages	37.65	40.66	23.18
Textiles	25.09	25.43	10.21
Wearing apparel	31.75	32.80	16.05
Leather products	12.10	20.94	17.02
Chemicals, refinery products, rubber, plastics	12.62	14.85	7.17
Steel refinery products	9.68	8.92	5.10
Nonferrous metal products	7.83	8.20	5.52
Motor vehicles and parts	34.42	38.65	15.41
Motor vehicles	70.50	70.50	25.00
Parts	23.40	23.40	10.00
Electronic machinery and equipment	11.93	16.90	9.62
Other machinery and equipment	12.83	15.37	10.14
Other manufactured goods	14.51	21.99	16.29
Services			
Wholesale and retail trade services	0.00	n.a.	0.00
Transportation services (land, water, air)	3.97	n.a.	1.99
Communications services	9.18	n.a.	4.59
Construction	13.68	n.a.	6.84
Finance, insurance, and real estate services	8.08	n.a.	4.04
Other commercial services	47.92	n.a.	23.96
Other services (public, health, etc.)	25.74	n.a.	12.87

n.a. Not applicable.

Note: Services barriers are based on gravity equation estimates. Accession rates reflect an assumed 50 percent drop in cross-border trading cost estimates.

Sources: China WTO accession schedule; GTAP data; Office of the U.S. Trade Representative. Gravity estimates are based on trade and macroeconomic data and cross-country regressions. See François and Spinanger 2001.

all firms are assumed to minimize costs, employing domestic production factors (capital, labor, and land) and intermediate inputs from domestic and foreign sources to produce goods and services. These technologies are modeled as constant elasticity of substitution (CES) technologies defined over primary inputs and Leontief processes defined over intermediate inputs. Products from different regions are assumed to be imperfect substitutes in accordance with the so-called Armington assumption. Prices on goods and factors adjust until all markets are simultaneously in (general) equilibrium, which means that we solve for equilibria

in which all markets clear. Although we model changes in gross trade flows, we do not model changes in net international capital flows. (This approach does not by any means preclude introducing changes in the level of gross capital flows.) Trade liberalization in the goods sectors involves a reduction of tariffs. This reduction involves in turn a shift from the model base rates in table 12.6 to the new bound rates. The new bound rates are generally quite close to our calculations of average accession rates, also shown in table 12.6. Service sector liberalization is modeled as a reduction in trading costs, reflecting the barrier reductions reported in table 12.6. These are modeled as Samuelson iceberg costs.

For the motor vehicle sector, we want to model the status quo in a stylized though representative way. One option is to implement imperfect competition in the model, but such an approach does not really deal with the primary issue at hand. Government policy has led to market segmentation, as well as to price setting and regulation. Although the best approach to use in this situation is ultimately something of a judgment call, we have chosen to focus on realized cost efficiency for the sector. The current cost structure of the motor vehicle industry reflects the net effect of a basket of policies. Like clothing in India and automobiles in Mexico before the North American Free Trade Agreement (NAFTA) the structure of the auto sector in China is a product of *regulated efficiency*—that is, the general regulatory and administrative environment. The critical issue is actually these collective inefficiencies, which follow from the full set of industrial policies. At the same time, an implication of the reforms that are being implemented alongside WTO accession seems to be restructuring and consolidation, leading to an improvement in regulated efficiency.

What shape will changes in regulated efficiency gains take? The industry, through rationalization, may move collectively down the relevant cost curves. A comparison of current average plant scale (table 12.2) with a global norm closer to 350,000 units per plant implies that average costs are roughly 20 percent higher simply because of inefficient scale. The 20 percent figure is based on the distribution of current plants in table 12.2. In particular, if we apply the formula $\Delta \ln (Average\ Cost) = -CDR \cdot \Delta \ln(Quantity)$, where CDR, the cost-disadvantage ratio, is the inverse elasticity of scale, defined as

$$CDR = -\frac{Average\ Cost - Marginal\ Cost}{Average\ Cost}$$

and where CDR is between 0.125 and 0.135 (the range of values found in engineering studies), we can calculate an average cost index for the industry. If such an index is 100 at 350,000 units per plant (the approximate norm for European and North American plants), current plant structure yields a cost index of roughly 120.

Data from interviews with industry representatives (Feenstra and others 2001) point to similar cost savings, with expectations even higher—in the range of 25–30 percent cost reductions. The World Bank (1993: 57) has described quite succinctly the expected gains from reaching MES: "If this cost-volume relationship is applied to the Chinese automotive industry, the passenger car segment has a cost disadvantage of 20 to 30 percent compared with the international producers having MES. This cost disadvantage could be an understatement, however, as there are already eight producers in the market."

These efficiencies are illustrated in figure 12.2, where we take sedan assembly as representative. In figure 12.2, individual plants are plotted relative to the cost:output mapping for an efficient plant. The figure depicts an expectation that significant cost savings may be realized if the government takes seriously its commitments to eliminate internal barriers, and if it responds by encouraging a restructuring of the domestic industry around a limited number of motor vehicle groups.

This net cost effect is stressed here and sets the treatment of motor vehicles apart from that of other sectors in the model. We work with the lower bound of these cost effect estimates. In particular, we focus on potential cost savings in the final assembly of autos (stemming from consolidation and rationalization at the plant level), which yields a higher regulated efficiency level for the industry. In addition, the differential treatment of parts and finished vehicles in the tariff schedule is tracked.

To set these issues in context, it may help to draw on developments in the automobile industry at an earlier point in time. That large gains can be achieved in rationalizing production and accordingly reducing costs in the automobile sector was most clearly demonstrated toward the beginning of the twentieth century. Henry Ford changed the parameters of producing automobiles radically by introducing the assembly line in 1910. By 1914, "13,000 workers at Ford were producing 260,720 cars. By comparison, in the rest of the industry, it took 66,350 workers to make 286,770 [cars]."[6] But it was not just the shift in cost parameters that was significant in transforming the sector. Demand factors were also important. Cars in the United States, as a result of Ford's new production methods, moved from being a scarce good to one affordable by large segments of the U.S. population. China is already in the process of moving into this phase, as is evident from figure 12.3.

FIGURE 12.2   Scale and Average Cost (with a CDR of 0.125)

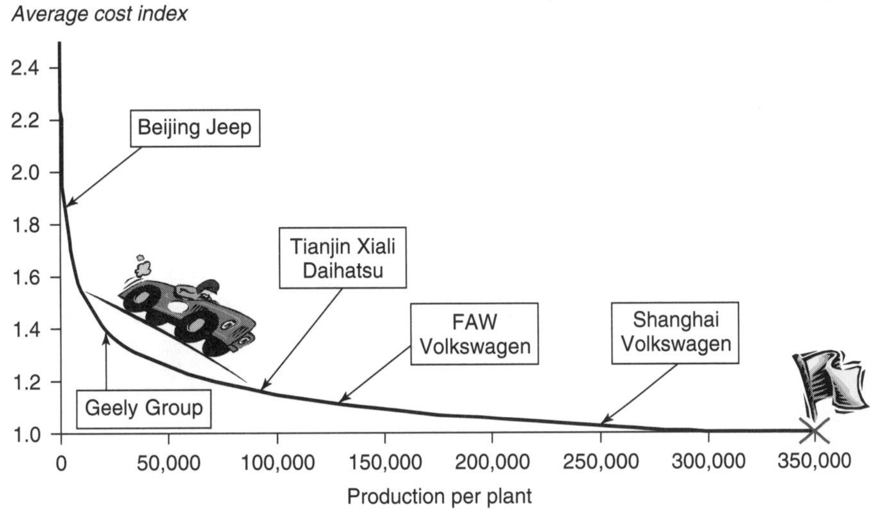

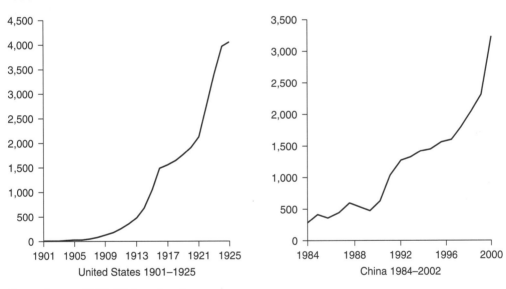

Note: Moving from the current range of output to plants with an average of 300,000 units implies a 20 percent cost savings.

Source: Author's calculations and data from table 12.2.

FIGURE 12.3   Motor Vehicle Production in China and United States

Source: Bessum 2002; VDA, various issues.

Experiments and Results

The experiments are directed at full accession to the WTO for Greater China (Mainland China and Chinese Taipei). The basic accession package covers the changes in tariffs detailed in table 12.3. For automobiles, we model the following effects:[7]

- Tariffs on motor vehicles will decrease to 25 percent.
- Tariffs on auto parts will decrease from an average of 23.4 percent to an average of 10 percent.

- Industry rationalization will implicitly involve the elimination of internal regional barriers and will allow for consolidation and rationalization within the domestic market. Small, inefficient factories will close.

To quantify the last effect, we take sedan production as representative. Given the typical scale of domestic production, we estimate that auto plants will realize a 20 percent cost savings in assembly if we move plants to efficient scale (see note 2 and the

TABLE 12.7   Impact of WTO Accession of Greater China on Output (percent change)

	A Impact of Eliminating ATC Quotas for WTO Members, Mainland China, and Chinese Taipei	B Impact of Mainland China and Chinese Taipei Accession, without Auto Sector Restructuring	C Impact of Mainland China and Chinese Taipei Accession, with Auto Sector Restructuring	D = A + B Total Impact, without Auto Sector Restructuring	E = A + C Total Impact, with Auto Sector Restructuring
Wool	12.80	18.26	16.84	33.40	31.79
Other natural fibers	12.11	17.86	16.41	32.13	30.51
Primary food	−0.43	−1.03	−0.92	−1.46	−1.34
Other primary production	−2.60	−3.57	−3.33	−6.07	−5.84
Sugar	−2.26	−7.93	−8.48	−10.01	−10.55
Processed foods	−1.02	−4.66	−4.74	−5.63	−5.71
Textiles	13.93	32.00	30.57	50.39	48.75
Clothing	50.26	75.46	73.03	163.65	159.98
Leather goods	−7.18	5.36	3.51	−2.20	−3.92
Chemicals, rubber, and refinery products	−2.03	−4.53	−4.27	−6.46	−6.21
Primary steel	−3.99	−9.13	−7.86	−12.76	−11.54
Primary nonferrous metals	−5.42	−9.24	−8.94	−14.16	−13.87
Motor vehicles and parts	**−4.11**	**−36.68**	**7.99**	**−39.28**	**3.54**
Electronics	−5.06	−3.91	−4.43	−8.77	−9.26
Other machinery and equipment	−3.80	−5.39	−4.84	−8.98	−8.46
Other manufactures	−2.16	−0.34	0.14	−2.49	−2.02
Wholesale and retail trade	−0.25	1.39	1.93	1.14	1.68
Transport services	−1.94	−1.95	−1.39	−3.85	−3.31
Communications	−0.51	0.06	0.99	−0.45	0.47
Construction	0.75	2.81	4.17	3.58	4.95
Finance, insurance, and real estate	−0.65	−0.40	0.22	−1.05	−0.44
Commercial services	−0.78	−5.85	−5.41	−6.58	−6.15
Other services	0.00	0.46	1.23	0.46	1.23

Source: Model estimates.

discussion in this overall section). This savings is modeled at the assembly level.

The overall sectoral effects of the experiments are presented in table 12.7. This table reports changes in the quantity of output under our alternative scenarios. Thus, as expected, the extension of the ATC phaseout to China and Chinese Taipei implies a rather dramatic expansion of the textile and clothing sectors—13.9 and 50.3 percent, respectively. There are important general equilibrium effects, because the resources needed for this experiment are drawn from other parts of the economy, including the motor vehicle sector.

The results in columns B and C of table 12.7 are very important for the motor vehicle sector. They reflect the incremental impact of China's market access commitments made as part of accession. Column B is a "business as usual" scenario, without the restructuring discussed elsewhere in this chapter. It reflects a domestic motor vehicle industry that continues to be fragmented, with favored producers in each region, small production runs, and

TABLE 12.8   Mainland China Motor Vehicle Market (millions of 1997 US$)

	1997 Benchmark	Impact of Mainland China and Chinese Taipei Accession, without Auto Sector Restructuring	Impact of Mainland China and Chinese Taipei Accession, with Auto Sector Restructuring
Values			
Imported motor vehicles and parts, world prices	3,607.71	10,595.68	6,967.97
Imported motor vehicles and parts, internal prices	4,806.39	12,080.71	7,995.72
Imported parts, internal prices	1,609.86	2,827.93	5,535.24
Imported motor vehicles, internal prices	3,196.53	9,252.78	2,460.48
Domestic autos, intermediates and parts	32,812.46	19,401.89	24,249.56
Domestic intermediate parts	10,896.15	4,493.95	5,189.12
Industry consumption of motor vehicles	21,625.50	14,698.79	18,785.03
Final consumption of motor vehicles	290.81	209.15	275.41
Indexes and shares			
Import share of total auto parts (percent of value)	12.87	38.62	51.61
Index of vehicle production	100.00	67.98	102.78
Index of parts production	100.00	41.22	56.28

Sources: Author's calculations and GTAP base data.

FIGURE 12.4   Import Share of Total Auto Parts

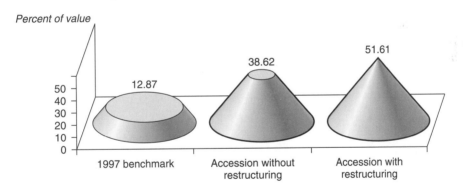

high costs. Such an industry is simply unable to compete with imports, and indeed is very hard-hit by imports, with domestic production falling by 36.7 percent. When that result is combined with the initial impact of the ATC phaseout, a rather dramatic retrenchment of the uncompetitive domestic industry occurs in the face of imports (column D).

The contrast is offered in column C and the corresponding total in column E. Column C represents the elimination of internal barriers, rationalization of plants (with smaller plants being closed), and a realized efficiency gain of roughly 20 percent as scale economies are realized. This industry is much different from the one in column B. Production actually goes up slightly (3 percent) in total, and the industry emerges as a relatively competitive one, despite the loss of protection.

More information is provided on the differences between the two scenarios in table 12.8 and figure 12.4. The table expands on the information originally provided in table 12.3, with a comparable breakdown corresponding to columns D and E

TABLE 12.9 Impact of Greater China Accession on Value Added (percent change)

	A	B	C	D = A + B	E = A + C
	Impact of Eliminating ATC Quotas for WTO Members, Mainland China, and Chinese Taipei	Impact of Mainland China and Chinese Taipei Accession, without Auto Sector Restructuring	Impact of Mainland China and Chinese Taipei Accession, with Auto Sector Restructuring	Total Impact, without Auto Sector Restructuring	Total Impact, with Auto Sector Restructuring
Wool	11.55	12.97	10.62	26.02	23.40
Other natural fibers	10.87	12.58	10.21	24.82	22.20
Primary food	−1.53	−5.46	−6.19	−6.91	−7.63
Other primary production	−3.68	−7.88	−8.47	−11.27	−11.84
Sugar	−3.34	−12.05	−13.36	−14.99	−16.25
Processed foods	−2.11	−8.92	−9.81	−10.85	−11.72
Textiles	12.67	26.09	23.62	42.07	39.28
Clothing	48.60	67.61	63.81	149.06	143.42
Leather goods	−8.20	0.64	−2.00	−7.61	−10.04
Chemicals, rubber, and refinery products	−3.11	−8.80	−9.37	−11.64	−12.19
Primary steel	−5.06	−13.20	−12.76	−17.59	−17.17
Primary nonferrous metals	−6.46	−13.31	−13.79	−18.91	−19.36
Motor vehicles and parts	**−5.17**	**−39.51**	**2.24**	**−42.64**	**−3.05**
Electronics	−6.11	−8.21	−9.52	−13.82	−15.04
Other machinery and equipment	−4.86	−9.62	−9.91	−14.02	−14.29
Other manufactures	−3.24	−4.80	−5.19	−7.88	−8.26
Wholesale and retail trade	−1.35	−3.15	−3.50	−4.46	−4.80
Transport services	−3.03	−6.34	−6.64	−9.17	−9.47
Communications	−1.61	−4.42	−4.39	−5.96	−5.93
Construction	−0.36	−1.79	−1.38	−2.15	−1.73
Finance, insurance, and real estate	−1.75	−4.86	−5.12	−6.53	−6.78
Commercial services	−1.87	−10.07	−10.45	−11.75	−12.13
Other services	−1.10	−4.04	−4.16	−5.10	−5.22

Source: Model estimates.

in table 12.7; table 12.9 portrays the results just for value added. The most striking difference between the two scenarios is the different impacts on intermediate parts production and final auto production, as illustrated in figure 12.4. Under the first scenario, characterized by a domestic policy status quo, imports of parts rise slightly and their share of the domestic parts market rises substantially. At the same time, there is a dramatic surge in imports of motor vehicles, which displace more than one-third of existing domestic production. The overall market for parts falls because of the decline in domestic

vehicle production. Under the second scenario, the final assembly sector is rationalized, allowing the sector to compete more directly with imports. The result is a shift to imported intermediates (rising to a market share of over 50 percent), a fall in domestic parts production (as they are displaced by imports), but a steady overall demand for parts. For the industry overall, although ground is still lost to parts imports, sales of domestic vehicles remain relatively steady in the face of imports.

One last view of the effect of accession is presented in tables 12.10, 12.11, and 12.12, which

TABLE 12.10   Impact of Greater China Accession on Value of Exports (percent change)

	A Impact of Eliminating ATC Quotas for WTO Members, Mainland China, and Chinese Taipei	B Impact of Mainland China and Chinese Taipei Accession, without Auto Sector Restructuring	C Impact of Mainland China and Chinese Taipei Accession, with Auto Sector Restructuring	D = A + B Total Impact, without Auto Sector Restructuring	E = A + C Total Impact, with Auto Sector Restructuring
Wool	−9.52	−18.73	−20.14	−26.47	−27.75
Other natural fibers	−4.67	−16.12	−16.67	−20.04	−20.56
Primary food	−4.16	−5.05	−7.29	−9.00	−11.14
Other primary production	−3.33	−2.98	−4.23	−6.21	−7.42
Sugar	−3.29	−5.19	−7.05	−8.31	−10.11
Processed foods	−4.99	−4.15	−5.96	−8.93	−10.65
Textiles	6.18	32.74	32.01	40.93	40.16
Clothing	87.81	80.03	77.48	238.11	233.33
Leather goods	−7.66	3.85	1.76	−4.11	−6.04
Chemicals, rubber, and refinery products	−3.29	−0.30	−1.01	−3.59	−4.27
Primary steel	−5.56	−3.00	−3.99	−8.39	−9.33
Primary nonferrous metals	−5.87	−4.05	−5.36	−9.69	−10.92
Motor vehicles and parts	−12.33	16.17	392.33	1.85	331.64
Electronics	−4.56	−0.86	−1.75	−5.39	−6.24
Other machinery and equipment	−6.69	−3.69	−4.52	−10.13	−10.91
Other manufactures	−5.74	−2.57	−3.69	−8.16	−9.22
Wholesale and retail trade	−4.79	−5.19	−5.82	−9.73	−10.34
Transport services	−3.31	−2.28	−2.44	−5.52	−5.67
Communications	−5.05	−4.38	−4.90	−9.20	−9.70
Construction	−4.92	−4.34	−5.62	−9.05	−10.26
Finance, insurance, and real estate	−5.33	−6.01	−7.10	−11.01	−12.05
Commercial services	−5.17	−3.00	−4.17	−8.02	−9.13
Other services	−5.59	−5.98	−7.04	−11.24	−12.24

Source: Model estimates.

reveal the export impacts observed under the various modeling scenarios. It is logical to expect some export response, both because of the general liberalization in trade and because pressure from imports may force firms to seek other markets. China exports less than 4 percent of its production in the motor vehicle sector, based on 1997 values. Of US$32 billion in production,[8] only $1.3 billion in products is exported. To put this figure in perspective, Australia has a comparable level of exports for an industry only one-third the size of

the Chinese industry. The export share for the Republic of Korea is 10 times as large. China's trade is therefore well below global integration standards as measured by exports.

Tables 12.10 and 12.11 compare export volume effects, as a percentage of base exports and in dollar terms. Clearly, restructuring accelerates the export orientation of the industry, with a rapid growth in exports. Exports rise by about 300 percent, or $3.8 billion, reaching roughly 10 percent of production by value. Although this expansion seems

TABLE 12.11 Impact of Greater China Accession on Value of Exports (millions of U.S. dollars)

	A	B	C	D = A + B	E = A + C
	Impact of Eliminating ATC Quotas for WTO Members, Mainland China, and Chinese Taipei	Impact of Mainland China and Chinese Taipei Accession, without Auto Sector Restructuring	Impact of Mainland China and Chinese Taipei Accession, with Auto Sector Restructuring	Total Impact, without Auto Sector Restructuring	Total Impact, with Auto Sector Restructuring
Wool	−4.95	−9.74	−10.47	−13.76	−14.42
Other natural fibers	−0.18	−0.63	−0.65	−0.78	−0.80
Primary food	−237.46	−288.39	−416.09	−513.86	−636.25
Other primary production	−153.94	−138.02	−195.70	−287.36	−343.13
Sugar	−4.58	−7.22	−9.82	−11.57	−14.08
Processed foods	−360.07	−299.33	−430.38	−644.47	−768.99
Textiles	1,356.02	7,186.55	7,026.81	8,986.47	8,816.86
Clothing	4,3997.88	40,096.19	38,820.21	119,303.97	116,907.51
Leather goods	−1,503.44	755.88	345.26	−805.49	−1,184.64
Chemicals, rubber, and refinery products	−560.97	−51.79	−171.59	−611.06	−726.91
Primary steel	−225.93	−121.72	−162.30	−340.88	−379.21
Primary nonferrous metals	−130.28	−89.89	−118.97	−214.90	−242.26
Motor vehicles and parts	**−141.58**	**185.76**	**4,505.86**	**21.28**	**3,808.80**
Electronics	−1,365.27	−257.74	−524.98	−1,611.25	−1,866.29
Other machinery and equipment	−2,145.66	−1,183.94	−1,450.56	−3,250.42	−3,499.21
Other manufactures	−2,183.35	−977.14	−1,403.76	−3,104.39	−3,506.52
Wholesale and retail trade	−338.09	−365.87	−410.81	−686.43	−729.21
Transport services	−278.13	−191.84	−205.06	−463.62	−476.40
Communications	−19.84	−17.22	−19.27	−36.20	−38.14
Construction	−25.88	−22.84	−29.53	−47.59	−53.96
Finance, insurance, and real estate	−26.63	−30.02	−35.49	−55.05	−60.23
Commercial services	−62.46	−36.25	−50.40	−96.84	−110.26
Other services	−78.30	−83.81	−98.61	−157.43	−171.40

Source: Model estimates.

dramatic, it should be kept in perspective. Export shares are shown in table 12.12. Currently, automobiles and parts are a small share of exports (0.6 percent in 1997), and they remain small (up to 2 percent) even with the growth in automobile exports. In addition, most of the restructuring remains focused on the domestic market.

Summary and Conclusions

In this chapter we examine the interaction between regulated efficiency and China's accession to the WTO, and its impact on China's motor vehicle sector. The approach we take is general equilibrium, requiring application of a global general equilibrium model.

We argue that regulatory reform and internal restructuring are critical to any realized effect on the auto sector. Such restructuring is represented here by a cost reduction that follows from consolidation and rationalization. This representation is supported by a comparison of scale in a typical auto plant in China with that in typical plants in North America and Europe, and by firm survey

TABLE 12.12   China Export Shares: Baseline and Scenario

Export Shares	1997 Baseline	Total Impact, without Auto Sector Restructuring	Total Impact, with Auto Sector Restructuring
Primary foods	0.046	0.033	0.033
Textiles	0.084	0.098	0.097
Clothing	0.102	0.303	0.298
Motor vehicles and parts	0.006	0.004	0.019
Electronics	0.133	0.100	0.099
Other machinery and equipment	0.146	0.104	0.103
Other manufactures	0.397	0.294	0.290
Services	0.087	0.062	0.062

Sources: Author's calculations; GTAP base data.

responses. We also draw on earlier similar estimates of the benefits to be had by achieving minimum efficient scale and by radically structuring production more efficiently.

The net result is movement of costs toward global norms. Without such restructuring, the domestic industry remains uncompetitive, and WTO accession will lead to a surge in imports of final vehicles, though imports of parts will fall as production moves offshore. With restructuring, the final assembly industry will become competitive by world standards, while the parts industry further integrates with the global industry through exports (and through higher imports of parts). As highlighted in figure 12.5, most automobile firms are located along the coast and thus are well placed to take advantage of global markets.

Two additional issues also require attention. First, as seen in table12.1, China's ratio of population to motor vehicles is far higher than that found in many other countries with similar income levels. Because this ratio reflects the impact of the existing policies, significant changes in these policies will shift demand back to what could be viewed as a normal pattern of consumption of cars, given China's geographic attributes. Second, improved access to car financing could further strengthen the demand for cars. Whereas about 75 percent of U.S. and European automobile purchases are financed through loans, only 15 percent of car purchases in China are financed this way (KPMG 2003, p. 7). Although China's protocol of accession to the WTO stipulates that automobile finance will be liberalized, only draft legislation has been presented to

date.[9] To the extent that this potential can be tapped, the pressure on automotive firms to be more productive and thus more competitive will be all the greater. This, then, would be another factor helping to ensure that the welfare gains calculated will come about.

The shortcomings of the analysis also need to be highlighted. We have worked with a very stylized model, even though we feel it captures important elements of the real world. Although restructuring has positive overall implications for the motor vehicle industry, significant adjustment costs not pointed to explicitly in the model are bound to emerge. Even if value added is preserved within the sector, there will most likely be a dramatic relocation of jobs toward a limited number of plants, with job losses in the other, smaller plants. The current regional scattering of final auto production (figure 12.5) will be replaced by a more geographically concentrated pattern. Parts production will also tend to concentrate. To the extent that parts suppliers are able to supply regional markets, this concentration is likely to mean an intensification of the clustering in the coastal regions, with parts shipments to Japan, Korea, the United States, and other regional centers of production.[10] This result is broadly consistent with the findings and recommendations of Takayasu and Mori (2004), who stress that the future of the automobile industry in the entire region, and not just China, hinges on the ability of local governments to adopt policies that help to better integrate national manufacturers into regional and global supply chains. Overall, a relatively large share of value added is kept intact with

FIGURE 12.5   Location of Automobile Production in China

Location of foreign production					Production capacities in provinces		
Producer	Foreign producer	Capacity (cars/year)	Production, 2002			Capacity (cars/year)	Production, 2002
1 SAIC VW	VW	450,000	278,890		Anhui	60,000	49,397
2 SAIC GM	GM	100,000	111,623		Bejing	115,000	10,408
3 FAW VW	VW	270,000	158,654		Fujian	80,000	16,935
4 FAW Toyota	Toyota/Mazda	70,000	30,165		Guandong	120,000	97,921
5 Dongfeng PSA	PSA/Citroën	150,000	84,378		Guangxi Zhuang	150,000	n.a.
6 Dongfeng Honda	Honda	60,000	59,024		Guizhou	10,000	1,831
7 Dongfeng Yulong	Nissan/Yulong	60,000	38,897		Hainan	50,000	11,989
8 Tianjing Toyota	Toyota	30,000	2,147		Heilongjang	30,000	14,577
9 Jiangsu Nanya	Fiat	100,000	23,393		Henan	30,000	n.a.
10 SAIC Chery	Daewoo	60,000	49,397		Hubei	180,000	84,378
11 Zehjiang Jili	Daewoo (geplant)	150,000	47,443		Jiangsu	130,000	38,460
12 Chongqing Chang'an Suzuki	Suzuki/Yanjin	150,000	67,846		Jilin	340,000	188,819
13 Chang'an Ford	Ford	50,000	n.a.		Liaoming	230,000	3,751
14 Dengfeng Yueda Kia	Kia	50,000	20,080		Shandong	80,000	n.a.
15 FAW Hainan	Mazda	50,000	11,989		Shanghai	550,000	390,513
16 Beijing Hyundai	Hyundai	30,000	1,356		Shanxi	50,000	20,080
17 China Guizhou Aviation Ind.	Wanhong/Chenchang	10,000	1,831		Sichuan	205,000	67,846
18 Shenyang Brilliance Junbei	BMW (mid-2003)	200,000	n.a.		Tianjing	50,000	2,147
19 Harbin Hafei	Mitsubishi	30,000	14,577		Zehjiang	150,000	47,443
20 Shangdong Yantei	GM	50,000	n.a.				
21 Southeast	Zhonghua	60,000	16,935		Total	2,380,000	146,495
22 Beijing Jeep	DaimlerChrysler	85,000	9,052				
23 Jinbei GM	GM	30,000	3,751		Other foreign firms	Employees	No. of plants
24 Hunan Changfeng	Mitsubishi	30,000	15,067				
25 Zhengzhou Nissan	Nissan	30,000	n.a.		Bosch	3,600	6
26 Rongcheng Huatai	Hyundai	20,000	n.a.		Kolbenschmidt	1,500	2
27 Jiangxi Fuqi	Golden Lion	20,000	n.a.		Michelin	4,000	2
28 Tianjing Huali	Golden Lion	20,000	n.a.		ZF/Sachs	2,100	2
29 SAIC GM Wuling	GM	150,000	n.a.				
30 Sanjiang Renault	Renault	30,000	n.a.		Total	11,200	12
31 Chengdu FAW	Toyota	5,000	n.a.				
32 Yizhong	SAIC/RDS	10,000	n.a.				

n.a. Not applicable or available.

Sources: VDA, various issues; Bessum 2002.

restructuring. From an employment perspective, value added results closely track the impact of restructuring on employment. Table 12.9, therefore, identifies a range of effects on auto sector employment, from −43 percent (without restructuring) to −3 percent (with restructuring). Needless to say, it is important that the structure of the industry be rationalized.[11]

Notes

1. Smith and Venables (1991) dealt with the benefits arising from such a situation, where access across the domestic market is improved, when examining the implications of the formation of the European Union's common internal market for domestic and foreign suppliers.

2. See, for example, China Online (2001). As WTO membership approached in late 2001, the opinions of the industry and related ministries, as reflected in the Chinese press, hinged critically on whether restructuring of the domestic industry would be allowed to proceed. Thus a report in *Touzi Yu Hezuo* (summarized in China Online 2001) stressed the expected injury to the industry, while the industry itself was indicating optimism that it could realize significant cost reductions, allowing it to remain competitive with imports (Feenstra and others 2001). In the meantime, price cuts by foreign producers in China have become commonplace, with some of them induced by increased import competition and others by more intense domestic competition. Buick, for example, reduced its prices on its domestically produced models by 12 percent, and VW lowered Passat prices by 6.5 percent (indiacar.net, May 3, 2002). But, even more important, nearly all major foreign producers have announced plans to sizably establish or increase production capacities. A recent major manufacturer to do so was DaimlerChrysler; in September 2003 it finally ratified plans to establish facilities to produce Mercedes C and E models in China (*International Herald Tribune*, September 9, 2003).

3. According to unnamed sources in Hong Kong, 100,000 or more sedans may have been imported into the country. Many of the smuggled cars tend to be luxury models.

4. In the past, foreign investors seeking partners frequently had to go to provinces other than those on the coast (see overview of policies). These provinces often tried to ensure that "buy local" conditions prevailed for local authorities. In Shanghai, taxi regulations "by chance" stipulated specifications that could be filled only by a Shanghai-VW model.

5. The model files themselves, along with the technical annex describing the model, can be downloaded from www.intereconomics.com/francois. The model is implemented in GEMPACK.

6. See http://inventors.about.com/gi/dynamic/offsite.htm?site=http://www.wiley.com/products/subject/business/forbes/ford.html.

7. We did not model the impact of the elimination of quotas for imported cars. Data on the value of quota rents could not be produced. Assuming that positive quota rents did exist the welfare gains would be all the greater. However, the qualitative message would not change.

8. All dollar amounts are 1998 U.S. dollars.

9. Nonetheless, some major car companies (VW and Ford) have reached agreements with Chinese banks (KPMG, 2003, p. 7). According to the *International Herald Tribune* (October 6, 2003), China has opened up this sector in line with its WTO commitments.

10. European manufacturers have already established 12 plants in China, and one large American company (Delphi) is shifting from Mexico.

11. Again, this is a message not unique to China. As emphasized by Doner, Noble, and Ravenhill (2004), the industries in China, Malaysia, the Republic of Korea, Taiwan (China), and Thailand all face significant pressure to restructure. In China's case, like that of the Republic of Korea, the relatively large local market offers the scope for increased presence of foreign producers through joint ventures and foreign direct investment. If managed properly (that is, if realized in a context of integration of China's internal markets), net efficiency boosts as modeled should be realized, with results as modeled in this chapter.

References

The word *processed* describes informally reproduced works that may not be commonly available through libraries.

Bessum, F. 2002. "Global Car Production Statistics." March. Available at www.geocities.com/MotorCity/Speedway/4939/carprod.html.

China Online. 2001. "How WTO Membership Could Affect China's Auto Industry." Available at www.chinaonline.com/issues/wto/NewsArchive/secure/2000/january/b200010319-3-SS.asp.

Chinese Motor Vehicle Documentation Center. 2002. *Catalogue of the Present Chinese Motor Car Production.* 2d ed. Aldeboarn: Netherlands.

Doner, R., G. Noble, and J. Ravenhill. 2004. "Production Networks in East Asia's Automobile Industry." World Bank, Washington, D.C. Processed.

Feenstra, R., D. Sperling, L. Branstetter, E. Harwitt, and W. Hai. 2001. "China's Entry to the WTO: A View from the Auto Industry." Mimeo, University of California Davis. Processed.

François, J. F. 2000. "Assessing the Results of General Equilibrium Studies of Multilateral Trade Negotiations." UNCTAD/ITCD/TAB/4, UNCTAD Policy Issues in International Trade and Commodities Study Series. UN Conference on Trade and Development, Geneva, October.

François, J. F., and D. Spinanger. 2001. "Greater China's Accession to the WTO: Implications for International Trade/Production and for Hong Kong." Paper prepared for Hong Kong Trade Development Council, December.

———. 2004. "Regulated Efficiency, WTO Accession, and the Motor Vehicle Sector in China." *World Bank Economic Review;* forthcoming.

François, J. F., and A. Strutt. 1999. "Post Uruguay Round Tariff Vectors for GTAP Version 4." Erasmus University, Rotterdam.

Huang, Y. 2002. "Between Two Coordination Series: Automotive Industrial Policy in China with a Comparison to Korea." *Review of International Political Economy* 9(3): 538–73.

KPMG. 2003. *China Automotive and Component Parts Market.* Hong Kong, August.

Li, Shantong. 2003. "Survey Report on Regional Protection." In *Workshop on National Market Integration*, proceedings of Development Research Centre Workshop, September 6.

Lopez de Silanes, F., J. Markusen, and T. F. Rutherford. 1994. "Complementarity and Increasing Returns in Intermediate Inputs." *Journal of Development Economics* 45: 133–51.

McDougall, R., ed. 2001. *The GTAP Database—Version 5.* Global Trade Analysis Center, Purdue University.

Smith, A., and A. Venables. 1991. "Economic Integration and Market Access." *European Economic Review* 35: 388–95.

Takayasu, K., and M. Mori. 2004. "The Global Strategies of Japanese Vehicle Assemblers and the Implications for the Thai automobile Industry." World Bank, Washington, D.C. Processed.

U.S. and Chinese Academy of Engineering. 2003. *Personal Cars and China.* National Academies Press. Washington, D.C.

VDA (Verband der Automobilindustrie). Various issues. *Tatsachen und Zahlen.* Frankfurt.

World Bank. 1993. *China Industrial Organization and Efficiency Case Study: The Automotive Sector.* Report no. 12134-CHA. Washington, D.C.

———. Various issues. *World Development Indicators.* Washington, D.C.

Zhang, W., and R. Taylor. 2001. "EU Technology Transfer to China: The Automobile Industry as a Case Study." *Journal of Asia Pacific Economy* 6(2): 261–74.

13

ECONOMIC IMPACTS OF CHINA'S ACCESSION TO THE WTO

Elena Ianchovichina and Will Martin

Trade policy reforms such as those flowing from accession to the World Trade Organization (WTO) lead directly to changes in policy instruments such as tariffs, nontariff barriers, and coverage of trade rules. The main policy concerns, however, are with the impacts on such economic variables as prices; output, employment, and trade volumes; factor returns; and household incomes. In this chapter we estimate the impacts on these key economic variables of China's accession to the WTO in 2001 as a guide to policy and as a basis for subsequent analysis at the household level.[1]

The obvious instrument for performing this type of analysis is the computable general equilibrium (CGE) model. Many such models now exist, and a cottage industry has emerged in estimating the impacts of trade reform in China (Gilbert and Wahl 2001).[2] The availability of the internationally standard database of the Global Trade Analysis Project (GTAP) has facilitated such modeling and reduced the burden involved in obtaining estimates of basic information such as trade flows and patterns of production and consumption. What standard models such as GTAP (Hertel 1997; www.gtap.org) do not do, however, is incorporate the nonstandard features of China's partially reformed economy, where many imports enter duty-free if used in the production of exports and labor market policies result in serious barriers between urban and rural areas.

Like Ianchovichina and Martin (2001) and Wang (2003), the analysis here explicitly allows for the duty exemption arrangements that result in close to half of China's imports entering as duty-free inputs into the production of exports. Recent work by Sicular and Zhao (2004) is drawn on to represent imperfect labor mobility and labor market distortions. This chapter extended our earlier work reported in Ianchovichina and Martin (2001) by moving to the GTAP version 5 database (Dimaranan and McDougall 2002) based on 1997 data rather than 1995 data; by incorporating

We thank Kym Anderson, Hana Polackova Brixi, Louise Fox, Thomas Hertel, T. N. Srinivasan, Alan Winters, and three anonymous reviewers for helpful comments, Prashant Dave and Zhi Wang for their generosity in providing data. Elena Ianchovichina is Economist with the Economic Policy Unit of the Poverty Reduction and Economic Management Network at the World Bank; her email address is eianchovichina@worldbank. org. Will Martin is Lead Economist at the World Bank; his email is wmartin1@worldbank.org.

improved estimates of protection in agriculture (Huang, Rozelle, and Min 2004)[3] and services (Francois and Spinanger 2004); by using measures of liberalization based on the final, multilateral agreement; by taking into account the restructuring of the automobile sector (Francois and Spinanger 2004); and by simulating the consequences of major labor market reform. This last issue is a particularly critical area for China, and there have been few simulation studies.[4]

This chapter first discusses the methodology and then the policy changes associated with China's WTO accession and the results of the simulation analysis. It then considers some possible complementary policy actions, such as reducing barriers to rural outmigration and expanding access to education.

Methodology

The standard GTAP model[5] was adjusted to incorporate China's important export processing arrangements. Ianchovichina (2003) documents the approach used and shows that failing to account for China's duty exemptions in analyzing WTO accession overstates the increase in China's trade flows by 40 percent and the increase in exports of selected sectors by 90 percent. The adjusted model (GTAP-DD) also incorporates some of China's key labor market mechanisms and institutions that related research has shown may have a major influence on the impacts of WTO accession (Sicular and Zhao 2002, 2004).

Export Processing Arrangements

Export processing arrangements in China take many forms. Most arrangements allow firms producing goods for export to import intermediate inputs at world prices. These arrangements were incorporated in the GTAP-DD model used in this study by creating two activities for each sector. For sectors covered—or potentially covered—by export processing arrangements, one activity is specialized in production for export, and one is specialized in production for the domestic market.[6] This separation is preferable to representations based on a single sector producing differentiated products for domestic and export markets because it allows the two sectors to use different input mixes, and it

allows export-oriented activities to use much more import-intensive means of production. It provides a reasonably realistic depiction of China's trade regime in the 1990s, when duty exemptions were used to facilitate exports while protection in the rest of the economy remained fairly high.[7]

The tax arrangements for export processing (duty and value-added tax [VAT] exemptions on imported intermediate inputs and VAT refunds on exports) discouraged export-oriented firms from using domestic intermediate materials and selling in the local market.[8] Furthermore, the vast majority of exports were produced using imported intermediates that were either exempt from duties or eligible for refunds on taxes paid.[9] China Customs data for 2000 show that 60 percent of imports entered duty free, 41 percentage points of which were imports used for export processing, 13 percentage points were capital goods, and 6 percentage points were goods in special categories, such as materials used by research institutes. Rough calculations based on input-output information from the GTAP version 4 database (McDougall, Elbehri, and Truong 1998) and data from China Customs suggest that 26 percent of imports were used to produce for the domestic market and only about 3 percent were used to produce ordinary exports.[10]

Intermediate inputs for domestic and export-oriented activities were initially estimated by allocating them to each sector in proportion to sales in export and domestic markets. However, this yielded unsatisfactory results, with the database showing much less use of imported inputs in the export sector than the reported imports of duty-free intermediate inputs for export production obtained from China Customs (Li Yan, China Customs, personal communication). To deal with this, increased use of imported intermediates was allowed for in export activities in accordance with the price changes involved in providing duty exemptions, and the elasticities of substitution between domestic and intermediate goods in the model.[11] This modification more than doubled the import-intensity of the exporting activities and reduced that of the domestically oriented activities.

China's Labor Market Policies

Perhaps the central labor market issue for the analysis is the barriers to mobility between rural and urban activities. Taking up employment in an urban area is inhibited by the need to obtain an urban residence permit (*hukou*). In addition, workers tend to be reluctant to permanently cut their ties with the rural sector because it is not possible to sell the land to which a rural family has use rights (Hussain 2004). Many workers move temporarily from rural to urban areas, although restrictions are frequently imposed on such movements, and social welfare benefits such as health care and schooling for children enjoyed by urban residents are typically not available to temporary migrants. While it is sometimes possible to overcome these problems by purchasing an urban residence permit, this imposes an additional cost on migrants from rural to urban areas, a group with particularly limited access to capital. Finally, as in all countries, rural–urban labor mobility is also inhibited by the sector-specific nature of farmers' human capital and a reluctance to cut family ties by migration to urban areas.

The per capita income of agricultural workers is only about one-third that of urban workers (World Bank 2002). Not all of this difference can be attributed to barriers to mobility between rural and urban areas, however. Urban workers typically have higher skills, work more intensively, and face higher costs of living than rural workers (Sicular and Zhao 2004).

To capture the effects of barriers to mobility, the model allows for both imperfect transformation between unskilled workers in agricultural and unskilled nonagricultural employment, and an implicit tax on nonagricultural employment. The imperfect transformation representation is designed to reflect the substantial differences in the characteristics of unskilled workers in rural and urban areas, and the ability, at a cost, to transform agricultural workers into nonagricultural workers through training, experience, and the creation of nonagricultural jobs in rural areas. The tax is designed to reflect the pure policy-induced barriers between rural and urban workers, such as the requirement for a residence permit in urban areas and the barriers to mobility created by the inability to sell farm land. It is specified as a barrier that raises the cost of labor to urban employers, with urban workers receiving the tax-inclusive wage.

The imperfect transformation between agricultural and nonagricultural workers is represented

using a constant elasticity of transformation between workers in agriculture and workers in other sectors in the following simple manner:

$$L_{NF}/L_F = \alpha(W_{NF}/W_F)^\sigma, \qquad (13.1)$$

where L_{NF} is the number of nonfarm workers, L_F is the number of farm workers, α is a constant term, W_{NF} and W_F are nonfarm and farm wages, respectively, and σ is the elasticity of transformation. The value of σ was set at 1.32, based on Sicular and Zhao's (2002) estimates of this parameter.[12] The tax reflecting pure policy-induced barriers between rural and urban wages was estimated at 34 percent by Shi (2002). While there is some level of unemployment in China, particularly associated with state enterprise reform and rural–urban migration, much of this unemployment is transitional, because of the weakness of the social safety net (Hussain 2004). Given the long-run focus of the analysis here, total employment is treated as exogenous.

Trade Policy Reforms

This section examines the implications of trade policy reforms in China and in its trade partners in the years leading up to accession.

Changes in China's Trade Policies

During the 1990s China made substantial progress in reducing the coverage of nontariff barriers, lowering tariffs, and abolishing the trade distortions created by the exchange rate regime. Lardy (2002) estimates that the number of tariff lines subject to quotas and licenses fell from 1,247 in 1992 to 261 in 1999. By 2001, 257 tariff lines were covered by a combination of licenses and quotas and 47 by licenses only, while 245 were subject to designated trading and 84 to state trading. Tendering and other registration requirements, primarily for machinery and electrical products, covered an additional 120 tariff lines. By 2001, nontariff barriers covered 664 tariff lines, or less than 10 percent of tariff lines (see Appendix table 13.A.1), with over a third of these being subject to designated trading, one of the less intrusive forms of quantitative restriction employed in China.

Data on nontariff barriers frequency alone may be misleading because of the enormous variations in the importance of tariff lines. To give some

TABLE 13.1   Import Coverage of Nontariff Barriers (percent)

Barrier	1996	2001
Licenses and quotas	18.5	12.8
Tendering	7.4	2.7
Licensing only	2.2	0.5
State trading	11.0	9.5
Designated trading	7.3	6.2
Any nontariff barriers	32.5	21.6
No nontariff barriers	67.5	78.4
Total	100	100

Note: For 1996 nontariff barrier coverage, the trade weights used were for 1992, while for 2001 the trade weights used were for 2000.

Source: For 1996, Lardy 2002; for 2001, Mei Zhen of the Ministry of Foreign Trade and Economic Cooperation during an internship at the World Bank, using data from WTO.

indication of the potential importance of nontariff barriers, the import coverage of the key nontariff barriers was calculated using data on nontariff barrier coverage of tariff lines and on import data by tariff line.

The import coverage of all nontariff barriers in China fell from 32.5 percent in 1996 (World Bank 1997, p. 15) to 21.6 percent in 2001 (see table 13.1). Coverage of import licensing and quotas fell from 18.5 percent in 1996 to 12.8 percent in 2001, and coverage of state trading from 11 to 9.5 percent. The import coverage of tendering requirements fell particularly rapidly, from 7.4 percent in 1996 to 2.7 percent in 2001. For more details on coverage by type and commodity, see Appendix table 13.A.2.

Oil was by far the most important import subject to nontariff barriers, accounting for almost half the value of imports subject to any nontariff barriers (see Appendix table 13.A.3). Ferrous metals, subject to designated trading arrangements, were the second most important category. Imports of oil and oil products accounted for 84 percent of total imports subject to state trading.

The average protective impact of the complete set of nontariff barriers in China was estimated (very crudely) to be 9.3 percent in the mid-1990s (World Bank 1997), with most of the protective effect arising from licensing and quota-constrained goods. The protective effect of these nontariff barriers has clearly declined since then because of a

number of factors such as the progressive phase-out of nontariff barriers, a standstill on new nontariff barriers during the accession process, the general WTO prohibition against nontariff barriers after accession, and a likely reduction in the severity with which many of these measures have been administered. A simple rule of thumb that protection provided by nontariff barriers declines with their import coverage would suggest that their protective impact has fallen to about 5 percent. However, given the large margin of uncertainty associated with this measure, the analysis here focuses only on tariff liberalization, implying that the results should be taken as a lower bound to the overall impact of liberalization.

The pace of tariff reform in China was also rapid during the 1990s. While average tariffs were very high in the early 1990s, they fell sharply after 1994 (table 13.2). A significant tariff reform in October 1997 reduced average tariffs well below 20 percent. Three subsequent reductions at the beginning of 1999, 2000, and 2001 further reduced tariffs on a wide range of items. The progressive reductions in tariffs between 1992 and 2001 lowered average tariffs by two-thirds, with larger than average cuts in the manufacturing sector, thereby ensuring that the future reductions in tariffs required under the WTO accession agreement are much smaller than the reductions occurring before accession. Another important feature of the reforms has been a substantial reduction in the dispersion of tariff rates—with the standard deviation falling from 32.1 percent in 1992 to 10 percent in 2001.

Examination of weighted average applied tariffs for 1995 and 2001 and after implementation of the final tariff bindings agreed in the accession schedule suggests[13] that substantial merchandise trade liberalization occurred in China over the period 1995–2001 (table 13.3). Weighted average tariffs dropped substantially for wheat, beverages and tobacco, textiles, apparel, light manufactures, petrochemicals, metals, automobiles, and electronics. Analysis by Huang, Rozelle, and Min (2004) suggests that some agricultural commodities such as vegetables and fruits, livestock and meat, and rice faced negative protection in 1995, generally as a result of restrictions on exports. Protection on these commodities rose (or negative protection fell) over the period 1995–2001. Accession is not expected to lead to a significant fall in protection on

TABLE 13.2. China's Average Statutory Tariff Rates (percent)

Year	All Products		Primary Products		Manufactures	
	Simple	Weighted	Simple	Weighted	Simple	Weighted
1992	42.9	40.6	36.2	22.3	44.9	46.5
1993	39.9	38.4	33.3	20.9	41.8	44.0
1994	36.3	35.5	32.1	19.6	37.6	40.6
1996	23.6	22.6	25.4	20.0	23.1	23.2
1997	17.6	18.2	17.9	20.0	17.5	17.8
1998	17.5	18.7	17.9	20.0	17.4	18.5
1999	17.2	14.2	21.8	21.8	16.8	13.4
2000	17.0	14.1	22.4	19.5	16.6	13.3
2001	16.6	12.0	21.6	17.7	16.2	13.0
After accession	9.8	6.8	13.2	3.6	9.5	6.9

Source: World Bank 1999, p. 340 to 1998. Authors' calculations for tariff lines with imports in 1999. Trade data come from COMTRADE. Protection data for 1999 to 2001 come from CDS Consulting Co. and after accession from China's WTO final offer.

most agricultural commodities after 2001. Import protection is expected to remain unchanged for most commodities except oilseeds, sugar, and dairy products.

Protection will continue to fall for all other merchandise commodities, with especially big cuts for processed food, beverages and tobacco, automobiles, electronics, and other manufactures. Francois and Spinanger (2004) conclude that the automobile sector liberalization will be accompanied by massive restructuring to realize economies of scale and improve structural efficiency, perhaps increasing productivity by 20 percent during the accession period (2001–07).[14]

A key element of China's accession agreement is the abolition of agricultural export subsidies. Huang, Rozelle, and Min (2004) estimate that there was a 32-percent export subsidy on feedgrains and a 10 percent export subsidy on plant-based fibers in 2001 (particularly cotton).

In addition to China's barriers on merchandise trade, border measures and domestic regulations on domestic service sectors and trade in these services have reduced the efficiency of services sectors. China has made substantial commitments to open its services sectors,[15] and critical services such as telecommunications, logistics, and finance are likely to benefit from inward foreign direct investment and rising productivity as they are restructured. Based on work by Francois and Spinanger (2001) reported in Francois and Spinanger (2004),

these measures are represented here as barriers to trade in services expressed in *ad valorem* terms. Following Francois and Spinanger (2004), the impact of accession is represented as halving the nontariff barriers to services trade. Efficiency improvements in the services sectors are not modeled since there were no reliable estimates of the likely productivity gains at the time this research was conducted.[16]

Changes in China's Trade Partners' Policies

The arrangements for textiles and clothing are a particularly important element of China's accession. Unlike most other developing economy exporters, China was excluded from the liberalizing elements of the Uruguay Round Agreement on Textiles and Clothing. This means that prior to accession China did not benefit from the integration of textile and clothing products into the General Agreement on Tariffs and Trade (GATT) or from the increases in quota growth rates provided for under this agreement. That placed upward pressure on the prices of these quotas in China, raising the costs of exporters just as an equivalent export tax would.[17] Under its accession agreement China benefited immediately from the integration of textiles and clothing into the GATT, leading to the abolition of quotas and increases in quota growth rates that have occurred since 1994 (WTO 1994). All quotas are to be phased out by 2005. Importing

TABLE 13.3   China's Import Protection before and after WTO Accession (tariff or tariff equivalent, percent)

Product	China 1995	China 2001	China Post-Accession[b]	Taiwan, China 1997	Taiwan, China 2001	Taiwan, China Post-Accession[b]
Agriculture						
Rice	−5.0	−3.3	−3.3	2.2	0.0	0.0
Wheat	25.0	12.0	12.0	6.5	6.5	6.5
Feedgrains	20.0	32.0	32.0	1.0	1.0	0.0
Vegetables and fruits	−10.0	−4.0	−4.0	35.7	36.9	16.0
Oilseeds	30.0	20.0	3.0	1.8	0.8	0.2
Sugar	44.0	40.0	20.0	21.9	25.8	22.7
Plant-based fibers	20.0	17.0	20.0	0.0	0.0	0.0
Livestock and meat	−20.0	−15.0	−15.0	7.5	6.5	4.0
Dairy	30.0	30.0	11.0	16.6	9.3	5.9
Processed food	20.1	26.2	9.9	14.9	14.2	9.9
Beverages and tobacco	137.2	43.2	15.6	48.1	22.0	13.0
Total	4.8	7.6	3.6	9.1	6.9	4.6
Manufacturing						
Extractive industries	3.4	1.0	0.6	5.5	5.5	4.1
Textiles	56.0	21.6	8.9	6.1	6.3	5.6
Apparel	76.1	23.7	14.9	12.8	13.4	11.2
Light manufactures	32.3	12.3	8.4	4.0	4.1	3.4
Petrochemicals	20.2	12.8	7.1	4.2	4.2	2.9
Metals	17.4	8.9	5.7	4.0	3.8	1.5
Automobiles	123.1	28.9	13.8	23.9	21.5	13.3
Electronics	24.4	10.3	2.3	2.9	0.5	0.3
Other manufactures	22.0	12.9	6.6	4.4	3.3	2.1
Total	25.3	13.5	6.9	6.3	5.2	3.5
Total merchandise trade[a]	24.3	13.3	6.8	6.5	5.2	3.6
Services						
Trade and transport	1.9	1.9	0.9	1.3	1.3	0.7
Construction	13.7	13.7	6.8	5.9	5.9	2.9
Communications	9.2	9.2	4.6	9.2	9.2	4.6
Commercial services	29.4	29.4	14.7	3.7	3.7	1.9
Other services	24.5	24.5	12.7	7.1	7.1	3.5
Total	10.3	10.3	5.2	3.2	3.2	1.6

[a]Those estimates are based on trade weights for the respective years. If trade weights for 2000 at the six-digit level of the harmonized system are used, the total weighted average tariffs in 2001 and 2007 are 12.2 percent in 2001 and 6.3 percent in 2007 for China and 4.5 percent and 3.1 percent for Taiwan, China.

[b]Applied rates at the end of the implementation period were estimated as the lesser of the bindings and 2001 applied rates. In virtually all cases the bindings were lower than the applied rates.

Source: Authors' calculations based on agricultural protection data from Huang, Rozelle, and Min 2002; manufacturing protection data from GTAP in 1995, from CDS Consulting Co. in 2001 and from China's WTO final offer for protection after accession; services protection data from Francois and Spinanger 2004.

economies will be allowed to introduce special textile safeguards during the period 2005–07, but these will be effective for only one year at a time.

The accession agreement includes a Transitional Product-specific Safeguard mechanism that allows China's trading partners to take safeguard actions under rules that are more permissive of protection than the usual WTO safeguard rules (Messerlin 2004). These provisions have the potential for introducing a new form of protection against

China. This potential danger needs to be weighed against the substantial gains to China from her trading partners being required to follow WTO rules in implementing contingent protection measures against China. For simplicity, these gains and losses are assumed to cancel each other out.

China's accession also triggered a liberalization of its partners' trade policies. The average tariffs of Taiwan (China) were estimated to fall by almost 1.5 percentage points, from 4.5 percent in 1997 to 3.1 percent after accession. Taiwan (China) committed to tariff reductions on thousands of industrial and agricultural product lines, a phase-out of tariffs on a number of products as part of the Zero-for-Zero program of the Uruguay Round, and reductions in tariffs on chemical products as part of the Chemical Harmonization program. Tariffs on the vast majority of products related to information technology were also reduced in 2000 and, once WTO accession commitments are implemented, the tariff on electronic products will fall to 0.3 percent (see table 13.3).

Taiwan (China) made horizontal and sector-specific commitments in the following service sectors: business, communication, construction, engineering, distribution, education, environmental, financial, health, social, transport services, and tourism and recreation. Like Francois and Spinanger (2002), we treat the WTO accession commitments of Taiwan (China) as halving nontariff barriers to trade in services.

Experimental Design

The impact of accession is evaluated here in the dynamic context of the growth and structural change expected in China and its trading partners during the period up to 2007, when almost all of the changes associated with accession will have come into effect. A baseline scenario is constructed under which the economies of the world grow and experience the manifold structural changes associated with economic growth up to 2007 (table 13.4 and Appendix table 13.A.5). The GTAP model includes key elements such as changes in demand patterns as incomes rise, changes in the industrial structure associated with changes in the stock of capital per worker, and changes in world prices resulting from changes in world supply and demand that allow the model to capture key changes in the world economy over this period. The

baseline broadly replicates World Bank projections for overall growth in each region and uses projections of factor input growth and a residually determined level of total factor productivity growth to ensure consistency between the two.

The model considers the effects of the WTO accession agreement signed at the Doha ministerial meeting in November 2001 on protection prevailing in 2001. In addition, it separately takes into account the liberalization in China during 1995–2001 since much of the liberalization during the 1990s was influenced by China's desire to prepare for the type of trade regime needed for WTO accession and to establish the credibility of its commitment to an open economy. These sharp reductions in protection are unlikely to have occurred without the prospect of accession to WTO, and they have been locked in by China's WTO commitments. Thus results are presented for both the accession period (2001–07) and the entire liberalization period (1995–2007).

The analysis starts with 1995 tariff levels because 1995 was a major turning point in the negotiations—the closing of the door on China's attempt to enter the world trading system by resuming its status as a Contracting Party to the GATT. As Long (2000, p. 43) emphasized, China focused more strongly on commercial considerations after 1995 than it had previously done—and its trading partners also strongly emphasized the commercial aspects of the negotiations. To capture the implications of WTO accession, 1997 protection data for China in the benchmark data (GTAP version 5) are adjusted to 1995 levels to obtain the initial base.[18] For Taiwan (China) liberalization is considered to have begun in 1997, the year for which tariff data are available in GTAP version 5.

Two experiments are conducted to evaluate the impact of WTO accession. The first assesses the impact of the fall in tariffs from 1995 to 2001 levels and the restructuring of the automobile sector accompanying the reductions in tariffs on automobiles and automobile parts during this period. The second assesses the impact of the fall in tariffs from 1995 to post-accession (2007) tariff levels, liberalization of the services sectors, continued restructuring of the automobile sector, removal of quotas on China's clothing and textiles exports, and removal of China's agricultural export subsidies. The productivity shock designed to capture the restructuring of the automobile sector is

TABLE 13.4   Projected Growth in Factor Inputs and Total Factor Productivity 1997–2007 (percent)

Trading Partner	Population	Unskilled Labor	Skilled Labor	Capital	Manufacturing Total Factor Productivity[a]
North America	11	11	12	49	High
	(1.05)	(1.08)	(1.11)	(4.07)	
Western Europe	0	−1	1	30	High
	(0.03)	(−0.08)	(0.07)	(2.69)	
Australia and New Zealand	10	12	10	55	High
	(0.98)	(1.14)	(0.99)	(4.45)	
Japan	1	−2	−7	35	Medium
	(0.06)	(−0.19)	(−0.71)	(3.02)	
China	8	13	50	174	High
	(0.81)	(1.26)	(4.15)	(10.62)	
Taiwan (China)	9	11	14	96	High
	(0.86)	(1.05)	(1.36)	(6.97)	
Other newly industrialized countries in Asia	10	−1	55	88	Medium
	(0.93)	(−0.10)	(4.47)	(6.53)	
Indonesia	16	17	123	25	Low
	(1.50)	(1.59)	(8.36)	(2.27)	
Vietnam	15	32	36	111	Medium
	(1.40)	(2.79)	(3.10)	(7.78)	
Other Southeast Asia	18	22	134	60	Low
	(1.70)	(2.04)	(8.87)	(4.83)	
India	18	23	78	88	Medium
	(1.67)	(2.10)	(5.92)	(6.54)	
Other South Asia	25	30	80	72	Medium
	(2.22)	(2.69)	(6.06)	(5.55)	
Brazil	14	19	72	31	Medium
	(1.31)	(1.77)	(5.60)	(2.75)	
Other Latin America	18	6	90	54	Low
	(1.68)	(0.57)	(6.65)	(4.42)	
Turkey	16	19	107	55	Low
	(1.47)	(1.75)	(7.55)	(4.46)	
Other Middle East and North Africa	24	37	67	28	Low
	(2.16)	(3.23)	(5.24)	(2.50)	
Economies in transition	−1	6	9	33	High
	(−0.11)	(0.56)	(0.90)	(2.88)	
South African Customs Union	15	31	47	34	Low
	(1.39)	(2.76)	(3.92)	(2.94)	
Other Sub-Saharan Africa	30	40	54	38	Medium
	(2.65)	(3.42)	(4.42)	(3.26)	
Rest of world	18	23	35	68	Low
	(1.63)	(2.10)	(3.05)	(5.32)	

[a]Low = average annual growth rates of 0.1 percent, medium = 1.0 percent, high = between 2 percent and 4 percent.

Note: Numbers in parentheses are annual growth rates.

Source: World Bank; GTAP data.

proportionate to the fall in tariffs on automobiles in each simulation.

The same macroeconomic closure is used for all experiments—full employment,[19] perfect mobility of skilled and unskilled workers between nonagricultural sectors, and perfect mobility of unskilled workers within agriculture. Based on the working assumption that trade balances are not changed significantly by WTO accession, trade balances as shares of GDP were fixed for China and Taiwan (China). While trade balances can be expected to vary during the transition, particularly if there are substantial changes in foreign investment levels, foreign investment levels are not determined within the model.[20]

Taxes lost because of trade liberalization are assumed to be replaced by a uniform, nondistortionary consumption tax affecting both private and government final consumption of all goods and services. This hypothetical tax is included to ensure that any adverse impacts of trade reform on government revenues, and hence on the ability to provide income transfers or public services, are allowed for in the analysis of impacts of the reform on households. Because the GTAP version 5 database appears to represent the VAT on domestic production as an output tax, the model generates tax losses from the contraction of industries such as tobacco and alcohol. These inward-oriented industries have higher VAT rates than export-oriented sectors such as apparel because exports are exempt from the VAT. When the export-oriented sectors expand, the net impact of WTO accession is a sharp contraction in tax revenues. In reality, such a contraction will not be observed because VATs of the same magnitude are levied on imports. To offset this impact, particularly in the poverty analysis, the consumption tax had to be adjusted downward. This was done by first computing the consumption tax that compensates for the loss in output taxes (this tax as a share of the total replacement tax is equal to the share of the output tax loss in the total tax losses) and then adjusting the consumption tax rate to eliminate the component due to the change in output taxes.

To reflect the long-run change in the stance of trade policy—phased in over many years—involved in WTO accession, most of the analysis uses a standard long-run specification, with capital and labor freely mobile between industrial sectors and labor freely mobile between industrial sectors and

within agriculture. However, barriers to labor mobility between rural and urban employment are incorporated.

Assessment of China's Accession

This section assesses the impacts of China's accession to the WTO on China and its trading partners.

Impacts on China

The focus here is on the impacts of the trade policy changes remaining after 2001. (Detailed results for the period before 2001 are presented in Appendix table 13.A.6). One important development in the period after 2001 is the removal of the quotas on apparel and textiles imposed against China and other developing country exporters by major industrial country importers. These quotas are scheduled for abolition in January 2005 for all WTO members. Abolition gives a significant boost to the textile and apparel sectors in China, which had been one of the countries most tightly restricted by the quotas.[21] Output in these sectors rises substantially (table 13.5). That in turn stimulates the production of plant-based fibers (mainly cotton), which increases by 16 percent.

Output and employment in the other agricultural sectors, with the exception of livestock and meat, are expected to fall as unskilled agricultural labor moves into the textile and apparel sectors and unskilled nonfarm real wages rise (table 13.6). Oilseeds and sugar contract more than other agricultural sectors as a result of falling protection. Tariffs on oilseeds fall from 20 percent to 3 percent, while tariffs on sugar fall from 40 percent to 20 percent. Protection in other agricultural sectors is assumed to remain almost unchanged. The automobile and electronics sectors also expand slightly, creating employment opportunities, particularly for skilled labor.[22] Results suggest that approximately 6 million farm workers in China will leave their farm jobs as a result of WTO accession reform after 2001 in pursuit of employment in the non-agricultural sectors.[23]

For most merchandise goods real wholesale prices fall as a result of trade liberalization after accession. Retail prices reflect a uniform consumption tax increase of about 1.9 percent levied to compensate for the loss of tariff revenue.[24] For some products, such as beverages and tobacco, automobiles, and

TABLE 13.5 **Changes in China's Key Economic Indicators after 2001 as a Result of WTO Accession (percent unless otherwise indicated)**

Product	Output	Employment	Exports	Imports	Trade Balance (Millions of US$)	Wholesale Prices	Consumer Prices
Agriculture							
Rice	−2.1	−2.3	6.1	−7.1	64	−0.9	0.9
Wheat	−2.0	−2.3	18.9	−10.1	174	−1.7	0.4
Feedgrains	−2.3	−2.6	−77.8	−2.4	−596	−1.9	1.9
Vegetables and fruits	−3.4	−3.7	14.6	−6.3	214	−1.9	−0.1
Oilseeds	−7.9	−8.4	29.8	20.9	−789	−2.8	−4.7
Sugar	−6.5	−7.4	13.9	24.1	−73	−1.9	−3.1
Plant-based fibers	15.8	16.4	−51.8	7.7	−189	0.1	3.1
Livestock and meat	1.3	1.1	15.5	−8.9	837	−1.6	0.2
Dairy	−2.0	−2.4	13.5	23.8	−143	−1.5	0.2
Other food	−5.9	−6.4	11.4	62.6	−3,460	−1.7	−1.8
Beverages and tobacco	−33.0	−33.1	9.7	112.4	−14,222	−1.8	−6.9
Manufacturing							
Extractive industries	−1.0	−1.3	7.5	−4.4	2,088	−0.7	1.2
Textiles	15.6	15.5	32.7	38.5	−10,366	−1.7	−3.2
Apparel	57.3	56.1	105.8	30.9	49,690	−0.5	−1.9
Light manufacturing	3.7	3.7	5.9	6.8	1,786	−0.9	0.0
Petrochemicals	−2.3	−2.3	3.1	11.8	−8,810	−0.7	0.8
Metals	−2.1	−2.1	3.7	6.8	−1,893	−0.4	1.3
Automobiles	1.4	−2.2	27.7	24.0	516	−3.9	−4.2
Electronics	0.6	0.4	6.7	6.8	453	−1.3	−1.7
Other manufactures	−2.1	−2.2	4.1	18.9	−11,291	−0.5	0.8
Services							
Trade and transport	0.0	0.0	0.8	−0.4	493	−0.2	1.6
Construction	0.9	0.9	2.7	17.5	−436	−0.2	1.7
Communications	−0.5	−0.5	−0.5	10.9	−56	0.1	1.9
Commercial services	−2.0	−2.0	−0.4	35.4	−1,749	0.2	1.9
Other services	−1.7	−1.8	1.4	33.6	−1,525	−0.1	1.6
Total	1.0	0.0[a]	16.8	17.3	717	−0.7	−0.2

[a]Reflects the fixed labor supply assumption.

Source: Authors' simulations with modified GTAP model; see details in text.

sugar, the fall in real retail prices reflects a larger than proportionate drop in protection.

Increased demand for nonagricultural labor means higher real nonfarm wages and higher returns to nonagricultural labor relative to agricultural labor. Removal of protection on some agricultural sectors additionally lowers the attractiveness of farming and implies falling returns to farm labor and land. Real farm wages fall 0.7 percent and the real rental price of land falls 5.5 percent. The decline in farm incomes and the rise in the real retail price of many nonfarm products mean that

some farmers may be hurt by WTO accession. Nonfarm wages rise 1.2 percent and skilled labor wages rise 0.8 percent, implying that workers in urban centers—and farmers who are able to engage in nonfarm employment—are more likely to be better off as a result of WTO accession.[25]

Accession will make China a much bigger player in world markets through three channels—the rapid growth and structural change of its economy; the liberalization undertaken in preparation for WTO accession; and the liberalization undertaken after accession in 2001. The liberalization

TABLE 13.6   Change in Real Factor Prices in China as a Result of Accession, 2001–07 (percent)

Item	Accession Alone	Accession with Labor Market Reform only	Accession with Increase in Skill Level only	Accession with Labor Market Reform and Increase in Skill Level
Farm unskilled wages	−0.7	16.8	1.6	19.4
Nonfarm unskilled wages	1.2	−3.8	2.7	−2.5
Skilled labor wages	0.8	−1.7	−6.3	−8.7
Rental price of land	−5.5	−9.7	−6.4	−10.5
Rental price of capital	1.3	−1.4	0.9	−1.8
Price of capital goods	−0.9	−3.6	−1.1	−3.9
Migration from rural to urban jobs (millions)	6	28	10	32.0
National welfare (billions of 1997 US$)	10.0	11.0	10.0	11.0

Source: Authors' simulations with modified GTAP model; see details in text.

undertaken after 2001 contributes to an increase in China's share in world exports from 4.4 percent to 7.8 percent upon completion of accession. Similarly, China's share in world import markets rises from 5.8 percent in 2001 to 6.4 percent in 2007. With the removal of textile and apparel quotas, apparel exports lead export expansion with an increase in export volume of about 106 percent, followed by textiles and automobiles. The dramatic fall in protection of beverages and tobacco results in imports more than doubling, followed by increases in imports of food products, textiles, agricultural products, automobile parts, and commercial services.

China's total welfare gain from WTO accession is estimated at $40.6 billion (in 1997 dollars), or 2.2 percent of per capita real income (table 13.7).[26] Most of the gain ($31 billion) was realized following the massive liberalization between 1995 and 2001 and the ongoing restructuring of the automobile industry. The remaining reforms will lead to an additional welfare gain of $9.6 billion. The largest part of this gain in welfare will come from further merchandise trade liberalization ($4.7 billion, nearly half the $9.6 billion), followed by $2.4 billion (25 percent) from the removal of quotas on textiles and apparel and $1.2 billion (12 percent) from services liberalization. Continuing automobile sector restructuring will generate $1.1 billion (11 percent), while the removal of agricultural export subsidies will provide only $275 million (3 percent) in additional benefits.

Impacts on China's Trading Partners

Among China's trading partners the largest absolute gains accrue to North America and Western Europe with close to half of the gains coming from elimination of the quotas they impose on China's exports of textiles and clothing—and thus elimination of their efficiency losses and rent transfers to China. North America, Western Europe, and Japan also gain from China's cuts in protection, which increase China's efficiency as an export supplier and its demand for their exports.

The welfare gain by Taiwan (China) from its and China's accession to the WTO is estimated at $3 billion per year—the second largest gain relative to the size of the economy after China's (see table 13.7). About half of the gain ($1.6 billion) was realized as a result of the liberalization in China and in Taiwan (China) during 1997–2001. Remaining reforms will lead to an estimated real income gain of $1.4 billion a year after 2001. Other newly industrialized economies also benefit from China's accession. Most of these benefits are associated with trade liberalization and removal of quotas on textile and apparel, which translate into gains from terms of trade improvements after 2001.

The world as a whole and key developing economies that trade directly with China benefit from China's accession, but developing economies in Southeast Asia, South Asia, and Latin America that compete with China in third markets may lose from the removal of textile and apparel quotas

TABLE 13.7   Welfare Change and Sources of Welfare Change as a Result of China's WTO Accession (millions of 1997 US$)

Country or Group	Total, 1995–2007	Tariff Cuts	Quota Reductions	Export Subsidy Reductions	Liberalization of Services	Auto Sector Restructuring	Impact 2001–07
North America	6,072 (0.0)*	3,207	2,713	24	172	−44	5,259
Western Europe	18,189 (0.2)	9,724	8,285	−51	338	−107	14,200
Australia/New Zealand	136 (0.0)	175	−47	2	18	−12	152
Japan	5,694 (0.1)	5,522	291	−22	5	−102	2,553
China[a]	40,552 (2.2)	29,452	2,389	275	1,160	7,276	9,563
Taiwan (China)	2,985 (0.6)	2,300	338	−4	265	85	1,376
Other Newly Industrialized Countries	6,831 (0.7)	6,539	−82	−185	49	511	1,456
Indonesia	−408 (−0.2)	−167	−216	−10	1	−16	−310
Vietnam	−453 (−1.4)	−63	−395	0	6	0	−405
Other Southeast Asia	−585 (−0.1)	−109	−464	−46	16	18	−268
India	−3,357 (−0.4)	−1,087	−2,338	−5	−23	96	−2,999
Other South Asia	−1,622 (−0.8)	−176	−1,427	−7	1	−12	−1,619
Brazil	−76 (−0.0)	−76	3	4	5	−12	359
Other Latin America	−32 (−0.0)	59	−171	20	32	29	−36
Turkey	−338 (−0.1)	−50	−295	−2	7	2	−327
Other Middle East and North Africa	368 (0.0)	675	−467	−13	57	116	−365
Economies in Transition	19 (0.0)	318	−321	4	15	3	−185
South African Customs Union	78 (0.0)	89	−18	0	5	2	13
Other Sub-Saharan Africa	−45 (−0.0)	71	−159	4	15	24	−78
Rest of World	155 (0.0)	330	−210	−15	27	23	−78
World	74,166	56,733	7,409	−27	2,171	7,880	28,261

[a]Impacts exclude output tax losses because of a compensating value-added tax levied uniformly on both imported and domestic goods.

Numbers in parentheses are percentage changes in per capita utility. The impact for 1995–2001 is the difference between the impact for 1995–2007 and the impact for 2001–07.

Source: Authors' simulations with modified GTAP model; see details in text.

after 2001. The losses will be largest for Vietnam—an economy that is following in China's foot-steps and has a similar pattern of comparative advantage in labor-intensive products. The welfare loss for Vietnam is estimated as a 1.4 percent drop in per capita income (see table 13.7). The loss to India is estimated to be considerably smaller as a share of per capita income, at 0.4 percent, while the percentage losses to other countries are very small.

Complementary Policy Reforms

While the overall effects of WTO accession on China's economy are generally positive, there are some concerns that declines in real returns to farm labor may exacerbate poverty in rural areas. Approaches that deal directly with these problems are more likely to succeed than approaches that attempt to water down China's trade policy reforms. Two policy tools that lend themselves to analysis within the model framework used here are relaxation of the barriers to labor migration from rural to urban areas and skills upgrading for workers in rural areas.

Impact of Reducing the Policy Barriers to Labor Mobility

Abolishing policy barriers to labor mobility from rural to urban areas—such as residence permits, differences in social insurance, and the inability to sell agricultural land—in conjunction with accession leads to a nearly 17 percent increase in real returns to rural workers (see table 13.6).[27] This contrasts sharply with the 0.7 percent reduction in real farm wages for accession without labor market reform. Rents to farmland would decline, with higher farm wages leaving a smaller residual return to farmland. Real urban unskilled wages would decline by an estimated 3.8 percent. Clearly, there would be scope for partial reform of these arrangements that could leave both farm and nonfarm unskilled workers better off than in the absence of labor market reform.

These results suggest that this reform would have significant impacts on the number of people leaving their farm jobs for jobs in the nonfarm sectors and on the industry composition of China's economy. Some 28 million people would leave their farm jobs if the government removed the policy barriers to labor movement from rural to urban areas[28]—several times the estimated 6 million people who would move as a result of WTO accession reforms alone between 2001 and 2007. The impact on the composition of Chinese industrial output would also be substantial (table 13.8). This would allow not only apparel production to expand more but also metals, automobiles, electronics, machinery, other manufactures, and construction, all at the expense of reductions in some agricultural sectors.

Impact of an Increase in Skill Levels

One of the central problems facing most rural workers is low levels of education. One way to get a sense of the likely impacts of improving access to education is to consider the impact of resultant increases in the skill levels of rural workers on the performance of the Chinese economy. This experiment looks only at the impact of improvements in education on the skills of rural workers. It ignores any potential benefits to rural households from improvements in access to education for their children—such as reductions in school fees—and any changes in the government budget associated with increases in government spending on education.[29]

An increase in the provision of education that would boost the annual growth rate for skilled labor from 4.15 percent to 5 percent and would lead to a decline in the annual growth rates for unskilled labor from 1.26 percent to 1.1 percent was considered. This was found to have important impacts on the structure of the Chinese economy. An increase in skilled labor leads to a stronger expansion, or a smaller contraction, in the manufacturing sectors that are skilled labor–intensive than does accession with labor market reform but no change in education spending (table 13.8, columns 2 and 4). Metals, automobiles, electronics, and other manufactures all expand.

While output in some sectors expands, the real wages of skilled workers fall as the supply of skilled workers increases (see table 13.6) and world prices of the outputs they produce decline. This contrasts with the case of accession alone, which results in an increase in the real wages of skilled workers. However, the real wages of generally much poorer unskilled workers rise with increased education, with the wages of unskilled nonfarm workers rising more than those of unskilled farm workers (see table 13.6). Of course, those who are able to transfer from agricultural to nonagricultural employment as a result of increased educational opportunities are likely to be substantially better off.

Overall, it is clear that increasing access to training and skills could substantially offset the adverse impacts on rural labor of the trade reforms associated with accession. Finally, increased education boosts the need for migration as demand for unskilled workers increases in large urban areas. An estimated 10 million farm workers are expected to exchange farm jobs for nonfarm ones (see table 13.6). The impact on consumer prices is small—with falling prices for farm products and rising prices for manufactured commodities.

Impact of Labor Market Reform and an Increase in Skill Levels

The combination of removing labor market barriers and increasing education spending creates the most favorable scenario for unskilled farm labor, leading to the largest increase in real farm wages (19.4 percent; see table 13.6). Farm output contracts more than in the case of labor market reform alone, while skilled labor–intensive industries such as metals, automobiles, electronics, other manufactures, and services expand more than in the case of labor market reform alone or increased education spending alone (see table 13.8). Under this scenario an estimated 32 million farm workers would leave their farm jobs for jobs in urban areas (table 13.6).

These results suggest that to generate pro-poor growth over the next decade, the government should consider both removing policy barriers to labor movement and changing the composition of spending to favor education. Not only would these policies facilitate the transformation of China's economy toward services and high-tech manufacturing sectors, but they also have the potential to more than offset any negative impacts of accession on rural wages and incomes.

Conclusion

The analysis suggests that the reforming economies and their close trading partners will be the biggest beneficiaries of accession to the WTO. China is undertaking the greatest reform and will gain the most. The North American and Western European economies that abolish their export quotas on textiles and clothing and increase their direct trade with China will gain the most in absolute terms. Taiwan (China) will benefit substantially, both as a consequence of its own liberalization and through strengthened trade links with China. Japan will gain substantially because of increased export opportunities in China and China's increased competitiveness as a supplier. Other industrializing and industrialized economies that are China's largest trading partners will also be substantial gainers.

China's WTO accession will have a noticeable impact on the level and pattern of global trade. With accession, China is becoming a much bigger player in world markets. Apparel exports will lead China's export expansion, followed by textiles and automobiles. In addition to being an important source of traded goods, China will become an important destination for other economies' products. Imports of beverages and tobacco will more than double, followed by imports of food products, textiles, agricultural products, automobile parts, and commercial services. The expansion of textiles, light manufactures, petrochemicals, and equipment exports from Taiwan (China) will be driven almost entirely by demand for these products in China.

Accession will have important distributional consequences for China. The wages of skilled workers and unskilled nonfarm workers will rise in real terms and relative to the wages of farm workers. An estimated 6 million people will leave their farm jobs in pursuit of employment in industry and services. Real farm wages and land rental rates will decline. The decline in farm incomes and the rise in the real retail prices of many nonfarm products suggest that some farmers may be hurt by WTO accession after 2001—an issue explored by Chen and Ravallion in chapter 15.

To help offset these adverse impacts on farmers, the Chinese government might make changes in its labor market policies. Abolition of the *hukou* system and reform of the labor market more generally would raise farm wages and allow 28 million people to migrate to nonfarm jobs in search of a better life. It would lead to an even bigger expansion of the labor-intensive manufacturing sector. An increase

TABLE 13.8   Change in Output and Employment in China as a Result of WTO Accession and Other Reforms (percent change over the period 2001–07)

Product	Output				Employment			
	Without Hukou Removal	With Labor Market Reform	With Increase in Skill Level	With labor Market Reform and Increase in Skill Level	Without Labor Market Reform	With Labor Market Reform	With Increase in skill Level	With Labor Market Reform and Increase in Skill Level
Agriculture								
Rice	−2.1	−4.3	−2.4	−4.6	−2.3	−7.4	−3.1	−8.2
Wheat	−2.0	−11.5	−3.3	−12.9	−2.3	−13.3	−3.9	−14.9
Feedgrains	−2.3	−7.8	−3.1	−8.6	−2.6	−9.7	−3.7	−10.6
Vegetables and fruits	−3.4	−7.1	−3.9	−7.7	−3.7	−8.9	−4.6	−9.7
Oilseeds	−7.9	−18.4	−9.4	−19.8	−8.4	−20.4	−10.2	−22.0
Sugar	−6.5	−17.1	−8.0	−18.4	−7.4	−22.4	−9.6	−24.2
Plant-based fibers	15.8	12.8	15.1	12.1	16.4	11.6	15.5	10.6
Livestock and meat	1.3	−3.3	0.6	−4.0	1.1	−7.0	−0.3	−8.2
Dairy	−2.0	−9.4	−3.1	−10.5	−2.4	−14.4	−4.3	−16.0
Other food	−5.9	−13.4	−7.0	−14.5	−6.4	−13.2	−8.9	−15.5
Beverages and tobacco	−33.0	−38.7	−33.7	−39.5	−33.1	−37.6	−35.0	−39.5
Maufacturing								
Extractive industries	−1.0	0.1	−1.2	−0.1	−1.3	0.2	−1.7	−0.2
Textiles	15.6	14.7	15.3	14.3	15.5	16.8	12.7	14.0
Apparel	57.3	61.4	56.7	60.7	56.1	62.6	52.7	59.1
Light manufacturing	3.7	−6.8	2.1	−8.5	3.7	−5.4	0.1	−8.9
Petrochemicals	−2.3	−1.3	−2.3	−1.2	−2.3	0.7	−4.4	−1.4
Metals	−2.1	0.8	−1.8	1.2	−2.1	2.4	−3.9	0.7
Automobiles	1.4	4.1	1.8	4.4	−2.2	2.3	−4.0	0.5
Electronics	0.6	4.5	1.1	5.1	0.4	6.3	−1.3	4.6
Other manufactures	−2.1	0.3	−1.9	0.6	−2.2	2.2	−4.0	0.3
Services								
Trade and transport	0.0	0.8	0.1	1.0	0.0	3.4	−3.1	0.4
Construction	0.9	2.0	0.9	1.9	0.9	3.4	−1.4	1.0
Communications	−0.5	0.6	−0.3	0.9	−0.5	3.4	−3.0	0.8
Commercial services	−2.0	−1.4	−1.8	−1.2	−2.0	1.0	−4.7	−1.8
Other services	−1.7	−0.5	−0.9	0.3	−1.8	1.5	−6.2	−2.9

Source: Authors' simulations with modified GTAP model.

in education spending, to improve skills, would have a positive impact on the structure of the Chinese economy. The real wages of skilled workers would fall, while the real wages of unskilled workers would rise with increased education spending. Thus, on the income side, improved skills would induce pro-poor growth and decrease poverty and inequality.

A number of caveats are important. The gains to China and Taiwan (China) are probably understated because tariff aggregation in the GTAP model hides

much of the variation in tariffs and the welfare gains from reducing this variation within the product aggregates used in the analyses (Bach and Martin 2001; Martin, van der Mensbrugghe, and Manole 2003). When Bach, Martin, and Stevens (1996) adjusted for this in a partial equilibrium context, gains to China almost doubled. The analysis here assumes flexible wages and full employment. However, trade liberalization and foreign competition may worsen unemployment and put downward pressure on the wages of unskilled workers in the short run. Furthermore, while the analysis here improves on Ianchovichina and Martin (2001), with better treatment of the extent of liberalization in agriculture and services and the changes in the automobile sector, there are still areas that have been ignored. One is nontariff barriers in the manufacturing sectors other than the quotas on apparel and textiles. Another is the impact of accession on foreign direct investment (FDI) and the hard-to-measure efficiency gains in services that are associated with this increased investment.

FDI has contributed significantly to China's economic growth and will play an important role as China continues to reform its economy. WTO accession is likely to increase FDI in China, as trade liberalization improves returns to investment and the liberalization of rules on investment eases financial flows into previously restricted sectors such as services and automobile production. The substantial productivity gaps between local and foreign firms imply that new FDI will raise productivity.[30] Walmsley, Hertel, and Ianchovichina (2004) take into account both the impact of FDI and increased productivity growth in services. They find that the impacts of accession are far larger than those predicted by earlier studies, including this one, which ignore the potential productivity gains in the services sector and are abstracted from capital accumulation and foreign investment.

TABLE 13.A.1   Tariff Lines Subject to Import NTBs, China, 2001

	Licenses & Quotas	Tendering	Licensing only	State Trading	Designated Trading	Unrestricted	Any NTB	Total Tarifflines
Paddy rice	0	0	3	3	0	0	3	3
Wheat	0	0	3	3	0	0	3	3
Cereal grains nec	0	0	1	2	0	9	2	11
Vegetables, fruit, nuts	0	0	0	0	0	109	0	109
Oil seeds	0	0	0	0	0	25	0	25
Sugar cane, sugar beet	0	0	0	0	0	1	0	1
Plant-based fibers	1	0	0	1	0	6	1	7
Crops nec	5	0	0	5	0	96	5	101
Cattle, sheep, goat, horses	0	0	0	0	0	6	0	6
Animal products, nec	0	0	0	0	0	62	0	62
Wool, silk-worm cocoons	3	0	0	1	2	9	3	12
Forestry	0	0	0	0	12	23	12	35
Fishing	0	0	0	0	0	57	0	57
Coal	0	0	0	0	0	6	0	6
Oil	0	0	2	1	0	1	3	4
Gas	1	0	0	1	0	1	1	2
Minerals nec	0	0	0	0	0	106	0	106
Meat: cattle, sheep, goats	0	0	0	0	0	26	0	26
Meat products nec	0	0	0	0	0	47	0	47
Vegetable oils and fats	0	0	12	7	0	32	12	44
Dairy products	0	0	0	0	0	24	0	24
Processed rice	0	0	2	2	0	0	2	2
Sugar	7	0	0	9	0	3	9	12
Food products nec	0	0	0	8	0	311	8	319
Beverages and tobacco	1	0	9	5	1	17	15	32
Textiles	39	0	0	3	25	711	46	757
Wearing apparel	0	0	0	0	0	289	0	289
Leather products	11	16	0	0	0	73	27	100
Wood products	0	0	0	0	18	106	18	124
Paper products, publishing	0	0	0	3	0	160	3	163
Petroleum, coal products	8	0	0	7	0	25	8	33
Chemical, rubber, plastic	35	0	15	21	5	1248	51	1299
Mineral products nec	0	0	0	0	0	198	0	198
Ferrous metals	0	0	0	0	181	49	181	230
Metals nec	0	0	0	0	0	190	0	190
Metal products	0	0	0	0	1	264	1	265
Motor vehicles and parts	64	0	0	0	0	93	64	157
Transport equipment nec	7	10	0	0	0	72	17	89
Electronic equipment	36	17	0	0	0	205	53	258
Machinery and equipment	39	77	0	2	0	1199	116	1315
Manufactures nec	0	0	0	0	0	219	0	219
Electricity	0	0	0	0	0	1	0	1
Gas manuf, distribution	0	0	0	0	0	1	0	1
Total	257	120	47	84	245	6080	664	6744

Source: WTO 2001. Commodity definitions are for GTAP-5, see www.gtap.org for concordances.

TABLE 13.A.2   The Import Coverage of Nontariff Barriers in China, 2001

	Licenses & Quotas %	Tendering %	Licensing only %	State Trading %	Designated Trading %	Any NTB %	Unrestricted Trading %	Total %
Paddy rice	100	0	100	100	0	100	0	100
Wheat	100	0	100	100	0	100	0	100
Cereal grains nec	0	0	0	0	0	0	100	100
Vegetables, fruit, nuts	0	0	0	0	0	0	100	100
Oil seeds	0	0	0	0	0	0	100	100
Sugar cane, sugar beet	0	0	0	0	0	0	100	100
Plant-based fibers	93	0	0	93	0	93	7	100
Crops nec	48	0	0	48	0	48	52	100
Cattle, sheep and goats, horses	0	0	0	0	0	0	100	100
Animal products, nec	0	0	0	0	0	0	100	100
Wool, silk-worm cocoons	0	0	0	0	95	95	5	100
Forestry	0	0	0	0	94	94	6	100
Fishing	0	0	0	0	0	0	100	100
Coal	0	0	0	0	0	0	100	100
Oil	100	0	0	100	0	100	0	100
Gas	0	0	0	0	0	0	100	100
Minerals nec	0	0	0	0	0	0	100	100
Meat: cattle, sheep, goats, horse	0	0	0	0	0	0	100	100
Meat products nec	0	0	0	0	0	0	100	100
Vegetable oils and fats	59	0	60	59	0	60	40	100
Dairy Products	0	0	0	0	0	0	100	100
Processed rice	100	0	100	100	0	100	0	100
Sugar	85	0	0	85	0	85	15	100
Food products nec	1	0	0	1	0	1	99	100
Beverages and tobacco products	20	0	16	20	0	36	64	100
Textiles	9	0	0	0	8	14	86	100
Wearing apparel	0	0	0	0	0	0	100	100
Leather products	0	0	0	0	0	0	100	100
Wood products	0	0	0	0	55	55	45	100
Paper products, publishing	0	0	0	0	0	0	100	100
Petroleum, coal products	58	0	0	58	0	58	42	100
Chemical, rubber, plastic prods	5	0	1	5	2	7	93	100
Mineral products nec	0	0	0	0	0	0	100	100
Ferrous metals	0	0	0	0	85	85	16	100
Metals nec	0	0	0	0	0	0	100	100
Metal products	0	0	0	0	1	1	99	100
Motor vehicles and parts	32	0	0	0	0	32	68	100
Transport equipment nec	1	3	0	0	0	4	96	100
Electronic equipment	9	5	0	0	0	14	86	100
Machinery and equipment nec	1	8	0	0	0	10	90	100
Manufactures nec	0	0	0	0	0	0	100	100
Total Import Coverage	12.8	2.7	0.5	9.5	6.2	21.6	78.4	100

Note: Based on WTO 2001 and import data from China Customs for 2000.

TABLE 13.A.3   Commodity Import Shares by NTB Measure

	Licenses & Quotas %	Tendering %	Licensing Only %	State Trading %	Designated Trading %	Any NTB %	Unrestricted Trading %	Total
Paddy rice	0.0	0.0	0.0	0.0	0.0	0.0	0.0	0.0
Wheat	0.0	0.0	13.0	0.7	0.0	0.6	0.0	0.1
Cereal grains nec	0.0	0.0	0.0	0.0	0.0	0.0	0.2	0.2
Vegetables, fruit, nuts	0.0	0.0	0.0	0.0	0.0	0.0	0.2	0.2
Oil seeds	0.0	0.0	0.0	0.0	0.0	0.0	1.7	1.5
Sugar cane, sugar beet	0.0	0.0	0.0	0.0	0.0	0.0	0.0	0.0
Plant-based fibers	0.5	0.0	0.0	0.3	0.0	0.0	0.0	0.0
Crops nec	1.1	0.0	0.0	0.8	0.0	0.0	0.1	0.1
Cattle, sheep and goats	0.0	0.0	0.0	0.0	0.0	0.0	0.0	0.0
Animal products, nec	0.0	0.0	0.0	0.0	0.0	0.0	0.5	0.4
Wool, silk	4.3	0.0	0.0	0.0	4.7	0.7	0.0	0.1
Forestry	0.0	0.0	0.0	0.0	11.7	2.4	0.1	0.3
Fishing	0.0	0.0	0.0	0.0	0.0	0.0	0.1	0.1
Coal	0.0	0.0	0.0	0.0	0.0	0.0	0.0	0.0
Oil	0.0	0.0	0.0	69.4	0.0	48.9	0.0	5.6
Gas	0.0	0.0	0.0	0.0	0.0	0.0	0.0	0.0
Minerals nec	0.0	0.0	0.0	0.0	0.0	0.0	2.5	2.2
Meat: cattle, sheep, goat	0.0	0.0	0.0	0.0	0.0	0.0	0.1	0.1
Meat products nec	0.0	0.0	0.0	0.0	0.0	0.0	0.4	0.3
Vegetable oils and fats	0.0	0.0	55.0	2.8	0.0	0.7	0.2	0.3
Diary products	0.0	0.0	0.0	0.0	0.0	0.0	0.1	0.1
Processed rice	0.0	0.0	9.9	0.5	0.0	0.5	0.0	0.1
Sugar	0.8	0.0	0.0	0.5	0.0	0.4	0.0	0.1
Food products nec	0.0	0.0	0.0	0.1	0.0	0.0	1.4	1.2
Beverages and tobacco	0.0	0.0	2.9	0.2	0.0	0.2	0.1	0.1
Textiles	16.2	0.0	0.0	1.3	8.2	0.7	7.1	6.3
Wearing apparel	0.0	0.0	0.0	0.0	0.0	0.0	0.6	0.5
Leather products	0.0	0.0	0.0	0.0	0.0	0.0	1.6	1.4
Wood products	0.0	0.0	0.0	0.0	8.8	0.8	0.6	0.6
Paper products	0.0	0.0	0.0	0.1	0.0	0.0	4.0	3.5
Petroleum, coal prods	20.8	0.0	0.0	14.8	0.0	3.4	1.3	1.6
Chemical, rubber, plastic	17.0	0.0	19.1	8.1	4.2	0.5	17.9	15.9
Mineral products nec	0.0	0.0	0.0	0.0	0.0	0.0	1.1	1.0
Ferrous metals	0.0	0.0	0.0	0.0	62.1	29.9	0.9	4.3
Metals nec	0.0	0.0	0.0	0.0	0.0	0.0	5.2	4.6
Metal products	0.0	0.0	0.0	0.0	0.3	0.0	2.0	1.7
Motor vehicles and parts	8.7	0.0	0.0	0.0	0.0	2.4	1.6	1.7
Transport equipment nec	0.2	1.6	0.0	0.0	0.0	0.1	1.8	1.6
Electronic equipment	26.8	41.1	0.0	0.0	0.0	6.0	23.8	21.7
Machinery and equip	3.8	57.3	0.0	0.3	0.0	1.6	22.2	19.8
Manufactures nec	0.0	0.0	0.0	0.0	0.0	0.0	0.7	0.6
Total	100.0	100.0	100.0	100.0	100.0	100.0	100.0	100.0

TABLE 13.A.4   Elasticity of Substitution and Changes in Real Consumer Prices due to China's WTO Accession

	Elasticity of Substitution between Domestic Products and Imports*	Short Run Closure		Long Run Closure	
		1995–2007	2001–2007	1995–2007	2001–2007
Rice	4.4	2.2	0.7	2.5	1.0
Wheat	4.4	−0.8	0.7	0.4	0.4
Feed grains	4.4	13	2.1	13.5	1.9
Vegetables and fruits	4.4	0.9	−0.6	1.4	−0.1
Oilseeds	4.4	−6.7	−5.9	−4.8	−4.6
Sugar	4.4	−2.1	−3.5	−1.8	−3.1
Plant based fibers	4.4	2.1	4.1	3.1	3.1
Livestock & meat	5.0	3.8	0.7	2.4	0.2
Dairy	4.4	2	−0.5	2	0.2
Other food	4.4	0.3	−2.7	0.4	−1.8
Beverages & tobacco	6.2	−14.3	−7.7	−10.8	−6.9
Extractive industries	5.6	2.5	1.7	2.3	1.2
Textiles	4.4	−10.3	−1.5	−10.5	−3.1
Apparel	8.8	−6.7	0.8	−8.6	−1.9
Light manufacturing	8.8	−2	0.5	−2.6	0.0
Petrochemical industry	4.1	0.7	0.8	0.9	0.9
Metals	5.6	1.2	1.3	1.3	1.3
Automobiles	10.4	−23.6	−4.0	−22.2	−4.2
Electronics	5.6	−5.3	−1.4	−5.8	−1.7
Other manufactures	5.5	0.5	0.8	0.4	0.9
Trade and transport	3.8	3	1.7	2.6	1.7
Construction	3.8	2.8	1.7	2.5	1.7
Communication	3.8	3.6	1.7	2.8	1.9
Commercial services	3.8	2.7	0.9	3.2	1.9
Other services	4.0	2.4	1.3	2.5	1.6

**TABLE 13.A.5   Changes in China's Key Economic Indicators in the Baseline,
without WTO Accession, 1995–2007**

	Output (Percent)	Employment (Percent)	Exports (Percent)	Imports (Percent)
Rice	63.8	−11.5	134.7	−8.8
Wheat	81.4	6.4	−15.2	126.3
Feed grains	109.5	23.8	−0.6	95.9
Vegetables and fruits	98.2	16.8	−10.8	122.1
Oilseeds	100.9	18.4	−36	151.7
Sugar	112.5	14.5	109.4	88.7
Plant based fibers	137.2	41.1	−8.5	146.1
Livestock & meat	121.9	25.6	12.8	135.3
Dairy	122.5	18.8	60.5	100.3
Other food	110.8	−1.5	76.8	58.5
Beverages & tobacco	114.6	−9	166.7	65.9
Extractive industries	77.8	67.2	−88	554.2
Textiles	142.2	−1.7	95	70.4
Apparel	110.5	−1.7	100.8	47.2
Light manufacturing	135.8	11	117.3	60.1
Petrochemical industry	126.7	−5.6	80.2	101.5
Metals	144.4	11.5	114.4	99.6
Automobiles	157.5	2.2	419.7	105.3
Electronics	186.5	13.1	168.1	112.1
Other manufactures	161.1	6.4	195.1	51.3
Trade and transport	129.4	−3.3	129.4	69.3
Construction	113.3	26.5	77.4	85.6
Communication	133.2	−12.4	452.9	11.9
Commercial services	133.4	1.8	211.7	55.1
Other services	113.6	21	101.1	75.1
Total	120.2	N/A	131.7	97

TABLE 13.A.6   Changes in China's Key Economic Indicators due to WTO Accession for the Period before 2001 (1995–2001)

	Output %	Employment %	Exports %	Imports %	Trade Balance US$ m.	Wholesale Prices %	Consumer Prices %
Rice	−0.7	−0.7	9.5	−11.3	101	0.5	1.5
Wheat	−2.8	−2.9	14.9	39.1	−484	0.1	0.0
Feed grains	2.3	2.4	2.5	−20.9	244	0.8	11.4
Vegetables and fruits	−0.6	−0.7	8.6	−26.5	486	0.5	1.5
Oilseeds	−1.8	−1.9	10.9	16.6	−549	0.5	−0.2
Sugar	−0.1	−0.2	9.1	3.3	8	0.6	1.3
Plant based fibers	−11.6	−12.2	29.6	−9.8	264	−1.2	0.0
Livestock & meat	1.3	1.4	8.7	−27.3	1888	1.1	2.2
Dairy	2.0	2.2	10.3	2.6	−10	0.8	1.8
Other food	4.6	4.8	10.9	−26.3	3537	0.3	2.2
Beverages & tobacco	−23.8	−23.8	16.8	614.9	−10656	−0.5	−4.2
Extractive industries	−0.4	−0.5	16.6	1.9	−781	0.1	1.1
Textiles	−12.1	−12.2	16.7	35.5	−9556	−3.0	−7.6
Apparel	−3.4	−3.9	23.7	344.6	−344	−1.9	−6.8
Light manufacturing	3.7	3.6	14.6	48.9	2008	−0.5	−2.6
Petrochemical industry	−0.7	−0.7	12.9	11.3	−4433	−0.6	0.0
Metals	−0.5	−0.5	20.9	23.5	−3051	−0.6	0.0
Automobiles	2.8	−13.2	326.8	195.5	2935	−15.9	−18.8
Electronics	3.8	3.6	18.4	16.2	2657	−1.8	−4.2
Other manufactures	1.9	1.9	17.6	22.2	8511	−0.8	−0.5
Trade and transport	1.3	1.3	10.1	−7.3	5284	−0.2	0.9
Construction	2.2	2.2	14.8	−6.3	301	−0.2	0.8
Communication	1.0	1.0	11.1	−7.4	229	−0.1	0.9
Commercial services	0.8	0.8	10.5	−6.3	798	0.3	1.3
Other services	0.3	0.4	12.7	−8.1	749	−0.1	0.9
Total	2.0	N/A	20.3	22.0	138	−1.4	−0.8

TABLE 13.A.7   Sensitivity Analysis with Respect to the Elasticity of Transformation σ (2.67) (percentage changes in China after 2001)

	Output (Percent)	Employment (Percent)	Exports (Percent)	Imports (Percent)	Wholesale Prices (Percent)	Consumer Prices (Percent)
Rice	−2.2	−2.5	4.2	−6.3	−0.8	1.1
Wheat	−2.4	−2.8	15.6	−9.2	−1.5	0.6
Feed grains	−2.5	−2.9	−78.2	−1.9	−1.7	1.8
Vegetables and fruits	−3.5	−3.9	12.3	−5.4	−1.7	0.1
Oilseeds	−8.3	−8.9	26.8	21.3	−2.6	−4.5
Sugar	−6.9	−8.1	11.8	24.4	−1.7	−3.0
Plant based fibers	15.7	16.3	−52.3	8.0	0.1	3.1
Livestock & meat	1.2	0.8	12.6	−7.6	−1.4	0.4
Dairy	−2.3	−2.9	11.5	24.4	−1.3	0.3
Other food	−6.2	−6.7	10.2	63.3	−1.7	−1.8
Beverages & tobacco	−33.2	−33.2	8.8	112.9	−1.9	−7.0
Extractive industries	−0.9	−1.2	7.6	−4.4	−0.8	1.1
Textiles	15.6	15.6	32.6	38.6	−1.8	−3.2
Apparel	57.4	56.4	106.1	30.7	−0.7	−2.0
Light manufacturing	3.3	3.3	5.5	6.9	−0.9	0.0
Petrochemical industry	−2.3	−2.2	3.2	11.7	−0.8	0.7
Metals	−2.0	−1.9	4.0	6.8	−0.5	1.2
Automobiles	1.5	−2.0	27.9	24.1	−4.0	−4.3
Electronics	0.8	0.7	6.8	6.9	−1.4	−1.8
Other manufactures	−2.0	−2.0	4.3	18.8	−0.7	0.7
Trade and transport	0.0	0.1	1.0	−0.4	−0.3	1.5
Construction	0.9	1.0	3.0	17.4	−0.3	1.6
Communication	−0.5	−0.3	−0.3	10.9	0.0	1.8
Commercial services	−2.0	−1.9	−0.2	35.4	0.1	1.8
Other services	−1.6	−1.7	1.7	33.5	−0.2	1.5
Total	1.0	0	17.5	17.2	−0.8	−0.1
Nonfarm unskilled wages	1.08	Migration	7*	Unskilled wage	0.7	
Farm unskilled wage	−0.02	Land rent	−5.7	Skilled wage	0.8	
Price of capital goods	−0.95	Capital rent	1.2	Welfare	9728**	

*1997 US millions.

**Millions of workers leaving their farm jobs for nonfarm jobs.

Notes

1. Because China's accession was a necessary condition for that of Taiwan, China, and because of the strong trade linkages between the two economies, the impact of Taiwan, China's accession to the WTO is also considered.

2. Among the studies using a general equilibrium approach to quantify the impact of China's WTO accession are Lejour (2000); Zhai and Li (2000); Li and others (2000); McKibbin and Tang (2000); Ianchovichina and Martin (2001); Walmsley and Hertel (2001); Deutsche Bank (2001); Wang (2002); Zhai and Wang (2002); Walmsley, Hertel, and Ianchovichina (2004); and Ianchovichina and Walmsley (2003).

3. Huang, Rozelle, and Min (2004) find that nominal rates of protection on important agricultural commodities (rice, vegetables and fruits, livestock and meat) were negative in 2001 and are likely to remain unchanged in the post-accession period. Consequently, the reduction in agricultural protection is likely to be far less than presented in earlier studies. Nonetheless, greater scope for imports is likely for a range of agricultural products (wheat, oilseeds, sugar, and dairy products), which are protected by tariffs that are scheduled to be reduced substantially and for products (cotton and feedgrains) for which export subsidies are ruled out. These important findings were not incorporated in earlier studies.

4. The current treatment differs from that in Zhai and Wang (2002), who represent imperfect labor mobility in a single country model with endogenous urban unemployment but do not differentiate between skilled and unskilled labor and employ a low level of elasticity of labor mobility between rural and urban areas (0.25). The results here are similar to those in Zhai and Wang (2002) in the case of WTO accession with high labor mobility (elasticity of labor mobility is doubled) and fixed urban unemployment (flexible urban wage).

5. GTAP is a standard global applied general equilibrium model with perfectly competitive markets and constant returns to scale technology. The model represents consumer demands through a constant difference of elasticities functional form and on the supply side emphasizes the role of intersectoral factor mobility in the determination of sectoral output. Product differentiation between imported and domestic goods and among imports by region of origin allows for two-way trade in each product category, depending on the ease of substitution between products from different regions. Land, capital, skilled and unskilled labor, and, in some sectors, a natural resource factor are used in production and are fully employed.

6. Some sectors, particularly the service sectors, do not participate in export processing arrangements and so are not exempt from duties on intermediate inputs used in the production of exports.

7. In a deterministic world, a producer of exports will always take advantage of duty exemptions or rebates unless the administrative costs are excessive, which does not appear to be the case in China. Many studies have either ignored the problem or, as in Lejour (2000), treated duty exemptions as simple reductions in initial tariffs, instead of exemptions on imports used specifically in the production of exports.

8. Export processors can sell locally, but they have to pay duty/VAT on the imported inputs used in the production of output sold on the domestic market.

9. The export processing arrangements did not prevent firms producing mainly for the domestic market from exporting. These firms produced exports, known as "ordinary" exports, using mainly domestic inputs and only a small portion of duty- or VAT-paid imported materials (Ianchovichina 2003).

10. According to GTAP version 4, 14 percent of imports were for final consumption and according to China's Customs 40 percent of imports were ordinary imports that were not duty exempt. This means that approximately 26 percent were ordinary imports used as intermediates. Also according to GTAP version 4, China's firms exported an average of 10 percent of their output, implying that only about 3 percent of imports were used for production of ordinary exports.

11. The GTAP version 5 database (Dimaranan and McDougall 2002) is the source for the elasticities of substitution between domestic and composite imported commodities in the Armington production structure of a sector. The values for these elasticities are shown in column 1 of Appendix table 13.A.4.

12. In a more recent work Sicular and Zhao (2004) estimate the responsiveness of rural labor supply to changes in agricultural returns. They present two "push" elasticities—2.67 for nonagricultural wage employment and 0.24 for nonagricultural nonwage employment. Focusing on the push elasticity for nonagricultural wage employment and testing the sensitivity of the results by replacing the elasticity of 1.32 used in our analysis with 2.67 leaves the aggregate results largely unchanged (Appendix table 13.A.7). The greater responsiveness of labor movement implied by the larger elasticity of transformation (2.67) translates into better poverty and inequality outcomes since farm wages remain nearly unchanged and an additional 1 million farm workers leave farming.

13. Applied rates at the end of the implementation period were estimated as the lesser of the bindings and 2001 applied rates. In virtually all cases, the bindings were lower than the applied rates.

14. Francois and Spinanger base their estimate of the 20 percent productivity increase on the distribution of current plants in China and apply the formula $\Delta \ln(AC) = CDR \cdot \Delta \ln(Q)$, where AC is average cost, MC is marginal cost, Q is the quantity produced, and CDR is the inverse elasticity of scale, defined as $CDR = -(AC - MC)/AC$, and varies between .125 and .135 (the range of values found in engineering studies). Then they calculate an average cost index for the industry. Assuming that the index is 100 at 350,000 units per plant, current plant structure yields a cost index of roughly 120.

15. Mattoo (2004) argues that China's commitments on services were the most comprehensive ever made in the WTO.

16. In a recent paper Mai, Horridge, and Perkins (2003) estimate productivity increases over 10 years at 1.8 percent a year for the strategic manufacturing industries and 2.7 percent a year for the services sectors as reforms take place under WTO accession.

17. These quotas are represented in the analysis as an export tax. In some cases the proceeds of this implicit export tax are redistributed to quota holders, who may be quite different from the producers and exporters of the goods. In other cases the quotas are auctioned, with the quota rents accruing to the government. In either case, the marginal return from additional output of textiles and apparel is net of the quota rent/export tax.

18. This adjustment was made with ALTERTAX (Malcolm 1998), so that the consistency and the shares in the GTAP database would be preserved.

19. The fixed employment assumption may understate the costs of accession to some degree. Zhai and Wang, who explore the impact of WTO accession on migration and unemployment (2002), conclude that structural unemployment may rise following China's WTO accession as farmers move to urban areas.

20. The assumption of fixed trade balance as a share of GDP is required when evaluating welfare impacts using a static trade model such as GTAP.

21. This is a consensus finding supported by Ianchovichina and Martin (2001), Deutsche Bank (2001), Wang (2002), and Ianchovichina and Walmsley (2003).

22. The model underestimates the potential expansion and efficiency increase in the service sectors. With its promise to eliminate over the next few years most restrictions on foreign entry and ownership, as well as most forms of discrimination against foreign firms (Mattoo 2004), China has set the stage for increases in foreign investment and productivity in these sectors. This in turn could lead to much larger income gains from WTO accession and larger increases in wages of skilled workers than shown here (see Walmsley, Hertel, and Ianchovichina 2004).

23. This estimate represents the number of "effective" farm workers likely to migrate from rural to urban areas based on employment data for 2000 from *China Statistical Yearbook* (NBS 2001, pp. 111–12).

24. The consumption tax is close to nondistortionary, because it applies at the same rate to all components of private and government consumption but not investment. Because the GTAP Version 5 database appears to represent the VAT on domestic production as an output tax, the model generates tax losses from the contraction of some industries (e.g., the tobacco and alcohol industries). These inward-oriented industries have higher average VAT rates than export-oriented sectors such as clothing because the VAT is exempted on exports. When the export-oriented sectors expand, the net impact of WTO accession is a sharp contraction in tax revenues. In reality, such a contraction will not be observed, because VATs of the same magnitude are levied on imports. To offset this impact, particularly in our poverty analyses, we had to adjust the consumption tax in a downward direction. We first computed the consumption tax that compensates for the loss in output taxes. This tax as a share of the total replacement tax is equal to the share of the output tax loss in the total tax losses. Second, we adjusted the consumption tax rate to eliminate the component stemming from the change in output taxes.

25. High unemployment due to the restructuring of state-owned-enterprises, privatization, and fierce competition in China imply that WTO accession may dampen the effect on the wages of unskilled workers. By assuming full employment, the model overestimates the increase in wages of workers in the nonfarm sectors, underestimates the fall in the wages of farm workers, and overestimates the increase in total welfare.

26. These estimates are in agreement with findings in Ianchovichina and Martin (2001) and Wang (2002). These are conservative estimates since they do not reflect income increases resulting from trade- and foreign direct investment–induced productivity gains, especially gains associated with liberalization of China's service sectors (Walmsley, Hertel, and Ianchovichina 2004). Transaction cost savings from developing institutions compatible with an open and modern market could be very large as well, but were not factored into the analysis.

27. Zhai and Wang (2002) obtained similar results for a combination of WTO accession and full labor market reform.

28. Since the tax on nonfarm employment of 34 percent represents a bundle of policies that act as a barrier to rural-urban migration, this estimate is representative of the likely impact and could change depending on the policy mix the government adopts.

29. The model does not track education spending as a component of the government budget constraint.

30. Claro (2001) estimates that in the apparel and footwear industries, the adoption of foreign technology raises productivity by 30–62 percent in collective enterprises and 20–59 percent in state enterprises.

References

Bach, C., and W. Martin. 2001. "Would the Right Tariff Aggregator for Policy Analysis Please Stand Up?" *Journal of Policy Modeling* 23: 621–35.

Bach, C., W. Martin, and J. Stevens. 1996. "China and the WTO: Tariff Offers, Exemptions and Welfare Implications." *Weltwirtschaftliches Archiv* 132(3): 409–31.

Bhattasali, D., Li, Shantong, and Martin, W., eds., 2004. *China and the WTO: Accession, Policy Reform, and Poverty Reduction Strategies.* Washington, D.C.: World Bank and Oxford University Press.

Chen, S., and M. Ravallion. 2004. "Household Welfare Impacts of China's Accession to the WTO." In Bhattasali, D., Li, Shantong and Martin, W., eds., *China and the WTO: Accession, Policy Reform, and Poverty Reduction Strategies.* Chapter 15. Washington, D.C.: World Bank and Oxford University Press.

Claro, S. 2001. "Tariff and FDI Liberalization: What to Expect from China's Entry into WTO?" Paper presented at the Eighth Annual Conference on Empirical Investigations in International Trade, Purdue University, West Lafayette, Ind., November 9–11.

Deutsche Bank. 2001. "Quantifying the Impact of China's WTO Entry." DB Global Market Research. [www.deutsche-bank.de/index_e.htm.]

Dimaranan, B., and R. McDougall. 2002. *Global Trade, Assistance, and Production: The GTAP 5 Data Base.* West Lafayette, Ind.: Purdue University, Center for Global Trade Analysis.

Francois, J., and D. Spinanger. 2001. "Greater China's Accession to the WTO: Implications for International Trade/Production and for Hong Kong." Paper prepared for the Hong Kong Trade Development Council, Hong Kong, December 2001.

———. 2004. "Regulated Efficiency, WTO Accession and the Motor Vehicle Sector in China." This issue.

Gilbert, J., and T. Wahl. 2001. "Applied General Equilibrium Assessments of Trade Liberalization in China." *World Economy* 25(5): 697–731.

Hertel, T., ed. 1997. *Global Trade Analysis: Modeling and Applications.* Cambridge: Cambridge University Press.

Huang, J., S. Rozelle, and C. Min. 2004. "The Nature of Distortions to Agricultural Incentives in China and Implications of WTO Accession." In D. Bhattasali, Shantong Li, and W. Martin, eds., *China and the WTO: Accession, Policy Reform, and Poverty Reduction Strategies.* Chapter 6. Washington, D.C.: World Bank and Oxford University Press.

Hussain, A. 2004. "Impact of WTO Membership on Inequality and Poverty." In D. Bhattasali, Shantong Li, and W. Martin, eds., *China and the WTO: Accession, Policy Reform, and Poverty Reduction Strategies.* Chapter 17. Washington, D.C.: World Bank and Oxford University Press.

Ianchovichina, E. 2003. "GTAP-DD: A Model for Analyzing Trade Reforms in the Presence of Duty Drawbacks." GTAP Technical Paper 21. Purdue University, West Lafayette, Ind. [www.gtap.org/resources/tech_papers.asp] and *Journal of Policy Modelling* (forthcoming).

Ianchovichina, E., and W. Martin. 2001. "Trade Liberalization in China's Accession to WTO." *Journal of Economic Integration* 16(4): 421–45.

Ianchovichina, E., and T. Walmsley. 2003. "Impact of China's WTO Accession on East Asia." Policy Research Working Paper 3109. World Bank, Washington, D.C.

Lardy, N., ed. 2002. *Integrating China in the Global Economy.* Washington, D.C.: Brookings Institution Press.

Lejour, A. 2000. "China and the WTO: The Impact on China and the World Economy." The Netherlands Bureau for Economic Policy Analysis. The Hague, Netherlands.

Li, S., Z. Wang, F. Zhai, and L. Xu. 2000. *WTO: China and the World*. Beijing: China Development Press.

Long, Yongtu. 2000. "On the Question of Our Joining the World Trade Organization." *The Chinese Economy* 33(1): 5–52.

Mai, Y., M. Horridge, and F. Perkins. 2003. "Estimating the Effects of China's Accession to the World Trade Organization." CoPS General Paper, no. G-137. Centre of Policy Studies and Impact Project, Clayton, Australia.

Malcolm, G. 1998. "Adjusting Taxes in the GTAP Data Base." GTAP Technical Paper 12. Center for Global Trade Analysis, Purdue University, West Lafayette, Ind. [www.gtap.org/resources/tech_papers.asp.]

Martin, W. 2001. "Implications of Reform and WTO Accession for China's Agricultural Trade Policies." *Economics of Transition* 9(3): 717–42.

Martin, W., D. van der Mensbrugghe, and V. Manole. 2003. "Keeping the Devil in the Details: Aggregation and the Benefits of Trade Liberalization." Presented at the Sixth Annual Conference on Global Economic Analysis, The Hague, June 12–14. Available at http://www.gtap.agecon.purdue .edu.

Mattoo, A. 2004. "China's Accession to the WTO: The Services Dimension." In D. Bhattasali, Shantong Li, and W. Martin, eds., *China and the WTO: Accession, Policy Reform, and Poverty Reduction Strategies*. Washington, D.C.: World Bank and Oxford University Press.

McDougall, R., A. Elbehri, and T. Truong. 1998. *Global Trade, Assistance, and Production: The GTAP 4 Data Base*. Purdue University, Center for Global Trade Analysis, West Lafayette, Ind.

McKibbin, W., and K. Tang. 2000. "Trade and Financial Reform in China: Impacts on the World Economy." *World Economy* 23(8): 979–1003.

Messerlin, P. 2004. "China in the WTO: Antidumping and Safeguards." In D. Bhattasali, Shantong Li, and W. Martin, eds., *China and the WTO: Accession, Policy Reform, and Poverty Reduction Strategies*. Washington, D.C.: World Bank and Oxford University Press.

NBS (National Bureau of Statistics of China). 2001. *China Statistical Yearbook*. People's Republic of China. China Statistics Press.

Shi, Xinzheng. 2002. "Empirical Research on Urban-Rural Income Differentials: A Case of China." Peking University, Beijing.

Sicular, T., and Y. Zhao. 2002. "Employment, Earnings and Labor Market Responses in Rural China." Mimeo, Peking University and the University of Western Ontario.

———. 2004. "Labor Mobility and China's Entry to the WTO." In D. Bhattasali, Shantong Li, and W. Martin, eds., *China and the WTO: Accession, Policy Reform, and Poverty Reduction Strategies*. Washington, D.C: World Bank and Oxford University Press.

Walmsley, T. L., and T. W. Hertel. 2001. "China's Accession to the WTO: Timing is Everything." *World Economy* 24(8): 1019–49.

Walmsley, T. L., T. Hertel, and E. Ianchovichina. 2004. "Assessing the Impact of China's WTO Accession on Foreign Ownership." *Pacific Economic Review* (forthcoming).

Wang, Z. 2002. "WTO Accession, 'Greater China' Free Trade Area and Economic Relations across the Taiwan Strait." Paper presented at the Fifth Conference on Global Economic Analysis, June 5–7, Taipei.

———. 2003. "The Impact of China's WTO Accession on Patterns of World Trade." *Journal of Policy Modeling* 25(1): 1–41.

World Bank. 1997. *China Engaged: Integration with the World Economy*. Washington, D.C.

———. 1999. *World Development Indicators*. Washington, D.C.

———. 2002. *China: Country Economic Memorandum*. Washington, D.C.

WTO (World Trade Organization). 1994. *The Results of the Uruguay Round of Multilateral Trade Negotiations*. Geneva.

———. 2001. "Accession of the People's Republic of China." WT/L/432 (www.wto.org).

Zhai, Fan, and S. Li. 2000. "The Implications of Accession to WTO on China's Economy." Paper presented at the Third Annual Conference on Global Economic Analysis, June 28–30, Monash University, Melbourne, Australia.

Zhai, Fan, and Z. Wang. 2002. "WTO Accession, Rural Labour Migration and Urban Unemployment in China." *Urban Studies* 39(12): 2199–217.

PART III

IMPACTS ON HOUSEHOLDS AND ON POVERTY

14

EARNINGS AND LABOR MOBILITY IN RURAL CHINA: IMPLICATIONS FOR CHINA'S ACCESSION TO THE WTO

Terry Sicular and Yaohui Zhao

The literature on trade liberalization in developing countries contains divergent views on the impact of liberalization on employment, incomes, and poverty. Although most studies find aggregate welfare gains, they disagree over the distribution of these gains among households. One view is that trade liberalization generates broad-based employment gains across regions for skilled and unskilled labor, and that consequently income gains are shared widely (Dollar and Kraay 2001). Under these conditions, trade liberalization contributes to reductions in income inequality and poverty. The alternative view is that employment and income gains go disproportionately to the already better-off groups, with negative implications for inequality and perhaps also for the poor (Rodrik 2000).

The reality probably lies somewhere in between, with the distributional outcome depending on specific conditions in the country in question (Winters 2000). First, it depends on the level and structure of pre-liberalization trade barriers, which determine the sectors that gain and lose. A differential impact on sectors holds implications for the distribution of gains among regions, skill levels, and income groups. Second, it depends on the preexisting distribution of assets—that is, of land, capital, and human capital. So, for example, if trade liberalization

benefits agriculture and if land holdings are highly concentrated, then inequality could increase. Third, the distributional impact of trade liberalization depends on the flexibility of domestic markets, especially for labor. Gains from trade liberalization are less likely to be shared equally where labor markets are segmented and barriers hinder the movement of labor among sectors.

These considerations are relevant to the impact of China's accession to the World Trade Organization (WTO) and its concomitant trade liberalization on employment and incomes in China. Indeed, the Chinese case has some interesting features. China's labor markets have historically (under socialism) been inflexible and highly segmented. Domestic economic reforms have allowed greater labor mobility, but many observers believe that substantial institutional barriers to the movement of labor persist. Also, in China certain assets such as land and education, while not equally distributed, are nevertheless relatively equally distributed by developing country standards. These two features would have counterbalancing effects in that the former would tend to cause the gains from WTO accession to be concentrated, while the latter would tend to cause the gains to be shared more broadly compared with the gains from similar liberalization in other countries.

239

This chapter examines the microeconomic determinants of rural employment and incomes in China. More specifically, using survey data we estimate income, wage, and labor supply functions for rural households. Because the households derive income from agriculture and sideline family businesses and since few households hire labor to undertake such activities (Bowlus and Sicular 2003), we must impute shadow wages derived from self-employment. Together, the income, wage, shadow wage, and labor supply functions empirically describe household income generation from employment.

Our analysis fills a gap in the literature. Even though the literature examining employment and earnings in rural China is now quite substantial, most studies of China's rural employment analyze the determinants of occupational status—that is, whether or not individuals participate in different types of work such as wage jobs or nonagricultural sidelines (examples are Hare 1994, 1999a, 1999b; Knight and Song 1997, 1999; Michelson and Parish 2000, Parish, Zhe, and Li 1995; Rozelle and others 1999; Zhao 1999a, 1999b). Relatively few studies estimate the rural labor supply per se—that is, hours or days worked (examples are Knight and Song 1997, and Yao 1999). Even fewer studies estimate labor supply as a function of wages, the relationship of greatest interest here.

To our knowledge, the only study that estimates labor supply for rural China and includes a measure of the wage as an explanatory variable is by Meng (2000). Like Meng, we estimate time worked as a function of wages and other variables. Unlike Meng, and indeed unlike the relevant literature for other developing countries (e.g., Jacoby 1993; Skoufias 1994), our labor supply functions allow for the possibility that wages or shadow wages, and labor's response to these wages, can differ depending on the type of wage. Thus it is possible for labor supply to be more responsive to the market wage than to the agricultural shadow wage, or vice versa. Finally, although other studies estimate total labor supply, we estimate total labor supply *and* its components—in this case, labor supply to household agricultural production, to household nonagricultural production, and to market or wage employment. By estimating the components of labor supply, we obtain information about how wages and other variables influence the composition of employment.

Our empirical results provide some of the underlying parameters needed to understand the effects of trade liberalization on levels of employment and earnings. The income generation functions give estimates of the impact of agricultural versus nonagricultural employment on income from labor. We find that nonagricultural employment generates substantially more income per hour worked than does agricultural employment. This result is consistent with the findings of other studies (e.g., Knight and Song 1997; Meng 2000; Michelson and Parish 2000), which generally conclude that income inequality among households reflects differences in access to higher paying, off-farm jobs.

We take this analysis one step further and decompose the income gap between households in richer and poorer subsamples. Our decomposition reveals that the income gap is accounted for by both differences in hours worked in different occupations and differences in the estimated returns to labor in different occupations—that is, poorer households are poorer both because they supply less labor to higher-paying wage employment and because the returns to the labor they supply in each occupation, and their returns to education, are lower. These findings suggest that the impact of China's accession to the WTO on income distribution will depend on how it affects the distribution of employment, wages, and the returns to education among households.

Our labor supply estimates reveal how work hours, and the composition of work hours, would respond to changes in wages for agricultural and nonagricultural work. We find that wages do not have a large effect on the total number of hours worked. They do, however, significantly influence the composition of hours worked. Our estimates of labor supply by type of employment—in household agriculture, household nonagriculture, and off-farm wage jobs—indicate that most own- and cross-elasticities with respect to the different wages are well below one. This finding suggests that although labor moves among these types of employment, mobility is limited.

A notable exception to this pattern is the cross-elasticity with respect to the agricultural shadow wage of labor supplied to the market. This elasticity is significant and large, indicating that differences in labor supply for wage employment among households is driven by differences in the returns to labor in household farming. Put differently, high market wages do not "pull" labor out of agriculture; rather, low marginal returns to work in agriculture "push" labor into wage employment. We discuss these results more fully later in this chapter.

The next section of this chapter presents an overview of aggregate trends in China's rural employment, earnings, and labor markets, paying special attention to the institutions and policies that affect labor mobility and the distribution of earnings. A description of the dataset follows. The next section examines household income generation and analyzes the income gap between richer and poorer households. We then turn to our econometric estimates of wage and labor supply functions.

Throughout this chapter our focus is on rural households. China's accession to the WTO is affecting both urban and rural households, but the institutional setting and economic behavior of these two types of households are substantially different and require separate analysis. Analysis of rural households is important because the rural sector contains most of China's population and also most of its poor. Indeed, a disproportionate share of China's poor population is located in rural areas.[1] Recent estimates for 1999 by Chen and Wang (2001) report a poverty rate (using the $1/day poverty line) of 24.9 percent in rural areas versus only 0.5 percent in urban areas. Despite increased urbanization, 64 percent of the population and 74 percent of employed persons are still classified as rural (National Bureau of Statistics 2001, pp. 37, 39). Average per capita income in rural areas is only about one-third that in urban areas, and evidence suggests a widening of the urban-rural income gap in recent years (Yang and Zhou 1999).

Rural Employment and Earnings in China in the 1990s: The Aggregate Picture

A review of aggregate trends in rural employment and earnings in China provides a broad context in which to interpret our microeconomic results. Aggregate trends reflect the impact of major policy reforms, including domestic market liberalization as well as trade liberalization in advance of WTO accession, and so they also provide some clues about the potential impact of WTO accession on employment and earnings.

Developments in the 1990s on both the supply and demand side suggest movement toward fuller employment and higher earnings in rural areas. On the supply side, in the 1990s China's labor force grew slowly both overall and in rural areas. Because of population planning policies and a marked decline in fertility in the 1970s, cohorts entering the labor force in the 1990s were smaller than those in the 1970s and 1980s. New cohorts entering the labor force should remain small or even decline further in the coming years because of the strict population control policies adopted in the 1980s.

On the demand side, macroeconomic growth combined with policy liberalization generated new job opportunities for rural workers. Rural nonagricultural employment grew substantially. The official data on such employment is problematic, but it does provide a rough indication of trends. Rural nonagricultural employment includes employment in township and village enterprises (TVEs) and in private and individual enterprises.[2] During the 1990s, employment in these enterprises grew, on average, 5.4 percent annually. In absolute terms, during the 1990s the increase in rural enterprise employment exceeded 66 million jobs, and by 1999 this employment was equivalent to one-third of the rural labor force.

A notable aspect of growth in rural enterprise employment is that nearly half of it stemmed from the expansion of private and individual enterprises. By 1999 these enterprises were employing over 45 million people, equivalent to about 10 percent of the rural labor force. Although some of this growth could be the result of reclassification of collective TVEs as private businesses, it also reflects the growing importance of household-based nonagricultural activities.

Also notable during the 1990s was a rise in rural–urban migration. After a relaxation of restrictions on labor movement, rural–urban migration appears to have grown substantially. Data on migration are spotty, and definitions of what constitutes migration differ (see Wu and Zhou 1996; Rozelle and others 1999), but most estimates suggest at least a doubling of the number of migrants between the late 1980s and the mid- or late 1990s. Sources suggest that by the mid- or late 1990s the number of migrants (excluding commuters) probably exceeded 50 million, or about 10 percent of the number of rural employed persons (Wu and Zhou 1996; Zhao 1999b).

Altogether, then, growth in employment by rural TVEs, by private and individual enterprises, and through migration increased from perhaps 130 million in the early 1990s to roughly 230 million in the late 1990s. By then, nonagricultural employment of rural residents had risen from less than 30 percent to nearly 50 percent of the number of rural employed persons.

This substantial expansion of nonagricultural employment has spurred some debate about the nature of labor markets in rural China. Some authors argue that labor markets are now fairly open and competitive, with considerable labor mobility (Rawski and Mead 1998). Others, however, argue that while open and competitive labor markets are emerging in some regional pockets, and while generally the direction of change has been toward more open, competitive conditions, rural labor markets nevertheless continue to be imperfect, and institutional and administrative barriers persist (Parish, Zhe, and Li 1995; Knight and Song 1999). These issues are relevant to our analysis and are discussed further later in this chapter.

Discussion of employment cannot be complete without mention of the largest employer, agriculture. Official statistics reveal cycles in agricultural employment. The number of rural employed persons rose to more than 340 million in 1991–92, fell to less than 325 million in 1995–97, and then rose again to almost 330 million in 1999–2000 (National Bureau of Statistics, various years). Interestingly, the upswings in these cycles occurred at the same time as downswings in rural enterprise employment, and vice versa, which suggests an inverse relationship between the two kinds of employment.

The official data on rural employment are, however, problematic. They simply count the number of people by primary occupation. They do not capture the fact that many rural workers engage in multiple occupations and that hours worked in any particular occupation can fluctuate over time. Some studies indicate that changes in hours worked in agriculture have been significant (Rawski and Mead 1998; World Bank 2001). Estimates of agricultural employment based on hours worked indicate that in the mid-1990s, when rural enterprise employment was expanding rapidly, agricultural labor days worked actually rose (World Bank 2001). These estimates indicate that growth in nonagricultural employment and agricultural employment can occur concurrently. The relationship between these two kinds of employment is important to our analysis, because the willingness and ability of rural residents to supply labor

hours to different sectors can affect the impact of trade liberalization.

What have been the effects of the just-described trends in employment on rural incomes and inequality? On average, the real per capita income of rural households rose during the 1990s. Between 1990 and 1999, net income per capita rose about 70 percent. This growth was derived from multiple sources. Wages contributed the largest share of the increase (38 percent), followed by agriculture (29 percent), and household nonagricultural sidelines and businesses (22 percent).[3] Although nonagricultural sources dominated, the fact that agriculture contributed nearly one-third of the increase in income is notable in view of the fact that, according to the official data, agricultural employment supposedly declined.

The average trends just outlined mask changes in distribution among poorer and richer households. The general consensus is that rural income inequality increased during the 1990s, while poverty decreased. These apparently contradictory developments reflect income growth for the poor, but faster income growth for richer groups.

A 2001 World Bank study outlines key aggregate factors underlying the recent decline in rural poverty, some of which are relevant from the perspective of China's accession to the WTO (World Bank 2001). First, aggregate growth in the gross domestic product (GDP) appears to be important. Nationally, the reduction in poverty coincided with a period of rapid GDP growth, and poverty reduction occurred more quickly in those regions that experienced the most rapid aggregate growth. Second, the composition of growth matters. The rate of poverty reduction has been faster in regions where agricultural growth has more or less kept pace with growth in other sectors. This situation reflects the fact that agriculture is the primary source of employment and income for the poor. These points suggest that the effect of WTO accession on poverty will be influenced by its impact on both aggregate growth and the sectoral composition of that growth.

The Survey Sample

For our empirical analysis, we use data from the China Health and Nutrition Survey (CHNS). CHNS data were collected through an independent survey conducted by an international team of researchers collaboratively sponsored by the Carolina Population Center at the University of North Carolina at Chapel Hill, China's Institute of Nutrition and Food Hygiene, and the Chinese Academy of Preventive Medicine. Data are available for four years: 1989, 1991, 1993, and 1997. The survey, which used a multistage, random cluster sampling method, covers about 3,800 households with 14,000 members in nine provinces with different geographic and economic characteristics.[4] The CHNS also offers information on community-level variables such as market prices, health facilities, and social services.[5]

The CHNS survey data are useful here because they provide detailed information on incomes and hours worked in different occupations as well as on a wide range of relevant individual, household, and community characteristics. The sample includes as household members migrant workers who work and live out of town, but whose earnings and expenses are considered part of the household's. The data do not, however, allow us to distinguish between work and income from migrant versus local employment. Thus although we are able to investigate mobility among types of work (in household agricultural production, household nonagricultural production, and wage employment), we cannot investigate geographic mobility.

For our estimations we use the most recent (1997) data, and we drop urban households—that is, we use a subsample of households that includes only those that reside in rural and suburban villages and in county towns. We include suburban villages and county towns because they have close ties with rural areas, and a significant portion of the population in these areas holds a rural residence registration or *hukou*. This subsample covers 3,239 households with 8,590 working-age adults. Because we are interested in labor supply, we further restrict our sample to households that contain at least one household member who works. This reduces the subsample to 2,998 households with 8,326 working-age adults. The number of observations actually used in our analysis varies among regressions, depending on the extent of participation in the activity being analyzed and on the prevalence of missing values in relevant variables.

Table 14.1 contains descriptive statistics for the nonurban subsample of the CHNS survey. It also gives some comparable statistics from the 1997 National Bureau of Statistics (NBS) official rural household survey, where available. Household size and structure are similar for the NBS data and for CHNS subsample. Income levels for the CHNS subsample are somewhat lower than for the NBS survey, but this disparity could reflect differences in how income is calculated. The structure of income also differs. In particular, agricultural income is noticeably higher in the NBS survey than in the CHNS samples. This difference could reflect the inclusion of households in suburban villages and county towns in the CHNS subsample but not in the NBS rural survey. For both the NBS and CHNS samples, the major sources of income are agriculture and wage employment.

The CHNS data provide some information about relative earnings in different sectors. Dividing average earnings by hours worked for each sector suggests that the returns to labor in agriculture are lower than in other occupations. Average net earnings per hour worked in agriculture are roughly 1.1 yuan as compared with 2.2 yuan in nonagricultural sidelines and 2.8 yuan in wage employment. When we use regression analysis to estimate the returns to labor in the next section, these earnings differentials become larger.

Income Generation Functions

A common approach to analyzing the determinants of income is to estimate an income generation function, where net income is a function of labor inputs, land and capital assets, and other household or regional characteristics that contribute to the generation of earnings. This approach takes income generation as a simple, linear accounting relationship, where income equals the sum of household labor and other assets times the returns to those assets. The regression coefficients provide estimates of the marginal returns to each asset. We use this approach both to examine income generation on average and to explore differences between poorer and richer subgroups.

The first columns (Model I) of table 14.2 contain results from income generation regressions for all households with at least one working adult in the CHNS nonurban subsample. The dependent variable is the sum of net earnings from the three occupations—that is, net earnings (revenue minus

TABLE 14.1   Descriptive Statistics, China Health and Nutrition Survey, 1997

Variable	NBS Rural Household Survey, 1997	CHNS Nonurban Households		
		Mean	Standard Deviation	Number of Observations
Household size	4.35	3.83	1.42	3,239
Number of adults	2.79	2.67	1.29	3,212
Number of dependents per capita		0.30	0.26	3,212
Number of male adults		1.36	0.80	3,212
Number of female adults		1.31	0.76	3,212
Number of male laborers (hours > 0)		1.18	0.73	3,239
Number of female laborers (hours > 0)		1.10	0.72	3,239
Mean age of working-age adults		35.39	14.30	3,238
Mean schooling of working-age adults		6.94	2.81	3,033
Ratio of male working-age adults to family working-age adults		0.51	0.18	3,041
Cultivated land (mu[a])		6.84	12.14	1,807
Household total income (yuan)		9,094	9,871	1,966
Household net earnings (yuan)	9,092	7,774	9,784	2,160
Household net earnings from agricultural sectors (yuan)	5,081	2,069	5,095	2,380
Household net earnings from nonagricultural sectors (yuan)	1,009	1,267	4,627	3,080
Household earnings from employed work (yuan)	2,240	3,830	7,835	3,069
Household nonlabor income (yuan)		1,397	2,868	2,808
Household total labor hours		3,786	2,874	2,904
Household total labor hours in household agricultural production		1,803	2,203	3,054
Household total labor hours in household nonagricultural production		572	1,504	3,170
Household total labor hours in wage employment		1,359	2,115	3,122
Heilongjiang		0.12		3,239
Jiangsu		0.12		3,239
Shandong		0.12		3,239
Henan		0.13		3,239
Hubei		0.12		3,239
Hunan		0.12		3,239
Guangxi		0.13		3,239
Guizhou		0.13		3,239

[a]The mu is a Chinese measure of area. Fifteen mu equal 1 hectare.

Note: The National Bureau of Statistics (NBS) data are taken from the *China Statistical Yearbook.* The NBS rural survey sample includes only households in rural villages but in all provinces, whereas the subsample of the China Health and Nutrition Survey (CHNS) data includes households in suburban villages and county towns but only in eight provinces. Note that income is calculated differently for the NBS and CHNS samples. Also, the NBS household income data are in per capita terms, and we calculate NBS household total income as mean household size times mean income. This method could create some bias, because household size and income per capita are typically inversely correlated. Nevertheless, comparison of the CHNS means with the NBS means gives a rough indication of how the CHNS sample compares with the official national rural survey sample.

Sources: National Bureau of Statistics, various years; authors' calculations using CHNS data.

TABLE 14.2 Income Generation Functions (dependent variable: household net earnings)

	Model I: All Households		Model II: Bottom 20 Percent		Model III: Top 20 Percent	
	Coefficient	Standard Error	Coefficient	Standard Error	Coefficient	Standard Error
Agricultural production labor hours	0.226**	0.101	−0.043	0.132	0.510*	0.274
Nonagricultural production labor hours	1.715***	0.137	1.266***	0.212	1.958***	0.304
Wage employment labor hours	2.372***	0.111	2.113***	0.153	3.004***	0.230
Mean schooling of working-age adults	241.438***	84.215	167.649	116.527	395.775**	188.010
Ratio of male working-age adults to family working-age adults	−206.177	1,185.776	3,709.768**	1,597.452	−447.157	2,679.677
Land	75.514***	17.636	200.764***	48.873	173.030***	37.720
Total equipment (1,000 yuan)	150.298***	16.869	231.095***	58.782	109.221***	26.446
Mean age of working-age adults	33.799	26.727	57.601	38.577	46.073	57.421
Heilongjiang	770.721	728.723	−3,922.149*	2,331.068	−4,998.626	3,416.966
Jiangsu	1,982.589***	717.698	−3,473.656	2,369.045	−3,594.468	3,386.499
Shandong	686.911	851.888	−4,332.018	3,374.844	−3,304.311	3,352.075
Henan	−1,015.651	748.158	−4,466.833**	2,288.171	−8,191.833**	3,658.165
Hubei	98.739	698.346	−3,145.446	2,242.68	−5,586.847*	3,375.095
Hunan	2,167.564***	905.101	−1,262.594	2,279.672	1,270.767	4,252.05
Guangxi	−480.419	750.139	−4,669.35*	2,502.903	−2,781.757	3,617.45
Guizhou	n.a.	n.a.	−2,520.564	2,185.661	−5,023.888	4,368.554
Constant	−1,083.532	1,517.58	n.a.	n.a.	n.a.	n.a.
Adjusted R-square	0.352		0.722		0.757	
Number of observations	1,671		333		349	

n.a. Not applicable.

***$p < .01$, **$p < .05$, *$p < .10$.

Note: Guizhou is the omitted regional dummy variable in Model I. In Models II and III all regional dummy variables are included, and the constant term is suppressed to allow analysis of the regional contribution in the Oaxaca decomposition. To minimize sample selection bias, we group households on the basis of average village per capita household income as reported by village leaders in a community questionnaire. Thus the bottom (top) 20 percent refers to all households that live in villages that have average per capita household net income in the bottom (top) 20 percent of the income distribution for villages in the survey.

Source: Authors' estimates using CHNS data.

TABLE 14.3   Descriptive Statistics for Variables Used in the Income Generation Functions, CHNS, 1997

Variable	All Households Used in the Income Generation Function		Bottom 20 Percent		Top 20 Percent	
	Mean	Standard Deviation	Mean	Standard Deviation	Mean	Standard Deviation
Household net earnings (yuan)	8,113.19	9,746.09	5,955.50	6,265.58	10,966.54	9,907.75
Household agricultural production labor hours	1,888.35	2,261.85	2,760.06	2,562.277	778.59	1,642.21
Household nonagricultural production labor hours	573.11	1,543.39	476.76	1307.40	529.67	1,484.76
Wage employment labor hours	1,578.73	2,093.83	1,127.63	1,883.53	2,525.19	2,217.55
Household total labor hours	4,040.18	2493.40	4,364.45	2,599.83	3,833.45	2,337.51
Mean schooling of working-age adults	7.20	2.83	6.77	2.91	8.17	2.55
Ratio of male working-age adults to family working-age adults	0.51	0.16	0.52	0.16	0.50	0.15
Cultivated land (mu)	4.80	12.16	4.85	6.75	5.72	13.75
Equipment (1,000 yuan)	2.24	11.64	1.06	4.36	2.92	15.18
Mean age of working-age adults	36.84	7.85	36.20	7.73	37.42	7.54
Heilongjiang	0.16		0.14		0.23	
Jiangsu	0.15		0.08		0.23	
Shandong	0.09		0.01		0.20	
Henan	0.11		0.17		0.04	
Hubei	0.14		0.24		0.14	
Hunan	0.07		0.10		0.03	
Guangxi	0.11		0.06		0.10	
Guizhou	0.17		0.22		0.03	
Number of observations	1,671		333		349	

Source: Authors' estimates using CHNS data.

nonlabor variable costs) from household agricultural production, net earnings from household nonagricultural production, and wage income. Explanatory variables include actual labor hours in each of household agricultural production, household nonagricultural production, and wage employment, as well as education, ratio of males to females, age, land and equipment assets to capture nonlabor inputs that contribute to income from household production, and provincial dummy variables. The mean values of these variables appear in table 14.3.

Of central interest are the returns to labor in different occupations. The estimated coefficient for agricultural hours of work is small, 0.23, and significant at the 5 percent level. The coefficient for labor hours in nonagricultural household production is 1.72, and that for hours in wage employment is 2.37, both statistically significant at the 1 percent level.

These results indicate that income differences among households are generated more by nonagricultural work than by agricultural work; furthermore, wage employment brings the highest returns.[6] These results are consistent with the findings of other studies for China (Knight and Song 1997; Meng 2000; Michelson and Parish 2000).

Education has a significant effect on household income. An additional year of average schooling for working-age adults in the household increases household net income by 241 yuan, roughly 3 percent of average net income. Again, this result is consistent with findings in other studies.

The average age of household workers and the sex composition of the work force do not have significant effects on household earnings. As expected, land and equipment assets have significant, positive effects. An additional mu of land (a Chinese measure in which 15 mu equal 1 hectare) increases net income by 76 yuan or 1 percent of mean income, and an additional 1,000 yuan of equipment assets increases net income by 150 yuan or 2 percent of mean income. The presence of significant, large coefficients on some provincial dummy variables indicates that location of residence is also important.

We explore differences between poorer and richer households using a modified Oaxaca-type decomposition. This method involves first estimating income generation functions for richer and poorer subgroups. To minimize the problem of endogenous sample selection, we divide the sample using average village incomes reported by village leaders in a separate community questionnaire. Models II and III in table 14.2 contain the results of income generation equations for households in villages in the top 20 percent and bottom 20 percent of the village average per capita net income distribution.

The two groups have significantly different coefficients. The returns to labor and education are substantially higher in the top 20 percent than the bottom 20 percent. For the bottom 20 percent, the returns to agricultural labor are not significantly different from zero. This finding would be consistent with a standard surplus labor story. By contrast, for the top 20 percent the coefficient for agricultural labor is positive and significant, albeit small. The nonagricultural and wage labor groups have positive and significant returns, but the returns are lower for the poorer subsample (bottom 20 percent).

Schooling has positive coefficients everywhere, but the return to education is smaller and insignificant for the poorer subsample. The ratio of males among working-age adults is insignificant except for the poorer group, for which it is large, positive, and significant. The presence of male workers thus appears to be most important in poorer areas. The returns to land and equipment are all positive and significant, with the magnitudes higher for the bottom 20 percent than the top 20 percent. This difference could stem from the greater scarcity of land and capital in poorer villages than in richer villages.

The Oaxaca decomposition combines these estimated coefficients with the mean values of the variables for the two groups. The mean values of household characteristics reveal substantial differences between households in richer and poorer villages (table 14.3). Average net earnings of the rich group are 1.8 times those of the poor group, and average

education is 1.4 years longer. Land assets are 0.9 mu larger (although not corrected for land quality), and equipment assets are substantially larger, too.

Employment also differs. Although both groups work in all three sectors, household agriculture dominates for the poorer group and wage employment dominates for the richer group. Overall, households in the poorer group work more hours. Total work time for households in the poorer group is 4,364 hours, about 14 percent higher than the 3,833 hours total work time for households in the richer group.[7]

Table 14.4 gives the results of our Oaxaca-type decomposition. Although conventional decomposition combines the contribution of regional dummy variables together with that of other characteristics, we separate out the effects of regional differences on the income gap. The overall difference of 5,011 yuan in mean net earnings is thus decomposed into three components: (1) the income gap due to differences in levels of household productive characteristics other than regional location, (2) the income gap due to differences in returns to these household productive characteristics, and (3) the income gap due to regional factors.

The results show that all three components contribute to the income gap, but the differences in productive characteristics are most important. This component explains 82 percent of the income gap between the two groups. The largest contributor here is the difference in wage employment hours, which accounts for 71 percent of the income gap. The richer households have fewer labor hours in agriculture (see table 14.4), which serves to reduce the income gap by 9 percent. Differences in education levels explain 8 percent of the gap. Differences in mean endowments of land and productive equipment, and in household structure and age, are relatively unimportant.

Differences in the returns to productive characteristics—that is, differences in the estimated coefficients of the two groups—account for 34 percent of the income gap. The largest contributor here is the difference in the returns to education, which by itself explains 34 percent of the income gap. Next most important is the difference in returns to wage employment, which explains 32 percent of the income gap. Differences in the returns to agricultural labor and sex composition of working-age adults are also important.

TABLE 14.4   Decomposition of Household Net Earnings Differentials between Households Belonging to the Top and Bottom 20 Percent

	Contributions to Income Gap between Households in the Top 20 Percent and Bottom 20 Percent of Villages	
	Yuan	Percent
Household net earnings, total gap	5,011.04	100.00
Amount due to		
(1) Differences in productive characteristics	4,116.19	82.14
(2) Differences in returns to productive characteristics	1,723.47	34.40
(3) Differences in regional location and returns to regional location	−828.61	−16.54
(a) Agricultural production labor hours	−462.40	−9.23
(b) Nonagricultural production labor hours	85.28	1.70
(c) Wage employment labor hours	3,575.93	71.36
(d) Mean schooling of working-age adults	394.56	7.87
(e) Ratio of male working-age adults to family working-age adults	−19.45	−0.39
(f) Land	162.50	3.24
(g) Total equipment (1,000 yuan)	316.56	6.32
(h) Mean age of working-age adults	63.22	1.26
(2) Differences in returns to productive characteristics (total)	1,723.48	34.4
(a) Agricultural production labor hours	978.92	19.54
(b) Nonagricultural production labor hours	348.15	6.95
(c) Wage employment labor hours	1,627.69	32.48
(d) Mean schooling of working-age adults	1,703.70	34.00
(e) Ratio of male working-age adults to family working-age adults	−2,121.71	−42.34
(f) Land	−146.48	−2.92
(g) Total equipment (1,000 yuan)	−242.43	−4.84
(h) Mean age of working-age adults	−424.36	−8.47
(3) Differences in regional location and returns to regional location (total)	−828.62	−16.54
(a) Differences in regional location	93.21	1.86
(b) Differences in returns to regional location	−921.83	−18.40

Source: Authors' estimates using CHNS data.

Regional location, like other household characteristics, contributes to the income gap in two ways. First, the returns to region of residence or estimated coefficients for the provincial dummy variables differ between the rich and poor groups. And, second, the regional distribution of the poor differs from the regional distribution of the rich. Together these regional factors explain about 17 percent of the overall income gap. Virtually all of this is due to differences in the returns to location.

In summary, our decomposition analysis shows that households in poor villages are relatively poor both because they have different characteristics than richer households and because the returns to those characteristics are lower. Here the key contributors to the income gap are a lower supply of wage labor by households in poorer villages, as well as the lower returns received by poor households for education, wage employment, and agricultural labor.

New Estimates of Labor Supply and Allocation

The estimates and decomposition just described indicate that returns to labor and pattern of employment are important factors underlying income differences. This finding raises questions about what explains the level and pattern of labor supply and why the returns to labor vary among sectors and households. Clearly, these two questions are interrelated, because household labor supply may depend on the returns to labor, and the returns to labor (especially in household production) may depend on household production decisions, including decisions on the allocation of labor. Here we pursue these questions by empirically analyzing the determinants of the returns to labor and of labor supply, and we employ instrumental variable methods to address the endogeneity of key explanatory variables.

We begin with a model of time allocation by rural households. The family is assumed to have endowments of workers, land, and other assets. The household may allocate its resources among three possible income-generating activities: agricultural production, nonagricultural production, and wage or market employment. In the first two activities, the household organizes production using certain quantities of family assets and labor and perhaps also purchased inputs, hired assets, and hired labor. In market employment the household faces an exogenous wage rate set by the market.

Labor supply decisions are the outcome of household utility maximization, where utility is a function of the consumption of leisure and goods and the budget constraint depends on full income, which includes profits from household production as well as the value of the household's time endowment. Where markets function well and factors are perfectly mobile, households maximize utility by first maximizing profits at market prices and then deciding on optimal levels of leisure and goods consumption given market prices and their endowments. Labor allocation to the different activities—hours worked in agricultural production (H_A), nonagricultural production (H_N) and wage or market employment (H_M)[8]—are the outcome of this decision process. In theory, the allocation of time among these activities should equalize the returns to labor in them. Optimal leisure consumption is the difference between the household's time endowment and total time worked in all the activities.

Where markets are imperfect, where transaction costs or barriers to mobility are present, or where households have preferences for certain types of work, the returns to labor in different activities may

no longer be equal. Moreover, in such situations the returns to labor in household production may not be observable. These returns or shadow wages will be endogenous and a function of both production- and consumption-side variables. Households thus may simultaneously face three different prices of labor: a shadow wage for labor in agricultural production (W_A), a shadow wage for labor in nonagricultural production (W_N), and an observed wage for market employment (W_M).

Factor markets in China are likely to be imperfect, so we adopt an empirical strategy that allows for this possibility. Specifically, we use the approach of Jacoby (1993), who notes that at the household optimum, the household's shadow price of labor would equal the value of the marginal product of labor in household production. Labor supply, then, can be modeled as a function of the shadow wages. We thus specify labor supply as a function of shadow wages, as well as of other relevant variables. Also, because we are interested in labor supply to three activities, we have three different labor supply functions. These take the form

$$H_i = f^i(\hat{W}_A, \hat{W}_N, W_M, I, X),$$
$$i = A, N, M \tag{14.1}$$

where $\hat{W}_A$, $\hat{W}_N$, W_M are the shadow wage in agricultural production, the shadow wage in nonagricultural production, and the wage rate in market employment, respectively; I is household nonlabor income; and X is a vector of household characteristics. Total labor supply is the sum of these three labor supplies.

Empirical Specification

The specification of our labor supply functions basically follows that of Jacoby and others,[9] except that we include multiple wages. The functions for labor supply to household agricultural production, household nonagricultural production, and wage or market employment are, respectively,

$$\log H_A = \alpha_0 + \alpha_A \ln \hat{W}_A + \alpha_N \ln \hat{W}_N$$
$$+ \alpha_M \ln W_M + \alpha_I I \tag{14.2}$$
$$+ \alpha_X X + \varepsilon_A$$

$$\log H_N = \beta_0 + \beta_A \ln \hat{W}_A + \beta_N \ln \hat{W}_N$$
$$+ \beta_M \ln W_M + \beta_I I \tag{14.3}$$
$$+ \beta_X X + \varepsilon_N$$

$$\log H_M = \gamma_0 + \gamma_A \ln \hat{W}_A$$
$$+ \gamma_N \ln \hat{W}_N + \gamma_M \ln W_M \qquad (14.4)$$
$$+ \gamma_I I + \gamma_X X + \varepsilon_M$$

Overall labor supply (H) is the sum of labor supply into three sectors. Alternatively, it can be estimated directly as

$$\log H = \delta_0 + \delta_A \ln \hat{W}_A + \delta_N \ln \hat{W}_N$$
$$+ \delta_M \ln W_M + \delta_I I \qquad (14.5)$$
$$+ \delta_X X + \varepsilon$$

The signs of the effects of the three wage rates on total labor supply depend on the relative magnitude of substitution and income effects.

The estimation of equations 14.2–14.5 requires knowledge of wage or shadow wage rates in all activities. For those engaged in agricultural or nonagricultural self-employment, shadow wages can be calculated using estimated parameters from household production functions (Jacoby 1993). We therefore begin with estimates of production functions in the next section. We then present our estimates of the wage and shadow wage functions. We use these estimates to project (shadow) wages for households that do not participate in one or more activities. These projected (shadow) wages are employed in our analysis of labor supply.

Estimation of Production Functions

We use the standard Cobb-Douglas functional form to estimate the production functions for agricultural and nonagricultural activities. For each of these activities the production function takes the form

$$\ln Q = \sum_{j=1}^{n} \alpha_j \ln M_j + \sum_{k=1}^{m} \gamma_k Z_k + \varepsilon \qquad (14.6)$$

where Q is the total value of output produced by the household; M is a vector of production inputs, which includes family labor hours, the value of variable costs (including materials and hired labor),[10] the value of fixed capital, and land used in agricultural production; and Z is a vector of other control variables, including average education of household workers, average age of household workers, and provincial dummy variables.

Each production function is estimated using three estimation methods—OLS, IV, and selectivity-bias

corrected estimation. In the IV or 2SLS estimations, labor and variable cost inputs are treated as endogenous. Instruments used in both the agricultural and nonagricultural production functions are exogenous variables for the household and the community, including household composition variables (number of working-age adults, children, and elderly) and local market prices of vegetables, pork, chicken, and gasoline. In the nonagricultural production function we also include as instruments the local market prices of honey-combed coal briquette, coal lumps, coal powder, and liquefied natural gas, and the market wage for unskilled labor. The selectivity-bias corrected estimation treats whether the household engages in the activity as an endogenous decision. The identification variable is the number of dependents in the household, and we use the Heckman method (Heckman 1979). As noted in tables 14.5 and 14.6, the IV estimation does not pass the Hausman joint exogeneity test for either agricultural or nonagricultural production. Selectivity terms in the selectivity-bias correction estimations (lambda statistics reported for Model III) are also statistically insignificant for both equations.

The first column of table 14.5 reports OLS estimates of the agricultural production function. The results indicate that variable inputs are the dominant contributor to agricultural output, with an elasticity of 0.46. Land is the next most important contributor to agricultural production, with an elasticity of 0.32, and labor hours have an elasticity of 0.19. The coefficient for agricultural equipment is also significant. These estimates are similar in magnitude to those in other studies (e.g., Yang 1997; Li and Zhang 1998). The coefficients of these inputs add up to 0.999, which indicates that agriculture displays constant returns to scale. Education is insignificant. A comparison of the first three columns of the table reveals that the instrumental variable and selectivity-bias corrected estimates are very similar to the OLS estimates.

The first column of table 14.6 reports OLS estimates of the nonagricultural production function. The elasticity of labor inputs is 0.62, more than triple the labor coefficient for agriculture. Output value is less responsive to variable costs in nonagricultural production than in agricultural production. The coefficient of equipment is the same as in agriculture, 0.033. Education is statistically insignificant. Interestingly, the nonagricultural production

TABLE 14.5 Agricultural Production Function (dependent variable: log of output value)

	Model I: OLS		Model II: IV		Model III: Corrected for Sample Selection Bias	
	Coefficient	Standard Error	Coefficient	Standard Error	Coefficient	Standard Error
Log of labor hours[a]	0.192***	0.035	0.260	0.197	0.179***	0.035
Log of variable costs[a]	0.458***	0.031	0.422**	0.177	0.449***	0.031
Log of equipment	0.035***	0.009	0.034***	0.011	0.034***	0.009
Log of land	0.317***	0.052	0.322***	0.107	0.314***	0.052
Mean schooling of working-age adults	0.010	0.012	0.014	0.016	0.009	0.011
Mean age of working-age adults	−0.0001	0.004	0.0002	0.004	−0.0001	0.004
Dummy: telephone present in local areas	0.095	0.062	0.089	0.064	0.104*	0.062
Heilongjiang	0.092	0.116	0.135	0.176	0.088	0.115
Jiangsu	−0.069	0.097	−0.026	0.154	−0.081	0.097
Shandong	−0.163	0.139	−0.116	0.198	−0.167	0.139
Henan	−0.623***	0.102	−0.617***	0.131	−0.614***	0.104
Hubei	0.023	0.090	0.005	0.108	0.046	0.090
Hunan	0.143	0.156	0.195	0.215	0.170	0.157
Guangxi	−0.312***	0.096	−0.310***	0.099	−0.265***	0.096
Constant	2.647***	0.350	2.323**	1.146	2.811***	0.353
Lambda	n.a.		n.a.		−0.091	0.096
Adjusted R-square	0.455		0.453		n.a.	
Log-likelihood	n.a.		n.a.		−1,393.699	
Number of observations	1,066		1,066		1,095	

n.a. Not applicable.

*$p < .01$,   **$p < .05$,   ***$p < .10$.

[a]Indicates endogenous variables. Instruments used are family composition variables (number of working-age adults, number of children, and number of elderly) and market prices for vegetables, pork, chicken, and gasoline. The Hausman statistic for the joint endogeneity test is 0.13, and the P-value is 0.937. Here and in later tables Guizhou is the omitted regional dummy variable.

Source: Authors' estimates using CHNS data.

function displays decreasing returns to scale. This finding suggests that rural households may encounter difficulties in expanding the scale of household nonagricultural production (or perhaps higher-income households underreport such income). Like in table 14.5, a comparison of the first three columns reveals that the selectivity-bias corrected estimates are similar to the OLS estimates. In the IV regression, the coefficients on labor and variable costs differ from those in the other specifications, but the Hausman test indicates that the overall the results are not significantly different from those of OLS.

Although the Hausman tests do not provide strong support for preferring the IV results to those of the OLS, we nevertheless use the results from the IV specifications to calculate shadow wages. We prefer the IV results because, in theory, output, labor hours, and variable costs are jointly and endogenously determined, and so in principle IV methods are needed to obtain unbiased results.

Estimation of Wages and Shadow Wages

We are interested in learning how rural households respond to differentials between agricultural and nonagricultural wages. Although we observe the hourly wage rates received by employed workers, the same is not true for workers engaged in household agricultural or nonagricultural production. We follow the approach of Jacoby (1993) and derive shadow wages from the production function

TABLE 14.6 Nonagricultural Production Function (dependent variable: log of output value)

	Model I: OLS		Model II: IV		Model III: Corrected for Sample Selection Bias	
	Coefficient	Standard Error	Coefficient	Standard Error	Coefficient	Standard Error
Log of labor hours[a]	0.618***	0.039	0.486***	0.183	0.656***	0.048
Log of variable costs[a]	0.167***	0.012	0.253***	0.069	0.154***	0.015
Log of equipment	0.033***	0.010	0.024*	0.014	−0.030	0.032
Mean schooling of working-age adults	0.012	0.016	0.007	0.019	−0.001	0.027
Mean age of working-age adults	−0.005	0.006	−0.007	0.006	0.012	0.008
Dummy: telephone present in local areas	0.075	0.098	−0.041	0.149	0.100	0.114
Heilongjiang	0.031	0.206	0.125	0.229	0.376	0.350
Jiangsu	0.159	0.144	0.201	0.155	0.123	0.205
Shandong	−0.271	0.188	−0.354*	0.209	−0.181	0.265
Henan	−0.008	0.125	0.016	0.133	−0.126	0.163
Hubei	−0.028	0.143	−0.092	0.159	−0.143	0.214
Hunan	0.066	0.135	0.059	0.142	0.223	0.241
Guangxi	−0.137	0.114	−0.128	0.120	−0.432***	0.169
Constant	2.968***	0.362	3.670***	1.136	2.985***	0.661
Lambda	n.a.		n.a.		−0.450	0.239
Adjusted R-square	0.603		0.561		n.a.	
Log-likelihood	n.a.		n.a.		−946.014	
Number of observations	507		507		1,611	

n.a. Not applicable.

***$p < .01$, **$p < .05$, *$p < .10$.

[a]Indicates endogenous variables. Instruments used are family composition variables (number of working-age adults, number of children, and number of elderly); market prices of honey-combed coal briquette, coal lumps, coal powder, and liquefied natural gas; and local market wage rate for the unskilled. The Hausman statistic for the joint endogeneity test is 1.77, and the P-value is 0.413.

Source: Authors' estimates using CHNS data.

estimates. Specifically, we calculate the shadow wage rates, or marginal products, of family labor hours from the IV estimates of the Cobb-Douglas production functions in tables 14.5 and 14.6 as follows:

$$\hat{W}_j = \frac{\hat{\alpha}_j Q_j}{L_j}, \tag{14.7}$$

$$j = \text{agriculture, nonagriculture}$$

where Q is the value of output and L is family labor hours.

Equation 14.7 allows us to calculate average shadow wages for households that engage in agricultural or nonagricultural production. These shadow wages are derived from household production functions and thus are at the household, rather than individual, level.

Households compare expected wage differentials among sectors when deciding their sectoral labor allocation. After a selection is made, only wages in the actually selected sectors are observed. To estimate the expected wage differential, we need the counterfactual wage rates for households not participating in a sector. To obtain these rates, we regress the shadow wages computed as just outlined against a range of household characteristics that potentially affect the productivity of workers. These include all exogenous variables in the production functions, the variables used as instruments for labor, and variable costs. We then use the results from these regressions to predict shadow wages for all households.

Note that the projected shadow wages are used later in our labor supply functions, and so some of the explanatory variables here will serve as instrument variables in our labor supply regressions. Therefore, because all second-stage variables should be included in the first-stage regressions, we also include all exogenous variables from the labor supply equations in the shadow wage equations. These variables include nonlabor income, number of dependents, education and age of workers, health status of household members, and a few community-level variables that measure the prevalence of nonfarm activities.

Table 14.7 reports estimates of the shadow wage equations for household agricultural production and household nonagricultural production. We use the OLS regression because, after including all the variables mentioned above, it is difficult to find additional identification variables for use in an IV or 2SLS regression. The agricultural shadow wage function has good explanatory power, and the results are reasonable. As expected, equipment and land are significant in enhancing the marginal productivity of agricultural labor. Average schooling of working adults is also positive and significant.

The explanatory power of the nonagricultural shadow wage function is low, perhaps reflecting the smaller number of observations and heterogeneity

TABLE 14.7 Shadow Wage Equations for Household Agricultural and Nonagricultural Production (dependent variable: log of shadow wage)

	Household Agricultural Production (OLS)		Household Nonagricultural Production (OLS)	
	Coefficient	Standard Error	Coefficient	Standard Error
Agricultural equipment (1,000 yuan)	0.020***	0.006	0.037	0.025
Nonagricultural equipment (1,000 yuan)	0.014***	0.005	0.018***	0.005
Land	0.012***	0.003	−0.016	0.012
Number of family working-age adults	−0.017	0.033	0.056	0.058
Number of dependents	0.045	0.036	0.104	0.064
Ratio of male working-age adults to family working-age adults	−0.281	0.207	0.656	0.399
Family nonlabor income (1,000 yuan)	−0.002	0.019	−0.052	0.033
Mean schooling of working-age adults	0.036**	0.015	0.008	0.031
Mean age of working-age adults	0.004	0.005	0.013	0.011
Dummy: all family members are healthy	0.220***	0.071	0.191	0.134
Dummy: telephone present in local areas	−0.008	0.084	0.330**	0.148
Market price of kerosene	−1.093***	0.229	−0.732*	0.402
Market price of rice most commonly used	−0.049	0.030	0.052	0.132
Dummy: TVEs present in local areas	0.138*	0.076	−0.084	0.136
Number of self-employed household enterprises in local areas	0.003	0.002	−0.003	0.003
Heilongjiang	0.604***	0.153	−0.058	0.443
Jiangsu	0.063	0.153	−0.266	0.296
Shandong	−0.057	0.236	−0.347	0.406
Henan	−0.653***	0.132	−0.186	0.217
Hubei	0.0002	0.114	−0.120	0.247
Hunan	0.949***	0.275	1.035***	0.360
Guangxi	−0.458***	0.135	−0.265	0.211
Constant	0.169	0.509	0.206	0.990
Adjusted R-square	0.274		0.076	
Number of observations	998		274	

***$p < .01$,   **$p < .05$,   *$p < .10$.

Source: Authors' estimates using CHNS data.

of labor inputs in nonagricultural activities. Here the most significant variable is nonagricultural equipment.

Not all households or individuals participate in wage employment. We therefore also need to predict market wages for nonparticipants. In addition, market wages are reported at the individual level, but to analyze household labor supply we need a measure of the expected wage at the household level. To address these issues, we first estimate a wage equation for all workers participating in wage employment. We then use these estimates to predict wage rates for all workers in the sample, after which we aggregate for each household the predicted individual wage rates of family members to obtain a household-level wage.

Table 14.8 gives the estimates of wage functions for the employed workers. Our specification follows the standard approach used in the labor litera-

ture, but adds some variables relevant to the China case. The dependent variable is the log of hourly wages. Independent variables include variables capturing individual human capital or labor quality (education, age, age squared, and health status), individual characteristics (marital status and sex), and regional dummy variables. We allow for possible sample selection bias by applying the Heckman method, but the results show that selectivity is not important.[11]

The employed wage function indicates that education receives a rate of return of 3 percent. This effect is statistically significant at the 1 percent level. The age-earning profile has a concave shape, with the maximum wage reached at age 48. Marriage has a positive but statistically insignificant effect on wage. Once given marital status, female workers earn 20.3 percent less than their male counterparts. Those who have urban *hukou* status earn 11.0 percent more

TABLE 14.8 Employed Wage Equation (dependent variable: log of hourly wages)

Independent Variable	Model I: OLS		Model II: Selectivity-Bias Corrected[a]	
	Coefficient	Standard Error	Coefficient	Standard Error
Female	−0.203***	0.029	−0.203***	0.033
Marriage status	0.012	0.046	0.012	0.058
Education level (years)	0.030***	0.005	0.030***	0.009
Age	0.029***	0.011	0.029**	0.012
Age squared	−0.0003**	0.0001	−0.0003**	0.0001
Health status	0.066*	0.040	0.066*	0.039
Urban *hukou*	0.110***	0.029	0.110***	0.029
Heilongjiang	−0.084	0.065	−0.084	0.064
Jiangsu	0.181***	0.058	0.181***	0.069
Shandong	−0.057	0.061	−0.057	0.070
Henan	−0.236***	0.072	−0.236***	0.073
Hubei	−0.043	0.064	−0.043	0.063
Hunan	0.229***	0.063	0.229***	0.065
Guangxi	−0.002	0.063	−0.002	0.062
Constant	−0.018	0.189	−0.018	n.a.
Lambda	n.a.		0.00005	0.084
Adjusted R-square	0.116		n.a.	
Log-likelihood	n.a.		−5,493.72	
Number of observations	1,910		8,123	

n.a. Not applicable.

***p < .01, **p < .05, *p < .10.

[a]The identification variable is the number of dependents.

Source: Authors' estimates using CHNS data.

TABLE 14.9 Summary Statistics for Wage Rates and Shadow Wages (yuan/hour)

Variable	Number of Observations	Mean	Standard Deviation
Shadow wage for agricultural production (W_A)	1,066	0.742	1.322
Shadow wage for agricultural production, predicted ($\hat{W}_A$)	1,500	0.517	2.197
Shadow wage for nonagricultural production (W_N)	507	2.383	3.243
Shadow wage for nonagricultural production, predicted ($\hat{W}_N$)	1,500	1.760	6.871
Employed wage rate (individual level) (W_M)	1,910	4.013	37.789
Employed wage rate, predicted (individual level) ($\hat{W}_{Mi}$)	8,270	2.239	0.554
Employed wage rate, predicted (household level) ($\hat{W}_M$)	2,755	2.271	0.526

Source: Authors' estimates using CHNS data.

than those who do not. Using the coefficients from the selectivity-bias corrected regression, we predict wages for all workers. To obtain a household-level wage, we calculate the weighted average of predicted wages for the workers in each household, where the weights are based on each worker's hours of work.

Table 14.9 shows the mean predicted shadow wages and market wages of all households and, for comparison, the computed shadow wages and observed market wages of participating households. Not surprisingly, the mean wages of participating households are higher than those predicted for all households. This difference reflects that participation is more likely at higher wage rates. The returns to labor are lowest for agricultural production, followed by nonagricultural production and wage employment. These numbers are broadly consistent with the estimated returns to work time from the income generation regressions reported earlier.

Estimation of Labor Supply Functions

Our household labor supply functions follow the form of equations 14.2–14.5. For the dependent variable, we use hours per adult rather than total hours to avoid possible correlation between household labor supply and number of working-age adults in the household. All specifications are estimated using IV (2SLS), with the wage and shadow wage equations reported earlier serving as the first-stage regressions. A large number of households supply zero hours to nonagricultural production and wage employment, and so for these functions

we also run Tobit regressions and report the marginal effects for all households and the standard errors of the marginal effects.

Our results appear in table 14.10. The first columns give estimated coefficients for total labor supply per adult. These results indicate that total labor supply is not sensitive to the marginal returns to nonfarm labor. The returns to agricultural labor have a coefficient that is negative, significant (at the 10 percent level), and small. This coefficient reflects the net impact of the agricultural shadow wage on the different components of the labor supply. This impact is positive for the agricultural labor supply but negative for the market labor supply (this is discussed later in this chapter). The effect of nonlabor income is negative and significant at the 10 percent level, indicating that leisure is a normal good. Interestingly, total labor supply per adult is higher the more dependents (elderly and children) in a household. This finding suggests that the need to earn income to support dependents outweighs the need to spend non-earning time caring for dependents. The effect of dependents also indicates that dependents cause households to reallocate labor away from higher-paying wage jobs to lower-income household production activities.

Although the nonagricultural wage variables do not have a significant effect on total labor supply, they affect the allocation of labor among different activities. The shadow wage for work in household agricultural production is significant for market employment, where it has a fairly large, negative coefficient. A 1 percent increase in the shadow agricultural wage decreases labor supply to market employment by 2.6 percent.

TABLE 14.10 Household Labor Supply Equations (dependent variable: log of working hours per adult)

| | Log of Total Hours IV | | Log of Agricultural Hours IV | | Log of Nonagricultural Self-Employment Hours | | | | Log of Wage Employment Hours | | | |
| | | | | | IV | | Tobit Unconditional | | IV | | Tobit Unconditional | |
	Coefficient	Standard Error	Coefficient	Standard Error	Coefficient	Standard Error	Marginal Effect	Standard Error	Coefficient	Standard Error	Marginal Effect	Standard Error
ln $\hat{W}_A$	−0.144*	0.084	0.025	0.098	0.141	0.304	0.008	0.376	−1.137***	0.335	−2.137***	0.485
ln $\hat{W}_N$	0.051	0.054	−0.123**	0.062	0.332*	0.194	0.389	0.247	0.617***	0.214	1.183***	0.296
ln $\hat{W}_M$	0.067	0.113	−0.120	0.129	0.577	0.400	0.791*	0.476	0.555	0.448	0.485	0.414
Log (nonlabor income)	−0.009*	0.005	−0.032***	0.006	−0.052***	0.019	−0.047***	0.018	0.118***	0.022	0.111***	0.021
Number of dependents	0.117***	0.020	0.140***	0.023	0.199***	0.070	0.141**	0.061	−0.318***	0.077	−0.310***	0.077
Mean schooling of working-age adults	0.009	0.010	−0.049***	0.012	0.088**	0.036	0.077**	0.035	0.236***	0.040	0.249***	0.040
Ratio of male working-age adults to family working-age adults	−0.128	0.125	0.261*	0.144	−0.292	0.445	−0.316	0.455	−1.598***	0.494	−2.078***	0.527
Mean age of family working-age adults	0.005*	0.003	0.007**	0.003	−0.013	0.010	−0.018*	0.010	−0.018	0.011	−0.026**	0.011
Dummy: good health for family	−0.012	0.045	−0.101*	0.052	0.145	0.160	0.075	0.145	0.180	0.177	0.249	0.171
Dummy: TVEs present in local areas	0.005	0.044	−0.206***	0.050	0.193	0.154	0.226	0.151	1.054***	0.171	1.279***	0.204
Number of self-employed household enterprises in local areas	−0.001	0.001	−0.006***	0.001	0.001	0.004	0.0003	0.003	0.010**	0.004	0.011***	0.004
Market price of kerosene	0.030	0.151	0.021	0.174	0.018	0.537	−0.272	0.501	−1.376**	0.595	−2.190***	0.627
Market price of common rice	−0.031**	0.015	−0.001	0.018	−0.095*	0.056	−0.139**	0.070	−0.158***	0.061	−0.208***	0.063
Heilongjiang	−0.054	0.111	−0.150	0.129	−1.204***	0.400	−0.944***	0.176	0.651	0.440	2.051**	0.903
Jiangsu	0.137	0.085	−0.258***	0.098	−0.387	0.302	−0.429**	0.199	1.684***	0.335	1.916***	0.529
Shandong	0.220*	0.113	−0.443***	0.130	−0.761*	0.389	−0.596***	0.176	1.770***	0.437	1.767***	0.696
Henan	−0.172**	0.085	−0.312***	0.098	0.475	0.304	0.304	0.369	−0.653*	0.336	−0.907***	0.247
Hubei	0.216***	0.064	0.344***	0.074	−0.607*	0.228	−0.529***	0.145	−0.111	0.252	−0.001	0.253
Hunan	−0.027	0.161	0.191	0.183	−0.385	0.554	−0.362	0.322	−0.220	0.621	0.521	0.792
Guangxi	0.329***	0.086	0.414***	0.099	1.234***	0.307	0.893**	0.410	−0.542	0.341	−0.621**	0.244
Constant	6.525***	0.268	6.881***	0.307	0.931	0.942	n.a.	n.a.	1.466	1.048	n.a.	n.a.
Adjusted R-square	0.098		0.198		0.105		n.a.		0.175		n.a.	
Pseudo R-square	n.a.		n.a.		n.a.		0.058		n.a.		0.073	
Observations	1,360		1,404		1,430		1,430		1,421		1,421	

n.a. Not applicable.

***$p < .01$, **$p < .05$, *$p < .10$.

Source: Authors' estimates using CHNS data.

The effect of the shadow wage for work in household nonagricultural production is negative and significant for agricultural labor and positive and mostly significant for nonagricultural and market labor supply. In other words, households with higher returns to labor in nonagricultural sidelines work fewer hours in agriculture and more hours in both nonagricultural and wage employment. Here the elasticities are small for agriculture and nonagriculture, and close to one for wage employment. The signs on the coefficient for the market wage are the same as those for the shadow nonagricultural wage, but this variable is significant in only one equation.

Overall, the coefficients on the wage variables reveal complementarity between employment in household nonagricultural production and off-farm wage jobs, but substitution between agriculture and both types of nonagricultural employment. Furthermore, the estimated coefficients on wage variables are larger in magnitude and more significant in the off-farm wage labor supply equations than in the household agricultural or nonagricultural labor supply equations. In other words, labor supply to household production activities does not respond much to wage levels; the supply of labor to off-farm wage employment does.

From the wage elasticities we can calculate the elasticity of labor transfers in response to relative wage differentials among sectors.[12] Subtracting equation 14.2 from 14.3 gives the following expression:

$$\log(H_N/H_A)$$
$$= (\hat{\beta}_0 - \hat{\alpha}_0) + (\hat{\beta}_A - \hat{\alpha}_A) \ln \hat{W}_A$$
$$+ (\hat{\beta}_N - \hat{\alpha}_N) \ln \hat{W}_N$$
$$+ (\hat{\beta}_M - \hat{\alpha}_M) \ln \hat{W}_M + \cdots$$
$$= (\hat{\beta}_0 - \hat{\alpha}_0) \qquad (14.8)$$
$$+ (\hat{\beta}_A - \hat{\alpha}_A + \hat{\beta}_N - \hat{\alpha}_N) \ln \hat{W}_A$$
$$+ (\hat{\beta}_N - \hat{\alpha}_N) \ln(\hat{W}_N/\hat{W}_A)$$
$$+ (\hat{\beta}_M - \hat{\alpha}_M) \ln \hat{W}_M + \cdots$$

Similarly, subtracting (14.2) from (14.4) gives

$$\log(H_M/H_A)$$
$$= (\hat{\gamma}_0 - \hat{\alpha}_0)$$
$$+ (\hat{\gamma}_A - \hat{\alpha}_A + \hat{\gamma}_M - \hat{\alpha}_M) \ln \hat{W}_A \qquad (14.9)$$
$$+ (\hat{\beta}_N - \hat{\alpha}_N) \ln \hat{W}_N$$
$$+ (\hat{\beta}_M - \hat{\alpha}_M) \ln(W_M/\hat{W}_A) + \cdots$$

Using these expressions and the results in table 14.10, we calculate the marginal response of $\log(\hat{H}_N/\hat{H}_A)$ to $\log(\hat{W}_N/\hat{W}_A)$ as 0.512 (5 0.389 1 0.123), and the marginal response of $\log(H_M/H_A)$ to $\log(W_M/\hat{W}_A)$ as 0.605 (5 0.485 1 0.120). These numbers imply that a 1 percent increase in the ratio of either nonagricultural wage to the agricultural wage raises the ratio of that nonagricultural work to agricultural work by about 0.5–0.6 percent.

Note that these numbers assume that the change in the wage ratio stems from a rise in the nonagricultural shadow or market wage, with the agricultural shadow wage remaining constant. Due to the presence of cross-wage effects, shifts caused by changes in the agricultural shadow wage (holding the nonagricultural and market wages constant) would be different. Here the relevant calculations are as follows: the marginal response of $\log(H_A/H_N)$ to $\log(\hat{W}_A/\hat{W}_N)$ is 0.017 (= 0.025 − 0.008), and the marginal response of $\log(H_A/H_M)$ to $\log(\hat{W}_A/W_M)$ is 2.165 (= 0.028 + 2.137). In other words, a 1 percent increase in the ratio of the agricultural shadow wage to the nonagricultural shadow wage would increase the ratio of labor in agricultural to nonagricultural production by 0.02 percent. For an increase in the ratio of the agricultural shadow wage to the market wage, the response would be much larger, 2.2 percent.

These numbers indicate that, for the most part, the effects of relative wages on sectoral labor allocation are not overly large or significant (relative to the standard errors). The one exception is the case in which a change in the agricultural shadow wage causes a change in the ratio of the agricultural shadow wage to the market wage. In this case, shifts in labor allocation between agriculture and off-farm employment may be relatively large.

These findings suggest that labor movement out of agriculture into other sectors is not driven by the "pull" of rising nonagricultural wages, but would be driven by the "push" of lower agricultural wages. Why would these pull-and-push effects differ? One explanation is that for rural families income from agriculture provides the base income that ensures that the household achieves some acceptable or minimum standard of living. If agricultural income falls short—for example, in the event of drought, which would reduce overall agricultural income as well as the returns to labor in agriculture—households may feel compelled to seek income from other sources. They do not typically seek that additional income from nonagricultural self-employment, because such activities usually require start-up time and some initial investment. Casual wage jobs entail lower initial costs and generate cash income more quickly. Field interviews with rural households that have experienced shortfalls in agricultural income indeed indicate that these households often send family members out to find casual wage jobs, sometimes seasonal, in construction, services, and other unskilled occupations.

Several nonwage variables have significant and interesting effects on labor allocation. Nonlabor income is significant and negative for labor supply to both agricultural and nonagricultural household production, but is significant and positive for wage employment. This result could indicate that higher income increases access to wage employment by, for example, providing the resources needed to cover initial and search costs associated with obtaining wage jobs. It could also indicate that households gain some status or utility from off-farm work. The magnitudes of these income effects, however, are fairly small. Not surprisingly, the number of dependents significantly increases labor supply to both types of household production, but reduces labor supply to off-farm jobs. One more dependent in the household increases working hours that an adult devotes to agricultural production by 14 percent, increases hours devoted to nonagricultural production by 14 percent, and reduces working hours in wage employment by 31 percent. Age has a marginally significant and positive effect on agricultural labor supply; for nonagricultural production and market employment, its effects are negative, and for the Tobit regressions, its effects are significant. This result is consistent with the observation that in rural China younger adults are more mobile than older adults.

Interestingly, a few household characteristics that do not significantly influence total labor supply have significant effects on the allocation of labor among activities. Education reduces hours worked in agricultural production by 5 percent, increases hours in nonagricultural production by 8 percent, and increases hours in wage employment by a substantial 25 percent. The proportion of males among working-age adults increases labor supply to agriculture, but reduces labor supply to wage employment.

Community-level variables also affect the composition of the labor supply. We use a dummy variable for the availability of TVEs and the number of self-employed household businesses as indicators of the prevalence of nonfarm activities in local communities. As expected, both variables are significant in reducing labor allocation to agricultural production and raising participation in nonagricultural production and wage employment. Also, the coefficients on the market prices for fuel and rice are in some cases negative and significant.

In general, our estimates indicate that labor supply to agriculture and labor supply to wage employment have opposite responses to most explanatory variables. In other words, factors that increase wage employment would tend to decrease agricultural employment, and vice versa. This conclusion is consistent with aggregate statistics that show such opposing trends in aggregate employment in the two sectors. Labor supply to nonagricultural household businesses, however, moves with agriculture for some variables and with wage employment for others. Thus, depending on which determinants of labor supply are driving aggregate trends, we might expect to observe concurrent growth in agricultural and nonagricultural household employment, or growth in one and decline in the other.

Conclusions

The impact of trade liberalization in China depends not only on the aggregate sectoral and price shifts that follow liberalization, but also on the microeconomic response of households and individuals to those shifts. In this chapter we have analyzed the microeconomics of household earnings and employment in rural China. Using household survey data with broad regional coverage, we have examined household incomes, wage determination, and labor supply in total and among sectors.

Our analysis of income generation provides information about earnings from labor. We find that the returns to nonagricultural labor hours are higher than for agricultural labor hours, a result that is consistent with other studies in the literature. We then decompose the income gap between poorer and richer groups. Key contributors to the income gap are the lower returns received by poor households from education, agricultural labor, and wage employment. Also important is the fact that poorer households work fewer hours in higher-paid wage employment. These results suggest that analysis of the impact of trade liberalization should consider not only the fact that the level and composition of employment differ among income groups, but also that the returns to employment in each occupation can differ among groups.

Our analysis of household labor supply provides some insights into how changes in wages after China's accession to the WTO might affect patterns of employment and thus earnings. Total labor supply is not sensitive to changes in wages, which suggests that any changes in wages resulting from WTO accession would not have much impact on overall employment. We also find that, for the most part, the allocation of labor among self-employment in agriculture, self-employment in nonagriculture, and off-farm wage jobs is not overly sensitive to changes in wages. In particular, labor supply to both agricultural and nonagricultural household production is inelastic with respect to most wages. Put differently, changes in wages do not cause large changes in the amount of labor supplied to household production.

The off-farm labor supply is more responsive, at least to the agricultural shadow wage. A lower agricultural shadow wage is associated with substantially increased employment in off-farm jobs. Thus if WTO accession raises wages for off-farm jobs, it would not "pull" labor into wage jobs; however, if WTO accession reduces the returns to agricultural labor, it might "push" labor into wage jobs.

Although in general labor supply is not overly sensitive to wages, it is sensitive to other variables. Household characteristics such as education, household composition, and regional location have significant effects on the level and sectoral composition of labor supply. Higher education is associated with less work time in agriculture and more work time in nonagricultural types of work. More dependents are associated with more work time overall, as well as with more work time in household production and less in off-farm wage employment. These findings suggest that labor mobility among sectors is significantly influenced by variables such as education, health, and demographic structure. Such variables are not directly affected by WTO accession, at least in the short term.

Notes

1. Official Chinese estimates show the number of rural poor declining from 65 million in 1995 to 42 million in 1998 (World Bank 2001), and show the number of urban poor ranging from 10 to 15 million in the mid-1990s (UNDP 1998; NBS 1998). These numbers may not be entirely comparable, but they indicate that roughly 75–85 percent of the poor are rural.

2. Official Chinese statistics distinguish between private and individual enterprises. Private enterprises are larger and rely on hired employees as the main source of labor. Individual enterprises are smaller and, although they may hire employees, rely largely on family workers for labor. Both types of enterprises are privately owned.

3. Income data in the text are deflated using the rural consumer price index and are taken from the National Bureau of Statistics (various years) and the National Bureau of Statistics Rural Social and Economic Survey Team (2000).

4. The CHNS survey covers the provinces of Guangxi, Guizhou, Heilongjiang, Henan, Hubei, Hunan, Jiangsu, Liaoning, and Shandong. The 1997 survey, which we use for our analysis, does not include Liaoning and so covers only eight of the nine provinces.

5. Detailed information about the CHNS is available at www.cpc.unc.edu/china/home.html.

6. Note that for agricultural and nonagricultural household production, these estimated returns are substantially lower than average earnings per hour worked given earlier (1.2 and 2.2 yuan, respectively). This finding could reflect the fact that in household production the average and marginal returns to labor differ and that the income generation function controls for nonlabor inputs. The estimated return to wage labor hours is also somewhat lower than average earnings (2.8 yuan).

7. Note that the difference in time worked per adult is similar to that for total hours, because the number of working-age adults in the two groups is similar—on average, the poor households had 2.74 adults and the rich households 2.71 adults.

8. Note that wage employment includes wage labor in agriculture, but in our sample hired farm labor is a small proportion of total wage employment.

9. Other studies taking this approach include Skoufias (1994) and Abdulai and Regmi (2000).

10. The CHNS data do not distinguish hired labor from other variable inputs.

11. Estimated coefficients for Models I and II are nearly identical despite the significance of the number of dependents in sector choice. Note that lambda is also highly insignificant. This indicates that there is no selectivity bias.

12. We thank Martin Ravallion for suggesting this approach.

References

The word *processed* describes informally reproduced works that may not be commonly available through libraries.

Abdulai, Awudu, and Punya Prasad Regmi. 2000. "Estimating Labor Supply of Farm Households under Nonseparability: Empirical Evidence from Nepal." *Agricultural Economics* 22: 309–20.

Bowlus, Audra, and Terry Sicular. 2003. "Moving toward Markets? Labor Allocation in Rural China." *Journal of Development Economics* 71 (2): 561–83.

Chen Shaohua and Wang Yan. 2001. "China's Growth and Poverty Reduction: Recent Trends between 1990 and 1999." World Bank, July. Processed.

Dollar, David, and Aart Kraay. 2001. "Trade, Growth and Poverty." Policy Research Working Paper 2615. World Bank, Washington, D.C.

Hare, Denise. 1994. "Rural Nonagricultural Activities and Their Impact on the Distribution of Income: Evidence from Farm Households in Southern China." *China Economic Review* 4 (1): 59–82.

———. 1999a. " 'Push' versus 'Pull' Factors in Migration Out-flows and Returns: Determinants of Migration Status and Spell Duration among China's Rural Population." *Journal of Development Studies* 35 (3): 45–72.

———. 1999b. "Women's Economic Status in Rural China: Household Contributions to Male-Female Disparities in the Wage Labor Market." *World Development* 27 (6): 1011–29.

Heckman, James. 1979. "Sample Selection Bias as a Specification Error." *Econometrica* 47 (1): 153–62.

Jacoby, Hanan. 1993. "Shadow Wages and Peasant Family Labour Supply: An Econometric Application to the Peruvian Sierra." *Review of Economic Studies* 60 (4): 903–21.

Knight, John, and Lina Song. 1997. "Chinese Peasant Choices: Migration, Rural Industry or Farming." Oxford Applied Economics Discussion Paper No. 188. October.

———. 1999. *The Rural–Urban Divide: Economic Disparities and Interactions in China*. Studies on Contemporary China. Oxford and New York: Oxford University Press.

Li Tianyou and Junsen Zhang. 1998. "Returns to Education under Collective and Household Farming in China." *Journal of Development Economics* 56 (2): 307–35.

Meng Xin. 2000. *Labour Market Reform in China*. Cambridge: Cambridge University Press.

Michelson, Ethan, and William Parish. 2000. "Gender Differentials in Economic Success: Rural China in 1991." In Barbara Entwisle and Gail E. Henderson, eds., *Redrawing Boundaries: Work, Households and Gender in China*. Berkeley: University of California Press.

National Bureau of Statistics. 1998. *Zhongguo Shehui yu Keji Fazhan Baogao* [China Social and Science and Technology Development Report]. Beijing: China Statistics Press.

———. 2001. *China Statistical Abstract 2001*. Beijing: China Statistics Press.

———. Various years. *China Statistical Yearbook*. Beijing: China Statistics Press.

National Bureau of Statistics Rural Social and Economic Survey Team. 2000. *Zhongguo Nongcun Zhuhu Diaocha Nianjian*

2000 [China Rural Household Survey Yearbook 2000]. Beijing: China Statistics Press.

Parish, W. L., X. Zhe, and F. Li. 1995. "Nonfarm Work and Marketization of the Chinese Countryside." *China Quarterly* 143: 697–730.

Rawski, T. G., and R. W. Mead. 1998. "On the Trail of China's Phantom Farmers." *World Development* 26 (5): 767–81.

Rodrik, Dani. 2000. "Comments on 'Trade, Growth, and Poverty,' by David Dollar and Aart Kraay." Available at http://ksghome. harvard.edu/~.drodrik.academic.ksg/papers.html.

Rozelle, Scott, Guo Li, Minggao Shen, Amelia Hughart, and John Giles. 1999. "Leaving China's Farms: Survey Results of New Paths and Remaining Hurdles to Rural Migration." *China Quarterly* 158 (June): 367–93.

Skoufias, Emmanuel. 1994. "Using Shadow Wages to Estimate Labor Supply of Agricultural Households." *American Journal of Agricultural Economics* 76 (May): 215–27.

UNDP (United Nations Development Programme). 1998. *China Human Development Report: Human Development and Poverty Alleviation, 1997*. Beijing: UNDP.

Winters, L. Alan. 2000. "Trade, Trade Policy, and Poverty: What are the Links?" Centre for Economic Policy Research Paper No. 2382. Centre for Economic Policy Research, London.

World Bank. 2001. *China: Overcoming Rural Poverty*. Washington, D.C.

Wu, Harry X., and LI Zhou. 1996 "Research on Rural to Urban Labour Migration in the Post-Reform China: A Survey." Chinese Economy Research Unit Working Paper 96/4. University of Adelaide, February.

Yang, Dennis Tao. 1997. "Education and Off–Farm Work." *Economic Development and Cultural Change* 45 (3): 613–32.

Yang, Dennis Tao, and Hao Zhou. 1999. "Rural-Urban Disparity and Sectoral Labour Allocation in China." *Journal of Development Studies* 35 (3): 105–33.

Yao Yang. 1999. "Rural Industry and Labor Market Integration in Eastern China." *Journal of Development Economics* 59 (2): 463–96.

Zhao Yaohui. 1999a. "Labor Migration and Earnings Differences: The Case of Rural China." *Economic Development and Cultural Change* 47 (4): 767–82.

———. 1999b. "Leaving the Countryside: Rural-to-Urban Migration Decisions in China." *American Economic Review* 89 (2): 281–86.

15

WELFARE IMPACTS OF CHINA'S ACCESSION TO THE WTO

Shaohua Chen and Martin Ravallion

There has been much debate about the welfare impacts of greater trade openness. Some argue that external trade liberalization is beneficial to the poor in developing countries, while others argue that the benefits will be captured by people who are not poor. Expected impacts on relative wages (notably between skilled and unskilled labor) and relative prices (such as between food staples and luxury imports) have figured prominently in debates about the welfare impacts.

What does the evidence suggest? One might hope to provide a conclusive answer by comparing changes over time in measures of inequality or poverty between countries that are open to external trade and countries that are not. A number of attempts to throw empirical light on the welfare effects of trade liberalization have been made using aggregate cross-country data sets that combine survey-based measures of inequality or poverty with data on trade openness and other control variables (see Bourguignon and Morisson 1990; Edwards 1997; Barro 2000; Dollar and Kraay 2002; Lundberg and Squire 2003).

However, caution in drawing implications from such cross-country comparisons is appropriate. Concerns have been raised about data and econometric specifications. Differences in survey design and processing between countries and over time

within countries can add considerable noise to the measured levels and changes in poverty and inequality. It is unclear how much power cross-country data sets have for detecting any underlying effects of greater openness or other covariates. There is also the issue of whether trade volume can be treated as exogenous in these cross-country regressions; it is clearly not a policy variable and may well be highly correlated with other (latent) attributes of country performance independently of trade policy. The attribution of inequality impacts to trade policy reforms themselves is clearly problematic. The correlations (or their absence) found in cross-country studies can also be deceptive because starting conditions can vary so much between reforming countries. Averaging across this diversity in initial conditions can readily hide systematic effects of relevance to policy (Ravallion 2001).

In principle, such problems in cross-country comparative work can be dealt with by better data and methods. However, the concerns go deeper. Aggregate inequality or poverty may not change with trade reform even though there are both gainers and losers at all levels of living. Survey data tracking the same families over time commonly show considerable churning under the surface.[1] The data show that many people have escaped poverty while others have fallen into poverty, even though the overall poverty rate is unchanged.

Numerous sources of such diverse impacts can be found in developing country settings. For example, geographic disparities in access to human and physical infrastructure affect prospects for participating in economic growth.[2] For China the economic geography of poverty and how this interacts with geographic diversity in the impacts of policy reforms are high on the domestic policy agenda. A policy analysis that simply averaged over such differences would miss a great deal of what matters to the debate on policy.

This chapter follows a different approach in which the attribution to trade policy changes is unambiguous and the diversity of welfare impacts is not lost. The article examines the welfare impacts at the household level of the changes in commodity and factor prices attributed to a specific trade policy reform, namely China's accession in 2001 to the World Trade Organization (WTO). For China, this meant a sharp reduction in tariffs, quantitative restrictions, and export subsidies, with implications for the domestic structure of prices and wages and thus for household welfare. Drawing on estimates by Ianchovichina and Martin (2002) of the impacts of reform on prices (for both commodities and factors of production), the following analysis applies standard methods of first-order welfare analysis to measure the gains and losses at the household level using large sample surveys collected by China's National Bureau of Statistics.

Measuring the Welfare Impacts of Trade Reform

Past approaches to studying the welfare impacts of specific trade reforms have tended to be either partial equilibrium analyses, which measure household-level welfare impacts of the direct price changes due to tariff changes using survey data (typically) covering many thousands of randomly chosen households, or general equilibrium analyses, which use a computable general equilibrium (CGE) model to capture second-round responses.[3] While partial equilibrium analysis requires little or no aggregation of the primary household data, it misses potentially important indirect effects on prices and wages. General equilibrium analysis has the power to capture these effects by simulating economywide impacts on markets. However, standard CGE models entail considerable aggregation across household types, with rarely more than six or so "representative households." Such models are crude tools for welfare-distributional analysis.

The challenge for applied work is to find an approach that respects the richness of detail available from modern integrated household surveys while ensuring that the price changes attributed to reform are internally consistent with economywide equilibrium conditions. In principle, the CGE model could be built onto the household survey, so that the number of households in the model is the number sampled in the survey.[4] For this study, that degree of integration would require an extraordinarily high dimensional CGE model, with 85,000 households. This is currently not a feasible route.

The intermediate approach used here carries the reform-induced commodity and factor price changes simulated from a general equilibrium model to the level of all the sampled households in the survey.[5] The welfare impacts are measured using standard tools of analysis familiar from past work on the welfare effects of price changes associated with tax and trade policy reform. This approach imposes minimal aggregation conditions on the survey data, within unavoidable data limitations. In addition to calculating the trade reform's overall effects on poverty and inequality, this approach provides a detailed socioeconomic map of impact, showing how it varies with other nonincome characteristics, such as location. This generates better insights to the questions policymakers ask about who gains and who loses from reform.

The general equilibrium analysis generates a set of price and wage changes. These embody both the direct price effects of the trade policy change and second-round, indirect effects on the prices of nontraded goods and on factor returns, including effects operating through the government's budget constraint. Ianchovichina and Martin (2002) use a competitive market-clearing model from the Global Trade Analysis Project.[6] The revenue implications of the trade policy change are reflected in changes in indirect tax rates.[7] Since the price changes are based on an explicit model, their attribution to the trade policy reform is unambiguous, thus avoiding the identification problems common to past attempts to estimate distributional effects of trade policy reform using cross-country comparisons.

The approach can be outlined as follows. Each household has preferences over consumption and work effort (under the standard assumption that goods have positive marginal utilities while labor supply has negative marginal utility) represented by the utility function $u_i(q_i^d, L_i)$, where q_i^d is an m-dimension vector of the quantities of commodities consumed by household i and L_i is a vector of labor supplies by activity, including supply to the household's own production activities. The household is assumed to be free to choose q_i^d and L_i subject to its budget constraint. Consistently with the general equilibrium model that generated the price and wage changes, there is no rationing at the household level; for example, involuntary unemployment is ruled out.

The indirect utility function of household i is given by:

$$v_i\left[p_i^d, w_i, \pi_i\right] = \max_{(q_i^d, L_i)} \left[u_i\left(q_i^d, L_i\right) \mid p_i^d q_i^d \right.$$
$$\left. = w_i L_i + \pi_i\right] \qquad (15.1)$$

where p_i^d is the price vector (of dimension m) for consumption, w_i is the vector of wage rates, and π_i is the profit obtained from all household enterprises as given by:

$$\pi_i\left(p_i^s, p_i^d, w_i\right) = \max_{(z_i, L_i^o)} \left[p_i^s q_i^s - p_i^d z_i - w_i L_i^o \mid q_{ij}^s\right.$$

$$\leq f_{ij}(z_{ij}, L_{ij}^o), \quad j = 1, \dots, m;$$

$$\left. \sum_j z_{ij} \leq z_i, \sum_j L_{ij}^o \leq L_i^o\right] \quad (15.2)$$

where p_i^s is the m-vector of supply prices, q_i^s is the corresponding vector of quantities supplied, L_i^o is the labor input to own-production activities, of which L_{ij}^o is used in producing good j, f_{ij} is the household-specific production function for good j (embodying fixed factors), and the z_i terms are the commodities used as production inputs, of which z_{ij} is used in producing good j.

Measurement of the welfare impacts is of course constrained by the data, which do not include initial price and wage levels.[8] However, this data limitation does not matter in calculating a first-order approximation to the welfare impact in a neighborhood of the household's optimum. Taking the differentials of equations 15.1 and 15.2 and using the envelope property (whereby the welfare impacts in a neighborhood of an optimum can be evaluated by treating the quantity choices as given), the monetary value of the change in utility for household i is given by:

$$g_i \equiv \frac{du_i}{v_{\pi i}} = \sum_{j=1}^m \left[p_{ij}^s q_{ij}^s \frac{dp_{ij}^s}{p_{ij}^s} - p_{ij}^d\left(q_{ij}^d + z_{ij}\right) \frac{dp_{ij}^d}{p_{ij}^d}\right]$$
$$+ \sum_{k=1}^n \left(w_k L_{ik}^s \frac{dw_k}{w_k}\right) \qquad (15.3)$$

where $v_{\pi i}$ is the marginal utility of income for household i (the multiplier on the budget constraint in equation 1) and $L_{ik}^s = L_{ik} - L_{ik}^o$ is the household's "external" labor supply to activity k. (Notice that gains in earnings from labor used in own-production are exactly matched by the higher cost of this input to own-production.)

Equation 15.3 is the key formula used in calculating the household-level welfare impacts of the price changes implied by the general equilibrium analysis of the trade policy reform. The proportionate changes in all prices and wages are weighted by their corresponding expenditure and income shares. The weight for the proportionate change in the j'th selling price is $p_{ij}^s q_{ij}^s$, the revenue (selling value) from household production activities in sector j. Similarly, $-p_{ij}^d(q_{ij}^d + z_{ij})$ is the (negative) weight for demand price changes, and $w_k L_{ik}^s$ is the weight for changes in the wage rate for activity k. The term $p_{ij}^s q_{ij}^s - p_{ij}^d(q_{ij}^d + z_{ij})$ is referred to as *net revenue*, which (to a first-order approximation) gives the welfare impact of an equiproportionate increase in the price of commodity j.

With the gain (or loss) to each household calculated based on equation 15.3, the covariates of those gains can now be examined. One covariate of obvious interest is income, needed to assess impacts on aggregate poverty and inequality. Ideally, one would use a money metric of utility based on equation 15.1. However, that would require an explicit model of the demand and supply system (that can be integrated back to obtain the indirect utility function). Again, feasibility becomes an issue because of the absence of complete data on price and wage levels. Thus there is little choice but to use income as the money metric of utility, in effect ignoring all geographic differences in the prices faced or in the extent to which border price changes are passed on locally. However, we make a seemingly plausible allowance for urban–rural cost of living differences in this setting.

Two further limitations of this approach should be noted. First, applying the calculus in deriving (15.3) implicitly assumes small changes in prices. Relaxing this requires more information on price levels and the structure of the demand and supply system.[9] This would entail considerable further effort, and the reliability of the results will be questionable given the problem of incomplete price and wage data.

Second, as already noted and consistent with the general equilibrium analysis, this approach also rules out rationing in commodity or factor markets or nonconvexities in consumption or production. In principle, these problems can also be handled through a completely specified demand model, which can be used to estimate the virtual prices at which the rationed demand or supply would be chosen. This is not feasible without data on price and wage level.

Setting and Data

While the official date of China's WTO accession is 2001, it is clear that the Chinese economy had already started to adapt to this expected change well before 2001. The trade reform can thus be thought of as having two stages, a lead-up period in which tariffs started to fall in anticipation of WTO accession and the period from 2001 onward. Ianchovichina and Martin (2002) argue for 1995 as a plausible beginning of the lead-up period. Their estimates of the price changes induced by WTO accession for the periods 1995–2001 and 2001–07 are used in this analysis. While the primary focus is on the second period, welfare impacts are also estimated for the lead-up period.

The measure of welfare impacts given by equation 15.3 is calibrated to survey data for 1999, two years before official WTO accession and a few years after the likely beginning of the lead-up period. The choice of 1999 was partly made for data reasons, since it was the most recent year for which the micro data were available. Choosing a year near the middle of the lead-up period (rather than a survey at the beginning or end) should also diminish biases due to any nonlinearity in the welfare impacts of price and wage changes.

Survey Data

The survey data used in this study are from the 1999 Urban Household Survey and the 1999 Rural Household Survey by China's National Bureau of Statistics (NBS). The sample size is 67,900 households for the rural survey and 16,900 households (out of the survey total of 40,000 households) for the urban survey.[10] Over the past 15 years, NBS has worked to improve both surveys, focusing on sample coverage, questionnaire design, methodology, and data processing.[11] The number of variables in the surveys has increased dramatically, with additional details on income, expenditure, savings, housing, and productivity, among others. NBS also provided micro data for three provinces (Liaoning, Guangdong, and Sichuan—the "test provinces"). The computer program to implement the estimation method was written for these data, after which the program was run by NBS staff on the entire national data set.

A number of problems remain in the 1999 surveys. For a sample frame, the rural survey relies on its sampled counties from 1985, which may no longer be representative. The urban survey excludes rural migrants, since the base of the sample frame is the legal registration system (*hukou*). As in other countries the rural survey gives data on the remittances of migrants workers, but it does not provide information about the migrant workers themselves, who (unlike in other countries) are not sampled in the urban survey either. This makes it difficult to measure impacts through labor mobility and rural-urban transfers.

Comparisons between the rural and urban surveys also present problems. For example, income in the rural survey includes in-kind income (such as from own-farm production and other household enterprises), but income in the urban survey ignores some in-kind components, notably subsidies from the government.

Sampling Weights

The population census puts the 1999 urban population share at 34 percent while the sample-based urban population share is 20 percent. To correct the rural and urban sampling weights, the urban population share from the *China Statistical Yearbook* (NBS 2000) was used to replace the survey sample weights to form the national figures.

Matching the Global Trade Analysis Project Model and the Surveys

There are 57 sectors in the Global Trade Analysis Project (GTAP) model. The China GTAP model used in this study regroups these 57 sectors into 25: rice, wheat, feed grains, vegetables and fruits, oilseeds, sugar, plant-based fibers, livestock and meat, dairy, processed food, beverages and tobacco, extractive industries, textiles, apparel, light manufactures, petrochemicals, metals, automobiles, electronics, other manufactures, trade and transport, construction, communications, commercial services, and other services. To these are added land, capital, and three types of labor (see below).

China's rural and urban surveys have about 2,000 categories for consumption and production. The variables from the household surveys are matched to the closest category in the GTAP model. For example, corn, millet, and potatoes are placed in the category "feed grains" and cotton and fiber crops are placed in the category of "plant-based fibers." The working paper version, Chen and Ravallion 2003 gives details on how the variables from the surveys are matched to the GTAP model sectors.

Definitions of Labor and Labor Earnings

The China GTAP model defines three types of labor: unskilled farm labor, unskilled nonfarm labor, and skilled nonfarm labor.[12] Since the rural and urban surveys have different questionnaires, rural and urban labor earnings are treated differently. In the urban survey three variables—sector, occupation, and education—are used to determine labor types. However, "sector" or "occupation" alone cannot indicate whether a person should be classified as skilled labor. For example, the financial sector may hire some unskilled labor while the services sector may hire some skilled labor. Similarly, a train driver in the occupation category "workers and staff-members in production and transportation" counts as skilled labor. Accordingly, education is also taken into account. Workers who have received education at the senior high school level or above are considered skilled labor. Others are classified as unskilled labor.

It is more difficult to determine the type of labor income for rural areas. There is no information on how much each person earns and from what work. Consequently, labor earnings can be classified only roughly by income source. For instance, all labor remuneration from agriculture is considered income from unskilled farm labor; earnings from industry or construction, grain processing, and the like are considered income from unskilled nonfarm labor; earnings from the services sector,

transportation and trade, and the like are considered income from skilled nonfarm labor.

Land

Under China's economic reforms, which began in 1978, all farmers have land use rights but not the right to sell, although they can subcontract the allocated land to other farmers. Therefore, the change in land prices from the GTAP model affects only the value of land rentals paid and received.

Household Income

For assessing the overall impacts on poverty and inequality, rural and urban households are combined. There is no cost of living index between urban and rural areas of China; urban and rural consumer price indexes are both indexed to 100 at the base date. The urban price level is assumed to be 15 percent higher than the rural price level. This differential is less than for other developing countries because subsidies to urban households in China help to compensate for higher housing and food costs than in rural areas.

Income per person is used as the welfare indicator (so that all households are ranked by per capita income, from the poorest to the richest). This is termed "net income" in the rural survey and "disposable income" in the urban survey. Post-reform income is then income plus the estimated gain defined by equation 15.3.

Measured Welfare Impacts of WTO Accession

Based on the predicted relative price and wage changes from the GTAP model for 1995–2000 (table 15.1) and 2001–07 (table 15.2) and production and consumption shares from the 1999 rural and urban household survey data, equation 15.3 can be used to compute the net gain for each household. The first panel in table 15.3 gives the mean gains for 1995–2001 and 2001–07, split by urban and rural areas. The second panel gives the Gini indices, both actual (for the baseline year, 1999) and simulated. The two simulated income distributions are obtained by subtracting the estimated gains over 1995–2001 from the 1999 incomes at the household level and by adding the household-specific gains from 2001–07 to the 1999 incomes. Thus the first simulation shows the distributional impact of the price changes during

TABLE 15.1   Predicted Price Changes from GTAP Model and Per Capita Net Gain or Loss for Rural and Urban Households, 1995–2001

Expenditures and Income Sources	Wholesale Prices (Percent)	Consumer Prices (Percent)	Rural Net Revenue (Yuan)	Rural Mean Welfare Change (Yuan)	Urban Net Revenue (Yuan)	Urban Mean Welfare Change (Yuan)
Expenditures						
Rice	0.5	1.5	73.66	0.15	−109.33	−1.64
Wheat	−1.7	−1.5	40.86	−0.74	0.00	0.00
Feedgrains	2.6	10.7	117.04	2.15	0.00	0.00
Vegetables and fruits	0.5	1.5	123.41	0.13	−378.69	−5.68
Oilseeds	−0.6	−0.8	37.05	−0.24	−1.04	0.01
Sugar	0.7	1.4	13.74	0.05	−174.06	−2.44
Plant-based fibers	−3.6	−1.9	36.84	−1.34	0.00	0.00
Livestock and meat	2.0	3.1	194.62	2.59	−500.65	−15.52
Dairy	1.5	2.5	2.50	0.02	0.00	0.00
Other food	1.2	3.1	−81.60	−3.39	−343.13	−10.64
Beverages and tobacco	−4.6	−7.2	−72.98	5.25	−197.20	14.20
Extractive industries	−0.2	0.8	17.99	−0.44	−173.03	−1.38
Textiles	−5.0	−8.9	−11.08	0.99	−53.50	4.76
Apparel	−2.7	−7.4	−64.13	4.75	−394.30	29.18
Light manufacturing	−0.3	−2.5	−16.15	0.40	−82.96	2.07
Petrochemical industry	−0.7	−0.1	−325.39	0.33	−398.23	0.40
Metals	−0.7	−0.1	−15.30	0.02	−24.02	0.02
Automobiles	−17.7	−20.4	−52.27	10.66	−37.76	7.70
Electronics	−1.5	−4.0	−24.27	0.97	−162.69	6.51
Other manufactures	−0.6	−0.3	−264.61	0.79	−431.16	1.29
Trade and transport	0.2	1.3	−18.70	−0.24	−110.53	−1.44
Construction	0.1	1.1	0.00	0.00	−31.11	−0.34
Communication	0.9	1.9	−16.72	−0.32	−152.04	−2.89
Commercial services	0.8	1.8	−61.37	−1.10	−533.33	−9.60
Other services	0.1	1.1	−414.45	−4.56	−680.99	−7.49
Income sources						
Farm unskilled labor	1.7	1.7	313.58	5.22	0.00	0.00
Nonfarm unskilled labor	1.7	1.7	287.19	4.78	1227.51	20.44
Skilled labor	2.0	2.0	360.87	7.09	3391.11	66.64
Land	1.3	1.3	17.08	0.22	0.00	0.00
Capital	1.3	1.3	21.14	0.27	126.01	0.77

Sources: Ianchovichina and Martin 2002; author's calculations from China National Bureau of Statistics 1999 Rural Household Survey and 1999 Urban Household Survey.

the first stage of the trade reform (what the baseline distribution would have looked like without the reforms) while the second shows the impact of the post-2001 price changes (how the changes are expected to affect the baseline distribution, looking forward). The third panel gives the headcount index of poverty for the official poverty line based on the poverty lines used by China's National Bureau of Statistics and for the $1 a day and $2 a day poverty lines from Chen and Ravallion (2001).

There is an overall gain of about 1.5 percent of mean income. All of this gain is in the period leading up to WTO accession. There is almost no impact on inequality, either in the period leading up to WTO accession or predicting forward. The aggregate Gini

TABLE 15.2   Predicted Price Changes from GTAP Model and Per Capita Net Gain or Loss for Rural and Urban Households, 2001–07

Expenditures and Income Sources	Wholesale Prices (Percent)	Consumer Prices (Percent)	Rural		Urban	
			Net Revenue (Yuan)	Mean Welfare Change (Yuan)	Net Revenue (Yuan)	Mean Welfare Change (Yuan)
Expenditures						
Rice	−1.4	0.7	73.66	−1.39	−109.33	−0.75
Wheat	−1.5	0.7	40.86	−0.92	0.00	0.00
Feedgrains	−3.7	2.1	117.04	−4.90	0.00	0.00
Vegetables and fruits	−2.6	−0.6	123.41	−4.02	−378.69	2.24
Oilseeds	−5.7	−5.9	37.05	−2.10	−1.04	0.06
Sugar	−2.8	−3.5	13.74	−0.34	−174.06	6.01
Plant-based fibers	1.6	4.1	36.84	0.56	0.00	0.00
Livestock and meat	−1.5	0.7	194.62	−5.21	−500.65	−3.40
Dairy	−2.4	−0.5	2.50	−0.09	0.00	0.00
Other food	−3.1	−2.7	−81.60	2.04	−343.13	9.32
Beverages and tobacco	−5.6	−7.7	−72.98	5.62	−197.20	15.09
Extractive industries	−0.4	1.7	17.99	−0.86	−173.03	−2.92
Textiles	−0.2	−1.5	−11.08	0.17	−53.50	0.82
Apparel	2.6	0.8	−64.13	−0.51	−394.30	−2.98
Light manufacturing	−0.6	0.5	−16.15	−0.08	−82.96	−0.43
Petrochemical industry	−1.1	0.8	−325.39	−2.60	−398.23	−3.19
Metals	−0.6	1.3	−15.30	−0.20	−24.02	−0.31
Automobiles	−3.8	−4.0	−52.27	2.09	−37.76	1.52
Electronics	−1.2	−1.4	−24.27	0.34	−162.69	2.20
Other manufactures	−0.8	0.8	−264.61	−2.12	−431.16	−3.46
Trade and transport	−0.4	1.7	−18.70	−0.32	−110.53	−1.85
Construction	−0.4	1.7	0.00	0.00	−31.11	−0.52
Communication	−0.4	1.7	−16.72	−0.28	−152.04	−2.54
Commercial services	−1.1	0.9	−61.37	−0.55	−533.33	−4.72
Other services	−0.7	1.3	−414.45	−5.39	−680.99	−8.76
Income sources						
Farm unskilled labor	−0.3	−0.3	313.58	−0.85		
Nonfarm unskilled labor	1.0	1.0	287.19	2.96	1227.51	12.64
Skilled labor	0.4	0.4	360.87	1.55	3391.11	14.58
Land	−4.7	−4.7	17.08	−0.80		
Capital	0.6	0.6	21.14	0.13	126.01	0.80

Sources: Ianchovichina and Martin 2002; authors' calculations from China National Bureau of Statistics 1999 Rural Household Survey and 1999 Urban Household Survey.

index increased slightly, from 39.3 percent without WTO accession to 39.5 percent after accession.

The incidence of poverty would have been slightly higher in 1999 if not for the trade policy changes in the lead-up to WTO accession, while poverty is predicted to increase slightly during 2001–07 due to the expected price changes induced by the remaining tariff changes during that period. The impacts on rural and urban poverty for a wide range of poverty lines can be seen in figures 15.1 and 15.2, which give the cumulative distributions of income for both the baseline and the two simulated distributions for the poorest 60 percent in rural areas and 40 percent in urban areas, respectively.

TABLE 15.3 Summary Statistics on Aggregate Welfare Impacts, 1995–2001 and 2001–07

Item	Rural	Urban	National
Mean gains (yuan per capita)			
1995–2001	34.47	94.94	55.49
			(1.54%)[a]
2001–07	−18.07	29.45	−1.54
			(−0.04%)[a]
Inequality impacts (Gini index as percentage)			
Baseline, 1999	33.95	29.72	39.31
Simulated: Less gains 1995–2001	33.90	29.68	39.27
Simulated: Plus gains 2001–07	34.06	29.65	39.53
Poverty impacts (headcount index, percentage)[b]			
Official poverty line			
Baseline, 1999	4.38	0.08	2.92
Simulated: Less gains 1995–2001	4.56	0.08	3.04
Simulated: Plus gains 2001–07	4.57	0.07	3.04
$1/day (1993 purchasing power parity)			
Baseline, 1999	10.51	0.29	7.04
Simulated: Less gains 1995–2001	10.88	0.28	7.28
Simulated: Plus gains 2001–07	10.81	0.28	7.23
$2/day (1993 purchasing power parity)			
Baseline, 1999	45.18	4.07	31.20
Simulated: Less gains 1995–2001	46.10	4.27	31.88
Simulated: Plus gains 2001–07	45.83	3.97	31.60

a. Percentage of mean income.

b. Official poverty line is from China National Statistics Bureau; poverty lines of $1 a day and $2 a day are from Chen and Ravallion 2001.

Sources: Authors' computations from China National Bureau of Statistics 1999 Rural Household Survey and 1999 Urban Household Survey.

FIGURE 15.1 Poverty Incidence Curves, Rural

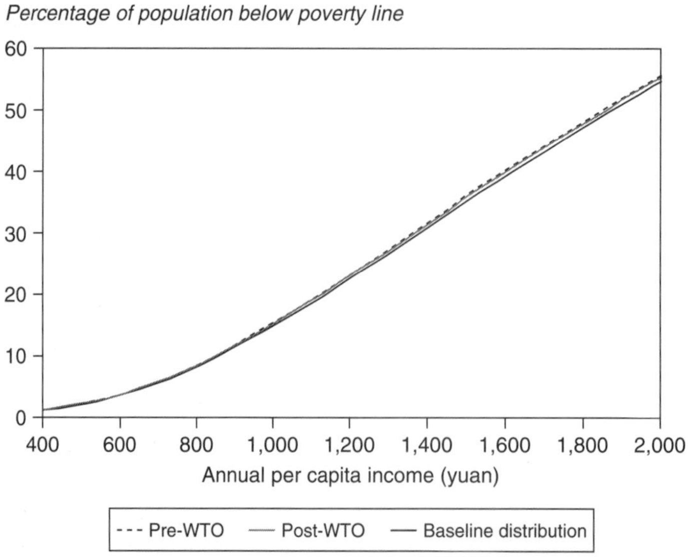

Percentage of population below poverty line

Annual per capita income (yuan)

--- Pre-WTO   — Post-WTO   — Baseline distribution

Sources: China National Bureau of Statistics; Chen and Ravallion 2001.

FIGURE 15.2   Poverty Incidence Curves, Urban

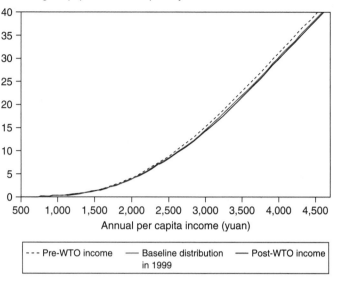

Percentage of population below poverty line

Source: Authors' computations based on data from China National Bureau of Statistics 1999 Rural Household Survey and 1999 Urban Household Survey.

While there is virtually zero aggregate impact when predicting forward from WTO accession, the disaggregated results show a more nuanced picture. The analysis focuses on three measures of impact at the household level: the absolute gain or loss, g_i; the proportionate gain or loss, g_i/y_i; and whether there is a gain or not, $I(g_i)$, where I is the indicator function. This third measure helps to determine where there might be high concentrations of losers, in specific areas or socioeconomic groups.

The results by provinces ranked by mean income per person are plotted in figure 15.3 for mean absolute gains (g_i in yuan per capita), in figure 15.4 for proportionate gains (g_i/y_i, as a percentage), and in figure 15.5 for the proportion of households that registered positive gains. The average gain or loss by province for urban and rural areas and the number of gainers in each case are shown in appendix tables 15.A.1 and 15.A.2, respectively; Chen and Ravallion 2003 give the province rankings.

The same results are also plotted in figures 15.6–15.8 against percentiles of the income distribution. So, for example, to see the mean impact in yuan per capita at the median income one looks at the 50th percentile of figure 15.6. (Notice that figure 15.6 gives the horizontal differences in figures 15.1 and 15.2 plotted against the point on the vertical axis.)

In the aggregate, about three-quarters of rural households and one-tenth of urban households will experience a real income loss. Farm income is predicted to drop by 18 yuan per person while urban income rises by 29 yuan per person. The breakdown by sectors in table 15.2 shows that the decline in rural income is due to the drop in wholesale prices for most farm products, plus higher prices for education and health care. Farmers will also benefit from the drop in some consumer prices and from the increase in nonfarm labor wages. In urban areas residents will enjoy lower prices for most farm products and higher wages, but they will also be hit by increases in service fees for education and health care.

Impacts differ considerably across regions (see figures 15.3–15.5 and appendix tables 15.A.1 and 15.A.2). The mean absolute gains tend to be highest in the richest provinces in both urban and rural areas (figure 15.3), though there is no correlation between the proportionate gains and mean income of provinces (figure 15.4). One spatially contiguous region—the northeast provinces of Inner Mongolia, Liaoning, Jilin, and Heilongjiang—stands out as having the largest loss from the reform. Both absolute and proportionate impacts are highest in this region—more than 90 percent of farmers in Heilongjiang and Jilin are predicted to experience a net loss.

Notice that these geographic differences in welfare impacts arise entirely from differences in consumption and production behavior. In reality,

**FIGURE 15.3   Mean Gains by Provinces: Absolute
              Gain in Yuan Per Capita**

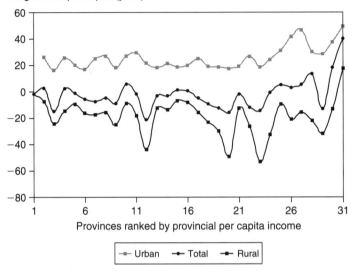

Source: Authors' computations based on data from China National
Bureau of Statistics 1999 Rural Household Survey and 1999 Urban
Household Survey.

**FIGURE 15.4   Mean Gains by Provinces: Proportionate
              Gains in Percent**

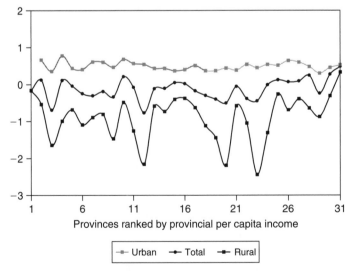

Source: Authors' computations based on data from China National
Bureau of Statistics 1999 Rural Household Survey and 1999 Urban
Household Survey.

FIGURE 15.5   Mean Gains by Provinces: Percentage of Gainers by Provinces

Percentage of gainers

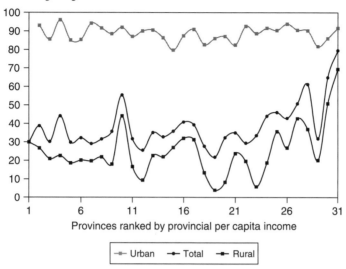

Note: Urban prices are assumed to be 15 percent higher than rural prices.

Source: Authors' computations based on data from China National Bureau of Statistics 1999 Rural Household Survey and 1999 Urban Household Survey.

FIGURE 15.6   Mean Gains in Yuan by Income Percentile

Net gain/loss per capita (yuan)

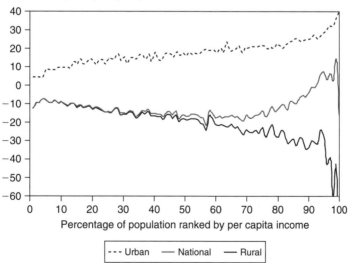

Note: Urban prices are assumed to be 15 percent higher than rural prices.

Source: Authors' compilations based on data from China National Bureau of Statistics 1999 Rural Household Survey and 1999 Urban Household Survey.

FIGURE 15.7   Mean Percentage Gain by Income Percentile

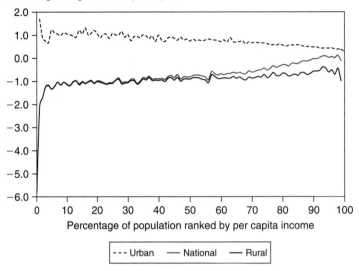

Note: Urban prices are assumed to be 15 percent higher than rural prices.

Source: Authors' compilations based on data from China National Bureau of Statistics 1999 Rural Household Survey and 1999 Urban Household Survey.

FIGURE 15.8   Percentage of Gainers by Income Percentile

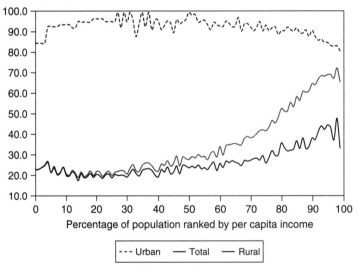

Note: Urban prices are assumed to be 15 percent higher than rural prices.

Source: Authors' compilations based on data from China National Bureau of Statistics 1999 Rural Household Survey and 1999 Urban Household Survey.

differential impacts on local prices are likely, due to transport or other impediments to internal trade. The analysis here does not incorporate such differences, and doing so would pose a number of data and analytic problems. This might, however, be a fruitful direction for future work where the necessary data on prices and wage levels are available by geographic area.

When households are ranked by initial income, there is a notable difference between urban and rural households, with absolute gains tending to be higher for higher income households in urban areas, but lower for higher income households in rural areas (see figure 15.6). Nationally (combining urban and rural areas with the corrected weights discussed above), there is the hint of a U-shaped relationship, though still with the highest absolute gains for the rich.

This picture is reversed for proportionate gains, which tend to fall as income rises in urban areas, but to rise with income in rural areas and nationally (see figure 15.7). In the aggregate the proportion of gainers rises with income, a result that is driven by the rise in the number of gainers as income increases in rural areas (see figure 15.8).

Explaining the Incidence of Gains and Losses

The way the problem of measuring welfare impacts was formulated in section II allows utility and profit functions to vary between households at given prices. To explain the heterogeneity in measured welfare impacts, these functions can instead be supposed to vary with observed household characteristics. The indirect utility function becomes $v_i(p_i^d, w_i, \pi_i) = v(p_i^d, w_i, \pi_i, x_{1i})$ where $\pi_i = \pi(p_i^s, p_i^d, w_i, x_{2i})$ for vectors of characteristics x_{1i} and x_{2i} that shift the utility functions in equation 15.1 and the profit functions in 15.2. Note that the characteristics that influence preferences over consumption (x_{1i}) are allowed to differ from those that influence the outputs from own-production activities (x_{2i}).

The gain from the price changes induced by trade reform, as given by equation 15.3, depends on the household's consumption, labor supply, and production choices, which in turn depend on prices and characteristics, x_{1i} and x_{2i}. For example, households with a higher proportion of children will

naturally spend more on food, so if the relative price of food changes, the welfare impacts will be correlated with this aspect of household demographics. Similarly, there may be differences in tastes associated with stage of the life cycle and education. There are also likely to be systematic covariates of the composition of income.

Generically, the gain can be written as:

$$
\begin{aligned}
g_i &= g(p_i^d, p_i^s, w_i, x_{1i}, x_{2i}) \\
&= \sum_{j=1}^{m} \left[p_{ij}^s q^s(p_i^d, p_i^s, w_i, x_{2i}) \frac{dp_{ij}^s}{p_{ij}^s} \right. \\
&\quad - p_{ij}^d [q^d(p_i^d, w_i, \pi_i, x_{1i}) \\
&\quad \left. + z_{ij}(p_i^d, p_i^s, w_i, x_{2i})] \frac{dp_{ij}^d}{p_{ij}^d} \right] \\
&\quad + \sum_{k=1}^{n} w_k [L_{ik}(p_i^d, w_i, \pi_i, x_{1i}) \\
&\quad - L_{ik}^o(p_i^d, p_i^s, w_i, x_{2i})] \frac{dw_k}{w_k}
\end{aligned}
\tag{15.4}
$$

Notice that the gain from reform is inherently nonseparable, in that it cannot be written as a function solely of p_i^d, x_{1i} and π_i because the gain also depends on production choices.

However, as noted above, household-specific wages and prices are not observed, so further assumptions are required. In explaining variations across households in the predicted gains from trade reform, wage rates are assumed to be a function of prices and characteristics as $w_i = w(p_i^d, p_i^s, x_{1i}, x_{2i})$, and differences in prices faced are assumed to be adequately captured by a complete set of county-level dummy variables.

Under these assumptions, and the linearization of equation 16.4 with an additive innovation error term, the following regression model applies for the gains:

$$
g_i = \beta_1 x_{1i} + \beta_2 x_{2i} + \sum_k \gamma_k D_{ki} + \varepsilon_i
\tag{15.5}
$$

where $D_{ki} = 1$ if household i lives in county k and $D_{ki} = 0$ otherwise and ε_i is the error term.

The characteristics considered include age and age-squared of the household head, education and demographic characteristics, and land (interpreted as a fixed factor of production, since it is allocated largely by administrative means in rural China). Also included are dummy variables describing some key aspects of the occupation and principle sector of employment, such as whether the

TABLE 15.4 Regression Results for Level of Gain (Yuan) in Rural Areas of Three Provinces, 2001–07

Variable	Liaoning	Guangdong	Sichuan
Log of household size	37.642 (6.42)	28.822 (2.64)	4.958 (2.16)
Age of household head	−2.425 (−3.11)	−1.783 (−2.60)	−0.548 (−1.51)
Age of household head squared	0.026 (3.36)	0.017 (2.66)	0.005 (1.30)
Agriculture household	−10.942 (−3.31)	−42.850 (−6.45)	−37.723 (−6.54)
Number of employees/ household size	12.665 (4.10)	−6.932 (−0.29)	12.652 (3.02)
Number of township and village enterprise workers/ household size	10.768 (3.13)	29.466 (3.06)	15.327 (4.26)
Number of migrant workers/ household size	5.399 (1.73)	7.798 (2.35)	7.067 (3.79)
Area of cultivated land	−0.027 (−5.73)	−0.002 (−1.00)	−0.001 (−0.28)
Area of hilly land	0.000 (−0.05)	−0.001 (−0.87)	0.002 (1.94)
Area of fishpond land	−0.001 (−0.94)	−0.070 (−2.85)	0.000 (0.04)
Highest education level			
Illiterate or semi illiterate	7.926 (1.04)	19.016 (1.25)	8.387 (0.92)
Primary school	0.071 (0.01)	−2.148 (−0.13)	9.694 (1.06)
Middle school	−0.755 (−0.11)	−4.261 (−0.26)	7.669 (0.84)
High school	2.125 (0.31)	2.806 (0.18)	9.675 (1.03)
Technical school	−3.096 (−0.44)	−36.482 (−1.09)	4.270 (0.38)
College (default)			
Labor force/household size	0.576 (0.08)	2.877 (0.15)	−4.995 (−1.16)
Children under 6/household size	46.999 (2.71)	8.109 (0.35)	−2.291 (−0.45)
Children ages 6–11/household size	1.414 (0.11)	2.247 (0.10)	−9.011 (−1.50)
Children ages 12–14/household size	−0.155 (−0.01)	−24.489 (−1.20)	−9.606 (−1.51)
Children ages 15–17/household size	−2.592 (−0.22)	−23.390 (−1.02)	−5.485 (−0.73)
Constant	−17.851 (−0.82)	−17.742 (−0.65)	−17.220 (−1.43)
R-square	0.278	0.116	0.116

Note: Numbers in parentheses are *t*-statistics.

Source: Authors' computations based on data from China National Bureau of Statistics 1999 Rural Household Survey and 1999 Urban Household Survey.

household is a registered agricultural household, whether there is wage employment, whether there is state-sector employment, and whether there is participation in a township and village enterprise. There are endogeneity concerns about these variables, but they appear to be minor in this context, especially when weighed against the concerns about omitted variable bias in estimates that exclude these characteristics. Under the usual assumption that the error term is orthogonal to these regressors, equation 5 is estimated by ordinary least squares. The model is estimated separately for urban and

rural areas in each of the three test provinces (Liaoning, Guangdong, and Sichuan) for which complete micro data are available.

There are some differences in the explanatory variables between rural (tables 15.4 and 15.5) and urban areas (tables 15.6 and 15.7). Results are presented for both absolute gains (g_i) and proportionate gains (g_i/y_i). Recall that these are averages across the impacts of these characteristics on the consumption and production choices that determine the welfare impact of given price and wage changes. This makes interpretation difficult. These

TABLE 15.5 Regression Results for Percentage Gains in Rural Areas of Three Provinces, 2001–07

Variable	Liaoning	Guangdong	Sichuan
Log of household size	0.768 (2.46)	0.022 (0.20)	0.030 (0.40)
Age of household head	−0.108 (−2.17)	−0.007 (−0.34)	−0.004 (−0.31)
Age of household head squared	0.001 (2.19)	0.000 (0.40)	0.000 (−0.02)
Agriculture household	−0.896 (−2.98)	−1.365 (−14.85)	−1.420 (−7.58)
Number of employees/ household size	0.630 (2.76)	0.271 (2.57)	0.444 (3.61)
Number of township and village enterprise workers/household size	0.669 (4.27)	0.585 (4.47)	0.548 (6.11)
Number of migrant workers/ household size	0.655 (3.59)	0.187 (3.59)	0.346 (7.08)
Area of cultivated land	0.000 (−1.77)	0.000 (−0.73)	0.000 (−1.61)
Area of hilly land	0.000 (−0.48)	0.000 (−0.35)	0.000 (2.20)
Area of fishpond land	0.000 (−0.17)	−0.001 (−2.23)	0.000 (0.55)
Highest education level			
Illiterate or semi illiterate	1.393 (2.18)	0.507 (1.26)	−0.013 (−0.05)
Primary school	−0.634 (−2.01)	−0.154 (−0.90)	0.069 (0.30)
Middle school	−0.891 (−3.08)	−0.023 (−0.14)	−0.011 (−0.05)
High school	−0.660 (−2.42)	0.010 (0.06)	0.006 (0.02)
Technical school	−0.573 (−1.87)	−0.229 (−1.18)	0.038 (0.14)
College (default)			
Labor force/household size	0.456 (0.85)	0.323 (1.81)	−0.099 (−0.71)
Children under age 6/household size	3.730 (3.61)	0.461 (1.49)	−0.169 (−0.78)
Children ages 6–11/household size	1.557 (1.41)	0.173 (0.72)	−0.275 (−1.48)
Children ages 12–14/household size	1.625 (1.54)	−0.477 (−1.60)	−0.343 (−1.85)
Children ages 15–17/household size	1.325 (1.80)	−0.289 (−0.91)	−0.192 (−0.88)
Constant	0.788 (0.69)	−0.709 (−1.39)	−0.584 (−1.68)
R-square	0.108	0.217	0.171

Note: Numbers in parentheses are *t*-statistics.

Source: Authors' computations based on data from China National Bureau of Statistics 1999 Rural Household Survey and 1999 Urban Household Survey.

regressions are mainly of descriptive interest, to help isolate covariates of potential relevance in thinking about compensatory policy responses.

For rural areas the results show that the predicted gain from trade reform tends to be larger for larger households in all three provinces. There is also a U-shaped relationship with age of the household head: the gains reach a minimum around 50 years of age (47 in Liaoning, 52 in Guangdong, and 55 in Sichuan). The gains are lower for agricultural households and higher for households with more employees and more township and village enterprise workers, with more migrant workers, and with less cultivated land (though significant only in Liaoning). The only strong demographic effect is that younger households (with a higher proportion of children under six) tend to be gainers in Liaoning. While the results for the county dummy variables are not shown (to save space), losses were significantly higher than average in six counties in Liaoning, seven in Guangdong, and six in Sichuan. Table 16.8 gives the mean losses in these counties for agricultural households.

TABLE 15.6   Regression Results for Level of Gain (Yuan) in Urban Areas of Three Provinces, 2001–07

Variable	Liaoning	Guangdong	Sichuan
Log of household size	−5.627 (−1.81)	5.289 (0.27)	−19.441 (−4.09)
Single household head	−1.366 (−0.4)	−37.216 (−2.06)	−17.369 (−3.61)
Age of household head	0.531 (0.92)	5.266 (2.43)	1.542 (2.34)
Age of household head squared	−0.001 (−0.24)	−0.040 (−1.8)	−0.015 (−2.22)
Highest education level (default is college)			
Primary school or lower	13.240 (2.95)	50.434 (2.4)	23.079 (3.11)
Middle school	19.104 (5.99)	56.659 (3.58)	26.096 (4.34)
High school	5.123 (1.62)	12.053 (0.95)	12.717 (2.39)
Technical school	11.086 (3.23)	11.075 (0.88)	9.552 (1.62)
College	3.974 (1.26)	3.447 (0.3)	11.013 (2.12)
Sector (default is government)			
Agriculture	−16.310 (−1.22)	−25.590 (−2.23)	17.293 (1.76)
Mining	−14.586 (−3.24)	19.351 (1.13)	−3.851 (−0.53)
Manufacturing	−9.231 (−2.59)	17.773 (1.28)	−4.634 (−1.2)
Utility	−9.387 (−1.63)	−10.816 (−0.42)	1.516 (0.13)
Construction	−6.394 (−1.18)	8.622 (0.63)	−4.409 (−0.92)
Geological prospecting and water conservancy	−27.422 (−2.62)	20.089 (0.92)	−16.585 (−0.83)
Transportation and telecommunications	6.368 (1.52)	16.525 (1.24)	1.644 (0.25)
Wholesale and retail	−3.184 (−0.61)	5.664 (0.45)	−1.983 (−0.4)
Banking and finance	−5.278 (−0.55)	3.888 (0.3)	9.491 (0.85)
Real estate	−11.708 (−1.71)	46.192 (1.35)	7.670 (0.37)
Social services	−5.542 (−1.02)	−4.186 (−0.33)	0.504 (0.1)
Health care	−9.260 (−1.93)	0.683 (0.04)	−1.049 (−0.17)
Education	−7.279 (−1.64)	7.649 (0.46)	−5.219 (−0.87)
Scientific research	−20.982 (−4.06)	17.882 (1.14)	−7.929 (−0.59)
Other	−7.784 (−1.42)	−24.851 (−0.75)	−7.012 (−0.73)
Type of employer (default is state owned)			
Collective owned	−1.927 (−0.76)	11.882 (0.54)	−5.946 (−2.09)
Foreign company	−3.138 (−0.72)	−10.988 (−1.22)	2.038 (0.31)
Self-employed	4.278 (0.6)	9.448 (0.64)	10.582 (2.08)
Privately owned business	−9.587 (−1.41)	−14.823 (−0.99)	−4.601 (−0.57)
Retirees reemployed	−13.333 (−2.45)	−35.591 (−1.82)	−6.752 (−0.99)
Retirees	−15.569 (−3.66)	−49.442 (−1.91)	−12.218 (−1.95)
Other	−10.350 (−1.36)	−6.568 (−0.34)	−16.796 (−2.06)
Occupation (default is retiree)			
Engineer and technician	10.244 (1.66)	3.479 (0.12)	10.179 (1.49)
Officers	12.747 (2.07)	17.701 (0.64)	10.564 (1.53)
Staff in commerce	11.742 (2.08)	18.553 (0.65)	12.734 (1.92)
Staff in services	19.940 (2.54)	3.380 (0.11)	4.057 (0.5)
Worker in manufacturing	17.484 (2.02)	13.151 (0.47)	13.810 (1.86)
Worker in transportation and telecommunications	21.469 (3.59)	9.637 (0.34)	16.117 (2.35)
Other	15.318 (2.05)	9.810 (0.27)	−6.141 (−0.77)
Constant	−10.744 (−0.77)	−164.442 (−2.43)	−17.611 (−1.1)
R-square	0.265	0.131	0.181

Note: Numbers in parentheses are t-statistics.

Source: Authors' computations based on data from China National Bureau of Statistics 1999 Rural Household Survey and 1999 Urban Household Survey.

TABLE 15.7 Regression Results for Percentage Gains in Urban Areas of Three Provinces, 2001–07

Variable	Liaoning	Guangdong	Sichuan
Log of household size	0.175 (3.54)	−0.038 (−0.4)	0.036 (0.46)
Single household head	−0.022 (−0.36)	−0.221 (−2.21)	−0.259 (−3.07)
Age of household head	0.000 (−0.01)	0.033 (2.55)	0.017 (1.53)
Age of household head squared	0.000 (0.1)	0.000 (−2.12)	0.000 (−1.46)
Highest education level (default is university)			
Primary school or lower	0.524 (6.43)	0.389 (3.7)	0.509 (5.15)
Middle school	0.539 (10.41)	0.583 (7.25)	0.591 (8.27)
High school	0.180 (3.56)	0.095 (1.46)	0.262 (3.83)
Technical school	0.214 (4.04)	0.076 (1.22)	0.120 (1.79)
College	0.054 (1.04)	0.015 (0.25)	0.125 (2.24)
Sector (default is government)			
Agriculture	−0.079 (−0.32)	0.166 (2.2)	0.338 (2.64)
Mining	0.183 (1.11)	0.346 (3.38)	−0.129 (−1.01)
Manufacturing	−0.015 (−0.27)	0.114 (1.41)	−0.021 (−0.34)
Utility	−0.040 (−0.36)	−0.144 (−1.18)	−0.134 (−0.84)
Construction	0.095 (0.91)	0.109 (1.19)	0.036 (0.51)
Geological prospecting and water conservancy	−0.407 (−3.06)	0.178 (1.03)	−0.228 (−0.53)
Transport and telecommunications	0.206 (2.93)	0.060 (0.79)	−0.036 (−0.4)
Wholesale and retail	0.060 (0.78)	0.081 (0.99)	−0.015 (−0.18)
Banking and finance	−0.088 (−0.47)	0.049 (0.53)	0.013 (0.12)
Real estate	−0.108 (−0.91)	0.222 (1.16)	0.106 (0.29)
Social services	−0.090 (−1.09)	0.065 (0.69)	0.148 (1.37)
Health care	−0.088 (−1.1)	0.007 (0.06)	−0.124 (−1.49)
Education	−0.057 (−0.75)	0.044 (0.44)	−0.031 (−0.39)
Scientific research	−0.454 (−4.09)	0.126 (1.11)	−0.082 (−0.73)
Other	0.012 (0.14)	0.034 (0.25)	−0.121 (−0.55)
Type of employer (default is state owned)			
Collective owned	0.053 (1.16)	0.008 (0.08)	0.137 (1.73)
Foreign company	−0.046 (−0.54)	−0.122 (−2.3)	−0.193 (−2.08)
Self-employed	−0.069 (−0.59)	−0.051 (−0.39)	0.317 (2.46)
Privately owned business	−0.182 (−1.65)	−0.231 (−1.96)	−0.037 (−0.22)
Retirees reemployed	−0.302 (−3.39)	−0.242 (−1.41)	−0.177 (−1.32)
Retirees	−0.341 (−4.2)	−0.452 (−2.37)	−0.359 (−3.42)
Other	−0.124 (−1.13)	−0.187 (−1.24)	−0.338 (−1.2)
Occupation (default is retiree)			
Engineer and technician	−0.015 (−0.14)	−0.141 (−0.69)	−0.036 (−0.29)
Officers	−0.044 (−0.43)	−0.063 (−0.31)	−0.045 (−0.36)
Staff in commerce	0.012 (0.12)	−0.036 (−0.17)	0.029 (0.24)
Staff in services	0.437 (3.08)	0.019 (0.09)	−0.011 (−0.08)
Worker in manufacturing	0.118 (0.82)	0.025 (0.12)	0.091 (0.56)
Worker in transport and telecommunications	0.209 (2.02)	−0.018 (−0.09)	0.130 (1.03)
Other	0.171 (1.33)	−0.069 (−0.27)	−0.636 (−4.2)
Constant	0.172 (0.7)	−0.623 (−1.68)	−0.197 (−0.71)
R-square	0.401	0.290	0.359

Note: Numbers in the parentheses are t-statistics.

Source: Authors' computations based on data from China National Bureau of Statistics 1999 Rural Household Survey and 1999 Urban Household Survey.

TABLE 15.8   Average Impacts for Agricultural Households in Selected Counties, 2001–07

Province	County Identifier	Gain		Provincial Mean	
		Yuan	Percent	Yuan	Percent
Liaoning	210181	−73.72	−3.07	−32.34	−1.29
	210212	−145.40	−2.99		
	210381	−172.01	−5.57		
	210921	−57.70	−5.21		
	211321	−45.58	−3.78		
	211322	−53.60	−3.23		
Guangdong	440111	−107.31	−2.74	−29.34	−0.81
	440126	−183.63	−2.64		
	440223	−102.33	−3.53		
	440523	−148.90	−2.55		
	440620	−227.23	−3.11		
	440621	−109.59	−2.64		
	441425	−316.49	−5.34		
Sichuan	510121	−130.46	−2.86	−12.31	−0.67
	510125	−63.19	−3.81		
	512425	−138.34	−5.71		
	512610	−52.23	−3.11		
	512825	−40.44	−2.80		
	513021	−93.02	−4.07		

Note: A negative sign means a net loss. Agricultural household means that more than 75 percent of income is from agriculture.

Source: Authors' computations based on data from China National Bureau of Statistics 1999 Rural Household Survey and 1999 Urban Household Survey.

In urban areas the gains tend to be higher for smaller households (except in Guangdong). As in rural areas there is a U-shaped pattern (except for Liaoning), with lowest gains at 66 years of age in Guangdong and 51 in Sichuan. While there is no pattern in the relationship between education and welfare gains in rural areas, the gains in urban areas tend to be larger for less educated households. However, this may be biased by the fact that education was used in identifying skilled labor (noting that unskilled nonfarm wages are predicted to increase relative to skilled labor; see table 15.2). There are some signs of sectoral effects, though only significantly so in Liaoning, with higher gains for those with government jobs. Retirees tend to have lower gains than others.

Conclusion

In the aggregate, the analysis finds that China's trade reforms have had only a small impact on mean household income, inequality, and poverty incidence. There is, however, a sizable (and at least partly explicable) variance in impacts across household characteristics. Rural families tend to lose; urban households tend to gain. Some provinces experience larger impacts than others; highest impacts occur in the northeast region of Inner Mongolia, Liaoning, Jilin, and Heilongjiang, where rural households are more dependent on feed grain production (for which falling prices are expected from WTO accession) than elsewhere in China.

Within rural or urban areas of a given province, the gains from trade reform vary with observable household characteristics. The most vulnerable households tend to be in rural areas, dependent on agriculture, with relatively fewer workers and with weak economic links to the outside economy through migration. There are also some strong geographic concentrations of adverse impacts. For example, agricultural households in some counties incur welfare losses of 3–5 percent of their incomes.

Naturally, the approach taken here has limitations. For example, there may well be dynamic gains from greater trade openness that are not being captured by the model used to generate the relative price impacts. Trade may facilitate learning about new technologies and innovation, bringing longer term gains in productivity. Trade reform may also come with (and possibly help induce) other policy reforms, such as in factor markets. The approach here has attempted to capture only the static welfare effects of WTO accession.

A further limitation was the need to make linear approximations in the neighborhood of an initial optimum for each household. In other applications this could be deceptive if price or wage changes are large or if the household were initially out of equilibrium, due to rationing (including involuntary unemployment), for example. In principle, there are ways of dealing with these problems by estimating complete demand and supply systems that allow for rationing. This may prove a fruitful avenue for future research, though it should be noted that these methods generate their own problems, such as those arising from incomplete data on price and wage levels at household level.

Despite these limitations, the type of approach followed here can usefully illuminate the range of welfare impacts to be expected from economywide reforms. By avoiding unnecessary aggregation of the primary household-level data, these relatively simple tools can also offer insights into the sorts of policy responses that might be called for to compensate losers from reform.

Appendix

TABLE 15.A.1   Rural Gains and Losses by Province, 2001–07

Province	Number of Sampled Households	Number of Gainers	Original Income (Yuan)	Post-WTO Income (Yuan)	Gain or Loss (Yuan)	Change (Percent)	Share of Losers (Percent)
Beijing	750	381	4,221.05	4,210.08	−10.96	−0.26	49.20
Tianjin	595	219	3,401.71	3,380.48	−21.22	−0.62	63.19
Hebei	4,200	1,310	2,441.50	2,426.82	−14.68	−0.60	68.81
Shanxi	2,100	926	1,772.62	1,765.13	−7.49	−0.42	55.90
Inner Mongolia	2,198	206	2,055.49	2,011.26	−44.22	−2.15	90.63
Liaoning	1,886	353	2,501.98	2,469.64	−32.34	−1.29	81.28
Jilin	1,598	132	2,260.12	2,210.46	−49.66	−2.20	91.74
Heilongjiang	1,997	115	2,166.59	2,114.18	−52.41	−2.42	94.24
Shanghai	600	416	5,409.11	5,428.79	19.68	0.36	30.67
Jiangsu	3,400	1,209	3,495.20	3,486.78	−8.42	−0.24	64.44
Zhejiang	2,693	1,148	3,946.44	3,934.92	−11.52	−0.29	57.37
Anhui	3,095	676	1,900.76	1,885.79	−14.97	−0.79	78.16
Fujian	1,750	469	3,091.39	3,071.40	−19.99	−0.65	73.20
Jiangxi	2,450	553	2,129.45	2,117.26	−12.19	−0.57	77.43
Shandong	4,200	822	2,520.76	2,494.89	−25.87	−1.03	80.43
Henan	4,200	828	1,948.36	1,931.70	−16.66	−0.86	80.29
Hubei	3,188	755	2,212.71	2,200.04	−12.68	−0.57	76.32
Hunan	3,700	1,181	2,102.98	2,095.39	−7.60	−0.36	68.08
Guangdong	2,560	514	3,628.95	3,599.61	−29.34	−0.81	79.92
Guangxi	2,310	309	2,048.33	2,025.75	−22.58	−1.10	86.62
Hainan	718	28	2,086.40	2,057.85	−28.55	−1.37	96.10
Chongqing	1,500	404	1,736.63	1,730.20	−6.43	−0.37	73.07
Sichuan	3,998	879	1,843.23	1,830.92	−12.31	−0.67	78.01
Guizhou	2,240	417	1,363.07	1,354.03	−9.04	−0.66	81.38
Yunnan	2,397	399	1,438.34	1,421.34	−17.00	−1.18	83.35
Tibet	480	143	1,309.46	1,307.41	−2.05	−0.16	70.21
Shaanxi	2,217	446	1,456.48	1,442.09	−14.39	−0.99	79.88
Gansu	1,800	479	1,357.28	1,350.34	−6.95	−0.51	73.39
Qinghai	600	135	1,466.67	1,452.61	−14.06	−0.96	77.50
Ningxia	600	108	1,754.15	1,729.05	−25.11	−1.43	82.00
Xinjiang	1,495	312	1,471.11	1,447.57	−23.55	−1.60	79.13
Rural total	67,515	16,272	2,257.15	2,239.08	−18.07	−0.80	75.90

Source: Authors' computations based on data from Ianchovichina and Martin 2002 and China National Bureau of Statistics 1999 Rural Household Survey and 1999 Urban Household Survey.
The ordering of provinces is the traditional administrative ordering as used in (for example) NBS 2000.

TABLE 15.A.2   Urban Gains and Losses by Province, 2001–07

Province	Number of Sampled Households	Number of Gainers	Original Income (Yuan)	Post-WTO Income (Yuan)	Gain or Loss (Yuan)	Change (Percent)	Share of Losers (Percent)
Beijing	500	430	9,388.88	9,431.72	42.84	0.46	14.00
Tianjin	500	451	7,323.57	7,358.47	34.91	0.48	9.80
Hebei	650	591	5,673.46	5,702.35	28.89	0.51	9.08
Shanxi	650	598	4,519.20	4,549.94	30.74	0.68	8.00
Inner Mongolia	550	495	4,491.87	4,516.19	24.32	0.54	10.00
Liaoning	1000	916	5,257.42	5,285.65	28.23	0.54	8.40
Jilin	700	610	4,630.13	4,650.46	20.33	0.44	12.86
Heilongjiang	1000	887	4,798.92	4,820.50	21.58	0.45	11.30
Shanghai	500	458	10,927.18	10,984.16	56.98	0.52	8.40
Jiangsu	800	723	6,933.07	6,968.78	35.71	0.51	9.63
Zhejiang	550	498	9,044.40	9,098.28	53.87	0.60	9.45
Anhui	500	458	5,159.46	5,190.37	30.91	0.60	8.40
Fujian	550	516	7,521.52	7,569.70	48.18	0.64	6.18
Jiangxi	550	498	4,762.78	4,783.38	20.60	0.43	9.45
Shandong	650	602	5,689.90	5,720.69	30.78	0.54	7.38
Henan	600	565	4,689.43	4,717.89	28.46	0.61	5.83
Hubei	750	619	5,743.18	5,765.29	22.11	0.38	17.47
Hunan	700	612	5,727.42	5,750.43	23.00	0.40	12.57
Guangdong	600	490	10,871.06	10,903.85	32.79	0.30	18.33
Guangxi	600	496	6,011.10	6,033.40	22.30	0.37	17.33
Hainan	200	172	5,766.33	5,787.64	21.31	0.37	14.00
Chongqing	300	239	5,910.18	5,931.90	21.72	0.37	20.33
Sichuan	800	691	5,610.29	5,634.60	24.30	0.43	13.63
Guizhou	450	383	5,324.43	5,347.71	23.27	0.44	14.89
Yunnan	650	566	5,939.69	5,973.23	33.54	0.56	12.92
Tibet				n.a.			
Shaanxi	500	427	4,768.99	4,788.25	19.26	0.40	14.60
Gansu	400	372	4,610.86	4,641.27	30.41	0.66	7.00
Qinghai	250	240	3,759.53	3,788.65	29.12	0.77	4.00
Ningxia	200	177	4,472.43	4,493.27	20.84	0.47	11.50
Xinjiang	250	214	5,277.25	5,295.94	18.69	0.35	14.40
Urban total	16,900	14,994	6,046.13	6,075.60	29.45	0.49	11.28

Source: Authors' computations based on data from Ianchovichina and Martin 2002 and China National Bureau of Statistics 1999 Rural Household Survey and 1999 Urban Household Survey.
The ordering of provinces is the traditional administrative ordering as used in (for example) NBS 2000.

Notes

1. Jalan and Ravallion (1998) report evidence of such churning using panel data for rural China. Baulch and Hoddinott (2000) review evidence for a number of countries.

2. For China's lagging poor areas see Jalan and Ravallion (2002).

3. Examples of partial equilibrium analysis of the welfare distributional effects of price changes include King (1983), Deaton (1989), Ravallion and van de Walle (1991), and Friedman and Levinsohn (2002). On applications to tax policy reform, see Newbery and Stern (1987). On CGE models see Decaluwe and Martens (1988) and Hertel (1997). For a useful overview of alternative approaches to assessing the welfare impacts of trade policies and examples from the literature, see McCulloch, Winters, and Cirera (2001).

4. The only known example of this full integration is Cockburn (2002), who built a classic trade-focused CGE model onto the Nepal Living Standards Survey covering about 3,000 households.

5. In an antecedent to the approach taken here, Bourguignon, Robilliard, and Robinson (2003) also take price changes generated by a CGE model to survey data (for Indonesia). Methodologically, the main difference is that Bourguignon, Robilliard,

and Robinson generate income impacts at the household level from a microeconometric model of income determination, whereas this study derives first-order welfare impacts analytically from a standard competitive farm-household model.

6. Hertel (1997) contains descriptions of the standard GTAP model with applications.

7. A full discussion of the assumptions of the general equilibrium model and the results of its application to China's accession to the WTO can be found in Ianchovichina and Martin (2002).

8. For food items, unit values can be calculated (expenditure divided by quantity) from the survey data, but there is no such option for food inputs to production, nonfood commodities consumed or used in production, or wages (the survey data do not include labor supplies or quantities consumed of nonfood goods, including production inputs).

9. Examples of this approach can be found in King (1983) and Ravallion and van de Walle (1991).

10. The full sample of the urban survey was about 40,000 households, but until 2002 the central NBS office kept individual record data for only 16,900 households.

11. For further discussion in the context of the Rural Household Survey, see Chen and Ravallion (1996).

12. By the International Labor Organization's definitions, *skilled labor* consists of managers and administrators, professionals, and para-professionals, while *unskilled labor* consists of tradespeople, clerks, salespeople and personal service workers, plant and machine operators and drivers, laborers, and related workers and farm workers.

References

The word *processed* describes informally reproduced works that may not be commonly available through libraries.

Barro, Robert. 2000. "Inequality and Growth in a Panel of Countries." *Journal of Economic Growth* 5: 5–32.

Baulch, Bob, and John Hoddinott. 2000. "Economic Mobility and Poverty Dynamics in Developing Countries." *Journal of Development Studies* 36(6): 1–24.

Bourguignon, Francois, and C. Morisson. 1990. "Income Distribution, Development and Foreign Trade." *European Economic Review* 34: 1113–32.

Bourguignon, Francois, Anne-Sophie Robilliard, and Sherman Robinson. 2003. "Representative versus Real Households in the Macro-Economic Modeling of Inequality." Working Paper 2003-05. DELTA, Paris.

Chen, Shaohua, and Martin Ravallion. 1996. "Data in Transition: Assessing Rural Living Standards in Southern China." *China Economic Review* 7: 23–56.

———. 2001. "How Did the World's Poor Fare in the 1990s?" *Review of Income and Wealth* 47(3): 283–300.

———. 2003. "Household Welfare Impacts of China's Accession to the World Trade Organization," Policy Research Working Paper 3040, World Bank, Washington, D.C.

Cockburn, John. 2002. "Trade Liberalization and Poverty in Nepal: A Computable General Equilibrium Micro Simulation Analysis." Processed. Quebec: University of Laval.

Deaton, Angus. 1989. "Rice Prices and Income Distribution in Thailand: A Non-Parametric Analysis." *Economic Journal* 99: 1–37.

Decaluwe, B., and A. Martens. 1988. "CGE Modeling and Developing Economies: A Concise Empirical Survey of 73 Applications to 26 Countries." *Journal of Policy Modeling* 10(4): 529–68.

Dollar, David, and Aart Kraay. 2002. "Growth is Good for the Poor." *Journal of Economic Growth* 7(3): 195–225.

Edwards, Sebastian. 1997. "Trade Policy, Growth and Income Distribution." *American Economic Review* 87(2): 205–10.

Friedman, Jed, and James Levinsohn. 2002. "The Distributional Impacts of Indonesia's Financial Crisis on Household Welfare: A 'Rapid Response' Methodology." *World Bank Economic Review* 16(3): 397–424.

Hertel, T., ed. 1997. *Global Trade Analysis: Modeling and Applications.* Cambridge: Cambridge University Press. [www.gtap. org.]

Ianchovichina, Elena, and Will Martin. 2002. "Economic Impacts of China's Accession to the WTO." Development Research Group, World Bank, Washington, D.C.

Jalan, Jyotsna, and Martin Ravallion. 1998. "Transient Poverty in Post-Reform Rural China." *Journal of Comparative Economics* 26: 338–57.

———. 2002. "Geographic Poverty Traps? A Micro Model of Consumption Growth in Rural China." *Journal of Applied Econometrics* 17(4): 329–46.

King, Mervyn A. 1983. "Welfare Analysis of Tax Reforms Using Household Level Data." *Journal of Public Economics* 21: 183–214.

Lundberg, Mattias, and Lyn Squire. 2003. "The Simultaneous Evolution of Growth and Inequality." *Economic Journal* 113: 326–44.

McCulloch, Neil, L. Alan Winters, and Xavier Cirera. 2001. *Trade Liberalization and Poverty: A Handbook.* London: Center for Economic Policy Research and Department for International Development.

NBS (National Bureau of Statistics). 2000. *China Statistical Yearbook.* Beijing: China Statistics Press.

Newbery, David, and Nicholas Stern, eds., 1987. *The Theory of Taxation for Developing Countries.* Oxford: Oxford University Press.

Ravallion, Martin. 1990. "Rural Welfare Effects of Food Price Changes with Induced Wage Responses: Theory and Evidence for Bangladesh." *Oxford Economic Papers* 42: 574–85.

———. 2001. "Growth, Inequality and Poverty: Looking Beyond Averages." *World Development* 29(11): 1803–15.

Ravallion, Martin, and Dominique van de Walle. 1991. "The Impact of Food Pricing Reforms on Poverty: A Demand Consistent Welfare Analysis for Indonesia." *Journal of Policy Modeling* 13: 281–300.

16

IMPLICATIONS OF WTO ACCESSION FOR POVERTY IN CHINA

Thomas W. Hertel, Fan Zhai, and Zhi Wang

After a decade and half of negotiations, the World Trade Organization (WTO) successfully concluded negotiations on China's terms of entry to the WTO at the end of 2001. China's accession is expected to lend a further boost to trade and foreign investment. China's foreign trade quadrupled from 1990 to 2000—growing much faster than world trade, which only increased 87 percent during the same period. By the year 2001, the volume of China's merchandise exports and imports had reached US$262 billion[1] and US$244 billion, respectively, ranking it sixth in world trade. China is also the largest recipient of foreign direct investment (FDI) among developing countries; over US$320 billion flowed into its economy during the last decade. Most studies predict that WTO accession will bring with it added benefits, both for China as well as for most of its trading partners (Ianchovichina, McDougall, and Hertel 1999; McKibbin and Tang, 2000; Wang 2001).

At the sectoral level, however, the effects of accession are likely to be quite different across economies. China's trade surplus in apparel products is expected to increase even more with elimination of the Multi-Fiber Arrangement (MFA) quotas under the Uruguay Round's Agreement on Textiles and Clothing, or ATC (Development Research Center 1998; Wang 1999; Walmsley and Hertel 2000). By contrast, the automobile sector is

likely to face substantial adjustments, because tariffs remain high and the scale of production is far below international standards to date (François, 2002). In addition, the imports of land-intensive agricultural products, including corn and soybeans, are expected to surge under the accession agreement. The services sector is also expected to face substantial expansion and restructuring. Such a broad structural adjustment is likely to have an effect on the distribution of income in China, potentially depressing rural incomes in some areas relative to urban incomes. Similarly, it is anticipated that coastal regions might benefit at the expense of the interior. Yet the rural–urban, interior–coastal income disparities in China are already at record levels (Yang and Zhou 1999).

Kanbur and Zhang (2001) track regional inequality over the past 50 years and find that there are three peaks over this five-decade period: the Great Famine of the 1950s, the Cultural Revolution of the late 1960s and early 1970s, and the period of openness and global integration of the 1990s. They also find that the interior–coastal disparities have especially contributed to the recent growth in inequality as the Chinese economy has opened up. Chen and Wang (2001) attempt to discern the separate impacts of growth and inequality on poverty in China since 1990. They find that the increase in inequality has contributed to greater poverty over the past decade. However, the beneficial impact of overall economic growth has dominated, and the absolute number of people in poverty (by several different measures) has been reduced.

For China's WTO accession, the same two forces are at work. On the one hand, further trade liberalization will accelerate the country's integration into the world economy and enhance economic efficiency (Yang and Huang 1997; Wang and Zhai 1998). On the other hand, the experience of the last decade suggests that such liberalization might also increase inequality (Kanbur and Zhang 2001). The goal of this chapter is to shed more light on this empirical question. Our approach is model-based. We use an applied general equilibrium model designed to capture the differential effects of accession on each of China's economic sectors. Special attention is paid to the disaggregation of households in order to permit us to say something about the likely impacts of accession on income distribution. In addition, we pay quite a bit of attention to the modeling of China's rural labor markets, which we see as the primary vehicle for poverty reduction in the wake of WTO accession.

This chapter is organized as follows. The next section provides an empirical overview of the Chinese economy—with a special emphasis on trade and poverty. This overview sets the stage for the computable general equilibrium (CGE) model described in the section that follows. We then turn to a discussion of the baseline scenario, against which China's accession will be evaluated, along with a description of the accession scenario itself. The next section uses simulation results to assess the impact of China's WTO accession on poverty, and the final section offers some conclusions and suggestions for future research.

Overview of the Chinese Economy, Poverty, and Trade

This section provides an overview of the Chinese economy. We start by looking at some stylized facts of household income and poverty and examining patterns of production and trade.

Households and Poverty

To facilitate analysis of the impacts of WTO accession on poverty, we obtained from China's National Bureau of Statistics aggregations for 2000 of the rural and urban household surveys for three provinces: Guangdong, Sichuan, and Liaoning. Together, these provinces are fairly representative of the diversity within China as a whole. Guangdong represents the relatively wealthy coastal region, which is heavily export-oriented; Sichuan represents the populous, relatively poor inland region in which agriculture plays a more important role in the economy; and Liaoning has a typical "old industrial base," which is heavily urban and highly dependent on state-owned enterprises. The latter are mainly concentrated in highly protected, heavy industrial sectors.

Within these surveys, we have aggregated households into several groups or "strata," according to their primary source of income. Recent analysis of trade and poverty by Hertel and others (2004) suggests the merit of distinguishing those households that are specialized—that is, they receive 95 percent or more of their income from one source: transfer payments, labor wages and salaries, or self-employment income. Because of the limited number of specialized, nonfarm households in the survey, as well as the absence of transfer- and labor-specialized households in the rural surveys, we end up with two strata in the rural survey—agriculture-specialized and diversified (all other)—and three strata in the urban survey—transfer-specialized, labor-specialized, and diversified. Within each stratum, we order households from poorest to richest, based on per capita income, and then group them into 20 vingtiles, each containing 5 percent of the stratum population. We then aggregate the three rural surveys, and the three urban surveys, before incorporating them into the national social accounting matrix. In this way, we obtain a disaggregated representation of households in the national model, wherein the earnings and spending profiles reflect the diversity obtained from the three provincial surveys.

Table 16.1 reports per capita income by stratum, location, and vingtile for the 100 representative households in the model. Using the $1/day level of poverty, Chen and Wang (2001) estimate that 24.9 percent of the rural population in China and 0.5 percent of the urban population are in poverty. Using these figures as a guide, in table 16.1 we place the rural poverty line in the fifth vingtile of the rural population and the urban poverty line in first vingtile of the urban population. The

TABLE 16.1 Per Capita Income by Location, Stratum, and Vingtile (1997 yuan)

Vingtile (Poorest = 1)	Rural Households			Urban Households			
	Agric.	Diverse	Total	Transfer	Labor	Diverse	Total
1	845	889	874	2,903	2,135	2,454	2,351
2	1,049	998	1,006	3,995	3,151	3,054	3,212
3	1,156	1,162	1,161	4,674	3,790	3,703	3,827
4	1,303	1,301	1,301	5,273	3,987	4,250	4,216
5	1,433	1,432	1,432	5,595	4,513	4,452	4,608
6	1,755	1,551	1,568	6,280	4,763	4,528	4,769
7	1,675	1,679	1,678	6,594	5,237	4,884	5,155
8	1,822	1,811	1,812	7,794	5,692	5,370	5,588
9	1,947	1,944	1,944	8,643	6,096	5,786	6,045
10	2,099	2,095	2,096	8,142	6,694	6,334	6,564
11	2,240	2,252	2,251	8,220	6,866	6,482	6,718
12	2,415	2,411	2,411	8,946	7,420	6,901	7,192
13	2,602	2,595	2,595	10,807	7,686	7,532	7,671
14	2,835	2,818	2,819	12,973	8,432	7,974	8,303
15	3,031	3,069	3,066	10,601	9,120	8,526	8,799
16	3,344	3,353	3,352	12,925	9,709	8,727	9,130
17	3,708	3,717	3,717	—	11,152	9,659	10,240
18	4,306	4,258	4,261	18,821	12,749	10,985	11,796
19	5,171	5,162	5,163	15,190	15,134	13,403	14,125
20	9,712	8,345	8,485	—	21,997	19,659	20,522
Share of population (%)	7.35	62.73	70.08	1.44	12.01	16.47	29.92

Not available.
Source: National Bureau of Statistics Rural and Urban Household Surveys 2000.

average income in each vingtile is much higher for the urban population, and even after adjusting for differences in cost of living, a far greater percentage of the rural population falls below the poverty line.

This preliminary analysis reveals that any policy that depresses incomes in agriculture is very likely to lead to a short-run increase in poverty. If opportunities arise elsewhere in the rural economy, however, it is possible that, after suitable adjustment, many of these rural households could be made better off. Such an adjustment will likely be most difficult for those households that currently do not participate in the nonfarm economy, either as workers or in a self-employed capacity. A critical determinant of farm households' ability to participate in the nonfarm economy will be their level of educational attainment. In general, the higher-income vingtiles in both rural and urban areas have a higher level of educational attainment. Within the

rural population, the average educational attainment of agriculture-specified households is lower than that of other households. There is also a significant gap in educational attainment between rural and urban households. Thus the most vulnerable farm households are likely to be those that are trapped in agricultural activity by virtue of their lack of education.

The impact of WTO accession on rural nonfarm households and especially urban households depends importantly on what happens to the manufacturing and services sectors. Here, we expect a mixed outcome, with profitability and employment in light manufactures rising, but the heavy industry and automobile sectors will be adversely affected. Households dependent on transfer payments are also potentially vulnerable after WTO accession, because reduced tariffs may bring additional pressure to bear on state-run enterprises and on government spending—and thus transfer payments.

Finally, by virtue of the way they have been defined, diversified households are likely to be little affected by trade liberalization. Decreases in one source of income will tend to be offset by increases elsewhere.

The fate of the labor-specialized households will depend on what happens to wages after accession. If educational attainment is used as a proxy for skill level, then the poor are most heavily reliant on unskilled labor. Therefore, from a poverty perspective, the key factor for labor-specialized households is what happens to wages for the unskilled after WTO accession. What are the likely factor market effects of China's WTO accession? These effects will depend on the pattern of production, trade, and protection in China, or the subject to which we next turn.

China's Production, Trade, and Protection

Having provided an overview of the Chinese economy from the household perspective, we now offer a perspective from the production point of view. table 16.2 has been assembled using the 1997 Chinese social accounting matrix developed by the Development Research Center (DRC) at the State Council. We used the most recent input–output table. One of the most striking points about table 16.2 is the very high share of employment in agriculture. This sector accounted for more than 55 percent of total employment in the Chinese economy in 1997, yet its contribution to economy-wide value-added (first column) is only about 22 percent. This finding is consistent with the low income levels observed in table 16.1 for agriculture-specialized households. Because this sector also relies almost entirely on unskilled labor, a reduction in the size of this sector will likely release additional unskilled labor into the rural—and possibly urban—labor markets, thereby depressing wages.

Table 16.2 also reveals a relatively underdeveloped services sector. For example, when compared with the 65 other regions in the Global Trade Analysis Project (GTAP) Version 5 database (Dimaranan and McDougall 2002), China ranks last in the share of economy-wide value-added generated in the services sector, and this share is scarcely half the world average: 37 percent versus 72 percent. The share of services in total employment in China is even smaller, amounting to less than 27 percent in 1997. This finding indicates the potential that may be realized by means of WTO accession as the rules governing foreign investment in the services sector are liberalized. In contrast to services, manufacturing's share of value-added is quite substantial—33 percent versus a global average of 19 percent based on GTAP data—placing China second, behind Thailand. Textiles, building materials, and chemicals lead the way, followed by sectors related to metals, machinery, electronics, and associated products.

An important factor in the growth of manufacturing activity in the past decade has been the rapid expansion of exports. Textiles, apparel, and leather products now account for more than one-quarter of total Chinese exports, and electronics account for another 11.5 percent. The export dependency of these sectors, as well as for crafts and toys and instruments, is high, with more than 30 percent of their output directed to foreign markets. (Textiles are important intermediate inputs, and so the export dependency ratio is somewhat less—about 18 percent.) Much of this export growth has been fueled by the export processing or export promotion regime introduced in 1986 (Naughton 1996). The enterprises operated under this regime have attracted a great deal of foreign investment as a result of special preferences—most important, the exemption from the tariffs on imported intermediate inputs to be used in the production of exports.

By 1997 the export processing regime had grown to account for 50 percent of China's total exports and 46 percent of its total imports. Nearly 80 percent of China's primary iron and steel, electric machinery, electronics, and instrument exports, and more than two-thirds of its leather, toys, and chemical fiber exports were "processing exports"—that is, assembling or transformation of imported intermediate goods and re-export. Export processing also constitutes a significant portion of China's exports of apparel, paper, and printing products. The high shares of processing exports in these sectors require a large volume of raw materials, components, and semi-processed products imported from abroad. Column 8 in table 16.2 shows that in textiles, apparel, and leather, ordinary imports constituted only 1–2 percent of total imports in 1997, and so almost all imports were used for the production of processing exports. Most imports of paper products, building materials, chemicals, basic metal and metal products, machinery, and electronics were also

TABLE 16.2 Economic Structure and Market Openness in China, 1997

	(1) Value-Added (%)	(2) Employment (%)	(3) Imports (%)	(4) Exports (%)	(5) Ordinary Imports/ Domestic Use (%)	(6) Total Exports/ Outputs (%)	(7) Ordinary Exports/ Total Exports (%)	(8) Ordinary Imports/ Total Imports (%)	(9) Net Exports (Billions of Yuan)	(10) Nominal Tariff Rate (%)	(11) Collected Tariff Rate (%)	(12) Collected As Nominal Percent (%)	(13) Post-accession Tariff Rate (%)
Rice	2.32	7.5	0.2	0.1	0.88	0.9	100	92	0.0	1.0	0.4	40.0	0.5
Wheat	1.27	4.1	0.9	0.0	6.93	0.0	—	78	−11.3	1.0	0.2	20.0	0.2
Corn	0.82	2.6	0.1	0.4	0.32	7.9	100	21	6.3	1.0	0.0	0.0	0.0
Cotton	0.62	2.0	0.6	0.0	2.96	0.0	100	17	−7.7	3.5	0.6	17.1	1.0
Other nongrain crops	7.35	23.8	0.5	1.1	0.22	2.3	100	25	12.8	5.7	5.7	100.0	4.1
Forestry	0.90	2.0	0.5	0.2	3.81	3.6	96	33	−2.6	28.6	8.3	29.0	11.5
Wool	0.03	0.0	0.3	0.0	29.65	8.9	100	6	−3.8	15.0	0.7	4.7	1.0
Other livestock	5.60	8.2	0.1	0.4	0.07	0.9	97	47	6.8	5.0	2.1	42.0	3.4
Fishing	2.07	3.2	0.0	0.2	0.19	1.2	92	77	2.5	0.8	0.5	62.5	0.2
Other agriculture	0.95	2.2	0.0	0.1	0.00	1.2	88	12	1.5	16.0	1.7	10.6	9.6
Coal mining	1.68	1.2	0.1	0.6	0.26	3.1	100	63	8.6	6.0	3.3	55.0	5.3
Crude oil and natural gas	1.67	0.2	3.6	1.5	19.07	14.4	100	71	−20.6	1.5	1.0	66.7	0.0
Ferrous ore mining	0.14	0.1	1.1	0.0	16.31	0.0	100	43	−14.4	0.0	0.0	—	0.0
Nonferrous ore mining	0.42	0.2	0.5	0.1	3.06	1.1	92	37	−4.9	0.0	0.0	—	0.0
Other mining	1.00	0.8	0.8	0.6	2.94	4.3	79	36	−0.5	2.9	0.9	31.0	1.2
Vegetable oil	0.28	0.1	1.2	0.3	8.41	4.3	19	46	−10.3	17.0	5.3	31.2	9.0
Grain mill and forage	0.78	0.2	1.1	0.3	4.08	1.6	76	94	−7.9	4.7	4.4	93.6	1.9
Sugar	0.05	0.1	0.2	0.1	3.07	3.3	12	36	−0.8	30.0	9.5	31.7	15.0
Processed food	1.72	0.6	1.0	3.3	0.74	9.7	72	18	42.4	23.2	3.7	15.9	10.4
Beverages	0.76	0.3	0.1	0.5	0.32	3.1	84	45	7.5	60.2	24.0	39.9	13.7
Tobacco	0.28	0.1	0.2	0.3	1.43	3.2	96	24	3.3	49.1	10.6	21.6	11.0
Textiles	3.25	1.5	6.8	11.4	0.41	18.4	60	1	104.5	27.5	0.2	0.7	9.9
Apparel	1.88	0.6	0.7	9.9	0.17	37.0	45	2	156.2	41.8	0.7	1.7	14.3
Leather	0.64	0.3	1.8	5.0	0.35	32.6	29	1	61.4	35.5	0.3	0.8	9.1
Sawmills and furniture	0.80	0.4	0.9	2.1	2.47	13.1	61	20	22.8	14.4	2.5	17.4	3.7
Paper and printing	1.45	0.6	2.9	0.5	4.88	2.0	35	33	−29.2	11.0	3.1	28.2	2.5
Crafts and toys	0.88	0.3	1.0	6.0	3.86	40.0	32	28	87.6	3.1	1.0	32.3	0.8
Petroleum refining	0.61	0.2	3.1	1.2	11.08	5.7	69	62	−19.6	8.7	4.8	55.2	5.1
Chemicals	2.52	1.0	11.8	4.2	8.48	8.3	80	31	−77.8	10.8	3.0	27.8	4.7
Pharmaceuticals	0.74	0.2	0.2	0.7	1.53	5.9	84	75	8.5	10.9	7.2	66.1	4.0
Chemical fibers	0.33	0.1	2.1	0.5	5.78	6.6	31	7	−17.4	15.5	1.0	6.5	3.8

TABLE 16.2 (Continued)

	(1) Value-Added (%)	(2) Employment (%)	(3) Imports (%)	(4) Exports (%)	(5) Ordinary Imports/ Domestic Use (%)	(6) Total Exports/ Outputs (%)	(7) Ordinary Exports/ Total Exports (%)	(8) Ordinary Imports/ Total Imports (%)	(9) Net Exports (Billions of Yuan)	(10) Nominal Tariff Rate (%)	(11) Collected Tariff Rate (%)	(12) Collected as Nominal Percent (%)	(13) Post-accession Tariff Rate (%)
Rubber and plastics	1.24	0.6	2.1	4.2	1.49	15.7	28	12	42.8	19.8	2.0	10.1	7.2
Building materials	3.54	2.1	0.8	2.1	0.60	3.4	82	20	23.9	20.8	3.6	17.3	9.3
Primary iron and steel	1.36	0.7	3.8	1.8	4.12	5.5	21	28	-17.5	8.1	2.0	24.7	4.2
Nonferrous metals	0.49	0.3	2.6	1.2	6.63	8.0	56	14	-13.1	7.1	0.9	12.7	2.9
Metal products	1.48	0.7	2.6	4.1	4.36	13.1	57	20	36.4	13.1	2.4	18.3	5.6
Machinery	2.36	1.0	5.6	1.8	11.16	5.9	61	35	-41.0	13.7	4.2	30.7	6.2
Special equipment	1.31	0.6	8.0	1.1	23.65	5.6	63	21	-82.9	14.1	2.6	18.4	5.0
Automobiles	1.09	0.4	1.1	0.4	4.11	1.9	63	73	-7.6	50.7	32.6	64.3	11.2
Other transport equipment	0.96	0.4	2.6	1.6	9.43	9.7	24	28	-5.8	5.6	1.3	23.2	3.3
Electric machinery	1.56	0.6	4.0	5.5	4.69	15.9	21	20	42.2	17.9	3.1	17.3	6.7
Electronics	1.63	0.4	13.2	11.5	13.27	36.3	9	20	25.2	11.8	2.1	17.8	1.6
Instruments	0.36	0.2	2.7	2.7	24.51	49.5	15	20	12.3	12.5	2.3	18.4	4.0
Other manufacturing	1.33	0.6	0.4	0.9	0.16	8.1	29	3	9.6	38.9	0.9	2.3	12.0
Utilities	2.45	0.5	0.0	0.2	0.00	0.9	100	—	3.8	0.0	0.0	—	0.0
Construction	7.03	5.8	0.4	0.1	0.28	0.1	100	100	-2.6	0.0	0.0	—	0.0
Transportation	3.91	3.1	0.7	2.8	1.83	9.4	100	100	38.9	0.0	0.0	—	0.0
Post and communication	1.61	0.3	0.2	0.7	1.27	5.7	100	100	8.7	0.0	0.1	—	0.1
Commercial services	7.47	9.0	1.2	0.7	1.31	0.9	100	100	-4.2	0.0	0.0	—	0.0
Finance	2.09	0.5	0.4	0.1	1.22	0.5	100	100	-2.7	0.0	0.0	—	0.0
Social services	5.17	1.6	2.9	4.5	5.17	10.1	100	100	38.8	0.0	0.0	—	0.0
Education and health	4.69	4.0	0.2	0.3	0.44	0.7	100	100	1.7	0.0	1.7	—	1.7
Public administration	3.06	1.8	0.2	0.0	0.45	0.1	100	100	-1.5	0.0	0.0	—	0.0
Total/average	100	100	100	100	3.59	7.7	51	32	409.5	11.2	2.7	22.3	4.0

— Not available.

Notes: Ordinary imports/domestic use and total exports/output are at domestic price. The sectoral share of imports and exports are at world price. The imports of rice, wheat, corn, cotton, grain mill and forage, and vegetable oil are the average of 1993–97.

The tariff rates are calculated based on the weight of ordinary imports for 1997 at the eight-digit level of the harmonized system. The average tariff rate is for merchandise only.

Source: Chinese social accounting matrix, 1997, Development Research Center, State Council.

used by foreign or joint venture companies as intermediate inputs to produce processing exports.

The dominance of duty-exempt imports is also evident when one compares the nominal tariff rate with the collected rate reported in table 16.2 (smuggling also plays a role here). The nominal tariff for textile products is 27.5 percent, but the collected tariff averages 0.2 percent. Similarly, dramatic differences appear in the apparel and leather sectors as well as many of the other export-oriented activities. The lowest nominal/actual ratios appear in the pharmaceutical and automobile industries where the nominal rate is only about twice as large as the actual rate. These sectors have relatively low export/output ratios.

Table 16.2 also reports the ratio of ordinary imports to domestic use (column 5) as an indication of overall import dependency. The sectors with the largest dependency on ordinary imports are energy and mining, machinery, special equipment, and electronics, all of which show import shares in excess of 10 percent of China's domestic use of these commodities.

An overall picture of China's trade is offered by the sector-specific net exports also reported in table 16.2 (value of exports minus value of imports in billions of yuan). By and large, these exports reflect China's comparative advantage. China is a net exporter of unskilled labor-intensive manufactures and a net importer of skilled labor and capital-intensive manufactures. The largest share of the trade surplus in China is attributable to apparel and textiles. Within the agricultural sector, China is a net importer of grains, but it has a trade surplus in other agricultural products.

China's nominal tariff structure is typical of that of many developing countries in that it provides high protection for the manufacturing sector, especially capital-intensive manufactures and final consumption goods. Automobile imports face one of the highest nominal tariff rates (50 percent), and the actual collection rate is also quite high (33 percent). The tariff rates in other manufactures and in the textile and apparel sector are also relatively high, but their effects are limited because the share of duty-paying imports (ordinary imports) is very small.

The final column in table 16.2 reports China's postaccession tariff rates, by sector. The trade-weighted tariff rate will drop by more than 60 percent

in the six years after China's WTO accession. The sectoral distribution of tariff cuts is relatively even. For most sectors, the tariff cuts range from 50 percent to 80 percent. Some light manufacturing sectors and capital goods sectors that historically have been highly protected—such as beverages, tobacco, automobiles, and electronics—will experience substantial tariff cuts. The dominant role played by the export processing sector will be very important in determining the impact of these tariff cuts. In sectors such as textiles, where virtually all imports come in under the export processing provisions, the impact of further tariff cuts on the cost of intermediate inputs will be negligible. The importation of consumer goods, as well as imported intermediates for domestic use, also will be affected by the WTO accession tariff cuts.

To the extent that accession leads to a decline in agricultural, relative to nonagricultural, profitability, we expect to see a rise in rural poverty and increased pressure on the rural population to migrate to urban areas. However, a definitive answer to the question posed by this chapter—Will China's accession to the WTO increase poverty—and if so, among which groups?—requires use of a formal model. We therefore turn next to a summary of the single-country general equilibrium model used in this paper.

Description of the Model

The CGE model of China used in this study is the latest in a long line of models developed and maintained by the Development Research Center of the State Council in Beijing. Earlier versions have been used to analyze the economy-wide implications of China's accession to the WTO (Development Research Center 1998), the consequences that accession might have for urban unemployment (Zhai and Wang 2002), and the income distribution consequences of trade and tax reform (Wang and Zhai 1998). The CGE model has its intellectual roots in the group of single-country, applied general equilibrium models used over the past two decades to analyze the impacts of trade policy reforms (Dervis, de Melo, and Robinson 1982; de Melo 1988; Shoven and Whalley 1992; de Melo and Tarr 1992). The China model began as a prototype CGE model developed for the Trade and Environment Program of the Organisation for Economic

Co-operation and Development (OECD) Development Center (Beghin and others 1994). Since that time, however, significant modifications have been made to capture the major features of the trading and tax system of the Chinese economy (Wang and Zhai 1998; Zhai and Li 2000), to add a full-fledged demographic module (Zhai and Wang 2002), and to introduce disaggregated households and an improved treatment of labor markets (this study). Here, we focus on the main features of the model, especially those relevant for assessing the consequences of China's WTO accession for poverty.

Modeling Household Behavior

To come to grips with the poverty question, it is critical that we disaggregate households to the maximum extent possible, subject to the limitations posed by survey sampling, computational constraints, and human capacity for analysis. It is particularly important to disaggregate households along those dimensions most likely to be affected by WTO accession. Thus, for example, one would not want to group together rural and urban households, or agriculture-and-nonagriculture specialized households. Otherwise, one would be introducing artificial diversification, thereby blurring the possible consequences of WTO accession. Accordingly, we have used the grouping of households in table 16.1: 20 vingtiles × 2 rural and 3 urban strata = 40 rural and 60 urban representative households. A total of 100 household groups are therefore used in the model.

Each household is endowed with three types of labor: unskilled, semiskilled, and skilled. These three types are distinguished by educational attainment:[2] unskilled workers are illiterate or semi-literate, semiskilled workers have a middle or high school education, and skilled workers have schooling beyond high school.[3] Households are also endowed with profits from family-owned agricultural and nonagricultural enterprises, property income, and transfers. Agricultural profits represent returns to family labor, land, and capital. However, because the land market is not well developed in China, the returns to land are effectively part of the return to family labor (Yang 1997). If a household migrates from the rural area and ceases to farm its land, the land cannot be sold or rented; Rather, it reverts to the state.

Households consume goods and services according to a preference structure determined by the extended linear expenditure system. Through specification of a subsistence quantity of each good or service, this expenditure function generates non-homothetic demands, whereby the larger the relative importance of subsistence consumption (e.g., importance would be high for rice and low for automobiles), the more income-inelastic is the household's demand for that good.

The other important dimension of household behavior is the supply of labor to off-farm activities. Whereas in developed economies this supply is typically modeled as a function of the relative wages in the farm and nonfarm sectors, in China the off-farm labor supply decision is complicated by institutional factors that have been built into the system to keep the agricultural population in place (Zhao 1999b). For example, the Chinese government has sought to make it costly for people to leave rural areas by tying incomes to daily participation in collective work. More recently, the absence of well-defined land tenure has raised the opportunity cost of leaving the farm. Because households that cease to farm their land may lose their rights to it, they have a strong incentive to continue some level of agricultural activity, even when profitability is quite low (Zhao 1999a). Low-skill farm households are prevented from moving to urban areas through denial of *hukou* (household registration), a government measure discussed in more detail later in this chapter. Because the growth in rural, nonfarm activities has been only modest, the factors just described seriously limit the ability of households to obtain off-farm work (Zhao 1999b).[4]

Our approach to modeling the off-farm labor supply is to capitalize on the econometric work of Sicular and Zhao (2002). They report results from a household labor supply model estimated using labor survey data from the 1997 Chinese Health and Nutrition Survey (CHNS) of nine central provinces. This survey measures the labor supplied by members of each household to farm and nonfarm activities. Sicular and Zhao estimate the implicit (shadow) wage for each individual in the sample if he or she were to work in agriculture or nonagricultural self-employment, and they also estimate the nonagriculture wage that this person could obtain. They then estimate labor supply equations for self-employed agricultural labor, self-employed nonagricultural labor, and wage labor. From these equations, it is possible to calculate elasticities of labor transfer between the farm and nonfarm sectors.

Because of the variety of labor supply elasticities produced in response to the three different wages, the authors obtain a variety of labor transfer elasticities, depending on the "thought experiment" being conducted. These labor transfer elasticities are asymmetric in their framework. For example, the responsiveness of labor transfers from agriculture to market wage employment based on a decline in the shadow wage of labor in agriculture is 2.67, whereas the elasticity of labor transfers in response to an increase in the market wage is only 0.6. Yet this response is symmetric in our model, for which only relative prices matter, and so it is difficult to choose the correct parameter for our analysis. For our base case, we adopt the "push" elasticity of labor transfer (2.67) (called here the high labor transfer elasticity). However, for purposes of sensitivity analysis we also report results from a simulation in which the "pull" elasticity of 0.6 is used (called here the low labor transfer elasticity).

Modeling Household Migration

Despite the large income and poverty differential between rural and urban households, China has limited permanent migration through a combination of direct and indirect measures. First and foremost, households must have an appropriate registration (*hukou*) to reside legally in an urban area. Without this registration, access to many of the urban amenities, including housing and education, is limited and quite expensive. Although highly skilled persons and investors can purchase a "blue stamp *hukou*" (Chan and Zhang 1999), this avenue is not available to the vast majority of rural residents. Because of these barriers to moving an entire household to an urban area, rural–urban migration is largely a transitory phenomenon— and one that is occurring on a massive scale. By most estimates, the number of "floating workers" (excluding commuters) exceeds 50 million, or about 10 percent of China's rural labor force. If commuters and mobile self-employed individuals are included, the figure doubles to about 100 million (Rozelle and others 1999).

For our modeling exercise, it is important to obtain an estimate of the wage gap motivating the temporary migration of workers between the rural and urban sectors in China. Zhao (1999a) documents an average annual wage gap between rural and urban work of 2,387.6 yuan for unskilled rural workers of comparable background and ability in Sichuan Province in 1995. Much of the wage gap stems from the social costs associated with migration, including the disutility of being away from family, poor quality of housing, limited social services for migrants, the danger of being robbed en route to and from the work location, and the general uncertainty associated with being a nonregistered worker in an urban area (Zhao 1999a, 1999b). Although these transaction costs are not observable, they clearly represent a very significant burden on the migrants and their families.

If there were no barriers to the movement of labor between rural and urban areas, we would expect real wages to be equalized for an individual worker with given characteristics. Shi, Sicular, and Zhao (2002) explore the question of rural–urban inequality in greater detail for nine different provinces using the CHNS. The authors conclude that the apparent labor market distortion is about 42 percent of the rural–urban labor income differential and 48 percent of the hourly earnings differential.[5] When applied to the average wage differential, this distortion amounts to an ad valorem "tax" on rural wages of 81 percent.[6]

We model these transaction costs as real costs that are assumed by the temporary migrants, recognizing that these migrants are heterogeneous and that the extent of the burden varies widely. Those migrants who are single and live close to the urban area in which they are working are likely to experience minor inconvenience as a result of this temporary migration. We expect them to be the first to migrate, other things being equal, in response to higher urban wages. As for migrants who have large families and come from a great distance, their urban living conditions are often very poor, and it is not uncommon for them to be robbed on the train when they are returning home from work. For such people, the decision to migrate temporarily is likely to be a marginal one—and one that they may not choose to repeat. With this heterogeneous population in mind, we postulate a transaction cost function that is increasing in the proportion of the rural population engaged in temporary work. This transaction cost function has a simple, constant elasticity functional form, which begins at the origin and reaches the observed wage gap (adjusted for transport and living costs) at the current level of temporary migration (about 70 million workers). We assume that further increases in temporary migration have only a modest impact on these transaction costs.[7]

In our subsequent analysis, these transaction costs associated with temporary migration will play an important role in the unskilled and semiskilled labor market. To the extent that WTO accession increases the demand for unskilled labor in urban areas, urban wages will rise and more rural labor will be drawn in. However, this supply of rural labor will come at some cost—both in terms of higher transport and living costs for the worker, as well as indirect transaction costs—because the additional workers are presumably being drawn from a greater distance or from less favorable family or social circumstances.

Modeling Production, Exports and Imports

An important characteristic of our CGE model is the explicit treatment of two separate foreign trading regimes. One is the export processing regime, discussed earlier in the context of table 16.2. This sector receives duty-free imports and is therefore extremely open, with considerable foreign investment. The other sector is the ordinary trade regime. Since the 1990s, processing exports have grown rapidly as a result of their preferential treatment. They now account for more than half of China's total exports. Obviously, any analysis of external trade and the impact of changes in trade policy must have an explicit treatment of this dualistic foreign trading regime in the model.

Trade is modeled using the Armington assumption for import demand and a constant elasticity of transformation for export supply. Thus Chinese products are assumed to be differentiated from foreign products, and exports from China are treated as products different from those sold on the domestic market. The small-country assumption is assumed for imports, and so world import prices are exogenous in terms of foreign currency. Exports are demanded according to constant-elasticity demand curves, the price elasticities of which are high but less than infinite. Therefore, the terms of trade for China are endogenous in our simulation.

Production in each of the sectors of the economy is modeled using nested constant elasticity of substitution functions, and constant returns to scale are assumed. Sectors differentiate between rural and urban labor that substitute imperfectly between them. This is an indirect means of building into the model a geographic flavor, because some sectors will be located largely in urban areas, while others will be predominantly in rural areas. By limiting the substitutability of rural and urban labor in each sector, we are able to proxy the economic effect of geographically distributed activity. Thus if WTO accession boosts the demand for goods that are predominantly produced in urban areas, then urban wages will rise relative to rural wages, and migration will be encouraged. Ideally, we would model the geographic distribution of industrial activity, but unfortunately the data do not exist to support this type of split.

All commodity and nonlabor factor markets are assumed to clear through prices. With the exception of the farm–nonfarm labor supply decision, labor is assumed to be perfectly mobile across sectors. Capital is assumed to be partially mobile, reflecting differences in the marketability of capital goods across sectors.

The current version of the DRC's CGE model has a simple recursive dynamic structure. Dynamics in the model originate from the accumulation of productive factors and productivity changes. The model is benchmarked on China's 1997 social accounting matrix and is solved for subsequent years from 1998 to 2007. We turn now to the details of the baseline scenario.

Base Case Projections and WTO Accession Simulation

China's WTO accession includes a complex package of trade and investment liberalization. In this chapter, however, only four aspects are considered:

(1) tariff reduction on industrial products
(2) agricultural trade liberalization (i.e., tariff reduction for agricultural products), introduction of the tariff-rate quota system for agricultural goods, and elimination of export subsidies for corn and cotton
(3) liberalization of direct trade in services

(4) phaseout of MFA quotas on textile and clothing.

Now that China is a member of the WTO, its exports of textiles and apparel products to North American and European markets are being subjected to accelerated MFA quota growth (from 2002 to 2006), similar to that affecting other developing countries that are WTO members. The remaining quota restriction will be eliminated in 2007, according to the ATC.[8] Therefore, the analysis at best captures only parts of the issue. It does not take into account other major aspects of WTO membership, such as reducing barriers to foreign investment, protecting intellectual property rights, securing market access, enforcing commitment,

and cooperating in dispute settlement. Because China's market accession commitments to WTO entry will be phased in over a seven-year transition period, a baseline from 1998 to 2007 is established using our recursive dynamic model under a set of assumptions: China will continue its grain self-sufficiency policy, and the import quota of agricultural goods will grow at 3 percent annually from 2000 to 2007. This calibrated "benchmark" will serve as a basis of comparison for counterfactual simulation conducted in the WTO accession experiments. Major results from the baseline calibration are summarized in table 16.3, and the key assumptions are outlined in table 16.4. The baseline uses the economy-wide total factor productivity (TFP)

TABLE 16.3 Summary of Baseline Calibration

	1997	2000	2001	2002	2003	2004	2005	2006	2007
Exogenous specified variables									
GDP growth rate (%)	—	8.1	7.3	7.6	7.8	7.8	7.8	7.8	7.8
Life expectancy (years)	70.3	71.8	72.0	72.2	73.2	73.4	73.6	73.8	74.0
Total fertility rate									
Urban	1.40	1.45	1.48	1.5	1.52	1.55	1.57	1.59	1.62
Rural	2.01	1.95	1.97	1.99	2.01	2.02	2.04	2.06	2.07
Calibrated results:									
Macroeconomic trends									
Growth rate (%)									
Total absorption	—	11.02	8.53	8.29	8.45	8.39	8.34	8.29	8.25
Labor force	—	1.23	1.21	1.17	1.15	1.17	1.16	1.15	1.15
Capital stock	—	10.08	10.51	10.45	10.28	10.18	10.08	9.98	9.88
Total Factor Productivity	—	2.87	1.74	2.16	2.43	2.44	2.49	2.53	2.56
Ratio to GDP (%)									
Private consumption	44.3	47.0	47.3	47.4	47.4	47.4	47.5	47.6	47.6
Investment	32.7	34.1	35.2	35.9	36.7	37.4	38.1	38.8	39.4
Export	21.7	25.5	25.7	25.7	25.7	25.7	25.7	25.6	25.6
Import	16.3	22.9	23.5	23.7	23.8	24.0	24.1	24.2	24.2
Urban/rural per capita income ratio	3.03	2.77	2.74	2.71	2.68	2.65	2.63	2.60	2.58
Population and labor force									
Population (millions)	1,236.3	1,269.9	1,280.5	1,290.8	1,301.0	1,311.5	1,321.9	1,332.4	1,343.0
Urban	369.9	397.5	407.2	416.9	426.6	436.5	446.4	456.4	466.5
Rural	866.4	872.4	873.3	873.9	874.3	875.0	875.5	876.0	876.4
Labor force (millions)	640.7	665.6	673.6	681.5	689.4	697.4	705.5	713.6	721.8
Urban	181.1	196.9	202.5	208.2	213.8	219.5	225.3	231.2	237.2
Rural	459.6	468.7	471.1	473.4	475.6	477.9	480.2	482.4	484.6
Grain self-sufficiency rate (%)	99.5	98.5	98.4	98.4	98.3	98.2	98.1	98.0	98.0
Share of rural labor force (%)	71.7	70.4	69.9	69.5	69.0	68.5	68.1	67.6	67.2
Share of agricultural employment in total rural labor force (%)	72.0	71.9	71.6	71.6	71.2	71.0	70.9	70.7	70.7

Note: — Not available.

Source: Authors' calculations.

TABLE 16.4   Summary of Experiments

Experiment	Description

Base	*Base case:*
	— Real GDP exogenous
	— TFP growth rate
	    — Agricultural sector exogenous
	    — Other sectors endogenous
	— Three percent growth rate of import quota for goods subjected to quantitative restriction (rice, wheat, corn, cotton, wool, vegetable oil, sugar, petroleum refining, automobiles)
	— Exogenous export quota growth for textiles (5.7 percent) and apparel (6.0 percent)—annual average
	— All tax rates fixed at their base year level
	— Balance of payments gradually declines to 40 percent of its base year level in 2007

WTO	*WTO accession* Tariff reduction — An average 60 percent cut in 2000 tariff level from 2000 to 2007 Agricultural trade liberalization — Quota restriction (10 billion yuan, 1997)

	Initial quota in 2000	Annual growth rate of quota (%)
Rice	1.073	26.4
Wheat	1.252	10.5
Corn	0.374	18.0
Cotton	1.153	4.5
Wool	0.665	6.5
Vegetable oil	3.706	27.0
Sugar	0.408	7.6

— Tariff cut for other agricultural goods
— Elimination of export subsidies for corn and cotton
Phaseout of MFA
— Acceleration of MFA quota growth rate from 2001 to 2004
— Zero export tax of textiles and apparel in 2005

Source: Protocol on the Accession of WTO; Authors' assumptions.

variable as a residual and adjustment mechanism to match the pre-specified real gross domestic product (GDP) growth rate under an exogenously specified life expectation rate and total fertility rate for both the rural and urban population.

The WTO accession scenario is described in detail in table 16.4. Import tariffs are reduced gradually, and the sectoral reduction rates are aggregated from the Harmonized Commodity Description and Coding System tariff schedules for the period 2002–2007 and weighted by 1997 ordinary trade data. The quota control system is introduced for rice, wheat, corn, cotton, wool, vegetable oil, and sugar. Moreover, the tariffs for other agricultural goods will

also be reduced. Following François (2002), we model the impact of service sector liberalization as halving the barriers to services trade. We also introduce a 20 percent productivity boost for the automobile sector to reflect the efficiency gain from industrial restructuring and realization of economic scale in this sector after China WTO accession.

Simulation Results

We now turn to the results of our analysis of WTO accession, beginning with the economy-wide effects, then turning to the disaggregated household impacts.

Economy-Wide Impacts of WTO Accession

Our results, which are directed at the outcome in 2007 when China's accession to the WTO is complete, are reported in terms of deviations from the baseline in 2007. The first column of results in table 16.5 reports the macroeconomic impacts of accession on China's economy under the high transfer elasticity assumption. Real GDP and welfare both increase by 0.65 percent and 0.73 percent, respectively, while consumption increases by over 1 percent and investment by only half as much. The reduction in trade barriers gives a substantial boost to trade in China, with both exports and imports rising by about 15 percent.

As for changes in factor prices, skilled wages rise more than semiskilled wages, which, in turn, rise more than unskilled wages. The relatively greater increase in skilled wages is fueled by the tendency for the manufacturing and service sectors to expand at the expense of agriculture. The manufacturing and service sectors are relatively intensive in their use of skilled and semiskilled labor, thereby boosting wages for these factors relative to unskilled wages. And then wages in the different markets are linked. In particular, urban and rural nonfarm wages are linked through the temporary migration of workers to the urban areas. Specifically, 1.46 million additional temporary migrants move to the city in response to the higher urban wages. As a consequence, the rural wage is once again equated with the urban wage, less the direct and indirect costs associated with migration. With transaction costs changing only modestly (–0.15 percent to 0.63 percent), the boost in wages is relatively more important for rural households, whose wages increase by a greater proportion because of the (nearly fixed) transaction costs.

Returns to labor in agriculture are also linked to the rural nonfarm wages via off-farm migration. As discussed earlier, this decision is based on the combination of agricultural wages and returns to land, because migrants risk losing the right to the land they leave. Because the returns to land fall, the returns to remaining in farming rise very little, thereby leading to additional off-farm migration (1.89 million).

Sector Impacts

Table 16.6 reports the impact of accession on output, imports, exports, and relative prices in the Chinese economy. To facilitate analysis, figure 16.1 reports the output changes in descending order, omitting the changes that are less than 2 percent in absolute value. Clearly, the largest increases in output stem from elimination of the quotas on textiles and apparel exports to North America and Europe; these products, as well as the production of synthetic fibers and cotton, increase by substantial amounts. On the other end of the spectrum, the most heavily protected sectors, which have sizable trade exposure, experience declining output. These sectors include wool, automobiles, vegetable oils, sugar, machinery, nonferrous metal products, special equipment, and wheat.

With the exception of a few mining products and transport services for which there is no cut in protection, import volumes increase for all sectors in the economy. The largest increases are for food and agricultural products (where there are deep cuts in protection), textiles and apparel (where the demand for intermediate inputs increases strongly), as well as automobiles (where there are strong productivity gains from the rationalization of production). Export volumes for most products also increase, fueled by cheaper inputs and real depreciation, as well as the elimination of textile and apparel quotas. Only cotton and corn, for which export subsidies are removed, and wool, which is used heavily in the expanding textile sector, experience reductions in export volumes.

Table 16.6 also reports the change in net exports for each of the product categories. It is not surprising that the largest increase in net exports is in the apparel and textile sectors because of elimination of the quotas under the Agreement on Textiles and Clothing. The net exports of apparel and textiles increase by 286 billion yuan and 61 billion yuan, respectively. Because chemical fibers and cotton are major intermediate inputs in the textile sector, their net imports also increase sharply. In addition, China's net imports of automobiles, chemicals, electronics, machinery, and commercial services also increase strongly, offsetting the increasing trade surplus from the textile and apparel sectors.

Finally, table 16.6 reports the percentage change in commodity prices relative to the Consumer Price Index in China. Wool, vegetable oil, and automobiles experience substantial relative price declines, because imports have a high market penetration ratio and their rates of import protection are cut

TABLE 16.5   Implications of China's WTO Accession, 2007 (percentage change)

	High Labor Transfer Elasticity	Low Labor Transfer Elasticity
Macroeconomic variables		
Welfare (Equivalent Variation)	0.73	0.62
GDP	0.65	0.54
Consumption	1.02	0.94
Investment	0.46	0.39
Exports	14.98	14.35
Imports	14.23	13.64
Factor prices		
Returns to agricultural land	−3.54	−1.65
Capital returns	−0.56	−0.35
Unskilled wages		
Urban	−0.30	0.24
Rural nonagricultural	−0.34	0.23
Agricultural	−0.76	−0.61
without land return	0.13	−0.08
Semiskilled wages		
Urban	0.37	0.69
Rural nonagricultural	0.26	0.64
Agricultural	−0.28	−0.54
without land return	0.66	0.00
Skilled wages		
Urban	1.11	0.89
Rural nonagricultural	1.11	0.89
Agricultural	0.42	−0.21
without land return	1.10	0.21
Inequality measurement[a]		
Urban/rural income ratio	0.0107	0.0167
Gini	0.0013	0.0012
Urban	0.0004	0.0002
Rural	0.0001	0.0003
Transaction costs		
Unskilled	−0.15	0.31
Semiskilled	0.63	0.84
Labor migration (millions)		
Agricultural-nonagricultural	1.89	0.54
Rural-urban	1.46	0.45
Unskilled	0.35	0.13
Semiskilled	1.03	0.29
Skilled	0.07	0.03
Labor migration (%)		
Agricultural-nonagricultural	2.42	1.55
Rural-urban	2.05	1.07
Unskilled	1.20	0.62
Semiskilled	2.86	1.75
Skilled	1.28	0.59

[a]Change of original value, not percentage change.

Source: Authors' model simulation results.

TABLE 16.6 Sector Impacts of China's WTO Accession in 2007: Percentage Deviation from Baseline

	Output	Import	Export	Net Trade (Billions of Yuan)	Prices (Relative to Consumer Price Index)
Rice	−0.8	151.7	2.3	−4.5	−0.4
Wheat	−4.2	50.9	—	−8.9	−1.8
Corn	−3.7	181.1	−66.5	−6.3	−0.2
Cotton	3.2	78.6	−23.8	−8.2	−0.5
Other nongrain crops	−1.0	53.9	2.4	−7.8	−0.3
Forestry	−2.9	16.9	−2.2	−2.9	0.3
Wool	−32.9	24.8	−19.2	−1.8	−14.6
Other livestock	1.3	1.6	3.5	0.3	0.2
Fishing	0.5	3.3	2.1	0.1	0.6
Other agriculture	0.1	5.7	6.2	0.1	−0.2
Coal mining	−0.8	−1.8	1.3	0.1	0.6
Crude oil and natural gas	0.3	−0.3	5.7	1.9	−0.4
Ferrous ore mining	−2.3	−3.6	3.6	1.3	0.3
Nonferrous ore mining	−4.1	−4.1	−0.5	0.7	0.6
Other mining	−0.4	1.3	3.5	0.1	0.1
Vegetable oil	−14.6	167.2	170.3	−20.1	−7.9
Grain mill and forage	0.8	5.1	27.9	−0.9	−0.6
Sugar	−10.9	180.1	295.5	−2.9	−4.5
Processed food	1.3	17.0	10.2	5.9	−0.3
Beverages	−0.6	130.0	11.2	−5.0	−0.7
Tobacco	−2.1	81.4	6.6	−6.1	−1.3
Textiles	17.9	62.0	45.3	60.6	−1.3
Apparel	38.6	54.8	102.2	286.2	−2.7
Leather	−1.3	19.7	1.4	−6.4	−0.6
Sawmills and furniture	−1.0	14.9	3.3	−3.5	−0.4
Paper and printing	−3.3	13.6	5.5	−16.3	−0.5
Crafts and toys	1.1	6.5	2.7	3.4	−0.2
Petroleum refining	0.0	1.0	4.8	4.8	−0.6
Chemicals	−1.8	7.9	3.0	−26.1	−0.7
Pharmaceuticals	0.3	14.1	5.2	0.3	−0.3
Chemical fibers	8.0	48.0	6.8	−28.7	−1.1
Rubber and plastics	−2.1	10.7	1.3	−5.3	−0.4
Building materials	−0.4	13.2	2.7	−2.5	0.1
Primary iron and steel	−3.8	2.4	1.3	−3.8	−0.1
Nonferrous metals	−4.8	1.7	−0.1	−2.1	−0.1
Metal products	−2.4	10.1	1.5	−11.4	−0.4
Machinery	−5.1	9.1	0.1	−21.8	−0.7
Special equipment	−4.6	7.0	1.1	−22.1	−1.6
Automobiles	−19.7	83.5	37.9	−50.1	−11.3
Other transport equipment	0.9	−0.1	2.2	1.3	−0.1
Electric machinery	−2.6	13.4	1.0	−21.0	−0.8
Electronics	−3.8	6.3	0.3	−29.2	−2.1
Instruments	−3.3	6.9	−0.3	−7.1	−2.0
Other manufacturing	−1.7	21.6	0.2	−2.4	0.5
Utilities	−0.6	16.5	2.9	0.4	0.1
Construction	0.3	10.3	3.1	−2.6	0.2
Transportation	0.3	−1.5	3.2	4.7	−0.1

TABLE 16.6   (Continued)

	Output	Import	Export	Net Trade (Billions of Yuan)	Prices (Relative to Consumer Price Index)
Post and communication	0.5	4.0	4.3	2.1	−0.4
Commercial sources	1.7	21.7	2.4	−15.8	−0.2
Finance	−0.5	17.4	1.7	−2.7	0.1
Social services	−1.0	14.9	2.1	−13.2	−0.8
Education and health	−0.3	18.6	0.9	−2.9	0.5
Public administration	−0.4	18.0	1.4	−1.9	0.3

— Not available.

Source: Authors' model simulation results.

FIGURE 16.1   Change in Sector Output due to WTO Accession, China

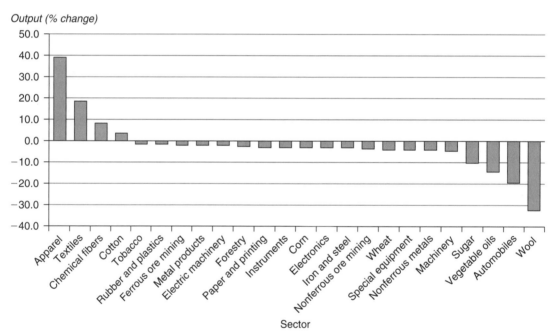

Source: Authors' model simulation results.

sharply. For most other sectors the price changes are quite modest.

Household Impacts

Table 16.7 reports the household impacts in 2007 of China's accession to the WTO. The first point to note in table 16.7 is that *WTO accession benefits all households, except those reliant on transfers.* The latter group, which receives much of its transfer income from state-run enterprises, is adversely affected by the decline in rents accruing to these enterprises. Government transfers are assumed to be constant in real terms and are indexed by the Consumer Price Index.

The smallest welfare increases for the other (nontransfer) households in table 16.7 are associated with agriculture-specialized households. They are adversely affected by the decline in returns to agricultural land, but rising returns to labor still boost the average returns to farming overall as some individuals leave the sector. Thus, even the agriculture-specialized households benefit from WTO accession. Figure 16.2 contrasts the gains for

TABLE 16.7   Household Impacts of China's WTO Accession, 2007 (Equivalent Variation as percentage of household income)

Vingtile (Poorest = 1)	Urban Transfer-Specialized	Urban Labor-Specialized	Urban Diversified	Rural Agriculture-Specialized	Rural Diversified
High labor transfer elasticity					
1	−0.274	1.217	1.044	0.446	0.534
2	−0.548	1.395	1.247	0.426	0.571
3	−0.450	1.533	1.279	0.343	0.606
4	−0.534	1.477	1.103	0.295	0.591
5	−0.584	1.451	1.252	0.366	0.609
6	−0.464	1.571	1.048	0.355	0.636
7	−0.397	1.631	1.315	0.320	0.658
8	−0.287	1.607	1.395	0.522	0.636
9	−0.381	1.706	1.295	0.370	0.623
10	−0.550	1.844	1.308	0.409	0.671
11	−0.457	1.709	1.269	0.316	0.650
12	−0.397	1.731	1.271	0.367	0.648
13	−0.356	1.766	1.267	0.345	0.635
14	0.263	1.719	1.224	0.421	0.683
15	−0.270	1.826	1.339	0.329	0.678
16	−0.190	1.768	1.204	0.654	0.664
17	—	1.631	1.102	0.782	0.749
18	0.052	1.682	1.230	0.629	0.642
19	−0.354	1.774	1.006	0.391	0.618
20	—	1.743	0.506	0.469	0.619
Low labor transfer elasticity					
1	−0.270	1.260	1.103	0.129	0.373
2	−0.566	1.418	1.272	0.090	0.411
3	−0.463	1.453	1.279	0.020	0.440
4	−0.553	1.471	1.128	−0.029	0.435
5	−0.596	1.393	1.212	0.037	0.464
6	−0.466	1.470	1.065	0.025	0.501
7	−0.437	1.520	1.264	−0.011	0.531
8	−0.291	1.526	1.337	0.188	0.510
9	−0.393	1.570	1.239	0.042	0.519
10	−0.566	1.689	1.217	0.064	0.573
11	−0.470	1.566	1.183	−0.014	0.559
12	−0.398	1.570	1.179	0.021	0.564
13	−0.369	1.570	1.186	0.021	0.550
14	0.326	1.562	1.123	0.068	0.588
15	−0.294	1.647	1.233	0.023	0.601
16	−0.185	1.547	1.126	0.253	0.596
17	—	1.488	0.996	0.410	0.672
18	0.073	1.490	1.082	0.309	0.598
19	−0.356	1.552	0.921	0.075	0.561
20	—	1.484	0.477	0.146	0.519

Note: — Not available.

Source: Authors' model simulation results.

FIGURE 16.2   Impact of WTO Accession on Rural Households

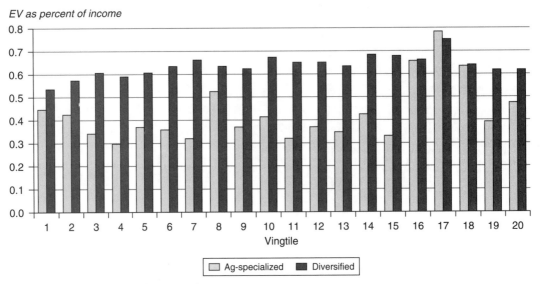

EV as percent of income

Source: Authors' model simulation results.

FIGURE 16.3   Impact of WTO Access on Urban Households

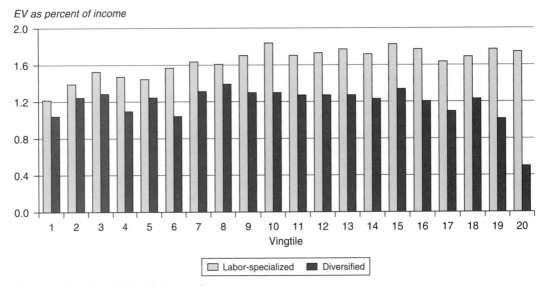

EV as percent of income

Source: Authors' model simulation results.

rural households specialized in farming with those that have diversified income sources. For the latter group, income rises more because of the increased role of nonfarm wage earnings. The largest increases in welfare after WTO accession accrue to the urban households—especially the wealthier, labor-specialized households. They benefit from the fact that, of all factor prices, skilled wages increase the most after WTO accession. Figure 16.3 contrasts these changes with the changes in EV (relative to the initial expenditure) for the urban

diversified households who also have significant income from capital. Because the latter rise more modestly, the highest-income, diversified households benefit proportionately less than the other nontransfer-specialized, urban household groups.

Sensitivity to the Elasticity of Labor Transfer out of Agriculture

As noted earlier, Sicular and Zhao (2002) provide several estimates of the labor transfer elasticity out of agriculture. In our base case results, we use the elasticity that relates the relative supply of labor to agriculture and nonagriculture (market wage) activities to a change in the relative wage rates—owing to a perturbation in agricultural returns. Our rationale for selecting this elasticity is that the largest relative factor price effect of WTO accession is the downward pressure on returns to agriculture. This "push" elasticity is 2.67. It is considerably higher than the "pull" elasticity engendered by an increase in the market wage for labor, which is estimated to be 0.6. For purposes of sensitivity analysis, we turn now to the second set of results in tables 16.5 and 16.7, which utilize the low labor transfer elasticity between agriculture and nonagriculture. The second column of table 16.5 reveals that the aggregate gains from WTO accession are somewhat smaller in the low transfer elasticity case—although not dramatically so.

The most important difference between the high and low labor transfer elasticity results is the impact of accession on the agriculture-specialized households (table 16.7). In the case of reduced off-farm mobility of labor, the gains of agriculture-specialized households are much smaller than those arising with a high off-farm labor transfer elasticity. In fact, a few of these farm household vingtiles now lose from WTO accession, because they are not able to take advantage of the improved opportunities outside of the farm sector and fall prey to depressed factor returns in agriculture. This finding confirms those of Chen and Ravallion (2003)—see Chapter 15 in this volume. By not modeling factor market adjustment at all, Chen and Ravallion have effectively assumed an even smaller labor transfer elasticity out of agriculture—zero. In their chapter, they conclude that the poor agricultural households will lose from WTO accession. This qualitative difference in findings on rural incidence highlights the importance of explicitly modeling labor markets in order to obtain an accurate assessment of the impact of WTO accession on farm households in China.

Conclusions and Policy Implications

The aim of this study has been to quantify the impact of China's accession to the WTO on income distribution and poverty. Toward this end, we have drawn on household surveys from three

diverse provinces in China: Guangdong, Liaoning, and Sichuan. Using these rural and urban surveys, we estimated earnings and spending patterns for 20 income vingtiles across five representative household groups in China. These groups were divided based on their location (rural versus urban) and their primary source of earnings, yielding five categories: agriculture-specialized, rural-diversified, urban labor-specialized, urban transfer-specialized, and urban-diversified. By embedding these disaggregated households in a national CGE model of China, we are able to identify the disaggregated household impacts of WTO accession.

We find that WTO accession benefits all household groups—with the exception of the urban transfer-specialized households, which experience modest losses because of the decline in rents accruing to state-run enterprises. The biggest gains go to urban labor-specialized households because of the strong rise in wages for skilled and semiskilled labor in urban areas. The smallest gains go to the rural agriculture-specialized households, which face declining returns to agriculture-specific factors and which have limited labor mobility out of farming. Indeed, some of these households could actually lose from accession under low values of the farm–nonfarm labor transfer elasticity. Because these households are also the poorest in China, WTO accession runs the risk of widening income disparities. Other studies that have abstracted from intersector labor mobility altogether have come to the same conclusion (Chen and Ravallion 2003).

The critical importance of labor markets to the rural impact of China's accession to the WTO suggests the potential for complementary labor market reforms to offset some of these adverse impacts. In a companion paper to this chapter (Zhai, Hertel, and Wang 2003), we find that reforms aimed at facilitating an improved flow of labor out of agriculture and between the rural and urban markets, can result in significant gains for rural households. In that study, we explore the following implications:

- reforming agricultural land markets to permit arms-length land rental in all rural areas, thereby facilitating the permanent movement of labor out of farming
- enhancing off-farm labor mobility
- abolishing the *hukou* system, thereby reducing the transaction costs imposed on rural–urban migrants.

When combined, these reforms reduce the estimated 2007 urban–rural income ratio from 2.58 (in the absence of WTO accession) to 2.09. When combined with WTO accession, the 2007 urban–rural income ratio is still reduced to 2.12 as a consequence of these three factor market reforms. Although these reform scenarios are perhaps more dramatic than those likely to be undertaken in the near term, even a small movement in this direction would clearly go a long way toward offsetting the potentially adverse consequences of WTO accession on rural–urban inequality.

Notes

1. All dollar amounts are current U.S. dollars.

2. We would have preferred to base this split on occupation—that is, what they actually do—rather than potential as determined by education. However, the rural household survey does not support this split.

3. Because the rural survey reports only the highest educational attainment of the household, attainment by worker is unknown. This factor biases the skill level of rural households upward, but, because the vast majority of rural households are unskilled, this bias is less of a problem in practice.

4. However, as noted by Parish, Zhe, and Li (1995), the rural labor market is looking more like a market all the time.

5. Other, unobserved factors inducing this rural–urban wage differential are likely. If so, estimation of the labor market distortion via subtraction of known factors is biased in the direction of overstating the *hukou*-related distortion. Therefore, it is useful to estimate as well the direct impact of household registration status on the observed wage difference among households. Shi (2002) takes this approach to the problem, using the same CHNS data set. He finds that only 28 percent of the rural–urban wage difference can be explained directly via the coefficient on the *hukou* registration variable. This figure is quite a bit less than the 48 percent left unexplained via the subtraction approach of Shi, Sicular, and Zhao (2002).

6. See Zhai, Hertel, and Wang (2003) for a detailed description of how this ad valorem distortion is obtained.

7. We assume that a doubling of temporary migration would only increase the marginal cost of migration by 10 percent.

8. On January 1, 1995, the ATC entered into force and replaced the old Multi-Fiber Arrangement. The ATC provides for elimination of the quotas and the complete integration of textiles and apparel into the WTO regime over a 10-year transition period, ending on January 1, 2005. All WTO countries are subject to ATC disciplines, and only WTO members are eligible for ATC benefits.

References

The word *processed* describes informally reproduced works that may not be commonly available through libraries.

Beghin, John, Sébastien Dessus, David Roland-Holst, and Dominique van der Mensbrugghe. 1994. "Prototype CGE Model for the Trade and the Environment Programme-Technical Specification." OECD Development Centre, Paris.

Chan, Kam Wing, and Li Zhang. 1999. "The Hukou System and Rural-Urban Migration in China: Processes and Changes." *China Quarterly* 160 (December): 818–55.

Chen, Shaohua, and Martin Ravallion. 2003. "Welfare Impacts of China's Accession to the WTO." World Bank, Washington, D.C. Processed.

Chen, Shaohua, and Yan Wang. 2001. "China's Growth and Poverty Reduction: Recent Trends between 1990 and 1999." World Bank, Washington, D.C. Processed.

de Melo, J. 1988. "Computable General Equilibrium Models for Trade Policy Analysis in Developing Countries: A Survey." *Journal of Policy Modeling* 10: 469–504.

de Melo, J., and David Tarr. 1992. *A General Equilibrium Analysis of US Foreign Trade Policy*. Cambridge, Mass.: MIT Press.

Dervis, K., J. de Melo, and Sherman Robinson. 1982. *General Equilibrium Models for Development Policy*. Cambridge: Cambridge University Press.

Development Research Center. 1998. The Global and Domestic Impact of China Joining the World Trade Organization, Research Paper, Development Research Center of the State Council, PRC, Beijing.

Dimaranan, Betina V., and Robert A. McDougall. 2002. *Global Trade, Assistance, and Production: The GTAP 5 Data Base*. West Lafayette, Indiana: Center for Global Trade Analysis, Purdue University.

Francois, Joseph F., and Spinanger, Dean. 2004. "Regulated Efficiency, WTO Accession, and the Motor Vehicle Sector in China." In D. Bhattasali, S. Li, and W. Martin, eds., *China and the WTO: Accession, Policy Reforms, and Poverty Reduction Strategies*. Washington, D.C.: World Bank and Oxford University Press.

Ianchovichina, Elena, R. McDougall, and T. Hertel. 1999. "China 2005 Revisited: The Implications of International Capital Mobility." Global Trade Analysis Project, Purdue University, West Lafayette, Indiana. Processed.

Hertel, Thomas W., Maros Ivanic, Paul V. Preckel, and John Cranfield. 2004. "The Earnings Effects of Multilateral Trade Liberalization: Implications for Poverty." *World Bank Economic Review*. Forthcoming.

Kanbur, R., and Zhang, Xiaobo. 2001. Fifty years of regional inequality in China: A journey through revolution, reform and openness. Working Paper 2001-04, Department of Applied Economics and Management, Cornell University, Ithaca, New York.

McKibbin, Warwick, and K. K. Tang. 2000. "Trade and Financial Reform in China: Impacts on the World Economy." *World Economy* 23(8): 979–1003.

Naughton, Barry. 1996. "China's Emergence and Prospects as a Trading Nation." *Brookings Paper on Economic Activity* 2, Washington, D.C.

Parish, W. L., X. Zhe, and F. Li. 1995. "Nonfarm Work and Marketization of the Chinese Countryside." *China Quarterly* 143: 697–730.

Rozelle, Scott, Guo Li, Minggao Shen, Amelia Hughart, and John Giles. 1999. "Leaving China's Farms: Survey Results of New Paths and Remaining Hurdles to Rural Migration." *China Quarterly* 158 (June): 367–93.

Shi, Xinzheng. 2002. Empirical research on urban-rural income differentials: The case of China. unpublished manuscript, CCER. Beijing: Beijing University.

Shi, Xinzheng, Terry Sicular, and Yaohui Zhao. 2002. "Analyzing Urban-Rural Income Inequality in China." Paper presented at International Symposium on Equity and Social Justice in Transitional China," Beijing, July 11–12.

Shoven J. B., and J. Whalley. 1992. *Applied General Equilibrium Analysis.* Cambridge: Cambridge University Press.

Sicular, Terry, and Yaohui Zhao. 2004. "Earnings and Labor Mobility in Rural China: Implications for China's Accession to the WTO." In D. Bhattasali, S. Li, and W. Martin, eds., *China and the WTO: Accession Policy Reform, and Poverty Reduction Strategies.* Washington, D.C.: World Bank and Oxford University Press.

Walmsley, Terrie, and Thomas Hertel. 2000. "China's Accession to the WTO: Timing Is Everything." Paper presented at International Conference on Global Economic Transformation after the Asian Economic Crisis, Hong Kong.

Wang, Zhi. 1999. "Impact of China's WTO Entry on Labor Intensive Export Market—A Recursive Dynamic CGE Analysis." *World Economy* 22 (3): 379–405.

———. 2001. "The Impact of China's WTO Accession on Trade and Economic Relations Cross the Taiwan Strait." *Economics of Transition* 9 (3).

Wang, Zhi, and Fan Zhai. 1998. "Tariff Reduction, Tax Replacement and Implication for Income Distribution in China." *Journal of Comparative Economics* 26: 358–87.

WTO (World Trade Organization). Protocol on the Accession of the People's Republic of China. Geneva: WTO.

Yang, Dennis T. 1997. "China's Land Arrangements and Rural Labor Mobility." *China Economic Review* 8 (2): 101–16.

Yang, Dennis Tao, and Hao Zhou. 1999. "Rural-Urban Disparity and Sectoral Labour Allocation in China." *Journal of Development Studies* 35 (3): 105–33.

Yang, Y., and Y. Huang. 1997. "The Impact of Trade Liberalization on Income Distribution in China." China Economy Working Paper 97/1. Research School of Pacific and Asia Studies, Australia National University, Canberra.

Zhai, Fan, and Shantong Li. 2000. "The Implications of Accession to WTO on China's Economy." Paper presented at Third Annual Conference on Global Economic Analysis, Melbourne, Australia, June 27–30.

Zhai, Fan, and Zhi Wang. 2002. "WTO Accession, Rural Labour Migration and Urban Unemployment in China." *Urban Studies* 39, no.12.

Zhai, Fan, Thomas W. Hertel, and Zhi Wang. 2003. "Labor Market Distortions, Rural-Urban Inequality and the Opening of China's Economy." GTAP working paper 27. Center for Global Trade Analysis, Purdue University, West Lafayette, Indiana. Available at http://www.gtap.agecon.purdue.edu/resources/res_display.asp?RecordID =1323.

Zhao, Yaohui. 1999a. "Labor Migration and Earnings Differences: The Case of Rural China." *Economic Development and Cultural Change,* 47(4): 767–82.

———. 1999b. "Leaving the Countryside: Rural-to-Urban Migration Decisions in China." *American Economic Review* (May 1999): 281–86.

17

COPING WITH AND ADAPTING TO JOB LOSSES AND DECLINES IN FARM EARNINGS IN CHINA

Athar Hussain

The knock-on effects of the conditions of China's accession to the World Trade Organization (WTO) on the labor market (including on farmers) are a major issue in analysis of the social impacts of WTO membership, in particular its impact on poverty and income equality. The nature of the labor market effects can be expected to differ in the short and the long run. In the short run, some of the effects will be adverse and will take two forms: (1) job shedding in particular industries, and (2) a reduction in the earnings of some farmers, depending on the region and the commodities produced.

Correlatively, the beneficial labor market effects will accrue in the form of expanded employment in the sectors opened wider to foreign direct investment (FDI). Additional beneficial effects would stem from job creation and the rise in earnings from the lower barriers facing Chinese exports. Broadly, the consensus is that product and labor markets effects all included, gains from WTO membership will far outweigh losses. Moreover, given the increased efficiency flowing from WTO accession in the long run the positive labor market impact (changes in jobs and earnings) would exceed the negative impact.

As for the social impact of WTO accession, the distribution of gains and losses is as important as the balance between the two. Even when gains exceed losses, there is a social dimension to be considered whenever the interpersonal distribution of losses and gains do not coincide. In the context of China's WTO accession, this might happen in the following four ways:

1. Because of a reduction in the prices of imported commodities, a large number of consumers gain, while a comparatively small number of workers lose jobs or farmers experience a decline in earnings.
2. Loss of jobs or decline in farm earnings precedes job creation or increases in farm earnings due to trade liberalization.
3. Those losing jobs or experiencing an income decline differ from those recruited into new jobs or experiencing an income rise.
4. Regions reaping gains from WTO accession differ from regions affected by the adverse effects of WTO accession.

All four scenarios involve noncoincidence between the distribution of gains and losses and thus create a potential issue for social protection. The first concerns the distribution of gains between consumers and producers (employees and farmers), and it arises from the simple fact that, for many consumer goods, the number of consumers

305

far exceeds the number of producers, including workers employed directly and indirectly. The implication is that adverse effects in the form of job losses or decline in earnings produced by WTO accession are likely to be far more concentrated than the favorable effects associated with a fall in prices dispersed over a large number of consumers. Such patterns of distribution of losses and gains are likely to arise for consumer goods such as passenger vehicles, making the adverse effects more visible than the favorable ones.

The second is particularly important because China had to start lowering barriers to foreign imports from the date of accession, December 11, 2001, but its exports will benefit from reduced barriers in other WTO member countries only after a time lag, in some cases a long and uncertain one. In short, whereas China's WTO accession involves an obligation to lower barriers to imports, it provides no more than a distant prospect of lower barriers on exports. The abolition of the Multi-Fiber Arrangement, from which China is expected to be a major beneficiary, is scheduled to take place in 2005, and Chinese textiles may continue to face special textile safeguards until 2008. Similarly, barriers on foreign farm imports began to fall immediately upon China's accession to the WTO, but it is uncertain when China's farm exports will face lower barriers; it is contingent on the outcomes of bilateral trade negotiations and of the Doha Round of trade talks, which will take some years to conclude.

In the third and fourth scenarios in the list, a mismatch occurs between the distributions of losses and gains over individuals and regions. In the first of two examples of likely outcomes of WTO accession, employment expands in the textile and clothing industry and the number of jobs in the vehicle and motor parts industries falls. Those getting jobs in the textile and clothing industries will naturally not all be just those losing jobs in the vehicle industry, even when both sets of industries are located in the same place. The second example concerns agriculture, where grain farmers, especially those heavily dependent on corn, wheat, and coarse grain, will likely be losers. These losers will be concentrated in the Northeast and Northwest. The gainers will consist of producers of export crops and animal products. Most of the gainers will be in the coastal provinces of the East and the Southeast. The Chinese economy is made up of numerous subeconomies that are loosely connected rather than fully integrated. Regional differences in factor endowments, labor productivity, or scale economies within China are arguably as pronounced as those between other countries. One implication is that the impact of WTO accession is likely to vary regionally. Moreover, the impact on the Chinese economy of WTO accession will depend crucially on what happens to internal trade barriers in the years after accession. A lowering of such barriers induced by China's membership in the WTO may have the effect of a geographic redistribution of production within the Chinese economy as well as between China and the rest of the world. It is conceivable that the impact of the removal of internal trade barriers may dominate the impact of lower international trade barriers.

Empirical evidence on the seriousness of losses in the Chinese context is not available. However, the evidence from the United States provides a benchmark for estimating losses suffered by adversely affected workers. The re-employment rates of workers displaced by competition from imports are typically low. The reason is not the nature of import competition. Rather, the explanation lies in the mismatch between the characteristics of laid-off workers and those of workers hired for new jobs. Workers to be laid off are not chosen randomly but selectively. In the United States, workers losing jobs are likely to be older and to have lower educational attainment. In contrast, new jobs tend to demand younger and better-educated workers. The patterns of selection of employees for redundancy and of new recruits are aimed at raising the efficiency of the U.S. labor force, and these patterns are likely to apply in China as well. Furthermore, the new jobs that laid-off workers find tend to be lower paying than the previous jobs.

In the United States, workers losing jobs because of competition from imports may experience a long spell of unemployment and a significant drop in wages when they find a new job (Kletzer 2001). Arguably, in terms of spells of unemployment, the losses suffered by Chinese workers losing jobs because of WTO accession are likely to be no less than those experienced by U.S. workers unemployed because of competition from imports. Indeed, they may be higher for three reasons. First, China, as a developing economy with a large pool of surplus labor, would have more job seekers per vacancy than the United States. Added to this, workers losing jobs because of WTO accession would be competing with the large numbers of workers laid off from the state sector. Second, barriers to labor mobility in China serve to prolong unemployment between jobs. Third, the problem of a lower re-employment rate among older workers, who are likely to account for a substantial share of employees selected to be laid off, is in the Chinese context compounded further by the fact they that they have much lower educational attainment than that of younger workers. Because of the adverse impacts of the Cultural Revolution (1966–78) on secondary and higher education, a large proportion of birth cohorts from 1955 to 1965 (ages 37–47 in 2002) missed out entirely on post-basic education and occupational training. As a result, the difference in educational attainment between younger and older workers in China is particularly wide.

A preliminary hypothesis is that China's WTO membership is highly unlikely to have an identifiable impact on the wages of skilled and unskilled employees—an issue that dominates the discussion of the impact of imports from developing economies on U.S. workers (Collins 1998). Likewise, a rise in the demand for unskilled labor because of a lowering of impediments to Chinese exports, such as textiles and clothing, is highly unlikely to translate into a rise in the wages of unskilled workers, as predicted by the standard international trade theory that proceeds on the assumption of full employment. In China, a developing economy, the supply of unskilled workers far exceeds demand, and a rise in demand induced by WTO membership is likely to be small relative to the excess supply. In fact, the wages of professional and skilled employees have been rising more than those of unskilled workers in China, and the trend is likely to continue. This pattern runs contrary to the expected change in relative wages, but it has little to do with international trade. Rather, it stems largely to a correction of the highly compressed wage structure inherited from the planning period. This chapter proceeds on the assumption that the impact of WTO entry on industry and services will principally be on jobs and that on farming will be on earnings.

For anyone studying the labor market impact of WTO membership, the principal problem is that this impact is intertwined with those of the two transitions under way in the Chinese economy: the transition from a planned to a market economy and the process of economic development that is seeing a transfer of labor out of farming. Both of these transitions involve job displacement and a redeployment of labor on a large scale. The labor recruitment practices of the planned economy left behind a legacy of surplus labor in the state sector, which, forced by competition, has been shedding this excess baggage. In just six years, from 1996 to 2002, the state sector (including enterprises, public institutions, and the government) has lost about 40 million jobs, or 37 percent of the total in 1996, and the trend is likely to continue for some years to come. The argument is that job losses or job displacement arising from WTO membership would simply be a part of the same phenomenon on a larger scale. Similarly, a reduction in income among sections of the farming population, which is likely to be one of the effects of WTO membership, has for other reasons been a common occurrence, especially since the late 1990s.

China's accession to the WTO in December 2001, although a historical landmark, was just one event in a series of step-by-step openings of the Chinese economy to international trade and foreign direct investment since 1979, referred to as the Open Door policy. From a historical perspective, the effects directly attributable to WTO accession may be seen as one chapter in the extensive story (i.e., ramifications) of the Open Door policy. Given the long time it has taken China to gain entry to the WTO, the event has been "expected" and "prepared for," at least to a degree. Some of the effects of WTO accession have preceded the cause itself. This is particularly true about the restructuring of industries over the last few years and perhaps also about the decision to convert marginal farming land into forests. This situation is akin to the observation that part of the relative decline in the wages of unskilled works observed in the United States may be attributable to employers securing restraint in wage demands by using the threat of developing country imports—that is, the expectation of heightened competition may have the same effect as the actual event. Most of the likely impact of WTO membership on the Chinese economy is attributable to sharper competition in product and services markets. In this respect, increased competition between domestic producers, which has risen sharply since the mid-1990s, has the same effect as that produced by heightened competition between domestic and foreign producers after WTO entry.

All this discussion leads to one implication and raises a question. The implication is that the adverse labor market impacts of WTO membership would be neither novel nor out of scale with what the Chinese economy has already experienced in recent years, or more specifically since the second half of the 1990s. This implication suggests that observers keep an open mind about the magnitude of the effects, at least at the national level. One important question is whether separate or special policies are needed to deal with the adverse impacts of WTO entry. Arguably, the policy responses to job losses or falls in farm incomes should be the same regardless of their proximate causes. A justification for special measures is that the adverse impact of the prescribed reduction in trade barriers after WTO entry may be concentrated over a short time period and fall heavily on particular regions, such as the rural areas of the already impoverished Northwest.

Social Protection and Adaptation

Schematically, the current social security schemes and policy measures that may be used to respond to the adverse impacts of WTO accession on the labor market (i.e., job losses and lower farm earnings in China) fall into four categories, depending on the policy aim and the target (table 17.1).

Excluded from table 17.1 are the social security schemes that are not directly related to a job loss or

fall in labor earnings, such as old-age pensions and health insurance. The category "social protection" covers various schemes differentiated by the target of assistance and the conditions attached to the provision of assistance, such as the requisite contribution record or insufficient means. These schemes do not prevent job losses or declines in earnings; they operate after the event and provide no more than partial compensation. Full compensation is ruled out in order to maintain economic incentives to remain employed and because of budgetary constraints. The category "adaptation" covers a diverse range of schemes with the common feature of facilitating individuals, localities, or industries to adapt to a new trade environment through labor redeployment and modification of the composition of economic activities. Most of the schemes falling under this category have not been introduced to deal with the effects of WTO entry, but they lend themselves to serving that purpose. A notable exception is the restructuring of various industries over the last few years in the expectation of WTO accession, such as those in the textile, steel, and vehicle industries. Some of the schemes, such as public works programs, contain elements of both social protection and adaptation.

Two gaps in the schemes and measures (table 17.1) that would provide protection and facilitate adaptation to the adverse impacts of WTO entry stand out. First, the schemes for households/individuals that fall under "social protection" vary greatly between rural and urban inhabitants, which leaves some groups such as migrants unprotected. Second, among the schemes for localities/industries

TABLE 17.1 Classification of Schemes and Measures

Target	Aim	
	Social Protection	**Adaptation**
Households/individuals	• Unemployment insurance • Poverty relief	• Job search facilities • Retraining • Assisted migration
Localities/industries	• Schemes to assist poor rural localities • Public works programs	• Development schemes for lagging regions • Assisted industrial restructuring • Assisted conversion of marginal forest land into forests

Source: The authors.

that fall under "adaptation," there are no assistance measures targeted at towns and cities adversely affected by industrial restructuring. These measures assume a special importance in the Chinese context because of impediments to labor migration. The problem of towns and cities caught in an unemployment-and-stagnation trap has come to the fore with the massive labor redundancies and layoffs in the state sector since 1996. The problem is particularly serious in medium and small towns heavily dependent on a few state enterprises that have been forced to shed labor because of financial difficulties. In such towns, job losses in a few enterprises accounting for a substantial percentage of local employment can generate significant negative pecuniary externalities. Such externalities arise whenever there is a combination of imperfect competition and increasing returns to scale. In the Chinese context, the negative regional impact of job losses is further exacerbated by the arrangement whereby urban income maintenance schemes are largely financed at the city level. Cities with a higher poverty or unemployment rate also tend to have strained public finances and therefore must reduce coverage or benefit levels. As described later in this chapter, there is a rural assistance scheme targeted at poor localities, but that scheme is of little or no use as a cushion against the adverse impacts of increased agricultural imports on farm incomes.

The framework employed in this chapter to analyze social protection measures is structured around the following questions.

- Do the beneficiaries (individuals/industries/localities) of a social protection measure overlap with those adversely affected by WTO entry? If yes, how significant is the overlap, and how effective is the targeting?
- How does the measure address the adverse impacts (e.g., assistance or facilitating adaptation)?
- How is the measure financed, and is the financing adequate to meet the measure's objectives?
- What effects does the measure have on incentive and efficiency? In terms of efficiency, would an alternative measure achieve the desired effect at a lower cost?

Instruments for Social Protection

Social protection schemes are intended to reduce the incidence of poverty and economic inequality. They provide a partial compensation for a job loss or fall in income, but on their own they do not facilitate a redeployment of labor, which is the ultimate aim. Following the usual convention, such schemes fall into two categories: social insurance and social assistance (social safety nets).

China, which has both types of schemes, has a more extensive social insurance system than those found in most developing economies. This system, then, provides the Chinese government with two types of measures to compensate, partially, the losers from trade liberalization. The differences between the two sets of schemes arise from two related features: first, the conditions attached to the provision of benefits (entitlement qualification) and, second, the method of financing. Under social insurance schemes, benefit payment is jointly conditional on the contribution record and on the occurrence of specific contingencies, such as unemployment. The first condition makes social insurance similar to commercial insurance and limits its coverage of the population. In China, as in many economies, social insurance is confined to the labor force in formal wage employment, and, unlike in other economies, is restricted to registered urban residents.[1] Under formal wage employment, it is easy to collect contributions in the form of a payroll tax and define and verify the state of unemployment, both of which raise difficulties in the case of informal wage employment or self-employment. The protective cover provided by social insurance in China is subject to two limitations. First, coverage is in practice limited to the labor force in urban areas in formal wage employment, which represents 14 percent (105.6 million) out of the total labor force of 737.4 million (National Bureau of Statistics 2003a).[2] Second, the contribution condition imposes a limit on unemployment compensation. In most schemes, the duration of compensation is linked to the duration of previous contributions and is subject to a maximum, which in China is two years. The implication is that unemployment insurance cannot be the sole mainstay of a comprehensive social protection system; it has to include a needs-based income maintenance scheme. Financed by contributions, social insurance resembles commercial insurance, but it differs in two respects, which help to extend its role in mitigating risks:

1. Participation is invariably mandatory for a designated section of the population, such as urban wage employees, which avoids adverse selection whereby low-risk groups opt out, thus raising the percentage of higher risk groups in the covered population.
2. The relationship between benefit and contribution in social insurance is typically looser than in commercial insurance and involves redistribution in favor of vulnerable groups.

In contrast to social insurance, social assistance is noncontributory and thus far removed from commercial insurance. A key distinguishing feature is that it can, in principle, provide protection to everyone in need in the relevant population. Normally, social assistance is available to all people whose resources fall under a specified minimum—for example, an income that falls under the poverty line. Furthermore, the benefit is available as long as the means test and some supplementary condition are satisfied.[3] China has several social assistance schemes, but each covers only a particular section of the population, which leaves some glaring blind spots in coverage (this is discussed later in this chapter). Table 17.2 presents the salient differences between social insurance, with reference to unemployment insurance, and social assistance.

Though overlapping in aims, social assistance and social insurance schemes are as much complements as they are substitutes. Developed and comprehensive social security systems invariably include both types of schemes. Does a low-income developing economy such as China need both types of schemes, especially social insurance that covers only a minority of the labor force, and usually that in regular wage employment? A low income does not constitute a barrier against the institution and functioning of social insurance, because benefits are tied to contributions that are usually a percentage of payroll. The principal advantage of social insurance is that, when well designed, it generates most if not all of the funds needed for its operation, which matters when possibilities for raising

TABLE 17.2 Differences between Social Insurance and Social Assistance

	Social Insurance	Social Assistance (Safety Nets)
Financing	• Self-financing, at least partially if not totally • Easy to combine with commercial insurance to cover additional risks	• Must be financed from general government revenue, which poses problems in low-income localities with a tight budget
Benefits	• Can be tailored to serve a range of objectives • Typically, benefits more generous than those under social assistance, but only available for a limited duration	• Usually set a level just sufficient to avert hardship, in some cases only severe hardship
Coverage	• Limited to those who can make the requisite contributions. By design, such schemes cannot provide universal coverage	• Restricted to those with insufficient income and savings to cover basic needs • In principle, can cover the whole population, depending on the budgetary constraint
Impact on poverty and economic inequality	• Provides protection against poverty to participants and those with an adequate contribution record • Reduction in inequality limited by coverage	• Can serve as social safety net to ensure protection against poverty • Limited reduction in economic inequality constrained by targeting

Source: The author.

revenue through alternative taxes are limited. The contribution condition that limits the coverage of social insurance also makes it attractive from a fiscal point of view. In contrast, social assistance schemes are, by design, not self-financing. The principal argument in favor of introducing and extending unemployment insurance is that it provides a first line of defense against poverty and reduces the task of poverty alleviation left for social assistance schemes. The latter is of particular importance when the coverage of social assistance is limited by budgetary stringency, as it is in China and other developing economies.

Overview of Chinese Income Maintenance Schemes

Table 17.3 presents an overview of various income maintenance schemes in China relevant to coping with job losses or declines in income stemming from WTO accession, excluding old-age pensions and disability compensation.

The land plots allocated to households are included as an income maintenance instrument in table 17.3 because of the importance accorded to them in providing income security for the rural population. Three features characterize Chinese income maintenance schemes. The first is the stark dichotomy between the urban and rural population. At present, no scheme covers both the populations, which are defined differently in China than elsewhere.[4] Second, the schemes aim to do no more than alleviate severe poverty. In the two urban schemes, the benefits are set at a flat rate either just above or at the local poverty line. The two rural assistance schemes are narrowly targeted, though in many cases inaccurately. The third feature is a high degree of decentralization. With the exception of the "Assistance to Poor Rural Localities" program, all schemes are in the first instance financed by low tiers of government: cities for the two urban schemes and villages for the "Assistance to Poor Rural Households" program. Higher government tiers contribute toward the cost of the schemes. But there is as yet no settled formula for cost sharing, and lower tiers of government end up bearing a share of costs that is too high to be equitable and consistent with the sustainability of the schemes.

TABLE 17.3 Income Maintenance Schemes in China

	Urban Schemes		Rural Schemes		
	Unemployment Insurance	Minimum Living Standard	Assistance to Poor Localities	Assistance to Poor Households	Allocation of a Land Plot
Coverage	Urban, formal wage employees	Registered urban residents	Designated rural localities	Usually restricted to very poor households and highly variable across localities	Long-standing inhabitants of the locality
Benefits	• Cash allowance • Health insurance • Free or subsidized services	• Cash allowance • Health insurance to cover large medical costs	• Investment in social services, infrastructure, and economic activities • Subsidies targeted at households	Benefits in cash and kind	A plot of land
Financing	Contributions and residual government financing	Central and territorial governments	Central and provincial governments	Locally financed	
Administering agency	City labor and social security bureaus	City civil affairs bureaus	Civil affairs bureaus	Villages	Villages

Source: The author.

BOX 17.1   Advantages and Disadvantages of Decentralization

Decentralization in the Chinese social security system offers both advantages and disadvantages.

Advantages:
- Decentralization allows flexibility to account for local variations and gives local governments the freedom to take initiatives. In fact, some local government initiatives have later been adopted as national policy. For example, the Minimum Living Standard Insurance (MLSI) scheme for urban areas, now a nationwide scheme, was first implemented in a few coastal cities. A uniform system for all of China runs the risk of being determined by the lowest common denominators.

Disadvantages:
- Municipalities and the tiers for the organization of rural social security are, in many instances, too small to provide sufficient risk pooling for maintaining the financial integrity of schemes. Decentralization is associated with variations in standards of provision that may go beyond the socially acceptable

differences. Furthermore, such variations may impede the transferability of social security entitlements (such as unemployment benefits) and thus impede labor mobility. Nontransferability is the principal barrier in bringing migrants under the social insurance cover.
- Decentralization accentuates disparities in social security provisions. Localities with a higher poverty level or a higher percentage of the needy in the population also tend to have more strained public finances and thus are forced to reduce coverage or the benefit level.

Planned Reform

The pilot program for improving the urban social security system, which is currently being tested in Liaoning Province, recognizes the problems created by decentralization. One of its aims is to upgrade the level of budgeting for social insurance from the municipal to the provincial level in selected localities, starting with the old-age pension scheme.

The rural–urban segmentation that casts a long shadow on the Chinese social security system has several facets. The urban and rural schemes not only are mutually exclusive, but also are structured differently. For the rural population, there are no equivalents of unemployment insurance (UI) and the urban Minimum Living Standard Insurance (MLSI), although the latter has begun to change. The explanation for confining UI to urban employees is not that the rural labor force, being self-employed, does not face the risk of unemployment. Although a majority of the rural labor force is engaged in the cultivation of its own land plots, a substantial percentage is employed in farming and nonfarming activities, and most of these are wage-employed. Over a third (35 percent) of the 490 million strong rural labor force is engaged full time in nonfarming activities, which says that in China *rural* is far from synonymous with *agricultural.* Leaving aside household units, town and village enterprises (TVEs) employ 133 million workers, or 27 percent of the rural labor force and far more than the total employment in the state sector (National Bureau of Statistics 2003a). The risk of unemployment facing TVE employees is just as

palpable as that facing their counterparts in urban enterprises; the labor retrenchment in TVEs in recent years is evidence. Additionally, many of the TVE employees are just as exposed to the impact of international trade as their urban counterparts. This being the case, the direct impact of WTO entry on rural China would not be confined to farming—it also would extend to rural industry. The impact of WTO entry on industry would straddle both urban and rural areas.

The MLSI, a social assistance scheme based on means, marks another major difference between social protection in urban and in rural areas. The scheme, which was introduced in 1997 and was by the middle of 2000 established and functioning in all towns and cities, aims to provide assistance to all registered urban residents with a household per capita income below the local poverty line. The number of beneficiaries under the scheme has risen sharply since inception, indicating improved coverage. The scheme marks a major change in the history of social security in China, in that until its introduction all social assistance was confined to a small section of the population characterized by the "three nos": no ability to work, no savings, and no relatives to depend on. Under the planned economy system, those physically able to work were expected to work and were provided with a job, which the government was able to do by virtue of its control of the economy. The introduction of the MLSI is underpinned by the government's recognition that it cannot provide a job guarantee to all in a market economy. With the combination of MLSI and UI, the urban population has all the ingredients of a comprehensive insurance against poverty, including that caused by the adverse impacts of WTO accession. As outlined later in this section, both schemes suffer from deficiencies, but those stem largely from problems in the design and implementation of the existing schemes. The lack of appropriate schemes does not create gaps in social protection for urban households, but it certainly does for the rural population.

Although the rural population benefits from numerous antipoverty schemes targeted at poor localities and at poor households (table 17.3), it does not enjoy the same degree of protection as the urban population. The program offering assistance to poor localities is a big one that dates back to 1994, when the government launched the so-called the "8-7" Plan.[5] The plan targeted the 592 poorest counties (designated as *national poor counties*) selected out of 2,000-plus rural counties. These counties, many of which were in the western region, contained, it was estimated, more than 70 percent of the 80 million people who remained poor. These counties were generally remote, characterized by backward socioeconomic conditions[6] and poor natural endowments—that is, they were areas in which geographic targeting is appropriate. The plan was financed entirely by the central government and backed by a multitiered administrative structure from the central government down to the counties. The principal instruments of assistance were tax reduction, financial grants, and a socioeconomic development program. The principal thrust was toward building infrastructure and developing the local economy rather than toward providing poor households with assistance. The program came to an end in 2000 and was replaced with a new one with similar aims and mode of operation, but targeted differently. Putting aside the issue of the appropriate territorial units for targeting,[7] these programs, though valuable in reducing severe rural poverty, are of little consequence, if

any, in cushioning the adverse impacts of WTO membership on income from farming. In general, the poor rural localities are remote and close to autarky. Market transactions with the economy outside the locality are sporadic and of low value. China's accession to the WTO would have little direct impact on such localities and their inhabitants. However, the program could be adapted to cope with the adverse impacts of WTO accession on rural areas by redefining its scope.

Also in rural areas is a wide range of assistance schemes that are targeting poor households. The oldest of these is the so-called Five Guarantees Scheme, covering food, clothing, shelter, health care, and funerals. The recipients of assistance under the scheme have been mostly elderly persons without means and relatives.[8] Therefore, the scheme is of little or no relevance in providing assistance to rural inhabitants adversely affected by WTO entry. Other rural assistance schemes cover a wider category of the poor than just the indigent elderly. These schemes have two features in common. First, they are highly decentralized, mostly organized and financed at the grass-roots level of villages. Second, associated with this high degree of decentralization, the structure of the scheme, funding, eligibility for assistance, and details of assistance vary widely. In contrast to the urban schemes (UI and MLSI), the rural schemes lack the underpinning of a national framework and are, as a result, far more variable in coverage and benefits. In localities, the spectrum runs from well-functioning schemes similar to the urban MLSI to no social protection scheme at all.

Decentralization has two related consequences, both of which erode the degree of protection provided by the rural schemes targeting households. First, localities with a higher incidence of poverty tend to have poorly financed and organized schemes, exactly the opposite of what is needed. Second, decentralized schemes are not able to cope well with correlated risks that adversely affect a substantial percentage of households in the locality. Competition from imports is an example of such a risk when households in a locality have similar or identical cropping pattern. The second feature of rural assistance schemes is that they are generally designed to provide assistance to those in extreme poverty only. The rural population is expected to rely on kin and community in case of all but dire contingencies. In sum, the rural areas lack schemes that can directly address the adverse impacts of WTO accession in the form of unemployment and a drop in farm earnings.

Land Plot as Insurance

One of the two rationales for the sparse and highly selective social protection cover in rural areas is that each rural household has been assigned a plot of agricultural land that serves as a floor to household income, a feature that is particular to China and a few other economies. The other is the high cost of introducing a social security regime comparable to the one in urban areas. In rural areas, there is a limited capacity to collect taxes and social security contributions, which is a common problem in developing economies. Agricultural land in China, compared with most developing economies, is very equally distributed. The removal of the adverse economic incentives that marred the collective economy and the provision of each rural household with a piece of land have together contributed to the dramatic drop in the (official) headcount of the poor, from 250 million in 1978 to 70 million in 1994, on the eve of the 8-7 Plan.[9] Landlessness and rural poverty do not go together in China, in marked contrast to the prevalent pattern in developing economies. However, in the present context the pertinent question is how much of a cushion do land plots provide against job losses in rural areas and a decline in farm income in general and those arising from China's accession to the WTO.

Controlling for the impact of input and output prices on farm earnings, income per capita from a land plot depends crucially on the land area per rural inhabitant, land quality and location, and technology. The constraint on income per capita imposed by the land–rural population ratio can be pushed back through investment in transport and other infrastructure and through technological upgrading, but it cannot be eliminated. The land–rural population ratio acts as a limit on the income security provided by land. Because of China's huge population, the cultivated area per rural inhabitant is slightly less than a fifth of hectare (0.19).[10] The cultivated land per rural person has been falling steadily since the distribution of land to households in the early 1980s because of the combination of rising population and various impediments to rural–urban migration. This trend may continue for some time.

After a sharp drop in the 1980s, the percentage gap between the rural and urban income per capita has been widening particularly rapidly in recent years. The implication is that the level of economic security provided by land plots, as measured by average farm income per rural inhabitant, has been falling relative to per capita income. Added to this, the level of income security land plots provide to rural households has been highly variable across localities. The distribution of land to rural households takes place at the grass-roots level of villages. As a result, the average area of land plot per household varies across villages even in close vicinity. Land plots have served to reduce the incidence of rural poverty but they have not been sufficient to prevent poverty, not even extreme poverty. Most of the rural population with a per capita income of less than 635 yuan per year—the official poverty line for rural inhabitants—has land.

It is also important to point out that not all rural households have a land plot, and the percentage without land has been rising. Two examples are described here—one from a prosperous region and another from a poor region. In rural areas of southern Jiangsu, one of the richest rural areas in China which covers 12 counties[11] known as Sunnan and has highly developed TVEs, a survey conducted in 1998 revealed that about 10.3 percent of households no longer possessed land. Reasons included the conversion of agricultural land to nonfarm uses and the relinquishment of land by households in order to opt out of liability for the agricultural tax. Furthermore, among the 89.7 percent of households with a land plot, another 3 percent planned at the time of the survey to give up their land plot in the near future. However, even in poorer rural regions not all rural households have a land plot. A survey of 1,500 households conducted in 1999 and drawn from 15 nationally designated poor counties in Gansu and Inner Mongolia found that about 3 percent of rural households for various reasons had no land. Most of the rural households without land had in the past given up land voluntarily and for good economic reasons. The important point is that on giving up land the households are not included in another income maintenance scheme.

How much of a cushion do land plots provide against a decline in household income from, for example, a job loss from a TVE or a fall in grain prices because of competition from imports? Land plots are not transferred to rural households in perpetuity but are leased for a definite period on a renewable basis.[12] In principle, the land lease can be sold or transferred, freely, but, in practice, it is subject to severe restrictions. One serious consequence of the limited tradability of land plots is that they cannot be used as collateral for loans. Land plots provide rural households with the option of an income generated by deploying household labor on their own land plot. It is this income that determines the value of insurance provided by land plots. In the event of the loss of a job in the nonfarming sector, households have the option of compensating for the loss of income by redeploying the now unemployed labor to their own land plot.[13] The important feature of this scenario is that income obtainable from the land plot remains unaffected by the adverse shock. However, when the decline in household income is the result of competition from cheaper agricultural imports, household land plots provide no cushion against the fall in income. Such competition reduces the insurance value of land. Because the competitive threat posed by agricultural imports varies across commodities, the extent of reduction would depend on the cropping pattern and the possibility of changing it. More specifically, in terms of the impact of WTO accession on farming, the Northeast and the Northwest would be losers and the East and Southeast would be gainers.

Anomalies in the Classification of the Population

As noted earlier, under the current social security arrangements any assistance that a person may receive after a job loss or reduction in earnings, for example, stemming from WTO entry would depend crucially on whether the person is living in an urban or rural area. The categories *urban* and *rural* are defined differently in China than elsewhere. This section will outline the anomalies created by the combination of the control on population migration and the rules governing household registration and will point to the implications of these anomalies for the incidence of the adverse effects of China's accession to the WTO.

Urban is both a spatial and a demographic category. According to the usual international usage, *urban* in its spatial sense denotes localities with a high population density and heavily dependent on industry and services as sources of income. In its demographic sense, *urban* denotes the population resident in an urban locality—that is, the spatial division *urban–rural* coincides with the demographic division of the population into *urban* and *rural*, and the two are interchangeable. In contrast, in China the spatial and the demographic divisions do not coincide, and the urban and rural populations, as officially designated, are intermixed and not mutually exclusive as they usually are. This situation creates anomalous divisions in the population and is associated with arbitrary exclusions or inclusions in the coverage of the social security schemes. Chinese cities are divided into urban districts (*shi qu*) and rural counties (*xian*). Similarly, the population is classified by personal registration status as agricultural (*nongye*) and nonagricultural (*fei nongye*). The spatial and the demographic divisions overlap, but only partially, producing the following anomalies (National Bureau of Statistics 2001):

- Of the 296 million people with nonagricultural registration (thus officially urban) living within the boundaries of 663 cities and towns in 2000,[14] 42.7 percent (126 million) were resident in rural counties, rather than in urban districts, and were covered by social security schemes confined to the urban population.

- Just as anomalous, 40.6 percent (116 million) of long-term residents in urban districts carried agricultural registration and were thus regarded as part of the rural population, even though most of them no longer had any relationship with farming.[15] They were still classified as *agricultural* because the occupational and residential shift from farming to industry and services does not automatically lead to a change in registration from *agricultural* to *nonagricultural*. These long-term inhabitants of urban districts are excluded from social security schemes for the urban population on the grounds of their registration status.

Thus the official designation *urban* in China does not denote the usual place of residence and work, such as urban districts of cities. Rather, it carries the label *nonagricultural* (*fei nongye*) on the personal register (*hu kou*). *Urban* is a personal attribute or status rather than a spatial designation. A striking example is provided by a comparatively common anomaly in China where some members of a household in an urban district are registered as *nonagricultural* and therefore regarded as *urban,* while other members of the same household are regarded as rural on the grounds of their registration as *agricultural.* Thus a household receiving the MLSI allowance may get less than the amount needed to bring its members up to the poverty line, as prescribed, because some of its members are not registered urban residents and so do not qualify. A frequent cause of such anomalies is marriage across the registration line. Similarly, migrants do not qualify for the MLSI allowance. Urban registration, if not inherited, is difficult to acquire, especially for large cities such as Beijing and Shanghai.

The control on labor migration and the rules governing assignment of the labels *nonagricultural* and *agricultural* to individuals produce two oddities at the aggregate levels of the labor force and the population. These oddities are important because they affect the pattern of incidence of impacts of WTO entry and also the coverage of social protection schemes. The first oddity is that whereas the gross domestic product (GDP) ratio of farming is a mere 15.8 percent,[16] similar to that in middle-income economies, the percentage of the labor force reported to be engaged in farming is almost three times higher, 47 percent, which is similar to that in low-income economies. Put together, the two percentages imply that the output per capita in farming, given by the ratio of its GDP share to its employment share, is less than a third of the average, or a mere 21 percent of that in the nonfarming sector.[17] A GDP share of farming that is a small fraction (say less than half) of its labor force share is a common feature of developing economies and corresponds to a wide gap between nonfarm (or urban) and farm (rural) per capita incomes in those economies. But with a GDP share of farming close to one-third of its labor force share, which implies that the urban GDP per capita is about four and a half times the rural GDP per capita,[18] the gap

between the two ratios in China is wide even for a developing economy. What factors explain the very low relative labor productivity in farming? Two explanatory factors are possible: low land productivity and a high labor-land ratio. The first does not have much explanatory power in the Chinese context. As in other East Asian economies, farming in China is intensive, and productivity per unit of land (e.g. hectare) is high by international standards. There is scope for raising land productivity further through the adoption of best-practice techniques, while keeping the labor–land ratio constant. But the principal explanation of the low labor productivity in farming lies with three impediments to the transfer of labor out of farming to nonfarming activities. The first impediment to rural–urban migration is the household registration system, which has diminished in rigor but not disappeared. The second impediment is the land tenure system in which rural households receive little or no compensation for giving up user rights on the allocated land. This arrangement is in effect tantamount to a tax on leaving farming completely. The third is the bias in favor of industry, which has tended to raise the investment cost of transferring labor into nonfarming activities and has therefore led to a higher land–labor ratio than it would otherwise be.

An important feature of the administrative control on rural–urban migration is that the impediment to the transfer of labor out of farming varies according to locality. It does not pose a serious impediment to the transfer of labor out of farming in localities with favorable conditions for the development of TVEs, such as a relatively high per capita income and educational level and good transport links. In such localities, most of which are in a few coastal provinces, controls on migration to cities have, arguably, spurred the growth of TVEs. In these areas, the result has been a substantial weakening of the link between labor outflow from farming and out-migration from the countryside. However, in localities where conditions for the growth and proliferation of TVEs are comparatively unfavorable, the control on labor migration bears down heavily and thus keeps a higher percentage of labor in farming. Such localities, which are poorer than those with developed TVEs, tend to be found in the interior provinces. There, migration control functions as a high barrier to the redeployment of labor out of farming. Given that, on average, income from farming is a small fraction of that from nonfarming activities, any measure that keeps a higher percentage of labor in farming in effect creates a trap that perpetuates low incomes and poverty.

What are the implications for the incidence of the adverse impacts of WTO membership? First, the larger the percentage of the labor force engaged in farming, the larger is the percentage of the population exposed to the risk of falling income due to competition from agricultural imports and therefore the more widespread are the adverse impacts. Second, among the localities reliant on crops especially vulnerable to imports, the adverse impacts would be variable. In particular, the impacts would be more severe in localities with less-diversified economies and those with an already low per capita income. The two tend to be correlated because less-diversified rural localities tend to be more dependent on farming activities that, on average, generate a lower income per capita than do nonfarming activities. However, low income per capita is also important in its own right because that heightens the vulnerability to falling into poverty after even a minor decline in income. On these criteria, the Northwest is particularly vulnerable. The region is reliant on crops at a disadvantage against imports, such as corn, wheat, and coarse grain; it has a very low income relative to the national average, and its rural economies are less diversified. Moreover, the shortage of water in the region limits the possibilities of changing the cropping pattern. The fact that the reduction in barriers to agricultural imports would be uneven and heavily concentrated in some regions that are already poor suggests the need for introducing assistance schemes that target particular regions.

The second oddity about the Chinese economy is the wide divergence between the sectoral distribution of the labor force and the division of the population into *agricultural* and *nonagricultural* (or urban and rural). The percentage of the labor force engaged in farming is 47 percent, but the percentage of the population/labor force designated as *rural* is 64 percent, 17 percentage points higher. The divergence has widened over the reform period because of the rapid growth of TVEs and the correlated expansion of nonfarm employment in rural areas. The divergence matters because the coverage of social security schemes is determined by the status division nonagricultural–agricultural, not the sectoral distribution. As a result, two individuals working in the same employment unit may have different social security cover simply because of their different designations in the household register.

Closing Loopholes in Social Protection

What feasible options are there for reducing, if not abolishing, the arbitrary anomalies in the coverage of social security schemes? An integrated social protection system that abolishes the urban–rural distinction as a consideration for the provision of assistance would eliminate the arbitrary anomalies altogether and immediately. Such an integrated system, however, although highly desirable on equity grounds, is not feasible for the foreseeable future for financial reasons. The tax system such a system requires is a decade into the future. A piecemeal and gradual elimination of the anomalies is the only possibility. Assuming that the fiscal constraint remains binding, piecemeal reforms along the following three lines appear feasible:

1. extending contributory social insurance schemes to regular wage employees regardless of personal registration status, which is losing significance because of changes in the household registration system
2. broadening the coverage of means-tested social assistance schemes targeting poor households, including the introduction of an integrated social assistance scheme covering urban and rural populations in selected localities with healthy public finances
3. overhauling the scheme, financed by the central government, to assist poor rural localities in order to extend coverage to localities seriously harmed by competition from agricultural imports, and introducing a similar scheme to assist towns and cities caught in a spiral of decline or in a stagnation trap.

The first would involve little, if any, extra expenditure, because employees brought under the social insurance net will be making advance contributions toward benefits. Such an extension will be largely limited to regular wage employees because of difficulty in collecting contributions and defining *unemployment*. The main groups brought under the umbrella of unemployment insurance would include migrants in regular employment and regular wage employees of TVEs. Some cities and provinces already include these groups in social insurance. For example, Guangdong Province extends social insurance to migrants.

The second recommendation covers both the MLSI for the registered population and the assortment of social assistance schemes in rural areas. A change in the coverage of MLSI to include all long-term urban residents regardless of their registration status will remove glaring anomalies in the way the scheme currently functions. The suggested change in the coverage will mean a greater expenditure, but it is likely to be only a small fraction of the current expenditure on the scheme. In rural areas, the priority is to institute a national framework for the provision of social assistance to poor households in order to set a minimum standard and put in place a mechanism to ensure that at least the minimum is reached. Some provinces are taking steps to abolish the urban–rural segmentation in social security. For example, Zhejiang Province has decided to extend the MLSI scheme, which had been confined to its urban population, to its rural population as well. Similarly, Shanghai is planning to introduce an integrated social security system for the whole population—both urban and rural.

The third recommendation is based on the assumption that an assistance scheme should target particular localities, thereby supplementing the social assistance scheme that targets poor households. As noted earlier, the current scheme to assist poor localities is of little use, if any, in assisting rural localities adversely affected by WTO accession. Furthermore, there is a strong case for introducing a similar scheme for towns and cities caught between the pincers of high unemployment and poverty rates, on the one hand, and strained public finances, on the other.[19]

The inclusion of migrants in social insurance and MLSI is of particular importance, because labor migration is one of the principal ways of adapting to changes in the structure of the economy, including that induced by trade liberalization. In the Chinese context, migrants form a heterogeneous group, but they differ in their length of stay. Some are visitors or short-term migrants, and some have resided in China for a substantial length of time. Six months is the cut-off period used in Chinese statistics to distinguish between short-term and long-term migrants. Correlated with this, migrants differ in their official status. A small percentage of migrants receive a new household registration and become indistinguishable from the local population. A proportion of them, usually long-term migrants, have temporary household registration. One set of social security schemes that covers all migrants regardless of differences among them is neither appropriate nor feasible. That would require an integrated social security system covering both the urban and rural population, which, as argued earlier, is not realizable is the foreseeable future. There is no doubt that for the purposes of social security long-term immigrants should be regarded as part of the urban population. However, for short-term migrants, it is far from obvious whether they should be regarded as part of the urban or the rural population. This decision takes on a special importance in China, because, according to the current official practice, the urban poverty line, 1,800 yuan per person per year, exceeds the rural poverty line, 635 yuan, by a very wide margin.[20] Therefore, a person who is poor according to the urban poverty line would be well off by the rural one.

The disadvantageous position of migrants is associated with the control on population migration, especially between rural and urban areas. Depending on the locality, immigrants are restricted to jobs and occupations that are not attractive to local residents. Furthermore, immigrants do not have the same access to public facilities, such as housing and schools, as local residents. With a few notable exceptions, migrants in cities are excluded from social insurance.[21] The notable exceptions are Guangdong Province and, to a lesser degree, Shanghai. The former treats migrants on a par with the local population for the purposes of social insurance, and the latter has begun to include migrants in particular social insurance schemes. The exclusion of migrants in cities from social insurance is not restricted to migrants from rural areas, but also extends to migrants from other cities because entitlements to social insurance benefits are not portable across cities. This arrangement reduces the benefits migrants, including those from another city, can derive from participating in social insurance schemes.

The official control on migration remains, but its rigor has diminished considerably. According a recent State Council circular, migration to county and some small or medium-size towns has been completely freed, in principle if not yet in practice. Moreover, the last few years have seen the introduction of assisted migration out of rural localities that have little or no prospect of emerging from poverty. However, while the focus of government policy and discussion has largely been rural–urban migration, urban–urban migration is assuming increased importance with the rise in urban unemployment and layoffs.

Two aspects of the participation of migrants in social insurance schemes are the collection of contributions and the disbursement of benefits. The problems raised by the first are, in principle, the same for migrants and residents. The only difference is that, compared with residents, migrants are more likely to be in jobs outside the coverage of social insurance schemes, such as casual or self-employment. The extension of social insurance schemes to the labor force in the informal sector, which includes not only migrants but also increasing numbers of local residents, would pave the way for wider coverage of migrants. But the aim should be not only collecting contributions but also disbursing benefits in return for contributions. Unlike collection, disbursement raises issues that can be solved only through some fundamental changes in the organization of social insurance. Aside from immigrants who receive a change in residence status, the rest are by definition temporary residents. This definition poses a particular problem for social insurance schemes, such as old-age pensions and unemployment insurance, in which contributions and benefits are separated in time. The problem arises because current social insurance schemes are largely organized and financed at the level of cities. Arrangements for the transferability of benefits between cities even in the same province are nonexistent or rudimentary. An integration of social insurance at the provincial level would make benefits transferable within a province, and it would go a long way toward addressing the problem of transferability because most migration is confined to one province. Such integration is planned, but it will take some time to implement. The portability of social insurance benefits also makes sense between urban areas that have comparable social insurance schemes, but it begs the question of relevance in the case of rural–urban

migrants because of the absence of social insurance schemes in rural areas.

The realistic options for extending social insurance to migrants have to take into account two considerations. First, restrictions on rural–urban migration, though considerably relaxed, are likely to stay for some time, especially for large cities. Second, urban and rural social security systems are likely to remain segmented for some time. It would then be inappropriate to apply one formula to all migrants. It is important to distinguish between social insurance schemes that (1) cover all migrants and (2) are confined to particular categories of migrants, such as those from other cities. The first set of schemes covers contingencies that seriously reduce a person's capacity to work such as physical injury and major illnesses. The implication is that the priority should be to extend disability compensation and insurance against large health care expenditure to all migrants. In these two sets of schemes, benefits are not deferred but run concurrently with the payment of contributions. The issue of the portability of benefits does not arise. The second group of schemes includes old-age pensions and unemployment compensation. These schemes involve deferred benefits and raise the issue of portability, which can be solved through a clearing mechanism. These are suitable for extension to city–city migrants, because all cities are covered by similar social insurance schemes.

Education and Training

Between 1978 and 2000, the portion of the labor force employed in the primary sector, most of which is farming, fell at an average rate of over 1 percentage point per year. This rate, although twice that in the planned economy period (1952–78), would have been even higher except for three factors: (1) the household registration system, (2) the land tenure system that provides little or no compensation for giving up use rights on allocated land, and, (3) the bias in favor of industry, which has tended to raise the cost of transferring labor from farming to nonfarming activities. However, as noted earlier in this chapter, all these factors are undergoing radical changes. Taking all the changes together, the implication is that the transfer of labor out of farming over the 20 years to 2020 would be at least as rapid as that seen over the

20 years to 2000. Added to this, driven by a more open international trade regime spurred by WTO membership and economic growth, the Chinese economy is likely to experience a more rapid redistribution of labor between occupations and sectors. In the Chinese context, the methods for adapting to the changes and reducing their cost in terms poverty and increased economic inequality fall into three broad categories:

1. improving the employability of the labor force by raising the general level of education and skills, especially in the rural population
2. facilitating the growth and proliferation of private enterprises
3. encouraging the adaptability of existing enterprises.

The remainder of this section focuses on the first point, education and skills. The literacy rate in China is substantially higher than that in many larger developing economies, especially low-income ones. However, the literacy rate is no longer an appropriate indicator of human development, nor are low-income economies relevant comparators in the field of human development for China. Thanks to the high growth rate of its per capita income after 1978, China graduated to lower–middle-income status at the end of 2000. The appropriate reference group for setting targets for human development and social security is not the present-day low-income economies but the middle-income ones. In terms of the average number of years of basic schooling for the current cohort of children, China lags behind many Asian countries, such as the Democratic People's Republic of Korea, Malaysia, Thailand, and Sri Lanka, as well as the Republic of Korea, Singapore, and Japan. Furthermore, as China narrows the technology gap with developed economies, the educational attainment of the labor force is assuming growing importance in determining the growth rate of the economy.

In China, nine years of schooling for all children has been a policy goal since 1986, but it has not yet been attained. The target is largely achieved in the urban areas, but is far from realized in rural areas, which is home to 64 percent of the population and an even higher percentage of those in the 15–16 age cohort. In the western and central regions, basic education in many rural localities falls far short of the prescribed nine years of schooling—in fact, about 26 percent of primary schools have a cycle of less than six years. Moreover, a significant percentage of children in poor localities drop out before completing the full cycle. The tenth five-year plan (2000–04) envisages that, by the end of 2005, at least 90 percent of those leaving school will have had nine years of education. The target date for achieving universal basic education (UBE) is set for 2010. However, according to the government's plan, the UBE does not mean a uniform length of schooling for all students. Depending on local financial resources and organizational capability, the UBE will actually mean less than nine years of schooling in some localities. For the poorest 5 percent of the population, all in the western provinces, the UBE will mean no more than three to four years of schooling.

With respect to post-basic schooling, the period since 1995 has witnessed a sharp rise in the gross enrollment rates in secondary schools (including vocational and regular schools) and in tertiary institutions. This trend is expected to continue. The tenth five-year plan (2000–04) envisages that almost 100 percent of children in cities and towns will go on to senior secondary and vocational schools after nine years of basic education. It is expected that by 2005 the percentage of the relevant age group in a tertiary institution would rise to 15 percent, from less than 10 percent in 2000. These trends will help to raise the average number of years of education to the level in East Asia, but they also will widen the gap between urban and rural areas, which has some adverse implications for the future.

What factors should be taken into account in deciding the appropriate general level of education for the population? Broadly, educational attainment influences labor productivity directly and the productivity of capital indirectly. An important feature of investment in formal education is that much of it precedes workers' entry into the labor force, and additional educational investment after entry in the labor market is, for most individuals, small. Moreover, learning through the work experience is crucially dependent on educational attainment prior to entering the labor force. The implication is that investment in education should be decided with reference to the likely course over the whole working life and to some sections of the population, especially poor rural communities, because of the high cost of education relative to current income.

A major determinant of labor market events over an individual's working life is the changes in the skills or the education level needed to perform work. Assuming a working life of between 40 and 50 years, most of the current cohort of school-age children in rural areas either would not be employed in farming or would switch to a job in industry or services fairly early on during the course of their working life. The implication is that the requisite level of education for rural children is not needed currently to get by with life in rural areas and work in farming, but that it would be needed in the future to live in an urban environment and take on jobs in industry or services. Viewed this way, the wide gap in educational attainment between urban and rural areas (especially the backward ones) is a serious deficiency that should be corrected quickly through a concerted policy. Comparatively low educational attainment among children in backward rural areas will in time act as an impediment to their out-migration or reduce their chances of getting or holding jobs when they migrate. Either way, comparatively low educational attainment among a group of children or a time lag in achieving the target of nine years of basic education for all has adverse implications for reducing poverty or income inequality in future. The policy implication is the importance of reducing the cost of basic education relative to average income for families in rural communities.

Conclusions

On the eve of its entry into the WTO, China presented a mixed picture of notable successes and some adverse developments. The Open Door policy, first introduced in 1979, has been a remarkable success. It has brought huge benefits and a few problems. China has faced no major balance of payments or currency crises. In the 24 years from 1978 to 2002, China's exports have grown at an average annual rate of 15 percent (in dollar terms), which points to its ability to adapt to and thrive in the face of foreign competition. With a foreign trade to GNP ratio of about 45 percent, the Chinese economy was on the eve of its WTO accession as open as any large economy.[22]

On the social side, China has also been remarkably successful in reducing poverty. The official headcount of the rural poor dropped from about 250 million in 1978 (31 percent of the rural population) to 32 million at the end of 2000 (3.5 percent of the rural population). The headcount of the poor and the poverty rate are highly sensitive to the poverty line. Both of these figures are much higher when the $1-a-day poverty line is used, but the reduction in poverty still remains dramatic. Unfavorable developments over the last decade or so include a sharp rise in interpersonal inequality in both urban and rural areas and a widening urban-rural disparity. Interprovincial inequality remains large, though falling in recent years. The urban unemployment rate has been rising since the middle of the 1990s and is high by historical standards. In recent years, rural household incomes have risen very slowly and have even fallen in some localities.

All the studies of the impacts of China's accession to the WTO agree that the overall benefits outweigh the losses. Although in the aggregate the population would benefit, losses and gains would not be evenly distributed, and there is little doubt that there would be a significant number of losers, at least in the short run. These will include workers displaced by competition from imported manufactured goods and farmers suffering a decline in income because of cheaper agricultural imports. Although it is difficult to foretell the losses precisely, evidence from the United States help in forming a rough idea of the magnitude. That evidence suggests that workers losing jobs because of competition from imports on average endure a significant spell of unemployment and also experience a decline in earnings when they find another job. Arguably, the losses suffered by Chinese workers who lose jobs because of WTO entry would be no less than those experienced by U.S. workers unemployed as a result of competition from imports.

This point raises the issue of compensation for workers and farmers adversely affected by WTO entry. What should be the magnitude of compensation relative to losses suffered? And what schemes or programs should provide the compensation? Full compensation for losses is ruled out on two grounds. First, it would be very costly to verify the true magnitude of losses, because full compensation would provide a huge incentive to exaggerate losses. Second, even when losses can be verified accurately, the opportunity cost of compensation may be prohibitive. On the grounds of feasibility, then, any compensation has to be partial, which raises the issue of the goal of compensation. The minimum goal for any compensation has to be the prevention of *poverty,* a term that can be defined in a number of ways. For the present purposes, *poverty* is defined as "inadequacy of command over economic resources," with "inadequacy" calibrated to take account of personal or household characteristics such as old age, ill health, or schooling age. A broader aim of compensation is to avoid relative poverty, which may be defined as a percentage (e.g., 50 percent) of average or median income per capita.

These goals remain valid regardless of the proximate cause of poverty. Adverse events such as a job loss or a decline in wages or in farm earnings can be produced by a wide range of causes, both internal and external. There is no general justification for special measures to deal with the adverse impacts of China's WTO membership. However, supplementary measures may be needed if the existing ones cannot cope with adverse impacts concentrated over a short time period or in particular regions, such as the rural areas of the already impoverished Northwest.

China has a range of schemes for income maintenance and poverty relief, and most of these share three characteristics:

- a stark dichotomy between the urban and rural population
- a goal of doing little or no more than alleviating absolute poverty, a feature that applies especially to the rural schemes
- a high degree of decentralization in financing and organization, which goes beyond the level consistent with equity and maintaining variation in provision within socially acceptable bounds. The income maintenance schemes for the rural population are supplemented with a scheme that provides each rural household with a land plot. The household land plots have played a crucial role in reducing poverty and in keeping rural poverty comparatively low, but they do not guarantee full protection against

poverty and cannot protect households from the lower earnings that might result from competition by agricultural imports.

The crucial question is how effective would the existing social security schemes be in preventing workers who have lost jobs and farmers who have experienced a decline in income (including their families) from falling into poverty, which is the minimum expected of any system of social protection? The answer depends crucially on whether the person is, officially, urban or rural. The (registered) urban population is covered by unemployment insurance, subject to the payment of the requisite contribution, and the Minimum Living Standard Scheme. Together, these schemes provide a fair degree of protection against poverty, although there are serious problems in the coverage of the health care and schooling costs of low-income urban households. In contrast, the provisions for income maintenance of the rural population are sparse and patchy. The employees of TVEs are excluded from unemployment insurance despite the fact that they number 128 million, which is about a quarter of the rural labor force. The rural social assistance schemes, which have goals similar to those of the MLSI, vary widely in coverage, benefits, and operation. They do provide a social safety net, but one that is ridden with tears. As presently constituted, the scheme to assist poor rural localities is not relevant because it is directed mostly at remote localities with little connection to the outside world, although the scheme can be altered to cover rural localities seriously harmed by competition from cheaper imports. However, there is at present no scheme to assist towns and cities caught in a high unemployment and stagnation trap.

Assuming that the aim is to close the major gaps in social protection against the threat of poverty, the priorities in urban and rural areas are different. In urban areas, the priorities are to alter the coverage of existing schemes, to institute a financing arrangement that ensures an equitable distribution of burden across government tiers, to make the contributory benefits portable, and to eliminate inadequacies in benefits. As for altering the coverage of existing schemes, all the major anomalies can be eliminated by extending the schemes to include all long-term residents, regardless of their registration status.

In contrast to its urban counterpart, the rural population needs additional income protection schemes. First, given the sizable labor force in TVEs, there is a strong argument for extending UI to wage employees in TVEs. Second, China needs a social assistance scheme that targets poor rural households, similar to the MLSI, backed by a national framework to ensure a minimum level of protection and equitable distribution of financial burden across government tiers. Third, the assistance scheme for rural localities needs to be recast so that it covers a wider range of disadvantaged localities.

There is a broad consensus on the value of raising the general education level and investing in skills, especially of the rural population, in order to mitigate the adverse impacts of WTO entry on labor and thus the population. However, these goals are not panaceas and they have their limitations. As pointed out earlier, most investment in education and much of the acquisition of skills take place before workers enter the labor market. Therefore, raising the level of basic education has little relevance for improving the employability of those who are already in the labor force, especially older workers. Raising the level of basic education should be viewed as a long-term measure that would be complemented by short-term measures, such as retraining adapted to the immediate circumstances of adversely affected workers.

Notes

1. That is, those with urban registration. Some rural social insurance schemes are in place, but none provides an unemployment benefit.

2. According to the regulation, social insurance applies in principle to the whole of the urban labor force of 247.8 million (34 percent of the total), but the actual coverage falls well short of that prescribed because of difficulties in collecting contributions. Some cities extend unemployment insurance to migrant workers in regular wage employment.

3. The supplementary condition is usually the obligation to take offered employment or participate in a training program.

4. This situation has begun to change. At the end of 2003, 11 provinces had some form of a minimum living standard scheme for the rural population, which creates the possibility of instituting one social safety net covering the whole population. On a similar note, Shanghai is planning to set up a unified social security system covering both the urban and the rural population.

5. The "8" in the "8-7 Plan" refers to the eighth five-year plan, which was under implementation in 1994, and the "7" refers to the seven years from 1994 to 2000. The plan expired at the end of the ninth five-year plan and has since then been replaced with the 2005–2010 Rural Poverty Reduction and Development Plan with the same aim.

6. The estimates of the percentage of the rural poor living in the selected counties vary over time. Recent estimates were 50 percent.

7. The program previously targeted the county level. It is generally accepted that counties are too large and differentiated for targeting. The proposal is to lower the level of targeting to the village, which would reduce the numbers of false negatives and positives.

8. In the past, the Five Guarantees Scheme also applied to urban areas, but since 1997 the urban Minimum Living Standard Scheme (MLSS) has superseded it.

9. As one might expect, the headcount of the poor is highly sensitive to shifts in poverty. However, the observation that rural poverty fell dramatically during the first 10 years of economic reforms remains valid even when a poverty line higher than the official one is used.

10. The actual figure depends on the definition of the land area (numerator) and of the denominator. Here, the land area is taken to be the sown area in 2000, and the total rural population serves as the denominator. The area of land per person is higher if the labor force employed in farming is used as the denominator.

11. These 12 counties include 6 within the administrative boundaries of Suzhou City and 3 each within the boundaries of Wuxi and Changzhou City.

12. In principle, land plots are leased for 30 years, but the actual duration in many localities is shorter than 30 years. Furthermore, at any particular point in time the remaining lease is generally a lot less than 30 years.

13. In considering the implications of the redeployment of labor to a household land plot as a way of coping with a job loss, one should also take into account any hired labor displaced as a result.

14. About 86 percent of China's 1.266 billion population in 2000 was living within the boundaries of cities and towns.

15. This situation arises largely from the expansion of city districts and the associated redesignation of some rural counties as urban districts.

16. This is the GDP share of the primary sector, which also includes activities such as quarrying.

17. If the share of farming in GDP is α and in employment is β, then labor productivity in farming relative to the average, which by definition is 1, is given by (β/α). Similarly, the ratio of labor productivity in farming with respect to that in nonfarming activities is $(\beta/\alpha) * \{(1 - \alpha)/(1 - \beta)\}$.

18. This is based on the assumption that nonfarming activities are confined to urban areas and farming activities to rural areas. The first part of the assumption is not strictly true for China. As a result, the urban–rural gap would be less than four and a half times.

19. The latter matters because social insurance and social assistance schemes are budgeted at the city level. The plan is to raise the budgeting to the provincial level. However, the plan has yet to be fully implemented.

20. The rural and urban lines, especially the latter, can vary across localities. However, the fact of a wide gap between the urban and rural poverty remains valid.

21. Social insurance covers the old-age pension, health care insurance, unemployment benefits, disability compensation, and maternity benefits.

22. The ratio depends crucially on how GDP is measured. However, the general proposition about the openness of the Chinese economy remains valid regardless of how GDP is measured.

References

Collins, Susan M., ed. 1998. *Imports and Exports and the American Worker*. Washington, D.C.: Brookings Institution Press.

Ehrenberg, R. G. 1994. *Labor Markets and Integrating National Economies*. Washington D.C.: Brookings Institution Press.

Fishlow, A., and K. Parker, ed. 1999. *Growing Apart—The Causes and Consequence of Wage Inequality*. New York: Council of Foreign Relations.

Kletzer, L. G. 2001. *Job Loss from Imports: Measuring the Costs*. Washington D.C.: Institute for International Economics.

NBS (National Bureau of Statistics). 2001. *China Towns and Cities Statistics Yearbook 2002*. Beijing: China Statistics Press.

———. 2003a. *China Labor Statistical Yearbook 2003*. Beijing: China Statistics Press.

———. 2003b. *Statistical Yearbook of China 2003*. Beijing: China Statistics Press.

Wood, A. 1994. *North-South Trade, Employment and Inequality—Changing Fortunes in a Skill-Driven World*. Oxford: Oxford University Press.